W9-BLE-438

NORTH
DAKOTA

MINNESOTA

SOUTH
DAKOTA

IOWA

NEBRASKA

MISSOURI

KANSAS

OKLAHOMA

ARKANSAS

ROHWER ■

JEROME ■

TEXAS

LOUISIANA

THE GREAT BETRAYAL

THE GREAT
BETRAYAL:

THE EVACUATION OF THE JAPANESE-AMERICANS DURING WORLD WAR II

BY Audrie Girdner *and* Anne Loftis

THE MACMILLAN COMPANY, NEW YORK, NEW YORK

COLLIER-MACMILLAN LTD., LONDON

Copyright © 1969 by Audrie Girdner and Anne Loftis

All rights reserved. No part of this book may be reproduced or
transmitted in any form or by any means, electronic or
mechanical, including photocopying, recording or by any
informational storage and retrieval system, without permission
in writing from the Publisher.

Library of Congress Catalog Card Number: 70-80791

THIRD PRINTING 1972

The Macmillan Company
866 Third Avenue, New York, N.Y. 10022
Collier-Macmillan Canada Ltd., Toronto, Ontario

Printed in the United States of America

940.531
G

Dedicated to Gerda Isenberg,
A Founder of the Palo Alto Fair Play Council
and friend to the American Japanese

24870

21310

Contents

Preface

ALTHOUGH UNIQUE in American history, the evacuation of the West Coast Japanese in 1942 resembled some of the epic banishments of more primitive times. The war dramatized the story, even as it distorted the issues. We now see what happened twenty-five years ago as a confrontation between expediency and liberty, prejudice and tolerance, and the individual and the state. Then, only a few voices of conscience insisted, "This is wrong!" Today the actions of the nation betraying its traditions and its constitutional guarantees appear, as more than one commentator predicted they would, as a black page in our history.

In writing this book, we have tried, above all, to tell the story of people, of their reactions and experiences in this cataclysmic uprooting. This would not have been possible without the help of many individuals. We would like to thank first those old and new friends who graciously allowed us to interview them, who opened their homes to us, and who made working on this project a rewarding experience.

We were fortunate in enlisting the advice of several experts while the manuscript was in preparation. Professor James M. Sakoda of the Department of Sociology and Anthropology at Brown University, who contributed to the studies in the University of California series on Evacuation and Resettlement, read all the chapters and corrected errors of fact as well as interpretation. Professor Don Fehrenbacher of the History Department at Stanford University, Professor John Kaplan of the Stanford Law School, and Allan Nevins, the historian, read portions of the book and gave us invaluable aid. We consulted the following individuals on major or minor factual questions: Professor Thomas Barclay, Bruce Bliven, Professor John Emerson, Miss Lisette Fast, George Fischer, Mike Masaoka, Professors Nobutaka Ike, Edgar Robinson, and Payson Treat.

Dr. Dorothy Swaine Thomas of the Population Studies Center of the University of Pennsylvania, who directed the University of California studies on Evacuation and Resettlement, responded immediately to the frequent queries and requests we put to her. Masao Satow, director of the Japanese American Citizens League, and Harry Honda, editor of the *Pacific Citizen*, were equally helpful. We thank Philip McLean, Mrs. Wendell Cole, Mrs. Arline Paul, and the reference staff of the Hoover Institution on War, Revolution, and Peace, the staff at the Bancroft Library of the University of California, Mrs. Kenneth Malavos of the Santa Clara County Law Library, Elizabeth Drewry, Director of General Services Information at the Franklin Delano Roosevelt Library at Hyde Park, and Mary Isabel Fry, head of the department of reader services at the Huntington Library in San Marino, California.

The late Francis Biddle, former United States Attorney General, Supreme Court Justice Tom Clark, Edward Ennis, formerly of the Justice Department, the honorable Spark Matsunaga, representative in Congress from Hawaii, and the honorable Charles Fahy, who was Solicitor General at the outbreak of World War II, were helpful in answering our queries. Joe Grant Masaoka of the Japanese American History Project at UCLA generously put his materials at our disposal. We are grateful to Kaz Inouye, Mrs. Hiroshi Ito, Toyo Miyatake, and Mrs. John Mayer for donating photographs, and to William Mason of the Los Angeles County Museum, Mrs. Toshio Hirata, and Mrs. Katherine Peterson for supplying information for captions.

We thank the following people for arranging interviews or lending us material: Hugh Anderson, Mrs. James Bowditch, Herbert Bretschneider, John Anson Ford, the Reverend Jun Fujimori, Mrs. Hiroshi Ito, Mrs. Louis Kaplan, Mrs. Roy Kepler, Mrs. Robert Kitaji, Mrs. Genevieve Lassere, Mort Lewis, Mrs. Hubert Marshall, Tad Masaoka, Mrs. William Mayer, Miss Helen Mineta, Dave Nakagawa, Mrs. Mary Richardson Nevins, Herbert Nicholson, Mrs. Grace Nichols Pearson, Mrs. D. C. Rust, Professor-emeritus and Mrs. Claude Settles, Mits Takasumi, Dave Tatsuno, Hike Yego, and Akiji Yoshimura. Rachelle Marshall gave special editorial assistance. Finally, we thank John Loftis and Bill Girdner for their unfailing support and encouragement.

Portola Valley, California   ANNE LOFTIS and AUDRIE GIRDNER

. . . in the total picture, the welfare of a negligible minority, of itself, is not important. Evacuation, when considered only in the light of 110,000 persons, looms small as an American problem. What should concern us is what is this thing that has happened to America?

—Togo Tanaka, 1943

THE GREAT BETRAYAL

ONE · CRISIS

On December 7, 1941, the Reverend Donald Toriumi, the first Japanese–American Presbyterian minister in the United States, was in Long Beach, California, assisting at a church service. A graduate of the San Francisco Theological Seminary, he was a youth worker in four Japanese churches in Southern California. On that Sunday morning following the service, a boy came running into the church to say he had just heard on his car radio that Japan had bombed Pearl Harbor.

The group standing in the vestry rushed out to listen to the terse bulletins of disaster that were being broadcast. Unidentified planes, presumably Japanese, had bombed Oahu. The surprise attack was launched against ninety-six American warships lying in the harbor and against Hickam and Wheeler fields where the planes were lined up on the runways. The Americans, caught off guard, had at first thought that the squadron swooping down from the northeast was one of their own units engaged in war games. At 1:45 P.M. (10:45 A.M. Pacific Coast Time), the news reached Washington. A Navy Department message read, "Air raid on Pearl Harbor. This is no drill." The war had started.

The American Japanese stood in the quiet sun-drenched street, two thousand miles from where a peaceful island had been turned into a battlefield. They stared at each other in disbelief. For years there had been talk about war between Japan and the United States. In the last few days the newspaper headlines had blazed with news of the crisis in the Pacific. The Secretary of State was at that moment discussing peace terms with the Japanese envoys in Washington. This news of an attack might be a false rumor. But the incredible report was verified when it was learned that President Roosevelt was telephoning members of his cabinet. There was no mistaking the reality of the crisis. Reverend Toriumi turned away, stunned and shaken. He wondered how the war would affect the people of Japanese ancestry living on the West Coast, two-thirds of whom were, like him, Nisei (second generation), born in America.

Later, while he was at lunch at the home of a church member, Mr. Toriumi was called to the telephone. The pastor of the First Presbyterian Church in Long Beach proposed that the two congregations hold a joint service at his church that evening. At eight o'clock Nisei and Caucasian youth marched down the aisle and sat together as a testimony to their friendship, Symbolically, they declared that they were all Americans, that the war would not divide them. Still moved by this experience, Mr. Toriumi was standing later that night on a street corner waiting to catch an electric train back to Los Angeles when an FBI man walked up to him, flashed a badge, and asked for his identification. The young minister, an American citizen, was startled. "It gave me a funny feeling, a very uneasy feeling."

David Sakai, a student at San Jose State College, spent the day with his roommate and three other Nisei students. "The news hit us like a bomb. We never left that radio the rest of the day. We were really shocked. We wondered what was going to happen to everybody, to friends and relatives in Japan."

Masao Hamamura was a high school student in Gonzales near Salinas. His initial reaction was like that of most Nisei: "*They* are attacking *us*." His mother was not surprised, however. She had recently visited Japan and thought that war was likely.

Monica Sone's father, a first-generation immigrant who ran a waterfront hotel in Seattle, would not believe in the attack until he heard the words in his own language on a short-wave broadcast from Japan.[1] Like the rest of the nation, the American Japanese spent the afternoon of Sunday, December 7, trying to dispel but only increasing their anxiety by listening to reports on the radio.

Interspersed with the news that the President was calling an emergency meeting of members of his cabinet and congressional leaders for eight-thirty that evening, came special bulletins from state governors and the mayors of large cities across the nation. Hawaii's governor announced that the islands were under martial law. In all West Coast cities extra guards were posted around harbors, airports, and defense installations. Telephone switchboards were jammed with calls from people wanting to talk to friends and relatives. Citizens rushed out to sign up for civil defense work. In Seattle a Marine Corps recruiting station was opened by demand at 6 P.M. and by nine o'clock, seventy-eight men had enlisted. Military personnel were ordered back to their bases.

San Francisco's mayor, Angelo J. Rossi, proclaimed a state of emergency and dispatched extra police to block off traffic in the Japanese sector of the city. Many Japanese-owned stores remained open, but in the residential area shades were drawn and people stayed indoors. In Los Angeles curious spectators flocked to "Little Tokyo" to see how the residents were taking the news. A policeman, no stranger to the district, fumed, " . . . these damn fool Sunday drivers have to come down here to have a look at it. Maybe they expect a bomb or some Jap to cut his guts out in the middle of First Street. . . . And the same guys would help lynch a poor bastard Japanese who might be trying to earn a living down here selling his countrymen's junk. We gotta protect the Japs against the Americans, not the other way around."[2]

In Seattle Kathleen Sonoda was taking a Sunday afternoon walk as a respite from her duties as a house girl for a Japanese family who ran a dry cleaning and laundry business. Her employer's wife came looking for her and told her to go inside. "She told me not to go out of the house because we were right in the town. The fact that Pearl Harbor was a sneak attack had a bad effect on the Japanese population here. At the time I thought, 'How could they do this, knowing what effect it will have on us?' "

Across the country, Larry Tajiri, a Japanese–American newspaperman, was walking up Times Square. "We may have been a little ashamed of our faces as we walked through those crowded New York streets on that December night," he wrote later. "We are Americans by every right, birth, education and belief, but our faces are those of the enemy. . . ."[3]

United States officials were immediately concerned about the safety of representatives of the Japanese government and posted guards around consulates. The State Department pledged full protection for all official Japanese and their establishments in the United States and its territories and at once considered the possibility of exchanging Japanese nationals in the United States, including diplomats and newspaper correspondents, for Americans in Japan. There were approximately five hundred Americans in Japan and five thousand in occupied China at the outbreak of the war. Before the President met with the cabinet on the evening of December 7, the Solicitor General, Charles Fahy, talked with him for less than ten minutes and afterwards divulged to the reporters, crowding outside the White House, "My visit had to do with the aliens—the Japanese—living in the United States."[4]

He was concerned with the drafting of a presidential proclamation regarding the status and conduct of aliens, both visitors from Japan and long-time immigrant residents, the Issei (first generation) Japanese. The 1940 census recorded 47,307 Issei (.0003 of the national population), most of whom had come to the United States before the exclusionary Immigration Act of 1924. The great majority of them lived with their American-born children, the Nisei, in the three Pacific coast states where in 1940 there were 112,353 persons of Japanese ancestry in a Caucasian population of almost ten million. The events of the first twenty-four hours of the war demonstrated that because, as Larry Tajiri said, their faces were those of the enemy, the public often failed to distinguish between a consulate staff recently arrived from Tokyo, and the resident Issei and their thoroughly American children.

In 1941, the average age of the second-generation Nisei was nineteen.

They were for the most part too young to exert the leadership that would have unequivocally stamped them as American citizens in the eyes of the general public. Most of them never expected to be identified with the enemy nation, which two-thirds of them had never visited. Almost overwhelmingly, their loyalty was to the land of their birth, whereas their parents, who were not allowed to become American citizens, had kept up strong ties with the mother country. The Issei's sense of *giri* (principle) demanded loyalty to Japan, yet as parents of Americans, they acknowledged ties to the United States. As law-abiding and somewhat elderly people (the average age of the first-generation men was fifty-five), they were not, in any case, inclined toward an active role in this painful conflict of national allegiance. Because of late marriages there was virtually a missing generation, a generation that might have challenged the Caucasian majority at the time the entire Japanese group came under suspicion because of their racial ties with the enemy. As it was, the Nisei, half of whom were students in 1941, were for the most part preparing to take their life roles, and the Issei, whose hard work in farming, fishing, and marketing paid for their children's education, were still laboring under the stigma of being "unassimilable."

Some of the Issei were immediately affected by the strenuous defense measures undertaken in the first twenty-four hours after the attack on Pearl Harbor. The Justice and War departments ordered the arrest of "suspicious enemy aliens" in Hawaii, Panama, and the United States. Puerto Rico, the Virgin Islands, Alaska, and the Philippines were later put under surveillance. Working from lists of doubtful individuals that had been compiled months before the war, FBI agents moved quickly. Some names were uncovered as the result of the confiscation of documents from the Japanese Chamber of Commerce in Los Angeles, which had lists of officers of Japanese organizations. After war was declared against Italy and Germany on December 11, suspected nationals from those countries were also taken into custody. Under wartime regulations, enemy aliens were not allowed to travel, to change residence without special permission, or to own firearms, bombs, explosives, short wave radios, devices which might be used for signaling, military maps, or cameras. The Japanese arrested were, for the most part, community leaders, businessmen, large-scale farm operators, who were officers in local Japanese associations. Implicating biographical data occasioned most of the arrests. Very few were actually enemy agents, but were suspected for past connections.

In the group of several hundred West Coast Japanese apprehended on December 7 was a eighty-year-old Issei from Pasadena who had served in the Japanese army in an earlier conflict with China. Another Issei detained in the first roundup fell under suspicion because he had withdrawn $10,000 from a Japanese bank in San Francisco several months before Pearl Harbor and deposited it in the Bank of America in nearby San Jose. He feared the outbreak of war and wanted to go back to Japan before it started. It was erroneously assumed that he and others knew in advance about the surprise attack. Subsequent evidence suggests that even the Japanese diplomatic personnel were not informed of their government's military coup, but at the time it was not surprising that American-based Japanese who had recently traveled to or had close business contacts in Japan should be suspected of having been fore-warned. Another of those first arrested was Seiichi Nakahara, a ship chandler in San Pedro. He was under suspicion because of his business connections. He supplied Japanese ships and had visited Japan in 1940. Other incriminating facts about him were his interest in short wave radios and his having recently received a telegram from Ambassador Nomura, who came from the same small town in Japan, as the latter passed through San Francisco en route to Washington for the peace talks with Hull.

Nakahara was detained with a group from Terminal Island in San Pedro Harbor where five hundred Japanese fishermen and their fami-lies lived in what had long been considered dangerous proximity to a United States naval base. As the Terminal Islanders crossed by ferry to the mainland on December 7, they were halted by Justice Department officials and put in a wire enclosure. Most of them were then taken to a detention center at Tujunga in the San Fernando Valley. Within hours after the attack on Pearl Harbor, the FBI also descended upon Guada-lupe, a small farming community in the Santa Maria Valley, which had a self-contained Japanese settlement living apart from the Mexican and "Anglo" families. A Nisei remembers, "Swiftly, silently, they sealed off the town, cut telephone lines to Japanese homes and spirited off a score of Japanese leaders. They left as swiftly and as mysteriously as they had come, leaving behind a stunned community." Many of the Issei group in Guadalupe were unabashedly pro-Japanese. When they heard the news of Pearl Harbor, "the men gathered at the farmers' association meeting house and cheered." One of the arrested Issei leaders wrote a farewell letter to his family from his jail cell, since he expected to be executed. "That he was soon removed to an Army camp where he re-ceived good treatment was one of the few pleasant surprises the white man had given him during the 40 years he had been in the United States."[5]

A few Nisei were also taken into custody. Togo Tanaka, the young editor of the English section of *Rafu Shimpo*, a bilingual Los Angeles newspaper, was served with a "presidential warrant" on December 8 and spent over a week in jail undergoing "some questioning by the FBI, mugging, finger-printing, mostly fraternizing with lots of familiar Issei." He had been sent to Washington in October by the *Rafu*'s publisher to ask the Attorney General, Francis Biddle, to allow the paper to continue publication after the war with Japan broke out. Biddle wanted to know how Tanaka knew that war was coming. Tanaka answered, *"Everybody* knows that."

In the G-2 section of the War Department Tanaka was shown slides of the *Rafu*'s English section, with his own "flag-waving, patriotic editorials on behalf of the Stars and Stripes . . . surrounded by the most ferocious fire-eating Tokyo dispatches in the Japanese language. . . . The contradictory editorials in the same issues floored me momentarily." On returning to Southern California he made a speech before a service club in Orange County two or three days before Pearl Harbor. This speech was covered by a local newspaper which inferred in its report that a Japanese editor predicted the outbreak of war. "In view of these circumstances, it probably isn't too surprising that I should have been arrested." After eleven days of incarceration he was released without explanation on thirty minutes notice.

The FBI arrests were largely precautionary and were accepted with the early blackouts and the air raid instructions as a necessity imposed by the emergency. On the Pacific coast the mood was extremely tense. On December 8 Mayor Fiorello La Guardia of New York City and Mrs. Eleanor Roosevelt, chairman and vice-chairman of the National Civilian Defense Council, flew west and in Los Angeles, San Francisco, and Seattle warned citizens to be prepared for the unexpected. "The situation in the Pacific is serious. It's bad, very bad," cautioned La Guardia. An invasion of the West Coast by the Japanese forces was considered not inconceivable as evidenced by the evacuation of Fort Ord and of forty miles of coastline near Santa Cruz, California, which was for a brief time cleared of all civilian residents.

On December 8 came a report, later discounted, of Japanese planes sighted one hundred miles west of San Francisco. Lt. General John L. DeWitt, commander of the Fourth Army, and military chief of the West Coast area (Western Defense Command), met with San Francisco civic leaders on December 9 and in angry tones castigated them for failing to take the situation seriously. "You people do not seem to realize we are at war," he stormed. "So get this: last night there were planes over this community. They were enemy planes. I mean Japanese planes. And they were tracked out to sea." Predicting a bombing attack, he advised those who "couldn't take it" to "get the hell out now, before it comes. . . . And remember, we're fighting the Japanese, who don't respect the laws of war. They're gangsters and they must be treated as such." Raising his voice almost to a shout, he suggested it might have been "a good thing" if the enemy had dropped some bombs. "It might have awakened some of the fools in this community who refuse to realize this is a war."[6]

On December 10 a treasury agent in San Francisco reported to the

Army that "an estimated 20,000 Japanese in the San Francisco metropolitan area were ready for organized action." At that time the city had a Japanese-ancestry population of approximately five thousand. The local FBI chief scoffed at the alarm, but an Army officer sent the report to Washington with a recommendation that "plans be made for large-scale internment" of aliens, and it was forwarded to the Provost Marshal General, Major-General Allen W. Gullion.[7] Carey McWilliams, who was then California Commissioner of Immigration and Housing, wrote that the crisis of December 7 "had the momentary effect of paralyzing public opinion on the west coast,"[8] but this incident shows that some of the military men were jittery enough to be thrown into panic by an implausible prediction.

Joseph W. (Vinegar Joe) Stilwell, who was then a major serving under DeWitt, made pungent comments in his diary on the atmosphere of hysteria in the Western Defense Command:

> Dec. 8 Sunday night "air raid" at San Francisco. . . . Fourth Army kind of jittery.
> Dec. 9 Fleet of thirty-four [Japanese] ships between San Francisco and Los Angeles. Later—not authentic. . . .
> Dec. 11 (Phone call from 4th Army) "The main Japanese battle fleet is 164 miles off San Francisco." I believed it, like a damn fool. . . .
> Dec. 13 Not content with the above blah, [the 4th] Army pulled another at ten-thirty today. "Reliable information that attack on Los Angeles is imminent. A general alarm being considered." . . . What jackass would sound a general alarm under the circumstances? The [4th] Army G–2 is just another amateur, like all the rest of the staff. Rule: the higher the headquarters, the more important is *calm*.[9]

In spite of the furor during the first weeks after Pearl Harbor, a climate of tolerance toward Issei and Nisei persisted. Officials were willing to comply with Biddle's directive that they should "take no direct action against the Japanese in their communities, but should consult with the FBI." The American Japanese may have remembered Mrs. Roosevelt's words, written with the authorization of the Justice and State departments just before the outbreak of the war: "I see absolutely no reason why anyone who has had a good record—that is, who has no criminal nor anti-American record—should have any anxiety about his position. This is equally applicable to the Japanese who cannot become citizens but have lived here for thirty or forty years and to those newcomers [refugees from Hitler's Germany] who have not yet had time to become citizens."[10] California's governor, Culbert Olson, spoke of action which should be taken to alleviate any tension in the situation created by the Japanese residents. He said that steps should be taken to prevent misunderstanding and injustice in reference to law-abiding Japanese here.[11]

Whatever their feelings of shame or fear, most American Japanese went on with their daily lives in the weeks following Pearl Harbor. Mrs. Fuji Takaichi, whose family ran an art goods store in San Jose remembers, "My brother opened the store as usual on Monday and nothing happened. Friends came around and that sort of thing. I was working for the County at the time. I was told on the Q.T. to avoid one supervisor because he had suddenly become very anti-Japanese, a super-patriot. Before the war he used to chuck me under the chin in the elevator. I guess I was about the only Japanese employee at that time; so they didn't want me to remind him that I was around. But I didn't lose my job or anything like that. . . ."

Dave Tatsuno operated a store in San Francisco which was closed temporarily a week after Pearl Harbor. "We were still hoping to salvage some holiday business. We did write to different wholesalers and asked for permission to send some goods back because of Pearl Harbor. . . . They said they would let us do so. . . . People were pretty well-behaved in San Francisco in spite of war hysteria."

In San Carlos, twenty-five miles south of San Francisco, Robert and Teiko Wada were not so fortunate. The Wadas operated a gas station and a fruit stand. On December 8 someone threw a rock through their window. About three-quarters of their Caucasian customers deserted them. Later, many told them they were sorry. They had been afraid of what the neighbors would say if they traded at a Japanese store. But the Wadas considered themselves to be Americans. The cleaning establishment owned by Kathleen Sonoda's employer in Seattle lost a lot of good customers. "I think they were afraid of us. I think it wasn't so much a matter of prejudice. I think they didn't know what to do themselves."

Yasuo William Abiko was the editor of the English section of the *Nichi Bei*, a newspaper started by his father in San Francisco in 1898. At the time of World War II the offices were on Ellis Street with a dormitory above them for the staff, which was large because the Japanese type was hand-set. When Abiko came to work on the morning of December 8, he found a coast guardsman standing by the front door. He was not allowed in the building, and the Japanese on the top floor were not allowed to come out for several days. Fortunately, they had an adequate food supply. The paper resumed publication on Christmas Day and continued to appear daily until May 15, 1942, five days before Abiko was evacuated.

Financial restrictions were imposed on the Issei in the first week of the war. When Japan invaded Indo-China the preceding July, President Roosevelt had issued an executive order freezing Japanese assets in the United States, a measure that brought all import and export trade transactions in which Japanese interests were involved under American control. On December 8 the Secretary of the Treasury ordered the impounding of the $131 million Japan had invested in the United States. The Japanese government, in turn, took over American banks in Japan. The Treasury Department also closed shipping companies operating between the two countries, revoked Issei business licenses, and blocked Issei bank accounts.

After four days, making a distinction between transactions that fell under the Trading with the Enemy Act and business conducted entirely on American soil, the Department unblocked bank accounts to the extent of allowing Issei to withdraw $100 a month for living expenses and also allowed alien truck farmers to sell their produce. By the fifteenth of December, except for banks and steamship companies which remained closed, the initial restrictions were substantially modified. However, Issei fishermen were not allowed to go out in their boats, nor were their wives allowed to work in the canneries. Alien Italian fishermen, on the other hand, were not thus restricted.

On that first Monday after Pearl Harbor, Nisei children went to school as usual. The superintendent of the Los Angeles schools commented that "the spirit was excellent. The children are Americans and we do owe them a square deal."[12] A short time later, Louis Fischer, in a report from the West Coast, wrote, "In Seattle, I saw a girls' school going on an excursion and smiling Japanese children were walking hand-in-hand and arm-in-arm with American children. Teachers and children in liberal Pasadena and Seattle told me that the Japanese students were often brilliant and always loyal. . . . The public is not showing hate or spite."[13]

This was true—with some exceptions. Masao Hamamura remembers that in Gonzales "some of the kids stayed home, but I went to school Monday, and we all went to the auditorium and heard President Roosevelt's speech declaring war." The next day in his home room class a Caucasian football player precipitated a fight by taking away his chair, saying, "I don't give up no chair to no Jap," while the teacher stood by, speechless. After inflicting black eyes and bloody noses on each other they were separated outside by the president of the junior class, a good friend of Hamamura's. "I think I would have killed him if they hadn't stopped me." The following day a Filipino boy pushed a knife against his back when he was sitting in another classroom. Again they were separated by a student officer while the teacher stood by. "He just stood there. I don't understand why. It was more of a shock to me than what the boys did." After the war, the Filipino boy sought him out to make friends with him. The feeling of some Filipinos, particularly in the Salinas area, was strongly anti-Japanese, but this was sometimes offset by individual acts of friendship and loyalty.

The faculty and student bodies of most West Coast colleges were markedly sympathetic toward the American Japanese on their campuses. The story is told that when Professor Yamato Ichihashi, a popular member of the History Department at Stanford, peered around the door of his classroom on December 8 and asked, "Shall I come in?", his students applauded. The International House on the Berkeley campus offered assistance to 315 Nisei students affected by a temporary travel ban. At San Jose State College the administration and faculty called together a student assembly at noon on December 8 to reassure Nisei students that they were welcome at the college and to enlist the sympathy of their Caucasian classmates. By December 11 the college had provided identification badges for 106 commuting Nisei students, and later a Japanese students' club distributed information sheets on the wartime status of Issei and Nisei that they could take home to their parents.

A student at Santa Ana Junior College, wrote about his experiences. On December 7 he was chatting with fellow students at the YMCA when they heard about Pearl Harbor. "No one ever questioned my viewpoint. I was one of them. We talked of 'those d— Japs' all day long. Monday I found out that a father of one of the Nisei had been taken away. I became a bit scared. Cutting class, I hitchhiked 40 miles to see my parents who were still there. With relief, I immediately 'thumbed' back to Santa Ana. Although three called me a Jap, the sympathy expressed by others more than made up for the slights. My anxious jaycee friends were glad to hear that my folks were still at home."[14]

An editorial in the Portland *Oregonian* of December 16 ran, "It should be our privilege as it is our duty to demonstrate to these young Americans in truth, as in theory, the democracy of which they were taught in our public schools. Here for our part is an opportunity to demonstrate that democracy really works—the rest is up to them."

The Nisei had accepted the challenge. Suburo Kido, national president of the Japanese American Citizens League, called an organization meeting immediately after Pearl Harbor and sent the following telegram to President Roosevelt:

> The Japanese Americans are stunned and horrified at this morning's unwarranted attack by Japan upon American soil, our country.
>
> We want to convey to you that we unequivocally condemn Japan for this unprecedented breach of good faith.
>
> In behalf of our 15,000 members in the 56 chapters of our Japanese American Citizens League, we unreservedly volunteer the facilities of our office to the defense of our land against this attack.
>
> In this solemn hour we pledge our fullest cooperation to you, Mr. President, and to our country.
>
> We appreciate the efforts you have made to preserve peace in the Pacific, but now that Japan has instituted this attack upon our land, we are ready and prepared to expend every effort to repel this invasion together with our fellow Americans.

Immediately American Japanese threw themselves wholeheartedly into the war effort. They bought defense bonds. They donated to the Red Cross. Two hundred Nisei in Seattle signed up for civil defense work. Nine radio operators from the tuna fleet in San Diego quit their jobs "so that there would be no suspicion of their integrity and loyalty to this country" and volunteered their services with the hope that "their knowledge of Pacific Coast waters and their ability to handle short-wave equipment might be of value to the United States" in its war with Japan.[15]

The West Coast Japanese were uncomfortably conscious of their racial and ethnic ties with the enemy and began to destroy what seemed, at the time, incriminating evidence against them. A Nisei mother in Santa Barbara asked to have a Japanese dance number in which her daughter was to appear canceled from a school program. "At this unhappy time," she said, "I'd like to keep all things Japanese as foreign to my children as is humanly possible."[16] Another woman remembers her anguish as a young wife when she and her husband destroyed their Buddhist family shrine. Some families burned ceremonial dolls and Japanese language books. A few buried money. Others gave their traditional costumes to the keeping of trusted Caucasian friends. A Nisei threw his souvenir samurai swords into the San Joaquin River.

There was some fear among the Japanese of going out into public places where they ran the risk of curious or hostile stares. Frank Bunya was riding home from school on a bus in Seattle when two men sitting behind two Nisei girls began to make loud derogatory remarks about them. "I was getting mad, but I couldn't do anything. Then when the bus stopped I had a sudden impulse. I took my school books and bashed them down on top of one of the men's heads and ran out the door. I could tell by the way he looked out the window that he wanted to catch me, but he couldn't. The bus had started off already." Some of the other Asians wore identity buttons proclaiming, "I am Chinese" or "I am Filipino." *Life* magazine ran an article in its December 22 issue, "How to tell Japs from the Chinese." The faces portrayed were those of a benevolent Chinese public servant, Ong Wen-hao, and a Japanese warrior, General Hideki Tojo. After discussing physiological differences, the article concluded, "An often sounder clue is facial expression, shaped by cultural, not anthropological, factors. Chinese wear rational calm of tolerant realists. Japs, like General Tojo, show humorless intensity of ruthless mystics." Little wonder that some Japanese were reported to be wearing "I am Chinese" buttons.

The New York Times published a commentary on this question in the column "Topics of the Times" also on December 22. The writer urged, "It is the uniqueness of the individual that makes one hope democracy can take hold east of Suez and west of Midway. . . . Meanwhile many of us may continue to have difficulty distinguishing between our Chinese friends and our Japanese antagonists. The best solution for that problem is to behave courteously to any law-abiding foreigner, whatever the slant of his eyes. It is the slant of the heart that counts—and that is no matter for offhand judgment."

A few instances were cited in the newspapers of Nisei children denouncing their parents as pro-Axis. Such open rebellion did not seem to fit a cultural group which placed strong emphasis on filial piety. In fact, one argument used later by the proponents of evacuation was that the Japanese community groups were so closely knit that one member would never inform on another. One of General DeWitt's top aides claimed that the Nisei had offered no data on pro-Japan sympathizers whereas a naval intelligence officer insisted that individuals had given valuable information. Some of the Issei felt that their sons were anxious to curry favor with the Caucasian authorities by disassociating themselves with their parents. A Nisei editor later accused his contemporaries of not defending their alien fathers interned by the FBI, thereby casting suspicion on them.[17] In general, however, whether or not they agreed politically and however widely divergent their attitudes about defending their liberties (for the Issei tended to submit and the Nisei to exercise their American-inculcated right to dissent) the younger generation sympathized with their parents in their time of trouble.

The mother of a Seattle-born Nisei had a brief nervous breakdown. The strain of the war added to years of overwork was too much for her. Her husband had died when her youngest child was six months old and she had run a residential hotel and worked in a restaurant while raising a family of five. Her son recalls, "It only lasted a few days, but she thought she was going to die, and she made us all promise we would make a trip back to Japan."

In Los Angeles three Issei committed suicide on account of the war. One of them, a sixty-seven-year-old retired cook who had lived forty-five years in the United States, said before he took his life, "I don't want to live any more since Japan has attacked this country, her friend. . . . I am a registered Japanese alien and I am ashamed."[18]

But these were isolated cases. The Japanese group as a whole, long accustomed to carrying on their lives in the face of discrimination, met the new difficulties with fortitude. Japanese farming and truck gardening, the most important occupations for the Issei, suffered a setback because of the war. Japanese growers supplied a considerable quantity of the fresh vegetables consumed in California and southern Washington. Japanese were also engaged in wholesale and retail produce selling, with some one thousand markets in the Los Angeles area alone doing a $25 million a year business in 1941.

After the first Treasury Department bans were lifted aliens resumed the management of their farming and produce businesses, but since there continued to be talk of farms being put in charge of an Alien Property Custodian some Issei entrepreneurs transferred their businesses at least on paper to the control of Nisei sons, a practice that had been going on for some time before the war to circumvent the alien land laws. In the first month after Pearl Harbor, business losses in the Japanese community were heavy. Profits were down more than 50 per cent over the previous year. Retail trade declined sharply.[19] Many insurance companies canceled their policies for Issei and marked up their premiums for Nisei. An insurance executive explained that his company "felt that Japanese, in view of the current affairs, were worthless risks." Another executive reported that the companies expected damage claims against the Japanese to go sky-high from injustice in the courts, from hooliganism, and other hazards.

Despite these ominous predictions, the atmosphere of tolerance that prevailed in the opening weeks of the war was marred by only occasional incidents of violence. George Shimada, fighting in a Golden Gloves championship in Seattle shortly after the outbreak of war feared he might be in for trouble when, as he stepped into the ring, a spectator yelled, *"Kill that Jap."* But the heckler was subdued. On December 12, a Chinese, presumably mistaken for a Japanese, was murdered in a particularly gruesome way and left on a street in Seattle's waterfront district. On December 27 there was a riot in Stockton, California, between Japanese and Filipinos who were angered by Japan's invasion of the Philippines. On January 1, thirteen bullets were fired into the Gilroy, California, home of Kazuo Ouchida, an incident which brought a protest from the Tokyo government. Attorney General Biddle reported thirty-six instances of crime and brutality against the West Coast Japanese between December 8, 1941 and March 31, 1942: "a sorry story of violence, but not one that told any tale of vigilante action. Seven killings in four months were not an indication that the entire Japanese population was 'going to be massacred,' as someone wrote to his congressman."[20]

Japanese, German, and Italian aliens continued to be arrested and held by the Justice Department. About 6,000 American Japanese, or 12.5 per cent of the Issei group, were apprehended. They were allowed a hearing before a civilian parole board at which they could be represented by a friend or a relative but not a lawyer. Eventually about ninety of these boards were set up under the direction of Edward J. Ennis, who had been named by the Attorney General to head the national enemy alien control program. Mr. Biddle wrote, "In all, about 16,000 were arrested . . . of whom 1,200 were German and Italian seamen. Only about one-third were interned, nearly half of them Germans, and the rest were paroled, released, or (in a few instances) repatriated."[21] Aliens who were detained were sent to internment camps in the middle west.

Fear but not general resentment was created among the West Coast Japanese by the FBI raids. When a leader of the Japanese colony in Redwood City, California, was arrested, his son, a Stanford graduate, said he realized it was the "proper procedure" during such a time of crisis.

Seiichi Nakahara was questioned so constantly that he did not recognize his son, Peter, when he came to visit. He thought Peter was an imposter trying to get information from him. When he was asked about his loyalty, Mr. Nakahara had answered frankly, "Of course, I am a Japanese citizen. My sympathies are with Japan, but my children are American citizens." In spite of this avowal he was cleared as a security risk and released, but gravely ill from stomach ulcers, he died a few days later.

The Japanese were confused because they could not understand why some Issei should fall under FBI suspicion while others were ignored. Often, those arrested had lived in Japan, had made a recent trip, or had close connections there. Some language school teachers, including women, were arrested. Leadership in the Buddhist or Shinto church was considered damaging. When Herbert Nicholson, a former Quaker missionary to Japan, and Floyd Schmoe, also a Quaker, traveled up the coast from Los Angeles to Seattle visiting Japanese homes where the fathers were in custody, they found frightened Buddhist priests hiding in their churches.

I. K. Ishimatsu, a busy San Jose grower, was active in the local Japanese Association in which he once held the office of treasurer. "Fortunately, I had many Caucasian contacts in the community at large such as officials, etc., who vouched for me." He was questioned many times by the FBI, particularly after he, along with others, formed a Japanese protective association against vigilantism and shootings with the blessing of the Santa Clara County sheriff. "This association was under suspicion by the FBI and many of us were called in for questioning. I had to explain over and over again that our organization was not to work against the U.S. or help the Japanese government as they seem to have suspected; that it was simply to help each other when an emergency occurred. This organization started after the wife of one prominent farmer in Coyote was shot in the chest in broad daylight and also there was a rumor that certain Japanese farms were attacked and there was a feeling among our community, 'Who's next?'

"The FBI refused to recognize our association, saying, 'if you need protection come to us, we can furnish you with the army,' and probably some of my friends were arrested by them for this but I was not arrested." Nor was a leading newspaperman in Portland, Oregon, who was convinced he did not have anything to worry about because he never belonged to any organizations. His daughter remembers he would go downtown when they were picking up people right and left and sending them to the Justice Department camp in Santa Fe, New Mexico, and he would come home every night.

The FBI visited the Sacramento home of another Issei newspaperman, Soichi Nakatani, one day when he was away in Stockton. The agents stayed at his house from 9 A.M. to 3 P.M. asking his wife questions and detaining anyone who came to the door. After a thorough search, they confiscated a toy sword, a picture of his brother in a Japanese army uniform, a portrait of General Tojo, and a children's book with pictures of toy soldiers. When Mr. Nakatani returned, he was arrested. He was suspected because he had invested his money with Japanese banks.

Actually, the Justice Department had established three categories for judging Japanese aliens: "A" (leadership, or in some cases, membership in Japanese organizations) to "C" which included individuals who had made a donation to a national cultural society. But these classifications were not, naturally, known to the Issei, many of whom lived in constant fear of being suddenly taken away. Monica Sone tells how her mother, frightened by the disappearance of her friends' husbands from their waterfront district in Seattle, packed a small bag with a change of clothes and toilet articles for her husband and kept it ready by the front door. But the knock they dreaded never came.[22]

The raids on suspicious aliens and the uncovering of contraband articles sometimes had pathetic and ludicrous aspects. In Mountain View, California, an old man over seventy, deaf and half-blind, was discovered in possession of a radio and some searchlights that were used on a tractor for night plowing. After deliberation, the officials decided he was harmless and "too infirm to plot anything."[23]

Helen Mineta, a teacher in San Jose, remembers that there were various stories as to what the FBI had used as evidence to pick people up. A lantern was considered to be contraband since it could be turned off and on as a signal. Knives with blades over six inches long were forbidden. A Japanese *sashimi* knife, used for cutting raw fish, has a blade about twelve inches long. "We had friends take care of ours. What a gift to give to friends! The man next door was apprehended with a flashlight and a boy scout knife. . . . We had bought flashlights to take to camp with us so when he was arrested my mother was particularly perturbed because we had misplaced the flashlights. Rumors were rife and there was a great deal of hysteria. It was felt that perhaps certain Japanese were marked for detention and the contraband items used as evidence were only excuses." The father in another family threw his automatic pistol into the outhouse and chopped up a brand new short wave radio, throwing the pieces into a canyon.

The Justice Department reported that during this period officers seized from enemy aliens a total of 2,592 guns, 199,000 rounds of ammunition, 1,652 sticks of dynamite, 1,458 radio receivers, 2,914 cameras, and 37 motion picture cameras. The Attorney General added: "We have not, however, uncovered through these searches any dangerous persons that we could not otherwise know about. We have not found among all the sticks of dynamite and gun powder any evidence that any of it was to be used in bombs. . . . We have not found a camera which we have reason to believe was for use in espionage."[24] The Army chief historian, Stetson Conn, has declared that, "In fact, no proved instances of sabotage or of espionage after Pearl Harbor among the west coast Japanese population were ever uncovered."[25]

In all probability, espionage was carried out by staff members of the Japanese consulates before the war. A list of the Japanese agents in the United States was found in June, 1941, in the Los Angeles apartment of a lieutenant commander in the Japanese Navy who was charged with conspiracy to obtain information for a foreign power. The consul posted bail for him. The consulates also served to strengthen ties between the disenfranchised Issei and the home country. In the late thirties, emissaries from Tokyo organized financial support among the Issei for Japan's war against China through such organizations as the Military Virtue Society and the Japanese Military Service Men's League. Many Issei said they wanted Japan to win the war, but they did not want the United States harmed. After all, their children were Americans. Some Issei would have gone into combat against Japanese invaders if they had landed on the West Coast. The Nisei who acknowledge pro-Japanese loyalty in their parents add that whatever their feelings, they would not have done anything subversive. Lieutenant Commander K. D. Ringle, a naval intelligence officer thoroughly familiar with the security problem on the West Coast, in an anonymous article in *Harper's* in October, 1942, estimated the potential saboteurs to be fewer than 3 per cent of the total Japanese-ancestry population.[26] The salient fact is that no resident Japanese, either in Hawaii or on the mainland, was convicted of being an unregistered agent of the government in Tokyo nor of having engaged in espionage activities. The Japanese agents were rather Caucasian Americans. Two were convicted before the outbreak of the war and at least three others were indicted later.

In his article Ringle urged a course of action that had already been supplanted—handling the Japanese problem "on the basis of the *individual*, regardless of citizenship, and *not* on a racial basis." This was essentially the method of the Justice Department while it was charged with the responsibility of keeping surveillance over the West Coast Japanese. If arrests resulted in inequities and hardships, it can be argued that during the sudden war crisis with the necessity for improvisation im-

posed upon bureaucratic procedures errors were inevitable. These precautionary arrests were probably justified by the gravity of the United
States' position in the Pacific. What is important is that individual Japanese, Germans, and Italians were given a fair hearing. They had a
chance to present their cases before civilian judges, and the majority of
them were exonerated and released.

It was during the next period when the handling of the Japanese
problem was transferred to the War Department that there occurred
the unprecedented abrogation of the civil rights of a racial minority. By
the time Lieutenant Commander Ringle's article appeared, there was no
longer in our national policy toward the West Coast Japanese any consideration of individuals, whether innocent or guilty, citizen or alien.
They were all subject to the control of the Western Defense Command.

In the first weeks of the war General DeWitt was satisfied to leave the
enemy alien problem in the hands of the Justice Department. Early in
January he told James Rowe, Jr., assistant to the Attorney General, that
any proposal for mass evacuation of the Japanese from the West Coast
was "damned nonsense."[27] General Gullion, the Provost Marshal General, began to press to have the alien program transferred to the War
Department and proposed eventually that the entire West Coast Japanese
population be moved inland. In a telephone conversation on December
26, DeWitt, who later was to stigmatize the Japanese–American group
with the oft-quoted indictment, "A Jap's a Jap. . . . You can't change
him by giving him a piece of paper,"[28] said to General Gullion, who at
the time expressed agreement, "An American citizen, after all, is an
American citizen. And while they all may not be loyal, I think we can
weed the disloyal out of the loyal and lock them up if necessary."[29]

General Gullion's representative at a West Coast conference on enemy
aliens early in January was Major (later Colonel) Karl R. Bendetsen,
the War Department's chief of Aliens Division, who would eventually
direct the evacuation. Bendetsen was, in the words of an observer, a
"remarkable young man . . . quietly compelling, his command of facts
and English so distinguished that without apparent effort he swung his
audience to his purpose."[30] The Justice Department's James Rowe, Jr.,
who was in San Francisco for this "on the ground" planning conference
agreed to General DeWitt's recommendations for a more stringent alien
control program. The head of the Western Defense Command was
irked by the fact that not until December 29 were enemy aliens within
his jurisdiction required by the Justice Department to surrender the
contraband articles prohibited by the presidential proclamations of December 7 and 8. General DeWitt wanted large-scale contraband raids, a
complete registration of enemy aliens, and the establishment of restricted
areas near defense installations from which they would be removed.
There was a conflict between General DeWitt and Mr. Rowe on "spot

raids" versus "mass raids," the latter considered unfeasible by the Justice Department. General DeWitt was also concerned with "what methods exist or what steps are in contemplation looking toward the control of (1) dual citizens, (2) disloyal, subversive citizens (where there has been no overt act detected)."[31]

The official and unofficial concern was with the Japanese population. A West Coast observer assessed the situation two months later, "Californians don't bother much about the German and Italian question,"[32] even though, according to Professor Conn, "there was a greater proportionate concentration of German and Italian aliens near strategic points than there was of Japanese."[33] An estimated 80,000 German and Italian aliens lived on the West Coast in 1940. Members of the Italian group had become wealthy and influential. The average age of the other aliens was sixty, and their average period of residence in the United States was twenty-five years. Under the Second War Powers Act, the Justice Department launched a program to naturalize aliens, but under existing laws, the Japanese were ineligible. In the West Coast hysteria that led to the evacuation, the Japanese, both aliens and citizens, were lumped together in a general racial indictment. German and Italian aliens were rarely mentioned, though DeWitt originally intended to remove *all* enemy aliens from a designated coastal area.

There is a hint of the furor to come against Nisei as well as Issei in the general's memorandum to Mr. Rowe on "disloyal, subversive citizens" which was written on January 5. Soon afterward feeling on the West Coast against the Japanese began to rise.

A still vivid sense of outrage over Japan's attack on Pearl Harbor was kept alive by the continued Allied reverses in the Pacific. The Japanese conquest of Guam, Wake Island, Malaya, and the Philippines, the Death March on Bataan, the fall of Hong Kong and Singapore crowded the headlines and added to the vague but potent fear that the enemy would come all the way to California. *Life* magazine described the mood in early January:

> Like characters in a tremendous and terrible mystery story the people of the United States Pacific Coast last week waited for SOMETHING. They didn't know what. They feared almost anything. Maybe the Japanese would bomb San Francisco, Portland or Seattle. Maybe Jap planes would hedgehop up from hidden bases on the peninsula of Lower California, attack the airplane factories of San Diego and Los Angeles. Maybe there would even be an enemy landing somewhere on the 1,300 mile coastline from Puget Sound to Mexico.[34]

However highly colored, this summary suggests some of the possibilities for enemy attack that were seriously considered by the defenders of the Pacific coast. The Western Hemisphere nations had either declared war or broken off diplomatic relations with the Axis powers. The Mexican government had removed the Japanese living in Baja California, to the mainland and sent troops to the Coast to guard against raiding attacks. The United States and Mexico were jointly patrolling an area from the Panama Canal to the Rio Grande looking for enemy submarine bases. Japanese colonies in Columbia and Peru were put under surveillance, as were 22,274 persons of Japanese ancestry in British Columbia, the majority of whom were Canadian citizens. Initially, only 178 Japanese were interned as "dangerous aliens" by the Royal Canadian Mounted Police after December 7, but in February Canada began a mass evacuation program more severe than that of the United States.

The multilateral efforts at Pacific coast defense were spurred by the occasional appearance of enemy submarines. On December 24 one surfaced within sight of the shore off California and torpedoed a freighter. Four days later a high-powered Japanese radio station, in an apparent attempt to create panic among Americans in the Philippines, broke into a program carried from San Francisco to Manila with an announcement in excellent English that Pearl Harbor was being attacked for the second time. These were trivial incidents compared with the intensive submarine warfare in the Atlantic, but the disastrous British and American defeats in the Pacific made them seem ominous. It was not until after the Battle of Midway in early June, 1942, that the West Coast felt itself fully safe.

Because of a false alarm sounded by the Secretary of the Navy, Frank Knox, who visited Pearl Harbor early in the war, the belief was widespread that Quisling activities such as had accompanied the Nazi invasions in Europe had occurred in Hawaii where one-third of the population was of Japanese descent. Since Knox's statements were not immediately refuted, it was assumed that some of these 159,534 people had assisted Japan in her attack on the American fleet. Nor were these fears allayed by the publication on January 24 of the Roberts Commission Report on Pearl Harbor. In its allegations of negligence on the part of the American military leadership, the Roberts Commission, headed by Supreme Court Justice Owen J. Roberts, which had been sent to Hawaii by the President, stated that two hundred consular agents of Japan on Oahu had not been required to register, because the American Army wanted to foster friendly relations with Japanese resident aliens and American citizens of Japanese ancestry in Hawaii. The Army was accused of imposing restrictions that prevented effective counterespionage; for instance, the FBI which was charged with "controlling all forms of subversive activity among the civilian population" was not allowed to intercept messages between Japan and the Hawaiian Islands. The report stated that Japan had complete information about the position of ships and planes at Pearl Harbor. It did not directly accuse the resident Japanese of espionage but said that of those spying for Japan "some were consular agents and others were persons having no open relations with the Japanese foreign service." The FBI, the chief of police in Honolulu, and other authorities later cleared the resident Japanese of any involvement in espionage or sabotage, but this was after the American public had misconstrued the somewhat ambiguous wording in the Roberts report. What came through clearly to everyone who read it was that the military command at Pearl Harbor had been "negligent" and "complacent." These were words frequently used in the press at this time.

The lesson was immediately applied to the situation on the West Coast. In writing his book *Americans Betrayed,* Morton Grodzins studied the editorial and Letters-to-the-Editor columns of 112 California newspapers for the period from December 8, 1941 to March 8, 1942. Beginning with the week of January 25 public opinion changed markedly and continued to mount against the Japanese. As the group was increasingly identified with the enemy, the distinction between aliens and citizens was ignored. This shift in mood was not confined to California, nor even the West Coast. *The New York Times,* which had declared editorially on January 9, "Here [in America] we have next to no Japanese hyphenate problem," in early February implied that the Western Defense Command was well advised in its close surveillance of the American Japanese. There were mass arrests by the FBI on Terminal Island on February 1 when nearly all alien males were removed and on Salinas and Monterey on February 10. As the Japanese diplomats who had apparently been temporizing with Secretary of State Hull while their nation's planes attacked Pearl Harbor were held up as examples of duplicity, so, suddenly, were the residents of the West Coast's little Tokyos considered to be potentially, if not overtly, traitorous.

The solution of "the Japanese problem" in Hawaii presents an ironic contrast to what happened on the West Coast. The Islands were put under martial law after the attack on Pearl Harbor, "As the full extent of the catastrophe became known . . . soon all sorts of wild rumors ran about. Some said that on the bodies of the enemy fliers had been found McKinley High School rings. People muttered behind their hands that the little Jap tailor had been shot in the uniform of Hirohito's navy, that the water supply had been poisoned. . . ."[35] A "Morale Committee" was organized by Caucasian civilians to protect themselves against the Japanese. Some of the Filipino plantation workers murmured threats and sharpened their machete knives. But the new military commander, Lieutenant General Delos C. Emmons who replaced General Short stood firm and reassured the Japanese population that they had nothing to fear if they obeyed the law. He implemented his statement that "We must remember that this is America and we must do things the American way. . . . We must not knowingly and deliberately deny any loyal citizen the opportunity of exercising or demonstrating his loyalty in a concrete way."[36]

There continued to be demands locally and in Washington for evacuating the entire Japanese population of Hawaii. Roosevelt and Knox favored the removal of all persons of Japanese ancestry from Oahu, but John McCloy, the assistant Secretary of War, urged that this was impractical. The relative assimilation of the group, their numbers, and their strategic importance to the economy of the Islands have been cited as reasons for the fact that their evacuation was considered unnecessary and unfeasible even though they were located in the active war theater. Under General Emmons' command they were allowed as much freedom as the rest of the civilian population, nor were any untoward incidents, either by or against them, reported except for one dramatic defection immediately after Pearl Harbor. A Nisei assisted a Japanese pilot who landed his crippled plane on Niihau Island and afterwards shot himself to avoid capture by Hawaiians.

On the West Coast, by contrast, after the first six weeks of tolerance, old anti-Asiatic antipathies were revived in connection with the military danger. Professor Grodzins in *Americans Betrayed* clearly demonstrates his thesis that "many traditionally anti-Japanese individuals and organizations realized that the war with Japan presented a natural opportunity to further their long-term aims. At the first meeting of the California Joint Immigration Committee (an old anti-Japanese propaganda group), after Pearl Harbor, the executive secretary remarked: 'I know that the Committee has received more active and more general support in the last month than it has received in the last thirty years of its existence, and what we want, we ought to get now.' "[37] Groups of this persuasion were aided by the early inflammatory broadcasts of John B. Hughes, the radio commentator, who drew attention to the danger inherent in the colonies of American Japanese near defense installations. He and the other alarmists did not mention that it was their occupations that had placed them close to strategic areas, the fishermen near harbor defenses, the truck farmers next to power lines and railroad rights of way because their methods of intensive cultivation enabled them to use small parcels of land in odd and assorted places, rejected by others. Rumors sprang up and were magnified out of all proportion. Mysterious arrows were reported in Japanese-owned tomato fields, placed so as to guide the enemy to American air force bases. Drew Pearson, commenting on this sort of alarm, reported that in Hawaii, after the Japanese attack on Pearl Harbor, people laughed at the stories of " 'arrows cut in the cane fields' to point the way to the naval base and similar phony yarns," when "Pearl Harbor, with its many anchored warships, was the most conspicuous spot in the tiny island of Oahu."[38]

There was much talk of Japanese discovered, both in Hawaii and on the mainland, with searchlights on cliffs near the sea, presumably signaling enemy submarines. A letter from General Gullion to the Attorney General on January 25 reported that the military were worried about shore-to-ship and ship-to-shore radio communications on the West Coast, although, according to Professor Conn, " . . . careful investigation subsequently indicated that all claims of hostile shore-to-ship and ship-to-shore communication lacked any foundation whatsoever."[39]

The Dies Committee in Congress (the House Committee on Un-American Activities) was busy spreading distrust against the Japanese. The chairman, Martin Dies, a Texas Republican, took an "I told you so" attitude after Pearl Harbor, claiming that the government had muzzled him when he planned an August, 1941, exposé of Japanese espionage activities. He promised to make public a "Yellow Paper" disclosing a spy ring of 150,000 members. Citing the two hundred consular agents on Oahu, he claimed that the offices of the power and water companies in Los Angeles had been infiltrated by Nisei agents planted by the Japanese government. Japanese–Americans owned radios capable of communicating with Tokyo; therefore, they were members of a vast conspiratorial network. They were accused of printing and sending to Japan books with aerial photographs of San Francisco and Los Angeles. Dies predicted that the West Coast was in for "a tragedy that will make Pearl Harbor sink into insignificance."[40]

That the general public was susceptible to war hysteria is illustrated by an early incident in Portland. During the first blackout there, a man answered a command to open the door to his house. There stood a Nisei soldier in American uniform. The owner took one look at him and rushed back shouting to his family, "The invasion is here!" The reporter commented, "The fact that the soldier was an American and that he wore a U.S. Army uniform wasn't nearly as apparent at first glance as the fact that racially he was Japanese."[41]

General DeWitt at first had scruples about the legality of any action against American citizens. So had many others. But the pressure was mounting to treat all Japanese, citizen and alien, as an adjunct of the enemy. Why should they be tolerated when they might repay that tolerance with treachery? So the argument ran. By the end of January a number of columnists were calling for wholesale evacuation. One of the more virulent ones, Henry McLemore, wrote in the Los Angeles *Times* on January 29:

> I am for immediate removal of every Japanese on the West Coast to a point deep in the interior. . . . Sure, this would work an unjustified hardship on 80 per cent or 90 per cent of the California Japanese. But, the remaining 10 or 20 per cent have it in their power to do damage—great

damage to the American people. They are a serious menace and you can't tell me that an individual's rights have any business being placed above a nation's safety. If making 1,000,000 [sic] innocent Japanese uncomfortable would prevent one scheming Japanese from costing the life of an American boy, then let 1,000,000 innocents suffer. . . . Personally, I hate the Japanese. And that goes for all of them. Let's quit worrying about hurting the enemy's feelings and start doing it.

This sort of attack had been predicted just before the outbreak of the war by Ernest O. Hauser, who, while stating unequivocally, *"The overwhelming majority of young and old Japanese–Americans stand with the United States,"* wrote in the *American Mercury*:

Japanese Americans are on the spot and they know it. All along the Pacific Coast, where practically all of the 150,000 descendants of Nippon reside, they are gravely charged with plotting against the United States. Alarmist patriots have figured it all out: when the Pacific zero hour strikes, Japanese Americans will get busy at once. Their fishing boats will sow mines across the entrance of our ports. Mysterious blasts will destroy Navy shipyards and flying fields and part of our fleet. Oil wells, situated near inconspicuous plots where Japanese truck gardeners tend their tomatoes, will turn into blazing torches. Sierra passes and tunnels will be blocked. To add the final demoniacal touch, Japanese farmers, having a virtual monopoly of vegetable production in California, will send their peas and potatoes and squash full of arsenic to the markets, throwing the population into panic.[42]

Columnists and politicians were also discovering insidious implications in the concentrated populations of the "Little Tokyo's" on the West Coast. Los Angeles had a Japanese population of 23,321; San Francisco had 5,280 Japanese; Seattle, 6,975; Portland, 1,680; and Tacoma 877. Patriots denounced the Japanese language schools that had been closed immediately after Parl Harbor. They were suspicious of the Kibei (translated "returned to America," Nisei educated in Japan) and they were alarmed by the fact that numbers of the Nisei held dual citizenship. That there were normal explanations for all of these circumstances, that, for example, many immigrant people other than Japanese held dual citizenship, did not occur to everybody, and these aspects of Japanese life in America which had always been strange to the Caucasian majority, now began to seem definitely suspicious.

The increasing hostility was reflected in official action and reaction against the Japanese. Mayor Fletcher Bowron of Los Angeles, a reform candidate who had been supported by the residents of Little Tokyo, switched markedly from tolerance of the Japanese to antipathy in mid-January. After the Los Angeles County Board of Supervisors on January

27 unanimously adopted a resolution favoring the transfer of Japanese aliens inland and ordered the dismissal of fifty-six Nisei employed by the county, the mayor announced that he was removing thirty-nine Nisei from the city payrolls, adding, "The temporary separation of city employees of Japanese parentage from their employment should not be regarded as a serious or significant matter."[43] Mayor Rossi of San Francisco made a distinction between German and Italians, the great majority of whom, he said, were "peaceful, law-abiding, and in complete sympathy with our form of government," and the Japanese. " . . . every Japanese alien should be removed from this community. I am also strongly of the conviction that Japanese who are American citizens should be subjected to a more detailed and all-encompassing investigation."[44] Eventually, every West Coast mayor of a large city with the exception of Tacoma's mayor, Harry P. Cain, favored evacuation.

California's liberal Governor Olson also abandoned his early espousal of tolerance under the mounting pressure. The State Board of Equalization suspended liquor licenses held by persons of Japanese ancestry. The State Personnel Board filed dismissal charges against several hundred Nisei employees. The board's directive was to forbid them to take civil service examinations, to refuse to certify them for state employment from the eligible list, and to investigate those already employed. The intended suspension of employees of German and Italian ancestry drew a protest from Earl Warren, who was then the state attorney general. Though he was simultaneously urging mass evacuation of the Japanese, he strongly denounced the action of the State Personnel Board as not sanctioned by any provision of the Constitution nor by any law. He also denounced the governor's authorization to the State Department of Agriculture to revoke the licenses of enemy aliens handling produce, but he did not succeed in reversing either action.

In January, a Nisei truck gardener, unable to prove his claim of American citizenship, was denied the use of the courts in San Diego. A Japanese leader in Seattle was held for three weeks on charges of subversive activity. All his funds had been frozen and he asked to be allowed to pledge his property in lieu of cash for the $25,000 bail which had been set by the judge. His request was refused and he spent a month in jail while the government prepared its case.

A group in the California legislature proposed to investigate violations of alien land law statutes by Japanese farmers. "Why choose this time to raise questions of no more significance now than they have been all along when nothing was done about them?", asked Chester Rowell, the liberal political commentator of the San Francisco *Chronicle*,[45] but the issue was kept alive and became a rallying cry for politicians in the next elections. Ironically, the Nisei were thwarted in their desire to prove their loyalty by aiding national defense. They had never been accepted in the Navy and they were now not encouraged to enlist in the Army. Eventually they were for a time categorized 4C, *i.e.*, ineligible because of ancestry. A California state senator, John Swan, demanded that every American-born Japanese air raid warden be suspended. "No loyal American-born Japanese," he said, "will want to help in any capacity where a blunder may always be looked upon as treachery."[46] At the same time that the avenues for rendering wartime service as citizens were cut off, the Nisei were being told they must prove their loyalty. A February 7 Los Angeles *Times* headline read, "Olson tells Japanese here they must help or get out." The California governor, who two months before had pledged tolerance and fair play, now made the fence-sitting declaration that he was opposed to evacuation but would recommend it to the federal government unless the Japanese showed they were 100 per cent behind the country.

Laurence Hewes of the Farm Security Administration described what happened at a farm meeting in Berkeley early in the year:

> . . . someone proposed barring all persons of Japanese ancestry from Federal agricultural programs; this would mean that they would receive no gasoline, baling wire, fertilizer, or other farm necessities; it would also mean that Japanese farmers would receive no benefit from meeting crop quotas. Although I spoke vigorously against it, the idea persisted among my colleagues and it was plain that my position was detested. A friend drew me aside: "You'd better pull in your horns and go slow; this thing can't be stopped and you'll soon be so unpopular you can't hold a job. Look at the politicians—they're falling into line everywhere!"[47]

A number of influential citizens rallied to the defense of the Japanese, among them prominent clergymen and journalists. The rights of the Nisei as citizens were upheld by such organizations as the American Civil Liberties Union, the American Friends Service Committee, and the Northern California Committee on Fair Play for Citizens and Aliens of Japanese Ancestry, which had been organized early in October, 1941. Among the original members of this committee were Dr. Robert Gordon Sproul, president of the University of California, Dr. Ray Lyman Wilbur, president of Stanford, Dr. Robert Milliken of the California Institute of Technology, Dr. Henry Grady, Chester Rowell, and Galen Fisher. The Japanese badly needed such friends who saw them as people rather than as an enemy enclave. The secretary of the Japanese YMCA in San Francisco had pleaded, "We need reassurance, courage, humanity, leadership!"[48] But the supporting groups seem to have been lulled by the first post-Pearl Harbor tolerance and did not rally in time to be effective when the tide turned. Locally and nationally, their voices were drowned out by louder clamor of the pro-evacuation faction.

The strongest and earliest agitation, as mentioned earlier, came from organizations that had a long history of anti-Japanese bias, such as the American Legion, the Native Sons and Daughters of the Golden West, the California Farm Bureau Federation, the California Joint Immigration Committee, the Western Growers Protective Association, and the Grower-Shipper Vegetable Association. Ironically, the American Legion had Nisei members who had fought in World War I, and some Japanese businessmen had joined the large farm entrepreneur organizations. An eastern observer commented, " . . . the reactionary politicians are out for blood and wholesale internment. Jingoes are endeavoring, under the cover of war-time flag-waving patriotism, to do what they always wanted to do in peacetime: get rid of the Japanese."[49]

Some of their competitors in the economic field openly admitted this. A representative of the Grower-Shipper Association of Salinas, lobbying in Washington for mass evacuation of the Japanese, said, "We're charged with wanting to get rid of the Japs for selfish reasons. We might as well be honest. We do. It's a question of whether the white man lives on the Pacific Coast or the brown men. They came into this valley to work, and they stayed to take over."[50] Later, the president of the Washington Produce Shippers Association, a cooperative of Caucasian and Japanese farmers, was to testify before the Tolan Committee on Defense Migration which met on the West Coast in late February and March, "I receive in the mail every day now, from these people in California, considerable volumes of propaganda on this point, seeking evacuation for commercial reasons."[51] The agitation was strongest in California but existed in the other Pacific coast states as well. Another witness before the Tolan Committee from Yakima, Washington, declared, "The great cry of 'kick the Japanese out of the Yakima Valley' is not due to fear of sabotage; it is due to economic reasons."[52]

The agitation against the Japanese promoted by their competitors and long-time detractors and fanned by newspaper columnists and radio commentators, spread like fire to West Coast congressmen and senators, both liberal and conservative. Senator Hiram Johnson, a venerable California reformer as well as a long-time anti-Japanese spokesman, headed the West Coast congressional delegation which urged the President to order the evacuation. "We are not in a position to look upon the situation with equanimity," he warned. "We cannot do so on the west coast. In the first place we have 130,000 Japanese, 30,000 of whom are citizens." Actually, the figure was approximately 112,000, of whom 71,484 were citizens. California's attorney general, Earl Warren, emphasized the danger of sabotage. The very fact that there had been none convinced him that the West Coast Japanese population was waiting for a signal from the enemy to go into action. At a meeting on February 2 he said, "It seems to me that it is quite significant that in this great state of ours we have had no fifth-column activities and no sabotage reported. . . . That was the history of Pearl Harbor. I can't help believing that the same thing is planned for us in California."[53] The mayor of Portland echoed this alarm, "I believe . . . that the only reason the fifth columnists haven't struck so far is because their respective governments haven't given them the go-ahead."[54] Among the few West Coast men in Congress who opposed evacuation were Senator Sheridan Downey of California and Representatives Jerry Voorhis of California and John Coffee of Washington. It is not surprising that General DeWitt, after talking to Governor Olson and others on January 27, was impressed by the weight of public opinion against the Japanese among what he termed the "best" people.

A western correspondent, John Bruce, writing in *The New York Times* after the evacuation order, conveyed some of the emotion that led the politicians, in the name of national defense, to press for it. "Californians are mad through and through, mad at the Japanese, that goes without saying. . . . We are part of the battlefront now. . . . We look across the Pacific as before, but there's a steelier glint in our eye and our carelessly welcoming, glad-hand smile has vanished. We were right, but what did it get us? We're kind of a dangerous people right now." He explains the antipathy: "We saw whole straw-hatted families laboring in the fields, women and children and grandmothers, saving patiently for the acre of rich loam which their peonage would buy vicariously; we saw them satisfied with the family pot of rice and the shack in the melon fields. We made their children go to school, but we felt that behind a façade of courteous reserve much of their loyalty, their affection and incidentally, their savings, was going back to Japan." The partial truths in this statement are revealing. The West Coast Japanese had never been fully accepted or understood, so it was an easy step to confer on them characteristics attributed to the enemy. They were the victims of the terrible anger that followed the shock of Pearl Harbor. In the eyes of many people, their very presence was a reminder of betrayal. John Bruce sensed the danger inherent in this situation, for he added, "There is an uneasy memory of the reproachfully worded tombstone in one of San Francisco's oldest cemeteries, a relic of vigilante days, under which the wrong man rests."[55]

Towards the end of January friction developed between the Justice Department and the Western Defense Command. On the twenty-ninth Attorney General Biddle announced that there would be a wholesale evacuation between February 15 and 24 of Japanese, German, and Italian aliens from twenty-seven West Coast areas which had been designated as sensitive by General DeWitt. Thomas C. Clark, later a Supreme Court justice, was appointed by Mr. Biddle to be coordinator of Alien Enemy Control for the Western Defense Command. As described by Professor Grodzins, Clark arrived in San Francisco, having been given only "the vaguest idea of the scope and complexity of the program he directed. 'I notice in the paper that I am supposed to be placing signs around these areas that the Attorney-General has designated,' he wrote in an early letter to the Director of the Alien Enemy Control Unit. 'I have no signs, nor do I have any personnel to put them up. I wondered just what the plan was.' "[56] To further complicate matters, General De-Witt kept adding to the areas to be evacuated until the program became almost impossible to carry out, and still it was not dealing with what was called the "Japanese menace." According to the Army historians' report, "Justice officials balked at accepting the very large Category A areas he recommended for Washington and Oregon, since they included the entire cities of Seattle, Tacoma, and Portland. The execution of this recommendation would have required the evacuation of about 10,700 additional enemy aliens and, as in the case of California, only about 40 percent of these would have been Japanese."[57]

Yet the Japanese were under constant scrutiny. A San Jose woman remembers that during this period her father went next door one night to see how their neighbor's garden was growing. People were very suspicious, and someone reported it. Officers came to see what he was doing. A woman riding in the hills behind Stanford University came upon a group of Issei gardeners chatting by a camp fire and she galloped home to report a spy ring.

By February 1 the Justice Department had arrested over one thousand Japanese aliens, but this did not satisfy the alarmists. Henry McLemore wrote four days later in the Los Angeles *Times*: "Mr. Biddle is the Attorney General in Washington, but he could run for office in California and not even win the post of third assistant dog-catcher. . . . All I know is that Californians have the feeling that he is the one in charge of the Japanese menace, and that he is handling it with all the severity of Lord Fauntleroy playing squat tag with his maiden aunt. . . . California wants the Japs put away until this thing is over." About the same time Westbrook Pegler commented, "The Japanese should be under guard to the last man and woman and to hell with habeas corpus."[58] In more restrained language, without mentioning the Japanese, the eminent political commentator, Walter Lippmann, who had talked to Warren, urged the evacuation of the West Coast, which he said should be treated like a warship with access barred to anyone "no matter what his citizenship or ancestry."[59]

The Justice Department was adamant. The Attorney General would not evacuate citizens. How were the Nisei going to be removed? On the West Coast and in Washington, the advocates of mass evacuation considered what steps should be taken. A parallel strategy developed. Considering the urgency of the situation, when a delay in taking action might, in the opinion of California's attorney general, "invite disaster," the solution would be to transfer the problem to the military. On February 7 Warren told the California Joint Immigration Committee:

> I think from now on the political approach for this thing is just too cumbersome: it is involved with too much red tape for us to do anything to protect our situation now . . . we are fighting an invisible deadline. There is only one group in the last analysis that can protect this State from the Japanese situation and that is the armed forces of this government. . . .
>
> What we need now it seems to me, is action, and I think we ought to urge the military command in this area to do the things that are obviously essential to the security of this State."[60]

Warren found an ally in the Justice Department. Tom Clark interpreted his new duties on the West Coast as being responsible to the military. He arrived on the scene at a time when emotions ran high and attended the conferences between General DeWitt and California officials. He seems to have wavered between the Justice Department viewpoint and the developing opinion that the Army should evacuate the Japanese. On February 10, he wrote to his colleagues James Rowe and Edward Ennis about the "clamor for the removal of all Japanese regardless of citizenship," adding, "I do not think such drastic steps are necessary."[61] A day later, after a high policy meeting in Los Angeles, he spoke of the possibility of "restricted martial law," declaring, "The Army has not yet asked for it, but if it does, I shall go to Washington and recommend it."[62] He saw the legal difficulty, "which means that the Nisei cannot be evacuated except under emergency orders." On February 16 he flew to Washington with Major Bendetsen. His final recommendation was for the removal of "all persons deemed inimical to the defense efforts," a stand which he has since publicly regretted.

On February 14 General DeWitt sent to the War Department a recommendation that the Secretary of War

> procure from the President direction and authority to designate military areas in the combat zone of the Western Theater of Operations (if necessary to include the entire combat zone), from which, in his discretion, he may exclude all Japanese, all alien enemies, and all other persons suspected for any reason by the administering military authorities of being actual or potential saboteurs, espionage agents, or fifth columnists.[63]

The War Department had cleared the way. John McCloy telephoned Bendetson: "We have carte blanche to do what we want to as far as the President's concerned."[64] Roosevelt had for weeks been receiving the complaints and warnings of the West Coast pressure groups, channeled through the Pacific coast congressional delegation. Representatives Leland Ford and Senator Johnson, both of California, were particularly active in transmitting the clamor of their constituents. Few anti-evacuation voices reached the White House. (The President did receive a cautionary letter from Robert Oppenheimer, the physicist.) On February 11, the President told the War Department to prepare a plan for wholesale evacuation of the West Coast Japanese. "Be as reasonable as you can," he added with unintentional irony. Bendetsen worked out the means to accomplish the purpose, through an executive order. General Gullion carried a draft of the order (which had in essence been approved by War Department officials and by Attorney General Biddle) to a meeting on the evening of February 17 at Biddle's home in Washington. Those present were, in addition to Biddle, his assistants, Thomas Clark, James Rowe, Jr., and Edward Ennis, and the military spokesmen, Major Bendetsen, General Gullion, and John J. McCloy.

General Gullion, interrupting the Justice Department officials who were explaining the impossibility of evacuating aliens from the large area requested by General DeWitt, reached in his pocket and brought out the draft for the presidential order which he read aloud to the astonished company. "Mr. Rowe didn't know whether the Attorney General had been informed that the citizen matter was going to be broached. Neither Ennis nor he had been informed it was coming. There was nothing they could do. Rowe was 'angry and hurt.' Ennis, as he made a last appeal for the individual examination of citizens, looked as if he were going to cry."[65] On February 19 the President signed Executive Order 9066, authorizing the War Department to designate military areas and to exclude any or all persons from them. The order was applied only in the Western Defense Command where the Secretary of War delegated the assignment for carrying it out to General DeWitt.

It is clear that the responsibility for the decision to remove the West Coast Japanese lies with several key men who either urged it or assented to it. General DeWitt, inspired to inordinate precautions by the example of Pearl Harbor, was particularly susceptible to pro-evacuation arguments. Just past sixty when the war came, he had had more experience as an administrator (he had been at one time Quartermaster General of the Army) than as a field commander. Despite his bluff, authoritative manner, he was swayed by General Gullion, who devised the strategy for the evacuation within the War Department, as well as by the alarm of West Coast officials. He was also prejudiced.

In this connection, we must consider what part anti-Japanese bias played in what was occurring in Oregon, Washington, and California. The hostile groups who espoused close surveillance of the resident Japanese were not directly responsible for the decision made in the national capital. Similar curbs against resident Japanese in Mexico, Canada, and Peru indicate a well-worked out hemispheric plan which must have originated with the military. But the clamor on the West Coast helped to convince the leaders in Washington that they need not scruple to use extreme measures in the name of defense. As California's attorney general, Earl Warren warned that the Issei and Nisei were potential saboteurs, while as a prospective candidate for the governorship (he was elected in November, 1942) he could be sure that such a hard line would be popular in the state. Political expediency also demanded that he press for exempting Germans and Italians from blanket restrictions against enemy aliens.

In the same way Roosevelt was open to influence from the Pacific coast congressional delegation. The evacuation decision offered an opportunity to bargain for their support though this was not a primary consideration. The proposal reached him in its final stages as a plan considered necessary by the War Department, endorsed by Stimson, and acceded to by the Attorney General with no opposing cabinet viewpoint presented. Yet the President bore the ultimate responsibility. He made the first transfer of power, enabling DeWitt to put the West Coast under what might become in effect martial law. Roosevelt knew how this extraordinary blank check was to be used. "I do not think he was much concerned with the gravity or implications of this step," Francis Biddle wrote later. "He was never theoretical about things. What must be done to defend the country must be done."[66] He apparently looked upon this as a tactical problem in the vast global war on which he was willing to take the advice of the military men. Secretary of War Stimson was reported to have been opposed to the racial exclusion aspect of the evacuation, but he was not brought into the question until it was drawing to a head because General Gullion had arranged that all the earlier discussion with the Western Defense Command be channeled through his office. John McCloy, who opposed the evacuation of the Japanese in Hawaii, urged its necessity on the West Coast. Biddle stated in his memoirs:

> If Stimson had stood firm, had insisted, as apparently he suspected, that this wholesale evacuation was needless, the President would have followed his advice. And if, instead of dealing almost exclusively with McCloy and Bendetsen, I had urged the Secretary to resist the pressure of his subordinates, the result might have been different. But I was new to the Cabinet, and disinclined to insist on my view to an elder statesman whose wisdom and integrity I greatly respected.[67]

If Roosevelt did not see Executive Order 9066 in terms of the rights of citizens, Chester Rowell of the San Francisco *Chronicle* was one of the first to point out its significance. On February 23 he wrote, "The order applies, in principle, to all of us, including American Indians, or those whose ancestors came over on the Mayflower. The rights of any of us, to live in our own homes, to move about, or the conditions under which we may do so, are subject to the sole will of the commanding general. It is presumed that he will exercise this authority with discretion. But if, in any case, he should not, the intent of the order is to close all individual legal remedy."[68] An editorial on the same page stated, "As a drastic departure from American habit, it is perhaps better for practical reasons if the order enforced is illegal. If so, it leaves an avenue open for recapture of rights suspended pending action by the courts. . . ."

The Nisei were not prepared to believe that their citizenship would count for so little. Before Pearl Harbor Helen Mineta, who was then a secretary in the speech department at San Jose State College, had once discussed with her Caucasian friends what she would do if war broke out between the United States and Japan. "It won't concern me," she had said flippantly, "because I'm an American!"

In the months that were to follow, this declaration of faith sounded ironic indeed.

TWO · BEGINNINGS

WHILE OBVIOUSLY RELATED to the attack on Pearl Harbor and its aftermath, antagonism towards West Coast Japanese was by no means solely the result of the war with Japan. International events only aggravated long-standing racial hostility. Like other manifestations of racism, the antagonism derived psychologically from a basic fear and suspicion of strangers—strangers who were different in skin-color, physiognomy, and culture. Secondly, and perhaps more importantly, the history of Caucasian–Japanese relations on the Pacific coast was characterized by economic conflict, by competitive clashes between interest groups as well as by pioneer rowdyism.

Anti-Japanese prejudice was in part an expression of American frontier behavior. In a western setting in which intolerance, vigilantism, and raw economic competition were the rule, the Asiatic immigrants, along with dudes, crooks, and fallen women, played the unwelcome roles of "strangers in town." In addition to normal immigrant difficulties resulting from the language barrier, cultural differences, and beginnings in poverty, these people were to have special difficulties heaped upon them as the years went on. Their story is one of a progressive heightening of discriminatory treatment from the turn of the century up into the nineteen-twenties. Ingrown group tendencies, which were held against them later, were one result of this treatment. As special targets of discrimination they were denied the privilege of becoming citizens of the United States, then denied the right to own land, and finally, after 1924, further immigration from Japan was shut off. At one point, during the San Francisco school segregation crisis of 1906, the problem was shifted to the national arena with the intervention of the federal government.

Oriental prejudice started with the Chinese who had preceded the Japanese as a source of cheap labor in the West. Beginning in the eighteen-fifties and tapering off in the eighteen-seventies, great numbers of men were needed for the clearing of forests and lands, for the building of railroads, in the gold fields, and for domestic work. This was the period of the cross-country race in railroad construction, culminating in the connection of east and west by rail. Federal rewards to the fastest and most efficient in the form of free land promoted great competition, and thousands of laborers were imported from southern China to do the backbreaking work. Some 25,000 Chinese arrived here from Hong Kong in the single year 1850. Three hundred thousand followed in the next thirty years. Subject to physical persecutions and cheating at the hands of rougher elements in the frontier population in California, the Chinese had no recourse to the courts. They were ineligible for citizenship, and since they were "heathens" they were considered unfit to testify truthfully in their own or others' behalf or to take court oaths. In the eighteen-seventies laws were passed in California prohibiting corporations from employing Chinese. There was a special tax on Chinese miners and a head tax, and licenses to do business were often denied. Agitators portrayed the Chinese as Asiatic hordes bent upon overtaking and destroying the white populace. In 1879 President Hayes vetoed an act of Congress that would have stopped Chinese immigration, but three years later Congress succeeded in passing the Chinese Exclusion Act. In the meantime, Japanese immigration had begun, and anti-Japanese prejudice was superimposed on the already existing anti-Chinese feeling.

The first contact between Japanese and Americans, however, after a long period of self-imposed isolation on the part of Japan, had been quite amicable. During the centuries in which intercourse with the Western world was forbidden by Japan, emigration was outlawed and for a time was even punishable by death. All American school children know the story of Commodore Perry and his opening of Japan's ports virtually at gunpoint in 1853.

A high degree of mutual curiosity was aroused in both countries. The three-volume diary of Norimasa Muragaki, one of a group of visiting Japanese dignitaries sent by the Shogunate to the United States in 1860, reveals the vivid impact of cultures: each found interest and amusement in the appearance and customs of the other. The foreign visitors were enthusiastically received. Ladies tossed flowers upon their carriages. A champagne reception and banquet given in their honor struck the delicate-mannered Muragaki as being as comical and as noisy "as the drinking bouts of workmen" in Tokyo.[1] He noted that in the Congress Americans made speeches at the top of their voices and talked in an excited manner, "some wildly brandishing their arms" as if they had lost their tempers.[2] However, the ceremonious, sword-bearing, and top-knotted visitors, regarded as charming curiosities by the Americans, had little relationship to the Japanese working people who arrived later as pioneer immigrants.

The first Japanese to take up residence in the United States were students. These young people came, presumably on a temporary basis, to study the American language, customs, and agricultural system in order to bring back information to their country. In the United States they sometimes lectured on Oriental culture and comparative government. Fifteen hundred of these students arrived within six years. Some had been chosen and subsidized by the government of Japan, some were sons of the wealthy sent here for a liberal education, and others were ambitious youths of scanty means with a good deal of adventurous spirit and determination to make their own way. These last, who become known as "school boys," lived with American families and engaged in domestic service as they furthered their education. They studied in different parts of the eastern and southern United States, and a few settled in San Francisco and elsewhere. Tadatsu Matsudaira, the first Issei engineer, was such a school boy. He came to this country with an ambassadorial party in 1872 and remained behind to study at Rutgers University. Another of these students was the noted bacteriologist, Hideyo Noguchi, who was to prove in 1913 that general paresis was caused by a spirochete in the brain.

Even before emigration from Japan was permitted, there had been some earlier chance entries—a few fishermen and shipwrecked sailors touching our shores. In 1869 a German fortune hunter named Eduard Schnell, operating on a Dutch passport, married to a Japanese girl of the Samurai class, and backed financially by one of Japan's feudal lords, established the first West Coast Japanese colony on Gold Hill near Sacramento. He had smuggled out his group of farmers and craftsmen in order to grow tea, silk, and bamboo in California. They planned also to manufacture lacquer and other products characteristic of Japan. Other groups were expected to follow, but the ambitious project failed.

During this whole period the Japanese, hardly known, were much preferred to the Chinese. It was not until they began to come in large numbers and to provide economic competition that amity changed to friction.

The first small group of imported contract laborers arrived in Hawaii in 1868 to work on the sugar plantations. The plantation owners had been exerting much pressure on the government of Japan and finally reached a special agreement with them, the Japanese government insisting on certain safeguards for these *"gannen mono,"* or first-year people, that did not apply to later contract labor.

In the eighteen-eighties, because of a population explosion in his country the Emperor removed the general prohibition against emigration. Those who came here from Japan at this time were, for the most part, of a higher occupational level than those who followed ten years later. Among them were clergymen, hotel keepers, metal rollers, and publishers. There were also cooks, students, and merchants, some laborers and household servants.

Japanese immigration figures rose from 186 persons in 1861 to a little over two thousand between 1881 and 1890 and over twenty-five thousand between 1891 and 1900. The figures reached seventy thousand by 1910. A large percentage of these immigrants, however, returned to their home country.

The contract system brought laborers in by lots, mostly to the Islands but also to California and the Northwest. The system was unjust and exploitive. Immigrants were indentured to their employers for a stipulated number of years at fixed wages, usually below those paid to other laborers doing the same kind of work. The work contract was exacted in return for the payment of a one-way passage to the new land, which had been depicted in glowing terms. Earning a living from the soil was a great struggle in Japan, and contractors told young men on the farms, "Why, in America at the end of the year you could have two hundred dollars saved!"

"Well, that two hundred sounded like a million dollars to the impressionable teen-age boys," according to the son of one venerable retired Issei, once a contract laborer. For this man the length of indenture in Hawaii was only a year. At the end of that year, he took the first boat headed for San Francisco. His story is typical. Countless Island laborers eventually made their way to the mainland. Others stayed and continued their lives in Hawaii, under environmental conditions that were more favorable socially but not economically.

A young immigrant to Hawaii who had become a Christian and learned English in Japan, was given a job immediately as an interpreter on a sugar plantation. He rode horseback with the overseers, who used bull-whips to make the cane workers keep up. He told his son in later years he thought that the men could manage, but one day when an overseer whipped a frail little man who was ill, the big and healthy interpreter beat the overseer into insensibility. The other workers hid him in the cane and later managed to ship him off on a freighter to the mainland, where he changed his name. In California he became a prominent Japanese community leader in the larger Sacramento area.

Among the contract workers, men trained in agriculture with approximately an eighth-grade education greatly outnumbered the illiterate peasant group. Japan was relatively advanced in the matter of general education. From the point of view of literacy, these contract workers averaged midway between the southern Europeans and the better educated northern European immigrant group.

Speaking of the art of Japanese calligraphy, Dr. James Higuchi, a California physician, comments, "Most of those old timers could write those fancy things with a pen, and that was quite an accomplishment. They could write almost anything they wanted to in a letter."

When Hawaii achieved annexation to the United States (and a free market for sugar) the islands came under American law, including the labor law of 1885 which prohibited importation of contract labor and which voided contracts previously entered into. Knowing that this supply of workers would soon be cut off, Hawaiian sugar plantation owners increased the importation of serf labor, getting them onto the island before the new law went into effect. After such contracts were outlawed, Japanese came to the mainland where wages were slightly higher and labor conditions better at the rate of approximately ten thousand a year.

They also went up into Canada, down to South America, and to the Philippines. Gradually, as Chinese immigration ceased and Chinese workers moved into other occupations, the Japanese took over the lowest paying jobs. The new immigrants satisfied the tremendous demand for cheap strawberry and tomato pickers, for domestics, for workers on railroads, in the lumber camps, in the salmon fisheries. For the Caucasian operators of the larger farms, the most profitable and comfortable arrangement was a readily available labor supply that disappeared from view and from conscience when not needed. Fruit and vegetable farmers required huge numbers of workers at harvest time, few during the growing season. So the immigrant farm hands were unsettled, kept on the move, following the harvests, planting, pruning, and hoeing.

Japanese immigrants who were able to speak some English provided workers for Caucasian farm operators. Often these labor contractors were lifelong friends and advisers to the workers they came to know. Other contractors were exploiters, some encouraging the workers to drink and gamble, with the result that due to their indebtedness to the contractor they found themselves unable to leave or to strike out for themselves.

A good many of the young Japanese, however, were not at all docile and accepting of near-starvation wages and bad working conditions. Many demanded more pay. Not allowed in white labor unions, the Issei laborers occasionally organized groups of their own, and thereby gained both collective advantage to themselves and the animus of Caucasians. A group of sugar beet workers, striking in California, were forced to disperse into other areas. Though officially unrecognized, the Japanese Hawaii Federation of Labor was vigorous and rebellious in the early days, and later Japanese participation in union life in Hawaii was a strong factor in forming an interracial society there.

Most of the Issei paid their own passage and came to this country with a little money in their pockets. The newcomers rarely made demands on charity. They paid their debts and rents, and, while most were poor, once established, there were few who could be classified as actually destitute.

The greatest single motivation for migration was economic, yet the most submerged economic class in Japan did not come. Of the people who emigrated, 90 per cent were country people rather than city dwellers. Farmers in Japan were considered middle class, just below the Samurai and above the merchant class. Agricultural skill was highly regarded. From a point of view of status, if not opportunity, going into farm work in America meant going down a step.

In the small country of Japan, land was at a premium. To keep a piece of land of usable size in the family, the primogeniture system was followed whereby the oldest son inherited the whole of the property, instead of its being divided among the children. Consequently, many younger sons who had little future at home migrated across the sea. They were eager for adventure and willing to take risks. Like other immigrants they wanted to see America, the land of "golden opportunity."

One such lad, Shinkichi (George) Okomoto, was about the fifth down in a line of brothers. He came to this country with his father who himself was not the oldest son, but was third down the line in inheritance; therefore neither had anything to look forward to in Japan. The older man found work on a farm in the San Joaquin Valley. The boy was left on his own at fourteen in San Francisco, where he was employed as a house-boy.

Shinkichi was a lively personality, and he must have been very bright, because he went from the first to the eighth grade in three years, without previously knowing English. On getting his first real job, as a messenger for an art goods store in San Francisco, the first thing he did was to memorize the map of the city. Many years later his daughter, Fuji Takaichi, recalls that if she told him the number of the place of destination he always could tell her what street corner it was closest to. His children also would watch in amazement when he wrapped packages neatly and perfectly. He could snap the string in two with the fingers of one hand very quickly. He had practiced that, too, because his ambition was to be a clerk in the store he worked for and he wanted to be a good one. Not very long afterwards, in 1906, he had his own art goods store, located in San Jose, where it was an attraction for many years. He died before the war and did not see the store's closing at the time of evacuation when his widow sold out everything and donated the proceeds to the community's war chest.

But G. S. Okomoto had developed one lifelong compulsion. He always bought the most expensive shoes and was very meticulous about polishing them every day. This concentration upon his shoes dated from his first months in this country when his father, because he had no money, made him wear girls' shoes to school.

One most remarkable mother of an unusual family had come to this country able to speak English, an advantage most Issei did not have. Having graduated from a Tokyo college for women where she learned to speak English with a British accent, she had taught school in Japan. She heard of a Protestant Japanese church in Placer County in California that had been established by a relative, and, being a person of independent disposition, she simply wrote that she was coming. There she later met her future husband, Shinzo Makabe, who had been sent to Tokyo as a boy by his family, supplied with dry groceries for the journey by foot from his home so that he could attend free school. When he came to mainland United States from Hawaii, he traveled from Salinas to San Francisco looking for work. There were no jobs to be had anywhere.

Once when he was down to seventy-five cents he bought some loaves of French bread, wrapped himself in a blanket and stayed in bed chewing on the bread, believing that if he drank enough water it would fill his stomach up. Traveling to Grass Valley, a California mining town, he worked as a cook and learned to prepare beans and salt pork, to butcher sheep, and cook mutton. Later he got a ride on a wagon into Placer County and got off in Loomis where he found the plum trees in bloom. This was in 1899.

The Makabe children were required to speak English in the home. The mother taught the children many things before they entered school. She could recite Shakespeare and could quote from the childrens' books when told the page numbers. The father was one of the few Japanese in the environs who could speak, read, and write English, and he worked as a court interpreter for the county. One of the children at the time of World War II was to figure in an unhappy incident of discrimination prior to being seriously wounded in the Army overseas.

The father of Minoru Yasui, a prominent Denver attorney who figured in a Supreme Court test case during World War II, came to the United States at the age of sixteen from a small farm in Okayama-ken. Two brothers had arrived before him to earn their "fortunes" as railroad section hands. The newcomer was too weak for such heavy work, and was assigned the job of water boy. This "offended his dignity," according to his son; so he went to Portland, where he worked as a school boy, aspiring to become a lawyer. But Oregon law prohibited aliens from entering the profession, "and since he could not be naturalized he started out for a fabulous place called 'Cincinnati'—only he had heard it as 'Shin-Shin-no-chi' which meant a new, new land." As the train passed through Hood River, Oregon, en route to Cincinnati, the countryside so reminded him of his home in Japan that he got off and decided to settle down there.

This Issei, like so many others, believed in the opportunities of America, especially for those who had had an education. He had seven children, two girls and five boys who together achieved a combined total of fifty-eight years of education beyond high school. One became an engineer, one a lawyer, one an orchardist, one a teacher, another a public health nurse, and two became doctors of medicine.

Like European immigrants, many of the Issei came to the United States to escape the universal conscription system in Japan. All kinds of people came: the honest and dishonest, the gamblers and the strait-laced, the dull and the bright, the aggressive and the retiring. There were merchants, thieves, Samurai, and especially farmers.

It was natural that these immigrants would be drawn to the American soil. Vast areas of virgin country lay as yet uncultivated. Even as the western population grew and the land was divided into smaller units, farming on the Pacific coast was still managed on relatively large acreages. And even the small farms were large compared with those of Japan.

After following the crops, some of the first generation began developing plots of their own, generally in places that few previously had been willing to work or known how to make productive. They demonstrated how small pieces of land could be developed and a respectable living made from them. Many Japanese farm laborers saved up capital with which they could lease property.

One Issei who would eventually become such a farmer had left the ken of Saga on the Island of Kiushu as a lad, because he was the youngest son and had no chance to inherit property. He first went to South America, to Peru and Chile, where he peddled housewares. He used to tell his children how he was chased through the cane fields by natives with knives. He could speak Spanish fairly well. A few years later he went to sea, and when his boat docked in San Francisco Bay, he jumped ship. He worked at various odd jobs and "batched" it with a friend. He went back to Japan to marry, and his son was conceived there but born in America so he always maintained that the boy was half-Japanese.

"The Issei who came to this country were a different breed to leave home and go to a strange country. America, after all, was settled by these kind of people," says Dr. Higuchi, the son. "You have to hand it to them. But my father felt discrimination very strongly—more so than my wife's parents. He resented it. He was not a happy man, but he got along pretty well with those he worked for. He share-cropped and made enough of a nest egg to buy his first piece of property. Whomever he worked for, he gave them their money's worth of work."

This Issei farmed in a fertile valley with an equable climate, but often Japanese farmers had to work land against almost insuperable odds, contending with many adversaries: the weather, the soil, the creditor, problems of water and drainage, drying heats, and destructive winds. In Guadalupe, near Morro Bay in California, Japanese farmers were digging the soil with pick and shovel and actually moving boulders by hand. There were areas in the San Joaquin Valley with perhaps only two feet of topsoil over hardpan. In Butte, Colusa, Yuba, and Sutter counties much of the soil was full of alkali and so brick-hard that no one but the Issei had considered it fit for growing purposes. They managed to start truck farms and rice fields. In some places they grew crops in desert and tule lands where nothing of use had grown before. In Walnut Grove, Sacramento County, Issei replaced a group of Caucasian gamblers who had settled there, and reclaimed the swamp lands, constructed roads, and did the meanest jobs at low wages. Often, what they began others later took over with profitable results. Hundreds of thousands of acres of unimproved western lands were eventually brought into cultivation by these people.

The story of George Shima is atypical of early California Japanese in one respect and quite typical in another. This farmer-businessman was unusual for this period in that he became very wealthy. Yet he epitomized Issei perseverance in the face of adversity and in his belief in the soil. Shima arrived in this country in 1890, and proceeded to earn his living as a labor contractor, supplying workers to Caucasian farmers. By saving his money and investing in property, he gradually built up his farmlands from the poorest of beginnings.

Shima became interested in reclaiming a barren delta in the San Joaquin River near Stockton, a sheet of water pockmarked by numerous islets covered with a dense growth of tule and other "wild vegetation . . . usually inundated during winter months."[3] The journalist and publisher E. Manchester Boddy, whose lifelong interest in the American Japanese began in the early nineteen hundreds when his mother held classes in English for immigrant Japanese in Washington's White River Valley, wrote of Shima's "precarious experiment": "Not only was the picture far from alluring, but the place was infested with malaria, and was considered too unhealthy for farming."[4]

There were close to thirty islands in the delta. First Shima diked one of the islets, draining the soil by means of a wide ditch cut across the land.

> Superfluous water in the ditch was pumped out into the river by engine. Thus the land was made to yield to the plough. . . . After the first ploughing the virgin soil was allowed to lie idle for a year or two, so that the brush and tule would rot under the sod. The soil thus prepared was found excellent for the cultivation of potatoes. . . .[5]

The whole delta system somewhat resembled the dikes in Holland. The farm area was actually below water level, and the water was simply pumped out. For irrigation they pumped water in again. Layer upon layer of decomposed material accumulated. Sometimes, according to one of Shima's relatives who worked there during the summers as he grew up, the material would get so dry that if one had thrown a match on it the whole area would have gone up in flames.

Dredgers and other machinery were expensive. A big company called the Empire Navigation Company financed Shima's capital equipment. He employed a large percentage of white workers, but most were from Japan. Those who came to work for him at first were friends and relatives from his own island of Kyushu, near Fukuoka. One would write the other, or they would hear about him, and they would come. Different groups operated different farms. Farming the islands meant cultivating up to ten thousand acres of land; even the smallest islands were three thousand acres. Shima's brother-in-law, who acted as his personal secretary, used to farm a number of the islands that were planted in potatoes and onions; later celery was grown. Today grain is the chief crop. The river bottom has come up, and the land is not as fertile as formerly.

The owners of the original development profited, and the vigorously handsome, mustached Shima, a millionaire, owned steamboats, barges, tugboats, and launches, on which he used to reach his delta ranches and with which he hauled potatoes to San Francisco. He became known as the Potato King, a name derived not from his top position in the business, though this is the present-day connotation, but because one year at a festival held in the Stockton area he actually played the role and was given the title of Potato King. In the Lodi area there was a Grape King.

Those who did business with Shima held him in the greatest respect, finding him "progressive and straightforward." He expected others to follow the same standards which he held for himself. He was not admired by everyone, however. A grudging note was sounded by a *Collier's* magazine writer, who commented that oil from Shima's steamers had been seeping into the tule grasses and killing mosquitoes "to such an extent that . . . in a very few years more of the delta will be comfortably habitable for white men, and they will be prepared to go back and contend with the Japs for a place upon this soil of Egyptian richness."[6]

Despite his many Caucasian friends, George Shima in his middle years found himself harassed upon buying a three-story mansion in Berkeley. There were insinuating headlines in Berkeley papers, and when he finally moved in over the protests of certain of his neighbors, he commented to a newspaper reporter that his neighbors should not worry, since he was putting up a high fence "to keep the other children from playing with his."[7]

He did construct a high wall, but it turned out he did not really need it for this purpose. The family had excellent relationships in the neighborhood and at school with his children's Caucasian friends. Although wealthy, George Shima did not cut himself off from involvement with the problems of his people. He devoted a large portion of his time and energy and used the power of his position to protest injustices done to the American Japanese group.

The history of the Japanese in the West is primarily an agricultural history. Countless first-generation Japanese immigrants challenged the soil and made their living from farming, though for most of them, as contrasted with the Potato King's experience, existence was a struggle.

In 1906 a group of California Japanese Christians established the Yamato farming colony in Livingston, a small town between Turlock and Merced in California's San Joaquin Valley. (Yamato was the ancient term for Japan.) Twelve years before an American colony on this tract of several thousand acres had simply been "blown away." The new settlers almost experienced the same fate. They suffered through disaster after disaster, coming close to starvation, surviving five lean and hungry years before making any headway at all. Winds swept away soil and dried up young plants. Grasshoppers, rabbits, and squirrels devoured what the winds left.

Buddy Iwata, the present-day general manager of the successful enterprise that developed from these pioneering efforts, recalls that his father, who used to deliver groceries from his store in nearby Turlock, frequently got his truck stuck in the same sand that kept burying the young plants. After every storm the farmers dug each plant out again with their hands, or planted anew, until at last they were able to get a crop started.

Water had to be carried in from two miles away. In 1909 the Japanese–American Bank in San Francisco, which held second mortgages on their lands, failed during a minor panic. After a number of the Yamato people banded together in 1915 for the cooperative purchasing of supplies and marketing, they began to ship grapes, figs, and almonds to eastern markets. From nonproduction in 1906, carload shipments rose to 260 in 1917. Some years later the farmers formed a true cooperative association.

Most Issei, particularly new arrivals, worked as farm hands or were wage earners in towns during the early years. As they competed in the labor market in increasing numbers, they began to draw the antagonism of Caucasians, who were also scrambling for a living in the survival-of-the-fittest atmosphere of the day. When Japanese immigration was at its peak, a labor leader by the name of Dennis Kearney began to gain prominence in California partly through his anti-Oriental activities. A recently naturalized citizen from Ireland, he had first engaged in a good deal of haranguing against the Chinese in the sandlots of San Francisco before whatever vagabond audiences would listen. Then he fulminated about his discovery that the Japanese were a menace. With the formation of the Workingman's Party by people of Kearney's point of view, attacks on the Japanese became organized and systematic.

In 1900 San Francisco was threatened with a bubonic plague epidemic, and, because rats carrying the fever were traced to ships coming in from the Orient, the city's Asiatic population was suspected of causing the disease. A rough and useless program of injections for Orientals was put into effect before Issei spokesmen protested, and an injunction put a stop to the practice. In the same year the San Francisco Labor Council and the Building Trades Council organized a mass meeting protesting Japanese labor in California.

The Japanese Association of America was formed at the time of the bubonic plague scare in response to the outbreak of anti-Japanese activity. In the months following the original crisis it grew rapidly. The association was largely a self-help organization resembling the chamber of commerce; it was made up of numerous, loosely connected local Japanese associations throughout California. Financial support came through memberships, donations, and fees. By providing a source of information and legal advice, the associations familiarized new immigrants with the laws, customs, and geography of the country. People learned to turn to the associations when they needed help. Over the years the associations assumed many new functions, from tending to welfare problems to giving aid in the filling out of income tax forms. The local groups sometimes served as focal points for social life, although this purpose was more often served by the *kenjinkais*, social clubs composed of men coming from the same kens in Japan.

One of the functions of the Japanese Association was to look after the deceased, there being a strong tradition in the Issei group of caring for the dead as well as the living. It was quite important to them to be buried with a certain amount of ceremony, and families spent large sums of money for memorial stones. The Japanese burial grounds were often segregated, like the one at Oakhill cemetery in San Jose, California, which was situated next to the generally unkempt paupers' burial ground. The Japanese Association took on the responsibility for seeing that their side was kept up, planting lawns and flowering cherry trees and keeping the grounds beautiful; the section became a source of pride.

Because they were not citizens, Issei were quite handicapped politically. Attempts at asserting political pressure were usually ineffectual since they could not produce a bloc of votes as a bargaining position. The Japanese Association to which most Issei men belonged raised sizable sums of money to prevent passage of anti-Japanese legislation, such as fishing restrictions, and in so doing wielded some influence, and provided a limited substitute for political activity within the Japanese group.

A Sacramento Issei community leader, who was active in work with the Buddhist church and the language school and who engaged in the semi-political activities typical of the group was contacted by the Japanese consul-general when he required information on Japanese problems in his locale. Like other leaders of his standing, one of this Issei's chief functions was to arbitrate disputes in the Japanese community.

But the Japanese Association gradually became an object of suspicion to the Caucasian majority. Critics felt it was under the influence and direction of Japan, and perhaps financially supported by the mother country. The central organization was closely associated with the consul-general's office. For many of the Issei's specific problems—immigration, picture brides, Japan–American commerce, military service, birth regis-tration, passports—representatives of the local associations dealt with the central association which in turn dealt with the Japanese consulate.

Occasionally, also, speakers came from Japan to address various groups, propounding Japan's China policy. As one Issei put it, "We listened, but did not necessarily accept what was said." Literature distributed under the Japanese Association's sponsorship pleaded Japan's cause in the Sino–Japanese conflict.

On the eve of American participation in World War II, because of such contacts, everybody active in these organizations came under scru-tiny and leaders in the Japanese associations were put under security arrest, although often they were soon released.

Despite an inclination among American Japanese to endure injustice quietly, looking to a better future for their children if not for themselves, those Issei leaders who could communicate in English did much to pro-tect the interests of their people. Resident Japanese, according to Roger Daniels, gave "thousands of speeches" and published "dozens of books" in their own defense.[8]

In general it was laboring people and small farmers who did not de-pend on Japanese workers but competed with them who tended to anti-Orientalism. Owners of big business enterprises, particularly those who profited from trade with Japan or by drawing from a large pool of labor, were Japanese defenders. Educated people like Dr. Charles Eliot of Harvard, David Starr Jordan of Stanford, and Chancelor Benjamin Ide Wheeler of the University of California, and travelers, particularly Asian missionaries, were also often defenders—when they were aware of the Japanese situation.

The prominent Protestant theologian Sidney Lewis Gulick, who re-versed the slogan by speaking of "The White Peril," devoted many years to a campaign for mutual understanding. He published over thirty books, fourteen of them in Japanese, explaining Eastern philosophy to Western-ers, and Western thought to Japanese, drawing the similarities and differ-ences between Buddhism and Christianity. He described variations in manners and physical appearance, pointing out how the shape and slant of the Oriental eye, for example, might be strange and disconcerting to Caucasians, but reminding the latter that their appearance often seemed fierce and rough to Orientals.

The Buddhism of the Issei—a foreign religion—was mistrusted by the

Caucasian community. As one Nisei, a Methodist, says, "Anything you do not understand can look mighty suspicious." Gulick pointed out there were more similarities than differences in the ideological teachings of Buddhism and Christianity; many of the values such as honesty and kindness, self-abnegation, and giving to others, were common to both. The East had the doctrine of Karma, the West the doctrine of inherited sin. The East said, "Do not unto others what you would not have them do unto you," whereas the West said, "Do unto others as you would have them do unto you." One religion was essentially reticent, or conservative, the other active. The Puritan ethic of hard work might almost seem to have been invented by the Issei. Differences lay in matters of legend, semantics, ritual, emphasis.

The Shinto religion, with an extremely small number of followers, was even less understood in America. Originally, village Shinto in Japan concerned the local gods who assisted with daily well-being. Many later sects, such as Tenrikyo, emphasized faith healing and resembled Christian Science in this country. Buddhist and Shinto practice overlapped a good deal, depending on the occasion rather than on membership. Certain Shinto festival days were dedicated to the harvest and shrines to healing. On the other hand, worshipers looked to Buddhist ritual for the well-being of the soul, and a Buddhist priest was ordinarily called in for funerals. State Shinto, as contrasted with village or sect Shinto was a relatively late development in Japan, not really a religion but a worship designed by patriotic philosophers to break the power of the feudal lords and to establish obedience to the emperor. Sect Shinto brought to this country, like Buddhist sects (Zen, Shin, Nichiren), was much altered in the new setting.

Toleration, a chief precept of the Buddhists, made adapting to the ways of this country easier. Certain forms characteristic of the new country were adopted, including church attendance, endeavor societies, hymnals, sometimes even Easter baskets, in keeping with the Buddhist practice of *dana*, or gift giving. Some Issei were converted to Christianity as a result of their earliest contacts here: missionary schools near ports of entry taught young immigrants English. Christianity was often associated with Americanism in the minds of Japanese immigrants (as well as many Caucasians) and participation in the dominant religion of the country aided assimilation by making Japanese Christians somewhat more at ease in the community than Japanese Buddhists. Sometimes children were sent to Christian Sunday schools with the idea that this would be some protection for them.

Sidney Lewis Gulick, Professor E. K. Strong, and others made case studies of predominantly Japanese communities, showing how Japanese families actually lived and worked, studying the expectations and abilities of their children, establishing facts and exploding myths. But many of their readers exposed to such studies resisted their conclusions.

The belief was general among white unionists that the Japanese actually preferred a low standard of living, would always accept low wages, and that Caucasians should not be forced to compete with them. There was truth to the charge that Issei often worked harder and faster than Caucasians, thus eventually lowering wage rates. A frequent complaint, also with a basis in truth, was that Japanese were used as strikebreakers, as Negroes excluded from unions have been similarly used in more recent times. While unions were concerning themselves with the task of raising wages and improving working conditions for laboring people in general, their reaction to the newcomers was often fanatically unreasonable, and they were careless with the facts. Among most white unionists the ideal of working-class solidarity did not include Orientals. Instead of pulling together for common betterment in a period of unlimited economic anarchy, it was a common practice, perhaps born of necessity, to try to rise by stepping on those below.

Not all labor men espoused racist doctrine. The United Mine Workers in Utah accepted Japanese members, and many unionists argued that the Japanese should have equal rights, but the anti-Oriental agitators had the ear of the rank and file. The Japanese and Korean Exclusion League (later the Asian Exclusion League), formed in 1905, was chiefly a propaganda organ. A number of other anti-Japanese societies followed.

A report of the United States Industrial Commission revealed the typical stereotyped, as well as contradictory, thinking of the time when it stated in 1900 that the Japanese were "more servile than the Chinese" but were less obedient and far less desirable. "They have most of the vices of the Chinese, and none of their virtues," the report read.[9] In 1905 the California legislature adopted a ten-point resolution condemning Japanese in the state. For the next several years, numerous anti-Japanese bills were proposed, seventeen of them in the single year of 1909, twenty in 1911. Up and down the state local ordinances were enacted against the group. Military and patriotic organizations and merchant associations joined the unions in declaring, "California shall not become the Caucasian graveyard."

Various newspapers found it to their advantage to keep the question boiling. The San Francisco Chronicle, which had modified its position by World War II, was the first to begin an unrelenting flow of propaganda against Japanese in America. The Call tried to outdo the Chronicle. The Hearst press raised circulation with articles crying "yellow peril." Demagogic politicians found the issue useful and attached themselves to it for their own devices. General John DeWitt's slogan, "A Jap is a Jap," can be traced to this earlier period. At the same time the Japanese were feared, they were derided: never, it was commonly believed, would they be able to do more than imitate American dress and customs.

The alarmists played upon the prejudices of many white parents of children attending the same schools with Japanese children. A fair number of older Japanese students attended school with the younger ones, in order to learn the language and get an education at the same time. Appealing to parental fears agitators made much of the problem of the overage student to illustrate the theory of biological inferiority.

Speakers often raised the spectre of intermarriage and the question of racial contamination and danger to pure white womanhood in arguing for restrictions on Japanese workers. Attempting to clinch their arguments with an appeal to science, Kearney and others warned that the blood of white people could not physically assimilate that of other races; therefore, the farther apart the two races kept, preferably with the Pacific Ocean between them, the better. On the East Coast where the Japanese population was sparse, Japanese–Caucasian marriages sometimes occurred, but not at this time in the West. (In an unusual match in 1906 a clerk in the office of the San Francisco police department had traveled to St. Louis in order to claim a bride of Japanese descent and brought her back to California.) Most Japanese spokesmen were careful not to propose intermarriage or even to bring up the subject. Intermarriage was frowned upon generally by the early Japanese settlers as well as by Caucasians. Those who broke the code were apt to find themselves living on the fringe of both Japanese and white society.

According to one Nisei, "If a boy ever married a non-Japanese, the folks would probably have met him at the door and said, 'Look, you're not our son any more.' If either of my sisters ever married a Caucasian, I'm sure my folks would have said, 'Don't you ever darken this door again!' Japanese people are probably just as prejudiced as anybody else when it comes to certain things, and this was one of the things."

However, on the grounds that they feared Japanese would try to take over the Caucasian race through intermarriage, California lawmakers passed an anti-miscegenation law in 1872 forbidding marriage between Japanese and Caucasians as well as between Caucasians and certain other racial groups. In the early nineteen-hundreds the California Civil Code was amended, declaring mixed marriages which had already taken place to be null and void.

Anti-Japanese polemics were larded with unsupported charges of immorality. The Japanese language did not even have a word for sin or for the home, one politician claimed—quite erroneously—in a speech before the House of Representatives.

Scorn and rough treatment came from many sources. Near Los Angeles a group of Caucasian girls employed at an ostrich farm settled the "yellow peril" question by going on strike when a Japanese was hired, fearing he would learn the feather business and teach it to others. He was discharged. One of the first physical attacks on Japanese occurred in San Francisco in 1890 when fifteen cobblers who had been working in a segregated shop below union wages were seized and beaten. They were forced to leave the city and change occupations. The year before, Tacoma natives attacked with clubs an incoming trainload of Japanese who were to work on a well. A train conductor named Kirkpatrick took the part of the Japanese and cowed the mob, but after the train left the Japanese were driven away down the track and told that if they returned they would be shot.

Much of the molestation, chronic and annoying, rather than dramatic, was suffered in silence. In the early days in San Pedro, California, the cannery "bosses" used to transport their Japanese employees to work in horsedrawn carts. Townspeople threw rocks at them and called them names. A young Issei laundry proprietor in San Mateo used to make his deliveries with horse and buggy. Growing tired of stones being thrown at him every time he passed certain groups, he took off one day and chased some of his harassers. But when he so reacted, according to his son, his own wife went after him with a pitchfork.

During the wild disorder in San Francisco the year of the Great Earthquake, which struck in April, 1906, the city collapsed politically as well as physically; a few months after the fire a corrupt city government toppled. The Asiatic population took an undue amount of punishment during the months following the tremor from both the toughs and the more respectable but prejudiced elements of the city population. Chinatown was completely destroyed, and, with emergency encampments all over the city, the Chinese emergency tents were moved several times, white residents in one section of the city objecting when a camp for the dispossessed Chinese was set up within view of their undestroyed homes. Attempts were later made to rebuild the original Chinatown on the extreme outskirts of the community at Hunters Point.

The predominantly Japanese section of the city was partially destroyed. Many of the buildings, like that of the *Japanese American News* (*Nichi Bei*) on Eddy Street, were gutted by fire, and 10,000 Japanese residents were rendered destitute. Traditionally cut off from the larger community and aware of hostility from a small but active element in the population, the Japanese organized immediately after the quake. A relief committee was formed under the direction of the local Japanese consul, K. Uyeno, and ten Japanese physicians worked around the clock at three encampments, one at Fort Mason, one at Lafayette Square, and one at the Japanese Tea Garden. Within ten days over 7,000 Japanese earthquake refugees were sent to interior points in California. Some returned. Contributions came quickly from various Japanese associations in the state and from other sources in Vancouver, Honolulu, and elsewhere. An emergency donation from the Japanese government of $25,000 was awaited in May. Japan, which only recently had been forced to ask Red Cross assistance of $16 million to save her own starving people after a rice famine, also donated close to a quarter of a million dollars to the general disaster fund, more than the donations from all other countries combined.

The American Japanese asked for little relief from the city. In July not over one hundred were receiving outside aid. Later, among the 30,000 earthquake victims who applied for rehabilitation there was not one Japanese.

Some of the Issei residents who were caught in the San Francisco disaster had experienced such things before since Japan was a land of tremors. "You know when there is going to be one because then the pheasants cackle," said the father of Kay Takemoto of Placer County, who was in San Francisco in 1906. "The reason there are so many earthquakes in Japan is because it is so small it shakes a lot." When a member of the Japanese and Korean Exclusion League (which had by no means been put out of operation by the calamity, which indeed seemed to have increased its agitation) expressed hope that the disaster would frighten Japanese residents from San Francisco, the president of the League reminded him that the Japanese were already familiar with earthquakes and would feel more at home than ever.

The Exclusion League, a latter-day form of Dennis Kearney's Workingmen's Party, was almost entirely composed of laboring people, who were at that time in control of the city government through their elected representative, Mayor Eugene E. Schmitz. Schmitz was a tall, bearded, appealing figure of a man, a former musician and the protégé and front man for Abe Ruef, political boss and a power in state Republican politics. The rank and file of union labor may not have shared in the tremendous returns from the graft that passed to their leaders from various city businesses and utilities which required licenses to operate, but they approved the anti-Oriental sentiment of the leaders who had played this refrain among other more righteous ones in their rise to power.

During a crime wave that swept over the city beginning in late August, nineteen beatings of American Japanese, usually with robbery as the motive, were later documented by the federal government. Most assaults went unreported, as when a world-renowned seismologist from the University of Tokyo, Dr. F. Omori, who was studying the earthquake, was attacked in the streets. Generally no police were present and when they arrived arrests were seldom made, although on occasion the victims who attempted to defend themselves were taken into custody.

In addition to these troubles, boycotts were organized by the Exclusion League and by various unions. The Carmen's Union distributed 10,000 copies of the league's pamphlet on the evils of Asiatic immigration. The Building Trades Council put pressure on liquor dealers to discontinue employing Mongolian help, and throughout most of October a boycott by the Cooks and Waiters Union of Japanese-owned restaurants was supported by other unions. As the restaurants were picketed, matchboxes were distributed, reading, "White men and women patronize your own race."[10] The boycott was most effective. Carpenters and mechanics employed in reconstructing shattered buildings who were found patronizing nearby Japanese restaurants were reported to the Building Trades Council. Sometimes photographs were used to prove that the men breaking the boycott were union members, and penalties were applied. George Sugihara, a restaurant keeper, was unable to stay by his cash register because rocks thrown through his window struck him. Customers, however, rather than proprietors were the intended objects of physical attack. White customers attempting to enter the place of business were struck by blows and bricks and stones were thrown at them when they left.

Between the tenth and fifteenth of October boycotters were active three times a day. When police officers friendly to the boycotters were on the scene, there was no violence; others were unfriendly and the boycotters left. On one occasion when a waiter asked the men how long they intended to keep up the boycott they replied: "Until the end—until the Japanese give up their business, pack up their goods, and return to the place whence they came." Eventually the president of the Japanese Restaurant Union paid $350 to the leaders, and the boycott ceased.[11]

Even before the unscrupulous Mayor Schmitz fled to Europe, the Board of Education had been planning to segregate Japanese school children in the public schools. On October 11 the Board removed ninety-three pupils of Japanese descent from over twenty different city schools, ordering them to a special, segregated school along with Chinese and Korean children, and theoretically, children of Indian descent. Only one Japanese child, however, enrolled at the school; the rest remained at home. The segregated school, which had been reconstructed in the burned section of Chinatown at Powell and Clay streets, was an adequate temporary structure and the teaching was satisfactory, but as the *Japanese American* editorialized, "to walk over miles of desolation through the burned district every day, among every possible form of danger, is indeed an impossible task even for the strongest adult." The editorial charged politicians with deliberately stirring up controversy for their own ends: "The Japanese colony here, under the prejudice of the public authorities, is utterly powerless to redress its own grievances."[12]

Immediately after the segregation announcement, Goroku Ikeda, Secretary of the Japanese Association, appealed to the school board. Two mass meetings were held; at the first, Japanese residents issued a manifesto and appealed to the President of the United States, "the undaunted friend of the opprest [sic] and suffering."[13] At the second meeting, held in Jefferson-Square Hall, "crowded to suffocation," some 2,500 American Japanese raised funds for injunction proceedings in the name of a Japanese youth, I. Yasuhara, who had been expelled from Pacific Heights Grammar School.[14]

But President Theodore Roosevelt first learned of the sudden segregation through the complaints of the government of Japan. Newspapers in Japan had publicized the story while the American press in general ignored it. Though at this point in history the United States was on excellent terms with Japan, Roosevelt having recently intervened helpfully in the Russo-Japanese War, the Japanese government, deeply offended, criticized the California school decision, as a violation of the United States–Japanese Treaty of Commerce and Navigation, under which nationals of each country were to enjoy rights and privileges at least equal to that of nationals of the most favored nation.[15] The United States had always insisted upon such nondiscriminatory treatment for its own nationals in other countries. Japan allowed all foreign countries equal rights in immigration and naturalization, and equal if not full rights in the use of land. Feeling ran so high in Japan on the school segregation issue that anti-American riots occurred. Although most Japanese newspapers cautioned restraint, some advised a show of military strength.

The President assured the Mikado of our good will and friendship, while privately, much incensed, he referred to the Californians as "idiots"[16] and called the "feeling on the Pacific slope . . . as foolish as if conceived by the mind of a Hottentot."[17] When Victor C. Metcalf, his Secretary of Labor and Commerce, who was about to go to California to investigate the situation, paid a call, Roosevelt called attention to his own children playing football with two children of the Turkish ambassador on the White House lawn and asked what was wrong with that! Arriving in San Francisco, Metcalf interviewed all parties to the controversy, including victims, and documented the details of the discriminatory acts leading up to the school decision. The problem of overage students, Metcalf suggested, could be settled by forbidding overage students of any race to attend public school. The Board of Education refused to budge, however, standing on state legislation passed in the early eighteen-seventies, that required equal education for non-Caucasian children, but made segregation or integration discretionary. The favored-nation clause was to be found in a treaty of commerce and navigation, argued the San Francisco *Chronicle*, a Republican labor paper, and going to school was a question of neither trade nor navigation.[18]

The federal government collected data in preparation for two test suits in the courts that were later dropped. In his annual message to Congress, December 3, 1906, Roosevelt, paying tribute to Japan's astounding development within a few years, said:

> They [the Japanese] are welcome, socially and intellectually, in all our colleges and institutions of higher learning, in all our professional and social bodies. The Japanese have won in a single generation the right to stand abreast of the foremost and most enlightened peoples of Europe

and America; they have won on their own merits and by their own exertions the right to treatment on a basis of full and frank equality. . . . But here and there a most unworthy feeling has manifested itself . . . in shutting them out from the common schools in San Francisco, and in mutterings against them in one or two other places, because of their efficiency as workers. To shut them out from the public schools is a wicked absurdity. . . .[19]

Noting the testimony in the Metcalf report on the brightness, cleanliness, and good behavior of Japanese children, he recommended legislation making naturalization possible. As for physical assaults on the American Japanese population, he promised the full weight of the federal government would be brought to bear in enforcing United States treaty obligations.

West Coast newspapers reacted with the same furor to the President's message as Japan's press had reacted to the segregation decision. Theodore Roosevelt became the butt of western ridicule. California's schools were a province of states' rights, not the concern of the federal government; Washington had exceeded its powers by intervening. The California congressional delegation expressed resentment at what they regarded as the President's intemperate language, presumably referring to the term "wicked absurdity." Defending San Francisco's honor, the *Chronicle*, which had long been exclusionist in policy, but in a milder tone, complained that the "little brown men were delighted at the rebuke which the President gave California." They were "secretly laughing at the people of San Francisco. . . ."[20]

Shortly after his return from Europe, Mayor Schmitz, charged with extortion on five counts, made a speech while out on bail decrying the coolie hordes that were threatening "to sweep away the very fundamentals of our civilization," and in an aside found fault with the judge who was to try him.[21] The *Chronicle* criticized these remarks, but not the anti-Oriental part of his address. In February, 1907, the President invited the San Francisco Board of Education to Washington for a friendly discussion of the issue, hoping the members would reconsider their adamant position. There being no objections from the local district attorney's office, the judge who sentenced him gave permission for Mayor Schmitz to accompany them. In Washington the board was persuaded to rescind the action, a capitulation which did not make the mayor or themselves popular back home.

In negotiations with the Emperor over the school crisis, Roosevelt managed to shift the focus from national origins which had derogatory implications to the question of social class. He persuaded the Emperor that the competition of the laboring classes represented a problem on the West Coast. The President and the Emperor came to terms. In an informal, extralegal, Gentlemen's Agreement, the President promised that Japanese children below the age of sixteen would be admitted into the regular public schools in return for Japan's agreeing to prevent emigration of skilled and unskilled laborers by refusing them passports. Agriculturalists and certain other groups, and the families of those already here, were still to be allowed to emigrate.

Later on its own initiative, the government of Japan showed further good faith by extending the emigration ban to include Mexico and Hawaii, an action that distressed the Island sugar planters. In a 1907 executive order, Roosevelt forbade Japanese migration into the United States by the indirect routes of Mexico, Canada, and Hawaii. Many Issei continued to slip in illegally, however, like the Mexican wetbacks of a later date.

Japanese immigration figures dropped immediately after the Gentlemen's Agreement, and because numerous Issei returned, there was an actual decrease in the Japanese population in the United States in the years following 1907. In 1909 the number of entrants was under a thousand. The Gentlemen's Agreement, which decided the controversy principally along economic and class lines, was honored for fifteen years.

Not everybody was happy with the compromise. Kyutaro Abiko, the dynamic editor and founder of the *Japanese American News*, who had been out of the state on business at the time of the earthquake and returned to see the distant flames of the city as his train crossed the Sierras, was chairman of the mass meeting called to consider the school crisis. He conducted a bitter campaign against official Japanese policy as expressed in particular by the Japanese consul-general in San Francisco, and condemned the Gentlemen's Agreement as a totally unnecessary capitulation.

An alien land bill introduced in the California legislature in 1907 failed to pass largely because President Roosevelt and Governor James Gillett joined forces in opposing it. Two years later the President used his influence to crush a similar proposal.

Under the Gentlemen's Agreement, Japanese who had come to this country alone to make their way were still allowed to send for their wives and families when they could afford to do so. Prospective brides were also permitted. Unattached Issei who had saved their money and wanted to settle permanently and raise families in the United States looked to their country of origin for wives. Some Issei returned to Japan to make their search. Countless others who could not afford the trip followed the age-old custom of letting their families arrange marriages for them just as they would have done had they never left home. They chose eligible girls from snapshots mailed to them. Sometimes they advertised.

The preliminaries to these arranged marriages were complicated. Besides the exchange of pictures and information, there were negotiations, investigations of character, family, and financial status. A mutual friend of both families diplomatically inquired into these matters and made sure the prospective mates did not have leprosy, tuberculosis, or police records, or come from the *eta* class (the *eta* were the "untouchables" of Japan). Since hard work was in prospect in the new land, the brides were expected to be strong and healthy as well as comely. Generally the couple were of the same or similar social standing. In order to prevent "white slavery" the Japanese government controlled the procedure closely. Intent of marriage had to be proved. Prospective husbands were investigated by the Japanese consuls here to see that they were morally and economically fit. Because the Issei had to work for years before they could afford a family, there tended to be an age gap between the grooms and their young brides.

The girls were married by proxy in Japan before they sailed to America. The United States government then required that the couples go through another ceremony here, the Japanese Association frequently helping with the arrangements. Thousands of brides came to our shores in this manner, and many Japanese–American families today are descended from them. The marriages were a stabilizing influence and established a family system among the Issei in America.

Not all picture brides found coming to this country as rosy an experience as they had anticipated. Some disappointed brides wrote back to Japan saying that they wanted to return on the next boat, but were discouraged by their families. Some did return. Some were divorced. A few drifted away from their marriages and the hard life involved and ended in the cities trying to find "easy" money.

Sometimes the pictures that the grooms sent were misleading. In order to appear as desirable as possible, some had their pictures taken in front of big homes they did not own. Other pictures were taken five or ten years earlier, when they were younger men. A bride may have dreamed of her future husband as tall and handsome and perhaps rich, according to the Reverend J. Fujimori of Alameda, California, only to be met at the dock by a short man in a borrowed suit without much money. Nevertheless, in his congregation today there are several such picture brides, still happily married.

Sometimes the brides arrived in beautiful traditional robes, their hair done high, and their faces powdered. One aged Issei couple, however, still laugh today remembering how he had looked up at the boat from the wharf and wondered about the girl up there who was dressed so oddly—she was a nonconformist and had on a *ha-ka-ma*, a kind of apron generally worn by men, over her kimona—at the same time she sighted him as the funny-looking man in her picture.

With traditional ceremonial costume and hair style, Mrs. Harry Iwagaki went through a typical Japanese wedding ceremony in the Wakayama-ken in the early nineteen-hundreds, without the groom present. An arranger took charge of the wedding, All the relatives of both families, who lived seven or eight miles apart, were invited. Before an elaborate feast, she signed marriage papers. Afterwards she lived in the household of her husband's parents for a time. When she arrived in San Francisco in a boatload of picture brides, she wore a Western-style suit.

Her husband-to-be was waiting on the dock. He had come to the country fourteen years before and had learned English—enough to get along in the white community—in a church-connected private school.

Iwagaki had searched for a wife for several years in California but had been unable to find a girl to suit him. Then he asked his parents to find him a girl, and they took their responsibility seriously, for they wanted him to have "love and a peaceful life with children." When they discovered the right girl at last, he and she corresponded for two years. He told her in these letters all about American life. He told her truthfully that money did not grow on trees, that he worked hard in an orchard with a shovel, and that he did not have a good house. In these letters they grew to know each other's likes and dislikes and reached an understanding.

After she arrived in San Francisco, they went to Monterey to be married. They became Presbyterians, and Mrs. Iwagaki was taught to sew, to cook, and to sing hymns. Her husband worked for a nursery and did gardening. It was very beautiful there, and she was happy. They remained ten months. Her mother had told her if they made ten thousand yen, approximately five thousand dollars, that they should come back to Japan, but if they did not, to stay in America, because with anything less than that it was not possible to lead a comfortable life in Japan. They eventually became Americanized and stayed in this country.

The first young Issei men to come to this country, like the first wave of western adventurers and settlers from the New England and middle western states, had rarely brought wives or families with them, and up to 1905 women therefore had constituted a small percentage of the Japanese population here. But by 1910 the male-female ratio of American Japanese had changed from over 2,000 males to 100 females, to 190 males to 100 females. Disgruntled Californians claimed that the increased number of female passports and the resultant increase in marriages and offspring was a violation of the spirit, if not the specifics, of the Gentlemen's Agreement. There was talk of an "invasion" of picture brides.

The fear was hardly realistic, considering the relatively small numbers involved. However, in 1919 the Japanese Association of America to help ease the tension passed a resolution against the importation of picture brides as being "out of harmony" with the changing ideals of the Japanese race. A year or two later Japan stopped issuing passports for picture brides.

From the time of the school crisis on, relations between Japan and the United States took a downward path. A vicious cycle began to operate: discrimination and hostile acts toward Japanese nationals on the West Coast produced fear of retaliation by Japan, and the fear of war was translated into alarm over "the yellow peril," increasing the hostility toward the Issei. Japan's expansionist policies in Asia increased American anxiety. Beginning with Japan's aggression in Korea in 1910, events in the Far East produced disturbing waves of reaction in this country. The line of distinction between a foreign government and our own immigrant residents and their children became blurred. For every transgression of the parent country, American-resident Japanese paid in some degree.

Children absorbed some of the adult attitudes toward Japanese. John Steinbeck recalled joining a schoolboy club dedicated to spying on American Japanese when he was about twelve. The boys in the club had their secret signs, messages, and codes, and prowled about Japanese farms in Salinas, California, arriving at the intelligence that Japanese farmers went to bed early and rose early. Then a Japanese schoolmate, who was very well-liked, asked to join. The club members were horrified. The whole structure of their racial dislike was torn "down to the roots." They explained to the boy that it would not be "cricket" for him to be a member because he was the enemy. Finally they allowed him to join when he offered to spy on his parents. "And because he was our friend we had to take him in, but it ruined the fine, ferocious quality of our club."[22]

Suspicion and criticism of resident Japanese was sometimes preached by otherwise enlightened men: Governor and later Senator Hiram Johnson, who had launched his Progressive reform career as one of the prosecutors of Ruef and Schmitz, and Senator James D. Phelan, a moderate reform ex-mayor of San Francisco were both forthrightly anti-Oriental, urging anti-alien land legislation and other restrictive measures. Drawing from a large store of misinformation and fantasy, Franklin K. Lane, Secretary of the Interior under Wilson, also a former San Francisco public figure, wrote a friend in the early nineteen-hundreds:

> The Japanese are reducing the value of California lands by buying a piece in a picked valley, paying any price that is demanded. They swarm then over this particular piece of property until they reduce the value of all the adjacent land. No one wishes to be near them; with the result that they

buy or lease the adjoining land, and so they radiate from this center until now they have possession of some of the best valleys. Really, the influx of the Japanese is quite as dangerous as that of the Chinese.[23]

The community of Florin, eight miles southeast of Sacramento, California, was cited by a *Collier's* writer, Peter Clark MacFarlane, as a "classic instance of Japanese agrarian aggression" that provided "an object lesson right at the doors of the legislature." A picture of a Florin schoolroom accompanying the article showed twenty-two Japanese pupils with hands folded, at least as starched and clean as the twenty white children in the room. "If present tendencies continue," the public was warned, "there will not be a white face in five years except those of the teachers." Nobody would socialize with these people, the author asserted. When "they" moved in, Caucasians moved out.[24]

Miss Alice Brown, a vineyardist of Florin, was one of many townspeople who had a different story to tell. "Adjoining my home," she said, "are eighty acres which for all these years had never been touched by a plough—so sloughy and shallow was the land that the white man set it aside as only fit for pasture. The Japanese turned it into the most beautiful vineyards and strawberry patches, and where the poorest of the poor soil lay is the finest berry patch in this vicinity."[25]

Researchers exposed as false some of the charges against the Japanese —low standard of living, lack of Americanization, and overabundance of children. The healthy birth rates, they found, stemmed from their being by and large a new marriage group. As one student investigator pointed out, children of Issei farmers playing in front of their small houses gave the appearance of being more numerous than actual count indicated. Nisei birth rates were on the average the same as those for other races of the same socio-economic level and the same new marriage grouping. As income rose, standards of living rose also, and birth rates decreased. The Issei had brought with them the tradition of ritual cleanliness from their homeland and introduced the daily hot bath to their frontier communities.

In some occupations Japanese were still working for lower wages than Caucasians, and in others, for example domestic and farm work, for slightly higher. When Issei were employers of others, they tended to pay higher wages than white employers for the same kind of work.

Their interest in Americanization and community action was on a general level with other groups of the same occupational standing in their farm communities. The Japanese, in the beginning, had often been eager to form community and business contacts. It had not been too difficult for them to make the transition from migratory work, following the crops and living in camps, to tenant farming, even though this upward move aroused the antagonism of certain big farm interests.

In the strawberry camps, the owner provided the land, the plants, and the house. The sharecropper supplied all the labor. About 40 per cent of the profit went to the cropper and 60 per cent to the owner. Later on it was 50–50. Although sharecropping was a definite step upward, the greatest ambition for many a Nisei son of such a sharecropper was to be able some day to work for a salary—to make perhaps $150 a month—rather than to take chances and wait and hope for a good crop and a good price. "If you could just get a job like that," one professional man says today of his boyhood dream, "you thought you'd be set for life."

As the movement grew among reactionary groups to hold down the Japanese to the level of seasonal laborers, competitors were searching for legal methods of preventing them from becoming farm entrepreneurs. Anti-Japanese land legislation began to be widely proposed. In May of 1913 California's attorney general, Ulysses S. Webb, arch foe of West Coast Japanese, successfully spearheaded the attempt to enact an anti-alien land law in the state. Like his predecessor Theodore Roosevelt, Woodrow Wilson fought the measure, hoping for a compromise, at the very least. He sent William Jennings Bryan, his Secretary of State, to Sacramento. Bryan was unsuccessful in his attempts to dissuade the legislators, and the Alien Land Bill passed. The only compromise was a mollifying matter of the wording: Japanese *per se* were not mentioned in the text.

All aliens who were eligible for citizenship, the Webb act read, could acquire, possess, enjoy, transmit, and inherit real property; aliens not eligible for citizenship only had such rights as were specifically defined by treaty obligations. The Japanese, like other Orientals, were not allowed naturalization privileges, and Japan–American treaty provisions did not specify agricultural land ownership. The Treaty of Commerce and Navigation had provided that Japanese nationals here and United States nationals in Japan could carry on trade, could own or lease and occupy houses, manufactures, warehouses, and shops, could lease land for residential and commercial purposes, and generally do what was necessary for trade, upon the same terms as native citizens or subjects.[26] Because it was not spelled out in the Treaty, the legislators made the interpretation that Japanese nationals could *not* buy land for the purpose of agriculture, and, under section two of the new law, they could only lease for a period up to three years. Further, although property already owned was not actually confiscated, Issei could not transmit it outright to their children as heirs. They could only will to them the proceeds of sales. Peter MacFarlane rejoiced: "In vain for Exposition Directors to protest, in vain for Presidents to intervene. . . . When the issue was raised there were but five men in the whole Legislature who dared to go home to their constituents and say:

The line was drawn between the white man and the brown and we voted for the brown."[27]

After the passage of this law there were hurt protests from Japan. A prolonged series of notes went between Bryan and Japan's Count Chinda. The United States attempted to assure the Japanese government that such a law did not really represent racial antagonism but was rather a purely local matter rising from business difficulties. Since Webb and other proponents of the act had flatly placed the argument on grounds of "race undesirability," and since even the otherwise liberal Wilson in a public speech the year before had claimed the United States could not make a "homogeneous population of a people who did not blend with the Caucasian race,"[28] this assurance was difficult for Japan to accept. Wilson pointed out that in the United States federal–state relations were such that the central government did not have power over state legislation. Eventually Japan accepted the second, though not the first, explanation. The land act of 1913 was a giant step backward in our relations with Japan.

Thousands of Issei were cut off from owning land, although some discovered legal loopholes in the new law which enabled them to control land without actually owning it. Caucasians and Issei sometimes formed land corporations in which Issei actually owned most of the stock. A typical corporation included two Caucasians, two Nisei children, the father, and another Japanese. Other Issei bought property, putting title in the name of a trusted Caucasian friend or employee. The method they gradually came to employ because it caused the fewest legal difficulties was that of leasing or buying property in the names of their American-born children.

During World War I there was a booming market for foodstuffs, and, while some lost heavily because of investment in land at high wartime prices in anticipation of stricter discriminatory legislation, many Issei farmers shared in the general prosperity. This good fortune seemed to revive anti-Oriental propaganda; the state seized land "in the public good" without remuneration when it was decided the land was held illegally.

At the peace conference after the war, Japan pressed hard for a clause in the League of Nations covenant that would insure equal and just treatment by all League members to all alien nationals, eliminating racial distinctions. This was voted down, the United States among those voting in the negative.

Demands to close the loopholes in the Alien Land Act of 1913 gained strength in California. Proposition One on the November ballot in 1920 called for prohibiting appointment of Issei as "guardians of estates of minors consisting wholly or partially of real property or shares in such corporations."[29] Once again the shaft was aimed at the Japanese, although again they were not named in the wording. The propaganda designed to promote passage was not so devious. The Los Angeles County Asiatic Association, for example, put out a pamphlet urging a yes vote, headlined, "SAVE CALIFORNIA—Stop Absorption of State's Best Acreage by Japanese Through Leases and Evasions of Law."

Fictional treatment of the problem, such as Wallace Irwin's "Seed of the Sun," appeared in the popular magazines. A serial in the *Saturday Evening Post* by the same author described a wealthy Caucasian family with good hearts and weak minds who were pressed to sell their valuable California land to apparently honest but actually sinister Japanese farmers.

In 1920 Japanese represented 2 per cent of the total population of California, and over 27 per cent of them were American citizens. Agriculture was the major occupation for 50 to 60 per cent of them. They were producing 92 per cent of the strawberries, over 80 per cent of the celery and asparagus, and 66 per cent of the tomatoes. This amounted to 13 per cent of the agricultural production of the state. Nevertheless, Japanese farmers controlled only 1.6 per cent of California farmland.

Proposition One, the addition to the alien land law, passed by a 3 to 1 vote. The loopholes were closed. After 1920 crop contracts had to be substituted for leases. The Japanese were deprived of the use of more than 300,000 acres of land which they had held by forms other than ownership. Many returned to tenant farming and sharecropping since the new law was generally interpreted in such a manner as to allow usage of the land.

The restrictions on leasing very often caused as much hardship as those on ownership, because most of the land worked by the Issei had been held through lease arrangements. Some crops demanded a cultivation process that took a number of years. Share leasing had previously been a profitable method both for Caucasian landowners, whose land was thus made use of in the fullest manner, and for the Japanese, who were rewarded for their effort. With the new restrictions against leasing, earnings in general took a drastic fall. Normally the term of the lease varied according to crop and area, but where Japanese were no longer allowed to stay long enough to plant, care for, and gather their harvests, they again had continually to be on the move, which made the cultivation of certain crops such as tree fruit an impossibility.

Two years later, the California legislature strengthened the land act still further, knocking down the last refuge, that of short-term tenant farming. Unless Japanese had previously legally owned property, they could only work the land as hired laborers. Sometimes wages were supplemented by gifts or scaled so high that Japanese were occupying the position of tenants or operators in fact though not in theory. But when contracts were broken by the Caucasians who had been willing or eager to make them, the Japanese had no recourse to the law. In many cases, also, banks were hesitant to make necessary loans since long-term prospects were uncertain.

Other western states passed discriminatory legislation similar to that of California. In 1921 Arizona, Texas (revising a 1911 law), Nebraska, and the state of Washington forbade ownership of land by aliens not eligible for citizenship. Arizona extended her law to apply to minors, and the Washington legislation clamped down tightly on corporations as well as individuals. Enforcement in Washington was strict: it was a gross misdemeanor for a citizen knowingly to hold land in trust for an alien, and property could be forfeited to the state for violation. All over the state of Washington ownership and operation of land began to be taken from Japanese hands and passed to others.

Nebraska tempered its alien land law by specifying that it was not to be enforced retroactively. In 1923 Oregon, Montana, Idaho, and New Mexico followed California's lead. Oregon's law was essentially a duplicate of California's. In 1924 Nevada struck from its constitution the clause guaranteeing the right of alien residents to own land on equal terms with others. With the exception of Utah, discriminatory legislation was passed in every state where there were Japanese, including Delaware, Louisiana, and Missouri.

Because of all this prohibitive legislation, land could only be acquired by evasive methods suggested by lawyers, and then not everywhere and not without considerable risk and anxiety. Community feeling was decisive. In many areas businessmen and district attorneys chose largely to ignore the letter of the law.

A second-generation Japanese says, "At first the only possible way to own land was to buy it in some citizen's name and just hope he was honest enough not to cheat you out of it. Some people took advantage of us."

Wayne Kanemoto, the third Nisei judge to be appointed in the state of California, can look out his courthouse window today and see the site of the family farm on which he worked as a boy. It is now an airport. "That's where I was born. I was born at home. I was a farmer boy until I was twenty-four years old. My father was able to lease land until the alien land laws were passed. In 1924 we moved to Berryessa, and the land was leased under the name of J. J. O'Brien." It was because of friends like O'Brien, who leased a good deal of land and supposedly employed Japanese to operate it, that these farmers were able to get by at all. "We stayed there one year. And then we came to East San Jose out on the King Road and then from there to the White Road farm, where we lived for ten years. The farmers moved about a good deal, because the land would play out, and fertilizer was prohibitive with the kind of prices you could get. When my sister became of age, my father had her lease the land. Businesswise, the oldest child may have been head of the managing department, doing the buying and selling and office work, but the father always remained head of the family."

The alien land laws were tested. In the state of Washington two American Japanese entrepreneurs who were citizens had formed a corporation under state laws in order to do farming. These men had not been born in the United States but had been naturalized. The Secretary of State in Washington took the matter to court, contending that the two should not have been allowed to become citizens in the first place, and therefore should not have formed the real estate corporation.

Eventually the case reached the Supreme Court where the noted George Wickersham argued for the Japanese—and lost. The Court decided that the naturalization certificates granted these men before 1906 were null and void. The corporation, therefore, was illegal.

However, since this case concerned race and citizenship it did not meet the question of the legality of alien land laws. A 1922 suit, long in the lower courts, tested the Washington law, at the same time that a companion suit from California was being heard.

The Washington case involved Frank and Elizabeth Terrace who wanted to give N. Nakutsuka a five-year lease on a tract of land they owned in King County. Lindley L. Thompson, the state attorney general, threatened the Terraces with criminal prosecution if they went ahead with the lease of their property. The Terraces asked the district court for an injunction to prevent Thompson from taking action. The injunction was denied. The Washington law, the plaintiffs believed, was repugnant to the due process clause of the federal Constitution and the Fourteenth Amendment. The requirement that Mr. Nakutsuka declare his intention in good faith of becoming a citizen was a legal impossibility; and because of this he had been denied his right to the occupation of farming. But the judge, in handing down his decision, reasoned the law was not really discriminatory, because Japan could discriminate also if it wanted to, and because not only the Japanese but also the Chinese were discriminated against. Further, he found yellow or brown skin to be the "hallmark of the Oriental despotisms"; people possessing it were not able to adjust to a republican form of government.[30]

The State Supreme Court upheld the district court. About the same time they considered a similar case, *Porterfield and Y. Mizuno* vs. *Webb*, which had been heard the year before in Los Angeles. The decision was the same. But the court added that the California alien land laws did not prevent aliens from engaging in agriculture for wages.

Eliot Mears, professor of geography and international trade at Stanford University, in 1927 pointed out that these decisions ran counter to what courts had usually decided in regard to other aliens. The Constitution, he reminded his readers, is meant not only to protect citizens against certain encroachments by the government, but alien residents as well. Federal and state constitutional law protects both against deprivation of life, liberty or property without due process, and upholds freedom of contract for both.[31]

The Terrace-Nakutsuka and the Porterfield-Mizuno cases set the general guidelines for later decisions on various aspects of the alien land laws affecting the Japanese. Some cases went through lengthy litigation before winding up in the Supreme Court; others were stopped early in lower courts of the various states. Some were heard simultaneously and cited each other for precedents. There were widespread prosecutions and threatened prosecutions. First outright ownership, then leasing, sharecropping, and stock-companies in which a majority of stockholders were ineligible aliens were struck down in turn.

An important respite came in 1922 when the California attorney general took two Japanese residents of Sutter County into court in a guardianship matter, one of many such cases. These residents were Hayao Yano and his minor daughter, who was two years old when the case began. Some Caucasian citizens had sold Mr. Yano a fourteen-acre tract of land worth $3,000, and water rights in Butte County. The contract was written in the name of the United States-born daughter. The Superior Court recognized that Mr. Yano was a man of good character, that he was sober and industrious. Nevertheless, it took away his right of guardianship over the child and appointed her grandmother as her guardian. The child had no property, the court stated, because property taken in a child's name solely to evade the laws of the state is not hers.

The California Supreme Court with one dissenting vote disagreed with the lower court. Mr. Yano had confessedly made this arrangement because he could not buy property otherwise, an act "in no manner unlawful." While the court did not feel the 1920 Initiative was a violation of the Japan–American treaty provisions, it held that that part of the law which disqualified Japanese aliens as guardians was clearly a violation of the Constitution. Parents had a preferential right to guardianship except when incompetent, and such guardianship was under the control of the superior courts. Mr. Yano must submit periodic financial accounts, however, he was to be allowed only a limited return on his investment, and was to give up the property to the girl when she became of age. Its legality thus established, this guardianship method of land operation became universally practiced by the Issei.

"I don't go so far as to say the alien land laws threatened our livelihood," says the Issei businessman, I. K. Ishimatsu. "But if you wanted to lease or own the land for any purpose, you had to use your children's name and if you didn't have your own children, you would have to take a risk and ask someone who was a citizen and hope everything worked out. A set of books had to be kept up for inspection by the state authorities in order to prove that you were an employee working for a wage. This caused quite an uneasy feeling because I was informed at the time that the punishment for alien land law violation was condemnation of all the subject's property and imprisonment.

"If it had not been for the anti-Japanese land laws, more people would have wanted to stay here. I, myself, thought this was a hopeless place to expand in. These were bad laws, I'll tell you that."

A Santa Clara Valley Issei woman, devoted as Mr. Ishimatsu is to American democracy, said, putting her hand to her heart, "When these laws were passed, it hurt here. It was like they were cutting off our arms. We had no power, we had nothing."

But more difficulty was to come. A new movement had begun with the aim of further restricting the Japanese group.

THREE · PUTTING DOWN ROOTS

SACRAMENTO-BORN Valentine Stuart McClatchy was publisher of the Sacramento *Bee* beginning in 1883, one-time director of the Associated Press, president of the California State Reclamation Board in charge of Sacramento River flood control involving the expenditure of some $32 million. A man of great publicity skill, McClatchy untiringly and over a period of many years turned out anti-Japanese propaganda in his newspaper, in briefs, and in well-circulated pamphlets. Not content with strengthening the alien land laws he and those who shared his convictions wanted nothing short of Japanese exclusion from the United States.

In 1920 and 1932 McClatchy represented the California Joint Immigration Committee before Congress and the State Department. This organization had arisen from the old Oriental Exclusion League. Its influence was far greater than the size of its membership indicated, and it had a persuasive lobby in Washington. McClatchy also acted as spokesman for the Native Sons of the Golden West, the American Legion, the California State Federation of Labor, and the California State Grange.

Immigration controls under the Gentlemen's Agreement were insufficient, it was held, and should be replaced by legislative restrictions. The committee also wanted to bar Japanese nationals already in this country and their native American children from citizenship forever, but they concentrated on exclusion as their immediate goal. Once again regional prejudice was carried to the national level, as they propounded the hoary argument that Japanese immigration and propagation of children in America was part of an organized, imperialist-inspired plot to take over the West.

McClatchy disputed earlier anti-Asiatic spokesmen on one point however: the Japanese were not immoral undesirables. On the contrary, it was precisely because they were not—because they were neither lazy nor immoral nor lawless—that they were so dangerous. They were part of an unbeatable economic machine.

The fact that he employed a more reasonable tone than previous race-baiters made his case more plausible. The exclusionists were not motivated by prejudice, McClatchy hastened to reassure his listeners. With so many people favoring exclusion, there could be no question of prejudice. Indeed, some anti-alien laws were passed in the legislatures "without a single dissenting vote." The pressure was not coming from extremists, but from the conversion of "the intelligent, conservative element."[1]

The pressure for exclusion at this particular period was curious in one way, because, in contrast to the general immigration trend, more Japanese were leaving the country in 1921 and 1922 than were coming in. The era of the influx of great numbers of laboring people from Japan was past. Nor did the Japanese group lack influential defenders. Many newspapers counteracted the tone of the Hearst and McClatchy chains. The Fresno *Republican*, for example, while favoring exclusion, editorialized in favor of civil rights and justice for the Japanese who were already here. The Monterey *Cypress* and the San Jose *Mercury* spoke well of the Issei as employers of labor. "The Japanese give their farm hands white sheets and treat them like white men," said a spokesman for the Municipal Employment Bureau of San Jose.[2]

Prominent Japanese made efforts to promote friendly relationships with the Caucasian community. A group of Japanese farmers in Colexico, California, gave a dinner and invited town businessmen and their wives. The vice-president of the local bank made a speech thanking the Japanese for their contributions to the community and spoke against exclusion. For this he and they were castigated by the American Legion. A similar incident occurred in Lodi, California.

But the Joint Immigration Committee had friends in Congress. Years of propaganda had prepared the public for this final, legislative step, and aided by the machinations of the powerful Henry Cabot Lodge, the Immigration Act of 1924 was brought into being, with its section 13C which stated that no alien ineligible to citizenship should be admitted to the United States, with the exception of a few nonquota immigrants such as government officials and returning nationals. This act nullified the Gentlemen's Agreement and by-passed diplomatic channels used for carrying out its principles. Further, it differed from the Agreement in that it was more obviously discriminatory against Orientals as a racial group and more stringent in its provisions. Thus the United States followed South Africa, Australia, and New Zealand in their Oriental exclusionist policies. President Coolidge signed the 1924 Immigration Act under protest, regretting that the exclusion provision could not be severed from the rest: "If the exclusion provision stood alone, I should disapprove it without hesitation. . . ."[3]

The affronted government of Japan reacted to the new act with disbelief. The Japanese press exploded, and one newspaper invited American missionaries in Japan to go home. " 'America was the first in helping and extending its sympathy to Armenians oppressed and treated inhumanely by the Turks,' " editorialized *The Japan American News.* " 'America did not hesitate to be the champion of humanity. They called the Turks barbarous but the Americans are the Turks now.' "4

The American ambassador in Tokyo and the Japanese ambassador in Washington resigned. There were mass prayer meetings throughout Japan as well as anti-American boycotts and demonstrations, one set off by a suicide in front of the American embassy in Tokyo.

Offsetting the jubilation of the anti-Oriental press, a few American newspapers, among them the Los Angeles *Express,* condemned the act, and the National Chamber of Commerce spoke against it. Charles Evans Hughes voiced strong objections. Apologetic New York business and professional men sent cablegrams to Japan, as did thirty presidents emeriti of leading United States universities. Ironically, a quota system had originally been proposed as a compromise solution by the Issei sympathizer and missionary-reformer, Sidney Lewis Gulick. His idea was perverted to deny to the Asiatic group any quota at all.

The Immigration Act of 1924, like the land laws, was aimed primarily at the Japanese, again on the grounds that they were not assimilable and could not become citizens. A naturalization case brought before the Supreme Court in 1922 had provided the hook on which to hang the argument.

In the days of the first Japanese immigration it had not been clear whether or not these newcomers could become citizens. A few had been naturalized, perhaps fifty or a hundred. James Mineno, who died in the Puyallup assembly center in 1942 at the age of seventy-eight, having spent most of his life in Alaska, was one of these pioneer citizens. He had left Japan at the age of eleven to go to sea. When his ship was wrecked, he had boarded a rescue cruiser bound for Boston. Finding his way to Washington, he obtained citizenship papers before it became a state. The first naturalized Issei was Joseph Heco, also a shipwrecked sailor who was rescued and brought to San Francisco in 1851 and who took an American name. Still another early American Japanese who was naturalized was the distinguished international lawyer, Misuji Miyakawa, who acted as counsel for San Francisco Japanese in the school crisis of 1906.

More often naturalization was discouraged, even though citizenship ineligibility was not specified in early laws. After the post-Civil War Fourteenth Amendment defined citizens as all persons born or naturalized in the United States, a naturalization act in 1870 granted rights to free whites and persons of African nativity or descent, omitting mention of Oriental races. Various courts classified Japanese and Chinese, along with Armenians and native Hawaiians, with the nonwhite races who were not to be allowed citizenship privileges. In his first message to Congress Theodore Roosevelt recommended that naturalization privileges be opened to Japanese nationals.

The California constitution of 1879 specified Mongolians as ineligible for citizenship. A federal act of 1882 prohibited Chinese from becoming citizens, but protests from the government of Japan had prevented Japanese from being named in the ban against the Chinese. In 1911 the Bureau of Immigration and Naturalization ordered that declarations of intentions to file for citizenship could not be received from persons other than whites or Africans, and the courts thereafter refused naturalization to the Japanese.

Often, the Orientals who wanted to be naturalized had been here a very long time—longer than many Caucasian immigrants granted this privilege. On the other hand, children of Japanese parents residing here permanently were American citizens by the "law of the soil." With the annexation of Hawaii, citizenship was conferred on Hawaiian-born Japanese, and in 1920 those of voting age began to exercise the privilege of the ballot freely and without fear. It was a different story in neighboring Canada: there Nisei were not allowed to vote.

Tokao Ozawa, the petitioner in the very important Supreme Court naturalization case of 1922 was a citizen of Japan and a twenty-year resident of Hawaii. He had been denied United States citizenship by a district court eight years before. Ozawa was a graduate of a Berkeley, California, high school and had been a student at the University of California for three years. He was educating his children in American schools, used English in the home, and was a person of intelligence and good character.

The main issue argued in this particular case, oddly, was whether or not Japanese were actually Orientals, and thus whether they were included under the permission for naturalization granted free whites. Though there were many exceptions, the Japanese and Chinese nationals had traditionally kept apart from each other, and certain Japanese spokesmen had attempted to disassociate themselves from the Chinese in the public mind. Now, part of their legal case was based upon this separation. Reversing the emphasis of most physical anthropologists, that the Japanese are Mongolian with a strong strain of Caucasian blood, the Ozawa lawyers argued that the basic stock was Ainu. Federal statutes used the word "white" merely to distinguish black people from others, they said. The Magyars of Hungary were freely admitted to citizenship, though they were of Mongolian origin. Were all whites really white, it was asked. Who could say what white was? What were the racial divisions? Did Japanese have yellow brains and hearts?

An opposition lawyer expressed surprise at the assertions of the experts called to testify. The Ainus left no traces of ever having possessed the art of writing, he said. Yet here were Oriental scholars professing to believe that the Ainus were a branch of the Caucasian race! Furthermore, the original natives of Japan had married freely with incoming Chinese and Koreans. The lawyers for the opposition admonished the Japanese to be proud of their Mongolian blood, without suggesting that this merited American citizenship. The Court decided against Ozawa.

Though the approach taken by Ozawa's lawyers was unusual, it may be that no argument they might have given before this Court would have made any difference. The judges defended themselves against criticism by maintaining that their decision did not imply "any suggestion of individual unworthiness or racial inferiority."[5] After the Ozawa case several Issei who had already been granted citizenship on the mainland and in Hawaii were taken to court and their papers declared null and void.

The Cable Act of 1922, which brought new protection to most American-born women who married foreigners by providing for retention of their American citizenship, did not protect Caucasian or Nisei women who married aliens ineligible for citizenship; until 1930 when the ruling was modified they lost their own citizenship if they so married and could not be naturalized. In 1924 clerks of courts with naturalization jurisdiction were ordered to refuse to file papers for aliens who were or whose husbands were of the Chinese, Japanese, or Hindu race.

The drastic exclusion law based upon various denials of citizenship had an immediate negative effect. The greatest immigration cutoff occurred immediately after passage of this legislation. Though the law was later interpreted more liberally, in the early nineteen-twenties, American Japanese men were suddenly forbidden to send to Japan for brides—a situation very damaging to a group whose culture stresses the importance of the family and the issue of children. At the time R. D. McKenzie pointed out that for Issei to fail in achieving a family succession was "to fail in life."[6]

Bachelor groups such as the gangs of fruit tramps who traveled up and down the coast following the crops and who never made the transition to more stable means of livelihood were looked down upon by more settled members of Japanese society. These bachelors seemed unamenable to social convention and most of their money went for *sake* or gambling.

Numerous suicides were known to have resulted from the new hardship imposed by the exclusion policy. The situation might have been more critical had not the ratio of men to women risen from 24 to 1 in 1900 and 7 to 1 in 1910 to almost equal numbers in 1920.

Established families were affected also. A number of persons who were visiting in Japan alone found that they could not reenter the United States. Although the law allowed some of those on temporary visits to come back, sixty-five cases were reported in which either the mother or one or more children were refused reentry. Proof of status and former residence was sometimes difficult to produce. Some Issei visiting in Japan could not bring back the wives they married there.

Throughout their history the West Coast Japanese have done a tremendous amount of transocean visiting, as well as changing residence frequently on this continent. Families remained close, if only through correspondence. Snapshots and letters continually traveled back and forth from America to Japan. A Placerville family took a yearly trip to Sacramento to have a formal family picture taken to be sent to relatives in Japan, an important and exciting occasion for the California children.

The principle reason for so many return visits, however, was that children, in particular the eldest sons, were traditionally responsible for the welfare of their parents. A son might return to Japan, for example, to care for the needs of an aged mother whose husband had died. Before 1924 under terms of the Gentlemen's Agreement one solution to this kind of problem was to bring aged parents as well as wives and minor children they might have acquired while in Japan back into the United States to live. After 1924 this was impossible.

An American Japanese farmer described his dilemma in a letter to R. D. McKenzie, who was making a study of the effects of exclusion for the Institute of Pacific Relations. The man's oldest son had been left with his grandparents in Japan. The boy, who was over eighteen, had been attending middle school when the exclusion act was passed suddenly, and the father did not have time to get him out of the country. The father suffered a great conflict of conscience, feeling it was his duty to take care of his six children in this country as well as his oldest boy and elderly parents in Japan.

Another farmer wrote that an important human right was denied because of exclusion. "I have been in this country seventeen years," he said. "In 1916 I went back to Japan and married, came back here with my wife and engaged in farming. We had a very peaceful and joyful home and were full of content in our lives. In later years we had two sons and two daughters whom we had great pleasure in making good American citizens. But about five years ago we had to meet with the destruction of our hopeful life. It was the death of my wife leaving the children motherless. . . . It is a world-recognized fact that the greatest education of children depends upon the loving hands of [the] mother. Recognizing this . . . I have been striving my utmost to get someone to take her place. . . . The only solution is the acquiring of a mother from Japan. But the present law does not allow that. . . ."[7]

Many Japan-oriented Issei who had acquired their "nest-eggs" returned permanently to Japan, but in general the exclusion act tended to stem the outward as well as the inward immigration flow. At first, because of the unpleasant experiences of others, most were afraid to visit at all. Many who had been uncertain before decided to stay permanently in this country, but not without considerable emotional conflict and a confusion of loyalties.

School children lived in two cultures, that of their parents, and that of the public school. Daily they shifted back and forth from one to the other. The winds of Caucasian feeling toward them blew now warm, now cold, now friendly, now unfriendly; sometimes it beckoned, sometimes it rejected. A Nisei boy wrote of his feelings: he wanted desperately to be an American, but he wondered, would America accept him? In school he learned about democracy and American history and to play baseball. Visiting Japan, he found much to laugh at. Reciting lessons in class back in this country, he found his fellow students laughing at him for mistakes in English. He experienced an almost schizophrenic pull between the two worlds. Here ". . . the strange people . . . had red hair, blue eyes, and white skin, just like the pictures of the ogres in Japanese fairy-tale books." They made him think he was living "in a story-book land."

When the first Alien Land Act was passed, the boy got the impression that the older Issei must have been bad people to have this happen to them, and he was angry with them. A Caucasian child called him names, and he cried. During World War I he and other Japanese were more popular. With Kibei college students, who had received a substantial part of their education in Japan, he felt a kind of hostile rivalry. Then as an American university student he came to realize how limited his own career chances here would be.

America, he said, had not been able to recognize him in high school. She had put the pictures of those of his race "at the tail end of the year book." By city ordinance, he could not play tennis on the courts in the parks. America would not let him own a house to live in. She would not give him a job, "unless it be a menial one." He began to wonder if a career in Japan might not be acceptable after all.[8]

Some Nisei in their frustration were morbidly unhappy, yet were paralyzed in taking initiative to better their group position. A Kibei girl told of her education and return to this country. She had wanted to leave behind her Japan's feudalism and all it implied and to jump immediately into another age, but on her return her father had expected to see a "little Japanese doll." There was "stormy weather" from the first night in her father's house, for he shared "the common belief that a person who raises questions over social problems is dangerous. . . ." Her only hope were the ideals she learned in American high school.[9]

Rejected by one society but not quite wanting to go back to the other, many Issei tried to prepare their children for a life in either country.

Future laws, even more discriminatory than the present ones, might one day make life in the United States impossible. Therefore many parents kept up their offspring's dual citizenship by active steps or by passive inaction.

Like France, England, Switzerland, the Netherlands, and many other countries, Japan had traditionally followed the code of *jus sanguinis* in regard to citizenship, laying claim to the children of all Japanese regardless of their country of residence or choice. American law does not recognize dual citizenship. In 1916 Japan passed an expatriation act, which allowed Nisei to renounce Japanese citizenship by petitioning the minister of foreign affairs or having their citizenship renounced by their parents, often an expensive process. Nisei between the ages of seventeen and thirty-seven, moreover, were not supposed to take these steps unless they had fulfilled a stint of military service in Japan. As long as Nisei remained on American soil, the Japanese government could not claim them for military service. The Japanese Association worked to terminate dual nationality and urged parents to expatriate their children from Japan, thus denying their allegiance to the Emperor. Many did so. Children over seventeen were registered as not available for active military service. Each year Issei men, being involuntary subjects of the Emperor, also had to file notice through the Japanese consul-general's office that they were not available for service.

In 1924 Japanese law was changed to read that Japan laid claim only to foreign-born children of Japanese parentage who were registered in Japan within fourteen days after birth, and even then this could be canceled by simple notification. Thus after 1924 most Nisei were outright American citizens, and in the nineteen-thirties, by most estimates, only 20 per cent of the Nisei group held dual citizenship.

With the relinquishing of dual citizenship, property rights in Japan and the right of succession were also lost. On the other hand, many Nisei, in the words of M. J. D. Negoro, writing in 1921, were "haunted by the fear of finding themselves . . . denied the rights of American citizenship" after they had given up their Japanese citizenship.[10]

The effect on the Issei of the series of drastic prohibitions in the form of alien land legislation, the exclusion law, and ineligibility for citizenship was to thwart their desire to merge in the general American community and to increase ingrown tendencies among them. The sort of activity that culminated in the Abiko resolution during the San Francisco school crisis, when the Issei group was younger and more hopeful, seemed long past by the nineteen-twenties.

It was difficult for Issei to think in terms of American ideals, civil liberties, and property rights since these principles so often did not apply to them. Issei frequently cite the legal situation involved in automobile accidents as an illustration of this: it was useless, they felt, to carry damage cases against Caucasians into the courts, because they "always lost." While the idea of a democratic society had appeal, legal barriers and lack of education stood in the way of involvement and understanding. "After the alien land laws," says one Issei who is politically active today, "we shied away when we saw Caucasians."

The Issei had tried to mingle in the beginning, according to George Shimada, a Nisei landscape gardener, "But when they were rejected, and all those things were written about them in the papers, they weren't powerful enough to fight it. So they just didn't try any more." Withdrawal and clannishness as a response to discrimination is a characteristic of all first-generation immigrant groups, but the problems of the Japanese in the West were in quantity and severity far beyond what European immigrant groups had to face.

According to Professor Eliot Mears, the Issei became abnormally shy and self-conscious. "The main idea of the older generation," says a Nisei businessman, "was never to make trouble." He tells how his parents were duped by an unscrupulous Caucasian door-to-door salesman. They bought a subscription to a group of popular American magazines written in Japanese, and then waited for months for the magazines to appear, but they never did—in any language. They did not report the fraud, nor would they have done so had it been a more unusual or serious offense.

When people got to know the Issei they got along well, according to another Nisei. Strangers were the problem. "My parents were pretty well educated in Japanese ways, I think, at least average or better, but they never became Americanized. If they went to some function they were uncomfortable as the dickens; so they hardly ever went anywhere. When things were going real well and Pa felt a little flush, we'd go to a Chinese restaurant. My folks didn't go to my high school graduation, partly because they didn't have decent clothes to wear, I suppose."

The Livingston Cooperative Society established by the Yamato group was frequently pointed out by well-wishers as a model enterprise and Livingston itself as a model Caucasian–Japanese community. Sociologists had observed that this of all areas was the most free of anti-Japanese prejudice. The colonists subscribed to the war loans during the 1914–18 conflict, to the Red Cross and the YMCA. They taught their children English before they entered school. Nevertheless, present-day descendants who testify to good relations with the Caucasian community recall seeing "No Jap" signs in Livingston before 1921, and there was no mixing in social life—an Issei attending a PTA meeting was "unheard of." One Nisei, a lifelong resident, feels that the older generation lived there without friction with the Caucasian segment because they made it a rule never to compete at all with the downtown merchants' community. Economic competition between the Japanese Coop and Caucasian farmers and farm organizations never led to trouble.

In the various West Coast towns when Japanese were denied admittance to theaters or public swimming pools, were refused haircuts in white barbershops, or underwent countless similar indignities, there was little outcry from them, and Caucasians in general either did not know about such policies or regarded them as normal. On being questioned, barbers gave a standard explanation of their discriminatory practice: Japanese hair was too coarse for their scissors.

Housing discrimination intensified concentration in certain areas and reinforced the inclination to withdraw. As the Reverend Jun Fujimori of Alameda, California, puts it: "We tended to stay where we were at ease." Restrictive covenants that covered Orientals as well as Negroes, Jews, and sometimes other groups were widespread in land deeds. Rentals in desirable areas were difficult to find, and are opening up only today for the American Japanese.

The alien land laws drove many farmers to the cities. Few remained in the Hood River Valley area in Oregon, for example, after this period.

Cut off from many areas of activity, the Issei directed their energies to bettering themselves and to raising their children. "Through all the discrimination," WRA head Dillon Myer commented later, "Issei were quietly and effectively carrying on their work. . . . It required a brand of courage . . . which very few people of any national origin could match."[11] In their work goals the first-generation Japanese often seemed indomitable. They appeared to embody the ideal of Japanese manhood symbolized by the carp, a fish "which swims upstream and which does not wriggle when laid on the chopping block."[12]

Their lives were not a series of crises or constantly threatening incidents, however. The nineteen-twenties and early thirties were characterized by a general lull in anti-Japanese agitation. Many Issei testify that while they worked hard and few got rich, the years were productive and happy. The Iwagaki family are a case in point. While living on a farm in Cupertino, California, they sent their children to public school and to a Caucasian church where they were well accepted. The parents themselves went in to nearby San Jose to the Japanese Methodist church where they could understand the services.

Their Caucasian neighbors were friendly, frequently dropping in on them to visit, as people do in small towns, helping when there was sickness, taking care of their chickens on occasion. The Iwagakis' experience was good, and their attitudes remained positive.

They kept up a correspondence with their family in Japan and maintained many Japanese traditions. Yearly they invited a large group of Japanese friends down from San Francisco for a picnic in the early spring when their orchard was in bloom, joining in the custom of all Santa Clara Valleyans in those days of touring the countryside in blossomtime by car.

Though the children shared the positive attitudes of their parents, one remarks that growing up they were always aware of a subtle feeling of being "not quite as good" as Caucasian children. For some Nisei discrimination was a cage with invisible bars; they experienced toleration rather than acceptance. Many Nisei, particularly those who had almost exclusively Caucasian friends and coworkers, remember no unpleasantness whatsoever in their relations with the dominant racial group. Parents rarely transmitted complaints to their children.

Shuji Kimura, writing in *The Tulean Dispatch*, an internment-camp publication, recalled neighborly interchanges between his family and Caucasians in their area. "The first of the vegetables would go to our neighbors, they in turn would bring their venison from their hunting trips and trout from their fishing trips. . . . The children would go Easter egg hunting together. Mother would exchange recipes." When it came to reminiscing, the Issei wanted to be with their own language group who shared common experiences. Nevertheless, their neighbors were important, and Kimura quoted an old Japanese saying, " 'The neighbor next door—more than the brother far away.' "[13]

Free from agitation and newspaper propaganda, Caucasians and Japanese generally worked well together. It was "not an assertion but a fact," according to K. K. Kawakami, that "left alone by busybodies" they toiled side by side in the rice fields and orchards without friction. Caucasians employed Japanese and Japanese employed Caucasians. In neither case was there trouble.[14]

Certain areas were worse than others in the matter of social prejudice, however. Walnut Grove near Sacramento had a long history of discrimination and segregation. Living farther north and west but about the same distance from Sacramento, Vaca Valley Japanese saw the prejudice they met with as tenant farmers gradually give way to toleration. Experiences could be different in fairly close-by areas and for different persons.

A Nisei surgeon who grew up in a relatively favorable area says, "Actually I really did feel that we were discriminated against. When I was going to grammar school, there were lots of Japanese there. When I went to high school in another town, about 1928, there was only one other Japanese boy and one girl in the whole school. When there are very few of you, people don't think of you so very much. When there are a whole bunch of you, people think, well, something's coming off."

Those who had lived both in the Japanese section of Seattle which was isolated and self-sufficient and in mixed or Caucasian areas found the city fairly accepting. The daughter of a Japanese-language newspaperman lived three or four miles from downtown Seattle in a cosmopolitan neighborhood among Negroes, Yugoslavians, and other Caucasians, as well as Japanese. "We never did think about race," this woman said. "I guess Seattle was more or less a melting pot. We all got on well together. In fact, when I was young I thought it was terrible just to go around with people of my own race. And yet as I grew older and started dating it was always with Japanese. So I had to change my tune."

A Nisei growing up in a small town in northern Washington, where there were very few Japanese, found early that he had to prove he could fight before he was accepted. "There really was prejudice there." His wife, from Auburn, Washington, felt that the frequency of contact between Caucasians and Japanese made for mutual understanding. "When they grew up with us, they tended to be on our side," she said. "More than the people who isolated themselves from us. They tried to learn about our ways, too. After all, it was sort of hard for us to learn the American way of life just during the school hours."

A Los Angeles Issei sent his five-year-old daughter to kindergarten in an integrated school. The child was bright, but she could not speak English and could not follow what was going on. In a later-day variation of the San Francisco school imbroglio, the Los Angeles administrators decided to send her by bus to a segregated school where there were solely minority-race children. She did not like being sent away from home to a segregated school and refused to go the next day. When her father found out what had happened and why, instead of punishing her, he took her out of school temporarily and decided that from that day forward they would speak nothing but English in the home, a decision influenced by the fact that he already had some knowledge of the language.

Issei who were restricted in their Caucasian contacts or who withdrew from English-speaking circles could not communicate well with the outside world, or even with their children, who were learning the ways, thought habits, and talk of their schoolmates.

The English that the Nisei children heard spoken all day at school was a simpler language than Japanese which many forgot and could not write at all despite attendance at language schools (*gakuens*). Sometimes they refused to speak it with their parents and would converse with their brothers and sisters in English which closed out their parents from their world. Or parents and children used an intermediary language with each other, a mixed English–Japanese with special words: for example, "bureddo," the Isseis' pronunciation of "bread." The children wanted to identify with their peers, and were often embarrassed by their parents' old-fashioned, foreign ways.

One girl was constantly chided by her mother for walking in the American manner rather than taking the tiny, ladylike steps thought proper for Japanese. "Why do you take such big steps," her mother would scold her. "You walk like a boy! Can't you be more feminine?" The same attitude held that smoking was also not ladylike.

"There's always a problem between the old and the young," Judge

Kanemoto points out. "There was a big gap between our parents and ourselves. They were educated in Japan. They had no opportunity to be oriented to our way of thinking. They were too busy eking out a living. We went to school here, and everything we learned was the American way of life and thinking. We couldn't speak Japanese, and they couldn't speak English. We knew the rudiments, but when you got to discussing anything you ran out of vocabulary before you got very far. So it was kind of a feeling communication that was all you had. But I'm still amazed that despite that tremendous gap they were able to communicate certain basic things to us. Among them: you don't do anything to hurt or disgrace the family, friends, or relatives. Education is important, and, by gosh, if you go to school, you don't go just to eat lunch. That's a favorite saying of the Japanese."

At the language schools the children were taught the old-fashioned virtues, morality and manners, as well as the fundamentals of the Japanese language. The schools preserved sources of pride, one reason, perhaps, for the notably responsible behavior of the Nisei group in difficult situations.

The teachers in these schools were well educated Issei, often trained in Japan. Particularly in the earlier schools, the teaching was ritualistic and strongly disciplinary, even feudalistic. The children went through books instead of grades, memorizing countless subtle aphorisms, often paradoxical or enigmatic, designed to develop a philosophical bent. There was a marked increase in student enrollment as well as the number of language schools immediately after the passage of the exclusion act.

Like all children, the Nisei students were tired after regular school and would rather have played. Often they were bored. One Nisei girl used to spend her time day-dreaming and poking her face with her fingertips in order to make dimples—until one day she discovered the teacher was standing behind her, causing the whole class to laugh.

Monica Sone gives a lighthearted description of these hours in Japanese school in her book, *Nisei Daughter*:

> Gradually I yielded to my double dose of schooling. . . . At Bailey Gatzert School I was a jumping, screaming roustabout Yankee, but at the stroke of three when the school bell rang and doors burst open everywhere, spewing out pupils like jelly beans from a broken bag, I suddenly became a modest, faltering, earnest little Japanese girl with a small, timid voice. I trudged down a steep hill to Nihon Gakko with other black-haired boys and girls.
> . . . At the beginning of each class hour, Yasuda-sensei [teacher] punched a little bell on her desk. We stood up by our seats, at strict attention. Another "ping!" We all bowed to her in unison while she returned the bow solemnly. With the third "ping!" we sat down together.

. . . I learned that I could stumble all around in my lessons without ruffling sensei's nerves, but it was a personal insult to her if I displayed sloppy posture. . . .[15]

During the Japanese writing hours, they leaned over their desks, painstakingly practicing the beautifully lined and shaded ideographs, in the old days using a brush, later a pen. There are three ways of writing Japanese, according to Yuri Katai, a young widow: the easy way, the hard way, and the middle way.

The easy way, *katakana*, puts together the needed number of signs for a word; the hard way, *kanji*, is one very complicated picture for every word, difficult to execute and difficult to remember. There are only fifty-one *katakana*, but thousands of *kanji*. Moreover, since each of its signs is a syllable, the *katakana* contains the clues for pronunciation. As a school girl Yuri used to write her lessons the easy way and the hard way side by side so that she could recite readily in class by reading from the simple side. If she was caught doing this she received a sharp rap on the head.

Teiko Wada, whose father-in-law taught in one of the language schools, says: "The children felt, 'It's not Japan here. It's America; so why should we have to learn and follow these stiff rules of behavior if we don't want to go back to Japan?' But we couldn't object. You didn't dare talk back to parents in those days. Not like the children of today." She now wishes, however, that she had learned more of the language and culture, because it would be "nice to have." Assimilation does not necessarily mean losing all the values of cultural diversity.

Some learned a great deal and took pride and pleasure in reading Japanese books and seeing Japanese movies. A good number of Nisei testify that they went to language school only to satisfy their parents and "did not learn anything." The fact that few of the boys exposed to this extra language education profited by it was demonstrated years later during World War II when Nisei soldiers in the intelligence service had to be retaught, "courtesy of the U.S. army language school." Despite the fact that in the nineteen-forties the number of language schools rose to 248, with 19,000 pupils between the ages of four and twenty, only 15 per cent of the Nisei tested in the evacuation camps passed the oral Japanese test and only 5 per cent were able to read a newspaper clipping which required a knowledge of from two hundred to three hundred characters.

Dr. James Higuchi had the equivalent of a high school education in Japanese. He went to Japanese class from grammar school days on, first in Los Altos, California, later in Campbell. The Los Altos school, not church connected, was a cooperative. The parents hired a teacher from Japan who had attended Stanford. He disciplined the children by hitting them on the knuckles with a ruler. "It was like the old-fashioned red school house—the whole range of classes from kindergarten on up through high school."

Somewhere between 1925 and 1930, all the textbooks were completely changed. The original writing in the books looked like characters executed with a brush. The new texts had a different paper, printed characters, as well as revised contents. Instead of the traditional Japanese stories (elementary stories were about the birds, and the spring) pupils began to get translations of foreign stories. Some of the old stories were about historical Japanese figures, and perhaps one reason for their being discontinued was to reduce the influence of Japanese history on the young.

Frank Bunya attended one of two language schools in Seattle, a large progressive school with eight grades. There was no physical punishment for pranks; rather students were given "the silent treatment" when necessary. If they liked their teacher, they were allowed to choose her for the next year. The school had only one purpose: to teach the language. "But now when I attempt to speak Japanese it is quite difficult."

One of the exceptions to those who "didn't learn much," was the attorney Peter Nakahara, who was raised in San Pedro, California, and grudgingly attended an unusually well-operated language school in nearby Compton. Although the teachers tried to instill precepts of Japanese nationalism, they also really did teach the language. "They taught that the Japanese war in China was a just war, that the Co-east Asia Prosperity Sphere was a beneficial concept for all of Asia. Most of the students weren't intellectually receptive to that propaganda, and it went in one ear and out the other. I think Compton was one of the few schools that made a serious effort to propagandize. I learned that the principal of that school was repatriated on the *Gripsholm*, subsequently sent by the Japanese government to the Philippines, and I'd also heard that he was killed in a bombing raid in the Philippines. But Compton a school of subversion? No. They did not attempt in any way to deny Americanism, to say that we owed a loyalty to Japan over and above that to the United States. They recognized that our allegiance was to the United States."

"Gee, I was in high school," comments another Nisei with a different language school experience. "I think I was old enough to realize if it was a propaganda sort of thing. It was purely educational."

The language schools were nevertheless historical objects of criticism. There was widespread suspicion that all the children turned out by the schools were potential traitors. A few of the schools were Shinto-run, and religious worship of the Emperor was part of the teaching. Most, however, were Buddhist, and many were nonsectarian or Christian. Some of the first schools also taught English to the Issei who were having assimilation problems. A superintendent of public schools in Fresno, California, G. P. Stafford, wrote in the Fresno *Republican* in 1920 that the language schools were an aid to the children's education, and that the ones he knew of emphasized Americanization.

A 1927 Supreme Court test case declared the schools constitutional. In Hawaii, where they were viewed as a stabilizing influence, sugar plantation money helped support them. James Michener wrote in his novel *Hawaii*, " . . . and it was a strange thing, but not a single child in later years ever remembered much of the jingoistic nonsense . . . ; few ever wanted to go back to Japan, but all learned respect for an established order of life. It was as if the great freedoms enjoyed in American school in the first part of the day insulated the child against the nationalistic farrago of the afternoon, so that most Japanese children . . . assimilated the best from both schools and were not marred by the worst of either."[16]

Increasingly, to American Japanese the United States meant home. The anti-Orientalists deplored this trend to Americanization and pointed rather triumphantly to the Japanese schools as proof that it could not occur. While making integration difficult by constant harassment and at the same time finding fault with the Japanese for being slow to merge, they declared that assimilation of nonwhite races was undesirable anyway. The "race-mongrelcy" phobia was even infecting the churches. The Melting Pot idea is "the great American illusion," wrote Montaville Flowers.[17] V. S. McClatchy was not quite so sweeping. There *was* an American melting pot, he felt, but the Japanese were not included in it.

The facts of history were beginning to erode the argument. As sociologists of the time pointed out, other immigrant groups did not assimilate any faster than the Japanese. Other groups did not adapt themselves to their new surroundings within a single generation, either. Indeed, in the early part of the century, according to an Immigration Commission report, the Japanese showed relatively rapid progress in attaining a speaking knowledge of English and were most anxious to assimilate. As far back as 1915 many households were subscribing to popular American magazines.

A study by the Stanford psychologist Edward K. Strong in 1933 showed a close correlation between students of Japanese and of Caucasian extraction in rating subjects in school that were most and least liked, with Caucasian interests showing only a slightly wider range. Just as the American environment was changing the weight and height of immigrant children, who were on the average larger and taller than their forebears, so also was it gradually modifying the cultural outlook.

Unlike many other immigrant groups, the Japanese desired rather than discouraged formal education for their young. The Nisei generation, accepting the wishes of their elders, were strongly motivated in this direction. California Nisei were taking "full advantage of the public schools." The average mainland Nisei boy, according to the Strong study, planned two years of college, although as he grew older, he modified his aspirations somewhat. Even so, expectations in the early nineteen-thirties averaged only 1.5 years over accomplishment. Intelligence testing helped dispel the notion of an inferior race.

Everywhere, but particularly on the West Coast, the Japanese were putting down roots—and roots much deeper than many Issei had originally intended. With the arrival of children and their involvement in the American scene, Issei were forgetting their young manhood dreams of getting rich, making a fortune, and returning to Japan. A 1930 survey showed only 5 per cent of the Issei hoped to return. Japan became for many a hazy dream, a dream that some who actually did return found to be so unrealistic that they turned around and came back again.

During these years persons of Japanese descent were trickling out into various parts of the country, as far from the West Coast as New England and New York. Some went to Canada and Alaska. Members of a group of Florida Japanese who had colonized to grow pineapples left that state because of heat and malaria for Chicago, New York, Boston, and states to the north. In Idaho, Utah, and Colorado Issei went into the sugar beet fields, and grew potatoes, tomatoes, cabbage, and other garden truck. They spread into the state of Washington relatively late. In 1920, besides raising the usual fruits and vegetables and running small businesses, Issei in the Seattle area owned 3,500 dairy cattle, supplying one-half of the city's milk. Washington and Oregon were second to California in Japanese population. In these two states the Japanese tended to be urbanites. Oregon Japanese lived almost entirely in Multnomah County. But by far the greatest number lived and were to remain in California.

Countless Issei raised crops in the hot, interior valleys. Large Japanese populations arose in the Sacramento, San Joaquin, and Imperial valleys. Certain small towns were predominantly Japanese—Vacaville and Florin, near Sacramento, for example. There were colonies in more temperate locations such as the Santa Clara Valley and San Benito County.

The most important occupation was truck gardening. In Santa Clara Valley, in Fresno, in Auburn, California, the Japanese were orchardists, too, growing peaches and prunes and apricots. They grew grapes in Lodi. They fished in Monterey and San Pedro. In Dos Palos they planted rice.

Japanese were collecting in Los Angeles and Monterey, in Fresno, Oakland, Sacramento, Santa Barbara, San Francisco, and Stockton. People from the same districts in Japan tended to congregate in certain areas. There were numerous natives of the kens, or prefectures, of Kumamoto and Wakayama in San Jose, while in nearby Mountain View there were a large number of immigrants from Hawaii. Many former residents of Hiroshima-ken lived in Alameda, California, and in Seattle. The San Francisco Japanese section was called Little Osaka, and the Los Angeles section, Little Tokyo—not because the residents came from these cities, but because they found a certain geographical similarity in them.

Ghetto life in the big cities was not always savory. There were gambling halls and brothels. Dissidents along the Nisei charged that Little Tokyo was riddled with rackets and a system of "kickbacks" in the small factories to supervisors or owners in exchange for low-paying employment. The city racial concentrations resembled small-town areas in one respect—the widespread prevalence of gossip. Further, some Issei associated themselves with the more reactionary groups in Caucasian society, often the very ones which denounced them.

Both light and heavy industry were being constructed in the nineteen-twenties and thirties within the Japanese sections of Los Angeles, but a good many who lived there worked outside the area. Some of these were contract gardeners who planted and kept up the gardens of Caucasian families throughout the city. They had gone into this new occupation as a result of the alien land laws and tended to maintain independent attitudes and such high standards that their reputation grew, and all Japanese gardeners came to be in high demand. Many other Japanese who lived in these urban areas worked on farms on the outskirts of Los Angeles, where the land was fertile.

One mother, who resided in Montebello County, a fringe area of Los Angeles, used to carry her baby on her back and take her little girl by the hand, walking two miles to the fields where she deposited them in a ditch to play while she did her work.

It was not the same as being left on a city slum street. This family moved about from one community to another without apparent adverse effects upon the children. "We were happy," recalls Yuri Katai, who was the second to oldest child.

The children in this family grew up self-reliant and resilient. There was no time for relaxation or talk in the evenings, for then schoolwork, chores, ironing and cooking had to be done. The mother, who came from the island of Kochi, was the reliable central figure in the family. They all worked hard. The girl, Yuri, was sometimes asked to do the washing—and sometimes forgot. Then the mother would have to wash diapers at night in the dark and the next day take the baby and wet diapers to the field.

Yuri, who now works in an electronics factory, recalls coming home during these earlier times after a first day's work in the strawberry season and being so sore and stiff that when she fell off her bed at night she was not able to get up. The Japanese, though many had great skill and love of farming, were not, contrary to popular belief, a breed born for stoop labor in the fields; they, too, suffered pain and exhaustion.

They developed great proficiency in harvesting, however, being particularly adept in growing strawberries, which take an unusual amount of care and practical knowledge in the growing and picking. It was hard to find qualified pickers who could keep up a momentum; if they did not, they broke down. When the plants were bearing heavily, they learned to sit carefully in the narrow space between the rows and pick the berries without crushing the plants in the other row. The undersized and rotten berries had to be thrown away, the runners trimmed, the plants hoed and sprayed constantly. The first crop sometimes produced immense strawberries. After picking, the boxes were filled and the fruit arranged artistically. Often families worked by artificial light, and at night they would irrigate as soon as the berries were picked.

In the orchards they would work late at night, too, taking flashlights and looking for breaks in the irrigation trenches, in order to find the small breaks before they could grow into huge ones. As a child, Yuri was afraid of the dark and shadows and had to be careful "not to think scary thoughts."

To harvest broccoli they would go out early in the morning in cold and rainy weather, build a fire and sit by it bunching the broccoli and tying it with raffia, which had to be untangled. It was piece work; the more you put out, the more money you made. Sometimes they would work soaking wet, but the children would be promised ice-cream cones if they kept up.

Yuri remembers planting celery. First the celery was seeded and then the very young shoots taken up and replanted in the mud. She remembers walking booted in a muddy trench and sticking in the young shoots. Today with the use of machinery celery can be planted by someone sitting on the end of a moving tractor. Today there are tomato picking machines and fruit pickers. In the old days it was backbreaking work all the way.

The fishing industry has traditionally been an occupational area of importance to American Japanese, even though a very small percentage were involved in it compared with farming. In Oregon and Washington there was too much discrimination for the Issei to make their living as fishermen. In Alaska there was no possibility at all, for only citizens were allowed to fish professionally, though many Issei worked in the salmon canneries. Some started out in Alaskan canneries just as they did on the railroads, before migrating farther south and going into farming.

Several thousand American Japanese were employed in the fish canneries in various coastal spots in California during the nineteen-twenties and thirties, and several hundred were employed in wholesale fresh-fish markets. Primarily, however, they worked from boats, fishing the ocean waters with very great skill.

Monterey was the earliest Issei commercial fishing area. The first fisherman in the Japanese community, which was settled before the turn of the century, was a Mr. Noda. At Point Lobos as in Southern California early fishermen used to find abalone, a Japanese delicacy previously unknown for eating purposes in this country. Cooperation between Caucasians and the Japanese grew with Monterey's fishing industry and relations between the two groups there were quite good. In 1927 Monterey Japanese had twenty-five boats for salmon fishing, the men making an income of about $500 a season. From July to November they fished for albacore, from May to January, for abalone. The most lucrative catch was sardines. Today for unknown reasons the sardines have disappeared from the area, and the canneries have closed down, but formerly the sardine canneries were quite important there.

San Diego Japanese operated about thirty boats in the years before World War II, trolling for albacore and netting sardines. In San Pedro they also caught yellowfish tuna with hook and line. When canneries feared passage of anti-Japanese fishing legislation they tried gradually to close out their contracts with these fishermen.

According to a veteran fisherman and buyer, the Japanese excelled at fishing, because they made a study of it. "When a Japanese goes into the game, he goes in with the idea of learning all that is to be known. He knows the currents, tides, temperature of the water, winds, etc., and the effect of each upon the fish." The same commentator felt they were able to withstand long hours and pressure better than other fishermen, because unlike the others they refused to become excited when they ran into a large school of fish. They remembered to eat and rest and to take care of themselves. They also kept their boats cleaner and delivered their fish "in A-1 shape" to the cannery.[18]

A typical skilled Issei fisherman worked as a mast-man on the boats that went out on trips from San Pedro lasting up to six months, fishing the waters of the Pacific coast down as far as South America. He climbed the mast and spotted schools of fish by changes in color and texture of the water, almost imperceptible to the uninitiated.

Sardine fishing was done in the dark of the moon. The season began in July in Washington, gradually moved south, reaching Monterey in October, and lasting until February in the waters of San Pedro and San Diego. When the moon was down the sardines would appear as phosphorescent areas at the water's surface. Dawn or the rising of the moon interrupted the search for fish. The return trip was "often a race," because the boats were unloaded in the order of arrival at the fish harbor.[19]

Most of the boats were owned by others, or Issei fishermen who desired independence were in the process of paying for them under financial arrangements with canneries that bought the fish. A certain percentage of the pay was taken out of the profit from each catch brought in and was credited on the boat mortgage.

There were three status levels among these fishermen, according to Leonard Bloom and Ruth Riemer who studied the prewar industry at Terminal Island. On the lowest level were crew members who did not own any of their equipment. Next were equipment owners, whose outlay often was considerable. Fish and bait nets might run from $500 to $10,000, and a huge tuna or sardine purse seine might cost $15,000 or $20,000. The top group were the boat owners or investors. In 1947 a large boat for sardine fishing might cost $30,000 or more.[20]

Although Japanese were not for many years allowed to join either of the fishermen's unions, they had their own arrangement: whenever they found a school of fish they let other Japanese know as soon as possible. "While prosperous, they stick together, and when in trouble, they do the same."[21]

American Japanese did not habitually, like the Chinese, go together in large family clans for the purpose of economic enterprise. The many Japanese business proprietors generally had small firms. In a town like Fresno, California, for example, there could be found a general store specializing in Japanese goods (since a competing store east of the tracks could undersell them on other items), fruit and vegetable stands, drug stores, grocery stores, pool halls, lunch counters and restaurants, fish markets, and movie houses.

In Seattle's Japanese town, which was close to the waterfront, there were restaurants, grocery stores, and a great many Issei-operated hotels, some on the waterfront. Farmers used to bring in their produce from outside to the big Farmers' Market. The district has changed now, and some of it is slum-like; before the war it was poor, but not a slum.

A hotel operated by the Issei mother of Frank Bunya was in an integrated area closer to the center of town but still with a fine view of the bay. Mr. Bunya remembers when the fleet used to come in, ships would shine their searchlights over the skies. The family would watch the lights from their window. The Seattle World's Fair was situated later about three blocks from the hotel.

His father died in Tacoma when he was about six months old. When he was five years old the family moved to Seattle. "My mother worked in the hotel in the mornings, making beds and cleaning up, then after lunch she went to work in a restaurant as a waitress until about one A.M. The two jobs were a necessity as there were five mouths to feed."

The children used to help, even before they were in high school. Frank Bunya had a frightening experience one day when he was changing towels. He opened the door to go into a room and discovered the man who was living there, a very good friend, on his knee by the chair. The boy thought perhaps he was looking for something, but when he went up and tapped him on the shoulder, he did not move. He had died of a heart attack.

This hotel did not have "riff-raff" or even many transients; most of their roomers, mainly retired men, were steady, friendly, and stable. They had about fifty-two rooms, and the hotel was 75 to 80 per cent full all the time.

Seattle, like most of the larger cities on the West Coast, had its Japanese language newspaper, the *Great Northern Daily News*. One of its editors, today over ninety years of age, had attended Keio University and arrived in this country carrying only a small straw basket with all his belongings. First he worked on the railroads, but he went into newspaper work when he was fairly young. He also wrote editorials for small newspapers as far from Seattle as Portland, Los Angeles, and Salt Lake City. In those days the Japanese language papers employed women typesetters.

Los Angeles and San Francisco each had several newspapers, sometimes with keen competition between them. San Francisco's *Nichi Bei*, founded by Kyutaro Abiko, the man who had acted as spokesman for the city's Japanese in the school crisis and later had led in the establishment of the Livingston Cooperative, enjoyed the largest circulation of any Japanese newspaper published in a foreign country. The *Rafu Shimpo*, established in 1903, was the first and largest Japanese and English language daily in southern California.

The flower industry is another field of enterprise associated with American Japanese. Although the culture of ornamental trees and flowers had been practiced to a high degree of perfection for centuries in Japan, two completely unskilled Japanese nationals were the first to enter the industry here near the turn of the century. Professor Yamato Ichihashi, writing in 1932, told the story of one of them, "a poor but ambitious student" who had migrated to California, made a return visit to Japan, and came back to this country with a bride and some seeds of a large Japanese chrysanthemum. He planted the seeds in the backyard of a family in Oakland where he worked as a domestic. These seeds led to the establishment by 1906 of fifteen Japanese nurseries, primarily around Oakland.[22]

Ryohitsu Shibuya, who landed in San Francisco in 1904, went to work for one of the earliest of these, the Domoto nursery in Oakland. His principal duty was to transport and merchandise the flowers in the San Francisco flower market. Every morning he loaded a small cart and pushed it to the station and then lifted it onto the train and took it to market.

A few years later Shibuya bought a piece of property in Redwood City and began to grow and develop chrysanthemums. He did a great deal of work in plant hybridizing and gained a widespread reputation in the flower industry in this country for his creations. According to his son, Takeshi Shibuya of Atherton, California, he had the temperament of an artist. He was "no joiner" and liked to work alone.

At first the relatively few Japanese flower growers displayed and sold their flowers alongside the Chinese and Italian growers in the basement of the Shasta Hotel and later in a new brick building by the fire station between Kearny and Grant avenues on Bush Street. Here they began their tasks before dawn, bunching and tying the flowers that were brought in from San Mateo, Santa Clara, and Alameda counties. The Chinese and Italian growers dominated the area industry in the early nineteen-hundreds. The Japanese established their own organization in 1924.

A city market established in 1909 for truck farmers and jobbers in Los Angeles was similar to the San Francisco flower market. Chinese, Caucasian, and Japanese held stock in the organization, with Japanese holding the smallest number of shares. The Japanese did not break away and form an independent group, however, as did the flower growers in San Francisco.

With the coming of the Great Depression in the nineteen-thirties, American Japanese, whatever their particular occupational situation, often suffered even more than others in the country—because of their handicap as latecomers, and members of a minority racial group. There were business failures, mortgages were hard to meet, and work hard to find.

Persons of Japanese descent were rarely on the relief rolls. To them public welfare was shameful. In Guadalupe, on the coast of California, a family was forced to go on relief because the father had ulcers and could not work, and the mother was a "weakling." The other Japanese in the town realized their plight, but condemned what they had done, and some of their children at school tormented the children of the couple who had accepted public charity.

There was always a great deal of mutual aid within the Japanese community which in the Depression became an acceptable substitute for public assistance. Issei helped each other when families suffered reverses without accepting IOUs. Sometimes bad feeling resulted, however. A very poor Issei couple loaned three hundred dollars to someone in a worse situation than themselves, but the borrower could not repay and later in a relocation center refused to speak to the donors.

No matter how difficult economic conditions were, unemployed Japanese living in the country areas and particularly on farms were generally able to subsist. "The Issei farmers were a self-sustaining people," a Nisei lawyer recalls, "I remember when supper was made from everything that grew on the farm."

Most Issei were extremely thrifty and had accumulated savings against such hard times as came with the Great Depression. Bankers did not necessarily foreclose on mortgages which could not be paid; for one thing it was not economic to do so. It was of greater benefit to everybody to let payments go until conditions improved. The Issei were good long-term risks. It was a matter of pride for them not to renege on their word.

One Santa Clara Valley farm family had raised prunes on a share basis during the nineteen-twenties and early thirties. It was hillside farming, on forty acres. They had to drive teams of horses on the sloping land, which was very difficult. After the first postwar years, the nineteen-twenties were poor years for farmers all over the country. A Dr. Mac-Dougal, who owned and shared with them, was "a nice person to work for." They had many friends and a fairly good life, but they did not make money and were barely able to pay the cost of living. In the years when prune prices were high, they did not have much of a crop, and in the low price years, they had bumper crops.

Previously they had saved $2,000 and so they decided to make a change and move to flat land. They did not want to raise their children in a shack in back of a Caucasian farmhouse as many Japanese had to do. They were proud and wanted their children to have a house of their own. Otis Clayton, a prominent banker and realtor, was willing to sell them ten acres of an eighty acre plot of land. They bought the property in the name of their underage son, with an older Nisei friend named as guardian, learning about the possibility of such an arrangement not from a lawyer of their own, but from the realtor's lawyer. When the 1929 crash came, banks closed, and they had difficulty paying off the capital and interest on their mortgage. One year they could not even meet the taxes, but the realtor took care of it. A kind-hearted man, he did not wish to foreclose. "You hang on," he said. "You keep it."

They removed one and a half acres of trees and planted raspberries in their place. This crop provided groceries and tax money. One year the government paid them not to pick, and the prunes were left to rot.

Like agriculture, Japanese business suffered from chronic depression even when the rest of the economy was prosperous. Particularly after 1924, according to R. D. McKenzie, business growth declined, because the exclusion law and assimilation problems forced many Japanese to turn to each other, relegating buying and selling to their own group.

Then, too, Japanese city business was in some ways tied to agricultural prosperity. The farmers who came in from the country to shop in the ethnic centers were a stable clientele but not one with much buying power. In small towns like Mountain View, California, which had a number of Japanese stores, as well as in the cities, trade tended to be sluggish. Profits often depended on whether the farmers did well enough to pay their bills. Weather and low crop prices could be calamitous for everybody. In the early nineteen-twenties after a season of heavy rains in the Sacramento area had damaged the rice and bean crops, many farmers went into bankruptcy. The Sacramento Nippon Bank was overextended and had to close, with consequent losses to depositors and borrowers, after which people used the Sumitomo Bank. Gradually times improved. The year 1929 was a good one. Many of the Issei who in increasing numbers moved from rural areas to the cities in the nineteen-twenties and thirties suffered from acts of harrassment, both legal and extra-legal, which were contrary to treaty obligations relating to commerce. Business licenses were sometimes refused. In 1923 anyone operating a fruit stand in Oregon with alien help had to display a large card stating that he was hiring noncitizens. In the West Coast states hundreds of city requirements made it impossible for Japanese to be employed in certain occupations. Some of these regulations were declared unconstitutional, but the courts were inconsistent.

City workers did poorly compared with farm workers. Few of them were able to earn over $18 or $20 a week. According to I. K. Ishimatsu, these Japanese working people "had to do a little better job than other people. Although jobs were scarce and pay was low, they managed to keep their jobs mainly as caretakers and houseworkers. Factory or white collar work wasn't generally open to them."

A few unions, such as the Garment Workers of America, began to admit Orientals. The attorney Peter Nakahara, who grew up in San Pedro, remembers the violent union strife there during the Depression. The two large ethnic groups in San Pedro, Italians and Yugoslavians, were fishermen (as were the Japanese on nearby Terminal Island) and belonged to two unions, the American Federation of Labor and the Council of Industrial Relations, the Italian fishermen to the AF of L and the Yugoslavians to the CIO. The Japanese at this time were not permitted to join either. During the great longshoremen's strike, the Yugoslavians struck in sympathy with the longshoremen, and Italians and the nonunion Japanese did not. A bloody struggle followed.

"We lived a block and a half from Union Hall. I remember several occasions when Yugoslavians chased us and tried to catch us. The young Japanese students going to school would have to go through a picket line. The Yugoslavian fishermen on the picket line threw a lot of the kids into the water at the ferry. Once in a while we'd go down to my father's market and would have to pass the picket line, and carry something to protect us. I recall occasions when they took ice picks and jabbed holes in my father's trucks, because they continued to work and unload the ships. Some of the Yugoslavian children whose parents were striking were hardpressed for clothes and for food."

International relations and world economic conditions complicated the Depression situation for American Japanese businessmen who were either directly involved in Japan–United States importing and exporting or who were tied to the self-sustaining Japanese community. Before 1929 Japan and the United States enjoyed an even exchange of cotton and silk. Japan was dependent upon an expanding foreign trade. In a crisis partly precipitated by the growing rayon industry in the United States, Japanese silk prices collapsed in 1930 and 1931, and the yen fell drastically in value. A sharp increase in Japan's cotton textile exports offset the loss. By 1936 Japan was the world's first exporter of cotton piece goods. She was dependent on the West in turn for machinery, wool, oil, and steel, and large amounts of raw cotton. One-fifth of Japan's exports came to this country, and one-third of ours went to her.

Part of the United States economy benefited from trade with Japan, but competitive industries suffered. During this same period when American textile manufacturers were in severe economic distress there was a flurry of sentiment in favor of curtailing Japanese cotton imports. The Hearst press decried the "floods" of imports, and blamed the nation's slow recovery from the Depression on Orientals.

Denunciations of Japanese imports were often couched in military semantics: an attempt by Japan to sell toothbrushes was termed a "foray" on the market, the sale of Japanese gloves an "invasion." An anti-New Deal news writer, protesting low tariffs on fish netting, described the goods as "hostile imports."

There were some reasonable men of internationalist persuasion in the government of Japan during this period, though the country was not a democracy and the military enjoyed power independent of civilian control. The titular head of the empire, the Mikado, was relatively isolated from the workings of his government. Some analysts feel that American treatment of Japanese nationals and American attitudes toward international trade hastened the decline of liberal influences and promoted the rise of the Imperialists to power in Japan.

Instead of economic dependence on the West, the Japanese militarists proposed to establish domination in Asia by whatever means they considered necessary. After almost a billion dollars in Japanese capital was invested in Manchurian industry *de facto* political control followed. When China's rising nationalism challenged Japan's economic interests, the resulting struggle culminated in various "incidents," some manufactured by Japan. All over China there were boycotts of Japanese trade. Japan bombed Chinese cities to force submission, and took one city after another until she commanded all Manchuria, changing the area's name to Manchukuo and establishing a puppet regime.

From the beginning of Japan's militarist activity in the East, even before the Manchurian crisis, there were sporadic boycotts of Japanese goods here. Individuals, sympathizing with China or reflecting old hostilities toward the Japanese, or both, would boycott silk stockings—or the local Issei florist. There were sometimes secondary boycotts. A Caucasian shoe store was put on a blacklist, because the wife of the proprietor was seen shopping at a Japanese store a block away. In the nineteen-thirties a Southern California "Committee of One Thousand," formed to boycott "all things Japanese," propounded their point of view in their publication, *The American Defender*.[23] At the same time these economic tactics were being pursued, the United States was engaging in large-scale Navy maneuvers in the Pacific.

In the years following the conquest of Manchuria, the Japanese government became nervous and fearful of spies. An American Quaker living in Japan found that life became too unsettling to remain there since he was followed every place he went. "Knowing you were being followed was not a very pleasant feeling," said a Nisei woman, who as a girl went to Japan to visit her grandmother with her oldest brother in the late nineteen-thirties. There they lived in a typically Japanese house with sliding doors, and slept on the floor, which was drafty and cold. Her brother worked as an architect in Tokyo at the time. She herself studied Japanese dancing and tea ceremony. Because they were Nisei, Japanese officials were worried about them, thinking they might be American spies. Her brother was something of a linguist, knew a little Russian, Italian, and had studied French, which probably added to the suspicions of the police.

"I remember their coming to the house and looking through my grandmother's desk to see what they could find. It was kind of ridiculous, really. They questioned us. My grandmother decided the place for my brother and myself was in the United States. We were going to come home anyway."

On this side of the ocean organizations and individuals tried to calm the tense atmosphere and to revive economic relations with Japan. A Pacific Oriental Trades Association was organized by Caucasian business interests to support repeal of the exclusion portion of the Immigration Act. Congressman Bertrand W. Gearhart was instrumental in the passage of the Veterans' Citizenship Act of 1935, which conferred citizenship on alien Japanese who served the American Army in World War I. Other groups proposed loosening the immigration restrictions at least enough to allow a small quota for Japanese, but V. S. McClatchy was still riding his charger, and the California Joint Immigration Committee flooded libraries with their literature and commanded the attention of key people, arguing that a quota for Japanese would open the way for Mexicans and some two thousand Chinese, as well. The Hearst press had not relaxed their campaign in forty years. The California Real Estate Association (CREA) which, urging a yes vote on the alien land proposition, had stated in 1920, "The ownership of our soil must not pass to an alien race," was advising its members in the nineteen-thirties on the proper methods of drawing deeds and erecting real estate signs advertising restrictions in order to confine occupancy to people of the Caucasian race.[24]

In Arizona, following anti-alien riots in Salt River Valley and a bitter controversy in the legislature over alien land legislation, several escheat actions against Issei were undertaken by the government. Crops and land were confiscated, and some corporations taken over by receivers. Various anti-Japanese bills were introduced in the California legislature in 1935, including one forbidding aliens to be employed by any department of the state, county, or city government. This failed to pass, as did the countless anti-alien fishing bills over the years directed at Japanese, who constituted only 15 per cent of alien fishermen in California.

Some of the same organizations that had promoted anti-alien land agitation worked for restrictive legislation against Issei fishermen. *The Grizzly Bear*, the organ of the Native Sons of the Golden West, played a familiar tune: it was "Jap" lobbies and "Jap" dollars that frustrated the plans for fishing restrictions for Issei. In Oregon and Washington (though not in California) fishing was forbidden to aliens who had not filed intentions to become citizens, which effectively eliminated Japanese.

The arguments against American Japanese as fishermen took on a military cast. There were rumors that the "gigantic" fleet of Japanese fishing boats could be converted instantly into mine-layers and torpedo boats (actually, only two of the larger and ten of the smaller boats of the West Coast fishing fleet were Japanese-owned) and that all the fishermen were disguised Japanese naval officers.

Because of such fears the California anti-alien fishing bill of 1939 was particularly fraught with heat and controversy. Three years later the Dies Un-American Activities Committee bitterly credited the Japanese American Citizens League with defeating the bill, a tribute which the organization acknowledged by giving Walter Tsukamoto, a Sacramento attorney and past national president of the JACL, a Nisei of the Year award in Chicago for his successful leadership in preventing its passage.

Despite these happenings, American Japanese before World War II were much more acceptable to the general public than they had been in previous years. The Depression had made common ground for many people. The fact that education was so highly regarded among the American Japanese, that they tended to be good business risks, that their delinquency and crime rate was low all disposed Caucasians in their favor. The low crime rate applied to Hawaiian as well as mainland Japanese. According to an authority cited by Professor Ichihashi, writing in 1932, the most common crimes among Japanese were gambling and drunkenness. There were few rapes, despite the enforced celibacy of the Issei when they first arrived in America. There were few heinous crimes, due, he said, to "effective ancient standards of conduct."[25]

Out of curiosity, a deputy in the sheriff's office in Auburn, California, where there was a sizable Japanese farming population, once went back through the jail register for the previous ten years looking for instances of juvenile and adult crimes among people of Japanese extraction and was unable to find any. A sheriff in Monterey County said that during twenty years as a deputy sheriff, "not five Japanese had been in jail."[26]

Although the Nisei's emphasis on education was approved, college graduates in the nineteen-twenties and thirties had much trouble securing employment in fields for which they were qualified. Sometimes they "could not even get in the door" for an interview. Replies to a job questionnaire sent to various colleges in 1927 elicited dismal comments. The University of Southern California replied that they never had any calls for Japanese graduates for teaching positions or for engineers. They did, however, have quite a number of calls from foreign departments of banks for accountants, statisticians, and office assistants. The University of California replied that they found a distinct prejudice against foreigners being hired as engineers in the public utilities and manufacturing companies. "It seems a tragedy that these intelligent men should spend four years in college to find there is no market for their qualifications." Stanford found it almost impossible to place a Chinese or Japanese of either the first or second generation in any kind of position in manufacturing, engineering, or business.

Some companies objected on the grounds that other men in the firms did not want to work with these minority persons. Washington State College reported that some of their Nisei graduates, speaking perfect English and knowing nothing about Japan, had nevertheless been forced to go there to find jobs they had been trained to fill.[27] There was still strong discrimination against Oriental clerks serving the general public in the nineteen-thirties. Many Nisei and some Issei went into medicine, but in order to get training they had to surmount numerous obstacles. Often good medical schools as well as general academic institutions set up a quota system for minority applicants, as they still do in some places. According to Dr. James Higuchi this was not the case at the University of California at Berkeley, a public institution. In his class at medical school there were five Japanese, three Chinese, and a large number of Jewish students, perhaps half the class, who "were just as discriminated against elsewhere as we were."

In 1927 there were only fourteen or fifteen dentists and twenty-six doctors of Japanese descent in Los Angeles. There were several graduates of law schools, but only one practicing lawyer. The nineteen-thirties showed only a slight increase of Nisei in the professions.

The statistical breakdown on occupations for Issei was almost identical with that of their fathers in Japan. Approximately two-thirds were engaged in agriculture, 7 per cent in fishing, 10 per cent in retail trades and professions. Agriculture was the chief occupation for Nisei as well as Issei, with business second, and skilled trades third. While still in school, however, Nisei occupational aims and desires were very similar to those of Caucasians.

As might be expected, college graduates were much less interested in agriculture and gardening, but because of the tight employment situation they frequently were forced to turn to this work. A brilliant University of California graduate in engineering found employment pruning grapes. The phrase, "the college graduate behind the fruit stand," was both symbolic and often all too actual. A Nisei joke ran that whenever you saw beautifully stacked apples in the grocery store you knew they had been arranged by a college-trained engineer.

A Bay Area man who had graduated from Stanford in engineering and was unable to find a place in the electronics industry typified the well-educated Nisei up against the problem of discrimination. After doing YMCA work, he became a Methodist minister. Countless young Japanese–American girls wanted to become teachers, but were discouraged by advisers from going into the profession. San Jose State College definitely tried to discourage these girls from even starting to take a teacher-training course, but if they went ahead with it the college tried hard to place them. In some colleges the girls took their four years' training only to find that their department refused to send them out for practice teaching. This was the experience at Fresno State College of the wife of the Methodist minister who had not been able to find an engineering position. Others did their practice teaching, but went through one interview after another only to be turned down again and again.

One education graduate, a talented artist, could not find public school employment and finally went to work in a private nursery school where she doubled as a nursemaid for the small children who boarded there. Helen Aihara (Kitaji), who had completed graduate work in education at Stanford University, eventually entered the public school system "through the back door" by first acting as a visiting school teacher for convalescent children in their homes.

Helen Mineta, who had been a secretary before the war and who today is a social studies teacher, had noted that her name did not sound particularly Japanese. Once, in applying for a teaching position she filled in the blank marked nationality as "American." When she went for an interview and the prospective employer was confronted with her obvious racial characteristics, the job became one for an algebra teacher, not a social studies teacher. "Their faces dropped a mile when they saw me. This was not what they expected. Realistically, I suppose I should have prepared them beforehand."

The appointment office at San Jose State College wanted to help Shiju Hirabayaski, who graduated in education in 1939, but told her not to raise her hopes too high. When she went out for interviews, she found everybody very polite, but they would say the positions were filled or give various excuses. Therefore, after earning her teaching degree, she attended Heald's Business College to prepare herself for another occupation.

Since many American Japanese had their own, usually small, commercial enterprises, business training looked like a promising field to Nisei. According to David Sakai, who after the war won the U.S. Junior Chamber of Commerce award as the outstanding young man of the year of Logan, Utah, the colleges did not discourage Japanese students from majoring in business. There were thousands of Japanese–American business students in the nineteen-forties. Yet even business graduates sometimes had to turn to companies in Japan or found themselves "clerking on Grant Avenue in San Francisco." Buddy Iwata of the Livingston Cooperative was more fortunate, finding a position after graduating from Stanford with the Mitsubishi Import-Export Company, a Japanese firm with operations in this country.

Despite the very great difficulty in procuring professional placement, the general unemployment rate among Japanese in 1940 was a good deal lower than that of whites and Negroes. In the lower occupational categories Japanese were in demand.

By 1940, 46 per cent of the sixteen- to twenty-four-year-old Nisei on the West Coast were students. There was a higher percentage of college graduates in this group than in any other racial division in the United States. Nisei at the University of Washington constituted only 2-7/10 per cent of the student body in 1941 and 1942 but almost 10 per cent of the Phi Beta Kappas.

Out of approximately fifty thousand Japanese workers in Washington, Oregon, and California in 1940, somewhere around four thousand were in manufacturing or trade, compared with twelve or thirteen hundred in the professions. In the same year almost half of this group in these three western states were engaged in agriculture, although few were doing low-paying migratory work. Many Washington, Oregon, and California agricultural entrepreneurs were shipping produce out of state. A Japanese-owned packing house, the Santa Clara Produce and Canning Company, shut down during the war and never reopened, was the first to send carloads of peas to eastern markets by rail in refrigerated cars. Over five thousand West Coast Japanese were farm operators, managing or owning some 226,000 acres valued at over $66 million. Nisei in 1940 held over 1,500 farms totaling 71,000 acres in the three West Coast states, representing 2/10 of 1 per cent of the total farmland there. The average Japanese farm was forty-two acres compared with the average West Coast farm of 231 acres. Japanese were cultivating 76 per cent of their acreage, while the average farmer cultivated only 20 per cent of his. There was a good deal of indirect control of agricultural economics by American Japanese which did not show up in statistical tables.

While most Issei held to individualistic, "go-it-alone" practices, some formed combines that were similar to the big Caucasian associations set up for marketing and purchasing advantage. These organizations provided credit to their members where the loan facilities of banks were not open to them. Fertilizer and farm equipment were bought wholesale through the organizations. There was some control of the market. The Japanese berry and vegetable growers' marketing association in California's Santa Maria Valley, termed "the yellow octopus," by a magazine writer, was described as a monopoly. Competitors accused, "When an outside grower-shipper tried to sell in Los Angeles, the syndicate froze him out by depressing prices till he quit."[28] The Southern Flower Market Association controlled members' operations from planting to distribution. The furor for the enforcement of the land laws had for the most part died down by 1940, and there was a great amount of business and agricultural cooperation between Caucasians and American Japanese, including joint Caucasian–Japanese ownership and control of many businesses—in San Luis Obispo, Fresno, Los Angeles, and elsewhere.

However, the new developments on the international scene threatened this interracial teamwork. The Sino–Japanese war, which in part provoked President Roosevelt's quarantine speech of 1937 condemning the world's aggressor nations and making reference to the "epidemic of world lawlessness," increased demands not only for embargoes on scrap-iron and war materials to Japan but for boycotts of Japanese goods here.

Tensions mounted in the American Japanese group in the decade between the Manchurian incident and Pearl Harbor. They felt the pull between America and Japan. Many Nisei were just coming of age and their organization, the Japanese American Citizens League, was beginning to gain in numbers and importance. The young organization was regarded as radical and bold by many of the older generation, but college Nisei sometimes criticized it as reactionary. It was essentially a moderate organization designed to fight injustices, but with the purpose of making it possible for Nisei to enter established American institutions.

In 1940 Japan joined the European Axis powers. The Japanese–United States treaty which covered commercial and agricultural rights of nationals in each other's countries was abrogated. California legislators Dillworth, Slater, and Tenney put through anti-spy, anti-sabotage, and anti-subversive legislation in Sacramento. Ugly cartoons of Japanese appeared in the newspapers, always the stereotype—near-sighted, bespectacled, bow-legged, and buck-toothed. In its October 14, 1940, issue *Life* magazine ran an article on "The Nisei—California Casts an Anxious Eye upon the Japanese Americans in its Midst." Despite the title, the tone was calm. The prevailing anxiety was attributed in part to previous West Coast prejudice and its possible effect upon the Nisei.

American sympathies went out to those countries invaded by the Axis powers, and with no strong international body operating under a rule of law, Americans felt threatened themselves. Some favored isolation, others preferred inaction; still others demanded limited economic sanctions or military reprisals. Nisei sometimes joined in the boycotts or picketed steamships loading scrap-iron for Japan. Two Caucasian college debaters, speaking in opposition to an embargo, recall that the strongest arguments they encountered favoring the quarantine for Japan were given by Nisei students. Among the demonstrators who paced the wharves during this period was a rather unique, colorful Issei of anti-Axis persuasion who carried his picket sign and wrote protest poetry.

Still, perhaps as many Nisei as Caucasians doubted that there would be war with Japan. It was "highly improbable," Dave Tatsuno, then a student at the University of California, had argued with impeccable reasoning in a speech class a few years before Pearl Harbor. "I laugh at myself. I'll always have great humility. I gave every reason—good customers, everything, and it sounded very logical, but war is not logical." Later many Nisei put their faith in America's naval blockade, believing that as long as the United States kept a blockade of strategic materials there could be no war.

The interplay of economics and international events affected Nisei as well as Issei suddenly that day in July, 1941, when they found that all the checks they had written "bounced back." Shuji Kimura wrote of this crisis:

> The commercial treaty between Japan and the United States had been abrogated, and the Nisei had to bring their birth certificates to the bank to prove that they were citizens and to have their accounts unfrozen. The Japanese ships suddenly ceased coming to the Pacific Coast ports. Communications became tenuous. Then throughout the summer, the American State Department began to urge Americans to leave the Orient.[29]

In November, 1941, Professor Yamato Ichihashi, of the Stanford history department, who was a dispassionate observer, not pro-Japanese, predicted an inevitable explosion between Japan and the United States if the latter continued to push Japan by "economic pressure."

Whether Professor Ichihashi's analysis of the situation was valid or not, the anticipated explosion soon occurred. A Japanese–American leader, Mike Masaoka, saw the war coming, and predicted that Nisei, blocked in so many lines of work and unable generally to enter the defense industries, nevertheless would be called upon to fight Japan or be put into concentration camps "of the Hitlerian model."[30]

FOUR · THE GREAT REJECTION

ON FEBRUARY 14, 1942, Robert Bendiner wrote in *The Nation*: "If the nerves of the Western Congressional bloc can be soothed, if inflammatory comment on the 'enemy-alien menace' can be diverted to more harmless pursuits, and if the press now working on Martin Dies's 'Yellow Book' happily breaks down, we may yet be spared a disaster on the West Coast." On February 19 Chester Rowell began a column on the demand for evacuation with the quotation, " 'Come now; let us reason together.' " The results of removing American citizens of Japanese ancestry "would be indubitably disastrous . . . not only against all law, morals and justice, but against our own interests. Those of us who still have functioning heads should keep them." As for aroused public opinion, he wrote, " . . . there has been little or no popular manifestation of it."[1]

The last statement was subject to question. Certainly there was little excitement about the Japanese before January 24, but immediately after the publication of the Roberts report on Pearl Harbor on that date, which indicted U.S. military men for negligence in controlling enemy agents, the Justice Department received several hundred messages urging evacuation or expressing alarm about possible Japanese sabotage or espionage. Between February 9 and February 22, 505 messages reached the Attorney General urging evacuation, while only 64 writers opposed it. Some of this agitation seems to have been organized. After the machinery for removing the West Coast Japanese was set in motion, the volume of mail dropped and 388 letters or telegrams were received on the subject between the end of February and the first of September, with 56 per cent of the writers approving and 44 per cent opposed.[2] From this we may conclude that though the groundwork may have been laid earlier by longtime opponents of the Japanese, the public demand for evacuation arose and reached its crescendo in two weeks. Because of this suddenness most of those who opposed evacuation protested too late.

Life magazine described the Pacific coast in the early months of the war as an armed camp with barbed wire on the beaches and troops and guns deployed from the Mexican border to Canada. Women were reported to be getting instruction in "How to Kill a Jap" in case of enemy invasion.[3] To espouse the cause of the American Japanese during this period of defensive preparedness was to expose oneself to the charge of being careless to the potential danger in the Pacific. The words "military necessity" were used effectively to counter arguments for human rights.

Norman Thomas on the national scene and a few influential Westerners, among them Carey McWilliams, Chester Rowell, Galen Fisher, and Louis Goldblatt of the CIO spoke out for the constitutional rights of Japanese–Americans. Professor Eric Bellquist of the University of California was particularly eloquent in a speech on war hysteria. "I would point out," he said, "that the United States is not merely a territory, a political unit, and a body of traditions, but a promise."[4] Unfortunately, there was no one in a position of authority on the West Coast who, like General Emmons in Hawaii, would implement the American precepts of fair play.

The furor in California, Oregon, and Washington had reached Congress through the West Coast congressional delegation. The day before the President signed Executive Order 9066 two California representatives, John Costello and Harry Sheppard, stood up in the house to warn the nation that the American Japanese were a "fifth column threat" and "a national hazard." They were joined by Representative John Rankin of Mississippi, who said Japanese should be removed "even to the third and fourth generation."[5] He added, "Once a Jap, always a Jap. You can't any more regenerate a Jap than you can reverse the laws of nature."[6]

Spurred by their angry clamor against what they termed the laxity of Attorney General Biddle, their colleagues adopted an amendment to an appropriations bill, allocating $300,000 of Justice Department funds to investigate Japanese activities on the West Coast. They might better have waited, for within forty-eight hours the President signed the order which took the primary responsibility for West Coast security away from the Justice Department and put it in the hands of the Army. General DeWitt, with the authority delegated to him by the Secretary of War, was permitted to establish military zones and to exclude from them any person, citizen or alien. Executive Order 9066 was applied only in the Western Defense Command since it was created to deal with the situation there. It was intended to supersede the previous Justice Department directives banishing enemy aliens from certain strategic zones. By including citizens, it allowed for the evacuation of the entire West Coast Japanese population.

At a Washington hearing before February 19 when Hiram Johnson recommended limiting the exclusion to the Japanese, Congressman Bertrand Gearhart is reported to have complained, "We can't single out a special class for evacuation. The law has to apply to all enemy aliens."[7] In theory, the presidential order could apply to anyone, "any person," but those close to the scene understood that, as the Attorney General said, "The problem is mainly a Japanese problem."[8] The Los Angeles *Times* heralded the new development with the headline, "PRESIDENT ORDERS JAPANESE MOVED."[9]

The Nisei had been taken by surprise by the whirlwind of agitation culminating in the government's decision to remove them. The *Rafu Shimpo*, published in Los Angeles, had begun only in mid-February to respond to the possibility that Japanese-Americans might be interned. "Wake up, Nisei," urged Togo Tanaka, editor of the English section, on February 14. "Write or wire to the President." In an angry letter printed two days later, a Mrs. Charlotte Susu-Mago opposed the suggestion of Representative Leland Ford of Los Angeles that the Japanese–Americans should be willing to let themselves be interned "as a contribution to this country." "Would you, Mr. Ford, . . . *be willing?*" she asked. "My answer is . . . it isn't necessary." The February 17 issue of the paper announced a mass meeting proclaiming Japanese loyalty to the United States to be held two nights later at a hall of the Maryknoll Catholic Mission, sponsored by the JACL, the Japanese American Legion Post, the California Young Buddhists League, and other groups. Urging all Southern California Japanese to attend, Tanaka warned, "Make no bones about it. The move is to deal with us as a group."[10] A February 19 editorial stigmatized the Japanese community for "bickering, back-biting, lack of leadership. . . . Who's going to speak up for us?", he asked. "If we're still hopeless adolescents in the most serious crisis we've ever faced, then God help us. We deserve to be kicked around."

An overflow audience of about 1,500 people attended the meeting at Maryknoll. "Tokie" Slocum, a local Nisei leader who boasted of his cooperation with the FBI, was one of the speakers. He pleaded, "We are not spies or stooges. . . . We've been fighting a moral war against the 5th column for years. We're still fighting that moral war. Your very presence here is a compliment to America and a sign you will fight with me to the end. . . ." With unconscious irony, since he could not have known what had just taken place in Washington, he continued, "Our greatest friend is a man who is the greatest living man today—our President, Franklin Delano Roosevelt." Another leader, Kay Sugahara, said, "If the Army and Navy say we are a menace, let's get out. But if it's merely a question of fighting politicians that would gain favor by hopping on 'those defenseless Japs,' we should fight them to a last ditch."[11] As if he foresaw what was coming, Saburo Kido, national president of the JACL, said, "We trust that the sacrifices which all of us may be called upon to make will create a greater and unified America when we have won the war."[12]

William Carr, a Pasadena real estate man, who felt that the evacuation was "an impossible injustice," attended another extremely tense meeting of Nisei leaders at this time. The morale of the Japanese group had been badly shattered by the events of the war: the FBI arrests, the economic restrictions, the boycotts, the widening schism between the generations as the Nisei loudly proclaimed their loyalty to the United States. Now that it seemed likely that the entire group was to be treated alike, the young leaders switched suddenly from protest to resignation.

The *Rafu Shimpo*, which had blazed with emotion before February 19, cautioned its readers a couple of days later, "Don't get excited about being evacuated overnight. Cool heads of the Army are in charge now."[13] This was followed next day by the plea, "Please keep our families together." The Nisei were adopting the fatalism of their fathers who used the expression *Shikataganai*, meaning, "it can't be helped." The public was not told what had happened behind the scenes to account for the startling change of tone. Some time during those two or three days JACL leaders had met with West Coast officials and learned that the die was cast. A Nisei, returning home after the meeting, summed it up for his family in two words, "We lost." But they had snatched a concession from defeat. In exchange for a promise of their active cooperation with the projected evacuation, they would be allowed to confer with General DeWitt's staff on how it was to take place in order to lessen the hardship for the people.

Some Japanese–Americans continued to protest. "Has the Gestapo come to America?" asked James Omura, an editor.[14] Lincoln Kanai of the San Francisco YMCA said that to confuse Nisei with enemy alien groups was "diametrically opposed to the Constitution and the objectives of the war."[15] The capitulation of the JACL was to be an underlying cause of the hatred many evacuees expressed toward the organization once the gates of the relocation centers had closed upon them. They felt that a small group of Nisei spokesmen had betrayed them. Mike Masaoka claims that the JACL, the only organized Japanese–American group to step forward at that time, had no choice but to accept the dictates of the Western Defense Commander. The Army had two evacuation plans, one to be used if the Nisei cooperated, and a second, to be enforced with guns and bayonets, if they did not. JACL officers had considered courting arrest as a means of protesting, but decided that such action would leave the communities leaderless since most of the prominent Issei had been interned by the Justice Department. They decided that the opposition, which consisted of the President of the United States, the War Department, and a majority of officials, civilian and military, on the West Coast, was too formidable. The organization was therefore at first not enthusiastic about supporting individual Nisei who resisted government policy.

During these days, the oppression increased. On February 19 Kilsoo K. Haan, a representative of the Sino–Korean Peoples' League, speaking in Seattle, predicted on the basis of "purported military documents" an invasion of the Pacific coast from Alaska to the Panama Canal by Japan, to be accompanied by local sabotage. He urged mass internment of American Japanese.[16]

There were frequent newspaper reports of Nisei losing their jobs. The International Brotherhood of Boiler Makers Local 6 in San Francisco refused to accept a Nisei into membership so he lost his job as a welder at a steel corporation. Caucasian employees of the Northern Pacific Railroad in Seattle and Auburn threatened to quit unless the Japanese were fired. But CIO mill workers in Portland unanimously voted to keep Nisei on the job.

Dr. G. K. Hashiba, a Fresno brain specialist, was dismissed from the staff of the Tulare County Hospital. Patients in other hospitals were refusing the ministrations of Japanese nurses. PTA leaders in Seattle forced the resignation of twenty-six Nisei girls who had been working in the offices of the city public schools by circulating petitions urging the schools "to remove these girls for the safety of our children,"[17] an action for which one newspaper reader proposed the ladies be rewarded by having their names engraved in bronze and left "on some stump in Okanogan County."[18] Agricultural specialists were actually testing Japanese grown vegetables for poison and a farmer who had innocently used too much spray was called in for questioning and paid a fine.

The Japanese farmers in the Salinas Valley began surrendering their leases because Filipino laborers would not work for them and shippers hinted they would no longer handle their produce for fear of being boycotted in the eastern market. The president of the Grower-Shipper Vegetable Association, E. M. Seifert, Jr., said at this time, "For the protection of future generations of Californians and Americans, no Japanese, even though he be born in America, should be permitted to own land."[19]

There seems to be a definite correlation between the President's order and the increase in discriminatory actions. The fact that the government had in effect branded the Japanese as dangerous and undesirable on the West Coast made them fair game for racial zealots and malcontents. It was reported that "when a Filipino took pot shots at Japanese near a Stockton filling station, no one interfered; instead, a

crowd gathered to laugh and make bets on how soon 'he'd get one.' "
Some people put "Jap Hunting Licenses" on their cars.[20] The stories
of Japanese atrocities in the war theater fanned a revengeful spirit
against local Japanese. Vigilante-type incidents were rare, but they were
the surface manifestations of an almost universal hostility. In the months
to come proposals were introduced to disfranchise the Nisei, to deprive
them of American citizenship, to deport all Japanese on American soil,
even to sterilize them. Two spokesmen for moderation commented on
the sudden intolerance of West Coast Caucasians. Francis Biddle said,
"In tense times such as these, a strange psychology grips us. We are oppressed and fearful and apprehensive. If we can't get at the immediate
cause of our difficulties we are likely to vent our clammed-up energy on
a scapegoat."[21] Dr. Henry Grady, the secretary of the Pacific Coast Committee on National Security and Fair Play said, "Our citizens of Japanese
parentage are just as trustworthy now as they were a few weeks ago when
Governor Olson and other publicists paid tribute to their loyalty and
civic devotion. Has the setback given to the Allied Arms by the military
machine of Japan made our political leaders in state, county and munici-
pality play the bully and turn against our Japanese citizens as a scapegoat for the remote culprits, in Japan, whom our Japanese–American
citizens have repeatedly denounced?"[22]

Until General DeWitt acted on the authority given him by the President through the Secretary of War, the West Coast was subject to the
restrictions imposed on all enemy aliens, and aliens only, by the Justice
Department. On January 29, the Attorney General had announced two
prohibited zones, the San Francisco waterfront and the Los Angeles airport from which Germans, Italians, and Japanese aliens would have to
move by February 15. Between January 31 and February 2, 133 additional prohibited zones were announced that had to be cleared of enemy
aliens by February 15 or February 24. In addition, twelve restricted
zones were designated in which enemy aliens were subject to a curfew
and a five-mile travel limit. While Tom Clark was supervising this removal program, the FBI stepped up its arrests. Agents were permitted
to enter the homes of noncitizens without a warrant, and the newspapers carried stories day after day of surprise raids on communities of
West Coast alien concentration.

The prohibited zones were small geographical areas, for the most part;
so some aliens moved just a few miles or even a few blocks. The parents
of the baseball player Joe DiMaggio had to leave the Fishermen's Wharf
area of San Francisco. There were about three hundred Japanese families
and some noncitizen Italians on Alameda Island near Oakland in the
San Francisco Bay. The older generation moved into San Francisco or
down the Peninsula to stay with relatives. The grown citizen children

could stay on and look after things. One Issei woman remembers how her sons and daughters, demonstrating true Japanese filial piety, brought meals over to her in East Oakland where she was living in a hotel room without adequate cooking facilities.

There was a good deal of anguish and uncertainty for those affected, most of whom were either elderly longtime residents or newly arrived refugees from Nazi Germany who, because they had not yet become naturalized, found themselves identified with the enemy they had just escaped. Of the ninety-two alien students at the University of California, seventy-five were Germans. One refugee, affected by the curfew and travel ban, which seemed all too reminiscent of the restrictions imposed on Jews in Europe, wrote bitterly, "Why is America called a democracy when it is not one?"[23] Thomas Mann, newly arrived in California, was an effective representative for the German refugees. The Italian group had influential spokesmen, including persons in public office. Forty residents of the North Beach Italian colony in San Francisco, including lawyers, bankers, and a few city officials, called on State Attorney General Warren to plead a reconsideration of hardship cases. In Stimson's letter to De-Witt, delegating to him the authority to remove people from the Western Defense Command, the Secretary of War asked that Italians be exempted.

The Federal Security Agency during this period opened an office in Los Angeles where ten thousand enemy aliens, mostly Japanese, were living in prohibited zones. At first no one came for assistance; so the FSA contacted ministers, the JACL, the American Friends Service Committee, to make known their availability to people who needed advice and financial assistance. Gradually one or another would come in to ask, "Am I living in a prohibited area?" "Shall I go ahead and plant my crop? If I plant I'm afraid I'll have to move before it can be harvested. If I don't plant I'll be accused of sabotage." Or, "Where do I register for employment?" The social workers knew it was futile to tell Japanese to register with the U.S. Employment Service since members of their race were being discharged in large numbers rather than being employed.

The FSA spent $300 on eighteen out of the 1,200 families who came to the Los Angeles office between February 9 and March 9. Only a fraction of a $500,000 assistance fund was used. The Japanese group, as always, was reluctant to accept public aid. They were taking care of each other. Their organizations had stopped raising money for bombers and ambulances and were soliciting relief funds for evacuees. George Nickel, who was involved with the FSA work with the Japanese in Los Angeles, wrote: "Most of the social workers assigned to the FSA offices never had encountered a comparable situation. They had difficulty with the language; they fumbled with the spelling of names. They were used to people coming in and pouring out their troubles, and they were awkward before reticence. Sometimes they didn't acknowledge the little bow that each Japanese woman made when introduced, or they seemed amused by unfamiliar mannerisms."[24] Social workers were disturbed by the plight of Nisei children: a boy of nine whose mother was sick, whose father was in the custody of the FBI, and a girl of fifteen in similar circumstances who had been investigated by the police because she was on the street late at night. They found she had taken upon herself the responsibility of closing her father's café at 1 A.M., opening it four hours later. A few Nisei girls were arrested for prostitution, a rare occurrence for which the turbulence and instability of their lives was blamed.

Unscrupulous individuals tried to capitalize on the uncertain situation of the aliens. Wearing false badges and claiming to be FBI men, extortionists attempted to frighten families into selling their possessions. Self-styled "immigration counselors" offered to give advice for exhorbitant fees.

It was during this difficult interim period before General DeWitt's first evacuation order superseded the withdrawal of enemy aliens as ordered by the Justice Department that a congressional group, the Tolan Committee on Defense Migration, arrived in San Francisco to hold hearings in four West Coast cities on the problems of moving aliens and citizens. The chairman was John H. Tolan of California. Other members were John Sparkman of Alabama, Frank Osmers of New Jersey, Carl T. Curtis of Nebraska, Laurence Arnold of Illinois, and George H. Bender of Ohio. The West Coast congressional delegation which had with fervor voted $300,000 to investigate Japanese activities on the Pacific coast was reported to be lukewarm about the "junket" of the Tolan Committee to their home districts. "Comment tonight indicated little interest in the committee's findings and considerable doubt as to the value of its proceedings," a Los Angeles *Times* newsman reported.[25]

It is significant that the Tolan Committee was urged to come to the West Coast by Carey McWilliams, a Nisei sympathizer, and was welcomed by the American Japanese press. The Army, the Navy, the Department of Agriculture, and the Justice Department requested that the committee, which was originally intended to study the migration of defense workers to the Pacific coast, be " 'a sounding board for facts, figures and fears' on the ground where Japanese invasion of the continent is expected first."[26] Tolan opened the hearings by expressing the conviction that "The Pacific Coast is in danger both from within and without."[27] But by the time the hearings were over, the committee declared in its report: "Serious constitutional questions are raised by the forced detention of citizens against whom no individual charges are lodged"[28] though it concluded "no alternative remains."[29]

Despite the fact that the committee arrived too late to alter significantly government policy, the hearings brought to public attention a

wide spectrum of opinion on the alien problem, particularly the
Japanese problem which had hitherto been covered in a more biased
way in most newspapers. The committee heard the testimony of mayors,
governors, the California Joint Immigration Committee, the California
American Legion, the State Federation of Labor, the JACL, the churches,
the Native Sons of the Golden West, and numerous private individuals.
Twenty-five years later a Nisei commentator, James Nakamura, wrote,
"The Tolan Committee Report to the Congress of the United States—
a credit to democratic America if there ever was one—gave the first
clear lie to the pressure group propagandists who made skilled use of
falsified reports to fan race prejudice to a high pitch."[30]

In the kaleidoscopic array of witnesses in San Francisco were Mayor
Rossi, pleading for the Italian aliens, and Attorney General Warren,
warning of a second Pearl Harbor. He cited California aircraft plants
"surrounded entirely" by Japanese-occupied land and recent Japanese
farm operations near air bases on arid tracts "on which hardly a jack-
rabbit could be grown."[31] Mike Masaoka, Dave Tatsuno, and Henry Tani
of the JACL told the committee that Nisei were loyal Americans. Masaoka said, "The Japan of our parents is not the Japan of today." He
pledged cooperation with evacuation but said Nisei would feel they had
"every right to protest" if evacuation was "primarily a measure whose
surface urgency cloaks the desires of political or other pressure groups."[32]

Professor Eric Bellquist blamed "inflammatory commentators" who
were undermining popular confidence. "I cannot believe that this is just
a matter of chance. The committee will do well to ascertain what lies behind the present clamor. What are the real motives?"[33] The prominent
churchmen Galen Fisher, Warren Chapman and Frank Herron Smith,
spoke for the Nisei. Louis Goldblatt of the CIO said, "This entire episode
of hysteria and mob chant against the native-born Japanese will form a
dark page of American history."[34]

The committee recommended hearing boards for Italian and German
aliens "most of whom were over 60 years of age and parents of American citizens of good standing in the community. . . . The Germans and
Italians do not have the original stratification of the immigrant group
such as the Japanese which has been kept intact by legal and social restrictions."[35]

Committee members saw immediately that simply to get rid of the
Japanese was not enough. Constructive plans had to be made for their
relocation and the care of their property. A telegram was sent to the
Speaker of the House of Representatives, Sam Rayburn, recommending
the appointment of an alien property custodian:

> We urge the immediate establishment of a regional alien-property custo-
> dian office for the Pacific coast area. We have learned of numerous

sacrifice sales by aliens: this office should have existed before the evacuation of February 15. It must be functioning before additional prohibited areas are evacuated. Many witnesses before this committee have urged this action. . . .

It is our impression that the need for an alien property custodian on the coast is but one example of a general need for advance planning for the civilian problems which are accompanying the evacuation of aliens and will accompany any future evacuations. . . .[36]

The telegram was forwarded to the Secretary of the Treasury who instructed the Federal Reserve Bank of San Francisco working with the Farm Security Administration to open offices in local communities to help with sales, creditors, and storage problems of evacuees.

While the Tolan Committee was holding hearings in San Francisco, two dramatic events on the West Coast distracted public attention. Confirming the fears of a nervous population, a Japanese submarine surfaced off the coast at Goleta near Santa Barbara on the evening of February 23 and began shelling an oil refinery. The fifteen-minute attack took place during a nationwide broadcast by President Roosevelt. No one was hurt and no fires were started. The end of a wooden jetty was splintered. Most of the twenty-five five–inch shells fired fell harmlessly into fields and canyons. But the attack, which seemed to many to presage the long-predicted Japanese invasion, sent residents of the area into a panic. Tokyo boasted, "This military feat has completely unnerved the entire Pacific Coast of the United States."[37] *Life* magazine commented: "No matter how comfortably Midwest and Mountain States continued to slumber, the West appeared now to be approaching a belated awareness that its murderous enemy was separated from it not by 5,000 oceanic miles, but by only a few feet of salt sea water, a few feet of dark night sky."[38]

Out of the dark night sky came an "air raid" on February 24 and 25 on Los Angeles which proved to be a false alarm. The submarine shelling, an actual enemy attack, however ineffectual, on the United States, may have been responsible for the excitement the following night. The military defense system of Southern California was on the alert. The appearance of unidentified aircraft touched off a barrage of sirens and anti-aircraft fire. "Madness was loosed. The city was blacked out. Searchlights stroked the sky. Anti-aircraft guns opened up. The night was laced with tracers and explosions."[39] Falling ackack damaged houses and autos. Two people died of heart attacks and three were killed in traffic accidents in what was described as "the worst transportation tieup in history."

The Secretary of War guessed that the unidentified planes were piloted by enemy agents. The Secretary of the Navy said the whole thing was a false alarm. According to the twenty-five-year commemorative report of the Los Angeles *Times*, "Months later, it was concluded that the great air raid was set off by nothing more than one small, lost U.S. weather balloon."[40] But with all the lights and furor, with banner headlines in one newspaper proclaiming, "I SAW WAR COME TO LOS ANGELES," nerve-wracked citizens poured telegrams into the governor's office urging him to get rid of all the West Coast Japanese immediately. A frightened woman sent a wire seven minutes after the all-clear sounded. "Each new hour that a single Jap is at liberty in this State is an hour we might tragically regret."[41] Japanese were reported signaling during the air raid and leaving their lights on during the blackout. Twenty were arrested in what were described as "extremely suspicious circumstance."[42] They were thought to be "spying or trying to signal the enemy aviators in the brilliant moonlit western sky."[43]

While the Tolan Committee was holding hearings in Portland there took place the first mass evacuation of a Japanese group, both citizens and aliens. One of the committee members referring to the shock that accompanied it, called the removal of the Japanese families from Terminal Island on forty-eight hours' notice a minor Pearl Harbor. It was the first episode in which citizens were involved and the first evacuation ordered by the military. Though only a few hundred people were affected, it is also remembered as the harshest and most arbitrary action taken against the West Coast Japanese during the war.

The fishing colony on Terminal Island, within rifle shot of a great naval base, had been a source of concern to military authorities even before December 7. There were originally about two thousand Japanese on the island, of whom eight hundred were aliens. Five hundred of the group were fishermen and many of their wives worked in the ten canneries on the island until war regulations prevented Issei from doing either. They were situated in a sensitive military zone because it was convenient for fishing and the canneries rented them houses in order to have their labor easily available on short notice.

The houses were really shacks with jagged shingle roofs and no yards. Five rooms rented for $15 a month. "The houses were awful" in the word of Virginia Yamamoto, then Virginia Swanson, who worked as a Baptist missionary on the island for five years before the war. "The Baptist Church was the one beautiful building on the Island, a symbol of hope for the people." There was also a Shinto shrine. The Terminal Islanders were unsophisticated people who worked hard and had little contact with the world on the mainland except for the high school age children who crossed by ferry to San Pedro daily to attend classes. The events of the war frightened them all the more because they had led such isolated lives.

Spies on Terminal Island figured importantly in the Dies Committee's "Yellow Book" which was by coincidence released to the press on February 27, the final date for the evacuation of the Island. The committee published the testimony of a Los Angeles police officer assigned to patrol Fish Harbor, who revealed his prejudice when describing a café which catered to a "class of trade which would be called 'low' such as Mexicans, Filipinos and Japanese." He claimed that before the war when Japanese ships docked at San Pedro, the crews went to homes on Terminal Island where they "spent many hours in deep conversation pertaining to the American fleet anchored in the harbors of San Pedro and Long Beach respectively."[44] He cited illegal gambling in pool halls, propagandistic Japanese movies, a pay-off man who rewarded spies, and a café proprietor who got American soldiers and sailors drunk in order to elicit information from them.

Another witness was a Yugoslavian fisherman who was asked, "Is it not a fact that these Japanese fishing boats, by employing Japanese crews, keep good American citizens from obtaining employment . . . ?" He answered, "Oh, yes; absolutely— The Japanese work cheaper and the canneries like to employ them in preference to us."[45] The fisherman answered affirmatively the question, "Therefore, you believe, do you not, that the concentration of a Japanese alien population in such close proximity to the national defense area and the principal fleet base of the United States is a definite menace?"[46] One of the witnesses, an attorney, Benjamin Harrison, though not indifferent to the possible danger said, "Personally, I am unable to testify to any acts of espionage nor do I know of any sabotage which has been committed by the group of aliens operating our fishing fleet. . . ."[47]

Carey McWilliams wrote in March, 1942, "Despite the fact that most of the residents are either loyal or quite harmless, nevertheless the colony provided a convenient screen for possible subversive activities. That Japanese spies were working among the fishermen was, in fact, pointed out years ago by some of the Japanese themselves."[48] He has since clarified this statement, "As to the Terminal Island incident, it is true that at one time individual Japanese officers tried to pick up whatever information might be available and may have used the Japanese–American communities as cover for their own activities, but I am sure that there was very little of this and that the resident communities themselves were not involved."[49]

In any case, most of the alien Japanese men on Terminal Island were apprehended by the FBI, some on December 7 and the rest in a mass raid on February 1. They had been under constant suspicion since the outbreak of the war. When an Issei fisherman on the Island, speaking in Japanese, tried to warn a friend who had moved for safety to the mainland that he would probably be arrested by the FBI in a roundup of noncitizen Islanders, the telephone operator interrupted, saying, "You cannot continue this conversation."

The sea log of another Island fisherman, with routine notations about the weather, tides, and channels, written in Japanese, was confiscated by a reporter for a magazine and photographed as a Japanese spy's diary. Virginia Swanson remembers that as the FBI swept onto the Island and took away the Issei men, the families huddled together sorrowing and weeping. The movie men were all set with cameras outside the cottages, hoping to catch a picture of a struggling Japanese. But people also remembered the bus driver who dropped his cap and picked it up slowly to give the women and children time to say goodbye to their men.

The total evacuation of the Japanese population on Terminal Island was expected, but it was assumed the residents would have a least a week's notice. About half the families had left in January or February to stay with relatives or friends. Most of the rest literally had no place to go. On February 14, anticipating a crisis, Virginia Swanson wrote a letter, copies of which she sent to the Tolan Committee, still in Washington, D.C., at that time, to Francis Biddle, Mrs. Roosevelt, Tom Clark, and various West Coast military men. In it she outlined the plight of the families who might be forced within thirty days to find homes in communities hostile to Japanese. Would the government help? She asked, "Could you work to find a place where they could move? Can you be sure families won't be broken up?" No one answered her letter.

The evacuation notices were served on the Islanders around noon on February 25. Miss Swanson phoned the Navy to try to get the deadline extended, but without success. She and Dr. Ralph Mayberry of the Baptist Mission Board, Esther Rhoads and Herbert Nicholson of the American Friends Service Committee, Allan Hunter, a Congregational minister, and some JACL members decided they would have to move the families themselves in the absence of any help from the government. They had located hostels. Some were former Japanese Language Schools, which they cleaned up and prepared as best they could. They managed to recruit volunteers with trucks to transport the Islanders and some of their possessions to the hostels. Joe Moody, the owner of a mattress company, who had had a Nisei roommate in college, donated mattresses and quilts and sent six of his trucks over to help with the moving.

On February 26 the narrow streets between the little shacks were jammed with trucks and milling women and children. Secondhand dealers, "descending like wolves to prey on the helpless," flocked in to take off the things people could not carry with them. They were reported to be giving a nickel on the dollar. A Nisei volunteer wrote later, "The women cried awful. . . . Some of them smashed their stuff, broke it up, right before the buyers' eyes because they offered such ridiculous prices."[50] Virginia Swanson remembers the beautiful wedding tea sets, saved for better homes, lying smashed to pieces on the floors of cottages.

She said, "The volunteers with trucks worked all night. The people had to go, ready or not. Some had to be pulled forcibly from their homes. They were afraid they were going to be handed over to a firing squad. Why should they have believed me, telling them to get into trucks with strangers?" The weeks of suspense with husbands gone, amid conflicting rumors and the badgering of profiteers, had frightened the women badly. The only representatives of the government they saw were the FBI agents who took away their menfolk and an officer from the State Board of Equalization who came to make sure the store proprietors paid their sales taxes before they left. He attached the property of a frantic widow who ran a beer parlor.

The refugees were thrust into hostels, only one out of seven prepared for them. Some people were dropped after midnight with no lights, nothing set up, no one to meet them. Esther Rhoads, in a letter to a friend, described the scene at the Forsyth School where she marked off floor space for families with chalk. "All afternoon trucks and Japanese kept coming. They were tired and dazed as a result of the sudden exodus. . . . We have old men over seventy—retired fishermen whom the FBI considered ineffective, and we have little children—one baby a year old . . . practically no men between thirty-five and sixty-five, as they all are interned either in Montana or South Dakota. . . . I feel especially sorry for the old men. They seem so lost in the high-ceilinged rooms of the Forsyth School. I think they long for the low ceilings and the cozy feel of their little homes back on Terminal Island." She asks, "Where are these people to go? There are many Japanese with young leaders able to face pioneer life, but those who have come to our hostels represent a group too old or too young to stand the rigors of beginning all over again."[51]

The refugees stayed on in the hostels or moved to temporary quarters, exhausting their meager resources, for in most cases their income had been cut off since the beginning of the war. They were among the first to go to the Manzanar assembly center. Back on the Island the looting of their homes began almost before they were out of them. Eventually the homes and shops were razed by the Navy. Bloom and Riemer wrote that the "Terminal Island Japanese Americans probably suffered more heavily in the Evacuation than any other occupational or locality group."[52] They had to abandon business property and expensive fishing equipment. The nets, even when safely stored, deteriorated without care and use. Many of the boats that were not owned outright had to be relinquished to the canneries.

After the Japanese left, it was reported that their places in the canneries would be taken by Filipinos, Yugoslavians, and Portuguese. Naval shore patrols stood watch on Fish Harbor. Virginia Swanson returned to the Island, where she had got permission to salvage a few personal possessions of the families, to find combat cars driving up and down the narrow alleys. As she entered the empty, silent church, she remembered the last communion service when people in the congregation had broken into sobs. On her way out she left the key on the table and the door open—for the Navy.

The Tolan Committee began hearings in Seattle on February 28. By this time its members were in the process of assessing the sort of welcome relocating Japanese would receive in interior areas. John Tolan came to the conclusion, "Nobody wants the Japanese. The committee has received numerous expressions from inland areas to that effect. Much of the population on the west side of the mountains [the Cascades] want aliens removed from the Coast, and of course, if they should be evacuated they must have some place to go."[53]

The committee heard testimony from a wide cross-section of Seattle's citizens. Two University of Washington students came to the hearings to register their opposition to the evacuation of Nisei, of whom there were about 250 in the student body at the university. JACL leaders spoke. Dr. Harold V. Jensen, a Baptist minister, said, "I don't see why we should send our Japanese out of Washington. . . ."[54] Like every West Coast churchman who testified before the committee, he advocated individual treatment of the Japanese.

The ever-vigilant Seattle PTA sent a representative to urge the evacuation of all aliens and their American-born children as a "protective measure for all children."[55] Governor Arthur Langlie wanted to reserve eastern Washington as an emergency evacuation area, presumably in case of enemy attack, for the state's Caucasian citizens, "our own loyal citizens."[56] The Seattle publisher Miller Freeman subscribed to a conspiracy theory. He told the committee: "Japanese are in America through fraud, deception and collusion. The Japanese government, ignoring the gentlemen's agreement, has accomplished the miraculous feat of permanently planting 300,000 of her people in this country, quadrupling the original number since the agreement was entered into in 1907, limiting the Japanese influx."[57]

The Seattle hearings were concluded on March 2, the day General DeWitt issued his first Public Proclamation. A few days before, John Tolan had predicted "a whirlwind of confusion . . . hardships, dislocations, perhaps to some people who have no wish to do harm. Perhaps the best observation is the old one: '*War is hell.*' "[58] DeWitt's proclamation divided the Western Defense Command into two areas. Military Area No. 1 included the western two-thirds of Washington, the western half of both California and Oregon, and the southern half of Arizona. The rest was designated as Military Area No. 2. A detailed map accompanied the proclamation. From Military Area No. 1 the following were to be excluded: first, persons suspected of espionage; second, Japanese aliens; third, American-born Japanese; fourth, German aliens; and fifth, Italian aliens. They were allowed to move into Military Area No. 2 where they were led to believe they would not be further disturbed, although as early as February it was planned that they would eventually be removed from the California portion of Military Area No. 2. While the "prohibited zones" of the Justice Department had been small areas, sometimes just a mile or two around military or defense installations, General DeWitt's proclamation covered almost a million square miles. The order set in motion a mass exodus that would take a great many people tremendous distances from their former homes.

The important question was how this was to be accomplished. Mike Masaoka said, "We trust that our government will treat us as civilian citizens who are voluntarily cooperating in national defense and not as military wards."[59] Dr. Henry Grady of the Pacific Coast Committee on National Security and Fair Play commented that it could be done by allowing evacuees free settlement, or by the government managing supervised work projects, or making the Japanese wards of the government. Actually, all three of these alternatives came to pass.

General DeWitt at first encouraged those who could make their own arrangements to move into Military Area No. 2 or out of the Western Defense Command altogether. But would the Japanese be welcome?

The Tolan Committee in February had sent wires to the governors of the states to the east and the replies were not encouraging. The governor of Arizona answered, "We do not propose to be made a dumping ground for enemy aliens from any other State. . . . I cannot too strongly urge that such aliens be placed in concentration camps east of the Rocky Mountains. . . ."[60] The governor of Arkansas replied, "Our people are not familiar with the customs or peculiarities of the Japanese. There will not be any way to employ these people in Arkansas. The only way I can visualize where we can use them at all would be to fence them in concentration camps under wire fence and guards."[61]

Governor Chase Clark of Idaho said, "Farmers here are very bitter against employing this labor. I am fearful such labor would get hurt. My recommendation is that if enemy aliens are brought to Idaho they be placed in concentration camps under military guard."[62] He was later even more vehement. In a speech at Grangeville in May, he said, "The Japs live like rats, breed like rats and act like rats. We don't want them buying or leasing land or becoming permanently located in our state. . . . I don't want them coming into Idaho and I don't want them taking seats in our university at Moscow vacated by our young men who have gone to war against Japan."[63]

The governors of Kansas and Montana were equally antagonistic toward the refugees from the West Coast. The only western governor to welcome them was Ralph Carr of Colorado who said, "If we do not extend humanity's kindness and understanding to these people, if we deny them the protection of the Bill of Rights, if we say they may be denied the privilege of living in any one of the 48 states without hearing or charge of misconduct, then we are tearing down the whole American system."[64] Other Colorado officials did not agree with him, nor did the general population in the state. There is a report of his trying to quell an angry crowd at a Navy rally in Durango, warning of possible retaliation by Japan if American Japanese were persecuted. "If Colorado's part in the war is to take 100,000 of them, then Colorado will take care of them."[65] Governor Carr was defeated in the next election, though this may have had no connection with his stand on the Japanese. Richard Neustadt, regional director of the Federal Security Agency, told the Tolan Committee, "I have seen representatives of the Governors, the chambers of commerce, and all the hospitality centers west of the Rocky Mountain States. They don't want them either."[66]

A JACL member had told the Tolan Committee in Seattle: "The Japanese feared with reason that, forced to vacate their homes, unable to find a place to stay, they would be kicked from town to town in the interior like the 'Oakies' of John Steinbeck's novel. Others went further and envisioned the day when inhabitants of inland states, aroused by the steady influx of Japanese, would refuse to sell gasoline and food to them. They saw, too, the possibility of mob action against them, as exhausted, impoverished and unable to travel further, they stopped in some town or village where they were not wanted."[67]

Only 4,889 Japanese left the Western Defense Command voluntarily. They relocated in various areas: mainly Colorado, Utah, Idaho, eastern Washington, and eastern Oregon outside prohibited zones.[68] A few also went to the Midwest and East. The reception was not hospitable. The *State Tribune* in Wyoming complained on March 5, "Every Congressman from beyond Salt Lake City is buried under an avalanche of mail protesting that the government is entirely too scrupulous in respecting the privileges of citizens of Japanese ancestry. We can't tell a good Jap from a bad one." When Thomas R. Bodine and a friend tried to stimulate a welcome for travelers to Idaho, people protested, "we're all white folks."

Japanese refugees were halted by patrolmen when they tried to enter Kansas. Arizona turned back many at the state line. When evacuees stopped to eat, they encountered signs saying, "This restaurant poisons both rats and Japs." An aged Issei couple who migrated to Santa Fe later petitioned the government for asylum in an assembly center because of the racial prejudice they encountered. It was estimated that 1,200 people turned around and came back to the Coast.

Among those who made a successful resettlement were the family of Seijiro Sugioka from Hollister. In three days they assembled a scattered clan, including grown children in San Francisco and Los Angeles, and started off in a caravan of five cars, accompanied by their minister, the Reverend Walter Girdner, whose church had voted to send him to help them on the journey. All during the trip Mrs. Sugioka took care of the minister's clothes and saw that he had the best chair to sit on. He thought he had never traveled with people who treated him better. He went in the lead car and when they stopped at a town he would get out and explain at gas stations, restaurants, and auto camps that these people, his good friends and members of his church, were moving inland on government orders, that they had decided to move themselves instead of having the government pay their expenses at a camp.

At times they met with hostility; at other times with friendliness. Tension was high, however, because they never knew what to expect. In Utah, a road construction crew picked up heavy rocks and threatened to stone them. But in Nevada, the owner of a motel where they stayed refused to ask them to leave, even though other overnight guests protested their presence.

Mr. Girdner's original plan was to take them to his home town of Mercer, Missouri, but a letter arrived at the parsonage after the caravan had left, warning them not to come there because feeling was running too high. With the help of Army officials this message was relayed to them by telephone en route. They then decided to go to Denver, Colorado, rather than to a small community where there might be more prejudice.

There they had some difficulty, what with anti-Japanese feeling and a housing shortage, in finding a place to rent, but finally located a large house on the east side of the city. A son-in-law set himself up in the photography business; a son took a position with the Christian Churches of Colorado. After the war, several members of the family returned to the West Coast. Others settled permanently in North Carolina, Indiana, Iowa, and Colorado.

The Hamamura family also went to Colorado in a group of seventy people from the Salinas area. The owners of the motels where they stopped en route were instructed to notify the local police and the FBI who "would come and check our luggage." They settled in Rocky Ford, about 130 miles southeast of Denver. The oldest son, Masao, remembers, "People were much nicer there, even nicer than in California, though our experience near Salinas was good. There were lots of Germans and Russians around Rocky Ford. We were actually comrades."

About fifteen California families settled in Grand Junction, Colorado, where they grew cherries, peaches, and onions. One group of about ninety Japanese under the leadership of Fred Wada of Oakland went to Wasatch County in Utah where they leased 3,800 acres of sagebrush-covered desert for $2 an acre and succeeded in making it yield good crops of vegetables and grain. The men were working sixteen to eighteen hours a day to clear the land and plant barley, peas, cabbage, lettuce, carrots, strawberries, and potatoes.

I. K. Ishimatsu of San Jose moved his entire clan of twenty-four people, including a four-month-old baby, to Cedar City, Utah. Before leaving, he gathered them together and told them, "Now we are taking a big chance. Do you want to go to camp? Or are you going to follow me?" And they all decided to go. He had friends in the produce business in Utah; so he thought he could get some jobs for himself, his sons, and the other men. Of the twenty-four in the family, half a dozen were able to work.

Mr. Ishimatsu recalls:

When we arrived in Utah, we lived temporarily in a motel, but this man had lots of pressure from the local people to keep us moving. (There were so many caravans of Japanese carrying mattresses and household goods it reminded you of covered wagons passing through Cedar City which is located on the main highway east.) At the same time, there were rumors reaching Utah that some Japanese spies were running out of California, so it was understandable to me that the innocent people of Cedar City began to feel concerned. Finally, the motel owner began to feel the pressure and asked us to find some other place to rent.

Before we left California, we were advised about the many restricted areas where aliens should stay out—one of which was the airport. Before we arrived in Utah the produce man had rented an old farm house with a barn full of hay for us to live in so we decided to move there. When we had unloaded half of our belongings I noticed an airplane coming in for a landing. I said to myself, "My God, we are too close to the airport; this must be one of those restricted areas." And I said, "Let's pack up again." And we went back to the motel which was expensive but we had no choice until we could find some other place to rent.

A couple of nights later townspeople who were representative of various clubs and lodges came to see me and told me that the councilmen had decided against having Japanese in town. Obviously, anti-Japanese feeling was rapidly building up in this otherwise peaceful town of Cedar City. I told these people I would appreciate it if they could make an appointment for me to meet with the councilmen so that I could honestly present my case before I left town. I showed them credentials I brought with me (bearing my picture attached to them) by the Santa Clara County sheriff, county auditor, prominent attorneys, and Union Pacific representatives, and they agreed to a meeting.

They made arrangements for me to appear before a group of city people who were member representatives of Veterans of Foreign Wars, Chamber of Commerce, lodges, and church people. I was introduced to them by the chairman of the meeting. I was shaking but I stood up because I was desperate to convince them of the fact that I was not one of those rumored spies seeking asylum in Cedar City. There were rampant rumors from California which had reached Utah accusing all Japanese of being spies or dangerous aliens.

It was nothing but lies! I said to them, "The U.S. government would provide us with free meals and free room if we wanted to go to a relocation camp, but the reason I want to stay here is to prove to you that I'm not a spy nor a dangerous alien. On the other hand, if I am accepted here, I can be helpful in the agricultural field because I am an experienced produce man." I even pointed out that many of their young men were being drafted so I was sure that they would face a labor shortage soon. After I had finished my plea I was called into another room where minutes later the chairman came and told me that they would make an exception and let me stay in the city.

You might say that was the happiest moment in my life when they told me that I could stay there.

Later I found an old brick house to which we moved. I was told the price we were paying for rent was outrageous but I didn't have any choice.

A couple times we had telephone calls during the night, apparently from a man under the influence of liquor, telling us to get out or they'd blast us with a shotgun. My wife became very nervous. I was scared too, of course. But somehow I was always ready for the worst so it didn't bother us much.

When you are in a position like we were you are prepared to meet any kind of persecution. Yes, I was frightened. But we didn't bother calling the sheriff's office. We just sat there and waited. The man who theatened didn't come. He didn't show up that night or any time.

The Ishimatsus stayed on and began contributing up-to-date California farming methods to the local fruit and sugar beet production.

Ishimatsu later brought in evacuees from the Topaz relocation center to help with thinning sugar beets and harvesting fruit. He persuaded some farmers near the town of Hurricane who were letting their peaches drop to the ground that he and his men would pick them at fifty cents an hour (the local arrangement was $2 a day plus dinner and lunch), and they would still make a profit on their peaches which they had never done before. Ishimatsu had some difficulty in persuading the farmers—who were "the nicest people . . . but they were more or less relaxed"—to accept his offer. When they did they made money. "They never saw such big money in their lives, I was told.

"I sound like I'm bragging, but I think I did something up there. I did what I promised in my first statement in Cedar City so I was proud of myself and grateful to those people who allowed me to stay and prove it."

Over five thousand Japanese moved into Military Zone No. 2. In California the line ran down the middle of the state. The Wada family moved from San Carlos to Fresno which is cut by Highway 99 because they "thought it would be far enough." They had been led to believe that no one would be evacuated from Zone No. 2.

The Geary Watanabes of San Jose, newly married, borrowed a truck, put in whatever they could and moved his relatives and hers to a farm near Orange Cove in the Fresno area. After they got settled they rarely went to town. In nearby Reedley a group of Koreans turned their backs on them and once a Caucasian woman spat at them.

Eastern Californians were vocal in their resentment of the Japanese refugees from Military Zone No. 1. In some places in the San Joaquin Valley there was as much antagonism toward them as there had been toward the Dust Bowl migrants of the thirties. In Del Ray, following a clash between a constable and three young evacuees, the townspeople smashed the windows of Japanese stores. A vigilante group called The Bald Eagles was formed in Tulare County in response to the arrival of 1,200 newcomers added to an original Japanese population of 1,800. Kern County farmers took their dissatisfaction to the governor. Farm groups from all over the eastern part of the state urged him to banish all Japanese from California.

On March 27 General DeWitt issued a freeze order on voluntary evacuation.

FIVE · EVACUATION

A GOOD MANY American Japanese left Military Area No. 1 quickly during the forty-eight hours before the freeze order on voluntary evacuation went into effect on March 29. There was an exodus from San Francisco's "Japan town" of "trucks of all sizes, station wagons and private cars, piled high with household and personal goods."[1] Mr. Kato, the proprietor of the El Camino nursery in suburban San Mateo loaded whatever possessions he could onto two trucks, sold the rest of his property, and started for Idaho. In his haste he probably overlooked the report of D. A. Storm of Monterey, who had gone to Boise to discuss the possibility of Japanese–Americans buying land in the state and who had reported being "thrown out" of Governor Clark's office.[2] However, Mr. Kato reached Idaho successfully even though he had trouble purchasing gas for his trucks en route, not because of the shortage, but because of his race.

Some Nisei girls from eastern Washington, who had been living with the Floyd Schmoes in Seattle, rushed 150 miles home across the mountains only to find that they were still in Military Area No. 1 and hence subject to evacuation by the government. Two Hawaiian Nisei girls were working at this time for Mrs. Gerda Isenberg of Palo Alto, who had been born in Germany. As she searched to find a means of getting them away from the West Coast, she thought how ironic it was that she, a naturalized citizen from an enemy country, should have to find a refuge for two Americans. She sent them to Philadelphia to the sister of Pauline Trueblood, the wife of the Reverend Elton Trueblood, the Quaker chaplain of Stanford University. Both girls found positions with families.

On March 27, almost simultaneously with the freeze order, General DeWitt announced that all Japanese in Military Area No. 1 were subject to a curfew and mileage restriction. They had to be in their homes at night and could travel no more than five miles from home without special permission. The curfew was later challenged in the courts as a violation of the rights of citizens. Some Nisei considered the curfew a nuisance; to others, it was a severe psychological blow. Yukio Okamoto, a young San Jose merchant, complained, "Gosh, what's a guy going to do if he works all day and has to stick around the house from 8 P.M. to 6 A.M.? I don't guess I'll be able to see much of my girl from now on."[3]

Two Nisei brothers from Stockton were students at the University of Southern California and the University of California at Los Angeles. No one could give them definite information about their status, but college administrators suggested they should go home. "We tried the different departments, the FBI and all that, to see if we could get a permit to travel, because they said travel was restricted to within five miles of where we lived. We went to four or five different offices, and they knew nothing about it. So we just hopped on a train and came home." Nisei soldiers still in the Army "defiantly stated [in Los Angeles] that if they could not be trusted enough to be permitted to walk down Broadway at 9:30 P.M., they might as well be told to turn in their uniforms."[4] Eiichi Sakauye, whose family had a pear orchard outside San Jose, was accompanying a farm bureau official at his request on an inspection tour of the acreage, when their car was stopped by a deputy sheriff who charged Sakauye with violating the curfew. He let the two Caucasians settle the question.

These restrictions paved the way for the first evacuation order. Since early in March when the Tolan Committee had assessed the hospitality of the mountain states toward voluntary Japanese migration, it was clear that some program of forced resettlement or involuntary evacuation (these were the euphemisms commonly employed) would have to be formulated if these unwanted people were going to be removed from the coastal area. The Tolan Committee petitioned the federal government to create an agency with a civilian coordinator to handle the problem. On March 18 through Executive Order 9102 President Roosevelt brought into being the War Relocation Authority which was empowered to set up and administer relocation camps for the Japanese. Milton Eisenhower, then with the Department of Agriculture, was appointed the first director of WRA.

Three days earlier General DeWitt had created the Wartime Civil Control Administration (WCCA) with Lieutenant Colonel Karl Bendetsen as chief. Working cooperatively, these two agencies transplanted the West Coast Japanese population not once, but in most cases, twice, in approximately four months—no small administrative feat. The operation cost the government several million dollars. What it cost the American Japanese in property loss and human suffering has never been accurately estimated. This extraordinary incarceration program was carried out in a smooth, efficient, and, on the whole, humane manner.

Laurence Hewes of the Farm Security Administration described an early briefing by Bendetsen:

> There on the wall was a map of the Pacific Coast with a new North-South line from British Columbia to Mexico. For our Japanese neighbors, America now commenced east of that line. We Caucasians, patriots by virtue of our skin, could continue to reside west of the line. With the deftness of a surgeon and with something of the same reassuring antiseptic quality, the young [then] major told us of evacuation proclamations to be followed by voluntary evacuation, followed in turn by involuntary evacuation, and mild detention for three or four years in a Federal institution. Bendetsen's tones made one think of restful, bucolic retirement, not of barbed wire or bayonets.[5]

As the evacuation of the entire West Coast Japanese population was being implemented, the restrictions on Germans and Italians were relaxed and eventually abolished. In March, General DeWitt announced that certain members of these groups could apply for exemption from curfew, travel restrictions, and evacuation orders: people who had applied for United States citizenship, those seventy years old or over, and the relatives (parents, wives, children, sisters, and brothers) of men serving in the U.S. armed forces. A Nisei from San Leandro, California, J. Harry Yanai, wondered why the parents of Nisei sons in the service were not exempted from evacuation. "Discrimination against the Japanese seems to be the order of the day," he wrote. "Whatever the source, it reeks of nothing but filthy politics—those who would benefit from the expulsion of their competitors by hook or by crook. . . . Now I know money talks."[6]

On May 26 after the Japanese from Military Zone 1 were safely interned in their first temporary prisons, the assembly centers, Bendetsen announced in a broadcast: "I am authorized to state that no further mass evacuation is contemplated either on the West Coast or on the East Coast."[7] (The Japanese from the California part of Zone 2 were, however, evacuated en masse.) Soon afterwards General DeWitt abolished the Justice Department's restricted and prohibited zones. On October 19 Attorney General Biddle announced a presidential directive by which all noncitizen Italians in the United States were freed of the stigma of being classified as enemy aliens.

Mexico and Canada were also carrying out restrictive policies toward people of Japanese ancestry while exempting Germans and Italians. The Mexican government created a sixty-two-mile barred zone adjacent to coastal areas and international borders from which all Japanese were to move by the end of March. Canada, as in the past following the anti-Asian policies of the United States, announced that the approximately 22,000 Japanese in British Columbia, the majority of whom were citizens, would be removed to the interior and used to help construct a highway through the Rockies. By November, 1942, some 19,867 people had been evacuated from a one-hundred-mile coastal strip along the Pacific; the majority of them were in interior housing projects, others in sugar beet camps, self-supporting projects, or industrial employment.[8] After they had left the "protected area" along the Coast, the government, which had promised to safeguard their property, proceeded to sell it. Discriminatory laws against them were passed by the Canadian Parliament. Ian Mackenzie, who represented British Columbia, favored mass deportation of Canadian Japanese to Japan after the war.

Under the authority vested in him by Executive Order 9066 General DeWitt designated about sixty individuals as "dangerous persons," and ordered them to leave the Western Defense Command. One of these persons was an Italian-American dried fruit merchant who continued to spend most of his time with his Japanese friends even after they were sent to an assembly center. He organized a drum and bugle corps and assisted with church services. His passion for Japanese culture as well as his interest in a Japanese lady led to the accusation that he was "too friendly with Japanese." The Caucasians who were required to move inland were not interned. The difference in treatment was noted abroad. After an Italian newspaperman reported that in the United States "Japanese, irrespective of whether they were Nisei or not, were being subjected to much harsher treatment than Germans and Italians and huge numbers of them were being interned in concentration camps,"[9] Tokyo threatened retaliation against Allied prisoners. An editorial in the Shanghai *Times* urged, "The Anglo-American nationals in Japan and occupied China should be herded together and driven into interior regions where there are no modern facilities."[10]

Japan's treatment of military prisoners was as a rule severe and on occasion cruel, as attested by those who survived the prison camps. Allied civilians interned in the Philippines and in other conquered territories suffered extreme deprivation. When the American ambassador to Japan, Joseph Grew, returned to New York City on the exchange ship *Gripsholm*, on August 25, 1942, he described in a CBS broadcast the experience of American missionaries, teachers, newspaper correspondents, and businessmen "who had spent the preceding six months in solitary confinement in small, bitterly cold prison cells, inadequately clothed and inadequately fed, and at times subjected to the most cruel and barbaric tortures." Several said as they waited for seven days in the harbor at Yokohama that "if negotiations for our exchange failed they would commit suicide rather than return to their imprisonment in Japan."[11]

On the other hand the Reverend A. K. Reischauer, who also returned on the *Gripsholm* after thirty-six years as a missionary in Japan, reported that Caucasian–American civilians in that country were in some cases interned or confined to their homes and in other instances allowed freedom of movement. Reischauer and other former missionaries as well as Grew, who had many warm personal friends in Japan, espoused the cause of the American Japanese. Japanese Christians and American missionaries kept ties of friendship as close as possible given the circumstances of two nations at war. In response to a request from the Methodist Bishop E. Stanley Jones, Japan's Toyohiko Kagawa, the renowned writer and preacher, in a vain plea for peace had organized a prayer vigil during the week before his nation's planes attacked Pearl Harbor.

In any case, the treatment of American nationals in Japan cannot justly be compared with the treatment of Nisei in the United States. More relevant is the estimate that if all the American-citizen descendants of enemy nationals had been interned during World War II, the United States would have had thirty million people in camps. The National Association for the Advancement of Colored People commented on the racial aspect of the evacuation: "It is significant that southern senators and congressmen are among the most rabidly anti-Japanese. For, if Asiatic-Americans be reduced to bondage, deprived of citizenship and of property, the same thing can be done to Afro-Americans and to Jews."[12]

On March 21 Congress passed Public Law 503, introduced in the Senate by Richard Reynolds of North Carolina and in the House by John Costello of California, which imposed a $5,000 penalty on anyone who violated evacuation orders. Included in the blanket banishment of a racial minority were people who had as little as 1/16 Japanese blood and Japanese who were married to Caucasians, Chinese, Filipinos, Negroes, Hawaiians, and Eskimos. A Nisei commented: " . . . there were enacted comic opera scenes in the Federal building [in Los Angeles], scenes too reminiscent of recent Europe. . . . I actually heard of Koreans and Chinese who wondered if they too might not be included because ultimately their ethnic origin and that of the Japanese were the same. A number of unemployed were heard discussing the possibility of 'getting interned' by claiming to have a great-grandfather who was a quarter Japanese. I know of a few cases in which half and quarter Japanese, who know nothing about Japan, Japanese, or the Japanese language, will be affected. Those of Luchuan origin [Luchu (Okinawa) was annexed by Japan in 1879] will be affected though they are not Japanese and are antagonistic to Japan though mixing with the Japanese because of convenience."[13] The only exemptions granted were to Nisei in uniform, a few civilian language interpreters, patients in hospitals, sanatoriums and insane asylums, jail prisoners, and orphans in institutions. The children were later moved en masse to the permanent relocation centers, and discharged hospital patients joined their families in camps.

As the Army prepared for what Dr. Paul S. Taylor called "the largest single forced migration in American history" friends of the Japanese protested. Professor Carl Dakon of the University of Washington urged Seattle families to adopt Nisei and Sansei children so that they "could be spared the suffering they are bound to experience through removal to inland points. I hate to see these young people oppressed with the feeling that there is no way to separate the good from the bad."[14] Professor Claude Settles of the sociology department of San Jose State College went up and down California speaking to luncheon clubs, church groups, and fraternal organizations, pleading the cause of Nisei citizens. Using the FBI and the Tolan Committee reports on American Japanese good conduct, he concluded, "The Japanese are not being shipped out because they are disloyal, but because their competitors covet over a hundred million dollars worth of land and crops." He named the names of those who profited. These statements did not endear him to certain members of the state legislature who were reported to have told the administration at the college, which was seeking an appropriation, "Unless you get rid of that man Settles, you don't get a cent." A Pasadenan with the same name as his father who espoused the rights of the Nisei so embarrassed the older man by his public declarations that he was ready to leave town. "Have you lost your marbles, helping the Japs?" he asked his son. It took real courage to speak for the unfortunate minority in the spring and summer of 1942. The wonder is not that more people did not see the issue clearly through the fog of wartime fear and overzealous patriotism, but that those few who did remained staunch and unswerving in their conviction of the rights of the individual.

Friends of a San Fernando Valley nurseryman, Sego Murakami, collected two hundred names on a petition, asking that he and his wife be allowed to stay. On March 21, Ray Lyman Wilbur, Chancellor of Stanford University, sent a letter to General DeWitt with the following message, "Whenever and wherever the constitutional guarantees are violated in the treatment of a minority, no matter how unpopular or helpless, the whole fabric of American government is weakened. . . . The test of America is the security of its minority groups." On April 27, the San Francisco *Chronicle* printed a letter signed by twenty-eight Protestant and Jewish clergymen pledging assistance to the Japanese. Members of various bar associations as well as the Pacific Coast Committee on American Principles and Fair Play repeatedly urged DeWitt to set up hearing boards to pass on individuals. But most of these efforts came even as the buses and trains were leaving for the assembly centers.

Many of the Nisei were trying not to lose faith in the America that rejected them. A Washingtonian recalled his feelings when he was challenged by a member of the older generation: " 'I told you so,' " old man Kawashima leered at me, baring his ugly yellow teeth. . . . "You *nisei* are a weak, spineless bunch. You boast about your citizenship, your rights and loyalty but look what happens. The government is going to throw you into internment camp with the rest of us like sheep and cattles [sic] and you still talk about faith in American democracy. Why do you keep kidding yourself?'

"I wanted to tell the old fossil to go lay a brick egg, but I sulked away with my soul half-crying, half-weeping because I wanted so much to keep faith. I see no logic in having to surrender my freedom in a country which I sincerely believe to be fighting for the same freedom. What, are we *nisei* so helpless?"[15]

Saburo Kido of the JACL said, "Never in the thousands of years of human history has a group of citizens been branded on so wholesale a scale as being treacherous to their own native land, regardless of racial descent." Still, he urged, "When we leave our homes, let us leave with a smiling face and courageous mien. Let us look upon ourselves as the pioneers of a new era looking forward to the greatest adventure of our time."[16]

The Seattle newspaper editor, James Sakamoto, petitioned President Roosevelt: "We have protested our loyalty in the past. We have not been believed. We are willing to assume the burden of continuing to demonstrate it under all but impossible conditions. We would be deeply grateful if you would point out to our fellow citizens that we are not traitors to our country. . . ."[17]

Sometimes the hurt and anger were less constrained. A resident of the White River Valley near Tacoma who had been locked out of his own packing shed by local police exploded: "These crazy bastards give me a pain! It's enough to drive a man nuts! It's bad enough to be herded off like animals without being locked out of your own business. Till Pearl Harbor we were respected people here: Joe played halfback on the football team, I was in the Chamber of Commerce, and Terry was in scout work. We were all active in our churches and we were friendly with everyone or thought we were. Now we can't step out of our homes to buy food without some hoodlum of a cop trying to run us in. By God! I'll be glad to get out of this place! I hope I never see it again!"[18]

While the WRA was locating and developing sites for permanent relocation centers, the WCCA was establishing temporary assembly or reception centers mainly in race tracks and fair grounds to house the West Coast Japanese until the permanent camps were ready. The WCCA set up sixty-four field stations from Arizona to the Canadian border, staffed by representatives of, among other agencies, the Federal Security Agency, the Farm Security Administration, and the Federal Reserve Bank in order to assist the evacuees with social welfare and property problems before they departed. Both Richard Neustadt, West Coast head of the Federal Security Administration, and Laurence Hewes, area chief of the farm agency, opposed the evacuation. Hewes wrote later, "A young Air Corps officer once said to me, 'In the military service you often get handed a lemon. Instead of crabbing about it the trick is to make lemonade out of it.' So, hating the evacuation, we made a game out of competing with the Army."[19] Hewes demanded and received a million dollar cash advance as well as the right to approve all property transactions involving Japanese and the power to freeze fraudulent sales (exercised just once) to protect the interests of the evacuees. He found it was an effective policy to staff his offices with Nisei who knew about farming and could act as interpreters.

> Results were little short of marvelous. . . . They could put a finger on just the right person to talk with tough old Mr. Watanabe, they didn't hesitate to scold mistrustful, fat Mrs. Takahashi, and they could locate exactly the boundaries of the Tanaka property. We never discussed with them the fact they too, must some day be evacuated, and, typically, they never brought it up.[20]

Hewes recalls that the registration of Japanese-owned or leased farms was mandatory. The Farm Security Administration report lists 7,076 Japanese farm operators and 6,664 Japanese-owned or leased farms totaling approximately 258,000 acres subject to relinquishment in Military Area No. 1. When the farms in Military Area No. 2 were added, the total was increased to over a quarter of a million acres. The farms in Military Area No. 1 alone were valued at $73,000,000.

The aim in transferring farms was to keep them in production so that the nation at war would be assured of the usual crop quotas. General DeWitt boasted that 99 per cent of all the acreage in the affected area owned or operated by the Japanese was kept in production.[21] This required cash for making loans to prospective buyers and a vigorous promotion program. Hewes wrote later:

> Our problems were manifold and complex: we needed time to plan. For we soon found that few Japanese farms met Caucasian concepts; many were small, with odd-shaped fields, and, contrary to popular belief, the soil was often poor. But somehow extraordinary skill had produced magnificent yields of highly specialized crops. . . . I called a meeting of packers and processors of these commodities; my message to them was: "If you people need these products then you should form industry-wide corporations to take over the farms of your Japanese suppliers. We'll furnish the financing.[22]

The soon-to-be-evacuated farmers were told by the Western Defense Command to keep on tilling their fields. "Ironically, to them, at least, General DeWitt asked them all to prove their loyalty to the U.S. by planting and cultivating, until the day of departure, the crops they could not return to harvest."[23] A Washington grower complained, "It is hard work. Why should we do it if it is not to be of any use? We can't get white men to work in vegetables, I guess they are built too far from the ground."[24] Takeo Yuchi, the "lettuce King" in Salinas, kept on filling orders from the Navy for onions while waiting to be evacuated. In the Puyallup Valley in Washington, which customarily shipped $3,500,000 worth of produce all over the United States, some of the farmers were returning fertilizer to the merchants to get some travel and subsistence money, but no one neglected the crops. A Nisei from Auburn was disgusted by the rumors that farm operators would cease to care for their crops when they had "so courageously plowed and planted in spite of freezing and lack of credit." He recalled:

> We began to plan our spring planting; we began to haul fertilizers for our acres again, for seasons will not wait. We helped with the work on the farms from which fathers had been interned [in Justice Department camps]. Being on the land is a source of strength in times of insecurity. We could not conceive of life on the farm which would be different because of the war. To plow, to plant seed, to weed—we felt as if they were an inexorable process of life which we could not change. As we worked in our fields, a man came in and talked to us. "I hear the government is going to take all you Japs away from here and send you to the sugar beet country. . . ."
>
> "Oh, yeah," I said and would pay no attention to him. Beer parlor talk. . . .[25]

Another Nisei wrote: "One man down in Imperial Valley [California] broadcast how much of a menace and danger the Japanese were. His brother was running up and down the valley buying up Japanese land cheap. In northern California they let the Japanese put in all their crops. Then about three days before harvest, when the Japanese had put in all the work and money, they discovered a 'military necessity' and evacuated them. Others got the benefit of their investment and efforts."[26] A family who eventually were sent to the Gila relocation center owned a vast acreage in California where they grew strawberries. For a number of years before the war a radio station had approached them about buying the land, but they refused to sell. Just before being evacuated they agreed to the transaction if the owners of the station would arrange to have the berries picked and send them the proceeds. Later, after they were in camp, they discovered that the berries had been bulldozed under before harvesting by the new owners.

The fact that West Coast Japanese cared for their crops until they left made more difficult the objective of the Farm Security Administration— to see that they got fair prices for land and equipment that they were using right up until departure. Though FSA agents spent over $4 million and earned the opprobrium "Jap-lovers" for fighting gougers and chiselers, the Japanese farmers still suffered incalculable losses. Losses could only finally be measured after the war when the farmers returned and assessed the deterioration of equipment, estimated income missed during the war years when prices were high, and added these figures to the initial losses suffered when they were forced to sell crops, land, and machinery in haste. The estimated loss on the strawberry crop in Elorin, California, was $150,000. A Salinas farmer sold his garlic crop for $100 an acre, when it had cost him $125 an acre to plant it. A Compton farmer sold a horse, three tons of hay, three-quarters of a ton of fertilizer, a harrow, a cultivator, and a plow for $100. These are only three of countless similar reckonings. As for those known as the "land vultures," Professor Settles had the following story to tell about the tactics of one of them in Santa Clara County, which he learned from John Rush of Gilroy:

> He has been an implement dealer in that region for a number of years. In that capacity he has taken mortgages on a great many farms belonging to Japanese people. In that way he has come to know these people very intimately and has learned that they can be trusted, if their name is ever put to a piece of paper, to a much greater extent than can their white fellow citizens. Now that this trouble has started, Mr. Rush has been approached by scores of people asking him to foreclose, in order that they (the urgers) may buy up these lands at a cheaper price.
>
> In the case of one Japanese who had to leave, he made Mr. Rush the trustee and guardian of his four children. Yesterday Mr. Rush was approached by a moneyed man of the community and was argued with for over an hour that Mr. Rush should persuade these children to sell their farm, so that the moneyed man could buy the lot, agreeing to split the profits handsomely with Mr. Rush if he would only do this for him.[27]

Many evacuees had to forfeit their leases, or they lost their land because they could not meet mortgage payments. A farmer in Wapato, Washington, was subleasing land for $800 a year. The owner ordered him to leave. When he protested that he wanted his money back, he was handed $100. In Los Angeles some Japanese had invested $92,000 in a commercial property. The lessor forced them to forfeit the entire amount before he would cancel the lease.

The Federal Reserve Bank had freezing power "designed to forestall unfair action by unscrupulous creditors which would be detrimental to the interest of the evacuees" but it was not once used. In fairness, it must be said that this was partly because many Japanese did not know of its existence. While the almost complete failure of the Federal Reserve Bank as an agency for safeguarding evacuee property was partly due to the fact that only 2,867 families took advantage of its storage facilities, the small number of those requesting help reflected the agency's policy of indifference toward the assignment. The Tolan Committee called the performance of the Federal Reserve Bank "deficient." The conditions under which the bank would accept property "have been cautious in the extreme."[28]

A Nisei remembers, "We asked if we could store some things with the government, and the official asked, 'Haven't you friends with whom you could store your things? We will not take responsibility for the things we take. However, if you do not have friends with whom to store things, you may bring them to the Western Producers' Exchange and we will take it away.' "[29] The government would only store cars at the owner's risk in open lots without insurance or sell them to the Army at the low wholesale Blue Book price. The evacuee didn't have much choice; he could take a chance with the government or sell the car himself for what he could get for it. "Whatever he did, he stood to lose," was the verdict of the *Pacific Citizen* in a twenty-five year commemorative essay.[30]

Many opportunists were waiting for the prices on Japanese-owned property to go very low before they bid on it. Henry Takemori and his wife owned a grocery store in Phoenix, Arizona, inside the prohibited zone. "When it came time to sell . . . potential buyers knew that the longer they held out, the less it would cost them. Finally, only two days before the Takemoris were scheduled to board the Greyhound buses leaving for Mayer [assembly center] with 242 bewildered passengers they sold the $15,000 property for $800—about the price of a new meat case."[31] The government told the Japanese, "All efforts to force the sale of property, equipment or other assets hurriedly and at a sacrifice should be reported to the service center," but either they did not see these warnings, since the vernacular newspapers were ceasing publication, or they had lost confidence in the government as a custodian of property. Their predicament attracted not only land speculators and rapacious secondhand dealers but also ostensibly charitable souls who, sympathizing with the "poor Japanese," helped them by buying a stove or a refrigerator or a washing machine for $5.

On the other hand, churches opened their basements, and true friends offered space in attics and cellars. In contrast to the half-hearted proposals of the Federal Reserve Bank was the indignation of Win Freitas of Hollister, who, when he heard that a family had been offered $35 for a new refrigerator, declared, "You're not going to take that. You pack it up and I'll take care of it till you get back." German neighbors of another family, mindful of the prejudice which hurt them during World War I, carefully cherished an antique doll case and *obis*.

People often sold at sacrifice prices because of panic. Some Alameda people who disposed of their parlor furniture, dining room set, and piano for $30 explained that they thought they could never come back. They thought Japan might bomb California, and nothing would be left. Or if Japan won the war they would be persecuted. Another couple who lost all their property stated, "It's better than losing your life." A woman said, "You had a feeling that if they could evacuate you and make it stick that they could also confiscate your property. There wasn't much difference. If they could take away your citizenship and move you bodily, there was no reason why they couldn't take over your business or your property or confiscate any warehouse holdings. . . . Whatever you saved, you were taking the chance that perhaps you wouldn't have it."

Another Nisei told the story of his father's panic:

> He almost gave the place away when he left. To him it was almost a relief. The property was in my name and my brother's name so I had to sign this thing when he sold it. I was pretty bitter about selling the place. I wrote to the lawyer, "Somebody's getting rich on somebody else's misfortune."
>
> He was just giving it away to have a few thousand dollars with him when he went to camp. He had fourteen acres near the county hospital, and he sold it for less than $6000. Even in those days it should have been worth at least a thousand dollars an acre. Ten years after the war every acre was worth ten or fifteen thousand dollars.
>
> I guess he got to the point where he was almost sick about the thing— he just had to sell it. The money wasn't so important. He probably was not one of these guys who thought Japan was going to win the war and that he would be a lord over here.
>
> He worried more about things like, if he left it there, just left it, there were people who might burn down the house or wreck the machinery. When you stop to think about it those things don't amount to a hill of beans. They can't take the property away. That would still be there. But he couldn't bear to leave his things there anymore. So he just got rid of them. And after all the trouble they had gone through to buy the property in the children's names, all the legal difficulties. He was a sick man from that day on.

As evacuation came closer a common greeting among the Japanese was, "Have you sold your furniture yet?" Cars appeared on the streets with "For Sale" signs attached. The San Francisco *Chronicle* under the headline "JAP TOWN SELLS OUT" described a scene in the city: "Along Post Street between Octavia and Webster, you can buy anything from a pool table to a begonia plant cheap, the signs tell you."[32] Junk men gathered to pick over the sales items. A Nisei remembers that second-hand dealers bought the papers and metal, "But we still had to burn big piles of things. I gave my pictures to the camera club friends, the piano I put into the church parlor, the washing machine and dishes went into the basement of one friend, the books into the basement of another friend. Here and there our boxes were scattered all over the town."[33] One man wrote philosophically: "There is an old saying. When your belongings become a worry, throw it away . . . so we don't seem to mind it like most of the people we know."[34]

Storage experiences varied enormously. Faithful friends guarded property; careless agents neglected it; opportunists exploited it; vandals destroyed it; thieves broke in and stole it. In some instances three years of moth and rust left little of value. The Japanese would not know the full truth until they returned. But occasionally possessions disappeared almost as soon as the evacuees departed. In Lindsay, Tulare County, California, George Kaku left his dry goods store to a Caucasian to operate on a lease, but before the man got ready to open it for business, some boys broke the lock, found stock they assumed was abandoned and told their parents. "A stream of people began to emerge laden with articles of clothing and other merchandise unused but mostly outmoded." The new manager heard about it and called the police who came and found fifty people inside the store going over the wares, selecting shoes. The police then went from home to home in a pickup truck bringing back items, including three typewriters and an adding machine. Most of the pilfered goods were recovered.[35]

On March 7 General DeWitt announced the acquisition of 5,800 acres in the Owens Valley 230 miles east of Los Angeles on which would be built the first reception center. Although citizens of Inyo County protested the prospect of a Japanese colony in their midst and Representative Leland Ford called the selection of a site close to the reservoir and aqueduct that stored water for the city of Los Angeles "an inexcusable piece of stupidity,"[36] the barracks of Manzanar began to rise from the valley floor. On March 21 one hundred soon-to-be-interned volunteers went to Owens Valley to help build their future homes, followed two days later by one thousand more. Five hundred of the second contingent took the train to Lone Pine. The rest assembled near the Rose Bowl in Pasadena at 6:15 on the morning of March 23, and the caravan of several hundred privately owned autos, from Motel Ts to 1942 sedans, driven by their owners and spaced by highway patrol cars and Army jeeps, started across the desert. Repair trucks to handle breakdowns on the road and an ambulance traveled in the procession. When they arrived, "prepared," according to *Life* magazine, "to wait out the war in willing and not unprofitable internment,"[37] Arthur Hirano, "who in the early depression years managed two restaurants in the 'Fifties' in New York City, fed the hungry newcomers a tasty dinner—beef stew, steamed rice, string beans, canned apricots, bread, jelly and peas."[38] Their wives and children joined them early in April.

The first family groups to arrive at Manzanar were some of the 258 evacuees from Bainbridge Island in Puget Sound who through General DeWitt's original Exclusion Order No. 1 were ordered to leave their homes by March 29. From start to finish, the Army took charge of this dress rehearsal for mass evacuation, posting the exclusion notices on the Island, then escorting families by ferry to the mainland where they boarded waiting trains and buses for Manzanar or the Puyallup assembly center, and finally accompanying them to their destinations.

The people, mostly farmers, had worked in their strawberries and peas up to the last minute, "in order to help save their crops for national defense."[39] Their Caucasian neighbors expressed different opinions about their departure. Some said they were "glad" and hoped they would never come back. Others were sorry for them and felt that they could be trusted. The high school superintendent promised to award diplomas to the thirteen Nisei members of the senior class no matter where they graduated. Kihachi Hirakawa, the pastor of the Island's Japanese Baptist church, which he had built with his own hands forty-one years before, faced removal alone since he had no relatives, but he said, "It is God's will." Pet dogs chased after the Army trucks transporting the evacuees to the ferry. The crowds of Caucasian friends bidding them farewell at the dock noticed the children carrying souvenir bunches of the grass from their yards to remember home by. The Japanese cried as the ferry carried them away.[40]

Thomas R. Bodine, who watched the Islanders board the train in Seattle, wrote later: "What impressed me most was their silence. No one said anything. No one did anything."[41] Other observers noted the kindness of soldiers, waiters, and porters on the train and remarked on the group singing led by the military guard. It took the evacuees two days on the train and four hours on a bus to reach Manzanar. Each one was given $2 a day for food. In the words of *Life* magazine, the Army had "extended the velvet glove. . . ."[42]

The Bainbridge Island exodus was the first of 108 separate evacuations. The "whirlwind of confusion" predicted by the Tolan Committee had begun. Throughout April and May the Civilian Exclusion Orders began to appear on electric and telephone poles throughout Military Area No. 1. Mrs. Josephine Duveneck, a Quaker, wrote, "As we went down California Street [in San Francisco] on the cable car . . . we saw soldiers nailing the evacuation orders onto telegraph poles at each street corner . . . the word 'Japanese' [was] written large so that it was visible from across the street. I couldn't help thinking of Munich in 1936 when the posters appeared overnight on the walls of buildings along the street, proclaiming various restrictions for Jews."[43] A Nisei from Washington remembered seeing an Army truck stop at a power line pole to tack up a proclamation for all Japanese residents of King County north of the Pierce County line. The notice said they would be evacuated in fourteen days.[44]

The evacuees received individual notices as well, telling them to send the head of the family to the local civil control station where they were issued tags with the family number which were to be attached to every individual and every piece of luggage in the family group. Evacuees were ordered to carry with them to the assembly centers bedding and linen for each member of the family, toilet articles, extra clothing, sufficient knives, forks, spoons, plates, bowls, and cups for every member of the family, and "essential personal effects," as much as could be contained in a sea bag and two suitcases for each person. "What kind of clothing shall we take?" people asked themselves. They did not know where they were going and with wild rumors circulating, some prepared as if for Alaska and others for the Mojave desert. "I'll bring some good books, games, lots of cigars I like, some of my choice delicacies to eat, a comfortable cushion to sit on, electric fan to cool me and other knickknacks," wrote a man who was looking forward to a vacation.[45] One family collected concentrates, powdered milk, raisins, cheese, vitamin pills, and chocolate, "all in anticipation of starvation. . . ."[46] Some parents from Lodi, California, decided to put packs on their children's backs so they could take care of themselves if they got separated. At the civil control station the head of the family was given specific instructions about the date, the time, and the place where he and his dependants must report for transportation to the assembly center.

The Civilian Exclusion Orders were issued on the basis of the military sensitivity of different areas in the Western Defense Command. Order No. 2 affected three thousand people in San Pedro and Long Beach. Order No. 4 cleared Japanese from the entire city of San Diego. On April 3, Good Friday, the first evacuees began to leave for the Santa Anita race track. On April 6 two more Los Angeles districts were ordered cleared by the fourteenth, three more by the twenty-eighth, and another 2,000 persons were ordered out of the city by the twenty-ninth.

The Reverend Allan Hunter, pastor of the Mount Hollywood Congregational church, and the Reverend Gurney Binford, a former missionary to Japan, using the title "The Sunday Before" collected the last sermons preached before evacuation by seven Issei and Nisei ministers who were influenced by Kagawa. The Reverend Lester E. Suzuki of the Japanese Methodist Church of Los Angeles cautioned his congregation, "try to make things beautiful where there is ugliness, love where there is hate, goodness where there is evil." The Reverend Royden Susu-Mago of the Japanese Independent church in Hollywood said, "We Nisei must not lose hope because present conditions check us temporarily. America needs us and we need America. . . . Under the pressure of this situation, some of us may be led to talk irrationally about packing up and going 'back' to Japan after the war. Go back? How can we go 'back' to a place we have never been? Where we can go back to is the very life of these United States. . . . This is a time of testing whether we are fit to be incorporated into the American pattern as an integral part."

The Reverend Hideo Hashimoto, pastor of the Japanese Methodist church in Fresno, declared, "In a sense, our being evacuated is the consequence of our sinfulness. As American citizens of Japanese ancestry, we had a great mission to fulfill. But we failed. In our self-centeredness, like Jonah, we ran away from our great mission." An Issei minister, the Reverend Sohei Kowta from Wintersburg, compared the trials of the Japanese about to embark on a new life in a strange place to the migration of Abraham leading his people to the land of Canaan. He spoke prophetically: "Give us a desert, we shall make it a beautiful garden; give us a wasted land, we shall change it into a productive field; give us a wilderness, we shall convert it into a beautiful orchard."

As the Japanese prepared to leave they thought of the neighbors who were staying at home. The Reverend Kengo Tajimi of Pasadena held an open house for his Caucasian friends before he was sent to Tulare. A Santa Barbara family asked their Negro neighbors if they could set out "a flower or two" for them as a parting gift. They transplanted their entire garden to the other yard. An Issei woman whose husband was interned in the Justice Department camp at Fort Missoula was told that fourteen soldiers from her town had been captured by the Japanese on Guam and Wake Islands. She called on all their mothers, presenting each with a cyclamen plant and in broken English tried to express her sympathy.

Japanese in Berkeley—1,319 of them—were ordered to Tanforan assembly center by May 1. On the eve of this evacuation a newspaper reporter called on the University of California artist Chiura Obata and found him sitting on the floor of his house, surrounded by the packed household goods, painting a watercolor of a redwood tree. He was to give a demonstration of watercolor painting at Berkeley's International House where the proceeds from the sale of 120 of his works would go to a university scholarship for the student, regardless of race or creed, who "has suffered the most from this war."[47]

A farmer in Mountain View who had sold his farm to a Chinese taught him how to transplant celery from hothouse flats to the soil and how to combat Blackheart and aphis. As a result of their communal activity, the ten-acre produce ranch "resembled a midwestern farm in the days of quilting bees and barn raisings."[48] A gardener issued a different sort of parting shot. He had decided to make a lot of money just to prove "he was as damn good as a white. I figured I could beat a big bunch of white gardeners out of their business . . . I acted just like a white man but I did it better, and my gardens are the best in town."[49] But he too relinquished everything.

At the peak of the evacuation, 3,750 people a day were being moved. Many of the Japanese simply could not stop working. A Nisei woman thinks her parents would never have been ready to leave if their deadline had not been extended when the younger children came down with chickenpox. Her father ran a wholesale-retail nursery and her mother worked right along with him, tending the bedding plants. In 1942 they had reached the peak of their money-making years. People streamed into the nursery all day long. She herself disliked working with dirt and fertilizer so she did the housework for the family, including sewing for four younger sisters. Every summer she made twenty school dresses. She grew up with Caucasians, though her father disliked "white" people. When she brought a Caucasian friend home for the night, he complained because "white" people exploited the Japanese. He was strongly pro-Japan in his sympathies. Still, he was pleased when a Caucasian neighbor, emigrating to Alaska, asked him to keep an eye on his wife and children who were being left behind. But soon he was gone himself, though the Seattle people were evacuated before the rural Japanese in Washington. Shuji Kimura wrote that buses with people on the way to Puyallup "would pass about ten in the morning in front of our house, rumbling lines of huge chartered buses loaded black with people, and waving as they passed our house. Sometimes I would be working, but I would not want to look up. I wanted to hide from them— perhaps because while they were being sent away, I was yet free, or perhaps because I wanted to flee from the thought of being sent away like them. Months later I was to understand the instant feeling of comradeship that one evacuee feels for another."[50]

By May 30 seven more California counties had been "cleared" of Japanese. Colonel Bendetsen issued a final warning "to dispel hopes of some evacuees that the Army will relax its regulations and allow certain groups to remain. . . . The removal of evacuees from designated areas is a matter of absolute military necessity. We have given repeated warnings, but apparently it has done little good. . . . Neglected personal and property matters will not for one moment obstruct the evacuation."

Engaged couples put forward their wedding dates so they would not be separated in the camps, though in planning ceremonies they had to work around the curfew and mileage restrictions. A Nisei, still on Alameda Island, ran across the Park Street Bridge to hand his wedding cake to his father who as an alien was banned from the "strategic zone." His bride had obtained special permission to travel up from San Diego for the wedding. The government had promised not to separate families. Many families collected together aunts, uncles, cousins, and grandparents, so they could be evacuated together. They often spent the last night in their homes rolled in blankets on the floor, because mattresses had been stored. Some people had to leave sick relatives behind in hospitals. Dr. Arthur Takii, a dentist who had just started to practice in

San Pedro when the war interrupted, left his hospitalized father in the care of Dr. Ralph Mayberry, a friendly minister, when he went to the Santa Anita assembly center just before Easter.

A young woman whose relatives were scattered asked a Caucasian friend, ". . . do you mind if we write to you and get in touch with each other through you? Otherwise, if we all move at the same time, which isn't likely, we would lose track of each other and be lost to each other until the end of the war and perhaps a great while after."[51]

The Aihara family in Sunnyvale were ordered to the Salinas assembly center on twenty-four-hours' notice, because one of the sisters, a nurse, was needed there immediately. Helen Aihara was teaching a convalescent child at his home when someone found her and gave her the message. They had already made arrangements to store their belongings with Caucasian friends; so they managed to meet the government's deadline without too much strain.

The Henry Tandas of Salinas will never forget their last day at home. They were so busy packing they could not take time to stop and feed their two-year-old daughter, who kept complaining that she was hungry. Shortly after they arrived at the Salinas assembly center, she became pale and listless and started vomiting. It was then they remembered the little packets of rat poisoning covered with what looked like bubble gum wrappers, which they had placed around their stored belongings. They obtained permission to rush her out to the hospital to have her stomach pumped. Her symptoms might have been a reaction to the typhoid and tetanus shots given at the center, but they were taking no chances.

People came to the rendezvous points, where the buses were to drive them to the centers, bearing prized possessions—a tiny child carrying a giant toy panda, a young couple with an infant in a pink bassinet "carried by the young father with first-child care." An observer noted how he placed his hat gently over the sleeping baby's head to protect her from the sun and wind.[52] Many were dressed in their best. A few wore tokens of their individuality such as golfing clothes and ski caps. School children waved the American flag. A little boy wore a cap stitched with the motto, "REMEMBER PEARL HARBOR." When Frank Duveneck of Los Altos, looking on at a departure scene in San Francisco, was struck by "a strange feeling that this could not be the America that I had fought for in 1918,"[53] he met an Issei wearing an American Legion cap. Another World War I veteran, Hideo Murata, had been given a certificate of honorary citizenship by the Board of Supervisors in Monterey County. When "E Day" was announced, he went to see his friend, the sheriff, "and asked if it wasn't all a mistake, or perhaps just a practical joke. Finding that the order meant what it said, he went to a local hotel, paid for his room and committed suicide. The sheriff found the certificate of honorary citizenship clutched in his hand."[54]

Army MPs supervised the loading of buses and trains. Mary Sutow saw a sentry come aboard the bus with his bayonet unsheathed. "They must have thought we were pretty dangerous people." A government official said, "We're trying not to treat these people like cattle." But the departing Japanese were tagged, in the words of an observer at the May 10 departure in San Francisco, "like checked parcels," and the women who were processing the lines of those departing "checked the called numbers in unsympathetic voices, as if they were handling a consignment of freight," while the occupants of the apartments nearby leaned out their windows watching the scene "with vacant or hostile expressions."[55]

In the confusion families were separated or mistakenly sent to the wrong centers. An old woman arrived at the Buchanan Street bus stop accompanied by her two Caucasian employers. Her son had just died after earning his doctorate, she told the officials, and she and her aged husband wanted to be sent to Tanforan with their only relatives, a niece and a nephew. But the Army could not comply with the request, and they were sent to the Pomona center. An eighty-two-year-old Issei from Pasadena was released from a Justice Department camp and arrived back at the Union Station in Los Angeles four hours after his wife was evacuated to the assembly center near Fresno. He was sent to Santa Anita, and it was several months before he was reunited with his family.

Two tiny children, one-eighth Japanese (one was blond and blue-eyed), were put aboard the bus in San Francisco by their Caucasian mother to go to the assembly center with their father, who had deserted the family and whom the children hardly knew. As the mother began to cry hysterically, an official cautioned the crowd, "Now, don't you people go and get into this."[56] In Seattle Quakers requested and were given permission to drive to the centers in private cars invalids who could not stand the bus trip. In this way, old couples were not separated. The Army had decreed that the husband could not stay behind if the wife was too infirm to make the trip. A Seattle observer wrote on May 11 that, beginning at nine in the morning, people were leaving by the hundreds. They were picked up as fast as the buses could turn around at Puyallup and come back for another load. He described a train from the White River Valley headed for the Pinedale, California, assembly center with "old ratty coaches . . . the roofs . . . covered with bird dung."[57]

Shuji Kimura described the last hours at home for their family, which was henceforth to be known as Family No. 16848:

> Now it was noon, and we did the last-minute chores. Father fed the horse an extra gallon of barley. Then we loaded our truck with our and a neighbor's luggage, and started for the train.
> The 18-car train was drawn up in the siding along the packing house from which we used to ship our peas and lettuce, and the place was full

of people. There was a tremendous line-up of trucks loaded with baggage.
. . . Many friends had come to see us off. We sat in the red plush seat of
the coach. "How's chances of getting a free trip with you?" "Tell us what
they feed you." "Don't forget to write."

We didn't feel so bad about leaving with all the excitement of leaving.
But soon when six P.M. came and the train began to move, and we saw
old Mr. Ballard waving his hat at us, his coat collar turned up against the
rain, Mother began to cry. I couldn't see through my tears either. I saw
the Main Street Crossing—there were more people waving. The train
began to go faster and the berry rows, the rhubarb, the lettuce fields, the
pea fields began to slip past our window like a panorama. My throat hurt,
but I couldn't take my eyes from the family fields and pastures slipping so
quickly away.[58]

Onlookers spoke of the dignity and patience of the departing Japanese. Yet in San Francisco "this confusion and uncertainty as to just
what day they were leaving and what their destination was, plus the
rush of packing and attendant exhaustion, apparently was the straw that
broke the camel's back for a lot of the people. A considerable number
of women were sobbing openly."[59]

A spectator in Sacramento wrote on May 13, "Today began the actual
evacuation of the Japanese. When I arrived at work this morning at 7 A.M.
there were several families and their luggage waiting to depart even
though their bus schedule called for 8:30 A.M. In fact, many of the nine
o'clock scheduled persons were patiently waiting. While we were loading the buses [for the Walerga center] all the Japs kidded each other.
As the last bus was ready to leave and there were several empty seats I
joined the nurse and social worker that is with every bus load and
went out to the camp. As soon as the bus started everyone became very
quiet and they didn't talk till they came in sight of the camp, then they
talked to each other for about a half second."[60]

Mrs. Duveneck wrote that the faces of the people entering the buses
in San Francisco "moved me deeply—a few grim and resentful, some
downcast, but most of them smiling with the self-control and gallantry
which is so characteristic of the Japanese people." She asked a military
guard, "Do you suppose we'll ever be able to live this down?" He
looked startled and did not answer.[61]

Church groups were frequently on hand at depots and bus stations to
serve tea and sandwiches and to pass out box lunches as well as take care
of last-minute emergencies. Grace Nichols Pearson described her difficulties in Santa Rosa as she tried to get permission to serve refreshments
to the evacuees. "Never too confident where the Army is concerned,"
she was surprised when an MP thought she was trying to sell sandwiches to the departing group. ". . . when we assured him we only
wanted to give them away, that was even harder to grasp."[62] Gerda
Isenberg, who helped at the Mountain View railway station, recalls, "Lit-

tle troubles were taken care of, like the forgotten teeth of an old man, the forgotten briefcase of a Japanese minister, a lost key. . . ."

Neighbors came to see them off. In Seattle, a Negro friend drove a Japanese family to the bus station in his new Plymouth, helped them unload their belongings, and then got down on his knees to tell the children goodbye. Helen Mineta recalls, "I was an honorary member of Players at San Jose State. Prior to our departure they asked if they could have a party at my house, since I could not leave it because of the 8 o'clock curfew, and they did. Then as we left for camp, they were at the station to see us off." Carey McWilliams spoke of "sentimental 'sayonaras' " for Japanese friends. "There was virtually no realization, among the generality of citizens, that they were witnessing a unique departure from American tradition."[63]

Helen Mineta's younger brother, Norman, a cub scout, served as a messenger on the train that took the family south. The San Jose *Mercury* commented, "For Norman it was an adventure of sorts." "We are all very anxious to leave," wrote an adolescent, "since it will be our family's first time to live out of Sonoma County."[64] The newspapers made much of the lightheartedness of the children and teen-agers, who were inclined to treat the excursions from home to assembly centers as an amusing junket. On an April 6 trip from San Francisco to Santa Anita, the younger generation entertained themselves with jitterbugging to swing music, impromptu picnics, and gin rummy games. Someone painted a sign on his truck: "CHUG CHUG TO SANTA ANITA." But one young girl of mixed blood wrote the following account of the train ride to her Caucasian mother, who was left behind:

Dearest Little Mother,
. . . after the trip, I know you would never have been able to stand it. 'Twas just a little *worse* than I expected. We reached San Jose and then had a very superficial medical exam. Then we sat in the train until 5 P.M. before we started. Some people who knew papa gave us some Japanese food to eat and I did enjoy it. . . . [After a box lunch was passed out] the odor of orange peels was overwhelming and later when bedtime came, offensive feet was the most obvious aroma in the car. Papa and I sat up all night in a single seat and it was pretty awful. Along about mid-nite the guards detected the strong odor of liquor in the car and on came all the lights. Then we were all threatened with having our baggage searched if the guilty party did not turn it in. It was an old guy who had been nibbling [sic] all day and to tell you the truth I could hardly blame him. However, I told my car captain who it was and told him to explain that the man must drink it up fast so as not to have it on him when we reached camp. I guess he did.
It was hot, and most stuffy all night and *very* uncomfortable. Papa dozed a bit, but I was on the qui vive all night. We were supposed to arrive at seven-thirty but the engine broke down and we lost 1000 gallons

of oil in a very little while. That held us up. We didn't reach here until nearly one—that meant being on the train for twenty-one or twenty-two hours. . . . Try to fancy riding on a day coach with one little toilet and wash basin and forty-three people to a car for that length of time.[65]

Takeshi and Ellen Shibuya boarded the train for Santa Anita at Mountain View. "The soldiers came aboard, and all had their guns. The window shades were drawn. We didn't know where we were going. It was just a horrible feeling, because we didn't know what was happening to us." Another woman recalls, "I was pregnant. I was supposed to be assured of a berth, or was it just a seat? I didn't get my berth. There was an Army officer or a nurse or someone who had that berth, and we had a big argument about that, I remember, because pregnant women were supposed to have special accommodations. I remember I thought it was terrible. I don't know whether I cried or not. The train trip is a perfect blank to me."

Doctors accompanied the trains. One of the sick passengers in a Pullman enroute to Santa Anita became worse in the night and was taken off the train at Santa Barbara where he died in a hospital. His family was not allowed to accompany him to the hospital. Kathleen Shimada says of the train trip to the Pinedale assembly center, "All I can remember is its being so dirty and rattly, miserable and cold. Day wasn't bad, but at night we had to sleep in the chairs, just sitting with the blanket we had with us, frightened and depressed. The whole thing was just miserable. I was bitter then for being uprooted from my home and taken off. We didn't know where we were going. I think it would have been easier if I had had my dad but, you see, I was the oldest of five with only my mother. The future is pretty bleak when you are uprooted from your home, not knowing where to go, and the responsibility lies on your shoulders."

Fuji Takaichi recalls not so much a feeling of fear and outrage but the fact of having been "so busy, so caught up in trifles we didn't have time to be too upset. I don't remember my mother being emotional. All she said was, 'Well, we're going to go together.' You had an uncertainty about where you were going and what was going to happen, but you knew you weren't going to be killed. . . . We went by train to Santa Anita about five o'clock in the afternoon. The train to Los Angeles goes down the coast by way of Monterey near the highway we had traveled so often. The sun was just going down. I remember looking out under the shade and saying to myself, 'This is mine, my country. I don't care, I'm coming back.' "

"There was nobody to hate," said a Boy Scout leader, "except General DeWitt, and he hated our guts anyway."[66] Another Nisei pointed out that they "could not let down the folks. Most of us wanted to be with our parents." Said another man, "We never thought that anything like evacuation would happen to either group." Mr. Shibuya recalls, "I joined the JACL as a way of protesting, but then our leaders told us we had no other alternative and committed us to the camps." Mr. Shimada felt, "In school we were taught about civil rights, the Constitution and all that. Then when they said evacuation it hit me kind of hard. What we learned was just washed down the drain. Most of us were pretty disappointed, because we didn't do anything to lose our civil rights, actually." Geary Watanabe concurred with this view: "We'd learned in school, 'You're innocent till proved guilty.' But what could minority groups do against the military?"

The general public missed the point completely. Newspaper readers were saying, "I hope those Japs are grateful for the way our Government is bending over backward to be considerate of them."[67] On May 28 the Bakersfield *Californian* editorialized, "California has shown an example of sanity. . . . Americans know how to treat even the unwelcome guest."

Sacramento's Little Tokyo had been "blitzed," the *Union* reported on May 14. "A few days ago lower Capitol Avenue and N street were chuck full of Japanese grocery stores, furniture marts, bait shops, restaurants, rooming houses and other businesses. But last night that district was full of 'for lease' signs on homes; 'new management' placards in stores; 'bargain sales' painted over the windows of other stores and heaps of receipts and other commercial papers piled on the sidewalks. . . . In a barber shop the aged proprietor sat alone in a room denuded of barber chairs, razors, brushes, hair oil and other appurtenances of his craft, and played solitaire." Herb Caen, the *Chronicle* columnist, wrote about San Francisco on April 7: "Saddest part of town right now, is, of course, Post Street from about Octavia to Fillmore—the heart of Japtown. No matter how hard-boiled and realistic you are, you can't help giving a second sober look to the padlocked little stores with their crudely lettered 'EVACUATION SALE!' signs in the windows."

No more Sukiyake restaurants "with their spider window scrawls," commented the Oakland *Tribune*, "no more Buddhist festivals with their lantern parades."[68] Ben Yoshioko, a WCCA employee exempted by Army permit from travel and curfew restrictions, was one of the last Nisei in Los Angeles. He described Little Tokyo in June: ". . . everything looks so deserted. . . . The Miyako Hotel is now the Civic Hotel. And the JACL sign, 'We Are Ready to Serve America!' is still hanging on the corner of First and San Pedro."[69]

By June 1 virtually all people of Japanese ancestry had been removed from Military Area No. 1. On June 3 General DeWitt proclaimed a curfew and travel ban affecting the Japanese in Zone No. 2. This was followed beginning at the end of June by Exclusion Orders 100 to 108, which banished 9,337 Japanese from Zone 2. About half the number were refugees from Zone 1, which meant that they suffered losses and uprooting twice. Herbert Nicholson was visiting east of Fresno when the group was ordered to leave. "I called on three doctors who had moved from Los Angeles to a small hotel in Sanger and had fixed it up as a hospital at a cost of $10,000. They were really mad. They asked me if I would lead the way and get them over into Utah. I said I would first try to get permission." Through the intercession of the father of one of the doctors in New York City, a message went from Mayor La Guardia to a military officer in San Francisco who wired his permission. They reached Salt Lake City safely.

The American Friends Service Committee had helped several farm families move from Palos Verdes near Los Angeles to a large plot of land near Porterville where they built shacks, dug wells, and planted many acres of tomatoes in virgin soil. They had a wonderful crop, but before they picked a single tomato, they were ordered to move to a camp.

On July 11 families from Lincoln in Placer County were leaving for Tule Lake. A young expectant mother was left behind to have her baby in a hospital near home. When she was taken there by a volunteer, an attendant said, "I don't see why we have to take care of you people."

"What are you going to do with me?" the mother-to-be asked.

"We'll take you but we don't want you," she was told.[70]

In the last registration were 3,000 people from Sanger and 1,300 from Reedley. By August 8, 109,650 people had been sent to assembly centers. Laurence Hewes wrote of the last days, "Sometimes a farm remained stubbornly untransferred. Then I was forced to inject problems of swine husbandry or goldfish-rearing ponds to circles of high military command. On these occasions the owner remained behind a day or two under special guard; then he too vanished. Finally, in August, the nasty business was over. . . . General DeWitt thanked me formally and told us we were through. Karl Bendetsen, who had become one of the Army's youngest full colonels, received a splendid military decoration. So at last the Pacific Coast was secure. . . . High up on San Carlos Hills, which stand above the lower [San Francisco] Bay, where once in Japanese nursery gardens a golden cloud of chrysanthemums bloomed against dark eucalyptus, there remained only blackened stalks and a tangle of dry brown weeds."[71]

SIX · CLOSING A FINAL DOOR

THE PRIMARY MOVEMENT to the assembly centers continued from March through May, 1942: 5,060 persons of Japanese extraction entered the center at Fresno from Zone 1 during this period, 2,447 were routed into Marysville, 4,453 into the Merced facility, thousands more into Pinedale, Pomona, Walerga, Salinas, Santa Anita, Stockton, Tanforan, Tulare, and Turlock in California, Portland in Oregon, and Puyallup in Washington. Some 200 persons were taken out to the isolated Camp Mayer in Arizona. More thousands were scheduled to be removed directly to Tule Lake in Northern and Manzanar in Southern California, and to Poston and Gila Rivers, permanent centers farther inland. By June 5 close to 100,000 had been moved, and by August 7, to use Army terminology, the first phase of the evacuation was completed. *Newsweek* magazine appeared to close the door ahead of the Army with the April announcement, "JAPS TRANSPLANTED."[1]

When a group of Bainbridge Islanders arrived at Manzanar after a forty-eight-hour trip in eight buses, they were met with a chorus of "hoorays" and a few scattered "banzais" from those who were there ahead of them.[2] What the newcomers saw was a "scenic spot of lonely loveliness."[3] A great, harsh piece of land, Manzanar occupied a 6,000-acre tract in Inyo County, Owens Valley. Beyond the desert Mt. Whitney and Mt. Williamson rose in the distance, protectively beautiful as well as useful for countless publicity pictures.

The area with its feeling of remoteness and desolation was actually but 280 miles from Los Angeles city hall. It was earthquake country. Dry, but arable, the land originally had held a river and a lake, but the lake disappeared and the Owens River went underground in 1872 during the most violent earthquake ever recorded in the West. When the first evacuees arrived, it was springtime. The hell of the desert summer was yet to come.

Unlike the other assembly centers this one was not enclosed by barbed wire fencing, although the gate and roads were guarded. The desert it-self was the barrier. The rows of tar-papered prefabs were like those in other camps except that here they had colorful red roofs rather than the usual black ones, and inside there was white plasterboard, rather than the customary walls of raw lumber. Manzanar was and remained the best-looking of all the camps. Throughout the evacuation period it served as the government showcase.

But despite the scenic beauty and lack of barbed wire fences, the new-comers soon found Manzanar was no "idyllic country club." It was rather, in *Life* magazine's words, "a concentration camp" designed eventually to incarcerate about ten thousand, in their words, "potential enemies of the United States."[4] With the closing of the gate behind them, the real shock of the evacuation came.

Immediately on entering each of the stockades called assembly centers, old men and grandmothers, the middle-aged, the Issei and the American citizens, children and babes in arms were "processed." This meant an inspection of belongings, a cursory medical examination, the filling out of forms. Often, crowds of resident evacuees stood about as the new ar-rivals came in, their faces "all blank and staring" as old people and others scrambled over the towering heap of baggage to find their belongings and struggled with heavy loads. Others pitched in and helped. Where they were better organized, JACL members and other Nisei were given the task of aiding women, children, and old people with their problems as they got off the buses, although official Army-posed photographs showed soldiers giving the evacuees a hand and carrying suitcases.

Once baggage was located the Issei often would sit down upon it, looking sober and tired, seeming to be overcome by the swift inevitabil-ity of events and waiting for the next thing to happen, while the young paced nervously about or talked with friends.

Chosen Nisei helped the personnel in other aspects of the processing also. At the Walerga center near Sacramento Nisei girl students, a prom-inent Japanese lawyer, and evacuee doctors wore arm bands imprinted with a w for Walerga as they directed people about.

Throats were scrutinized, tongues and arms stuck out, shots given. Men were examined for venereal disease. Baggage was inspected for contraband, sometimes perfunctorily, and men were "frisked" like movie gangsters by inspectors running their hands over their clothing. The evacuees had been ordered to bring only the belongings they could carry. Everything else was to be left behind, and no household goods were to be shipped in, though this rule was changed later as was the rule forbidding pets. Cars and trucks of those who had supplied their own transportation were impounded to be held for them or disposed of at the owners' risk. The vast majority of evacuees obeyed the orders quite literally, but some were shocked as at Tanforan to see that a group of

San Francisco people, who had arrived first and were helping check others in, had brought trunks full of things—supplies, radios, golf clubs— and at Salinas a wealthy vegetable corporation operator drove in with a truck "loaded to the gunwales" and "got by" with it. After the preliminaries, Caucasian administrators took a lengthy social and occupational history of each arrival and explained some of the rules of the camp. Then members of the personnel or selected Nisei directed them to their quarters.

Fumi Ihsida, who was at the Tanforan center, later recalled very little of the family preparations or the trip to camp. It was when they gave her family a number that the incarceration "really hit" her. In addition to being numbered, they had been lettered: her father was A, her mother was B, the oldest child was C, she was D, and so on. She was quite angered that her family should be numbered and lettered "like criminals." The initial uprooting, according to James Sakoda, had been accomplished "swiftly and mercifully," and it was not until they had poured into the temporary centers that many of the evacuees felt anguish and deprivation.[5] According to Mrs. Dorothy Tada, executive director of the Pasadena YWCA, "It was a very deep blow that leaves me a bit insecure today to think that people in times of hysteria and pressure do not behave in the most rational way."

What struck most of the internees was the sudden horror of the watchtowers, the soldiers with bared bayonets, the searchlights at night ceaselessly playing over the grounds. A Nisei wrote to a friend outside, "This evacuation did not seem too unfair until we got right to the camp and were met by soldiers with guns and bayonets. Then I almost started screaming. . . ." He was made to feel like a convict, dragging chains. He wondered, would he and his people ever be able to throw off the chains?[6]

The philosophically inclined more often had feelings of mild anger. "It was all so ridiculous." What did the Army people think they intended to do, anyway? A Nisei teen-ager in a spirit of black humor cavorted silently in the glare of the spotlights the evening of his arrival, spreading out his arms and pantomiming, "Shoot me!"

At the opposite extreme from the people who made the long trip to Manzanar, one suburban family after extensive preparations disposing of their property, breaking relationships with their friends, and saying goodbye to their native San Mateo, perhaps forever, found they had merely been transported across the Bayshore Highway to be quartered at the race track in nearby San Bruno, where they could climb the bleachers and watch the familiar "DRINK ACME BEER" sign at night.

In the Los Angeles area "Luxurious Santa Anita Race Track" awaited the evacuees, according to an Army release.[7] There were lawns by the entrance, some trees, even flowers. But to a distracted father, whose family had entered the center on Good Friday, everything might have been all right except that, as he told a Caucasian friend, he did not know how to quiet the crying of their children. "When we left early this morning to come here it was just a picnic for the youngsters, but now they think the picnic is over. They are asking us to take them home."[8] The perhaps apocryphal story was much repeated about a child in this new, strange place with its monoracial atmosphere, its marching soldiers instead of pets and playmates, who was heard to inquire, "When can we go back to America?"

Shown to their quarters, each family was presented with a broom, a mop, and a bucket—when they were lucky—for most of the camps were inconceivably dusty. "Yesterday," a young evacuee wrote to the Reverend Allan Hunter in Los Angeles, "there was so much dust that ten feet up in the air I saw a mole digging his burrow."[9] On receiving their mops and their brooms evacuees busied themselves scrubbing down floors and putting away their belongings. Water had to be hauled in from a long way as the block laundry rooms and mess halls were a good distance off. Water from these sources was cold as often as warm. "There is running hot water in every apartment," a Nisei wrote, "that is, you do the running . . . and hope that the water is still hot by the time you reach your . . . apartment."[10] Mothers with infants and the attendant laundry problems had to go through the same procedures. One Nisei mother, who had exhibited flower arrangements in the county fairgrounds at Merced and who now found herself locked in where the animals had been penned before, felt considerable anxiety for her new baby because of the lack of sanitation, but though there was much inconvenience, no medical troubles materialized.

Tomiko Sutow, who had been processed at Masonic Hall in San Mateo and then processed again at Tanforan, seems to have experienced the same thankful amnesia during the evacuation preliminaries as Mrs. Ishida. She recalls nothing whatsoever before the moment she was handed a long bag made of mattress ticking containing straw, a method of mattressing the cots in the centers. Most new arrivals stuffed their own casings with straw, making not too uncomfortable beds at first—before they began to mat down and turn to dust, requiring them to be refilled every couple of weeks.

Tohio Endo remembers hearing some of the Issei talk as they filled their straw mattresses. "*Nasakenai*," they kept saying, meaning, "how sad, how futile everything is, but we have no choice, we are forsaken." Then someone said, comparing the bags to shrouds, "Now we fill them to lie down upon; soon they will put us inside and take us away." Many of the old did not live to leave the camps and go home again.

Evacuee quarters were located in units or "apartments," a euphemism for single rooms, four to six of them to a 20′ x 100′ long shack called a barrack. There were rows and rows of these barracks, stretching in some centers as far as the eye could see. Fourteen barracks composed a block. There were up to forty-eight blocks in the larger centers, each serving almost eight hundred people. Each block had its own mess hall, its own laundry, and, at least theoretically, its own recreation room. Evacuees frequently became confused and could not find their way home; one place looked like another. Santa Anita was the largest center, occupying twenty-five acres divided into seven sections, each with a post office, a store, a mess hall, and showers. The Portland center in the Pacific Livestock Pavilion housed substantially all its inhabitants under one roof.

In May there were 169 new buildings at Tanforan. Trucks constantly drove up and down. The rough dirt roads were deeply rutted. The clubhouse entrance was headquarters for the police department; the first deck hall the recreation room, and the bar was boarded up like a huge box in the middle of the floor. At Santa Anita church services were held at the bar. At the Salinas center children spent time fishing in the marshes and puddles. When it rained everybody slipped around on the treacherous adobe.

A typical single family unit had one window that looked out on the street. Some quarters had no windows at all. An exceptional room at Pomona had three windows. There were no shades or curtains except when people were able to find goods with which to make them, no shelves, closets, or lockers, and to keep their places neat evacuees stored their belongings under the beds.

Originally, living units housed up to eight persons per family in a 20' x 20' room. If families were small, other persons were often moved in with them. Extra children might be housed next door. Three families might live in one room. At the Fresno center one entire building was occupied by a twenty-two member family from Madera County who took up all the units, since the objective was to keep families together.

A newly married young woman, Fuji Takaichi, was farsighted enough to resist registering with her mother and sisters or her husband's family.

Her mother was disturbed for fear their family would be separated eventually if they did not register together, but Mrs. Takaichi decided that if they did it that way they would all end up in one unit "with mama and papa," which is what happened to others.

Shizu and James Hirabayashi were married at Tanforan in the first wedding at that center. A friend who was the same size as the bride sent her the wedding gown, another friend whose parents owned a nursery made arrangements to have flowers sent in and a cake was delivered from San Francisco, but no outsiders were allowed at the ceremony. Newlyweds were granted separate quarters for a brief time, sometimes known as honeymoon cottages. The first evacuee wedding at Manzanar, when Howard Kumaji married Kimiko Wakumauri, was described in the Berkeley *Gazette* in April with the comment, "A honeymoon trip isn't contemplated for the present." But they, too, were given separate quarters.

Life's dramas of birth and death continued in the centers. The first baby born at the Santa Anita center was a boy; so the father, Roy Yoshida, was not able to name it Anita as planned. But shortly after this the first girl child at the center was born to a prominent Terminal Island physician, Dr. Mitonori Kimura and his wife, and was named Katherine Anita. The camp's first twins were born to a couple who occupied appropriately numbered quarters 52-32-2.

As new people poured into the centers, the larger family-sized rooms often became a memory. Carpenters came in, excused themselves, and proceeded to partition them in half making them 8 or 10 by 20 feet in order to house twice the number of people. Single iron beds with link springs lined the walls of the apartments. Sometimes they were army cots, mostly in bachelor quarters. A few of the beds in some centers had cotton-filled rather than straw mattresses. Evacuees were issued two or three army blankets, often used.

Barracks were constructed of rough green lumber. These thin pine boards buckled and separated, and large spaces grew between them. The tar paper glued on the outside of the barracks did not keep the searchlights from shining between the boards at night, and one girl felt she was in a cage with the lights coming through between the bars.[11] Doors might or might not fit the openings meant for them. Sometimes they were at least two inches too small all around. Floors made of the same raw lumber developed cracks between the boards, although in some camps the government eventually laid linoleum. One enterprising young woman, Helen Aihara commandeered some discarded cardboard boxes, cut them into rectangles, and covered the floor to keep the Salinas winds from coming up into the room. "The floors looked like a mosaic," she wrote Clara Hinze, her former teacher.[12] On very cold days she practically sat on the hot plate given her by her teacher-friend. "It is and has been a life-saver in many ways. We use it to try to heat this sieve we call our home. . . . It really is bitterly cold here at night." She worried about large families with infants and the aged and infirm under these conditions.[13] Cold entered the cracks at night and dust in the daytime. At Tanforan watering trucks wetted down the roads twice a day; later some roads were spread with gravel. People there put up wind breaks, but they were ordered down because the administration said they made the camp resemble a "Hooverville."[14]

Barracks, including those at Tule Lake, were constructed for the temperate California climate, which was sometimes more theoretical than real. In the Tule Lake center where the weather could go to eighteen degrees below zero large pig-iron stoves stood in the center of the rooms, their chimneys going straight up through the roof. Here car-

penters began to line the walls with plywood for the winter. On entering the camps the evacuees would scramble about looking for lumber
scraps left over from the building. With these they built shelves, closets,
coal boxes, tables, and chairs. Where lumber piles existed it was a matter of first come, first served. There was no official go-ahead on the use
of lumber, and the more timid were left out since there was nowhere
enough to go around.

Many of the women were in a run-down condition when they arrived,
yet they immediately set about sewing curtains, putting up coat hooks,
and generally making conditions more livable. "Now that I am here,
what can I do?" one public-spirited woman asked herself as soon as she
had stuffed her mattress with straw. She went out and volunteered for a
job. For these people there were no more surprises, and they tried to
make the best of things as they found them. They had an unusual
strength according to a former missionary worker, and they coped in a
constructive way. Miraculously, they kept themselves and their quarters
looking neat and clean.

At the Santa Anita and Tanforan race tracks and at various fairgrounds
and stockyards horse and cow stalls had been refurbished for human
habitation, chiefly for bachelors and small families, and at Puyallup
evacuees were even housed in former pigpens. At the Stockton fairgrounds, housing was erected in the main race track area, and the former hog farms became the recreation and baggage center. Except for a
certain olfatory unpleasantness, stables frequently provided better housing than the hastily constructed barracks, and according to one former
stable occupant, they were actually warmer than other units. The stable
rooms which housed up to seven people might be 12' x 24'; some were half
that size. The partitions between units were "horse-high." The walls had
been haphazardly hosed down and whitewash hurriedly applied over the
cobwebs and the fly specks. Disinfectant was sprayed on. A bachelor
recalled that from every splinter a horse hair hung, and the walls were
scarred by horseshoe marks where the former occupants had kicked at
their confinement.

Sometimes linoleum was laid over floors which had not first been
properly cleaned of manure. Sometimes floors were merely covered with
straw. During the summer the stench rose through the asphalt. "Have
you ever slept in a stable?" asked Ernest Fukuda, now a Los Angeles
civil engineer. "Many of us did at Santa Anita, and believe me, they
need more than clean straw."[15] At Santa Anita where 8,500 people lived
in the stables there had been but a four-day interval between the hurried evacuation of horses on March 24 and the arrival of people on
March 28. At first the odor bothered them considerably, one Nisei
wrote in a letter in May, but then either they became accustomed to it,
or it no longer existed. "We hope that it is the latter."[16]

Twenty-five stalls were condemned at Tanforan by San Mateo County Health officials as unfit to live in, but they still remained in use. Women were sometimes afraid to go to bed at night in the reconverted stables because of cockroaches and other living things. "How I wish we had traps or cats for the rats and mice who play tag all over us in the dark!" someone wrote.[17]

Some wrote their friends that they found living accommodations acceptable, though at least one person added that perhaps that was because he was not used to much in the labor camps where he had lived previously as a farm worker. It was felt that a great many of the poorest people who had been farm or migratory workers were living better than before, and for many the burden of worrying about a livelihood was lifted. But most evacuees found camp conditions a shock. A Southern California pastor, apologetic over his predicament and that of his people, was dismayed to see the expressions on the faces of the Japanese "women folk" as they first glimpsed their new homes at the Tulare center, but he commented on the characteristic fortitude and quietness with which they faced their situation: it could be worse, they said, and they were "thankful" this much was provided. He himself "apologized" that they were causing the nation and the Army so much "trouble," and he was looking forward to self-forgetfulness in church work.[18] When a block monitor calling at the quarters of an Issei family discovered they had no bedding, the head of the family replied that they would make out some way, perhaps by throwing a coat over themselves to keep warm. The Nisei monitor saw to it that the uncomplaining couple received blankets.

Bachelors at Tanforan who did not live in stables occupied a huge dormitory under the race track grandstand, an enormous room with 350 to 400 beds along one wall. There was less than two feet between each bed, and ventilation was bad. About thirty single women originally placed in another dormitory eventually dispersed to live with families.

At Tanforan status was conferred by housing areas, desirable or otherwise. Some persons occupying quarters in relatively favorable sections were suspected of looking down upon those in other areas. There was much joking about the situation. Yasuko Ann Ito, today a member of the San Mateo City Human Relations Commission, remarks: "We were the infielders—the others were the stable people!" The section by the railroad tracks was called "Skid Row." Though stigmatized, Skid Row people were compensated by convenience: they lived nearer the laundry room. As if in some country village, Issei, Nisei, and Sansei (third-generation children) promenaded around the track each morning before breakfast and greeted each other through the fog.

Nomenclature was a favorite occupation at the Santa Anita center. Signs of all kinds from the homey to the sardonic were tacked to dwelling places. All the avenues between the barracks were named after the famous horses; there was Bridle Path and Seabiscuit Avenue. Various people at different times had the "honor" of occupying the stall that had belonged to the famed Seabiscuit—Barrack 28, Units 24 and 25. At Manzanar, signs were tacked to barracks: Dusty Inn, Manzanar Mansion, Waldorf Astoria, and La Casa de Paz (House of Peace), which an Army release found "most puzzling."[19] A Pomona street was named Burlap Row.

But such levity had its limitations—Army imposed. Revealing a sensitivity hitherto unsuspected, the WCCA Operation Manual, Paragraph XXIV, stated in no uncertain terms: "No store, highway, public road, buildings, site or other object in any Assembly Center will be named after any living military or naval person of the United States of America. . . ."[20]

The very great congestion in the centers came partly because some West Coast communities had not allowed additional sites to be developed in their areas as the Army had planned and was also the result of the great hurry involved in building. Most camps remained unfinished as the arriving waves of evacuees moved in. They were not quite the twenty-eight-day miracle of accomplishment by Army engineers that official releases described. Thousands of carpenters worked on each of the original centers through March and April, and thousands more continued to build as summer came on. In June, when Manzanar, the first camp to operate, was officially changed from an assembly center to a relocation center, half its buildings had been constructed. Some centers still had open ditches into which people fell at night, and residents fashioned makeshift steps to get into their barracks.

As would be expected under such circumstances, mail and medical facilities were incomplete as well, which further added to the personal dislocation. Despite the government's sincere attempt to keep families together, some had been separated and were still corresponding in order to bring all the members into one place. Lines had been drawn down the middle of towns and farm districts, and people often went in different directions, the movement depending primarily on priority in the order of evacuation. Many Washington and Oregon people went to Fresno. Thousands from Sacramento and Marysville found themselves at Tule Lake. Acquaintances, like property, were lost, some to be glimpsed months or years later in a mountain state relocation camp or on a city street, heard of through friends, or never seen again. Even as evacuees moved in others were moving out: as early as May some were moved to Tule Lake from the Portland center, which had just opened; by the beginning of June Camp Mayer was closed down, its inhabitants transferred to Poston, a former Arizona Indian reservation.

In late March Thomas Bodine and Floyd Schmoe of the American Friends Service Committee drove to Camp Harmony, the Puyallup center, which was forty miles from Seattle and fifteen from Tacoma. They found it a madhouse of swarming carpenters. Puyallup differed considerably from the show place Manzanar. Untar-papered, boxlike buildings had been thrown together on a huge field that was formerly the fairgrounds parking lot. The grass had been scraped off the surface of the field with steam shovels, and two by fours laid on the ground with planks nailed onto them. Barrack walls were unpainted and pitch-smeared with one tiny window every twenty feet in the rear wall, no windows on the side, and a small windowless door at the front. "There will be approximately forty rows of these rabbit hutches," Schmoe and Bodine reported, "four hutches to a row, six rooms to a hutch." The center would house eight thousand human beings. "Army barracks," they concluded, "are palaces by comparison." Furthermore, these were not to be filled with healthy young men, but with women, children, and old people.[21] One group of evacuees mistook the buildings for chicken houses rather than rabbit hutches. "They sure go in for poultry in a big way here," Monica Sone reported someone's serious comment as the bus on which she traveled to Puyallup turned into the wire-fenced area that they thought was a chicken farm.[22]

The units were supplied with kerosene or wood stoves. Bachelor quarters, as at Tanforan, were located under the grandstand where there was neither daylight nor air and only one entrance for two hundred boys and men. It was too stuffy for sleeping so they played poker all night. Because of the constant darkness an electric light had to be kept on morning and night. At first these quarters were condemned by the Health Department, but Puyallup became so crowded they had to be used. Fuses blew out constantly since the Army could not get priorities for heavy enough wire for these camps except by act of Congress. Therefore heating appliances, tea stoves, and the like were forbidden.

Internees at Puyallup found themselves behind an eight-foot fence; in some places it was a solid wall up to thirty feet high. There was no shade and little real open space between buildings. "This encirclement tends to rapidly produce a prison psychosis," another investigator stated.[23] Internees were not to walk on the grass within ten feet of the fences. There were no orders to shoot, however, and the rule was frequently disobeyed. Inside the towers, guards with machine guns sat watching the children at play.

Confinement at Payullup was compounded because due to the peculiar layout of the fairgrounds the camp was divided into four separate areas, with fences and guards around each one, making prisons within a prison. The city streets and highways marked the boundaries between. Rules forbade passage from one area to another except for funerals and weddings. Area A had showers but no recreation hall, and Area D had a hall but limited showers. The people in Area D who in the beginning were unable to wash were later taken under guard to showers in other areas. The year-round rains of the state of Washington kept Puyallup in a perpetual sea of muck. Residents had to struggle against sinking into apathy on the inside of the barracks and into mud on the outside.

On June 15, *The New Republic* published an article by a young man named Ted Nakashima, entitled, "Concentration Camp, U.S. Style." It was a succinct and angry piece. The writer was an architectural draftsman who had been working on a defense housing project design for the Army engineers before being assigned to Puyallup. When he left home he still had 391 defense homes to detail and later was allowed to work on the drawings in camp but at center pay of less than twenty dollars a month. Nakashima was born in Seattle, and his parents had come to this country in 1901. His father, an editor, had "spoken and written Americanism for forty years." Now his parents and sister were interned in the Livestock Exposition Building in Portland. He discussed the military atmosphere of Camp Harmony (Puyallup) and the fact that no one was allowed to take the two-block long hike to the latrines after nine at night under any circumstances because of curfew. He had left "a fine American home" built with his own hands where he enjoyed highballs with Caucasian friends—a carpenter, a laundry-truck driver, an architect, an airlines pilot—good friends, friends who would swear by him. "I don't have enough of that Japanese heritage 'ga-man' [a code of silent suffering and ability to stand pain]. . . . What really hurts most is the constant reference to us evacuees as 'Japs.' 'Japs' are the guys we are fighting. We're on this side, and we want to help."[24]

The Army complained about the article, according to the editors, and the magazine sent out a man to investigate Nakashima's charges. The editors reported back to their readers that things were not as bad as Nakashima said, but were in the nature of temporary hardship. Food was adequate, and most of the rules they found to be reasonable.[25]

Meanwhile scouts for the American Friends Service Committee had been worrying about another camp in the process of construction. The forty-acre site called Topenish was located in the midst of the Golden Hop Yards near Yakima, Washington, and was spotted with dark huts used by Indian hop-pickers during harvest season. Most of the huts in a long row of sheds had dirt floors and no windows except for a small, unglassed, and unscreened square at the rear. Temperatures here went to 110 degrees in the summer in the shade of the buildings, and hopyards on all sides shut off the breeze. After sending out very unhappy reports to their membership, the scouts returned in May and were not allowed inside. Conflicting announcements began to come from the government. One spokesman denied that it was being considered for the Japanese, while a colonel stated it would be used as soon as it was improved. The worst buildings, it was explained, would not be used by Japanese but would be "kept for Indians."[26] For whatever reason, the Topenish center project was abandoned after an expenditure of $47,018 and American Japanese were never sent there.

Evacuees longed for letters and visitors. But during the first days and weeks after they arrived at the centers, visitors except for Sunday preachers were only able to enter under unusual circumstances. One outsider who transported some medical cases got into Puyallup accidentally. (Very sick people had not been evacuated and were left behind in hospitals, and the Friends Service Committee in Seattle had pleaded for permission to transport by car some of those who had not been able to withstand the trip by bus or train and thus reunite them with their families. When an Army captain thanked the drivers for their assistance, these Quakers made use of the opportunity to say that they were glad to relieve human suffering but that they objected to the whole evacuation.[27])

Perhaps because there was still a good deal wanting in the camps and much disorganization, administrators were anxious to prevent the public from getting an unfavorable picture. One observer felt the administration was doing what it could "through the JACL" to keep the internees from writing to outsiders what their center was really like. "Conditions are worse than even we had expected," he said. But a colonel told him he was proud of this particular camp—that he had "seen them all" and this was the best of all the assembly centers up and down the coast.[28] In July, the WCCA headquarters refused a request from a sociology professor at San Jose State College to view the barracks, the hospital, and the educational facilities at the Tanforan center.[29]

After the first period, visitors were allowed to see their friends at the gate or through the barbed wire fences. To do this they had to secure a permit by writing five days in advance of the day of the intended visit. Barrack and unit numbers were required so messengers could be sent to notify the evacuees that they had visitors. Often visitors were turned away after a thirty or forty-five minute wait in line because they did not have the required information. In May half hour visits were allowed once a week at the Santa Anita gate. On receiving notifications, evacuees at this center would leave their quarters and go through a gate and across a clearing of about half a mile where they came to another fence. Then they passed through another clearing to still another fence where they met their friends. "You stick a foot over the line, and you get a bawling out from the M.P.," a Nisei college girl wrote. "One man got a bottle of beer from one of his friends, and the M.P. came along and took it from him and emptied the bottle at his feet. . . ."[30] At Puyallup the internees and their visitors talked through the barbed wire within hearing distance of a soldier.

People brought gifts and comforts, and provided a line of communication with the outside world. They could accept money from the internees to buy them cokes, candy bars, or potato chips, although vendors and salesmen could not approach the fence. Later this was forbidden in some places.

By July reception rooms had been provided in most places, and visiting through the boundary fences was then forbidden. But the system at the visitors' house at Santa Anita somewhat resembled that in a penitentiary: internees were seated on one side of a table, friends on the other. They were not allowed to embrace, touch, shake hands. Visits were brief. According to a San Jose Nisei, "Most visitors were appalled." At Tanforan the routine was similar at first. Guests were taken upstairs and gifts inspected. Long tables were arranged in a line through the center of the room, making a barrier, guests on one side, evacuees on the other. They could not hand things across the table, not even notes. Evacuee spokesmen protested to the administration, who said the orders came from WCCA headquarters in San Francisco. The system was changed, tables were rearranged at random in the room, friends at last were allowed to shake hands.

At the Fresno center the visiting hours from two to four were described as a happy time with excitement in the air. The visitors' reception hall was always filled to capacity.[31] In one ten-day period at Tanforan 1,135 individual visitors were recorded, in addition to 654 who came in groups. Some evacuees at the Merced center and at nearby Pinedale, however, recalled few visitors. "Nobody came to visit us there, anyway," one woman who had been at Pinedale said, "It was such God-forsaken country."

All kinds of people came to visit at the other centers: schoolmates and former teachers, Caucasians and non-Caucasians, tenants and landlords, representatives of concerned organizations such as the Fellowship of Reconciliation, a pacifist organization, the YWCA, and liberal church groups. One evacuee experienced a surprise that was not uncommon: some of those he had considered his best friends never appeared, and one person he hardly knew, a poor boy who perhaps had a basis of identification or sympathy, was his most faithful caller. A dealer who used to deliver Coca-Colas at Tanforan recalls seeing chauffeured limousines lined up with the Buicks and Chevrolets and Fords: these belonged to wealthy Hillsborough women who came bearing gifts to visit their maids for whom they had a good deal of affection. Mayor Revolta of Pleasanton and Mrs. David Starr Jordan called on evacuees. An elderly humanitarian was heartened to see Chinese coming to see their former Japanese neighbors.

Kenneth Hansen, a vice-president of Syntex Corporation and former

Assistant Director of the Budget under Kennedy, a man who was viewed throughout the country on television opposing Senator Joseph McCarthy in defense of the Eisenhower Administration's China trade policy, was a freshman student at the University of California at Berkeley at the time of the evacuation. He and a roommate, John Cleary, who was a teaching assistant in psychology, went to the Tanforan center to call on some Japanese friends from Commerce High School in San Francisco who were confined there. One of these friends, Eiji Fugita, was a brilliant student and some members of his family were United States junior and senior fly casting champions. Other chums were Robert Yamasaki, Harry Oda, a girl who had been a student body officer, Pat Maruki, and a Nisei girl, Suzuki, who used to help Hansen in mathematics. Cleary and Hansen were able to visit them but briefly, and Hansen recalls his friends' acute embarrassment, not because of the visits, which they appreciated, but because of their circumstances of internment. It was a period of great uncertainty for them, and they were terribly uncomfortable.

Hansen and Cleary were very aroused about the whole matter, and on returning to the campus they mimeographed a statement protesting the evacuation, using equipment in the university mailroom where Hansen worked. The argument they employed revolved chiefly around the government's judgment on individuals, made in a wrong way, and ignoring due process. They did not protest the constitutional violation, the fact that the Nisei were American citizens. The full impact of the constitutional question did not come to Hansen until later. He feels that the evacuation was generally approved of or relatively ignored. "Even today people don't register when you mention it," he says.

The boys marched up and down, passing out their statement at Sather gate, the main campus entrance. The city police, not the university administration, asked them to go with them down to the station. There they answered questions, filled out forms, and left some pamphlets. They were subsequently called in three times. The situation was somewhat ambiguous. It was never made clear whether or not the boys had violated any law. Nevertheless, throughout the years this small incident has been checked out by security field investigators in loyalty checks of Hansen for various sensitive jobs, and apparently it was still in his dossier as late as 1961.

In June, the entire faculty of the Raphael Weill Elementary School in San Francisco visited 250 former students at Tanforan. "The smartest pupils were these Japanese children," Miss Brady, the vice-principal, said. "We miss them horribly, and we hope they will come back soon."[32] Countless teachers experienced a similar feeling of loss and kept up contact with their former pupils, many of whom were in the top group in their class.

Mrs. Frank Duveneck, obtaining a permit for visiting Tanforan as a representative of the American Friends Service Committee, reported fair conditions and good personnel in charge. She requested stoves from the committee for small babies who were endangered by the damp chilliness of the center. The Friends also sent in a truckload of recreational materials and reading matter. They dispatched another truckload of things, including a piano, to Manzanar. Cottie Keltner and his brother Orval brought personal belongings that had been stored at the Lincoln Avenue Presbyterian church gym in Salinas to Japanese friends in the center there. He made many trips with papers and documents.

Among the numerous gifts that visitors were forbidden to bring was uncooked food (sometimes any food), as well as contraband articles. A cake taken into Santa Anita was so thoroughly inspected by knives stuck through it at one-inch intervals that it looked like a sieve by the time it was turned over to the family for which it was intended. With other guards or in other places inspections were lenient. Center couples were unable to buy contraceptives since evacuees were forbidden to bring in or purchase drugs. Visitors occasionally smuggled them in to those who did not want to produce and raise children under camp conditions. After a visit at one camp by General DeWitt, where he "raised Cain" because of managerial inefficiency and sloppiness, various improvements were made, such as a visitors' hall, flush toilets, and a change in the rules about gifts. Uncooked food, flowers, and fruit were afterwards allowed.

Residents gave their friends money and lists of things they wanted: wash boards, soap, towels, clothing, brooms, games for the children, monk's cloth, and garment bags, double sockets, electric cords, straw hats for the sun, deodorant, thumbtacks, moccasins because heavy duty shoes made their feet sore. Their needs were never-ending.

Gerda Isenberg used to stop by at Tanforan on her way up to San Francisco where she worked with Jewish refugees. She was not allowed to visit inside at the time, but one of her friends used to give her long shopping lists. In later years, when the friend returned to Palo Alto, she asked Mrs. Isenberg, "You didn't think I wanted all those things for myself, did you? You were buying for the whole camp!" Residents particularly wanted lumber in order to make boxes for packing and storage. One could not park at the race track, and Mrs. Isenberg remembers carrying lumber across El Camino Highway.

Many of the evacuees excused the primitive conditions due to the fact that the camps were still in the process of organization. They expressed confidence that at least the WCCA men were trying and felt they would "hate to be in their shoes." A young fruitworker wrote in his diary: "But it sickens me inside to watch women and children standing in line at the mess halls with the wind and dust blowing in their faces."[33] Everyone had to stand in long lines for services—for meals, for showers, mail, laundry tubs, the clinic. A couple with small children might stand in line for an hour and twenty minutes in the valley heat before they could be fed. At the opposite climatic extreme, a Salinas evacuee wrote, "I have seen many pathetic sights and I can't hold back the tears at times. . . . If it was warm it wouldn't be so bad [for the aged and babes in arms] but it's bitterly cold from fog or wind; or so dusty you can't keep your eyes open. These people should be fed in a special hall and served by waiters and not forced to stand in long lines suffering all the time. . . . There should be a social hall where it is warm and heated. . . ."[34] After complaints to the administration, some centers allowed mothers with infants to be given their rations first. And individuals were often helpful: one young man took it upon himself to stand in line for others for coupon books, for mail, or other things; he found lumber for an old man so he could make a little bench. There was a great deal of mutual aid.

After lining up for meals three times a day, internees again lined up to wash their own dishes in a washtub with soapy water, then put them through two tubs of greasy water for rinsing. By the time they were through after breakfast it might be about time to line up for lunch. At Tanforan during the 4:30 to 6 P.M. dinner hour, about 4,000 of the 6,000 evacuees could be seen standing in their silent queues waiting to be served. In April, at Santa Anita, the largest center, an official reporter for the Army told of all the internees being fed in one hour at the mess halls. The relative efficiency of this center was verified by other observers. All supplies were procured through the Army Quartermaster Corps rather than through bidding or concessions, thus eliminating one possibility of profiteering. Cooks, like members of the administration, were often taken from former WPA employment.

Descriptions and evaluations of the food varied from person to person, and camp to camp. Generally the food situation improved as time went on. From Army field rations they changed over to "B" rations, and eventually there were fresh food supplements. A doctor of Japanese extraction evacuated from Hawaii described his first dinner at Tule Lake after a long train trip as appetizing: canned weiners, sauerkraut, potatoes, bread pudding, bread with oleomargarine. A noon mess at the Stockton Center consisted of boiled rice, potatoes and gravy, string beans, bread without spread, and "coffee." An "incredible" Pomona supper offered a bowl of cold canned tomatoes, a scoop of rice, and a bread custard pudding. A Tanforan boy reported beans on the menu all week and made a frequent center complaint: the coffee was so vile you could not tell what it was. Cooks at another camp told an evacuee that what they served was not actually real coffee but a substitute. An anthropologist at the Poston center described a first day's meal as potato hash and stale bread with mold on it. A special treat of Jell-O elsewhere was so hard it "was bouncing on the floor." It was odd to live in the middle of the "salad bowl of the world" wrote a Salinas evacuee to a friend, and yet never even see a salad green.

Many of the great number of complaints were standard response to institutional cooking. The food was adequate in most places, and some found it tasty, particularly after the first weeks. "The food seems to be improving, although not to the point that it is good," a girl wrote.[35] Saltpeter was liberally applied in the kitchens to all the residents' food, in order to decrease their sexual urges. Outbreaks of intestinal disturbances were common due to inadequate rinsing of dishes or to the food itself. The *Walerga Wasp* gave medical advice for what to do in case of food poisoning.

Traditionally, the Japanese not only cooked their food in certain ways and with certain flavorings, but always arranged it beautifully on the plate or in separate dishes; this was part of cooking—to make the food appealing to the eye as well as the palate. In camp the food was scooped out of large garbage cans, which, while clean, were never very appetizing to look at. At Salinas the dishpans from which some of the foods were served were also used to hold mop water for the dining room floors. Then the cooks heaped the different kinds of food all on the same plate so that everything mixed together. "Now," wrote a Nisei youth, "I can [at last] understand the word Mess."[36] Some felt, as they lined up cafeteria style, that they were holding out their dishes like beggars. After a time Santa Anita eliminated the long lines and served meals family style with large bowls of food on each table. Rice had been the main item in Japanese cuisine, and changes were made in order to include it in the main meals, and in April, soy sauce was provided for flavoring.

Insufficient quantity was sometimes a problem for teen-age boys and those who did heavy work. Sometimes the last persons in line did without until the next meal. One hundred were turned away at Tanforan one day with only rice on their plates. Much inedible food was thrown into the garbage. Inspectors, measuring the garbage and noting this, misinterpreted the reason, thinking the evacuee people were getting too much and that was why they threw it away, and so quantities were decreased. (Meals at first averaged thirty-three cents per evacuee per day, but this was found to be too conservative an amount and costs increased to a thirty-nine cent average in a maximum allowance of fifty cents.) Around the middle of May at Salinas just as food was becoming more plentiful and more palatable, new groups arrived from Hollister, San Juan, and Gilroy, and again quantities for each individual were decreased.

Scarcities of certain items occasionally developed. An evacuee wrote that the cooks at Puyallup were "getting disgusted" and did not know what was holding up supplies.[37] Milk shortages were a source of great complaint, more so at some centers than others. A Fellowship of Reconciliation Bulletin reported no milk at Tanforan for persons over three, no butter, no eggs.[38] The commissary department attempted to rectify the situation by providing dry milk for children four to seven years of age and increased the bottled milk supply by 62 per cent. Milk, they promised in the camp newspaper, would be sold at the canteen later.[39] All in all, per capita milk consumption for the total period was higher in the camps than for the American population as a whole.

There were rumors of food scandals and graft. It seemed inconceivable to many that they should not be eating more and better food on the fifty-cent allotment. "The papers say we are being fed as the army is fed, but don't you ever believe it," wrote an evacuee. A warehouse worker spoke of "lots of graft and politics" in the distribution of food. Whether or not all these rumors were true, there was often ample cause for complaint. At one center evacuee suspicions were eventually confirmed, as a Caucasian food employee was arrested and removed just as the camp was to close.[40]

Visiting officials, according to a Nisei critic, were always given better food than the evacuees, and were fed at separate tables and waited upon. Evacuees themselves were likely to receive better fare on such a day, also.[41] When Representative Leland Ford of Los Angeles, a conservative Republican and strong critic of the American Japanese, went on an inspection tour at the Manzanar center in July he chose not to eat with the federal employees who were enjoying steaks and fried potatoes, but instead took evacuee rations with the internees. One of his findings was that it "did not look good" for administrators sitting next to the Japanese to have different menus and service. The rations, however, he found ample as did others at this center. An official Army reporter lined up with evacuees at Santa Anita in April to partake of the mess. To a menu of butter, cream, fruit, canned meat, and vegetables would soon be added fresh produce and meat, he announced.[42]

A far more serious hardship situation existed in the area of medical care and hospitalization. No fees were paid for medicine or medical and dental services. The enormous problems of organization and supply produced by the suddenness of the evacuation, were eased by the great amount of talent and spirit of cooperation among the internees themselves. There were a good number of Japanese doctors and nurses in the evacuee group, particularly at the Tanforan center where they drew from nearby universities in Berkeley and San Francisco. But even at Tanforan for the first ten days there was only one doctor and one graduate nurse to take care of 3,000 people. By the time there were 6,000 residents, three doctors, three practical nurses, and three graduate nurses were working in a twenty-bed hospital. Still later there were four doctors. Chronic cases such as diabetics and paralytics were cared for in their own lodgings by their own families. The very ill and surgical cases were at first sent out to San Mateo Hospital. A twenty-year-old woman who contracted lung trouble in her drafty room at Tanforan was taken to Canyon Sanitarium where she later died. The sheriff of San Mateo County placed guards over Japanese hospitalized in the sanitarium as well as over those in the Community Hospital, despite WCCA assurance that the Army would provide a guard if it was deemed necessary. A pneumothorax case was sent to Community Hospital in Tanforan, and his wife and children sent on to Topaz.[43] Much red tape was involved in bringing in a county ambulance for transportation out to the county hospital. By May they had managed to acquire one ambulance for the whole camp.

At all the centers the medical staff was inadequate, at least at first, and nurses' aides and orderlies were trained as rapidly as possible. Dentists and optometrists were called upon to help physicians administer medical aid, in fact all the skill at the command of the center doctors was tapped. Doctors and nurses worked day and night. At Walerga near Sacramento a small unit under Dr. George Iki examined incoming residents and gave 20,000 hypodermics with remarkable efficiency. The job was made easier by the fact that the first group of arrivals had been unusually free from disease. An Army release told the story of a young Japanese physician, Dr. James Goto, who had been a house surgeon at the Los Angeles County Hospital and who saved the life of J. Marvin Kidwell, the service director at Manzanar. Stricken with acute lobar pneumonia while supervising the arrival of a thousand evacuees, Mr. Kidwell was taken to the hospital. There was no oxygen tent, but Dr. Goto treated him with sulfa and pulled him through.

During the evacuation the policy had been to leave very ill persons behind in local hospitals, but some were sent to centers by mistake. One such case was an elderly woman with cancer of the breast who was not aware of her advanced condition. She had not gone to a hospital as yet, and was put on board a Greyhound bus that was supposed to leave her at the San Mateo County Hospital, but which took her instead to Tanforan. Some concerned individuals who knew about her condition checked the hospital, then tried to find where she had gone and what was happening to her. They found the camp officials cooperative, but there was not one grain of narcotics in their hospital for her or for anyone else, nor in any doctor's kit. The woman was not put in the hospital but in a stable. She wrote to a friend a short time later that she was awakened in her stall bed on a Sunday night, the rain was coming in, and all her clothing was wet. In the morning she tried to go to the latrine, but the mud around it was so deep she could not get in. She went to the next one and found the roof had blown off of it. Blankets that friends had sent never reached her. But a friend called General DeWitt's headquarters daily until her release was secured.

From another center an evacuee wrote home to her Caucasian mother who had to remain behind: "I'd rather see you in your grave than trying to accustom yourself to the conditions here. . . . It is just cruel, I think." The girl's aged Japanese father would cry whenever he thought of his wife back home, and he thought of her day and night.[44]

Poor sanitation and the possibility of epidemics were an ever present worry. The Turlock center launched a "Swat the Fly" campaign in June. All the camps had a program of inoculations for typhoid and smallpox. When measles broke out in several centers, there were no facilities for isolation, and the patients' families continued to eat in the common dining halls and washed in the common sinks. In North Portland a mild measles epidemic claimed the life of a six-year-old boy. Some feeling was aroused by the incident, but cooperation was maintained. When a Japanese physician asked for an isolation building due to a measles outbreak at Tanforan, a public health doctor said, "Well, they all have to get measles sometime; so let them get it."[45] Nor was any attempt made to find and segregate cases of active tuberculosis.

Despite the large number of pregnancy cases, it was difficult to induce the mothers-to-be to register for care. Five babies were born in one month at Tanforan, and one, which was premature, died. There was no incubator. The 2 A.M. formula feedings for babies were delivered; otherwise prepared formula was picked up at stations set up throughout the camps.

A young woman physician named Dr. Fujita walked miles every day at Tanforan center to make calls on patients. She also organized a public health program among mothers with babies to give instructions on infant care and feeding, and to launch a vaccination program. A small amount of serum was on hand, but there was neither time nor adequate personnel to administer it. There was no cod liver oil, although the Army promised to obtain some. The San Francisco poet, Kenneth Rexroth, and his wife, Marie, a public health nurse, worked with the evacuees at Tanforan as members of the Fellowship of Reconciliation, and Mrs. Rexroth volunteered to spend her vacation to aid Dr. Fujita's project.

Another remarkable woman, Mrs. Yamashita, a registered nurse from San Francisco Hospital, was charged with the responsibility of heading the well-baby clinic at Tanforan where she made up formula for sixty to eighty babies. An energetic and busy person, she had been born in Denver where she had experienced none of the racial prejudice associated with the Pacific coast. At camp she was rethinking the racial problem. According to a newspaper report she was burdened not only with the care of the infants, but with the "social and historical implications of her internment." She felt the experience of evacuation, while interesting, was going to make a difference in her attitude, and that all the evacuees were " . . . a kind of lost people."[46]

The Tanforan hospital as it finally developed contained a men's ward, a women's ward, an obstetrical ward, and maintained a clinic and an out-patient service. The hospital was a fairly good one and eventually adequately staffed. It had an optometrist, a dentist, and even a student mortician. Many medical and nursing students worked there. By the time Tanforan was closed, 1,000 prescriptions for glasses had been dispensed. The Santa Anita center hospital, located beneath the pastel blue grandstand, had excellent facilities and new equipment. It was clean, and the beds had inner spring mattresses. Dr. Arthur Takii, a dentist there, had sold all his equipment on being evacuated from San Pedro, but managed to get hold of a school dental unit and practiced in a primitive way. In July there were six dentists practicing in the clinic, the largest of its kind. Not all centers were so fortunate as the two located at the racetracks.

Puyallup was slow in opening its hospital. When the building was finally ready, the green wood shrank, and wind and rain came in through the large cracks. Evacuees waiting in line for their second medical examinations were exposed to the elements, and there was a small virus epidemic. The hospital at Turlock was also said to be inadequate.

County governments were solicited, sometimes in vain, to open their hospitals and public health services to evacuees for emergency surgery and medical treatment. More serious cases could be sent to government hospitals. But county facilities, suffering from shortages also, were taxed by the number of evacuees needing treatment.

Two nurses at Salinas struggled to bring efficiency and proper care to that center. Improvising cans for pitchers and thermometer holders, they kept more medicine in their first aid kits than was to be found in the rest of the hospital. Some of the personnel were authoritarian and resistant to change, others too frightened of the camp administration to make demands. The only way to accomplish anything, these girls found, was to insist they were acting in the interest of others.

The single greatest complaint among camp inmates was lack of privacy. There was no privacy in evacuee quarters, in the showers, in the latrines. The noise level of all the camps was very high, and babies and old people suffered from this. There was no way of getting away from people; everywhere one went there was a crowd. Up to eight beds lined the walls in some units, and partitions between living units extended only to the beginning of the roofline which slanted to a peak in the middle of the room. The upper triangle was open. Everything could be heard from one room to another: a neighbor's most intimate secrets came through very clearly, another neighbor's snoring was in one's ear, quarrels were heard everywhere.

When the man next to the Takaichi's stall would come in a little late and his wife would start berating him in Japanese, Mrs. Takaichi would jab her husband who could understand the language and ask, "What's she saying? What's she saying?" At Santa Anita one soon forgot that the Japanese husband was always head of the house and that all Japanese were quiet and submissive. "Or a baby would begin to cry and pretty soon there'd be six babies crying all the length of the stable area." A few people built up their barrack partitions to the roof, but there was not material enough for many to do this.

"You may feel assured on this point," an information circular read. "There is no reason whatever for interfering with normal family arrangements," and the government had no intention of doing so.[47] But for obvious reasons, normal marital life was difficult, if not impossible. The only seclusion within an "apartment" was provided by flimsy curtains that residents might put up between the crowded beds. Children, it was reported, did not get their proper sleep at night, and there was a good deal of restlessness among them. Grown children, too, lived with older parents, and sometimes a family contained more than one generation of couples. The searchlights that swung monotonously around an arc periodically lit up the rooms and seemed to rout out any final illusions of privacy.

The communal shower rooms were equally disturbing to many reticent people. A typical center had one open shower room with perhaps eight shower heads jutting out from the walls. Here again long lines of people awaited their turn. Later doorless stalls were erected, and some residents obtained shower curtains which they carried with them. Others bathed in their underclothes. Occasionally family members would circle around the person taking a shower. A few washed between twelve and one at night when they were not likely to find other people about. Some were so shy they chose to go dirty rather than shower in front of others. The shadeless shower-room windows looked out on the road. The plumbing had been installed in accordance with Army plans designed originally for soldiers. Faucets were too high, and only taller people could use them. Washbasins were also too high for women of average Japanese height. Children could not manage at all without help.

Occasionally women took sponge baths in the sinks of the lavatories when the showers were full. Hot baths were a ritual tradition with the older group, and they missed their bathtubs. At Tanforan a woman was reported to be taking daily baths in the washtubs to the embarrassment of the men who helped their wives with the washing. "[I] never had a chance to check on this," commented a member of the governing council in a report to his friends outside.[48]

The community privies had the same drawbacks as the showers. The older models consisted of two long wooden planks made of fresh-sawed, unsandpapered wood, with six holes each and no plumbing connections. Newer models with plumbing connections flushed automatically about every fifteen minutes and might be lined up ten to a row. Inhibitions had to be left at the gate when people came to the camp, one evacuee wrote. Women, in particular, were not happy sitting back to back and side to side with strangers. The rooms were so designed that if a door was left open, moreover, they could be seen from the outside.

It was promised that more privacy would be provided. At the Salinas center partitions were built at last in the latrines, but at some centers the situation was never corrected. No special provisions were made for children. A woman walking by a men's room one day heard a small boy screaming for help. She got a man to go in, and the child was found hanging by his elbows in the overlarge hole. It was a good twenty-foot drop to the bottom.

Living quarters were often a considerable distance from the rest rooms, showers, and laundry rooms. This was tiring for mothers with babies who had to wash diapers every day. There were no washing machines, and clothes were scrubbed on washboards. If the faucets in the showers were too high, the laundry tubs were too low. A Nisei college girl described the laundry room at Santa Anita: "There are two long tables, and underneath there is a sort of water trough. On both sides of the tables are faucets and little platforms to put your tub or bucket. The people who built them must have thought the Japanese women were awfully short for they're only eighteen inches from the ground."[49] A long room contained rows and rows of ironing boards. One middle-class Nisei woman with rheumatoid arthritis, who like countless others had never been used to heavy lifting or field labor, states that many women began to have health problems during this period.

Nevertheless, friends outside received as many cheerful letters as unhappy ones from the assembly centers. The evacuees began to be commended for their cooperation and compliance. Nils Aanonsen, manager of the Tulare center, told his group of internees, "It has been a revelation to me to see how you have adapted yourselves to this strange and difficult life, and to watch the many ingenious ways in which you have found outlet for your energies. . . ."[50] A Federal Reserve Bank official was surprised and enlightened by the way in which the American Japanese were taking the situation. Some religious workers who had been present at almost twenty evacuations commented, "Everywhere the Japanese cooperated 100 per cent, and the officials had nothing but praise for them."[51]

These people had gone into Santa Anita "with no more fuss than once attended the surge of railbirds through its turnstiles," the Los Angeles *Times* commented approvingly.[52] "Everything is functioning smoothly," a WCCA spokesman said. "There have been no complaints, strict discipline is being maintained and the Japanese are keeping their quarters spotlessly clean. They are all anxious to work and we have not yet been able to find tasks for all of them."[53]

A newspaper reporter, surveying the center at San Bruno, was glad to find nothing disturbing to him: "No neurotics, brawlers, political troublemakers or quiet weepers defaced the gathering places. . . ." Everybody was busy and seemed to "understand the government's position."[54] *Business Week* magazine described evacuees as "philosophical" and "even pleased" about their lot.[55] A Sacramento reporter observed that the demeanor of Walerga evacuees showed their "utter confidence" in America. " . . . the whole kit and kaboodle took to their new homes as ducks take to water."[56] "JAPANESE FIND ASSEMBLY CENTERS HOMELIKE," the Fresno *Bee* headlined a report.[57] "You may find that the internment will be a 'stablizing' experience," a hopeful clergymen told some evacuees, not meaning to pun, but causing his audience to be convulsed with laughter, since many of them were living in horse stalls. The evacuees were "fed up" with people who came in to do them good, said a person who overheard the minister's remark.

Romanticized stories about the centers abounded, particularly about Manzanar, which was a photographer's paradise. Pictures taken there revealed uncrowded families eating together, thus illustrating government efforts "to preserve family life." Camera shots of evacuee quarters at this center were taken from such an angle—the middle of the street toward the ends of the barracks—as to make the living units appear to be family cottages.[58] One writer went so far as to assert that evacuees were afforded "complete privacy in their barracks."[59] A reporter for the *Christian Science Monitor* pointed out that Tokyo's descriptions of the "indescribable humiliation" of Japanese in the camps were grossly exaggerated.[60]

The realities hardly bore out these sanguine reports. The early stage of the internment brought some physical hardship and much mental cruelty. The degrading communal life, the loss of freedom and individuality, the sense of injustice were corrosive to the human spirit. There was no physical brutality; in this sense, at least, the assembly centers and later relocation centers were not equivalent to Nazi concentration camps for Jews. The WCCA was doing the best job possible; both the Army and the civilian personnel worked hard to handle the tremendous undertaking, to control a situation of a kind they had never encountered before.

Assembly center administrators and the Army authority over them often demonstrated a certain arbitrariness. The standard answer in most centers to disturbing problems that arose was to clamp down, to cut off two-way communication, to take away privileges, or to use other disciplinary measures. Complaints by evacuees in one camp that packages were not being delivered, for example, were answered by an administration threat to stop visitors from bringing any packages at all. An evacuee block manager resolved the situation by volunteering to take over package delivery. In general, however, the administrators seemed to be trying to be fair, at least by their own standards.

But this over-all humane treatment and Army efficiency were diverting the minds of concerned citizens from the main point, according to Thomas R. Bodine, reporting to the American Friends Service Committee. "Many soft words are being spoken about the evacuation of the West Coast Japanese," Mr. Bodine wrote, "not only in the government's press releases, but in reports from Christian observers and others, even among Quakers. 'A soft answer turneth away wrath.' It also lulls the uneasy conscience back to slumber. . . . What we are denouncing are not the men in charge but the circumstances."[61]

The WCCA operation was highly centralized. Assembly center administrators were responsible to the chief of the Assembly Center Branch, Rex L. Nicholson, who in turn was responsible to Colonel Bendetsen at the WCCA headquarters in the Whitcomb Hotel in San Francisco. Over-all plans were made in Washington. The executive setup in the camps involved a manager, an assistant manager, clerical staff, and four operating divisions: work and maintenance, finance and records, feeding and lodging, and service. There were, further, two divisions at management level: supply and storage, and internal security. The United States Office of Education assisted with technical standards and the general plan for schooling, and the United States Public Health Service with hospitals and sanitation. Most of the staff administrators had been brought in from the Works Progress Administration established in the Depression period.

Efficiency and intelligent handling of evacuee problems varied considerably from one camp to another. The Santa Anita camp, with rules stricter than others, nevertheless received praise for its miracle of organization. Visitors were heartened by the high caliber of the men in charge of Manzanar. The Turlock center, under the management of Ernest Pinella, was one of the better camps, more intelligently run by an administration that seemed to be genuinely interested in people. With only 3,500 residents, officials there were considered friendly and helpful. It was the most democratic and the most lenient of the centers. Sources of grievance such as bad sanitation, existed, but due to management attitudes evacuees tended to complain less.

Yet everywhere the Caucasian personnel were a class apart: their quarters were generally located in a separate, guarded section, and even where not rigidly separated were noticeably better built and furnished than those of the evacuees, with individual bathrooms. Fraternizing with the Japanese group was forbidden by written rule.

The assembly camps were like small towns, needing every kind of service. Evacuees themselves performed all phases of the actual work under Caucasian supervision. "We all got busy and built up the center very quickly," said Yasuko Ann Ito. "We made a quick adjustment." Persons with skills were much in demand and were put to work right away. YMCA boys, members of the JACL, Issei who generally had strong feelings against remaining idle, those who called themselves "progressives" or "anti-facists," all were eager to begin working, to become involved, to illustrate their compliance. The first volunteers among the girls worked as waitresses, a few as stenographers, and the men as cooks, dishwashers, and in various utilitarian roles. Men were needed to keep the fires going in the laundries and the kitchens. Electronics technicians were needed to run the public address systems. A small amount of job training was begun. Tohio Endo, in charge of maintenance at one of the centers, did carpentry, made partitions for the schools and repaired equipment when it broke down. Later he was one of the few allowed to go outside, with a guard, to buy camp necessities. His job was complicated by the fact that much of the equipment sent in on order was faulty. The boilers started exploding one day so that there was only cold water in the showers. He discovered that a truckload of water tanks had been delivered without stay bars inside. Mr. Endo feels that many dealers unloaded their defective merchandise on the centers.

Workers were not paid at first, and in April wage policies were still being decided. A storm of anti-Japanese protest had broken out in March when it was announced that evacuees at Manzanar would get "security wages" of between $50 and $95 a month, with $15 a month deducted for subsistence. Evacuees, it was thought, should not be treated so well while soldiers were fighting and dying, and this plan was soon abandoned. Compensation scales that were finally arrived at were $8 a month in the unskilled category (including gardeners, junior typists, attendants, laboratory helpers, wood-cutters), $12 a month for skilled workers (bakers, barbers, butchers, senior typists), and $16 a month for professional and technical help (accountants, dentists, registered nurses, teachers, and doctors). In June the scales were raised to $12, $16, and $19. Wages were paid out in script. A $20 charge was to be levied against evacuees eligible for the work corps who chose not to join. While a subsistence allowance was not deducted, no provision was made for compensation for accidents while working. In publicity releases the unheard-of low wage rates were often cited with pride rather than apologies, as an example of the sacrifice evacuees were making like soldiers in the service of their country. White workingmen and staff employees doing the same or similar jobs received the going community wage. Frequently the Nisei doing tasks side by side with Caucasian workers or under them were more skilled and better educated and were at least as intelligent.

As time went on jobs became scarce, and many put themselves on the long waiting lists for openings. A typical college student studied three hours a day as she waited for a job, hoping for something to do, for the chance to be productive and for interesting companionship.

Criticism of workers who had made their way into supervisory positions arose in the evacuee community. Some of the less favored evacuees felt many of those in authority were officious and misused their power. Although exhaustive social histories on all evacuees had been compiled which included vocational data, work was to be found chiefly through "knowing somebody." Those who were "on the ground floor" had better jobs and found them for their friends. Issei and Kibei often felt discriminated against by Nisei job holders and dispensers. The employment office, one Nisei wrote to a friend, was merely "a filing case."[62] This was demoralizing to the reticent and to those who were used to more orderly procedures. A girl of fifteen managed to get an office job because she had a relative who "was somebody." The girl gave dictation to a woman who had had ten years' secretarial experience. The woman resigned.[63]

A YMCA boy agreed: "Sure there's quite a bit of string pulling," but those like himself who had started working early on a volunteer basis naturally were familiar with the requirements and automatically got the jobs when badges were issued. And they in turn tried to give out work according to ability as they saw fit.[64] Others felt there was a maldistribution of work loads—that young men loafed while nurses and office staffs toiled "like horses." There was enough dissatisfaction so that at least one camp administration announced that from May 23 on work assignments would go through regular channels: the administration would use the files and inform persons of employment by means of messengers.

While residents of the centers as a whole were notably adaptable to new conditions, individual responses varied a great deal. All, even those who responded by throwing themselves into the life and work of the camp, shared to some degree the underlying current of anxiety and resentment. The youngsters and teen-agers tended to regard the experience as something of a lark; they enjoyed the communal life. The slightly older Nisei of the official leadership group, though badly shaken, constantly voiced their desire to cooperate and their faith in American institutions. On leaving San Francisco JACL leaders thanked the city for its understanding treatment: "We especially desire that you do not cast upon us the stigma of guilt. Ours is only the hope that by wholehearted co-operation with the proper authorities, our victory may be sooner and more complete. . . ."[65] This group wanted desperately to believe in America's fairness, and they did not want their already precarious position endangered by rebellion or opposition to government policy.

Leaders cautioned, "Don't rock the boat." One JACL leader, Fred Tayama, was reported by the Los Angeles *Times* as saying, "I don't like the word 'evacuation'; it would be better to say co-operation, because we all want to co-operate with the government."[66]

The majority of the evacuees tried to hold in their feelings, to mind their own business, to concentrate on keeping their families together. They told themselves, as the authorities told them, that they were doing their part for the war effort by complying and not questioning. This was an extremely difficult role for Nisei who had been at the beginning of their careers and now found themselves uprooted and completely uncertain about the future. And since they were citizens, they were shocked by the way the government had treated them. But the evacuation was a *fait accompli,* and one Nisei wrote Tom Bodine there was "no use hollering."[67]

Other Nisei felt they had been betrayed by their leaders, who had put up no resistance to the evacuation. Many were extremely cynical and found the overadjusted "super-Patriots" in their group objects of amusement or anger. Such attitudes were at first expressed in remarks and grumblings, and were to come out more into the open later in the more permanent relocation centers. The cooperators, in turn, were apt to feel those who grumbled were "cry babies." Some camp "progressives" disapproved of the American Civil Liberties Union, church groups, and "the Norman Thomases" who were attempting to publicize and fight the injustice involved in the evacuation; they even disapproved of the *Pacific Citizen,* the JACL organ, which, while it preached cooperation, was criticizing evacuation on constitutional grounds.

The Issei, who more or less had expected something like the evacuation program in case of war between Japan and the United States, were offering no resistance, but morale among them was poor. Issei who had migrated to America had largely been an adventurous lot, anxious to escape the extreme rigidity of village life in the old country. Nonconformists in Japan, according to the anthropologist John Embree, had been conspicuous misfits in country life, and the only solution for them was to emigrate.[68] In the West they had been able to exercise greater initiative. In the assembly centers these individualistic people fell back into older patterns of conformity.

A Nisei remarked that in her weeks at Puyallup his mother aged as she never had before. An observer reported that at the Tanforan center many elderly Issei with poor memories would arise in the night and try to get out.[69] One half-Caucasian, half-Japanese who had been turned down by both the Army and the Navy because of his race, somehow escaped from Tanforan and walked into the WCCA headquarters at the Whitcomb Hotel, requested release, and, on being refused, drank a bottle of poison.[70]

"Probably the most sorrowful evacuee I met," Richard Donovan wrote in the San Francisco *Chronicle* after his visit to Tanforan, "was a middle-aged professor of history, who said that the war had put off his dream of internationalism for another hundred years, at the least. 'We will all make a fetish of our own little boundaries now,' he said, 'and to hell with the brotherhood of man.' " One thing he hoped was that the war would end quickly, whoever won it. " 'If it goes on too long, everyone will lose and there may never be an end.' "[71]

The feeling of isolation was very strong. The young particularly felt the loss of outside contacts. Many Nisei had, like the Issei, the uneasy feeling they were not really part of America even though they regarded Japan as an alien country. A sense of purposelessness haunted them which many forced to the back of their consciousness by involving themselves in various activities. One Nisei described himself as numb—he could not look to any future; he could only concern himself with present bodily comfort.[72] Under the hustle and the stoicism, Richard Donovan detected much aimlessness and unrest. Residents seemed more like "people in a railroad station." Issei seemed to be "thinking long and private thoughts."[73] A Nisei mused, "Today is the Sabbath. People are wandering back and forth, back and forth. There is no pattern to the movement . . . no purpose, no significance . . . only movement."[74]

Evacuees had not greatly feared the movement into the assembly centers. There had been a sense of unreality, a feeling that the government was not really doing this to them, that it was not really happening. But once inside the centers as time passed, the anxiety and uncertainty increased tremendously as to where they would be sent next and more permanently. They had little information as to where they were headed. In the absence of official announcements, rumors ran rampant—that they would be released and allowed to earn their living, that people who complained about conditions would be sent into the desert where there were poisonous snakes. Some of the internees who got the idea they were going to be sent to Siberia, bought cold weather clothes. Some said the assembly centers were to become permanent. The fear was widespread that they would be moved into inland camps and left there in the wilderness for many years, isolated and forgotten. To help alleviate these fears, a group of Quakers visited the relocation site at Minidoka, Idaho, where a more permanent camp was being constructed, and came back to describe it to the inmates at Puyallup. The reality of the description vastly relieved their anxiety. " . . . if you could have seen their faces beam," one of the Friends wrote, "to have some real first-hand news from the outside world of what is happening beyond the barbed wire."[75]

In the circulation of rumors, the centers were like small towns. Tales spread of nonexistent riots outside the camps, and shootings of evacuees and rapes inside. New rumors denied the first; some undoubtedly authentic. The rigid center enclosures intensified small-town gossip and introversion. Different groups with divergent interests were forced to live close together without the possibility of escape. A Nisei Christian woman did not attend church services on Sundays because she felt as soon as she did she would be placed in a fixed category. She approved the tolerance of Buddhists who did not insist, as did some of the Christians, that theirs should be the only church in the camp.

Like countless others coming from cosmopolitan communities, an evacuee from a college town was struck by the monoracial appearance of his camp. He felt strange in a sea of black-haired, dark-skinned people. He was not used to this. "What I wouldn't give just to see one blonde!" he exclaimed to his sister. Actually, a number of race mixtures were in the camps since persons who were 1/16 Japanese were interned, and even the pure Japanese were diverse in appearance. Skin color varied as in Japan. A girl who kept a diary commented on the many interesting faces: there were stunning-looking Eurasians, there were part-Chinese and part-Filipinos, there was even a group at Puyallup who were part-Eskimo and who could speak neither Japanese nor English. There were close to one hundred partners of mixed marriages at the Tanforan center alone. At Pomona there was a large family of twenty-one persons, known as the "Hayward tribe." (Hayward, the father, originally named Hayoshi, was part French and one-quarter Japanese.) Before the internees went to permanent camps, several hundred persons of part-Japanese descent as well as partners in mixed marriages were released.

Among the throng of internees were educated professionals and unlettered laborers, liberals and conservatives, young and old, the gentle-mannered and the roughnecks. Co-existing with hearty farmers was an important poet, the father of the sculptor Isamu Noguchi, noted for his delicate, old-fashioned verse, who had written of children of the darkness who were afraid of the light because it might "change their darkest hair to red and dust."[76]

The presently well-to-do manager in the floral industry who had been taken from a large home in Mountain View and "thrown into" one of the stalls at Santa Anita feels he absorbed the shock only because he was young. If he had been middle-aged, as he is now, it would have been a problem, "because we think a lot more." A girl of mixed Caucasian–Japanese descent, acutely unhappy away from her old contacts and the intellectual stimulation of her former Bay Area community, had been engaged to a Caucasian soldier in the American Army. She found out that if she had made the proper request at the proper time before evacuating she could have been married and following her husband like other Army wives. In a Kafkaesque series of errors she and those who tried to intervene for her kept making appeals in letters that never reached the proper authorities or that reached them too late. Her letters to her fiancé trailed behind his movements from camp to camp, and when they finally reached him the couple were told no more appeals could be made. Being in the midst of apparently well adjusted country people made her that much more despondent. Her Japanese father was made ill from living in drafty quarters and was also in a state of mental depression.[77]

A rumor of pilfering in the Santa Anita camp was relayed to a small-town Japanese woman. On hearing the report, she declared flatly, "Japanese don't steal." But when she hung out her sheets on the community wash line, hers were the first to disappear. "Oh, she was furious!" her daughter says, "but, you see, some of the people didn't have sheets, didn't have anything, didn't even have clothing enough and no way to get any. They helped themselves." At another center, possibly in reaction to such instances of petty theft, there was a passion for honesty. Chiaki Koji-moto, chief clerk at Tanforan, reported that the inhabitants were "either very honest or very careless," because in a two-week period over two hundred articles were turned into the Lost and Found: money, jewelry, toy pistols, even one open can of milk.[78] But an idealistic Nisei wrote of "lifting" materials in order to improve the family quarters, a common practice.

Assembly center life sharply increased the crime rate of the American Japanese group. From a rate of 4.5 per 1,000 persons in 1941, it rose to 20.6 in six months. Most of the infractions were of a minor nature, however.

Although horse-racing disappeared from Santa Anita when it was turned into an assembly center, gambling persisted. Big-time gamblers from the Los Angeles ghetto set up equipment and created a scandal by "making book" on the races in Aguascalientes, Mexico. These opera-tors ran dice games, chuck-a-luck, blackjack, and poker until thirty-five persons involved were taken into custody in June. Another professional ring was operating at Turlock. Some of the games involved large amounts of money. These, too, were raided, and both operators and customers were fined $100 or sentenced to the county jail in Modesto. In July a new regulation from San Francisco came into effect: there was to be no more card playing in any of the centers in the evacuee rooms; residents could play cards only in assigned locations. But at at least one center the administration's chief of police felt that it was unduly harsh to deprive ordinary residents of this pleasure because of a few gam-blers and did not enforce the ruling. (All of the centers had police or-ganizations in addition to the soldiers.)

In the assembly centers there began a reverse-Americanization proc-ess. Mutual understanding between Caucasians and Japanese groups in the American population as well as involvement of Japanese–Americans in democratic government was completely cut off by isolation from the larger community. Parents grew concerned because their children were beginning to speak Japanese rather than the English that they had learned in school.

The political spectrum in the camps had as wide a range as the community outside. At one extreme were the pro-Japan partisans; on the other a small number of Communists. During the reception center period Nisei Communists were suspended from the party as alien Japanese had been earlier, an action that seemed to reflect the Communists' fervid pro-war position at that time. Democrats and Republicans made up the largest active citizen groups. There were a few pacifists at the centers, chiefly college students. The largest group was politically inactive, even more than in Caucasian communities outside, because the Issei had little experience in civic participation. This inexperienced mass had small interest in the policies of the government except to feel resentment with their common lot.

Camp programs intended to Americanize the internees featured much patriotic ritual. When a new American flag was hoisted at Tanforan, the entire camp turned out for the ceremony, and the camp administrator gave an address on the significance of the flag. Drum and bugle corps were formed. Nisei at Santa Anita sent in entries to a war poster contest. A great number of service flags could be seen displayed in the windows of the little dwelling units. Often these had two or three stars. At Santa Anita twenty-nine World War I veterans, twenty-two of them citizens, started an American Legion post. Internees wearing MacArthur buttons were a common sight.

In connection with the voluntary camp beautification program at Tanforan, a Nisei councilman gave a speech at a bridge opening ceremony. "It is because we, in the United States, have the opportunity and freedom to use these talents that we develop our cultures," he said, adding, "although our freedom, here in the center, is limited to some extent. . . ."[79]

An alert college girl with a sense of irony noted down a sign on the post office in her area, which was "too good to go disregarded":

Democracy Training Program
1. What is democracy?
2. What effect did the articles of confederation have on our thirteen colonies?
3. Learn parliamentary procedure and its significance to an active citizenry.[80]

But camp administrations regarded evacuee forums and meetings with visible signs of nervousness.

At first, camp self-government consisted largely of Issei and Nisei who were appointed or elected for each block and who were responsible for enforcing curfew regulations. The block managers came around to count heads every night at six. Residents had to eat quickly in order to return home in time for this check. Teen-agers and adults, too, frequently resented this man with the unpopular duties and referred to him as "the block-head."

Restrictions seemed to be tighter in areas close to the administration headquarters in San Francisco. While many internees felt the soldiers who guarded the camp as a whole had been "taught to regard us as the enemy," and while they were not supposed to fraternize, occasionally certain soldiers made friends with the residents. They were, after all, boys in uniform, all kinds and from all backgrounds. At Puyallup it was remarked that the guards and evacuees were on somewhat intimate terms. Hiroshi Ito, a Nisei soldier in the American Army whose family was interned at Tanforan, obtained information about the center chiefly from some Caucasian soldiers who came up and talked to him one day, asking if he was Japanese. Why did they want to know? he demanded, but they were friendly and said they had become acquainted with Japanese while guarding them at Tanforan. "They thought the evacuation was wrong," he says.

There was some question as to whether the soldiers were there chiefly to guard the Japanese from the hostile persons on the outside or to keep evacuees from escaping. One night at the Puyallup center a soldier on duty saw a shape moving outside the fence. "He commanded it to halt. The something moved on. So the soldier lifted his rifle and shot the something dead. It was a cow. But," according to the person reporting the incident, "it could have been a child . . . a twelve-year-old out on a spree."[81]

At the same center at about the same time, Tom Bodine investigated a rumor of a riot between loyal and disloyal internees said to have been quelled by soldiers. He found that on the particular night involved the residents in Area A had been served some bad canned fish at supper and had been stricken with food poisoning. Off and on throughout the night they had turned on their lights and rushed for the latrines. A soldier on duty in the guard tower saw the lights blinking on and off and the internees running about, and, thinking there was an uprising, he turned on the siren. Soldiers came pouring out, and for a short time there was wild disorder. Nobody was hurt.[82] With the bombing of Dutch Harbor by the Japanese, the guard was increased at the centers.

Searches for contraband and confiscation of property were an irritating feature of center life. Evacuees had been told when they left their homes not to bring in weapons, knives, cameras, short-wave radios, and so on. Since camp administrators individually extended the list, the rules were not clear. Some evacuees thought no radios of any kind were allowed, yet clearly many had commercial band radios. Each guard seemed to use his own judgment on what should be confiscated, and some took away scissors, screw drivers, knitting needles, baseball bats, saws, and rubbing alcohol. When these possessions were confiscated, some evacuees retrieved them off the vehicles as fast as they were taken away. A Salinas center family were allowed to keep a two-celled flashlight. Some women had their sewing machines and forbidden hot plates. One lady who enjoyed her cup of tea in the middle of the afternoon brought her hot plate and teapot. When her teakettle would start whistling, there would be a mad dash to turn it off before the supervisor came in.

The knitting needle ban did not apply everywhere: at the Tulare center, for example, many women knitted for the Red Cross with lend-lease yarn. Some through foresight had brought in canned goods and had been allowed to keep them. At Salinas coffee and other beverages brought from the outside were approved, but not eggs or other uncooked foods. The kitchen help all had knives, though sometimes these were locked up at night. A girl requested her hand clippers which were being held in storage, because she wanted to cut her father's hair. Surely, she felt, the administration could not believe she would run about cutting up the camp with a pair of hand clippers. When she went down to get them and saw all the unidentified knives taken from residents, mostly paring knives which anyone would bring in, and also a blackjack, she agreed that some of them were wicked-looking. Men hid the tools with which they improved their living quarters, and sometimes when these were found and taken away they used great ingenuity in making new ones in the shops or boiler rooms, using the heat to forge the metal.

When it came to books and other reading matter, and records, the confiscators often showed poor in judgment. Books of Japanese poetry and textbooks on European government were seized. Sometimes the manner of the search and seizure made people angry. Occasionally a large group of Caucasians, perhaps aided by a Nisei, would sweep through all the areas simultaneously for checkup raids. People did not know whether they would ever again see some of their confiscated valuables.

An outspoken young woman from a university community commented that most people did not dare say much. Some evacuees were reported to have been sent to Poston for trying to escape or for wasting the food. "Well, I am not doing anything like that," she wrote in a letter, "but if I can do anything to help these people I am going to do it. No one in this world will shut my mouth as long as I tell the truth."[83] An editor said, "What one evacuee might call an outrage another might regard as an inconvenience."[84] A Nisei school teacher wrote, "If you know anything about the Japanese, they are capable of taking a great deal of punishment without a word of complaint and many are taking punishment. They say to the American officials that things are fine and they know they aren't. What fools these mortals be!"[85]

While there were differences in attitude in the matter of compliance, as well as in pro-Japanese versus pro-American sentiment, these differences did not polarize the evacuee community in the assembly center period. There were political overtones when trouble arose, but the causes were more often mundane than ideological. Dissension followed incidents that brought to the surface all the underlying grievances at once.

SEVEN · THE INSIDE
AND THE OUTSIDE

A SIZABLE MANUFACTURING operation for the supplying of war-time camouflage nets to the Army was carried on at Santa Anita under the direction of the United States Engineers. During the relatively brief period that the Santa Anita camp was running, project workers there garnished and completed more than 22,000 nets. So great was the savings to the government through use of evacuee labor in this project that General DeWitt was able to report a profit that more than offset the cost of feeding the whole camp.[1]

The Geneva Convention forbade the use of prisoners of war in forced labor; therefore the government did not put foreign-born Japanese nationals into this work for fear of their possible classification as war prisoners. Only interned American citizens were so employed. During the period in which the WCCA was in charge, a total of 2,718 man-months of labor went into the production and packing of these huge drapes used to cover over war equipment and structures, blending them into the surrounding landscape and disguising them from enemy view. Evacuees worked a forty-four-hour week in eight-hour shifts and at one time were producing 250 to 260 large nets a day. A young man wrote with pride of the high production achievement at Santa Anita: "The officials claim this project of ours to be one of the most successful undertakings in any of the assembly or relocation centers thus far," and he experienced "great satisfaction" working on it.[2]

The basic nets were manufactured on the East Coast out of hemp twine. At Santa Anita they were spread out and tacked to wooden frames laid on the floor ramp of the grandstand area where the internees knelt, weaving in four-foot long colored burlap strips, patterning contrasts in tone and form. The nets varied in size from 22' x 22' to 36' x 60'. After a time, machinery arrived to hang additional nets vertically from beams, and workers stood up to garnish them. At least one bleacher romance which ended in marriage began as men and women and boys and girls over sixteen worked side by side breathing the burlap dust that rose in a great, hovering cloud from the materials.

After lunch one Tuesday afternoon in the middle of June a camouflage net garnisher stopped weaving in his strips of cloth. The foreman spoke to him and asked that he resume what he had been doing. The worker replied that he was hungry; how could he be expected to continue working? Hearing this, other members of the crew stopped work in sympathy. Soon 800 evacuee employees joined in a sit-down strike, and the whole Santa Anita operation came to a halt.

The strike, a simple act, spontaneous—almost casual—in origin, was fairly quickly, fairly easily ended. Later that afternoon and the next morning, self-appointed representatives from the workers, foremen, and supervisors of the camouflage operation met with the camp administration. They presented lists of requests to Russel Armory, the project director. A few workers returned to their jobs before lunch on Wednesday. By afternoon all the people were working again. On Thursday Mr. Armory spoke at a mass meeting. Concessions were made which did not —perhaps could not—take into consideration the complicated nature of the grievances which lay behind the sudden act of protest.

The voiced complaint about insufficient food had triggered the strike, and general but not unanimous dissatisfaction with the food was a factor. (The newspapers dismissed the strike as a result of the internees being served sauerkraut, and one journalist fancifully explained that the objection was due to the fact that it was a "Nazi" dish.) There were the widespread but unpublicized charges that Caucasian stewards were engaged in food profiteering—selling evacuee rations to the outside. A rumor spread that an optometrist had been moved to the Poston center for being too outspoken in requests for food improvement. While it was explained that the optometrist was sent to the other camp simply because he was needed there, a slogan was circulated, "Remember Dr. Ishimaru."[3]

Many camouflage workers were allergic to hemp, and the thickness in the air from the burlap dust as well as fumes from the dye irritated eyes and lungs. Added to this was the rumor, later shown to be baseless, that a poisonous dye was being used and that the reason the project had been given the evacuees at Santa Anita was that San Quentin prisoners had refused it, thus making the evacuees not only prisoners but prisoners second-class. Working for long hours on the hot cement floor was backbreaking and hard on the feet. There was no protection from the Los Angeles summer sun which beat down upon them. After standing or kneeling all day the crews had to wait in long lines for food, while lines of white collar workers moved faster. The $8 a month originally paid for this work amounted to four and one-half cents an hour. Later this wage was raised very slightly. After the strike was underway a pamphlet of unknown origin was circulated apparently attempting to capitalize on the ferment, but it did not reach more than a portion of the workers.

A particularly tender area of resentment was the administration's use of pressure tactics in recruiting people for this job. The evacuees were required to sign a paper stating that they were making a "voluntary" request for camouflage work, but this was hardly the case. In May, when the people from San Jose arrived at Santa Anita, most Nisei from areas evacuated earlier were already employed in the more desirable jobs. The San Joseans, as a whole an educated, well assimilated group, were unable, therefore, to obtain work for which they felt they were qualified. On May 30 when the camp administration suddenly received orders from the Army to put 800 to 900 workers on the camouflage project by the following Monday, it was the San Joseans who were chiefly tapped for the project. Many hundreds of evacuees were called into the personnel office. High school classes, which were being held on a seminar basis, were abandoned as both students and teachers were recruited. All other new jobs were frozen until the quota was filled.

On June 9 the center manager denied, through the *Pacemaker*, the camp newspaper, that there was a blacklist of the hundreds who turned down camouflage work, but this was widely believed. According to the administration there was no draft; it was rather the moral duty of the residents to work on the nets. Male workers were hard to find, so particular pressure was put upon women and girls. Evacuees asserted that they were intimidated into acceptance; they were told if they did not accept this particular work they would probably not receive another chance for a job for the duration of the war.

One woman who was a high school girl at the time says, "My mother and I would not volunteer. They locked us in here—now they should not expect us to sign up." A college girl who was a member of the Fellowship of Reconciliation was handed a notice telling her to report in to the office. She gave conscientious objection to war as her reason for not signing. The Caucasion interviewing her accepted this explanation, but asked her if she did not have an additional excuse. She answered that she was susceptible to hay fever, but please to note her first objection on her card, which he did.

During the strike various requests were made, including a demand for improvement in quality and increase in quantity of food for workers, issuance of medically approved masks for working on the burlap, a four-hour workday for mothers, regular Army pay of $41 a month, clothing allowances because of the rapid deterioration of clothing and shoes, and injury compensation. The Health Department which was called in found no serious health hazards, but suggested the establishment of grievance committees. Some of the requests were acted upon. Girls could work half a day if they chose. Camouflage workers no longer had to stand in regular mess lines. Overnight there was a marked improvement in menus for everybody. But the greatest dissatisfaction of all remained: only token wages were paid for unpleasant and essentially involuntary labor.

Though the episode was not apparently directly related to the strike, two days later six men were arrested who had attended a meeting called to discuss general camp conditions and to make recommendations. Shortly afterward the number arrested rose to eleven persons. Several of those who faced possible prison terms were members of the newly elected "self-governing council," including the camp "mayor." Six were aliens. Five were citizens. Politically they represented varying points of view, from conservative to left-wing, and while there was considerable tension and disagreement among them, arrests were not made on account of their politics or their incompatibility but rather because in exercising their limited self-governing prerogatives, those seized had made three mistakes: (1.) They had neglected to have a policeman present at the gathering, in violation of a rule against secret meetings; (2.) Those attending had spoken Japanese, a language forbidden at such meetings; and (3.) Certain of the prisoners had conspired to circulate a petition asking for the publication of a Japanese section in the camp paper, violating a prohibition against petitions. But for a time nobody, including the families of those arrested, knew why they were being held, where they had been taken, or what might become of them.

By this action the camp administration diverted attention from the camouflage dissatisfaction, bringing the full weight of authority to quash the least suggestion of trouble, and perhaps preventing Army officers from assuming direct control of the camp operation. Some of the charges against the prisoners were vague, such as conspiring to create a troublesome situation at Camp Santa Anita. The Southern California ACLU pointed out that the "illegal" meeting held on June 18 had preceded by seven days the formulation of the rules that made it illegal.[4]

It had been proposed at the meeting in question that the Spanish ambassador be asked to investigate conditions at Santa Anita. (Under the rules of war the Spanish ambassador, representing the government of Japan, could be appealed to by those held in actual prisoner-of-war camps.) This was quickly protested by an "anti-Fascist" alien as a disloyal suggestion. However, the protestor as well as the speaker he criticized were among those arrested.

The target of various charges and rebuttals, the eleven men were first held in jail, then cleared by the State Attorney General's office which had brought the charges, then seized again by the military authorities. The former editor of the controversial prewar newspaper *Doho*, dedicated to "complete Victory over Japanese Militarism and Nazi Fascism," was held in jail and charged in a federal court with circulating the language newspaper petition. Eventually, Elmer Davis of the Office of War Information intervened for the editor, a Nisei, secured his release, and put him to work doing propaganda translations in Washington. The five elected councilmen who were accused of holding the secret meeting were removed to other centers.

The Southern California branch of the American Civil Liberties Union decided to defend several of those charged. After many months, A. L. Wirin, attorney for the ACLU, succeeded in reducing individual bail from $10,000 to $2,000 each and in securing a writ of *habeas corpus*, the first since the evacuation began, for one of the defendants, Ernest Wakayama, a Nisei Republican, American Legion leader, and former AF of L official, and his wife, Toki. These two were chosen for the purpose of developing a federal test case to challenge the constitutionality of certain aspects of the evacuation. The defense contended that the Army action constituted imprisonment without hearing or trial and that the petitioners were being held solely because of their ancestry and thus were illegally discriminated against. The national ACLU and Walter Tsukamoto of the JACL joined in this particular action which did not challenge the constitutionality of Executive Order 9066 nor the congressional legislation making disobedience to the military proclamations a crime. The Wakayama case was eventually dropped by the ACLU as other cases which more directly challenged the evacuation came into prominence.

From the beginning, there was very little opportunity for acquiring information or engaging in free discussion in any of the assembly centers. Evacuees could subscribe to magazines and their hometown newspapers, except for certain banned publications. The JACL organ, the *Pacific Citizen*, which had a remarkable wartime coverage of news and problems of concern to American Japanese, was allowed. At first regular Japanese language newspapers still being published were allowed in the camps. Not a very large percentage of internees took newspapers, however, and few had radios. For most, subscriptions were a luxury they could not afford. Because of the limited circulation of these available sources of news there was a feeling of isolation and uncertainty.

To compensate somewhat, mimeographed camp papers were started in fifteen centers, often staffed by persons with talent. The managing editor of one was the former English editor of the *New World* in San Francisco; the adviser for another was a distinguished professor. Former staff members of the University of California's *Daily Californian* helped run the Tanforan *Totalizer*. These papers were begun with enthusiasm and high hopes. Circulation, as General DeWitt pointed out, was free. There was the *Mercedian*, the Walerga *Wasp*, the Turlock *Fume*, the Pinedale *Logger*, and in Fresno the *Grapevine*.

The papers provided camp information, improved morale, and helped restore a feeling of normalcy. Releases ranged from advice and rules about fire prevention to procedures for the obtaining of marriage licenses. Songfests were announced and directions given for obtaining tables for bridge, *goh*, and *shogi*. Administration warnings were printed: no more soft drinks would be available until missing Coca-Cola and milk bottles were returned. *Haiku* and doggerel appeared. Friendly rivalry developed between papers of different camps.

Yet certain aspects of these ventures were discouraging to conscientious editors. One editor was quoted in the San Francisco *News* as discovering that Japanese reticence was "no myth." Nobody wanted to be quoted, especially block leaders. " . . . if the leaders themselves feel that they must remain silent, then there's something wrong somewhere."[5]

Censorship was the rule. Each Santa Anita *Pacemaker* underwent administration examination three times before publication. The same held true at Fresno. A Tanforan paper came back to the editors for redoing because minor, last-minute corrections had been made and therefore the paper did not follow approved copy. A YMCA mimeographing machine was confiscated, because the evacuee group had published an information bulletin without permission. Nothing was permitted to go into the papers that did not meet with center management approval. Discussion of the international situation, war news, national news, even hometown news and politics was taboo. Not only was a Japanese language section for the older people prohibited, but commonly used expressions such as *kifu*, meaning donation, and *bon*, meaning memorial services, were censored.

"We don't have a policy. Politics are out! We don't have to worry about what our advertisers think," the first editorial in the Manzanar paper had rejoiced. "This is plain Utopia."[6] But by June one of the editors commented privately that the only thing free about the Manzanar *Free Press* was its subscription fee. "Morale is low in some of the centers," a Nisei leader living outside the camps wrote, "especially in view of the stupid censorship imposed upon the center newspapers which precludes their publishing anything outside of matter fit for a high school paper."[7]

In other matters, too, freedom of expression was circumscribed, more so, as a matter of fact, than in the Justice Department camps for "dangerous" aliens. One center official forbade the production on the Fourth of July of an historical play about Valley Forge because it contained lines in which soldiers condemned the Continental Congress for sending them bad food. This, they feared, might be interpreted as a reflection on the center food. Adult forums at the Fresno assembly center presented programs on "How Evacuees Can Improve Their Center Life," on "The Constructive Use of Leisure," and on "Post-War Reassimilation." A second center's first topic in a Town Hall series for adults was, "How May

We Better Cooperate to Improve Tanforan?"[8] Meetings for the purpose of discussing international problems or politics were not authorized.
Other centers did not encourage any programs at all. The trouble with
forums, one educational director worried, was the ever-present chance that
radical elements might control them. Radical, in the center terminology,
did not imply left-wing politics, but rather any kind of critical or disrup-
tive attitude. Except for religious leaders of chosen denominations, no
outside speakers on any subject whatsoever were allowed.

Business Week reported in July, 1942, that camp mail was censored but
that there was no limitation on the right to send and receive it. Carey
McWilliams, investigating the question of mail censorship at Pomona,
reported in *Harper's* that he had been able to verify a military censorship of outgoing and incoming mail at that center.[9] An evacuee wrote
that the administration did not so much censor the mail as sample it
occasionally. Some evacuees at Tanforan reported that their mail coming
from Tule Lake had been censored. Even employees in the postal departments of the different centers were not always aware that this took place,
however, and at least one official denied it explicitly. The evacuee population in general was never conscious of the large amount of censorship
that was practiced in the assembly centers and even today are unaware
that it existed.

In all the assembly centers evacuees had been allowed to plan and
put into operation self-governing councils, however anomalous in the
context of internment these bodies might be. It was felt that self-governing councils would develop a needed "sense of social obligation and
responsibility."[10] Each block was allowed one delegate, the delegates in
turn electing temporary and permanent councils. The councils, acting
together, or sometimes special committees made up of council members
drafted constitutions and by-laws.

At Tanforan the night before the big election for council delegates
to draft the constitution, all the candidates paraded, carrying banners
in Japanese and English. One had made a two-foot stove pipe hat; another wore a woman's nightgown over his jacket with a number of
signs and slogans pinned to it. A sixty-year-old Legionnaire carried a
tub and drummed on it all around the camp. The election the following
day was difficult and challenging. Most Issei and many women were
voting for the first time in their lives. Even in Japan many had never
voted because they had not been able to afford the poll tax. Issei, excited
over the experience and the idea of self-government, took pains to vote
seriously. All adult residents were permitted to vote, but in one camp
only 47 per cent actually did so. Many of those who stayed away from
the polls, surprisingly, were not the politically uninitiated but rather
the more disillusioned Nisei.

It was a shock to some of the Nisei helpers at the polls to discover how little most of the Issei knew of the procedures involved. Some brought down their wives' ballots for them; others brought ballots for the whole family. The poll workers explained to these new voters the meaning of the secret ballot. Voter education is generally a slow process, one center election board member reasoned, and she was dismayed to hear other young helpers remark that the Issei were not very bright since they did not understand. Voters who confessed that they had lost their ballots wanted to know if they would be put on a blacklist as a consequence. A great many had been frightened by the instances of people being sent to Poston for wrongdoing. The average Issei had never had an opportunity to develop the idea that government was part of himself, something he could participate in, manipulate, change.

Nevertheless, certain Issei in the assembly centers were a great deal more knowledgeable in organizational matters than the Nisei, who had risen to prominence by way of Boy Scout or YMCA work. According to one politically active Nisei at Tanforan, these Issei "knew all about preambles and by-laws and practical politics" having learned through participation in labor unions and organizations such as the American Legion. It was from this small older and more sophisticated leadership group that council membership was largely drawn. At one center an elected committee was composed of six men, only one of whom had ever voted before. Several of the others, however, were Issei who had graduated from American colleges and universities.

Civic-minded leaders plunged into council work with energy and enthusiasm with the expectation that these bodies would be a means of preserving the democratic spirit of the people. Everyone could do something useful, said the chairman of the council at Fresno, Dr. T. T. Yatabe, a dentist and public speaker of intelligence and wit. He warned against lack of confidence and against selfishness. All should pull together.[11] Lively discussions developed on how much power the councils should have, whether they should have both legislative and administrative power, and whether there should be elected legislatures. Arguments occurred sometimes on the position of the Issei; some Nisei fought having Issei represented at all. There were struggles for power typical of any political group: when an overbearing chairman tried to cut short a meeting because someone began to question the election manager of his brother who was running for office, there was a good deal of shouting in behalf of "freedom of speech," and the meeting went on.

Some attempts were made to draw women into council participation, but these efforts were not too fruitful. According to a Nisei school teacher, the Army dealt with only one sex. Then, too, the older generation of Japanese women had never taken an interest or been allowed real participation in government. A version of the women's auxiliaries of Japanese villages that aided and cooperated with the men's governing groups were proposed in some assembly centers, though they were never brought into being.

From the WCCA point of view the primary purpose of the councils was to act as liaison between the center population and camp administration as well as clearing houses for welfare matters. The notable reforms that took place at Tanforan occurred largely through the suggestions of the local councils to a receptive project director.

Councilmen themselves often conceived of their roles as being far more significant. Some even believed that if they did a good enough governing job, transfers to new centers inland might become unnecessary. But the Caucasian personnel tended to mistrust too much ambition or initiative on the parts of these leaders. Councilmen were often caught between pressures from the people they felt they represented and limitations imposed from above. Though the councils often achieved a great deal, some councilmen resented being treated as if they were mere messengers from one group to the other. Leaders in a northern camp complained across the barbed wire that they always got the "run around" when they tried to put their ideas into effect. Project directors pleaded for time to make desirable changes.

It is interesting to note that the Nazi concentration camps also had their parallel lines of authority, one dominated by the SS, the other by prisoners. This kind of arrangement was characteristic of Japanese and other prisoner-of-war camps as well, the prisoners having only nominal power that could be snatched away by the guards.

Suddenly late in June sweeping orders came from Army headquarters increasing censorship and imposing strict rules for the camp councils. For a time evacuees and their representatives were plunged into uncertainty but on July 18 a summary of the rules and new additions was issued. Henceforth telephonic communication to the outside would be strictly limited to emergencies and transacted under supervision. Visiting privileges among evacuees could be changed at WCCA discretion. Lights must be out at 10:30. Tools would be kept in custody and checked out as used. Bicycles were restricted. There would be no fraternization between internal security police and evacuees who were to stay at least ten feet back from all outside fences. The WCCA would continue to provide funerals and religious services.

August regulations forbade all literature written in Japanese except for Bibles, hymn books, and dictionaries. At some centers, however, duty-bent military police appropriated Bibles and dictionaries as well as textbooks in comparative government and books on Japanese and Chinese poetry. Newspapers from Colorado and Utah were intercepted. All Japanese records, whether speech or music, were ordered turned in. More general resentment was aroused over the seizure of records than of books. And with these other rules came the most shattering directive of all: self-government at every WCCA assembly center was dissolved forthwith. While there might be advisory committees in the future, these, if allowed, would be chosen by center managers. "Immediately upon receipt of these instructions," the new regulation stated, "all reference on the part of the administrative staff to evacuee self-government in Assembly Centers will cease."[12]

The chief of the internal security police came into the council chambers of a Northern California center to read to the members the directive to disband. One Nisei member, a dedicated cooperator who believed in and wanted to keep believing in the benign purposes of internment as something that would "help win the war," and who further had developed a gratifying personal relationship with the project director now found silence and a closed door when he tried to make an appointment with him. Day after day he and the other members of the council attempted to see the head man, wanting to express their appreciation to him for past harmony in working together. The young man, who had often defended the administration's policies among the more critical elements of the resident population, was very shaken by the rebuff. Discouraged, he sat in his stable and wrote: " . . . there is to be another election next Tuesday [for an advisory body]. They asked me to be election chairman. But I refused. . . . I told the fellow who came to talk to me that I couldn't help in an election where the center manager could pick anyone outside of the 27 elected on the panel [or] kick out any of the members if he dislikes them.

"There is no feeling for the election. No one even talks about it. As far as I know there aren't any candidates."[13] Later overtures reinvolved him in camp life.

Some camp directors at first withheld the news of the mandatory dissolution of self-government, and when they did announce it, did not, perhaps could not, explain how it had happened or why. Buddy Iwata the young "mayor," or council chairman, at the Merced center, a Stanford graduate who had helped others with their property and moving problems up until the moment of evacuation, was asked to submit a letter of resignation. He and the other council members were astonished and disturbed by the request though the center manager seemed very reluctant and embarrassed and expressed confidence in his leadership and abilities. After the elimination of the council, Mr. Iwata was asked to take a purely liaison job, which he accepted, but he found it "rough" to be a go-between and try to please everybody, so rough, indeed, that when he was transferred to Amache, he turned down all similar positions, choosing to devote his university education to digging ditches instead. As advisory committees took the place of councils, Issei participation was forbidden—except at the Merced center where the manager persuaded the WCCA to allow him to appoint one Issei official. But self-government in the assembly centers had been eliminated, and would not be revived again.

A respite from these denials and disappointments came from outside the centers as the California elections approached. The Hearst press, incorrectly guessing that citizens of Japanese descent would all vote alike, feared that 20,000 Nisei voters might determine elections in California. If they were allowed to vote, said Leland Ford, they could outvote the rest of Los Angeles County and elect a Japanese to every office and thereby bring on "civil war."[14] In July the Fresno registrar refused to send someone to register Japanese–Americans, who were largely from Fresno County, at the nearby center. There were no funds to pay for the gas, he explained. The distance was three miles.[15] State Attorney General Warren ruled that evacuees could not vote in their new locations. Later the WRA, endorsing this decision, pointed out that the interned citizens could register by mail in the areas of their former residence.

Beginning early in May, American citizens of Japanese descent began sending for absentee ballots. Registrars in Los Angeles, Sacramento, San Francisco, and elsewhere were kept busy with increasing numbers of ballot requests for the August elections, which in many areas, notably Fresno County, exceeded the requests of service men. The JACL distributed 15,000 ballots. A record 6,000 were sent from Los Angeles. It was not only their privilege but their duty to keep up participation in democratic government, one Nisei wrote, expressing the viewpoint of the majority. But even as these preparations were made, the right of franchise for the Nisei was under severe legal attack.

Two suits had been filed early in May, one in Alameda County and one in San Francisco, asking the federal court to order registrars to strike from the books the names of all voters of Japanese ancestry. Cameron King, registrar of voters in San Francisco, was the defendant in *Regan vs. King*; Regan, the Grand Secretary of the Native Sons of the Golden West, being the challenger. A suit filed previously by James K. Fisk, state adjutant of the American Legion, against G. E. Wade, registrar, was dropped in favor of concentration on the Regan case. Regan was represented by Ulysses S. Webb, an old foe of the Japanese and the former attorney general of California, who had retired. (Commenting on his influence, a critic said, "You cannot defeat in election a man with the initials U. S. in his name.")

According to Webb, the suit should determine, "if any Jap is entitled to be a citizen."[16] The Sacramento registrar, informed of the move to disenfranchise the Nisei, told newsmen he would keep issuing absentee ballots until he was instructed not to. Meanwhile, at their respective national conventions the Native Sons and the Native Daughters set aside a thousand dollars apiece to promote an amendment to the United States Constitution to exclude from citizenship persons of Japanese ancestry everywhere in the country.

Civil libertarians assisted Cameron's lawyers, Walter Dold and John Tool, in countering these onslaughts against Nisei voting rights. Ernest Besig, executive director of the Northern California ACLU, described the Regan suit as "a cruel and preposterous attempt to nullify express constitutional guarantees" and an attack on the rights of all minorities.[17] Those who had brought the action had chosen "a strange time" to assail our cherished constitutional rights and liberties, Wayne Collins, who wrote the ACLU *amicus curiae* brief, commented, but such persons were true to type: they fished in "troubled waters"; they exhibited the "typical courage" of opportunists and oppressors—they kicked the weak, the helpless, and the prostrate.[18]

Webb argued the case on the basis of white supremacy. Only white persons, he declared (erroneously), were present at Bunker Hill, Lexington, Valley Forge, and at the drafting of the Declaration of Independence and the Constitution. "This is a white man's country. . . ."[19]

Judge A. F. St. Sure, before whom *Regan* vs. *King* was argued, described the case as exceptional, since the question of citizenship of natural-born Americans had definitely been established through a long line of Supreme Court decisions, including *Morrison* vs. *California*, which specified American-born Japanese. He agreed with counsel for the defense and dismissed the action. Judge St. Sure gave his decision on July 2, one day after the WCCA had eliminated all assembly center self-governing councils, thus somewhat mitigating that blow.

Ulysses S. Webb appealed. The judges of the state circuit court of appeals, appreciating the widespread importance of the proceeding, heard the case *en banc*—all seven sat in hearing. After a hurried conference with the other judges, Senior Judge Curtis Wilbur, without giving Webb sufficient time to develop his arguments, spoke for the Court, upholding Judge St. Sure and dismissing the suit in an abrupt, one-sentence decision. The United States Supreme Court refused a further appeal.

The JACL had filed a belated *amicus curiae* brief in self-defense against this final thrust at Nisei citizenship—and under considerable difficulty since their two principal attorneys, Walter Tsukomoto and Saburo Kido, were both confined in evacuee camps at the time. More of a public relations effort than a constitutional argument, their brief dealt with the sociological history of the Japanese in America and the moral questions involved in discrimination. The Lawyers Guild also filed a brief.

With the elimination of the self-government councils and the tightening of all rules, a more definite concentration camp atmosphere began to permeate the centers. Democratic correctives through council action, however circumscribed the councils had been, were no longer possible. Without such a check camp administrations could be as arbitrary as they chose. Minor incidents occurred in some camps having to do with graft or personality conflict, but these were confined to limited areas and did not become known to the general camp population. At the Santa Anita center, however, widespread feelings erupted again as at the time of the camouflage strike.

General DeWitt ascribed the cause of the new crisis to an "overzealous" search for contraband.[20] On the fourth of August, three days after the abrogation of the camp council, the interior security police instituted a camp-wide search for contraband articles. In two of the center's seven districts, according to DeWitt, the searchers were "overbearing" in their manner. "Added to this was an order from the center manager to pick up, without advance notice, electric hot plates which had previously been allowed on written individual authorization . . . for the preparation of infant formulas and food for the sick." Legitimate complaints about the search failed to reach the chief of interior security police until the middle of the afternoon, according to DeWitt, and by the time the search was stopped the whole camp was in a state of anger, and crowds had begun to gather.[21] There was an incident of violence in which a suspected "informer" was attacked. But most of the crowd stood in cold, silent fury. Two hundred soldiers were called in, and martial law lasted three days.

As in the play *Roshomon*, there are different versions to the story, depending upon the vantage point from which the action was viewed. Many evacuees contend that certain camp police officers had locked the doors when they made their search and had taken money and valuables. (Some evacuees, mistrusting banks, had brought all their worldly goods with them.) An evacuee remarks today: "Some of the m.p.s looked a lot like the deputy sheriffs you used to see in the old days in the county jail—you couldn't tell the inmates from the deputies." Letters to the outside insisted that only a minor part of the story was published in the newspapers. (During the search an editor of the *Pacemaker* was taken to the station for possession of literature which the arrester suspected as subversive, and his books were confiscated.)

Fuji Takaichi who was in a position to see a good deal of the action recalls it vividly. She was an office worker at the time and had not known what was happening in the morning. When she went out at noon to get some lunch, she saw that something unusual was going on, that people were standing around in groups. She went home quickly, because she knew her mother had been knitting some socks, and people were not supposed to have knitting needles or scissors. "When I got home, here was my mother sitting perfectly relaxed. So I said, 'You know, mother, they're going to take your knitting needles away.' All she said was, 'Well, it's all taken care of, dear.'" Her mother, who was an amateur gardener, had brought cuttings of her pet geraniums and planted them out in front of the stable area. Now each plant suddenly had a stake—a knitting needle.

When the daughter arrived back at work in the office under the grandstand, she noticed that no one else had returned, but she went to work and was busily doing her typing when suddenly the door opened, and a uniformed soldier came in. He had his helmet on and pointed his bayonet in her direction. She let out a yell, "Oh!" He told her she would have to evacuate the building. She went outside. The whole area was covered with people. She had never seen a mob before. There was the most frightening sound—a kind of undercurrent in the vast silence. One could hear the silence. And there was a feeling that came with it, that one did not know what was going to happen. She was terrified.

Another evacuee arrived late upon the scene to observe hundreds of people walking up an eighty-foot-wide street, picking up stones and bottles. He did not know why everybody was so enraged, but as he walked along he heard various stories, many of which he felt later might have been rumors, and he also began to get angry.

The active elements of the crowd had chased a suspected informer, a Korean, into a building where a large number of people saw him beaten and a typewriter thrown at him. Then they saw him go down in an attitude of prayer. As the aggressors left they piled all the office furniture on top of him.

The Reverend John Yamazaki, a newly ordained Episcopal priest, accompanied by a Buddhist layman, had gone to the administration building to see if the contraband search was official, and they were trapped between the military police and the crowd. They saw some security officers who had been searching the barracks running for their lives and escaping through the fence. They themselves were under suspicion for communicating with the project director. They knew it would be fatal to tell the crowd to calm down so they tried specific suggestions. They told them, "If there has been an unwarranted search in your barracks, please bring evidence, description of the officer, list of objects taken, details, witnesses. Complete this objectively so we can turn it over to the Administration."

Mrs. Takaichi saw about half a dozen of the officers whom the crowd had cornered. As she came out the door, they were directly in her line of vision:

> And their faces were green. They were absolutely terrified, because they suddenly realized, they could have one little gun, you know, but there was nothing to keep this tremendous horde of people from tearing them limb from limb. Just then the Army arrived. I couldn't move, because there

were so many people. There was no place to go. I saw them come up the main avenue which hits the grandstand there, the trucks with the mounted guns, and they all had their helmets on and their bayonets. A group of them jumped off and started coming. They were trying to make a pathway, and I'll never forget—I think what broke the whole thing up was a little old lady with a cane. She was so old that she leaned on a cane, and she was right in the middle of one of these bridges. One of the bridges that went across a moat. The soldiers were trying to get across, and here they were four abreast with their bayonets fixed, and there was this little old lady, and she'd turn around, and she'd look at them, and then she'd take her own time—she wasn't going to be rushed—she'd go a few steps, and then she'd turn and she'd look at them, just as if to say, "Well, who do you think you are?"

They were trying to rush, and she wasn't going to rush. Do you know, everybody started laughing, and that was the thing that broke the tension.

"The soldiers were shakier than we were," says Eiichi Sakauye, a San Jose orchardist, who had taxied members of the personnel in the motor pool pick-up from eight in the morning until eight at night, traveling one hundred miles back and forth over less than 7/10 of a mile route, because no Caucasian personnel had been permitted to drive their cars in that morning.

An investigation was made of irregularities, and the offending policemen were discharged. A number of others resigned. As in the case of the camouflage strike, about two weeks following the contraband riot disciplinary actions began to occur, on charges apparently completely unrelated to the riot. This time the Army came into the camp and started arresting young Nisei, removing and taking them for separate and individual relocation. Eventually twenty youths and three young wives were sent away to unknown destinations. No reasons were given. Some of those picked out had been involved in a mess hall skirmish a while before after one had demanded more food; yet all but the one had been cleared of charges. One innocent bystander was arrested and was considerably upset not only by the arrest, but by the exaggerated stories about what he had done to occasion it and the feeling of shame that followed. Ironically, real mischief-makers among the young were left in camp. People gathered near the tower gate as the youths were put onto trucks were bewildered and asking, "Why?" Families were being broken up, and it had been promised that this would not happen. Evacuee spokesmen had pleaded with the administration all the previous night to stop what they regarded as a grave injustice to most of those being shipped out. The assistant project director said the orders had come from the Army, which kept its information secret. Finally persuaded that what was being done was a mistake, he made five phone calls to different WCCA officials but was turned down.

An evacuee wrote to Claude Settles, her former teacher, "People have had to put up with so much here, most of which was unnecessary: the ban on Japanese literature; Japanese records; and the denial of free speech, assembly, press, freedom of religion . . . the search, and many other things. I feel that the sooner everyone is relocated the better it will be for everyone concerned. If things continue like this, I fear that there will be something that will make August 4 look silly."[22] But Santa Anita was exceptional, as has been stated, from a point of view of dramatic social crises, and in other centers life went along as best it could.

Many things that started in the assembly centers were expanded later in the relocation centers: the short-lived self-government councils, recreation programs, beautification projects, camp food production, the rudimentary beginnings of an educational system, and legal aid.

Evacuees had come into the centers with a tremendous number of legal problems, chiefly relating to property, and the WCCA set up legal aid departments to help answer questions, often manned by youthful Nisei attorneys or attorneys-to-be. The evacuees were at a loss as to how to go about tending to their affairs from within the confines of the centers. What, for instance, could they do about rents, profits, dividends, and royalties? Securities and investments? Mortgages? Before evacuation, JACL lawyers had tried unsuccessfully to get a moratorium on mortgage payments and insurance premiums. American Japanese had already lost 50 or 60 per cent of their assets. The problem now was how to protect themselves from further losses. The young lawyers aided in adjusting differences arising out of hastily made or indefinite agreements. They tried to obtain proper accounting for amounts due evacuees from the operation of their farms and businesses outside. They tried to find out whether property was being satisfactorily cared for. The question of collecting unemployment insurance was unsettled. When the legal aid offices were first set up, before the *Regan* vs. *King* decision, the voting question was still a matter of debate.

There was uncertainty over use of the courts: could they sue or be sued? Could they defend themselves in suits brought outside the centers? Could they obtain interlocutory decrees of divorce? Several judicial decisions between June and September determined certain legal rights of evacuees. Three long-time residents of California who had been injured in an automobile accident two years previous to evacuation were awarded damages. In another case an alien from the Los Angeles area, a fisherman by the name of Kumezo Kawato, had been unable to collect wages and injury damages from his employer. He sued, but federal Judge Yankwich, a Romanian-born Unitarian naturalized in 1912, refused to hear his plea, because Kawato was an enemy alien. In a unanimous decision, the United States Supreme Court eventually upheld the right of peaceable, law-abiding enemy aliens to seek justice in civilian courts.

A. L. Wirin, who had lost the CIO as a client because of his defense of Japanese–Americans, commented for the ACLU that the decision was a bright page in American legal history: a fisherman had the right to sue "a wealthy American corporation." Now, he wondered, what about the rights of 70,000 American citizens evacuated and interned "solely because their ancestors were born in Japan?"[23]

Fishermen were far removed from the ocean that had given them their life work, and businessmen were not allowed to ply their trade in the centers, but farmers and gardeners and housewives sometimes found spots for the growing of a few vegetables and flowers, although they realized that they might not be there to enjoy the harvest. Outside barrack homes vines and flowers and vegetables began to sprout. Evacuees grew morning glories, cactus, and violets. A man at the hot Sacramento center planted zinnia seeds the first day he arrived, as well as gladiola bulbs shortly thereafter. "We are hoping to see the bloom before we are relocated again," his daughter wrote. "We left our garden at home with just rows and rows of different flower plants with buds and berries which we were planning [to use] to make jam."[24] One group of Issei produced 161 lugs of squash, string beans, and corn at a farm project at the Fresno center. Otamatsu Uyemoto, who had raised tomatoes for thirty years in the San Pedro hills, made a 6' x 15' vegetable garden at Santa Anita that flourished in May with green onions, Chinese *nappa*, radishes, *daikon* (used for Japanese pickles), and tomatoes, and in July this center had several acres of vegetables for use in the kitchen. George Yano spelled out "Victory" with pebbles in the garden in front of his Tanforan quarters. Another man made a rustic ornamental fence from eucalyptus limbs. At every center volunteer crews kept busy landscaping grounds. They built fish ponds and rock gardens. Small parks sprang up out of the sand and the dust.

Men attempted to conquer their environment here through symbols. A noted plant developer collected Santa Anita's horseshoes and mounted them on a board. Gentaro Shimo, an artist, had no materials with which to work, so he looked near the camp incinerator and found a sack of leftover fire clay that he could use for sculpture. He also made soap miniatures. Using a pocket knife he hollowed out bars of soap, which when held to the light revealed clean-cut profile silhouettes.

Time was the great vacuum. Methods of filling it varied, some original and creative, others the way of least resistance. At first there was no school. "We mostly walked around," says a Nisei woman who was in the eighth grade at the time. "We went to bed early." Boys played all day, stopping only to sleep. A harmless old Issei from San Pedro in a Salvation Army uniform used to preach and play taps on the bugle. He had injured his leg and believed he had been cured by a miracle. Before evacuation when the police used to come to take him away in San Pedro he would employ Judo techniques and throw them "right and left." But at Santa Anita he was left undisturbed to address his first big audience. Everybody would listen as they sat in the bleachers resting after doing their laundry, though nobody could understand him after the first few words, "God is love, God is love," for he would lapse into a stream of incoherence. But the longer he went on with his gibberish, the more people clapped when he paused for breath.

At some centers there were outdoor symphonic concerts in the evening when records donated or lent by outside groups were played over the loudspeakers. Movies were a rarity. The need for recreation and recreational equipment was critical. Most of the materials were sent by interested individuals. Gradually a recreational system was built up, and plans were made for an official program. Many activities began spontaneously.

Persons with established hobbies like bridge were fortunate. One of a group of expert bridge players at Tanforan, Paul Kasugai, had translated all the works of Culbertson into Japanese before he had played more than a hand or two of bridge. Letters sent to the bridge column of the San Francisco *Chronicle* from Tanforan, asking for information, were treated warily at first. Their initial impulse, the columnists wrote, was not to answer, for they wanted "no friendly traffic" with the "enemy." After consulting the Army, they decided to answer the letters.[25]

Japanese board games underwent a revival. Hundreds of women signed up for needlecraft, and there was a model airplane craze among the youngsters. Boys went frog hunting with homemade nets. *Sumo* experts organized Japanese wrestling squads.

Talent shows were frequent. "Woody" Ichihashi, the son of the aristocratic Stanford professor, Yamato Ichihashi, organized a swing band at one center, and at another Dick Miyagawa, a singer from San Jose State College, entertained frequently. Miyagawa also taught boxing, starting a program meant for 1,000 youths with three sets of boxing gloves. Tanforan contenders for local Golden Gloves tournaments trained by running around the track. Competitive sports were organized for Issei men. While many of these programs started spontaneously, they were all under the supervision of Caucasian personnel.

Softball was popular everywhere. There were the Rough Riders, the Dodgers, the Indians, the Peanut League, and countless other teams. Balls were in short supply, and evacuees wound gunny sack threads into baseballs during rest periods or while standing in mess lines. Gifts of basketballs, baseballs, and horseshoes were welcome, but volunteer assistance with the recreation program by an outside church group was refused by camp administrators because of concern that this might stimulate subversive activities in the camp.

Women at the Tulare center, wanting to keep fit, rose at five in the morning to do exercises. At another center, an eighty-three-year-old, five-foot, ninety-five-pound woman, a physiotherapist, demonstrated such feats as standing on her head and "leg raising."

Rudimentary adult education classes were started through the impetus of a few active Nisei. One of these leaders had a particular interest in the Americanization of the Issei and began government and English classes for them. He also organized a private dancing group among these older people, believing that folk dancing was the first step toward Americanization. The Issei displayed great enthusiasm for these classes, and at one center two-hour courses in comparing American and Japanese Constitutions which started with thirty people soon attracted two hundred daily. Several notables, among them the artist Chiura Obata, devoted their talents to teaching fellow inmates. Another university professor organized graduate courses and a normal school.

Hundreds of Japanese–American students had missed the last weeks of high school in their own communities and received their diplomas in absentia. Some attempts were made to simulate home ceremonies. In one mass ritual, graduates of twenty-four different high schools sang the "Star Spangled Banner" and listened to a student speech, "We Face the Future."

Education programs in the assembly centers like recreation programs started with no plans and no materials. Since the centers were considered temporary, no initial budget for education was provided. But the education-oriented parents were anxious that their children continue their schooling. Programs were needed if only to keep them out of mischief. In some places, the children themselves pressed for some kind of school. Though progress was discouraging, evacuee teachers and undergraduate amateurs drew up a curriculum, begged materials from outside sources, scrubbed down bare rooms for classes.

A letter from a preschool supervisor at Manzanar read, "I know they would love to do cut-out and paste; making things with their hands is really the most fascinating thing they can do, but we don't have any scissors or paste, let alone bright paper. . . . Children lose interest very quickly . . . we need everything."[26]

Used textbooks slowly began coming in. Fresno State College donated used drawing paper, crayons, water colors, and molding clays. Teachers were waiting for promised educational supervisors hired by the WCCA to arrive—some were expected in May, then in June, some as late as fall. Halen Aihara (Kitaji) recorded the gradual setting up of a nursery school and the training of girls as teachers at the Salinas center day by day in her diary. From discouraging beginnings she built up the little school in a laundry room, until she could write, "The room is beautiful now. It has a real child's room look. . . . Little Gingi became greatly excited when he saw the pictures on the wall. It was a real test for me. . . ."[27] Mae Hirake of San Jose State, "a live wire with good ideas,"[28] began a primary group at Salinas.

At Fresno, Rose Matsumoto and eight girls who had had scout leadership training taught nursery rhymes and games behind the laundries and under the fig trees. Eventually 14,000 Nisei, Sansei, and Issei went to the "Little Black Schoolhouse," using discarded textbooks from the Fresno city schools.[29]

Immediately on arriving at Tanforan, three evacuee teachers drew up a professional outline for an informal elementary school program, using imagination in the absence of supplies and books. They used newspapers to teach children to form complete sentences, to spell and pronounce. To "counteract bitterness" in the minds of the youngsters, they told flag stories and historical incidents. They taught arithmetic by letting the children play buying and selling at a grocery store. For art, they observed together colors and proportions in nature. On the first day of school two children, one fourteen years old and one sixteen, tried to enroll in the first grade. They were gently told the class was only for six- to eight-year-olds. The girls burst into tears. They had only recently arrived from Japan, wanted to learn English and were willing to sit with the first graders in order to do so.[30]

The Los Angeles superintendent of schools lent textbooks to Santa Anita, where an educational project resembling a correspondence school was organized with college students as tutors. Three interned Walt Disney artists put their imaginations to work to make learning to read a game for some 1,500 children. But accredited teachers were scarce.

Kyoko Hoshiga, a Mills College graduate, set up a library at Tanforan, which opened its doors in May with sixty-five books and a mass of inconsequential periodicals. Eventually she managed to accumulate several thousand volumes. The most popular book with borrowers there was William Shirer's *Berlin Diary*. Hugh Anderson, later with the WRA at Poston, purchased an Encyclopedia Brittanica for the Santa Anita library.

Temporary canteens and small stores sold limited amounts of merchandise at Army post prices on a first-come-first-served basis, accepting coupons in lieu of money. Major purchases were made through catalogues to mail order houses, which did a huge business both during the assembly center and the relocation center periods. Banking was also done by mail. Centers were in drastic need of shoe repair and similar services. At one camp, amateur barbers could be seen plying their trade on the streets.

As camp internees worked to make their lives as duration prisoners more bearable, their absence from the West Coast made an impact on the economy. Over 100,000 consumers were gone from the Pacific slope. *Business Week* had pointed out as early as February that evacuee expulsion from defense areas would force business to cope with "a serious problem of dislocation," particularly in factories and food-processing plants.[31] Field laborers were hard to find. The San Mateo County agricultural commissioner, Max J. Leonard, reported in August that the total production of chrysanthemums would decrease by $300,000. "About half the acreage once cultivated by the Japanese is now idle." But someday, he believed, chrysanthemums would again reign supreme in San Mateo County.[32]

The chief casualty was vegetable production. The United States was losing millions of dollars worth of vegetables and the work of thousands of skilled citizens. American Japanese had farmed about one-third of the truck crop acreage. They had produced 40 per cent of the California carrot crop, an important item in the diet of night fighters. In Los Angeles County, at the beginning of the assembly center period, where 18,000 farms and nurseries had once been operated by American Japanese, the County Department of Agriculture was desperately trying to find Caucasians to take over this enormous industry. In March they had only 165 offers. Laborers were being drawn into more lucrative factory work in war industries so that many housewives, school teachers, and retired persons had to pick prunes, cut apricots, or work in the canneries. Attempts were made to draft workers from other racial minority groups, with limited success. Late in the season the first trainload of five hundred imported Mexican laborers arrived in California to work in beets. The Mexicans were told they were "good will envoys." An Army release advised, "Our own welcome to these allies must be equally cordial and sincere."[33]

The wartime food shortage and the resulting high prices which imposed a hardship on military and civilian consumers was often a windfall for producers. The large land-owners became wealthier, when they could find workers, and many who for years had existed on a ragged financial edge achieved affluence. American Japanese had been an important part of the California economy. Now Caucasian operators had the field to themselves. Some areas adjusted fairly rapidly to the dislocation that followed the departure of the Japanese. Salinas, for example, increased its 1942 lettuce production by 6,000 acres over the previous spring.

Certain crops, however, faced countrywide failure for lack of harvest hands—particularly sugar beets. A number of prominent persons, among them California's Democratic Governor Culbert Olson, proposed a program of temporary work leaves for camp farmer workers in order to save this critical crop. Republican Attorney General Warren, who was soon to defeat Olson in the gubernatorial race, came out in opposition to this plan. Newspaper editorial writers as well as Olson's critics charged that he, knowing General DeWitt would never allow such a program, was simply playing for the Nisei vote. Others worried that American Japanese, allowed passes to work in the fields, might be offered the going wage in agriculture. LeRoy McCormick, district attorney of Tulare County, also argued that employers should not have to pay the expense of transporting internees back and forth between assembly centers and their work. Nevertheless, despite a good deal of sound and fury from a small segment of the population, including San Francisco Greek–American societies, a work leave program got underway in other states but not in California. In May Milton Eisenhower of the WRA announced a furlough plan, and work recruiters canvassed the centers.

At this time very few persons of influence on the national scene spoke out against the evacuation itself. "The history of these people [the American Japanese] is a history of betrayal," Wayne Collins, the indomitable San Francisco attorney who championed many American Japanese in their period of trial, says today, citing instance after instance of the indifference of otherwise liberal persons. Their attitude seemed to be, "It's too bad about the 'poor Japanese,' but what can you do?" They told themselves that these Americans of Japanese ancestry were a necessary sacrifice to the war emergency or that the program was "good for the country," or that one could not or should not "fight the Army," no matter how mistaken its action might appear to be.

Norman Thomas, a cofounder of the American Civil Liberties Bureau (later the Civil Liberties Union), many-time socialist candidate for President, and one who consistently throughout his career gave himself to the cause of the underprivileged and the oppressed, was probably the first national figure to speak out on the central issue of the evacuation—the fact that it threatened the democratic principles of the nation; that Americans were taking away the liberties of Americans. In predicting the coming of the war, which he feared, he had worried about a possible discrepancy between ends and means, in engaging in armed combat for a just cause. Propaganda and the authoritarian controls imposed by modern warfare would force us into imitating our enemies, he warned. Since he was on the side of the democracies as against the totalitarian countries, he promised that if war should nevertheless come no one would work harder than he to prevent his own dark prophesies from coming to pass. And no one did.

Reacting swiftly to the evacuation crisis, in speeches throughout the country, on radio, in articles, in a widely circulated pamphlet, he argued for reversing or stopping what was happening. In March of 1942 he wrote that the drastic handling of the Japanese problem on the West Coast was "a good deal like burning down Chicago to get rid of gangsters. . . . It sets an enormously dangerous precedent for military dictatorship over our own liberties. It will be taken in other countries as another proof of racial arrogance. The worst feature of the whole bad business is the small volume of protest and the considerable volume of applause from the West Coast for this establishment of military despotism. What a way to defend democracy."[34]

A letter signed by Thomas, John Dewey, Harry Emerson Fosdick, Reinhold Niebuhr, Harold Rugg, Clarence Pickett, Oswald Garrison Villard, and many others, asked President Roosevelt to rescind the evacuation order. At a special conference of the Post-War World Council a compromise resolution framed by Thomas and passed by a narrow margin urged keeping evacuation confined to its present geographical limits, taking the entire matter out of military hands, exempting Nisei from the orders, and establishing boards for individual hearings for both aliens and civilians. Ironically, the most vociferous group opposing the resolution was the Japanese–American Committee for Democracy organized in New York, which declared that the government's action was a contribution to victory for the Allied nations.[35]

Even in the American Civil Liberties Union which might predictably have taken the lead in challenging the evacuation, Thomas had to contend with those he called, "totalitarian liberals." The Union commented on the President's Executive Order: "Unquestionably the most serious violation of civil rights since the war began will arise with the enforcement of the President's order permitting military authorities to establish zones from which all aliens and citizens alike may be evacuated."[36] But taking a cautious position, the national director, Roger Baldwin, said the Executive Order was "undoubtedly legal in principle, but may readily result in illegal action."[37] The fact that the Executive Order was issued by Roosevelt significantly altered the protest. Roosevelt was a figure of great personal appeal with a deserved reputation as a champion of the underdog. It seemed inconceivable to civil libertarians, some of whom were his personal friends, that he could be taking such a drastic step on inadequate evidence. Having approved the President's order the national board then turned around and found fault with most of the particular Army directives issued under its authority. The President's order, though it gave power over civilians to a military commander, had not specified evacuation on a racial basis. Arthur Garfield Hays, Osmond Fraenkel, and Roger Baldwin wrote later, ". . . we opposed from the beginning the exclusion of any persons on racial grounds. . . ."[38]

The Northern and Southern California branches of the ACLU, showing the same inconsistency, reported that 144 of their members favored the President's order, as against 84 opposed, while only 110 favored an order of DeWitt's, which 113 opposed. There were 117 who favored testing the constitutionality of the orders as applied to citizens, with 120 opposed, and 188 who favored the establishment of hearing boards, with 67 opposed.[39] Later that month members of the national ACLU, in a statement signed by John Haynes Holmes, Arthur Garfield Hays, Roger Baldwin, A. L. Wirin, and Carey McWilliams, among others, urged the President to institute a system of hearing boards to test the loyalty of Nisei. In Northern California Ernest Besig and Wayne Collins took the position that hearing boards were not a valid solution to this civil liberties problem since under American law it is presumed that all citizens are loyal except when by acts they prove otherwise.

Although some civil libertarians had attempted to persuade their Japanese friends to resist evacuation when they were first sent to assembly centers, most of the Nisei were loathe to add to their troubles by becoming guinea pigs for a legal principle. A few resisters had "disappeared." A thirty-seven-year-old man had hidden for twenty-one days in his employer's basement, where he was found in June. A retired Navy seaman had been removed by force to an assembly center. A twenty-one-year-old Irish Japanese who had been posing as a Mexican was sentenced to six months in a county jail. His Irish mother had accompanied his father to a center.

In the state of Washington, a Nisei woman, Mary Asaba Ventura, and her husband, a native of the Philippines, had appealed to the law to prevent her imminent evacuation so that she would not have to disobey orders. But the judge in this first test case stated that she was making a premature complaint, that she was trying to be relieved of imprisonment before it occurred. In regard to Mrs. Ventura's application for a writ of *habeas corpus*, the judge declared that since curfew orders applied at night and there was nothing to prevent her freedom of movement during the day such a writ was unnecessary. She could, if she wished, come into the courtroom or listen through the open door. If she violated the orders later, she would be assured of a fair court trial and all her constitutional guarantees. The judge continued, "How many here believe that if our enemies should manage to send a suicide squadron of parachutists to Puget Sound that the Enemy High Command would not hope for assistance from many such American-born Japanese?"[40]

Lincoln Kanai, a San Francisco YMCA secretary, analyzed the Nisei predicament in a long, mimeographed letter sent to friends early in the spring of 1942. He was in sympathy with the United States war effort, but the evacuation orders were a "tragic error." He predicted that American Japanese would cooperate despite everything that had happened to them in order to win the war. They were prepared to accept the temporary loss of rights and privileges. In time, the hysteria would change to "right thinking."[41] Then shortly afterwards he left the evacuation zone, disregarding freeze orders, going about his business as if the orders had never been issued. Already active in the relocation of Japanese–American students, he went from city to city tending to various matters, sounding out important people on evacuation and arguing its injustice. He made no attempt to hide, but wrote a number of detailed letters back home concerning his activities. He was arrested in Milwaukee while attending a YMCA conference. Perry J. Stearns and other liberal lawyers in Milwaukee attempted to procure a writ of *habeas corpus* for him. This was denied, and the judge sent him back to the Coast. There he was sentenced to a six-month prison term. Since Kanai was a foundling raised by Hawaiians, there was some question as to whether he was actually of Japanese descent and therefore properly subject to the Army orders. But he cared little about this point. The emphasis in his prepared statement was on citizenship. Evacuation was a "domestic problem of civil liberty, not a problem of loyalty," he argued.[42] The aims of democracy were embodied in the Constitution, and whenever discriminatory measures which ignored due process of law were "made by a numbered few," then he would oppose them. He made his confession "willingly and without duress."[43] Optimistic communiqués were issued regularly from his places of confinement. He found the experience of being imprisoned "socially unique and interesting,"[44] while sitting in a cell gave him a "chance for meditation" and sharpened his convictions.[45] He served time in the federal penitentiary at Dupont, Washington.

On the evening of March 28, 1942, the day Kanai wrote his last letter from the San Francisco YMCA, Minoru Yasui, a twenty-five-year-old Nisei attorney, walked into a Portland police station at 11:20 P.M., well after the eight o'clock curfew hour. Yasui was presenting himself for arrest in order to test curfew regulations. He was a reserve officer, a second lieutenant in the United States Army, having taken ROTC training at the University of Oregon. He had been employed as an attorney by the Japanese consul in Chicago, but had resigned on December 8, 1941, and immediately offered his services to the Army only to be rejected for active service like many other Nisei at the time.

In deciding his case, Judge James A. Fee of the federal district court ruled that DeWitt's curfew order was unquestionably illegal when applied to citizens. While acknowledging a danger of invasion to the Pacific coast, Judge Fee pointed out that the perils facing the nation were "not more dreadful than those which surrounded the people who fought the Revolution and at whose demand shortly thereafter the ten amendments containing the very guarantees now in issue were written into the Federal Constitution." The civil power in this country is supreme, Judge Fee maintained. Military power, even in wartime, cannot be allowed to become dominant.[46] But in the same decision Judge Fee then asserted that Yasui himself did not come under this guarantee of justice to citizens because he had by the act of being employed as attorney for the Japanese consulate intended to renounce his citizenship.

Yasui's Issei father, who had come to this country to get away from the restraints of Japan, had sent his son a telegram urging him to go into the (American) Army and to serve his country. This was used against him; it was made to appear that he had been urged to serve the Emperor, the reverse of his father's message. Yasui realized that his former affiliation with the Japanese consulate was a handicap in his case, but no one else had "seemed willing" to violate the law in order to test it. For his stand, he wrote, "I have been formally and officially repudiated [in a JACL bulletin] as a glory-grabbing, self-styled martyr."[47]

Yasui was fined $5,000 and sentenced to twelve months in a road camp. The following year, the United States Supreme Court reversed both parts of Judge Fee's ruling, deciding that the citizenship matter was irrelevant, and that the Army curfew order was valid. The case was sent back to the district court to give it opportunity to strike its findings as to the appellant's loss of United States citizenship. Yasui was re-sentenced to eight months and ten days, the time he had already served, and was taken to the Minidoka center. While in the Multnomah County jail in Portland he had written that he felt like a "lonesome cowboy";[48] at Minidoka three hundred fellow detainees gathered in the dining hall and pledged him support. Nevertheless, he would have preferred "a thousand times" dying as an American citizen on the field of battle to enjoying the comparative comfort of the center.[49]

A young man with idealism equal to that of the militant patriot Yasui, but of different philosophy, Gordon Hirabayashi was a student at the University of Washington when war broke out. A year younger than Yasui, he was vice-president of the campus YMCA and a senior in the Arts and Sciences school. Hirabayashi described himself as a "conscientious objector to evacuation," and voluntarily surrendered to the FBI after refusing to register for evacuation from Seattle.

A Quaker whose immigrant parents had come to the United States for religious freedom, he said: "If I were to register and cooperate . . . I would be giving helpless consent to the denial of practically all of the things which give me incentive to live. I must maintain the democratic standards for which this nation lives. Therefore, I must refuse this order for evacuation. . . . I am objecting to the *principle* of this order which denies the rights of human beings, including citizens."[50]

In May, Hirabayashi was held in the King County jail in Washington for $5,000 bail, and it was anticipated that the Civil Liberties Union would make his a test case. "I think it is about time that this whole matter of what citizenship implies be cleared up and if there are any civil rights inherent then they should be observed and protected," wrote Grace Nichols. "If not, it is time we found out about it and ceased to live under such grand illusions as to what it means to be an American citizen."[51] Federal district Judge Lloyd Black, before hearing the Hirabayashi case in July, indicated he intended to uphold evacuation and internment. This he did, citing *Yasui* and *Ventura*.

The Supreme Court of the United States, deciding the *Hirabayashi* appeal in a companion case with that of *Yasui*, upheld the constitutionality of the curfew order as applied to Americans of Japanese descent. Concurring in the unanimous report delivered by Chief Justice Harlan Stone, Justice Francis Murphy nevertheless noted the "melancholy resemblance to the treatment accorded to members of the Jewish race in Germany" and said that the decision took the justices to "the very brink of constitutional power."[52] Justice William O. Douglas expressed somewhat mutually contradictory opinions. "It is true that we might now say . . . there was ample time to handle the problem of the individual rather than the group basis. But military decisions must be made without the benefit of hindsight. . . . Loyalty is a matter of mind and of heart, not of race. That indeed is the history of America. Moreover, guilt is personal under our constitutional system. Detention for reasonable cause is one thing. Detention on account of ancestry is another."[53] Nevertheless, he, too, concurred in the judgment. The Court took advantage of the fact that Hirabayashi had been sentenced concurrently on two counts—violation of curfew and violation of evacuation orders—to avoid the issue of the constitutionality of evacuation and internment entirely. The decision was on the curfew order alone. Hirabayashi served a three-month sentence in a prison camp near Tucson, Arizona, in the fall of 1943.

According to most judicial thinking at the time, idealists like Hirabayashi, Yasui, and Kanai should not set their personal principles against official military judgment. Americans had to trust in the good faith of the Army commander—to believe that he was acting not from reasoning based on race prejudice but on military necessity. In the Hirabayashi case, as in others, the judges attempted in their statements to disassociate the decision from the question of racial prejudice, though in view of what had happened to the Japanese and to no other group as well as General DeWitt's statements connecting disloyalty with racial inheritance, this was difficult to do.

Another evacuation resister stayed behind for more earthly considerations—for romance rather than principle. Fred Korematsu, a graduate of the public schools in the Oakland area of California, employed as a welder at a trailer company, was arrested in May as he came out of a post office. He was charged with violating curfew regulations and failing to leave a restricted area. A reticent person of unquestioned loyalty, Korematsu had previously attempted to enlist in the United States Army and had been turned down because of stomach ulcers. For a time he worked in an Oakland shipyard, but was discharged when the Boiler-makers' Union canceled his membership for racial reasons. He was not a dual citizen, did not speak Japanese, and most of his acquaintances were Caucasian. Because he was romantically interested in a Caucasian girl and did not want to leave the area, he had undergone facial plastic surgery, had changed his name, and had been posing as a Spanish–Hawaiian.

He was held in the San Francisco County jail. The Northern California branch of the ACLU posted a bail bond, but instead of releasing him on the bond, the jailer phoned the Army and military police took him to Tanforan. When the bond was raised to $2,500, Korematsu refused to sign it. He was put in jail once more, and thus his counsel was able to file a demurrer with the intention of challenging the congressional statute under which he was arrested.

As has already been noted, the national office of the Civil Liberties Union generally took a more cautious approach toward these viola-tions, deliberate or otherwise, than did its Northern California branch, or at first, the Southern California branch. The thinking of most young Nisei prominent in the JACL was similar to that of the ACLU during this period. The Reverend George Aki of San Luis Obispo, who feels today that it is "sometimes a disservice to your country to bow the head," reflected the Nisei leadership's thinking at the time of evacuation and in-ternment. Those who defied orders were an embarrassment, he felt then; they were making it worse for the rest. Nisei should be law abiding whether the laws were just or not.

Leaders in both organizations wanted to wait for some more propitious moment for challenging the evacuation orders. An exchange of letters between a Southern California ACLU attorney and a JACL official also indicated a desire to find persons of a more conventional stamp to offer themselves for test cases. Since the JACL civil rights fund was suf-fering a severe deficit the ACLU underwrote their expenses though the Northern California branch of the ACLU barely had a budget during these years. Its executive director and a longtime woman member of the board sometimes supported the branch and its cases from their own pockets.

While the JACL and the national ACLU confined themselves to questions of due process and hoped for a change in the fortunes of war and the American temper, cases were being heard in lower courts on their way up to the Supreme Court. After the referendum vote which had revealed the membership's reluctance to test the constitutionality of the evacuation orders, the national ACLU office had prevailed upon the Seattle branch to withdraw from the Hirabayashi case, and to sub-mit a "friend of the court" brief on limited grounds instead. The na-tional office had also attempted to prohibit the Northern California branch from challenging the revocation of Yasui's citizenship along with curfew regulations. To prevent controversy, the Northern California ACLU had filed their brief in the name of their attorney, Wayne Collins. Later the national office filed an *amicus curiae* brief for Yasui in the Supreme Court. When the national office sought to persuade the Northern California ACLU to withdraw from the Korematsu challenge, a committee from the San Francisco office decided that, since they had already agreed to undertake Korematsu's appeal, they could not withdraw in good faith. Consequently, the group took on the responsibility for the case until it finally reached the Supreme Court in 1944 along with a companion case—that of Mitsuye Endo, a young Nisei woman who challenged the detention program. These two cases were the most important of the evacuation years.

Throughout the assembly center period many friends outside continued to hope that there might be a rescission of the Army orders for mass imprisonment, particularly after the first months of the war were past and the fear of invasion relaxed. Though often subject to harassment, these friends of the American Japanese held to their positions—in speeches, in daily contacts, in letters to public officials, and to editors of newspapers. Sometimes they were rewarded with a hearing, more often their appeals met with no reply. Caleb Foote, today a professor of criminology at the University of California, urged people to write letters of protest. "These are our brothers, in deep distress," he said. Alleviation was not enough; the government should admit its mistakes before the program went on any longer.[54] But—although he pointed out that the matter was no longer "in his department"—United States Attorney General Biddle, in answering questions toward the end of August, regarded the release of Japanese–Americans as "highly improbable."[55]

Instead of leaving camps for freedom, internees were being moved into more permanent camps farther inland. Aliens and citizens were boarding the trains once again. Doctors and administrators left with advance units to prepare the new centers. As preparations were made for the second uprooting, everybody became upset and nervous once more. By July, Marysville, Sacramento, and Pinedale, delivered of their thousands, were ghost towns.

The last day at Tanforan all the remaining evacuees ate in the same mess hall. Because something was wrong with the food, many became violently ill from their final meal. On October 30, its last evacuee resident closed the halls, locked the buildings, and checked to see that everything was in order. When they were gone the Navy occupied the center. Various Army agencies moved into other centers, which were "more ideally suited for troop use than . . . for housing of families," according to General DeWitt.[56] Walerga, the first to shut its gates, became an Army signal corps replacement depot. As Salinas detainees were leaving, linoleum was laid in the kitchens and the infirmary.

The Santa Anita center took the longest to empty, from April until October when the only reminders of its 18,000 former occupants were deserted barracks and a message scribbled on a building, "Left for winter resort."[57] The Fresno center was the last to be cleared. On Friday, October 30, a young Fresno woman, Hiroko Kamikawa, a former junior at the local state college and daughter of a grocery store operator, took the train to Jerome. On leaving, the Fresno people were thanked by the cigar-smoking center manager for being "good soldiers" and for obeying the rules without question.[58]

By November 1, the transfer was completed. After the Army had seen to transporting the evacuees into the new centers, their major duty in the evacuation program ceased, and 120,313 persons came under the custody of the War Relocation Authority. Mrs. Mary Tsukamoto, ready to leave for Jerome, wrote, " . . . frightened as we are . . . there is no room for tears. . . . Idleness and bitterness will deaden character."[59]

Teiko Wada, who had not been in an assembly center but had evacuated to Zone 2 thinking that would be far enough, boarded the train for some place in Arizona; that was all she knew of her destination. "I thought I was going in there to die . . . [that] they were putting people there and would just starve them to death. You know, you read so much about other countries that that's all I thought of."

EIGHT · A BAD DREAM GOES BY

OFTEN MISTAKING the freedom of the outside as the sign of a new start, like a sick man looking out his window and interpreting a day in autumn as the coming of spring, the evacuees had poured out of the assembly centers at the rate of five hundred a day. "It was the first time I had been outside that gate and it was a very unusual feeling," an evacuee wrote. "Beyond that gate one [felt] free, as though the air was fresher and more invigorating. It can't be explained. . . . Driving through the gate at Salinas Assembly was like breathing fresh air again after holding our breath for ages."[1]

Settling down in the ancient trains, they passed forests and towns and orchards, as they traveled through the green valleys of Washington and Oregon or the orange groves of Southern California. Everywhere they saw people going about their daily lives. One woman, passing near her own farm, caught sight of apricots on the trees, soon afterwards the Navy hangars at Moffett Field, and then the dry Mount Hamilton range. To many of the travelers the scenes outside the windows, so familiar at one time, now began to seem unreal as once again the strangeness of what was happening to them contradicted the every-day quality of the land-scape. The sights and sounds did not "ring true," as one of them said; there was a divorcement, a separation.

Sometimes they took a zigzag route and did not know why. Up north, back south, and then climbing and going through mountain passes, Altamount, Tehachape, feeling the pull of the heavily laden cars. As before, some trains traveled with the blinds down, or the blinds were pulled down when they entered a town. "It was like the secret move-ment of troops," the wife of a printer observes. "It took us five days to get where we were going. You weren't even supposed to know where you stopped—where you were. Well, we knew [when] we were in Albu-querque. We could read the signs; we peeked. We stopped in the Al-buquerque station. Pretty soon there were two troop trains on either side.

One was filled with Navy men; the other, Army. All of them wanted to know, 'Where are you going?.' We said, 'We don't know where we're going.' The soldiers and sailors flirted with the girls."

The evacuees became aware of the cars in which they rode—rickety and ancient. "They must have got them out of the relic pile," a grammar school teacher remarks. Some were equipped for gaslight and had mohair seats.

Status privileges were granted a Nisei business manager who helped the commander see that all the travelers were comfortable. He ate special food in a special coach with the Caucasians. Milk formulas for babies were prepared in the women's rest rooms. A newlywed teacher traveling in the fall boarded the train bound for Utah wearing a white sweater. It was charcoal-gray from soot when she arrived. An Inglewood nurseryman, mourning over the war, had let his beard grow since Pearl Harbor. He would not shave until the war was over, he said. "Nobody win war. Everybody lose."[2]

The weather turned hot as they entered the wastelands, feeling that, instead of going forward to something new, they were hurtling back into some forgotten past. The West Coast had disappeared, and this was primitive country. "Going across the Mojave Desert it got hotter and hotter," Mrs. Henry Tanda remembers. It had begun to get warm in the San Joaquin Valley for groups traveling to Poston from Salinas. The trains kept stopping for ice to keep the food fresh and the cars tolerable. Even so, much of the meat spoiled. People began to perspire profusely. Traveling from Salinas to Poston meant changing from 65° to a possible 130° in the shade. On Easter Sunday Poston temperature was already 110°. Exiles traveling to the wilderness from Merced or Turlock did not experience so drastic a change.

There were long waits at desert stations. In one party some students getting off for cold drinks in Barstow got lost, boarded the wrong train, then eventually found their own. As travelers got closer to Poston after miles of barren land, relieved here and there by sagebrush and mesquite, they could see a few cotton fields and herds of cattle. Then suddenly an oasis appeared just across the Colorado River. The Indian agency near Parker, Arizona, was located there, between Wickenburg and Needles. There were lawns, eucalyptus, and oleanders planted near the painted buildings where government employees worked and lived. Parker was a former mining town and still contained some of the remnants of its past—stores, covered sidewalks and saloons, rubbish and decay, "which the desert bleaches, but does not absorb."[3] Besides the government colony, ranchers and 1,200 Mojave and Chemehuevi Indians lived nearby. Also in this war year, 1942, husky Army troops were encamped for desert training.

At Parker, evacuees, mopping their faces and fanning themselves, transferred from trains to buses for the eighteen-mile trip to their camps.

Beyond the agency, the ground dropped almost to the level of the Colorado River and widened out into a great plain dotted with occasional tamarisk and cottonwood trees, and farther off a wilderness of "dust laden mesquite and creosote bushes."[4]

The three camps of Poston, later nicknamed Roaston, Toaston, and Duston by the internees, lay farther south, on the middle-western section of the 90,000-acre Colorado Indian reservation. The camps were to contain from five to 10,000 inhabitants each. Three miles lay between Poston I and II to the north, and between II and III to the south. Unlike the other centers, Poston was run primarily by the Indian Service headquarters at Parker and only indirectly by the WRA. Situated two hundred miles from Phoenix, the center was named for Charles Poston, the "father of Arizona," who had originally envisioned a great agricultural valley crossed by an irrigation system, a dream which "had never become a reality."[5]

An evacuee, coming in to Poston under the equatorial sun of July, found that people were suffering from nosebleeds and from heat prostration. Another said, "People kept falling down. We thought it was Devil's Island!" Cots were provided for the faint. Sunstroke cases were hospitalized. In a short time there were seven deaths among the travelers from Salinas. Those who greeted the newcomers during "the intake" dispensed ice water, salt tablets, and wet towels in the mess halls. New arrivals were constantly urged to hurry along.

Issei going through the "intake," according to Dr. Alexander Leighton, a Navy psychiatrist who was sent to Poston to study the evacuees in their concentration camp environment, were "weary, sweating and polite."[6] They went through the registration lines with their heads held high. He also observed that, despite the long trip, there were "remnants of daintiness among the women."[7]

Immediately after being fingerprinted, before people could go to their quarters, work corps enlistment forms were put into their hands for signing. Swearing loyalty to the United States "in thought, word and deed," enlistees agreed to serve as members of the corps "for the duration of the war and fourteen days thereafter."[8] They swore further to accept "whatever pay, unspecified at the present time, the War Relocation Authority determines. . . . In doing this I understand that I shall not be entitled to any cash or allowances beyond the wages due me at the time of discharge from the work corps; that I may be transferred from one relocation center to another by the War Relocation Authority; that medical care will be provided, but that I cannot make a claim against the United States for any injury or disease acquired by me while in the Work Corps." They pledged financial responsibility for use of all government property while working and acknowledged themselves liable to trial and punishment for infractions of rules.[9]

Some, suffering as they stood from clutching their bundles and children, tried to puzzle out the form. Most, however, "even lawyers," signed without reading, according to Leighton. A "very few" refused.[10]

Shown to their barrack rooms, they found them almost identical to those in the assembly centers they had left—the same lack of protection from the elements, sacks to be filled with hay by the first arrivals. A man, writing in Japanese to a friend soon to be moved to a relocation center, urged him to do all in his power to be sent to some camp other than Poston. Go to Tule Lake, he advised. He himself had vomited blood on smelling the unfamiliar desert. He had feared consumption, but the doctor told him it was an upset stomach.

"We spray water in the rooms and wet our cots and we carry wet towels over the head whenever we go out," he said. "Thus, we are really having a duck's life here. The people [have] lost their smile in their faces . . . they are panting and panting. . . . The other day one of the guards died of heat prostration."[11] Ice ran low and people petitioned for the immediate erection of an ice plant. Then the temperature which had killed babies and the aged dropped to 110° for a few days, and they heard of nose bleeds that did not stop. "Truthfully, I must say this scorching Hell is a place beyond description and beyond tears."[12]

Sitting in a puddle on the floor with a wet towel across her shoulders and on her head, a school teacher made entries in her diary: "Haven't had enough energy to write or do anything but try to keep cool and keep going. . . . Arrived Sunday afternoon in Parker at one P.M. It was exactly 24 hours on that terrible train."[13] A small child across the way had been stricken by the heat. Next door, another girl suffered heat prostration and delirium. "She fought furiously." She was taken to the hospital in Camp I where she was unconscious for more than a day. "There are so many people just collapsing." The previous evening they had had a severe electrical storm and downpour of rain. "It twisted awnings and window coverings away." The dust had been bad, "but it is a little settled now. . . ."[14]

The internees all slept on cots out of doors, some between wet sheets. Hot winds blew at night, almost taking their sheets away. To cool the poorly ventilated rooms closely quartered with people, which increased the discomfort, the evacuees kept the floors wet, constantly pouring water upon them. In a letter to a Caucasian friend, the teacher asked to be sent an old white sheet that her family had left in Salinas to use for awnings; also a garden hose, a carpenter's plane, and a large square from their ranch. She desperately needed a straw hat with at least a six-inch brim. Packages had arrived addressed to her, but she had not had energy to open them.

People came out of the hospital looking rested, but thinner and weaker. Heatstroke in those who survived could waste muscle tissue and make walking difficult. One young couple used to leave their babies asleep on the couch while they went to the mess hall for lunch. If the babies wet their diapers, they would be dry by the time the parents returned.

The teacher made an air cooler and a dressing shelf with the tools sent her from home. " . . . it fell down one day when the neighbor next door was trying to put up some shelves, too . . . my jar of melted cream spilled all over my things. I laugh when I think of it now, but it wasn't funny when it happened. That's been the extent of my carpentering."[15]

The suffering at Poston from the heat and elements was perhaps the most severe of all the desert camps, although a Caucasian employee at the Gila River center where the temperature could climb to 125°, reported that at times you could not take hold of a doorknob without a handkerchief in hand. Gila residents sometimes prepared baths by leaving buckets of water out in the sun to heat. At other camps, too, salt tablets were dispensed, and heatstroke victims were hospitalized. It was "hot enough" for Mary Adachi at Topaz in Utah. Her family was allowed to purchase an air cooler since her mother was ill. "It didn't help much unless you were right in front of it." Electrical appliances were not generally encouraged because they blew fuses, although the fuse problem was not so great at Topaz as it had been at Tanforan. People without the money to spend on professional models often fashioned their own. Robert Wada, a member of the internal police at Gila River, made one of these coolers for his family quarters. A primitive version of today's air conditioners, it consisted of a three-foot square box and a fan. Inside the box was hardware that held water. The fan drew cooler air into the house.

People carried umbrellas against the sun. Some dug cellars four to six feet deep below the black tar-papered barracks that absorbed the heat and there spent the hottest hours of the day. Parents created shade areas for the children so that they could play outside without getting sunstroke. At Poston, unlike Topaz and other places of almost total barrenness, there was some green to be seen in the distance: sagebrush, arrowwood, willow, and cottonwood trees grew nearby. Some of the more energetic men went into the brush to clear little shelters and retreats. Slowly the area began "to look like a park, with crude benches, tables, and chairs appearing every so often." Sometimes they caught a glimpse to the "many shaded blue mountains . . . through natural arches made by the mesquite trees."[16] But a volunteer party going out to work in the brush found the arrowwood so high they could hardly breathe, and the fluff from the cottonwood trees got into everyone's eyes; they enjoyed a respite as they swam in the river.

The dust that had been an omnipresent annoyance in the assembly centers proved nothing in comparison with the sand and dust in the wasteland camps. In trying to get about in some of these places, people were apt to sink ankle to knee deep in sand. In the powdery soil at Topaz they walked "with slow, deep steps," pulling their legs way up with each step.

On the terribly hot September day, when Esther and John Sills, well-known ceramists today, drove to Gila River where they were to work and teach, they were greeted as they came down from the Salt River Canyon by a "whopping sand storm." Being met by fierce desert dust storms was a common experience of evacuees entering the desert camps. Leighton described a bus with forty passengers coming into Poston as "plowing through the dust, like a ship in a choppy sea."[17] Poston residents dubbed the dust "Arizona fog." Mary Adachi, who arrived at Topaz in one of these storms unable to see more than two or three feet ahead, recalls, "Everybody's hair and eyebrows would be snow-white with sand." A Terminal Islander remembers walking around at Manzanar "with towels over our noses and faces, eating sand by the mouthful." A Poston girl complained, "Our mouths are always gritty."[18]

Evacuees learned to live with the ferocity of the dust and winds. When a wind storm came, they covered everything over if they had time and "stayed put" until it went away. Watching a baseball game at Topaz they could see the dust coming; in about two minutes nobody at all was there, they had run for cover so fast. Sometimes they were blinded by the sand and found they had run into the wrong room or barracks. Motor traffic came to a standstill during the sudden storms which hurled particles of sand so hot they burnt into the skin. An evacuee ascribed to Satan a great wind traveling about seventy miles per hour which struck Poston about eight o'clock in the evening on the twenty-second of July the year of arrival. It was another of the devil's tests upon them, he felt. Roof tops were ripped off and went sailing through the sky "like giant leaves."[19] Stopped only when they collided with poles and wires, the roofs dropped to the ground. So did the power lines, and the next day the camp had no electricity and water. This particular storm caused $50,000 worth of damage, but there were no human casualties. Were it not for the storms at Amache, the relocation center at Granada, Colorado, a man wrote, the climate would have been fine, because they were 3,600 feet above sea level. It reminded him of Sonoma County in California.

But none of the housewives living in the desert could ever sweep their floors clean, although the knotholes and the shrunken boards with spaces between them were sometimes a help. Too, the holes were useful as ashtrays. "During a windstorm, which was quite frequent, the rooms were as dusty inside as out," according to Mary Watanabe who was at Poston and later at Topaz. When it rained the fine silt turned the camp into a mudpuddle. The roads were sprinkled and later hardsurfaced, which helped. A Minidoka resident says, "Nothing would grow. I can remember only one garden, other than that, nothing. . . ." Dust settled on the typewriters and was noticeable even while writing a letter."[20] Dust and heat raised havoc with watches and clocks.

Togo Tanaka recorded his thoughts during a dust storm at Manzanar: "It was mostly in such moments as these, when our eyes became bloodshot with the fine dust, our throats parched, and I suppose our reason a little obtuse, that we fell into the common practice of trying to figure out just how in the world we would find our way out of this manmade hell. As I think back now, I must admit it was a most stimulating occupation. . . .

"I am glad that throughout our eight months of residence . . . we never for a moment within our hearts accepted our internment with any degree of resignation. For to do so would have meant that we had reacted either with bitterness or with the loss of that spirit which drove us relentlessly to seek our way out."[21]

The Reverend Allan Hunter recalls that Manzanar churchgoers advised preachers to avoid the text, "I shall lift up mine eyes unto the hills." They had heard it before. As they pointed out, during the dust storms they could not see the hills, anyway.

Near most of the desert camps evacuees found those creatures which lived in heat and sand: land turtles and centipedes, rattlesnakes, black widow spiders, scorpions, and mosquitos. The little reptiles which stood stationary and stared as people went by were not lizards; they were poisonous baby gila monsters. A teen-ager watching a truckload of boys being taken from the Gila camp during the segregation program of a later period stepped on a venomous scorpion and was stung. She soaked her foot in a bucket of ice for hours and recovered.

According to one Nisei the stories that had come to them in the assembly center of rattlers and poisonous insects were all true; however there was a good deal more fear than there were casualties. Not being allowed hunting weapons, the braver Issei men would go out into the desert with forked sticks to capture the rattlers, bringing them back alive to display in camp, the length of the reptile and the number of his rattles being equivalent in sports prowess to antler points on a deerhead. Using a long pole Hawaiian Kibei boys from Okinawa captured snakes seven feet and over just out of hibernation. Others used two sticks and their bare hands. At Jerome, Gila, and elsewhere gourmets would skin and broil the glistening white flesh of the snakes, seasoning it with *shoyu*. At swampy Jerome a cage was exhibited in a recreation hall containing ten to fifteen rattlesnakes, many copperheads, and one beautiful coral snake. An evacuee at Gila managed to finagle an egg a day from the poultry project for his pet gila monster.

But the average residents directed their energies to such matters as procuring mosquito screens. At Poston the screens lay in warehouses for months, finally to be released in November at the end of the mosquito season. Flies which crawled all over perspiring faces were perhaps of more concern than snakes. Residents sent away for muslin and netting with which to screen their rooms. Crickets crawled through the cracks between the floor boards and ate people's clothes.

"Clothing wore out fast in the Arizona sun and with the harsh water," according to Mrs. Ray Okamoto, "and the clothing allowance was totally inadequate." The Okamotos had been evacuated from Visalia, California, to Poston, and had been forced to leave a daughter behind in a Fresno hospital because she had whooping cough. When she recovered, the child was sent on to Poston. Another baby was born in camp during the winter. As the next summer came on, the government shipped Mrs. Okamoto's refrigerator to her so that she could keep the milk fresh. She used to get up at 4:30 in the morning to wash diapers ahead of the crowd. It was noisy on summer nights, and the children played and cried all around them. There was little sleep to be had. She and her husband wanted to leave as soon as it would be possible, but it was two and one half years before they could do so. Of her Poston experience, Mrs. Okamoto says, "A bad dream went by."

The total list of these more permanent, prison-like camps was ten: Manzanar and Tule Lake in California, Poston and Gila River, both on Indian reservations in Arizona, Topaz, which was sometimes called Central Utah, Amache in Colorado, Heart Mountain in Wyoming, Minidoka in Idaho, and two camps in Arkansas—Rohwer and Jerome. Plans for an eleventh, Otwell, also in Arkansas, were dropped. Construction on Heart Mountain and Amache did not begin until the end of July. Topaz, Jerome, and Rohwer were finished even later, with residents streaming in heavily in the autumn.

The ten had been culled from a possible three hundred sites by a number of cooperating government agencies, including the relocation authorities, the office of Indian Affairs, the Soil Conservation Service, the Bureau of Reclamation, the Bureau of Agricultural Economics, the Farm Security Administration, the Forest Service, the Public Health Service, and others. The sites had to be remote from military zones but accessible to railyards or highways, had to have adequate water and power and at least 7,500 acres of land with agricultural possibilities. The land had to be government owned or controlled, and the projects were not to displace white settlers. As a result the tracts selected were places where no one else would choose to live.

Physically and psychologically, the camps were much alike in their isolation, in the ruggedness and primitive character of the terrain, in their confinement and almost total lack of conveniences at the start. Topaz, with a population of 8,000, was perhaps the most barren of all the camps in appearance. The terrain was absolutely flat, and residents, looking in one direction, could see apparently forever into the horizon.

Looking the other way they could see a mountain range, very small and far away. There was nothing but sagebrush for vegetation; there were no trees at all until later a few were planted around the hospital and the administration buildings along with some sunflowers. After that it was not quite so dusty. There were twisters or whirlwinds and heat in the summer and snow in the winter, but the spring was fairly nice, at which time the sagebrush appeared to be a little greener than in the winter. Topaz was near the towns of Abraham and Delta in Utah's Millard County. It was 140 miles south of Salt Lake City. Most of the San Francisco Bay Area people had been transferred there from Tanforan. Like city real estate developments named after imaginary lakeviews, the streets running north to south at this center were a study in overcompensation: Ponderosa, Locust, Cottonwood, Greasewood and Elm, Tamarisk, Willow and Juniper, named for the trees indigenous to the area but actually too far off from the camp to be seen. The soil was too alkaline even for greasewood. The area in the environs of Topaz was rich in gems and minerals, however, as the camp name itself and its streets running east and west attested—Alexander, Malachite, Jasper, and Obsidian. Climatically speaking, Topaz was improved by its 4,561-foot altitude.

The camp itself was crowded into a typical square-mile barbed wire enclosure. The barracks were the familiar black tarpaper; there were forty-two blocks, twelve barracks per block, here and there a recreation hall—the usual picture. But to one of the residents who had come from Santa Anita, even as she slept in an unfinished room with the rain showering upon her bed, Topaz represented comparative freedom: to her it was "a haven of peacefulness."[22] Despite crowded conditions, she commented that at Topaz there was at least no everlasting emphasis on "cooperation," a word of which all had become very tired. But a Topaz bachelor did not find much comfort in his unfinished room with its open roof: he was badly burned when hot roof tar fell on him.

The desert camp at Gila River was physically better appearing than Poston or Topaz. Teiko Wada, who had believed they were all being sent away to die, perhaps of starvation, found the camp at Gila was not so bad as she had anticipated. The buildings were whitewashed and, like those at Manzanar, they all had red roofs, not black. The soil was good enough for residents to achieve favorable results from their gardening efforts. The Superstition Mountains rose in the distance, and the hardier residents scaled them for exercise, though the rocks broke off in their hands as they climbed.

Yuri Katai recalls watching outside movies at Gila River. "We would all sit on a hill on an army blanket. A big cactus was sometimes in our way when we tried to see the screen. Once in a rain storm the lightning hit this cactus and smashed it to smitherines."

Amache near Granada in Colorado with its sagebrush and cactus, its cottonwood trees, its rattlers and prairie dogs, was arid and dusty like the others, but the camp was on a little hill surrounded by flatland at a 3,500-foot elevation. The heat, while considerable, was not quite so intense as at Poston. In October the snows began. Amache was located in Prowers County in the Arkansas River Valley, 130 miles east of Pueblo. The nearby town was Lamar where "Japs Not Wanted Here" signs were posted.

Melons and fruit grew on nearby farms. Half of Amache's 10,000 acres were under cultivation when the center opened, the land being reasonably fertile, though sandy. Water came from wells which had a pumping capacity of 1,000 gallons a minute.

To the north of these centers, Camp Minidoka in Idaho was a crescent-shaped site fifteen miles across set in an area described optimistically as "virgin desert sageland." The 68,000-acre tract was broken up by huge outcroppings of lava. Well guarded and drab, it housed approximately 9,000 evacuees. From extreme heat in the summer, temperatures dropped to twenty-five below zero in winter. Minidoka was later called Hunt after the town that supplied its postmark which was named for the first white man to explore the Snake River.

Because of the name, Tule Lake, George Shimada, on being evacuated from Burlington, Washington, had visualized a pretty spot in the woods. Located on a 26,000-acre tract of land in California's Modoc County owned by the Federal Bureau of Reclamation, Tule Lake, thirty-five miles south of Klamath Falls was actually a hot and dusty desert-type area covered by a sparse growth of tule and grasses. "All I saw for trees," he reports, "were watchtowers and chimneys sticking up out of the barracks." There was no lake, only a reclaimed lake bottom 4,000 feet above sea level. While the winters were long and cold, with temperatures that fell to twenty-nine below zero, from the point of view of climate, Tule Lake was probably the most pleasant of the ten relocation centers. The temperature never reached unbearable degrees in summer, and the air was dry. The black barracks-covered land stretched out for miles with two "mountains," Castle Rock and Horse Collar, in the distance, one shaped like an abalone shell, neither larger than a hill. But in appearance, according to Irene Takemoto, Tule Lake was "a pretty sad place."

A sense of isolation, a feeling of being forsaken pervaded all the camps. At Jerome and Rohwer, which were located in the swampy lowlands of Arkansas where there were trees and lush vegetation, the Caucasians who lived nearby, the hill people, were not themselves in the mainstream of American life. Internees in Arkansas were often better informed about the world and the war through their camp papers and radios than many of these natives. Jerome was near the town of Dermott, which was put off-limits after a visiting Japanese–American soldier was shot at by a local person. Rohwer was near McGehee in Desha County in the Mississippi River Delta of southeast Arkansas. The town of Little Rock was about 150 miles from Rohwer, but the evacuees never went there.

Clearing away the forest and brush was one of the first objectives at Rohwer, and the administration began sending evacuee surveyers to the wooded areas outside the camp. One such engineering party, working in the forest, was suddenly shocked to see shotguns pointing in their direction from out of the trees. The bearers of the guns stepped forth. They were local people, apparently unaware of the existence of the relocation camp close by. They thought the members of the surveying party were Japanese paratroopers who had been dropped onto their countryside, and they marched them into town, and down the street, to the city jail. There was no reasoning with them. The project director was forced to go down and get his evacuee surveyers out of jail.

As at the other centers, advance medical groups had come in early before there were even floors in the barracks. Camp Rohwer experienced the usual outbreaks of measles and mumps and some food poisonings. Epidemics though greatly feared did not occur but some former swampland internees, presently afflicted with arthritis, feel their disability began at Rohwer because of the unaccustomed heavy work and the sultry climate.

Jerome, in the low delta country, was likewise beautiful and damp. The heat and the penetrating "damp cold" were felt more. Rains were frequent with the result that most of the inhabitants were struck by the tropical beauty about them. Barrack gardens were rewarding, and great blossoms showed through their windows. "Between the barracks," according to Sada Murayama, "there was a trellis with morning glories, forming a tunnel of flowers. One block in particular was a showplace. Any outside visitors were taken there."

There was no need for guards in the towers at Jerome, and the fences were not high. The camp was surrounded by swamps infested with water moccasins. Four of the most deadly snakes in America were indigenous to the area. There was continuous danger of malaria, even though the Army had sprayed the swamps with DDT. Evacuees sometimes got permission to go beyond the fences to pick up wood or to gather mushrooms. But there was no telling what they might encounter when reaching for the mushrooms. A cartoon in "Lil Dan'l," a mimeographed booklet covering one year at Rohwer, showed frightened residents with rattlers all around them, and a little boy holding up a small snake. The boy was saying, "What are you afraid of? It's only anopheodrys aestivus."[23] Despite the beauty of the surroundings and displays of humor and fortitude, it has been noted that there was a low state of morale in the Arkansas camps.

While living facilities presented essentially the same picture as in the assembly centers, they sometimes varied in one place or another in certain details. Poston rooms were slightly larger than those at Heart Mountain. Generally of cheap, single-wall construction, some camp barracks had double walls, ceilings and closets, celotex, even occasionally linoleum. Other camps had none of these things. When floors were finally laid in Arkansas, they were of hardwood—made from native red oak cut from the surrounding forests. Floors at Amache were lined with brick, and the rooms had set-in heaters.

The problem of privacy remained. When families consisted of fewer than five persons, they had to be prepared for others to move in with them. Two small rooms on the ends of the barracks were reserved for couples. Walls were not built to the ceiling, but sick persons or parents worrying about their children overhearing people next door sometimes obtained special permission to put on their own sheet rock and to close up the openings between the rooms.

Again, as before, necessities were provided, but living was Spartan. Changes in regulations under the WRA allowed a certain amount of equipment and personal belongings to be shipped in at no extra cost from government storehouses—chairs, tables, sewing machines, but only occasionally refrigerators or stoves. A certain number of nonperishable foods were also allowed. Family washes were done on scrub boards, although Heart Mountain possessed a very few plunger-type machines. To do their washing or to take showers, internees might have to walk a mile in rain, snow, or dust, and "by the time you walk back you need another shower."[24]

A government information circular put out during this period implied the evacuees were fortunate. "Had canvas for great tent cities been available it would have been used. Tents would have been pitched and evacuees would then have gone to work building their new wartime homes. . . . The houses [as actually built] might be called 'basic' structures; they are soundly constructed and provide the essentials for decent living. They are not fancy, but they are good. . . ."[25]

Facilities were much improved by 1943. Nevertheless, a great many people were anxious about the cheap structures. If the barracks stood up for the duration of the war, they felt they would be lucky. The outbreak of fire in these flimsy buildings jammed close with people was an ever present concern. In a fire the shacklike structures of tar paper, celotex, and pinewood would burn to the ground within six or ten minutes. A strong wind at such a time might mean a major catastrophe. Fire hazards were numerous. At Topaz, stoves were close to the walls, and difficult disposal of hot ashes compounded the danger. People shoveled ashes out to the bare ground and wetted them down with water supplied by three deep wells. Personnel and evacuees there as elsewhere carried on extensive fire prevention programs. Posters and bulletins were displayed throughout the camp; warning articles appeared in the papers.

Until people learned to run the stoves inside their rooms at Heart Mountain properly there were a number of fires, none of them serious. A stray spark from burning rubbish at Manzanar ignited a brush fire which swept two hundred feet before twenty workers working frantically to clear a firebreak in front of the advancing flames got it under control.

All camps developed fire departments, giving evacuee firemen appropriate training and gradually building up equipment. Fire fighters received $16 a month and the captain $19. A canteen fire broke out in Block 41 at Tule Lake on the first of September, 1942, and families in the vicinity had to haul out their belongings. In November of the first year Topaz residents turned out to celebrate the construction of their fire station with a dedication ceremony. In June, 1944, Topaz had a $5,000 warehouse fire which started by spontaneous combustion in the paint shop. There were other fires, but due to luck and foresight they were not calamitous. The evacuees had feared fire and plague, but they were spared these disasters.

An important factor in fire prevention was the land improvement program—the establishment of adequate water facilities, brush clearance, repair of canals, roads. A typical operation in basic fire prevention combined with clearing and subjugation of the land was carried on at Poston I where a group of men, mostly Issei over fifty, made up what was known as the "firebreak gang." Richard S. Nishimoto, a highly intelligent, middle-aged, college-educated Issei with agricultural experience, was the project foreman. He was often mistaken for a Nisei. His group was expected to accomplish a number of monumental tasks. They were to clean up piles of scrap lumber left over from construction, separating out the usable material and burning the remainder. Between certain blocks there lay five acres of ground densely covered with refuse. Huge quantities of highly inflammable dry trash littered the area, some of it within twenty feet of the combustible barracks. The engineering department had first suggested clearance for dust control and to have cleared land on which to build a lateral system for farm irrigation so that vegetables could be grown.

Block managers were instructed to put all idle men to work on the project. A call went out for 250 workers. Of the one hundred who volunteered about thirty men stayed and labored to the end. When Nishimoto was first put on the job, he walked into a beehive of activity. Elderly Issei were energetically working, picking up lumber off the ground and throwing it into trucks and trailers, raking the remainder into piles. They worked fast. But it was June, and the heat was already considerable. No drinking water was available. Pretty soon the men began to complain and the pace of work slacked off. "Who do they think we are?" some said. "Hell, we're no slaves. We don't have to work if we don't want to."[26]

Men began to leave the job. Nishimoto sent boys out for pails of drinking water and talked to the men, advising them to rest between loadings, to slow up and set their own pace. Only forty-five came back after lunch. The foreman determined to try to get higher wages for them. He tried treating them with more respect, by addressing them in Japanese, in the polite form. He wanted them to forget their bad experiences and to have faith in democracy.

A new kind of difficulty arose when Nisei boys were hired to drive heavy equipment. They appeared to derive a thrill from riding the tractors and liked to keep them moving. Often they did not wait for full loads but raced down the road, bouncing up and down, their loads scattering about them, "throttles wide open."[27] There were seven young drivers. Some of the machinery was disabled from this kind of use, and tires were punctured. The foreman solved the problem by discharging the youngest driver and making each of the others responsible for his machine for the day.

In July the thermometer was registering 110° in the shade at 10:30 in the morning. Men dropped out until only fourteen remained. The foreman ordered a fifteen-minute rest every hour in a shady place. This was appreciated by the men, and gradually the crew began to increase again. The trash was finally raked up. The job of burning it was complicated by dust storms and whirlwinds.

Farther off they began to dig out tree trunks, dragging them with heavy cables. They piled up branches and bushes of mesquite and cottonwood, which they had knocked down with the heavy tractors, and burned them, too. As they worked in the open, temperatures rose to 120°, 128°, and even higher. The men built a hut from scrap lumber and tar paper big enough for forty people where they could rest in the shade.

Nishimoto was under great pressure from the administration to work the men harder. They were supposedly to get $12 a month for this work. But when the foreman took a time sheet to a Caucasian supervisor, he refused to honor it, telling Nishimoto that the "Japs" were only volunteers and did not qualify for compensation.

The foreman fumed to himself, "God damn it! So we are Japs, are we? Ignorant bastard!"[28] Outwardly he remained calm and reminded the man they had been promised pay, even though they had no work cards. Receiving no satisfaction, he spoke to various people and finally found a woman employee who said she would see to it that these men—some in their sixties—were paid.

One day toward the end of July a number of the men were affected by the extreme heat. One became dizzy; others were nauseated. They went to the hut and lay down to sleep. A Caucasian came by and demanded to know "the meaning of all this."[29] The foreman had to make up an excuse: they were waiting for a tractor. The Issei workers were normally gentle in nature, according to Nishimoto, but they "could get quite excited and rebellious when people were authoritarian in manner." Hearing the foreman's answer they seemed to gain confidence in his sincerity with them and thenceforward developed a real *ésprit de corps.* Toward the end of August the weather cooled a little, and they were able to cover five to seven acres a day.

The men received their first pay checks to the tune of a "flowery speech" on August 27.[30] Several were disappointed and angered when they read the figures on their checks. Two had received only $7.83 for 196 hours of work, and another $10.81 for 180 hours. Two others were not compensated at all. One of them was destitute and needed the money badly. When he put up an objection he was mocked by one of the appointed personnel, but a top administrator, who was more reasonable, gave him a loan.

One of the most important projects at Poston was the construction of an irrigation canal that was to take water to the relocation city. On the hot morning of the fourth of July in the first year, 9,000 Camp II residents gathered near the firehouse to celebrate the canal's completion. To commemorate the event, some evacuees had purchased a number of small mulberry trees and planted them in a circle. In the evening when it was cooler, they gathered on the banks of the canal for a water festival. However, there was no water. It would not appear for some time until it was diverted from the Colorado River.

Once a training plane from a nearby Air Force base crash-landed at Poston II. Seeing the canal, the pilot mistook it for a landing strip. All the evacuees came running out, while a Nisei commented, "He must have thought he was in Japan."

The building or repairing of existing canals in other camps was often a part of the vast reclamation projects internee farmers were expected to accomplish. The swift-running Milner-Gooding canal adjacent to the Minidoka center, which was owned by the Federal Bureau of Reclamation, was in need of extensive repair. The canal was losing half its water through seepage. After fixing it the WRA planned on large-scale production of root and other vegetable crops on the wasteland thus reclaimed through irrigation.

As they proceeded to dredge and reline the canal with bentonite, a kind of clay that expands when it gets wet, evacuees simultaneously began to clear seventy acres of land by grubbing out sagebrush, so that the ground might be planted the following spring, in 1943. The work was done by hand, using a mattock, or grubbing hoe. It was a slow process. Finally, someone devised a contraption with rows of V-shaped iron bars three-quarters of an inch wide to be pulled by tractor over the sagebrush, breaking it off at the ground. The garage superintendent built the rig to specifications, and it worked fairly well except that occasionally the bars would become bent, because the ground was so hard. Later heavier equipment was brought in. A high school organization known as the "Hunt Ag Club" did a good deal of volunteer work after the roughest part of the clearance was accomplished.

In October swift-flowing water poured from the canal into a ditch to irrigate the arid agricultural land near the two-mile long living area of the community. Quick-growing seed was planted for dust control. Eventually more permanent laterals were constructed, and more acreage was brought under control.

Outside contractors employing Caucasian labor and bringing in their own machinery did the actual dredging of the main canals constructed or repaired at various other centers. At Gila River the government had made arrangements with the Pima Indians to turn back the reclaimed reservation land to them after wartime use. Vast acreage in the woods of Arkansas was cleared for agriculture. As might be expected, drainage rather than irrigation was the most important engineering problem in the swamplands. In November, 1942, a huge, eight-mile-long canal was completed at the Jerome center which carried off surplus water from the farmland, running it into the Boeuf River. Thirty varieties of vegetables were planned for the following spring on about 1,000 acres of cleared land, in addition to alfalfa and long staple cotton.

At first it was suggested by some officials that if evacuees were successful in land reclamation at Poston, some might be able to lease acreage from the Indians after the war. The plan was dropped, however, and no evacuee applicants were allowed to lease any part of the 90,000 acres they developed. Repeatedly as the work progressed the WRA publicity department beset by pressure from legislators and growers, reassured the general public that none of the wasteland being transformed by their labor would be made available to the evacuees after the war. "Evacuees will not be eligible for any rights or interest in the land they work," official spokesmen made clear."[31] Nor, the agency promised, would any of the vegetables they grew be sold outside the projects to compete with outside farm entrepreneurs, whatever the war emergency. Originally, the government had anticipated that not only would sufficient quantities of food be produced by the evacuees for use in the centers but that surpluses would help offset wartime shortages in the country as a whole. The Japanese could also experiment with rubber and silk. Some of these plans were spectacularly carried out, marvels of ingenuity and hard work. Many were not, in the words of a JACL official, "what they were cracked up to be." Some were abandoned entirely. While production was never so grandiose in most centers as originally anticipated, many miracles, both large and small, were accomplished during these years.

It was not only the idealists in government who imagined that out of the evacuation would come the transformation of the wilderness through the use of American Japanese labor, causing wasteland and desert to burst into bloom. Many evacuees had similar dreams. Isamu Noguchi, distinguished artist and celebrated designer of furniture and stage sets, as well as one of America's foremost sculptors, although from the East Coast accompanied his father, the poet Yoné Noguchi, to Poston. While there Isamu Noguchi worked on a number of ideas to promote group enterprise in what he hoped would be a model community. As chairman of the landscaping and park areas he drew up beautifully conceived plans. Finding clay in the soil suitable for pottery, he hoped to see established ceramic and woodworking apprenticeship guilds. A cooperative pottery factory would give people training, put them to work in a creative way, make use of native materials.

Many of his plans did not come to fruition. Man and nature and the difficult environment, proved resistant. The whole operation of getting the camps set up and running, the struggle to make a hostile land productive, all took time, concentration, and effort. Some had enthusiasm and understanding for the advanced and imaginative ideas of persons like Noguchi; others, including many evacuees themselves, often were indifferent.

The idea of using native materials was adopted at Poston when it was decided that adobe mud would be used for bricks in building the schools. Adobe provided good insulation, and schools made from it would be more permanent than the usual prefabs. Such construction, according to the engineer employed for the project, would make use of Frank Lloyd Wright's principle of allowing buildings "to slide over the undulating motion of the earth."[32] An Indian school made of adobe was situated seven miles away and was described as charming by an evacuee teacher with an artistic sense.

Building with adobe was time consuming. Mixing and molding the bricks in the desert heat, laying them out to dry and stockpiling them for eventual construction took months. Brick molders worked in sheds at the end of the firebreak in Camp II, and on the site of the future grammar school. Like the firebreak crew, they were paid $12 a month. Education for their children, always a positive value in the American Japanese culture, was held out as an additional reward. But many adobe workers had misgivings. Most had no desire to kill themselves in the heat. Some had a feeling that this particular kind of work was degrading. (At Poston there was a general feeling among the evacuees that the Japanese were being classed with a people whose culture they considered to be more primitive than their own. Anthropologists came to study them on the reservation. Teachers took training in Indian schools. The Director of Education of the Indian Service spent weeks in Poston working out school plans.) The workers had no real idea of what would become of them or their children after the buildings were built and the war was over. In August, 1942, fifty-six adobe laborers at Poston II voted to strike for the $16 a month pay they had been led to believe they would receive for the work. Concessions were made, and the strike was settled. Kitchens, recreation halls, and other spare places were to be used in the fall for classes until school buildings were ready.

A summer school was set up for seventy-five young evacuees, giving them a rapid teacher education course. Three times a week these teacher training students as well as accredited teachers went from Camp II to Camp I for lectures, where they perspired "like fountains," despite electric fans sent by friends. Speakers of high caliber lectured to them— an instructor in psychology from Oakland, John Collier, Commissioner of Indian Affairs, and others in the Indian Service. Dr. Miles Carey, former principal of McKinley High School in Honolulu, arrived to take charge of the schools.

Helen Aihara (Kitaji) who had helped build a school system at the Salinas assembly center, now began working again on a more permanent system here. She attended the classes at Poston I, gathered difficult to come by materials once more, and prepared herself not only to teach primary grade classes, but to do speech correction and remedial reading, new fields for her. Again she asked her San Jose teacher and other friends for materials—newsprint, speech correction, and drama books stored in the barn on her farm. "I'm ashamed to have to ask all this of you, but I see no way out."[33]

In between courses she hovered anxiously over the workers making bricks for the school. She wished the job would go faster. She would have liked to join in and help make them herself if they would only let her.

School began in September without buildings and with a teacher shortage. There were about 175 teachers in the Poston system. Those of Japanese descent were for the most part very young and barely trained. The fourth grade teacher, a Salinas Junior College graduate, faced each day a class of seventy-eight children without assistants. Helen Aihara had sixty-seven children in her first grade. "I have a great deal of respect," she wrote, "for all of these inexperienced youngsters who are courageously trying to give the children a chance to learn. All the other classes are much too large for good teaching."[34]

Teachers spent their time off scrubbing down classrooms and washing window sills and floors, carrying heavy buckets of water though the dust came in again as fast as they cleaned. The janitors were not very efficient. "We now have tables, twenty inches tall and home made chairs eighteen to nineteen inches high, so children keep toppling over. Pulling slivers has become an avocation."[35]

At last, in November John Collier broke ground for the first Poston school building. Eventually there would be seventy of them, built at a cost of $350,000.

During the course of her evacuation experience, Helen Aihara was trained as an Indian Service teacher and spent six months working with Navajo children at Fort Defiance. "It was another world, very interesting." She traveled a good deal during this period and saw "unbelievably beautiful country torn by over-grazing." She perceived the similarities in the problem of teaching American Indian children and American Japanese children: both were isolated in camps away from the general culture. Sometime later she was married and was allowed to leave Poston to be with her husband. When he was drafted, she returned to camp to rejoin her father. She must have had positive feelings about her teaching of the Indian children, because when her first boy was born at Poston, they called him "little Indian."

While Helen Aihara had arrived in Poston in the blaze of desert summer, others had arrived at their destinations amidst the chill portent of winter. When Eiichi Sakauye reached Heart Mountain on an evening in September it was twelve degrees below zero, and there was snow on the ground. Mr. Sakauye and his family were shown into a finished but bare barrack. They had no blankets that first night; so they cuddled up together and tried to keep warm. Several hundred later arrivals faced the same situation, sleeping on floors until center officials went out and bought bedding for them in nearby towns, because expected shipments had not come. Late arrivals were generally unequipped with the proper clothing, but at Heart Mountain and various other camps those who worked were given a limited amount of GI issue clothing and World War I Navy pea jackets weighing about twenty pounds each. Evacuees bought most of their cold weather clothes from the Sears Roebuck catalogue, although some clothes were issued through a welfare agency set up in the camp.

This northernmost WRA community, at 4,600 feet higher by over a thousand feet than Minidoka, had many of the same characteristics of other desert camps when there was no snow—the same flat, treeless scene, dry bushes, and raging winds. The Heart Mountain center was almost completely colorless. The landscape was "a dull, gray brown tinged with faint green during spring and early summer."[36] "I'd never seen such desolate country," Lily Aratani told newspaper reporters in Los Angeles.[37] The desolation stretched out many miles until it reached a group of low, shelf-like hills and the odd, flat-topped Heart Mountain that jutted up beyond. The camp itself was all black, the sides of the barracks and the roofs as well covered with black tar paper, except for the administration buildings, the hospital, and nearby soldiers' barracks. A high school built after October had tan walls and a red roof, which "stood out like an island in a sea of blackness."[38] A mile away was the muddy Shoshone River. Except for the warehouses, soldiers' barracks, and administration buildings, the camp was out of sight from the highway that ran from Cody to Powell.

The surrounding country was as barren of people as of vegetation. At night coyotes crept into the camp. The nearest towns had populations of 2,500, and although Heart Mountain became the third largest city in Wyoming it did not reach the 11,000 population first anticipated. When the temperature was around 75° or 80°, the air in this high place could be clear and bracing. The weather was "very good," an Issei, expressing himself with difficulty, wrote to an English-speaking acquaintance. But the water was "no good," and he was discouraged by the lack of green. "I making garden. But no good. I Bring plant from Pomona. Please sento to me Seed next Springtime."[39]

Evacuees and gardens alike suffered from frost. Very often the ground was so icy people fell down. Evacuee weather observers watched the changes of season, the snow, the rains, the winds, and kept temperature records. The lowest temperature recorded by one observer was over thirty degrees below zero.

Colonists at Heart Mountain described waking up at dawn in winter to the chorus of dishpans, the "roosters of a concentration camp." Inside the barracks people would stir. "Some groan and roll over. Others push back the covers and slip quickly into their clothes. Grabbing towel and toothbrush they go outdoors where the bits of snow and ice crunch under their feet. 'Cold,' they say to one another, and hurry towards the warmth of the latrines. . . ." Later, puddles of water which had been frozen hard all night begin to melt. When a boot lands on them they crack and break, and muddy water spurts up over the toe of the boot.[40]

Another wrote in a letter, "For the last few days we've been having a real taste of Wyoming winter. It started out with a blizzard—and, oh, what a blizzard! It's just like the kind we see in the movies. I never thought I'd really be in one. . . . The laundry and latrine barrack is about fifty yards away from our doorsteps. Dad wets his hair there and by the time he comes back to our barrack, his hair is frozen to ice!"[41] Hands would stick on doorknobs, and a damp towel carried outside for a short time would freeze so stiff it could be broken over the knee. School children at another camp held cans of hot ashes between their legs to keep warm in unheated classrooms, but coal was plentiful at Heart

Mountain. Volunteer carpenters began to line barrack rooms with celo-tex, and the administration's friendliness offset the chill weather. A group of Santa Anita arrivals who had been greeted personally by admin-istration officials immediately volunteered for disagreeable tasks which had been almost completely shunned at the assembly center.

There was a high rate of illness due to the cold, and the hospital was overcrowded in 1942 and 1943. The Caucasian administrator and the American Japanese head of the hospital were dedicated and humane, but the problems were great. An overwrought letter of grievances written on a very bad typewriter in the winter of 1942 by the chairman of an agitation group at Heart Mountain was sent to both the project direc-tor and to Dillon Myer, the head of the WRA. The letter, which differed considerably from antiseptic official reports by members of the camp health department, referred to an epidemic of colds and pneumonia, to the hospital bed shortage, the doctor shortage, to unbalanced diets, stomach ailments, and the frequent nausea of the residents. The ele-vation, the writer pointed out, was too high for many, and caused heart trouble. Arthritics and rheumatics were suffering.[42]

The work and the weather produced a great interest in meals. At ten in the morning people would start getting hungry again after early breakfast. And when they met they "did not say good morning. . . . We all [asked what there was] to eat and when,"[43] an evacuee wrote. Dur-ing a food shortage during the first months, one ladle of food was put on each plate at each meal. A generally uncomplaining, hard-working evacuee remembers going to bed hungry every night, "and I wasn't a big eater." The community protested, Caucasian kitchen personnel were investigated, and a number of workers were discharged for profiteering. "After that they gave us two ladles of food." Ranchers came from sur-rounding areas to sell chickens and eggs, which were cooked on hot plates. But after the first year, as the food production program began to be successful, most evacuees found the food plentiful and generally of good quality.

Heart Mountain was in Buffalo Bill country. Colonel Bill Cody him-self was said to have promoted the idea of the Shoshone irrigation proj-ect many years before American Japanese were set down in the Big Horn Basin to develop it. The project, like those in the other camps, was to serve several purposes—to be a genuine and permanent benefit to the whole area after the Japanese were gone, and aid in preparing some 27,000 acres of the total 46,000 in order to feed the camp, and, hope-fully, to provide surplus crops to exchange with other camps. Before the arrival of the evacuees, farming areas nearby were used mainly to graze cattle and sheep; the ranchers knew little of truck farming, or intensive cultivation of the land. Government plans anticipated the production of alfalfa, small grains, sugar beets, beans, potatoes, seed peas, and later possibly truck crops.

In the spring of 1943 the canal repaired by evacuee and outside labor finally flowed with water from melted snows stored in the reservoir, the water traveling over a twenty mile, twisting course to a spot four miles from the planned farming project.

Other challenges had to be met before food production plans could get underway. The weather station was set up under the direction of James Ito, the Nisei assistant supervisor in the agriculture department, a graduate in agriculture of the University of California. Soil analyses were made. A thousand acres of sagebrush were grubbed out, and manure was extensively applied to compensate for the lack of organic vegetable matter in the dehydrated soil. Then came the disking and plowing. Evacuee spirits rose as the smell of the fresh-plowed earth filled the air, and vast acres lined with furrows could be seen where only scraggly bushes had grown before. The building of greenhouses, designed by Toru Ino, was delayed due to slow action from Washington but they finally appeared on a slope south of the Heart Mountain *Sentinel* building. A reporter was able to write late in spring of the hotbeds "green with cabbage, broccoli and cauliflower seedlings."[44] The 6' x 48' beds produced many thousands of plants.

An urgent call went out for at least a hundred men to get the land ready for the drilling of the soil and the transplanting of the tender young seedlings. Glenn Hartman, who had been a professor of agriculture at the University of Wyoming, was chief of agriculture and industry at the center. The farm operation was headed by a Caucasian superintendent and his Nisei assistant, Eiichi Sakauye. About seven hundred men worked on the farm project. Some of the crew were former seedmen from Los Angeles, some were experienced farmers from Washington; others were from Santa Clara County.

According to Sakauye, the Nisei superintendent, the first year presented unusual difficulties, some unforeseen, because of the peculiar Wyoming farming conditions. The growing season was short—ninety to a hundred days. Snow lay on the ground occasionally at the beginning of June. The first snowfall of winter came in September. The short season was offset by the long hours of daylight in the desert summer at this far northern location. The first year, not having made allowance for the warm nights and long days, the evacuee farmers found that many crops matured twice as fast as they anticipated.

Because of the rapid maturation of crops, large numbers of harvest hands had to be recruited rapidly, and this was always difficult because of the low wages paid. "We worked harder than we were working on our own farms," said Mr. Sakauye. "In order to get out and harvest the crop we had to be on the ball. Once we had sixty acres of sweet corn to be canned. We went to the canning company to contract for having the corn processed, and that night it froze, and that was the end of the sixty acres of corn. That's why timing was very important."

In general, according to a block manager, evacuees tended to lose their enthusiasm for work in the camps. "Environment changed people." This did not apply to the farm crew, but "700 applicants out of 10,000 people is not a very big percentage." Sometimes, however, on the warm days which reminded them of spring back home, men would flock to the employment office, and mere onlookers at the farm project could be seen voluntarily "picking up shovels and hoes to help. . . . When asked about it later, they said they just wanted to get in and help without knowing what had made them want to. . . ."[45]

James Ito recalls that not only was the farm project able to call upon government agricultural experiment stations for aid and advice but it also received a good deal of help and advice from the scattering of neighboring farmers of Japanese descent who were permanently located in the surrounding Big Horn Basin. Evacuee farmers met with these neighbors to study local dry bean production; they, in turn, raised onions following the example of the evacuees. Mr. H. Kawano, one of these ranchers from Powell, gave the Heart Mountain farm project a start in string beans and *azuki* bean production by donating 150 pounds of beans.

The neighboring Issei, so hungry to speak Japanese, visited frequently in camp. The families were glad to find Oriental girls as marriage prospects for their sons. At least one evacuee girl married a farmer's son, a veterinarian.

Food production workers on the thousand-acre Heart Mountain development grew many varieties of vegetables never before seen in this part of the country—cucumbers, tomatoes, even cantaloupes and watermelons—and all types of Japanese vegetables, *gobo, karashi* (a mustard), *shirouri* (a white melon used for pickling), Japanese rice, *daikon, nappa,* and *takana.* Many of the vegetables, such as celery, were of prize-winning size and quality. The growing season was too short for soy beans. While the center never became quite self-sustaining, the farmers were able to produce a substantial supplement for their tables and to send some of their surpluses to other camps as well as store them for winter. One year because of an early frost the high school students, including girls, were released from classes to harvest potatoes fast enough to save them and store in the root cellars.

Daikon was always stacked in circles as it was picked, leaves to the outside, so that if a frost came this special radish would not be ruined before being taken to the commissary department for pickling which was done in a huge tank set in a hole dug in the floor of the warehouse. As in other centers, the commissary department also produced their own *moyashi* (bean sprouts). The mung beans for the sprouts had to be sent in, they could not be grown at Heart Mountain. But at Topaz 125 pounds of beansprouts had been grown on an experimental basis by Mr. and Mrs. S. Taguchi so successfully that the commissary department was soon producing 1,800 pounds per week. Heart Mountain, Topaz, and other centers also had their *tofu* factories which produced the soft-curd soy bean cakes that are a standard delicacy in Japanese diets.

Mr. Yuki, a former Seattle *tofu* manufacturer, built up this operation at Minidoka to the point where the supply allowed for servings twice a week in the mess halls. At another center a renowned dietitian who was interested in the bland *tofu* for ulcer diets studied its effect on hospital patients.

Storage cellars and pickling and canning for food preservation were common to all centers. Some centers had specialties: mulberry tea was dried at Manzanar on a small scale, and a contest was run to name the soy sauce produced there. It was called Manza. Sauerkraut was made at Tule Lake, the cabbage imported from the Gila River center. Sixty employees at Poston produced 1,200 to 1,500 pounds of chow mein and Japanese noodles daily. A few Topaz evacuees drank soy bean juice rather than milk during the war, and some made ice cream from it. Sometimes experiments got evacuees into trouble: some kitchen workers were caught making *sake*, a Japanese wine brewed from molds off steamed rice or soy bean paste. Liquor was forbidden in the camps.

Relocation center food was similar to that in assembly centers, especially at first. A Nisei newspaperman reported food at an unnamed center as "substantial, healthy, and not very appetizing . . . a combination of American and Japanese dishes and tastes like something bought for about thirty-eight cents a day—which is what it happens to cost."[46] After food production programs were in full swing, adequate supplies of vegetables, meat, and poultry appeared on most tables.

Sizable shipments of surplus crops in season were often sent from one center to another. Because of a transportation failure, Poston evacuees were forced to eat their surplus watermelon themselves, even at breakfast. Vegetable production at Poston was generally disappointing, however. The soil, while good, contained alkali which had to be leached out. The first year many acres of tomatoes died. At Gila River, corn grew taller than a man's head, and watermelons were shipped to Army camps. Topaz farmers experienced similar difficulties to those of Poston. An evacuee wrote a friend, "My next door neighbor is a soil chemist that leaves every morning looking for less alkali and finding more."[47] Another remarks, "At Topaz even the Japanese could not grow anything except morning glories." It was not quite that bad, actually. At first nothing would grow, but productivity gradually increased until one-fifth of all the food consumed was grown there. Amache, though it was only a few miles away from the farming community of Granada in Colorado, experienced equal difficulties.

Camp Rohwer in Arkansas was subject both to excessive heats and to unpredictable rains. After the swamps were drained, an unexpected drought made it necessary to import water from a nearby bayou. Severe storms in the spring raised havoc with planting schedules and forced evacuees to plant in mud. The delta soil was fertile but had been poorly farmed for a number of years. After the internees weeded and reconditioned it, crops, including soy and mungbeans, eventually did well there.

The undeveloped soil on the farms near Tule Lake was converted to rick, dark loam several feet deep. Plants grew in great abundance. Here the wasteland did become a garden, as in the dream.

Evacuees tended successful egg and poultry projects, including turkey farms, and raised and processed porkers, sheep, and even cattle. "They made cowboys out of the Japanese," comments a former Topaz internee. In February, 1943, 720 steers were unloaded and let out to graze on the alfalfa pastures of Heart Mountain. Many Japanese learned meat-cutting for the first time, a skill that was useful to many later. "You had the opportunity to learn any skill," according to Kay Takemoto.

Since in Japan, only the lower "eta" caste engaged in meat handling, some evacuees at Amache objected to volunteering for butchering operations. The project director, James Lindley, announced flatly that if no butchers could be found, there would be no meat. Volunteers came forward.

A milk shortage in Arizona in the fall of 1942 was commonly blamed on evacuee consumption alone, despite the fact that many farmers in the area neighboring the Gila River center were contributing to the shortage by slaughtering their dairy cows and drying the meat, due to the scarcity of beef. After a complaint from Mayor Newell Stewart of Phoenix about evacuee milk consumption and a demand for an investigation by the Arizona Senator Carl Hayden, Donald Nelson, head of the War Production Board, ordered canned and powdered milk to be substituted for fresh milk at Gila. By 1943 fifteen cows were supplying residents with forty or fifty gallons of milk a day—a small percentage of the amount of fresh milk they had previously consumed.

At Minidoka, 62,730 dozen eggs were produced in a single year. Experienced Japanese caponized the chickens there, and 7,215 meat birds were slaughtered. Anticipated large-scale fish production at Poston resulted in a display of a single tankful of fish. Fish for center menus was generally shipped in frozen. The nation's surpluses were sometimes unloaded on the camps, and there were long runs of certain foods such as fish or lima beans.

With all the center projects going at once it was possible to bring about an almost self-perpetuating system. The large amounts of garbage from the mess halls fed the pigs, fertilizer from the barnyards fed the soil, and while in the beginning feed was purchased, eventually crops and silage fed the cattle.

Relocation center land not devoted to the growing of vegetables was given over to certain experimental projects, principally long staple cotton, castor beans, and guayule. The growing of castor beans at Gila River for the purpose of making castor oil was abandoned early because of a wave of opposition from people outside who feared competitive commercial ventures. The spectacularly leafed plants, left to nature, grew wild and scattered color about the center.

From the beginning of evacuation, Dr. Robert Millikan, famed physicist, head of the California Institute of Technology, and a member of the Pacific Coast Committee for American Principles and Fair Play, had been concerned lest American Japanese evacuee scientists have no projects on which to devote their skills. Under his impetus, Dr. Robert Emerson, an authority on protosynthesis at Cal. Tech., was lent to Manzanar during the WCCA period. Experiments were made on the guayule shrub, a source of second-grade rubber and a subject for minor experiment since the early 1900's. With the rubber shortage during the war, interest in guayule increased.

The evacuee chemists worked on a $750 budget. Their equipment was makeshift, their table a door placed atop the frame and legs of an old kitchen range. "For glassware we have accumulated some jam jars and we are eating peanut butter like mad so that we can use the jars that come with it,"[48] wrote one of the chemists. The laboratory director was Dr. Kenzie Nozaki, who had earned his PhD in chemistry at Stanford University. The guayule was grown at both Manzanar and Poston.

Hugh H. Anderson, who had been very active in helping American Japanese in the Pasadena area with their evacuation problems and who later was to work as an adviser on cooperatives at Poston, was asked to go to Salinas on behalf of the scientists at Manzanar to obtain toppings from guayule seedlings being transplanted to the fields by the USDA Emergency Rubber Project. No one at Manzanar had the gasoline rations to make the long trip for this purpose.

These toppings were the initial material out of which grew an extraordinary development in rubber at this center. While thousands of seedlings were planted at Poston, these plants died, and the primary accomplishment in guayule production occurred at Manzanar, not only in the growing of the plant hybrids but more importantly in the innovation by scientists there in extracting the rubber from the shrub, resulting in a product of high tensile characteristics and low production costs. The scientific personnel for the guayule experiments at Manzanar were under the supervision of Dr. Shimpe Nishimura, one of the designers of the cyclotron with Dr. Lawrence at Berkeley.

An unusual undertaking at Gila River produced miles of fragrant stock fields, rows and rows of marigolds. Although not a WRA idea, the government nevertheless paid old-time expert growers who had brought special strains with them from Los Angeles the usual ten cents an hour to labor in these huge desert gardens set against a background of the Superstition Mountains. Masses of blossoms in season decorated center weddings and special occasions, and sometimes the growers gave bunches of flowers to members of the staff of whom they were fond. But marketing of the flowers was forbidden.

Artists and artistic souls like these growers were among the most fortunate of the evacuees at Gila River or other centers in which beauty could be found in the midst of an unpleasant climate and imprisoning conditions. The beauty of scene could be a mockery, or it could be a solace. Many letters coming out of the camps described the subtle colorations of the desert, its brilliant skies (dust in the atmosphere makes the evening sun red), the changes of season. "The country—what I have had strength enough to see is beautiful," Helen Aihara had written on first seeing Poston. "The mountains to the North West are rugged, beautiful and stony, but oh so treacherous looking."[49] As time wore on, she was asked one evening to drive to a distant plateau with her brother and friends. "From the hill on the plateau where the others were digging a large, partially petrified log, I saw Poston II three miles away enveloped in columns of dust. . . . People in Poston were breathing the dust and sweltering. We on the plateau were cool. . . ."[50]

Professor Chiura Obata wrote optimistically of a daybreak at Topaz, a golden sun shining through a vermillion sky. He painted a little water color illustration on his letter to accompany his words. To him this daybreak symbolized the "bright future of new life."[51] Another evacuee wrote in Japanese that, while living at Heart Mountain was petty and tiresome, "when I see some artists drawing or poets writing the poems I feel something different and . . . glad in my heart."[52]

A group of Issei men used to go out on the buttes near Camp Gila River as the evening cooled the air, and their mannered, highly trained, quavering voices would rise in "long songs" (naga-uta). Internees and personnel below could hear the songs floating down but could not distinguish the singers among the jagged peaks.

As Thanksgiving and Christmas approached, volunteer woodcutters were dispatched to the hills of Arkansas to chop wood for barrack stoves, and as marrow-freezing cold came to Heart Mountain and Tule Lake, there was soon nothing left on the coal pile but dust. Stoves had to be kept going day and night to keep the rooms warm. "There is a lot of difference between being cold in your own home and cold in drafty barracks," says a JACL leader. Issei at Poston chopped mesquite for braziers they had constructed. Outdoor bonfires became a feature of the landscape in November. Women donned slacks at Heart Mountain so that their legs would not bleed from frostbite, while pipes froze and broke.

At Poston turkeys were slaughtered and dressed for Thanksgiving dinners, and families sat together for the holiday occasion. Besides the turkey there were cranberries and dressing. "Though we haven't eaten too well since then," someone said, "it was good." The women had fashioned peach and cherry blossoms out of citrus fruit wrappings and attached them to trimmed mesquite branches for table decorations.

At Gila River the evacuees had a choice of turkey at Thanksgiving or at Christmas. They voted for Christmas and made Christmas trees out of sagebrush and juniper. Those with friends back home received packages. Protestant churches chose camps and sent money to ministers at the centers for the purchase of Christmas gifts for the children. At one camp when a group of high school youngsters serenaded the guards in the patrol towers with Christmas carols, they were driven away. These soldiers "had been taught to regard us as the enemy."

The traditional New Year's *Mochi-gome*—a feast dish made from rice —was provided for the first New Year. At Poston, 14,500 pounds of it were cooked in the mess halls.

A New Year's poem by Miyuki Aoyama was published in the Heart Mountain *Sentinel*:

> Snow upon the rooftop,
> Snow upon the coal;
> Winter in Wyoming—
> Winter in my soul.[53]

The Tule Lake site was a bird sanctuary. In the winter there were snow ducks and geese. Millions of birds—gulls, pelicans, and others— migrated annually. The center itself was a preserve, but the Caucasian personnel who could hunt outside brought in gorgeous birds for their own consumption. Deer were plentiful in season. According to Mrs. D. C. Rust, who worked there as a teacher, it was a hunter's paradise. However, the Caucasian hunters were not allowed to share their bounty with the internees.

The Japanese made small wood carvings of the geese they could see flying overhead and sold them for a dollar apiece. Sumio Doi wrote a letter during his confinement at Tule Lake to the editor of the Sacramento *Bee*, "As the sun rises and sets in this vast concentration camp for the Japanese people here in Newell, Modoc County, once the home ground of Indians, we envy the proudly flying ducks in mass V formation looking for newer feeding grounds. Where these ducks are flying no one knows. Looking through the wire nets, what of our future?"[54]

NINE · STORM CLOUDS GATHER

INTO THESE TEN AREAS of desolation an extraordinary mixture of human beings—evacuees and administrators—were thrown together and expected to create some form of society. Was their relationship to be one of jailers and captives or of working partners building self-sufficient communities? This question, which had arisen in the makeshift assembly centers, had to be confronted more fully in the relocation camps. The transition from Army control in the assembly centers to civilian management under the War Relocation Authority meant a changeover from what Mike Masaoka has described as "quasi-military prisoner of war operation" to a more democratic treatment.

Most evacuees in retrospect, and many while they were in camps, have given the WRA credit for an enlightened attitude. A Manzanar resident expressed a feeling that was common, but by no means universal, when he wrote in 1943, "All of us in the camp feel, I'm sure, that the WRA is doing a thankless job well."[1] About the same time Galen Fisher made an evaluation of the agency: "Some day the job done by the WRA in creating these centers will be recognized as a marvel of social engineering."[2] He went on, however, to point out the fatal flaw in the administration of the camps, the reason why they must inevitably fail as democratic communities. "The odds were stacked against success. The patient, so to speak, had been inoculated with a malignant germ before the doctor [WRA] took the case."[3] It was impossible to imprison people without trial and then expect them to act as members of a free society.

A Nisei wrote from Poston, protesting that though the President had the right to remove him from Los Angeles on the grounds of military necessity, " . . . after being moved from the nerve centers of the defense area, the President had overstepped his power in continuing to hold me a virtual prisoner on these premises."[4] Though Roosevelt called the centers concentration camps in an October 20, 1942, press conference, the WRA insisted they were not. "No," says Professor Roger Daniels the historian, "just a place where you got shot if you stepped outside." The government preferred to call the centers "wartime communities" and the evacuees "residents" or "colonists." A pamphlet of "definitions" was distributed by the WRA in an attempt to clarify evacuation semantics, but it failed to mollify prejudiced Caucasians and irritated the Japanese. All the euphemisms disregarded what was to them the central fact—they were being held involuntarily.

Togo Tanaka, after his release from Manzanar, spoke of this anomalous situation. "My constant and repeated reference to that fence," he told an audience in Chicago, "is perhaps unfair because it seems to leave so little room for all the happy things that went on and continue to go on within the relocation center. But these happened in spite of and not because of it. The relocation center, though geographically located in free America, spiritually belongs to the oppressed lands we are fighting to liberate."[5] Carl Mydans, the photographer, wrote in a similar vein about the evacuees at Tule Lake: "Because the problems which have arisen to plague the camp stem fundamentally from their loss of liberty, these problems can never really be solved. Their life cannot be made pleasant. It can only be made endurable."[6]

To be herded together, offered subsistence, and deprived of any reward for initiative was a spiritual death sentence. No matter how benign were the policies of the WRA, the situation was humiliating to all, intolerable to many. "Psychologically, it was a concentration camp," said Mich Kunitani, who was at Poston. It is to the credit of Dillon Myer, who succeeded Milton Eisenhower as director of the WRA, that after a short time in office he realized that the relocation centers were unworkable and turned his efforts to getting people out of them. He said, "Internment camps were never *intended* in relation to this program."[7]

They had not originally been intended by Milton Eisenhower, either, who, after three stormy months on the West Coast, had resigned in June, 1942, to take a job with the OWI in Washington. Laurence Hewes tells of meeting him on Market Street in San Francisco in a downcast mood shortly before he left for the East. "I'm getting out of all this," he said. "I guess I'm not a grassroots boy. I know my Washington, but out here I'm lost."[8] He had nothing but praise for the cooperation of the Japanese he was evacuating, but he found himself in the middle of a hurricane in dealing with the local politicians. "We are going to do this the American way," he had once proclaimed hopefully, but at the Western Governors Conference in Salt Lake City in April, he had been impressed with the futility of getting general acceptance for any plan for free colonization. The governors would accept Japanese only in government reservations. As the center sites were developed and built, he had the painful duty of urging the evacuees to consent to the injustice that was being done to them. He assured them that the WRA "would be tolerant, patient, and considerate in handling this human problem of wartime migration and resettlement."[9]

Dillon Myer also experienced far more difficulty with hostile congressmen and West Coast politicians than with the evacuees. Recurrent investigations of the relocation centers by teams of visiting legislators inevitably produced charges of WRA pampering and laxity. WRA policy was formulated in a public arena. Every response to evacuee demands was interpreted by critics as a concession to captives. The fact that the Japanese were behind barbed wire, though not charged with any crime, was proof to a good many people that they were guilty. The Army stood always just outside the gates, ready to come in to enforce martial law as it had at Santa Anita, as it would again at Manzanar and Tule Lake. The WRA as a New Deal agency, suspected of being a testing ground for radical theories, was an anathema to the powerful groups who wanted the Army to resume control of the "enemy."

With the exception of the Los Angeles *Daily News*, the San Francisco *Chronicle*, and the San Francisco *News*, most of the West Coast newspapers and the Hearst press nationally assisted this viewpoint by converting rumors into facts and inflating small happenings into full-scale alarms. The hostile newspapers, including the Los Angeles *Times* and those in the McClatchey chain, appeared to carry on an unremitting campaign to villify the interned Japanese and the agency that treated them as American citizens and loyal aliens against whom there was no charge or suspicion of subversive activity. Dillon Myer has said that before 1942 he had been occasionally shy and unsure of himself. But his baptism by fire as defender-advocate of a despised minority converted him into a fearless fighter.

A former official in the Department of Agriculture, he had had little training in handling the human problems that he encountered in the WRA. He had to improvise policy from first to last. There was no blueprint to follow since aside from the Indian reservation system there was no precedent in America for detaining and governing several thousand people.

As the WRA policy shifted from creating self-sufficient communities to getting the evacuees out of the camps, the change in directives from Washington further disillusioned the Japanese who felt themselves to be helpless pawns in the hands of a capricious government. In the assembly centers, the self-governing councils had been quashed. In the relocation camps, the early ambitious plans for creating industry and agricultural projects were reduced and modified in response to pressure from the outside. At a 1943 investigation a senator asked, "Do they put anything out that can be used elsewhere?" The committee chairman answered, "No, they won't let them do that."[10]

On the one hand, rival Caucasian groups feared Japanese enterprises would offer unfair competition. On the other, farm interests, which had led the movement to put the Japanese into camps, soon pleaded to have them released as farm laborers. Ten thousand men left the centers on short-term leaves to save the harvest throughout the western states in the summer and autumn of 1942. The success of this program as proof that the Japanese would be accepted outside the centers, however self-interested the motivation for receiving them, further encouraged the WRA to shift its emphasis to relocation, at a cost of abandoned plans and deterioration of morale in the centers. Disorganization was inevitable in an agency so beset by pressures from within and without. The WRA performance improved as it went along. Dillon Myer's leadership in the relocation program, when he worked tirelessly to change public opinion, won him the "undying respect and admiration" of the Nisei, according to Bill Hosokawa, a Denver *Post* editor.

Dillon Myer recruited an unusual number of fair-minded administrators, whose efforts to some extent softened the harsh measures they enforced. But for them, a larger number of evacuees would have become completely disenchanted with American life. Mich Kunitani characterized WRA personnel as "dedicated, sincere, anxious to equate action with their values." This was the WRA at its best. Other administrators were poorly educated, inflexible, and inclined to look on the job as custodial in nature. According to one evacuee, they varied from being "completely competent to overtly psychotic."

They were recruited through the civil service and drawn from many sources, from the CCC and WPA programs, from the Indian Service, and other branches of government. Former missionaries and compassionate individuals volunteered their services. Women were hired as teachers, social workers, and office workers. With headquarters in Washington, the WRA had three chief field offices, in Little Rock, San Francisco, and Denver. Later many smaller offices were created to assist with relocation in cities throughout the country. At each of the ten centers there were less than a hundred administrators overseeing 5,000 to 10,000 evacuees.

Idealists on the staff, like some of the evacuee idealists, believed in the possibility of building showcase democratic communities along the lines of the first WRA plan. At the centers they worked side by side with people who were taking advantage of a comfortable sinecure, sometimes at the expense of the United States government or of the evacuees. The chief officials at each center tended to be fair and open-minded, though not uniformly so; the more prejudiced and unscrupulous administrators were apt to be found in the lower echelons.

In several centers black marketeering on the part of food stewards was exposed. A notorious instance occurred at Tule Lake where the thefts of the warehouse manager were brought to light when his station wagon en route to nearby Klamath Falls was hit by a slow-moving train which scattered far and wide a load of Grade A meat, pilfered from the camp mess hall supply. The property officer at another center was arraigned for taking financial advantage of the evacuees whose property he was supposed to be protecting. (The functions performed by the Federal Reserve Bank and the Farm Security Administration in holding and transferring evacuee property were assumed by the WRA in 1943.) Some staff members were drawing larger salaries than they had received in previous jobs and were enjoying a few fringe benefits such as a modest gas ration and inexpensive servants close at hand. A Department of the Interior pamphlet, designed to attract personnel to Tule Lake, pictured a scenic environment, a recreation club and domestic help for child care and general housekeeping. There were illustrations of evacuee women in dust caps, wielding mops and brooms. The Northern California branch of the ACLU exposed what they termed the "slave labor racket" at Tule Lake. Evacuee cleaning women, cooks, and men servants were paid the usual WRA pittance for a forty-hour workweek. They were hired through the recreation club built by the Japanese and operated for the benefit of Caucasians. The ACLU charged that the club received $30 from members desiring servants, out of which the evacuee received $19 plus a $3.75 clothing allowance.[11]

Though living conditions were somewhat Spartan at the ten centers, similar to the atmosphere of an Army or CCC camp, at the relocation centers the administrators were quartered in white compounds where the houses were furnished, and ate in separate mess halls where the fare was more ample than that served in the evacuee dining rooms. "We had too much," said a teacher at Poston, "and they didn't have enough." As governors and governed, the Caucasians and Japanese lived in a framework that enforced their differences. The consciousness of barriers was expressed in the terms they used for each other. The WRA people were *hakujin* or whites or occasionally *keto* (hairy foreigners) to the evacuees. The word "Jap" was outlawed by the administration, but it recurred in moments of tension. When a teacher at one center used it, her class walked out and she was later fired.

Dr. Alexander Leighton, who studied the Poston community, classified the administration there as consisting of two groups, what he called the "people-minded" officials who saw the Japanese as individuals and the "stereotype-minded" personnel who looked on them as a separate caste. Dr. Robert Billigmeier, a sociologist, who was an observer for a University of California study at Tule Lake, finds this a valid characterization. Some of the stereotype-minded administrators, he found, were not initially hostile to the evacuees. He remembers a staff member who arrived at Tule Lake well disposed towards the inmates, saying, "I really love these people. They're so clean and law-abiding." But when the evacuees working with him became critical of him and when evacuees in general criticized the operation of his department, the man reacted with "hurt paternalism. He understood little of the strains they were experiencing in camp."

Similarly, an official at Poston, on first arriving "had spoken with enthusiasm about building the community and of the skill and aptitude of the Japanese people. In fact, he went so far as to suggest grading the bank of the Colorado and spreading sand to create bathing beaches for the residents. At the same time, he appeared mistrustful, and for a while it was difficult to understand his apparent inconsistencies. By October, however, he was expressing considerable fear and hatred of the residents and insisting that a 'Jap was a Jap' and none could be relied upon. He carried small arms and advised other employees to do the same. To the Military Police he talked at length of his fears, and wrote a letter to the commanding officer, urging him to tell his men to shoot to kill, so that in the event of trouble in the camp they would not be held back by humanity or any pangs of conscience."[12]

The military police who guarded the camps, and who were generally quartered separately from the WRA personnel, might be expected to be among the stereotype-minded in their attitude toward the evacuees. In fact, the Army tried to indoctrinate them in this point of view, not always successfully. Chet Huntley, the newscaster, reported a "good-natured camaraderie" at Poston between the GIs and the Nisei in 1942. "I wrote that Japanese kids could be seen riding the backs of GI-driven trucks inside the barbed wire . . . but the Army major scornfully red-penciled it. The Army had to be revealed as an agency with drawn bayonets guarding the Japanese."[13] A teacher at Poston thought that on the whole the evacuees preferred the guards to the WRA "appointed personnel" for the reason that the soldiers, like the "colonists," were serving at the camp involuntarily.

At the Gila center, five Nisei, assisted by an Indian mule skinner, were credited with saving the life of an Army private whose car went out of control and ran into a canal, pinning him under mud and water. They ran from a neighboring field and dragged him from under the car. For their prompt action, they were "publicly thanked by Captain Van Pelt of the 319th Military Escort Guard Company in a statement to the press."[14]

Armstrong Hunter of New Milford, New Hampshire, who worked during one summer at a church in Delta, Utah, near Topaz says, "One strong recollection I have is that there were real differences in attitude between the soldiers who were providing the security for the place . . . and the administrators. The soldiers seemed to be poor white, without advantages; the administrators were generally college people. I believe there was little contact between them." At some of the centers, the guards and the women teachers went to nearby towns on dates; some of the romances resulted in marriage. One young teacher, a 1942 college graduate, away from home for the first time, preferred to attend parties with Japanese and Caucasians in the company of a conscientious objector, who was also assigned to teach at her camp. The teachers who dated the guards were often incompatible with the teachers (some of whom were accused, correctly, of being members of the Fellowship of Reconciliation) who enjoyed the company of the Nisei.

Leighton describes how some of the sentries at Poston became agitated during the strike in November, 1942, and "talked excitedly with torrents of abuse against the evacuees and expressed the desire for an opportunity to shoot them."[15] Though no shooting took place at Poston three shots were fired at a youthful evacuee at Manzanar, wounding him. A sixty-two-year-old evacuee at Topaz, James Wasaka, was shot and killed by a guard on April 11, 1943. According to an Army report, he was attempting to leave the center and failed to heed the warnings of sentries in two of the towers. At Tule Lake an evacuee construction crew worker, Shoichi James Okamoto, was shot at close range by a sentry on May 24, 1944, and died the following day. Witnesses reported that the attack was unprovoked. Though WRA officials expressed regret and indignation, the sentry was acquitted in court martial, a verdict which was "kind of expected," in the words of a Nisei girl at the center. "They knew the result before they even started. All those things are whitewashed." An older evacuee was more angry. "Their laws are mockery to civilization," he declared. "They can shoot and kill an innocent man for no reason whatever and be acquitted. . . ."[16]

There were emotionally disturbed and potentially violent people working at the various centers, the more so since recruiting had been necessarily hasty. Lower-echelon WRA officials muttered threats against the evacuees in the bars of nearby towns; poor demented souls on the teaching staffs indulged their eccentricities, and occasionally, as in the case of an elderly lady who swallowed castor beans, had to be relieved of their duties. Some of the personnel "didn't know what it was all about," in the words of one evacuee.

"I'm quite aware that among them were some reactionaries," said Sada Murayama about the Tule Lake administration. "But they didn't have much to do with the evacuees. The staff as a whole were very human, with many professional and college-educated people who gave us a great deal of support and encouragement. They deserve credit for the fact that so many of us emerged from the experience with a minimum of damage to our egos." Her friend, Jeannette Smoyer, later Mrs. D. C. Rust, conducted a typing class without typewriters. She improvised paper keyboards. She also helped with the high school newspaper and was an adviser to the Little Theater. "Supposing Samuel French finds out about this and wants to collect royalties?" asked Sada Murayama, who was directing the plays. Jeannette Smoyer answered, "You people are behind barbed wire. Let Samuel French come in!"

Talented individuals were attracted to the centers. The California artist, Ynez Johnston, taught art at Tule Lake. Edythe N. Backus, who catalogued the music collection at the Huntington Library, volunteered to teach at Poston because, as she was of German origin, she sympathized with the plight of the Japanese. She was a friend of the accomplished Nisei musician, Ruth Tayeko Watanabe. Kay Damon, now Mrs. Harry Prochaska, also applied to teach at Poston because she was incensed at the fate of her friend, Grace Fujii, who, twenty-four hours after taking her comprehensive examinations at Mills College and winning a diploma and a Phi Beta Kappa key, "was taken off to a horse stall at Tanforan."

Grace Nichols (Mrs. Wilfred Pearson) wrote an eloquent letter to the WRA applying for a teaching job but "finally learned from friends in Poston that the people who got jobs were the ones who appeared in person on the project, ready to go to work, so I went and found they were correct." She was soon assigned a class of over thirty rambunctious first graders with whom she gradually established a warm relationship.

> . . . I knew little of teaching methods and less of handling six-year-olds in quantity, but I did love them, and they returned my affection warmly. Somehow, with that as a basis, learning took place in spite of all the obstacles and deficiencies the situation afforded.[17]

Kay Damon improvised a curriculum for her eighth-grade class at Poston in a bare room. The class sat on the floor while she directed singing, told stories, and led nature study. By November 1 the parents had built school furniture and she had one book for each subject which she used herself. The class was sometimes noisy and wild. Some of the students were taking their feelings out on the situation. She felt that she succeeded "in the field of relationships, and that was important, helping kids feel like people." She was also an adviser to a high school girls club. "I loved them," she said.

In the center atmosphere where students laughed when teachers spoke of the United States Constitution and the Bill of Rights, and scrawled the words "Jap Prison" on their tar-paper school walls, the presence of this sort of person was decisive. "I cried bitterly as I corrected my eighth graders' essays on 'The Saddest Day of My Life,'" said Ruth Fischer, who taught at Tule Lake. "This was, of course, the day they were evacuated." A Heart Mountain evacuee wrote about a teacher there who was asked why she had volunteered:

> . . . she felt the most constructive thing she could do was to show the Japanese in America that there are some Americans who care and who do not blame the war on them. And so she came way out to this forlorn un-

inspiring country to add her mite toward maintaining the true American spirit of living. That was the most beautiful thing I have heard since being interned.[18]

"Working in a relocation center was rewarding to many of the teaching and administrative staff," said Robert Billigmeier, "because the fruits of their concern were so apparent in the response of the evacuees and because they believed that the harm done by the evacuation had to be reduced as much as possible and that this could be done by their individual contributions. It was also a terrifying experience because of our personal involvement with the evacuees. Through our close association with the Nisei we were aware of their anguish and uncertainty. What seemed most threatening to us was the thought that the Nisei might have grave difficulty in reintegrating into American society, or, indeed, might not even have the chance to attempt re-integration."

Mrs. Billigmeier was also a teacher and their apartment was a "neutral island" for the Nisei at Tule Lake. "There were so many agreeable young people it was exciting to be with, people of considerable talent." Mich Kunitani found friends on the staff at Poston among people "who had an interest in other things beside evacuation." Dr. Victor Goertzel came with his family to be the vocational director of the high school at Topaz and their room, with its pot-bellied stove became a social center.

The Fourth of July, 1942, was celebrated memorably by a group of evacuees and staff at Tule Lake at the apartment of the late Corliss Carter, director of community services. An East Indian friend of Sada Murayama came up from San Francisco to cook a chicken dinner with spices. "Such hilarity!" Jeannette Rust recalls. "The Caucasians practised bowing, Japanese-style." Some of this group still meets once a year "because we're people who like each other."

John and Esther Sills exchanged visits with evacuee friends at Gila. Mr. Hasegawa, head of the center's cooperative store, "often visited us in staff quarters, and we met his wife and children but only at his house, or in his surprising little garden. . . . One thing we both regretted and resented, was that our high school age daughters were sent about twenty-five miles to school, so that they would not 'have to' mingle socially with the adolescent Japanese boys and girls. When they attended a high school dance at the center, unfavorable comments were made by members of the Caucasian staff."

Until he was felled by a polio attack, Hugh Anderson worked from 8 A.M. till midnight developing the cooperative store at Poston. When he "hit a psychological low" he would take a walk, find an old Issei sitting and smoking and sit down beside him for a few minutes. The silent communication refreshed his spirit. So the barriers of race and position continued to be ignored by warm-hearted people.

Studying the administrators, as well as the evacuees at Poston, were the team of social scientists directed by Dr. Alexander Leighton, a psychiatrist and a lieutenant commander in the Navy Medical Corps, and Dr. E. H. Spicer, an anthropologist, later on the faculty of the University of Arizona. They were assigned to Poston because it was administered under the Indian Service, and John Collier, the commissioner of Indian Affairs, was interested in its possibilities as a demonstration colony. The purpose of the study was three-fold, to apply psychological tools to assist in easing conflicts at Poston, to evolve methods for handling people that would be useful to the United States later in occupied territories, and to train Nisei in social analysis so they could give service in occupied areas of the Pacific, during or after the war. This last is another example of the inconsistency in the government treatment of the Japanese. Though initially denied any substantial participation in the war effort as a group, they were selected when individually useful. Leighton's book about Poston is called *The Governing of Men*, and one section of it is a manual of principles for handling subservient peoples under stress. Poston was a laboratory to prepare administrators for the subjugation of Okinawa or Japan.

Conrad M. Ahrensburg, then on leave from Brooklyn College, and Elizabeth Colson of Radcliffe, and at least a dozen Nisei were on Leighton's staff. According to Mich Kunitani, "anthropologists were running around on the roofs" at Poston. "Constructive evacuee spies," as Hugh Anderson called them, studied and reported on the behavior of their fellows. "They had their fingers on the pulse of the people. If it hadn't been for this group the Army would have been in the camp half the time." Leighton and his staff made a real contribution in providing a wide-angled view of conflicts at the center. As dispassionate observers, they helped to neutralize antagonisms. Because Washington administrators felt that the program proved its efficacy during the Poston strike, it was decided to form a community analysis section of the WRA, directed first by the anthropologist John Embree and later by Spicer. Community analysis studies were begun in other relocation centers. The Washington office produced the eminently fair and informative report *Impounded People*, published in 1946. At least ten postwar reports were published by the WRA, among them, *Wartime Exile, Impounded People, The Relocation Program, Wartime Handling of Evacuee Property, Administrative Highlights of the WRA Program, Community Government in War Relocation Centers, Legal and Constitutional Phases of the WRA Program, Token Shipment, The Evacuated People*, a statistical analysis, and *People in Motion*.

Another group of social scientists used the centers as a laboratory. A University of California study of Japanese evacuation and resettlement, under Professors Charles Aikin and Dorothy Swaine Thomas of the

Berkeley campus, was financed by grants from the Columbia Foundation in San Francisco, the Rockefeller Foundation, and the university. Three books were produced, *The Spoilage* (1946), about evacuees who returned to Japan, *The Salvage* (1952), about those who relocated successfully in the United States, and *Prejudice, War and the Constitution* (1958) about the legal and historical significance of the evacuation. The University of California researches were not undertaken, as was Leighton's, for the purpose of influencing human relationships in the centers, but were intended to explore the impact of a traumatic experience on a cultural and racial group. Dr. Thomas assigned Caucasian staff members to Poston, Minidoka, and Tule Lake. Robert Billigmeier was one of them. She also recruited evacuee observers at Tule Lake and other centers. They had to work clandestinely. They avoided taking notes at meetings, for instance, in order not to arouse the suspicions of their neighbors. Many evacuees express resentment at having been used as free guinea pigs for these studies.

Joe Grant Masaoka, now administrator of the Japanese American Research Project at UCLA, and Togo Tanaka were observers for the WRA at Manzanar. Tanaka also reported for Dorothy Thomas. He said that since the FBI continued to arrest loyalty suspects in the relocation centers, the observers were suspected of being traitors to their own people. The word *inu*, meaning "dog" or "informer," was occasionally written on the doors of the Nisei who described events for the administration.

If the staff members were a disparate group, the evacuees were even more varied. "The fact of common ancestry, which was the basis of the evacuation, subsequently proved to be a shallow common denominator," WRA analysts concluded in a report published after the war.[19] Every camp had its own atmosphere that depended to some degree on the previous experience of the people who went there. The centers where dissension was strongest had a diverse cross-section of the prewar West Coast Japanese population. At Tule Lake, late-comers from the Sacramento area challenged the already entrenched first arrivals from Washington and Oregon. At Manzanar, Terminal Islanders, a vociferous, tight-knit group, clashed with people from West Los Angeles and Bainbridge Island. The Northwesterners at Manzanar found the Californians "very Oriental." Poston, as an experimental community, attracted social theorists and intellectuals. Certain evacuees, strategically placed in prewar government service, had been allowed to choose Poston, but they were a small minority among farmers and workingmen.

There was less trouble at the Arkansas centers, at Gila, at Amache, at Heart Mountain, which was sometimes praised as a "happy camp," and at Topaz where the people were considered "docile." Mrs. George

Aki sensed "there was more of a feeling of helpfulness there" when she visited friends in Utah than at Jerome where she and her husband were living. Minidoka, which had a relatively homogeneous population from the cities of the Pacific Northwest, was often rated as the "best" of the ten. At first the evacuees cooperated well with an enlightened staff in a relationship which E. H. Spicer, in a community analysis report, described as a "benevolent dictatorship."[20] Minidoka, which was not in the Western Defense Command, had less rigid military supervision than Manzanar, Tule Lake, and Poston. In fact, the electrified fence at Minidoka was disconnected at about the same time that more searchlights and guard towers were being added to the other centers. It is not clear whether this was a cause or effect of the good conduct which the project director praised in the following "report card" issued when Minidoka was less than a year old:

Major crimes	none
Petty cases	two
Disloyal activities	none
Factional strife	none
Unreasonable complaints	none
Breach of trust	none
Moral flagrancy	none
Cooperation in civic affairs	excellent
Response to food rationing	good
Cooperation with Administration	excellent
Religious endeavor	good
Volunteers to armed services	excellent
War bonds and Red Cross contribution	good[21]

Later, the situation deteriorated markedly because of staff changes, a more rigid administrative policy, and the resentment felt toward some 1,700 former residents of Tule Lake who were transferred to Idaho. At a time when the previously strife-torn centers, Poston and Manzanar, were settling down, the Minidokans were beginning to be a great deal less cooperative, and the project director, reacting to what had happened in the other camps, decided that a more arbitrary type of government was called for.

At almost every center there was a period of initial harmony. In the first weeks when the staff worked closely with evacuee volunteers on the urgent common problems of building and equipping the new communities, a harmonious pioneering spirit prevailed. "During the early weeks," says a community analysis report, "the WRA staff in the centers had more of a sense of unity of purpose and satisfactory relations with evacuees than at any time thereafter."[22] Dissension was inevitable, however.

The mass removal of everyone on the Pacific coast with Japanese blood contributed to the diversity in the centers. The approximately 22,000 Japanese–Canadians moved inland from British Columbia never crossed the border and the substantial number of Japanese arrested in Panama, Brazil, Peru, and other Latin American countries were sent to United States Justice Department camps where they were treated as prisoners of war. But about 150 Japanese from Alaska, more Eskimo than Oriental, were sent from Puyallup to Minidoka and around a thousand Hawaiian Japanese were scattered in other centers. Many of them were more belligerent and aggressively pro-American than the average mainlanders. Robert Billigmeier described a group of seamen and longshoremen at Tule Lake who had been caught in West Coast harbors when the war broke out, as "a no-nonsense group nobody fooled with. They were political radicals. Japan was a fascist country. They supported the democratic country." Other Hawaiians were vociferously anti-American.

Hawaiian Japanese who had been interned in Justice Department camps in North Dakota, New Mexico, or Texas were sometimes paroled to the relocation centers and joined by their families. In November, 1942, General Emmons announced his intention of sending a few—1,037—voluntary evacuees from the Islands to the mainland camps. They were, he said, "chiefly those whose presence here is not useful to the war effort . . . elderly people. . . . No stigma or suspicion should be attached to the individual,"[23] though among the group were Shinto priests, language school teachers, and militant Kibei, educated in Japan. Except for members of the 100th Infantry Battalion, the Hawaiians were never an important group in numbers or influence on the mainland during the war, but coming from a place where Japanese were more assimilated in the culture, their attitudes were different.

Another distinct group were the former Okinawans and descendants of Okinawans from Southern California, some of whom had been associated with the left-wing newspaper *Doho*. They were historically opposed to the rulers in Japan and had brought their rebellious tradition to the United States. A group of Okinawans had protested the evacuation before the Tolan Committee.

Among the farm laborers and "fruit tramps," the old railroad hands and mine workers, many of whom had lived too migratory, unsettled a life to form a political orientation, there could be found an occasional Socialist or "Wobbly." Yohio Nishimura, one of the oldest Japanese labor leaders, planned to help organize a cooperative and a Japanese language press at Topaz.

Isamu Noguchi hoped to help build a democratic society at Poston in conjunction with his other creative ideas. As chairman of the Nisei Writers and Artists Mobilization for Democracy, his aim was to "be useful to our American homeland during and after her struggle against the

Axis." He wrote in a letter from Poston, "I came to this particular relocation area voluntarily, knowing that it, if any, had a real chance of success. I wished to experience at first hand what were the actual possibilities of planned economy, and what were the effects of forced racial segregation under even the best of circumstances."[24]

An evacuee from Heart Mountain wrote to a Caucasian friend expressing her hope for some stimulating friendships. "There are a number of other interesting people, artists, writers and very Americanized Nisei, who are congenial and we have the nucleus of an interesting artistic and intellectual group if we ever get organized here into a club or circle of some kind."[25]

But the atmosphere of the centers blighted these hopes. Larry Tajiri wrote, "Evacuation destroyed the 'Little Tokyos' of far-western America. But relocation established racial islands in the desert and on the Arkansas bottomland. Instead of Americanizing the aliens, as hoped, there was an indication that the reverse was true and that young Americans were being 'Japanized' through daily and enforced co-existence with their elders and their loss of normal contact with other Americans."[26] After a short time at Poston, Noguchi wrote, "Personally, I feel very deeply isolated from America and her war effort . . . the more truly American we were, the more must we feel the strangeness of the surrounding faces— the unfairness of the situation."[27]

Through letter writing the Nisei clung to their friends outside with the fervor of prisoners straining for a glimpse of freedom. The messages and gifts that reached them were a tangible link with the world they belonged to, enabling them to put their present fate in some sort of perspective. The reminders that they were not forgotten helped them to fight their way out of their "man-made hells." An embittered man at Jerome would not allow his wife to acknowledge the packages and letters sent to them by their daughters' teachers and friends. "He did not want us to have anything to do with *hakujin*."[28] But despite the rumors that letters were censored and packages examined, the evacuees who had at least one trusted Caucasian friend were given some encouragement to hope for a friendly America to which they might some day return. These whose previous experience had been positive were sustained by the promises of democracy, elusive yet still remembered.

The reports they received in the newspapers, on the other hand, might have led them to believe that there was some truth in the argument that they were being locked up for their own protection. The *Pacific Citizen*, published in Salt Lake City, wartime headquarters of the JACL, as well as their home town newspapers brought constant reminders of the hate campaign that ironically continued to grow as the gates of the centers closed upon them. There was still some nervousness on the West Coast about the enemy of the Pacific. Japan had invaded the

Aleutian Islands in early June; the Oregon coast suffered a slight bombing raid on September 9 which provoked Representative Homer D. Angell to predict "an all-out attack" in a speech in Congress on September 22. Responsible military opinion, however, had never seriously contemplated a Japanese invasion of the three West Coast states and confidence in American ability to turn the tide in the Pacific war increased after the victory at Midway in June. Still, some people expected Japan would retaliate on the West Coast for General Doolittle's raid against Tokyo.

With the Issei and Nisei behind fences, the rationale for a general alarm against them no longer existed, yet the clamor continued. Morton Grodzins wrote, "How far the regional demands frequently were from this issue of national defense was best illustrated *after* Japanese had been removed from the West Coast and incarcerated. Though further repressive measures against Japanese Americans had no direct relationship to the national safety, it was at this time that the greatest regional effort was made to have the group treated as one of special iniquity."[29]

The Japanese question was argued in the California election campaigns in the summer and fall of 1942. Earl Warren's stand in the gubernatorial race has already been discussed. The evacuees read that the Republican candidate to succeed him as state attorney general promised to "sound the alarm against future inroads by these Asiatics, who are, every one, capable of spawning trouble after the war."[30] Fortunately, he was defeated by the Democrat, Robert Kenny, who used the power of his office in a number of instances to insure fair treatment for the Japanese. A congressional candidate, Al J. Dingeman, also happily defeated, declared himself in favor of deporting all Japanese from the United States.

As at the time of evacuation, these regional sentiments were carried to the floor of Congress where certain southern politicians allied themselves with the West Coast race haters. At the time of the assembly centers Representative Jack Z. Anderson of the 10th Congressional District in California, a frequent spokesman for farm interests and a pear farmer himself, proposed depriving the Nisei of citizenship. Perhaps the most inflammatory proposal, because it was more widely publicized, was the so-called "concentration camp" bill, introduced by Senator Tom Stewart of Tennessee. Its progress was reported in detail in the *Pacific Citizen*. During the same time that the Regan suit in California attempted to challenge the legality of Nisei citizenship, Senator Stewart introduced S. 2293 "to provide for taking into custody certain persons who are citizens or subjects of, or owe allegiance to, any nation or country with which the United States is at war."[31] The bill would have extended the removal, already in effect in the Western Defense Command, to "any or all Japanese residing in or found in the United States."[32] This would have included those in Hawaii. It struck at the legality of Nisei citizenship. "There is no such thing as a Japanese not being a subject of the Emperor of Japan," Senator Stewart insisted.[33]

Shortly after the Stewart bill had been introduced in the Senate (on the same day that Roosevelt issued Executive Order 9066), Togo Tanaka, still in Los Angeles editing the English section of *Rafu Shimpo*, on hearing of it, had reacted with fury. "This is the last straw," he wrote. "You can rob us of all our worldly goods. You can drive us from our homes. You can kill the incentive for clean, hard work. You can do all these and more. But you CANNOT stop us from thinking. You cannot crush the spirit of liberty and the American tradition on which we were nurtured and raised."[34] But as the months passed in the centers, a defeatist attitude often replaced the earlier anger. A WRA pamphlet, commenting on the effect of reported attempts to deprive the Nisei of their citizenship, said, "Some did not see what difference it made. It seemed an unnecessary irony."[35] When S. 2293 came up for a vote on the Senate floor in late June, it was challenged by Abe Murdock of Utah and Joseph Ball of Minnesota, with minor protest from Robert Taft of Ohio and D. Worth Clark of Idaho. "I think we are treading on very dangerous ground when we pass a bill of this kind," said Senator Murdock, and the bill was tabled.[36] It was revived some months later, in the Senate by Stewart, in the House by Representative Rankin, again unsuccessfully.

The active dissent of only two senators resembled the first qualified attack on evacuation by the American Civil Liberties Union. At a time when winning the war took precedence over every other consideration, the danger of suppressing minority rights was not widely recognized. William Henry Chamberlin became alarmed and wrote that civil liberty should be given "an A-1 priority, in war as in peace."[37] This was an opportune warning at a time when Los Angeles American Legion Post members were trying to ban a blandly objective pamphlet on evacuation by Dr. George Gleason, a churchman and former YMCA official, as being too favorable to the Japanese. When the ACLU attorney, Al L. Wirin, was interviewed in Los Angeles over radio station KFBW on the 151st anniversary of the Bill of Rights, all his references to the privileges of American citizens of Japanese ancestry were deleted from the script by the station management.

As the moderate spokesmen were silenced, the voices of hate filled the air waves and the newspaper columns. Nisei well remember Dr. John Lechner, Austrian-born founder of the Americanism Educational League "to promote the American constitutional form of government and expose subversive propaganda."[38] He impressed California Legionnaires with his plan to deport the Japanese. Though by implication unsafe for America, "These repatriated Japanese, Issei and Nisei alike," he said, "can do more to Christianize Japan than 1,000 missionaries and 10,000 Bibles."[39] A Nisei minister asked, "Why don't they send me to Siberia? I don't know anyone there either."

The OWI released a short film entitled *Japanese Relocation*, with a commentary by Milton Eisenhower,[40] and the Quaker Floyd Schmoe filmed the relocation centers sympathetically. But the general public was being given a picture of American Japanese as spies and enemies in such war motion pictures as Twentieth Century Fox's *Little Tokyo, U.S.A.* which was being shown in the summer of 1942. It was the story of a Nisei spy ring in Los Angeles, with the Japanese played by Chinese actors. The Chinese consul in Los Angeles had decided it was all right for Chinese actors to play Japanese roles as long as the Japanese were portrayed as villainous characters who met a violent death before the end of the picture.[41] Another film on Japanese American treachery was RKO's *Betrayal from the East*, in which a cheerleader at Stanford was revealed as a Japanese naval officer in disguise. Drew Pearson gave an introduction to the effect that the picture was based on fact. *Air Force* by Warner Brothers perpetuated the myth about Nisei sabotage and espionage in Hawaii. In *Across the Pacific* by the same studio, a Japanese–American acted as an agent for Japan in a plot to blow up the Panama Canal. *Black Dragon* and *Behind the Rising Sun* also portrayed the Nisei as spies. The scripts for these movies seem to have been concocted from some of the more lurid accusations in the Dies Committee's "Yellow Book."

Portrayals of this sort may have contributed to some of the clamor right outside the gates of the relocation centers. When a train wreck occurred near Parker, the evacuees at Poston were immediately implicated and were never fully absolved in the minds of the local residents even though an investigation by railroad officials and the FBI uncovered no evidence of sabotage. Representative Leland Ford warned of the danger of allowing Japanese workers to till gardens at Manzanar at some distance from the camp "with no fence around them and apparently no guards. . . . The people in the Owens Valley know what could possibly happen to those small communities. There are 9,800 people in the Japanese camps and there are only 7,500 in the whole county of Inyo. I was told that sometime there might be a lot of dead Japanese found in the valley if conditions did not change. . . ."[42]

George Savage, publisher of the Lone Pine *Progressive-Citizen*, addressing a newspaper conference at Stanford University in June, 1942, uttered an often to be repeated criticism of the WRA. Politics and the "social worker approach" so popular with many New Dealers have no place in the management of such an institution as Manzanar.[43] He urged that the Army be put in charge once more. Critics claimed that the Japanese were being "coddled" by the WRA, a charge, wrote one Poston humorist, that he and his friends "were having some difficulty reconciling . . . with the existing conditions in the relocation centers," unless "what they meant by 'coddle' was the alternative definition: 'To cook slowly and gently, as eggs or fruit, in water just below the boiling point.' "[44]

George Savage, from his vantage point near Manzanar, evaluated the attitude of the American Japanese: 30 per cent were disloyal, 30 per cent were opportunists, and 40 per cent were loyal.[45] The evacuees evaluated themselves and their lives in camp in quite different terms. "We merely vegetated," said one person. "There was no incentive to live or to work. We were clothed and fed by the government. There was no need for making any effort for improvement of our standard of living."[46] A young cook's helper, and a high school drop-out (one of the opportunists), said, "We fed ourselves well; in fact, we were liberally fed since we helped ourselves to the food in the kitchen. When the bell was rung we served the people the minimum amounts on their plates. . . . When the chief cook caught on to what we were doing, he laid down the law to me. I got angry and I remember chasing him with a butcher knife. . . . We broke up dances, everyone cutting in on one girl."[47]

Fuji Takaichi remembers a World War I veteran, a member of the American Legion. "They had a service [in camp] and there he was in his old uniform with an American flag, just as proud as he could be. I thought it was the saddest thing because he was so pathetic looking. Somehow or other he got into some difficulty. I don't know with whom or what. They took him away from his family. I don't know what the reason was. They accused him of being an agitator or something and I understand he completely went to pieces. He was institutionalized." Would he have been classified loyal or disloyal? The same summer he was marching with his flag, the California branch of the American Legion revoked the charters of the all-Nisei Townsend Harris Post in San Francisco and the Commodore Perry post in Los Angeles. And at the same time Representative John Rankin of Mississippi suggested that Negro and Japanese blood donations to the Red Cross be labeled so as not to contaminate Caucasians. "I wouldn't want any Japanese blood," said a commander of the Veterans of Foreign Wars, "and I don't think our servicemen would."

"With the undercurrents of terror and destruction," commented Jeannette Rust, "it took a pretty well-poised, inventive person to turn it into a creative experience." "I had to be a tower of strength for my children," explained Mrs. H. T. Nakamura who did not become bitter even after her small son died of meningitis at Heart Mountain. Kay Prochaska thinks that her friend, Grace Fujii, who organized a nursery school at Topaz "used her resources in a way she probably wouldn't have but for the challenge. She made the most of what could have been a very negative experience."

Sada Murayama, whose legal status as an alien limited her rights in time of war, said she "expected nothing, so everything that came was to the good. For me every situation has an element of humor or humanity. That side of things interested me. Inasmuch as I accepted the challenge of looking on the positive side, I had a wonderful time!"

She had been tied to a family business before the war but at Tule Lake she found her future vocation, social work, through a volunteer assignment. Her job mainly involved interviewing elderly people who came to see her about medical problems, clothing allotments, and such matters. "Nobody came angry and resentful to vent this on me." Then, as director of the little theater she began to work with young people. "We specialized in one-act plays. We put on one Chekhov play, *The Boor*, about a blustering, noisy Russian. Can you imagine a withdrawn, shy Japanese boy attacking a part like that? The aim was not to put on a finished performance, but to help young people who were unsophisticated socially. They could lose some of their self-consciousness. Sometimes the performances were so bad they were almost a satire, but the experience did something for the actors."

The Tule Lake administration gave her a paid staff, a secretary, and a whole barracks as well as free access to the scrap lumber pile, and the labor of people in the maintenance department. Her greatest triumph was a sunrise effect for a Boccaccio play, a muted increase of light, produced by the camp electricians. She worked under Harry Mayeda, the evacuee chairman of the Community Council, a "natural leader."

Another charismatic personality who led youth to outgoing, constructive channels was Mary Nakahara, who grew up in San Pedro. As Mrs. William Kochiyama, an activist in the black power movement, she no longer subscribes to the ideas she held twenty-five years ago though she has always totally immersed herself in causes she believes in. At Santa Anita and Jerome she saw that it was of paramount importance to keep adolescents from becoming embittered about their imprisonment. With experience in Sunday school teaching and scouting, she organized "The Crusaders," a youth group, who wrote and sent gifts to Nisei soldiers, to the orphans at the Children's Village at Manzanar, and to the Japanese TB patients left in sanatariums on the West Coast. "Service to others is life's most satisfactory experience," was the philosophy of "The Crusaders."

Because she wanted the teen-agers to rise above their own adversities, she rewrote the words to hymns and patriotic songs to fit the camp situation. "I was a super-patriotic American," she explains. "In other words, I was a naive, apolitical, provincial, idealistic do-gooder." Her barracks room was honeycombed with cubicles for ingoing and outgoing mail to soldiers. She went to the camp gate every day with her "Crusaders" to sing "booster" songs to the people who were leaving to relocate outside the center and to Nisei GIs departing for overseas. "She was indefatigable," remembers another evacuee, "inspired to the point of obsession."

The relocation center experience was a great equalizer. Each evacuee brought only himself, his skills and attitudes, the emotional residue of his previous existence. In the communal society of the camps none, theoretically, had more status than any other. The first leaders who emerged were the men who could address themselves to the perplexing and frightening environmental problems. But as these were solved, gradually previous ties as well as antipathies to family, generation, and former associates began to reassert themselves in the new setting. Groups began to work together—and against each other.

Daisuke Kitagawa, an Episcopal priest at Tule Lake, had found many tensions in the prewar Japanese communities. These he characterized as "tame, decent, and orderly" on the surface, but internally "quite neurotic." The West Coast Japanese, largely because of ostracism, had lived in what was in effect an *apartheid* society which "was not participating in the ongoing life of either America or Japan." He noted, among the Issei "a poverty of ideas," "extreme divisiveness," and an "irrational sense of inferiority" towards whites, coupled with "an irrational sense of superiority" toward other ethnic or racial minorities. The Issei "continued to hope to reach America long after he had arrived," reverencing his Nisei son who, striving to prove his Americanism, adopted a grudge against his parents as "almost his union card for belonging to his circle." Surface behavior was correct; the Nisei "internalized" his "terrible tension."[48]

It was inevitable that this generational conflict would be renewed once the crisis of the evacuation, which had consolidated families, was past. As in the assembly centers, the Nisei tended to take the first leadership positions because it was easier for the administration to work with them. The Issei were reported to be infuriated at the sight of officious youngsters, untried and unfit, in their eyes, ordering around their elders as they licked the boots of the WRA men. In most of the centers a ruling was adopted that only Nisei could be elected to the community councils. The ruling, which was an important factor in conflicts at Poston and Tule Lake, was later changed. Staff-evacuee relations got off to a good start at Minidoka where, though there was no community council, the Issei held positions of leadership. Serving on the informal block councils in many of the centers were family heads, occasionally bachelors, and very rarely, women, who met together to discuss matters of common concern such as how they would use a common plot of land or whether Japanese or American dishes should be featured in the mess halls.

Self-expression and self-government were encouraged by the WRA.

"There is . . . a wonderful opportunity here to practice a democratic civil government," wrote a young Nisei from Poston.[49] But remembering the capricious dissolution of the camp councils in the assembly centers, many evacuees were reluctant to commit themselves again or were afraid to take the appointed position of block manager—which involved relaying directives and complaints back and forth between the staff and the residents—for fear they would be blamed for unpopular decisions from headquarters.

Daisuke Kitagawa found many of the Issei, deprived of their traditional role in the household and community, overwhelmed by "a sense of futility."[50] The early WRA emphasis on community enterprises failed to capture the enthusiasm of self-made men who would rather grow vegetables for their own consumption than work for the grandiose schemes of the administration. The men interned in Justice Department camps had been treated as prisoners of war and were not required to work. When they were paroled to the relocation centers they persuaded some of the other Issei that the government, having imprisoned them, had no right to expect their labor.

The conviction of many of the older people that "If we are treated as Japanese to such a degree so we will become Japanese in fact" led the residents to look on the centers as duration arrangements and not to exert themselves except to make their quarters as comfortable as possible. Their viewpoint was diametrically opposed to that of the citizens who followed the JACL position that cooperation with the government might bring release. They believed that their future in America depended on the record they made in the centers. To them it was an acknowledgment of their status as citizens that the WRA should ask them to cooperate in building democratic communities.

This was not entirely a generational conflict, and by no means the majority of the center populations subscribed to these two extremes of viewpoint. But as the weeks went by and it became apparent that living conditions were not consistent with the roseate schemes envisioned by the WRA, the evacuee cooperators began to lose face.

Grievances against the administration mounted. As mentioned earlier, the work program and the low and unreliable wage payments drew heavy complaints, especially as evacuee experts, including doctors and agricultural specialists, were forced to work under less competent Caucasians at a humiliating wage differential. When the hospital equipment, ordered through the Army, in several instances did not arrive on time and medical supplies did not meet the health needs of the people, when the food served in the mess halls was not sufficient for the evacuees who were asked to do heavy work, the discomforts endured, added to the insecurity of being uprooted, caused intense fearfulness in many people. The lack of privacy, the high noise level in the camps were tiring. A teacher at Poston noticed that the children escaped by daydreaming or falling into a deep sleep when engaged in quiet activity. When Daisuke Kitagawa returned to Tule Lake after conducting the funeral of a TB patient in Kent, Washington, he "was immediately struck by the tension in the air."[51] The administration at Tule Lake catalogued the fears of the people, listing economic worries, mistrust of whites, fears about the postwar future, fears of a food shortage at camp, concern over the education and control of children, sectional rivalry, dread of stagnation, and sensations of claustrophobia.[52]

The dependency of evacuees increased their fearfulness. "One did not choose what he might eat at breakfast, but ate what someone else had ordered and the evacuee mess crew placed on the board table. One did not select a doctor, but went to the hospital and waited for whatever service was available. This dependence on people whom one had never seen before was definite enough from the first. It was clear that food, shelter and medical attention depended on a group of Government employees who were to be found at the edge of the camp in the administration buildings, but what kind of people they were and how they would use their authority remained to be seen."[53]

As the evacuees felt the full impact of the conditions under which they were expected to live, their anger began to grow. In almost every center there was some incident, major or minor, in which the accumulated tension exploded. The strike of the adobe brick workers at Poston was mentioned earlier. Sometimes it was an uprising against a mistrusted white overseer or an attack on an evacuee thought to be a WRA spy. At Poston II in August the Issei met in a serious, dignified conclave to protest the ruling that only citizens could hold office. In the same month, a "Kibei meeting" was held at Manzanar to protest a WRA ruling that Kibei could not leave the center on temporary work leaves to help with the harvest like other Nisei. A torrent of grievances against the administration came pouring forth at this meeting, which also revealed the deep fissures with the Japanese group.

A Citizens Federation had been formed at Manzanar in July to press for reopening the selective service to Nisei. This group, with a JACL viewpoint, clashed with the vehemently anti-administration Kitchen Workers Union. According to a WRA report, *Impounded People*, the "incidents" cleared the air and made the administration aware of the evacuee viewpoint, but these minor explosions were warnings of major dissension to come. The battle lines began to form.

The Nisei-governed JACL was a convenient scapegoat. Its leaders were hated for being close to the administration. It was well known among the evacuees, as the Dies Committee later disclosed, hoping to alarm the public over proof of collusion between captors and captives, that JACL officials worked closely with Dillon Myer in helping to formulate WRA policy. The leaders had won their favored position by actively cooperating with evacuation and bringing the rest of the Japanese group with them. Their pragmatic stance of conciliating the Establishment won them privileges. Saburo Kido, the national president, and other officers were allowed to leave the centers to attend meetings in Salt Lake City, the JACL headquarters during the war. Yet some of the Issei who had set them the example of aligning themselves with the sources of power in the prewar Caucasian community, such as chambers of commerce and marketing associations, were now critical as were anti-JACL Nisei who had complained of the group's "Tammany Hall" tactics at the assembly centers.

The JACL policy was to fight against all odds for acceptance and reinstatement in American life. The Japanese–American creed, written by Mike Masaoka, says, "Although some individuals may discriminate against me. I shall never become bitter or lose faith, for I know that such persons are not representative of the majority of the American people." Though JACL policy worked for the long-range benefit of the evacuees, to some it seemed to be a betrayal of their rights as Americans when Saburo Kido said in June, 1942, "At the present time . . . we are not questioning the legality or sagacity of the steps which have been taken. The army must be given full rein to carry out its task of waging and winning the war."[54]

A number of idealists denounced the JACL position on the grounds that it whitewashed their treatment by the United States. Though the action of rebels had divisive and often tragic results, they were motivated by an integrity that would not condone a wrong and a loyalty to principle that despised power politics. One of the angriest of these men, doomed by his position, yet respected by the administration that was forced to punish him, was Joe Kurihara, an Hawaiian-born Nisei. As an intensely patriotic World War I veteran and a devout Catholic, he was deeply hurt when the Merchant Marine Corps refused to accept him after Pearl Harbor. Some time after witnessing the forty-eight hour evacuation of Terminal Island, he was sent to Manzanar where he made a vow to crush the JACL-dominated Manzanar Citizens Federation "wherever I meet them." In August, 1942, he spoke of his disgust and disaffection: "I was wounded fighting for the United States. I draw compensation for my wounds from the United States government while rotting in a United States concentration camp." Then, ripping open his shirt, "These are the scars I have, keepsakes of my army service for this country. It is no longer my country. I am now a hundred per cent Japanese. I spit on these scars of the United States."[55] Some of the WRA people found Kurihara's speeches "subversive," but one staff member said, ". . . he is bitter and sore in quite an American way." The assistant project director said, "If I were Joe Kurihara, I'd be mad too. He was a veteran of the World War, was discharged from the United States Army honorably, had done his part as a citizen. It's just as if I had saved one of you guys from getting stabbed or killed in a street brawl, and you rewarded me by kicking me into the gutter. Hell, sure I'd be bitter."[56]

Evacuees with intense grievances about the conditions of their imprisonment translated anti-administration feeling into anti-American feeling. When some of the wrongs were righted after strikes and other expressions of rebellion, they felt more tolerant toward the democratic system. In almost every center there was the equivalent of the "boilerroom crowd" at Minidoka which consisted mainly of Issei bachelors who had little stake in America, who were unsympathetic to the Nisei, lacked occupational or educational status in the community, and kept up a "sentimental attachment" to Japan. They spent a good deal of time embroidering rumors of Japanese military victories supposedly based on illicit short wave broadcasts.[57]

Some of the Kibei were flag-waving idolaters of the Emperor who had lived their formative years in Japan during the militaristic era. Rejected by their Americanized families and by other Nisei as ridiculous and incomprehensible, they adopted roles as troublemakers in the centers. The centers gave them scope (as well as a chance to recruit converts) for their activities that they could not have had in a free society. As feelings polarized, the pro-Japan Kibei and the "boilerroom" bachelors assumed an importance disproportionate to their numbers.

Many Kibei were indistinguishable from other Japanese–Americans. Quite a few of the older ones were completely at opposite ends of the political spectrum. Some were Trotskyites and left-wing sympathizers. Many were taken out of the centers for government service with the OWI, the OSS, or as military language school teachers. Leighton described the group as follows:

> . . . even though in many cases the maladjustment in the United States may be due to Japanese training, there is evidence that some Kibeis did not get along well in Japan either. The attitudes which give trouble are domineering or superior airs, gambling and drinking, going about in gangs, inability to speak English and a tendency to vaunt all things Japanese. . . . In addition to the type just outlined, there is another sort of Kibei little mentioned. . . . These persons seem to stress the advantages of their marginal position between two cultures rather than the hardships. . . . Their tendency seems to be toward living peacefully with all types and if they become active at all, it is to promote understanding and expansion of common ground. Some of these Kibeis are loyal to America, some to Japan, while very many are torn between the two.[58]

A Kibei, who later renounced his American citizenship, made a revealing statement: "Before evacuation I had no feelings of identification with Japan or America, because I had dual citizenship. I think that most of the Kibei did not have particular feelings one way or another until they got into camp."[59]

Lieutenant Commander Ringle, the West Coast intelligence officer, had advocated a close surveillance of Kibei despite their American citizenship, though he urged that they be judged individually, estimating, as noted earlier, that only 3 per cent of the West Coast Japanese population was potentially dangerous. The Manzanar administration first estimated that 99 per cent of the people were loyal. In contrasting this with George Savage's figures about Manzanar (40 per cent loyal, 30 per cent disloyal, and 30 per cent opportunists), and the later and somewhat similar estimates of Senator A. B. Chandler's investigating committee, even allowing for the distortion which incidents in the relocation center must have provoked in the minds of people outside, one must come to the conclusion, as Senator Chandler did, that the relocation centers were *creating* disloyalty.

Yet the troubles that developed at Poston, Manzanar, and later at Tule Lake were given a propagandistic oversimplification by the press. The incidents were the result of many grievances and not simply an expression of the pro-Japan versus pro-America factions. Mobs were formed of the usual inflammatory material, including bored, excitement-loving youths, unstable, uncommitted, easily manipulated. The majority of the evacuees remained neutral because their inclination was to accommodate to circumstances. In this they were following Buddhist and Christian precept as well as adhering to the behavior pattern of their immigrant struggles.

The affair at Poston, which occurred in mid-November, 1942, was quite accurately called a labor strike. On Saturday night, November 14, a thirty-year-old Kibei was attacked by unknown assailants and severely beaten with a piece of pipe. Of fifty suspects arrested, two were held for further questioning, both twenty-seven-year-old Kibei. One was the ex-brother-in-law of the victim and a popular figure at Poston and the other was a judo instructor, who also had a following. When it became known that these men would be tried in an Arizona court, evacuees objected strenuously, on the grounds that a fair trial would be impossible in so prejudiced an atmosphere. An Issei delegation visited the project director on November 17 and requested their release. The director, Wade Head, refused. On November 18 a second delegation petitioned him, again unsuccessfully.

Shortly after seeing them Head and his associate director left Poston to attend a WRA meeting in Salt Lake City, leaving the assistant director in charge. A strike was called by Issei leaders, who, in the crisis, had displaced the legitimately elected all-Nisei Community Council. Several thousand people gathered in front of the jail where the two men were being held. The assistant project director tried to enlist the aid of the

Community Council in arbitrating the situation, but the council resigned as a body after its chairman said, "If you cannot trust us, then we have nothing more to do. We feel you should give us self-government."[60] The Issei Advisory Council and the block managers also resigned and informed the administration there would be a general strike beginning the following day.

The assistant project director, left in charge of the developing crisis, which he had inherited without much knowledge of the first stages, was faced on the one hand with a united protest from the evacuee population and on the other with divided counsel from his fellow administrators. A number of them, as well as the FBI men waiting to hear the charges against the prisoners, were in favor of calling in the Army, which stood outside the gates, to restore order with martial law. The assistant director, backed by a majority of his staff, took the more difficult course of negotiation with the strikers. He and his team reasoned that if force was applied, "the fire would be driven underground rather than quenched and that the hitherto collaboratively minded residents would be alienated from the administration and moved deeper into the arms of the oppositional group by what they would regard as high-handed injustice that gave the lie to all the administration had said about self-government."[61]

The presence of the community analysts, Leighton and Spicer, doubtless influenced this decision. It was severely tested in the next few days when all services except the police, fire department, and the hospital were curtailed. The initial act of rebellion by evacuees was expressed in pro-Japanese symbolism. As the strike leaders stood around bonfires, they played Japanese music on a public address system set up near the jail, flew block flags of red painted on white. Sunrise pickets shouted, *"Dai Nippon Teikoku Banzai!"* (Banzai to the Great Japanese Emperor).

Tales of this activity reached the public through the newspapers. Reporters were not allowed at the center and gathered their copy, to some extent, by interviewing prejudiced rumor-mongers in a tavern in Parker. A distorted view of the events occurred also right on the scene at Poston among the military police guarding the camp as well as among the residents. "Things were seen in terms of plots, secret agents, and the strength of Japan pitted against the greatness of the United States. One might have thought that the Burma Road went through the adjacent mesquite," Leighton wrote.[62]

Eventually, the administration conceded to the strikers' demands to the extent of releasing one prisoner outright and agreeing to try the other, the judo instructor, in the center. The evacuees, on their side, agreed to initiate a closer working relationship with the administration. The Nisei, tired of the strike, which had lasted ten days, began to tear down and burn the nationalistic block flags. The music on the loud speaker shifted from "*Aikoku Kyoshinkyoku*" to "Don't Sit Under the Apple Tree."

When he returned to Poston, Wade Head approved the action taken by the assistant director. "We will just have to settle this ourselves," he said. "If we handle it right, we will come out of it in a much stronger position."[63] He decided to give recognition to the Emergency Executive Council, formed during the strike, that included Issei, on the ground that they represented the people. It was a far-sighted decision. The leaders of the strike emerged as the leaders of Poston, and at the same time became collaborators with the administration. The extent to which feeling died down afterwards is illustrated by the fact that when a short time later the judo instructor was taken outside the center and held briefly by the Yuma County authorities and then returned, no one protested.

Assessment of the strike varied. Helen Aihara (Kitaji), a resident of Poston II, described her reaction in a letter to a friend.

> The affair in I was settled. The accused is released under custody of his lawyer. They had demanded unconditional release for him, but you can see how very bad that would have been. It would make beating one's enemy easy, just as long as one had many friends. . . . This has brought out into the open agitators and trouble makers. We saw them for what they were and that helps us to be on guard.[64]

The following year two WRA officials who were at Poston at the time of the strike, after leaving the administration, expressed the "white backlash" viewpoint before the Dies Committee. One estimated there were six hundred spies among the evacuees at Poston; the other said that supervising the center had been transformed "from a custodial job to a social experiment honeycombed with silly sentimentalism."[65] Isamu Noguchi, who had left Poston before the strike, wrote that he thought some good would come of it. In addition to focusing attention on the need for relocation and assimilation, Poston had achieved a priority rating for building materials![66]

The incident, properly called a riot, at Manzanar early in December, 1942, was handled quite differently from the Poston strike. Trouble broke out around the first anniversary of Pearl Harbor, between pro-American and pro-Japanese factions. Antipathy between the two groups had been simmering for months. Tom Yamazaki, a twenty-eight-year-old graduate of the University of California, who had served on a committee of six to draft a constitution for Manzanar, wrote a nineteen-page report to the project director in May, urging some sort of segregation policy. "One cannot expect peace when Slocum [Tokutaro] a strong Legionnaire and pro-America man lives next to an equally strong Axis man." Another participant in drafting the constitution, Karl Yoneda, a Kibei CIO official, had left the center with two other militant citizen leaders, Koji Ariyoshi and Sho Onodera, to enlist in the United States military intelligence, which angered the opposing faction.

The incident that precipitated the riot was the attack on Fred Tayama, at that time chairman of the southern (California) District Council of the JACL. According to a Nisei observer, he and other JACL leaders who had urged cooperation with evacuation and become involved in evacuee property problems "had to pay heavily" for their roles when they got to camp. Tayama was severely beaten by six men on the night of December 5. Three suspects were taken into custody at the center, and one of them, a cook, was transferred to the Inyo County Jail in nearby Independence.

The Los Angeles *Times* account which may have been fanciful or at least exaggerated, says that Tayama had tried to stop a pro-Japan demonstration. "Shouting 'Pearl Harbor, banzai, banzai' an estimated 1,000 pro-Axis Japanese, many of whom are Kibei, adherents of Japan, demonstrated in a firebreak and hooted down Japanese–American Nisei . . . who protested their antics."[67] On Sunday morning, December 6, a crowd gathered at the main gate and a committee demanded of the project director, Ralph Merritt, that he return the prisoner from the Independence jail. Merritt agreed to do this provided the crowd dispersed.

At this point there seems to have been several mob actions. One group rushed to the hospital where Fred Tayama had been taken, to attack him again. Frank Chuman, who was the business manager of the hospital, and Dr. James Goto hid Tayama under a bed in one of the postoperative rooms. His enemies broke into the building of the hospital wards and came looking for him through the corridors, but failed to find him.

They then joined the crowd that had gathered in front of the jail where the prisoner had been returned, and spokesmen demanded his release. When Merritt refused, the crowd began to throw stones at the evacuee police. At this point the project director called in the military police who ordered the assembly to disperse. They used tear gas, but it was ineffective because of a high wind. The story differs as to what provoked the soldiers to open fire. One account says an empty car was pushed toward them. Another says someone exploded a lightbulb. After a warning, the military police shot into the crowd, killing one man outright and wounding eight or nine others. Ambulances carried the victims to the hospital. Frank Chuman remembers the group of friends and relatives collecting at the hospital entrance while he screened those who were called in to help care for the wounded. "The crowd was quiet, more concerned than angry. Some wanted to go in."

Meanwhile, at another gathering, a "death list" of *inu* (informers) who were going to be attacked was read aloud. Togo Tanaka's name was on the list. A neighbor, an elderly Issei, warned him. Tanaka left his barracks on Block 36 to seek out his older brother on the other side of camp. As the noise and confusion of the rioting spread, he left his brother's barracks and headed for his own.

Because it was a dark, windy, and cold night, he was muffled, like everyone else, in a government issue Navy surplus pea jacket. No one recognized him. His face was not well known, though his name was. He joined the mob and marched with them to the door of his barracks, 36-12-1. His wife and baby daughter were inside with her parents. The ringleaders went inside. Angry threats were uttered by the mob, but no physical harm came to his family.

"I stood frozen with horror at the rear of the milling mob, not a single friend in sight. I died a half a dozen times wondering what I would do if they attacked my family. My father came from a proud Samurai family. I was armed with a deadly looking butcher knife my brother had given me; it had been purloined from the kitchen mess hall where he was night watchman. When the ringleaders failed to find me in the barracks, the mob finally moved on.

"I knew then I could never stay another night in Manzanar. I threw the knife under the barracks and sought out a neighbor, the Reverend Ralph Smeltzer, a Brethren minister and volunteer camp worker, and a pacifist. He took me out of camp and into the custody of the U.S. Army."

Later that night, Togo Tanaka and his family and others on the "death list," including Fred Tayama, the victim of the beating, were spirited by the administration to a barracks outside the main camp. The next day they were taken to a former CCC camp in Death Valley, where they lived for a couple of months under the jurisdiction of park rangers from the National Monument before being relocated. Tokutaro Slocum, who had received some publicity because he had served with Sergeant Alvin York in World War I, was allowed to relocate in New Mexico. The chief agitators, including Joe Kurihara, were also moved from Manzanar and sent to "isolation centers" at Moab, Utah, and Leupp, Arizona.

During a period of martial law, all but essential services were curtailed at the center. Even with the removal of the chief contestants, the unrest did not subside for some time, since violence had been met with violence and two evacuees had died, one immediately and one later. A report says that residents were coerced into wearing mourning bands for the victims. Dorothey Tada arrived at Manzanar from Amache shortly after the riot when she received word that her father was very ill. The feeling of the residents was still strong. Women were making paper flowers for the funerals.

An evacuee wrote, "A lot of young boys of high school age, probably Nisei, go about whistling Japanese military tunes. They weren't that way before. The Kibei . . . are very troublesome because they are so openly pro-Japanese. Not all Kibei are that way of course. Some have returned to Japan and come back disgusted at Japanese fascism. . . . Practically all the Issei . . . are passive. . . . The thoroughly American are very quiet because they have no basis on which to preach Americanism . . . [they] are always in danger of being beaten up by pro-Japanese gangs if they should openly express their pro-American sympathies."[68]

Interpretations of the Manzanar incident vary even more than the assessments of the Poston strike. Wayne Collins, the San Francisco attorney, maintained, "There was nothing sinister in the assemblage. They were merely trying to petition the WRA for redress of wrongs. The right of assemblage to petition the government or its agents for redress of grievances is a right guaranteed by the First Amendment of the U.S. Constitution." But a man at the center thought ". . . the disturbance reaches deep into the psychological climate which has been going from bad to worse. We all expected some sort of disorder to break out, for the air has been tense and explosive for the past several months. . . . Small pro-Japanese minorities are trying to have their own way in the various relocation centers by a reign of terror. . . . The disturbance at Manzanar and the earlier disturbance at Poston are the results of this forced association of mutually incompatible groups in the restricted atmosphere of a concentration camp."[69]

The Manzanar incident provoked a storm among that section of the public who found their worst suspicions of the Japanese confirmed. It hastened a policy that the WRA and the JACL had been formulating— the segregation of the "loyal" from the "disloyal." This was in theory a forward step, but in its implementation it was unjust and heartbreaking.

TEN · THE LOYALTY QUESTION

A SEGREGATION POLICY finally developed as a consequence of events that took place early in 1943. In February the evacuees were asked to declare their loyalty to the United States by repudiating Japan. The controversial loyalty oath was part of a questionnaire introduced in connection with Army recruiting for an all-Nisei combat team. The WRA decided that all center residents over seventeen should fill out similar forms in order to expedite the relocation program. The resulting information would also be the basis for clearing evacuees for work in war industries.

The registration was instituted for the welfare of the evacuees, but the questionnaire itself revealed the mistrustful attitude of the government toward the American Japanese. In turn, the negative response of the evacuees showed how irrelevant were the demands of the United States to their situation as they saw it and to what extent the experiences of a year's imprisonment had destroyed their faith in the beneficent processes of democracy. The registration and the segregation that followed is the tragic story of groups and individuals working at cross purposes. It began with an announcement by the War Department late in January, 1943.

The Army had undergone a change of heart in its policy toward the Nisei in the year since Pearl Harbor. That the policy was still ambivalent in early 1943 is evidenced by the fact that volunteers for an American fighting unit were required to foreswear allegiance to the Japanese Emperor, an allegiance that only the dual citizens among them could have held even nominally. When the war started there were approximately 5,000 Japanese–Americans in the military service. For the most part, they had not been disturbed in areas outside the Western Defense Command. But on the West Coast, where from time to time an enemy attack was feared, their racial visibility made them suspect and led to repressions that were never imposed on second generation Germans and Italians.

Like other young Americans, Nisei rushed out to enlist when the war started. Several thousand were turned away. Walter T. Tsukamoto, an Army reserve officer since 1927, wired the Secretary of War, complaining that he had requested immediate active duty five times but was advised by his commanding general that "my Japanese ancestry precluded such assignment."[1] A West Coast university dean in charge of draft deferment on his campus reported that practically no Nisei asked for deferment or for special jobs before Pearl Harbor. After the declaration of war he discovered that eighty-three members of the Japanese Students Club had volunteered or were already in the Army.[2]

One youth, who wanted to enlist, by pretending to be a Mexican lied his way aboard a bus going from Sunnyvale to San Jose, California, more than the five miles distance from home that Nisei were allowed to travel. At Jefferson Barracks when it was discovered that he was a Japanese–American he was thrown into an isolated cell. His morale disintegrated. "From then on," said his sister, "he decided he wasn't going to put himself out."

Nisei continued to be drafted until June, 1942, when they were categorized either 4-F, "undesirable," or 4-C, "aliens not acceptable to the armed forces." Arthur Garfield Hays, general counsel for the ACLU, protested this 4-C classification to General Lewis B. Hershey, head of Selective Service; it was, he said, a contradiction of citizenship status and a penalty not applied to descendants of other nations with which the United States was at war.

Nisei servicemen in the Western Defense Command were transferred to inland posts. Several hundred were given honorable discharges. The rest were assigned to noncombatant duty. The Army took the "gun away from most of us and replaced it with a broom or a mop, a pencil or a typewriter," in the words of Pfc. Vincent Tajiri.[3] By June only three Nisei remained on special duty at Fort Ord near Monterey, General DeWitt reported, "in cautioning citizens to be on the lookout for Japanese in U.S. Army uniform."[4] He did not specify whether he expected imposters would be landing from enemy-based submarines. He felt he was minimizing the danger by keeping the number of Nisei in uniform allowed in the Western Defense Command to under ten and refusing to allow Nisei servicemen on furlough to visit their families at Manzanar and Tule Lake. These precautions seem to have been dictated more from fear than from logic. For the very reason that they were distinct racially, the Nisei were easier to superintend in the United States than were descendants of Germans and Italians. The difficulty came in the Pacific war theater where they had to be closely guarded, not because they were mistrusted, but in order to protect them from their fellow soldiers who might mistake them for the enemy and shoot them. Yet when interpreters and translators were needed, the Army was willing to take Nisei to the Pacific.

A military board, which convened in Washington after Pearl Harbor, had decided against accepting Nisei volunteers. A March 1 report states that the Army was discharging Kibei. Yet a short time later, impelled by the acute shortage of men who could speak Japanese, the military intelligence was recruiting Kibei and Nisei reasonably fluent in the language from the relocation centers. Lieutenant Colonel (now Brigadier General) John Weckerling and Captain (now Colonel) Kai Rasmussen, who were in intelligence work with the Fourth Army at the Presidio in San Francisco are considered responsible for the program to enlist Nisei to serve in the military intelligence. Some months before the attack on Pearl Harbor, Captain Rasmussen, a naturalized citizen from Denmark with some knowledge of Japanese, pointed out the serious problem that could arise in the event of war because of the fact that there were so few Japanese-speaking people in the United States. He persuaded the War Department to recruit Nisei (and Kibei) as most likely to be knowledgeable in the language, but he soon discovered that only 3 per cent of the 3,700 men he interviewed could speak Japanese fluently.

The War Department gave Weckerling and Rasmussen $2,000 to start a school in a converted hangar at Crissy Field in San Francisco, which was opened five weeks before Pearl Harbor with hastily mimeographed texts and orange crates for chairs. Of the sixty hand-picked students in the first class, fifty-eight were Nisei. The Los Angeles Superior Court judge, John Aiso, was on the original faculty.

Rasmussen later gave a testimonial to the Nisei before the Chandler Committee in Washington: "Their record for loyalty, in my opinion, is unquestioned. We have carefully screened them. In my own case I have found it necessary to separate from my command approximately four or five per cent, who were definitely disloyal. . . . Their loyalty to the commanding officer, aside from their loyalty to the United States . . . is probably the most complete of any group in the United States."[5]

"All day and late into the night they studied Japanese reading; writing; interrogation; translation and interpretation; analysis of captured documents; Japanese geography and map reading; Japanese military organization and technical terms. For good measure they were given lectures on the social, political, economic and cultural background of Japan."[6] The pace was grueling, and fifteen of the sixty men had to drop out. Of the graduates, thirty-five were divided between service with the marines at Guadalcanal and the 7th Division in the Aleutians. The remaining ten were added to the faculty. With the evacuation of the American Japanese population in the spring of 1942, the Western Defense Command was not a hospitable place for Nisei, even in military training. The school was moved to Camp Savage, Minnesota, and eventually to Fort Snelling in the same state. On June 1, 1942, a second class of two hundred men, most of them Nisei, began the six-month course of study.

Hoichi Kubo, an Hawaiian Nisei who came to Camp Savage by way of Camp McCoy, Wisconsin, where he was based with the 100th Infantry

Battalion, recalls that there were about twenty-seven sections at the language school, graded on ability as shown in an aptitude test. Some of the Kibei were in Sections 1, 2, and 3 for those most fluent in Japanese, but since they were apt to be weak in English they were later teamed with bilingual men in a combat situation where immediate translation was required.

The War Department became thoroughly convinced of the value of the program, though one graduate pointed out that in the intelligence school the Caucasians were officers and the Nisei were noncommissioned men. Many Caucasians were later trained in Japanese. Buddy Iwata left Amache very shortly after arriving to teach at the Navy language school in Boulder, Colorado, where some sixty-six of his students, "a brilliant group of Phi Beta Kappas," were former Stanford classmates.

Except as teachers in its language schools, the Navy refused Nisei throughout the war. Secretary Knox had said, "The rights of Japanese–Americans cannot be recognized without great risk to our military operations. . . . It would be quite possible for disloyal Japanese to impersonate these naval personnel (Nisei) with highly damaging results."[7] Two board members of the ACLU wrote to Knox's successor, James V. Forrestal, pointing out that this objection could not pertain in the case of the WAVES, the women's branch of the Navy, which also did not accept Nisei applicants. Acting Secretary Ralph Bard replied that "it is impossible to accede to the proposal that the Japanese–Americans be made eligible for any of the various branches of the Naval service, including the Women's Reserve. . . . This policy is dictated not by any fundamental distrust of the loyalty of this group as a class, but because of the peculiar conditions which are encountered in present Naval warfare and which would make their presence particularly troublesome in active areas of combat, such as in the Pacific."[8]

The *Pacific Citizen* of April 1, 1943, reported the story of the only Nisei in the United States Coast Guard at that time, Hawaiian-born Toshio Shimabukuro, who left Springfield College in Massachusetts in the middle of his junior year to volunteer. His request for combat duty in the Pacific was denied temporarily while he accompanied the exhibit of one of the first trophies of the war, a midget, two-man suicide submarine captured by the Americans at Pearl Harbor on December 7. Apparently, the Coast Guard was not unmindful of his propaganda value.

Very few Nisei managed to get into the Air Force. Sargeant Ben Kuroki, much decorated and renowned as a turret gunner in many European bombing missions, was an exception. Another young man, who had scored the highest in the class in his aeronautical course at the University of Washington, thus qualifying for pilot training, was told bluntly, "We don't want any Japs in the Air Force."

George Yonehiro, now a judge, was a nineteen-year-old student in aeronautical engineering in the civilian pilot training program at Sacramento Junior College. After Pearl Harbor he was grounded and two policemen were assigned to follow him around.

Another California Nisei, who had a civilian pilot's license, was serving in the Air Force when war broke out. After one month, he was given his papers and told to go home. "We thought he'd go out of his mind," his sister recalls. "He was extremely depressed. He wrote to his congressman. He wrote to the FBI. He wrote to everyone." Finally, from Poston, he was cleared for counterintelligence work in the Pacific. It is interesting to note that among those who answered "no" to the loyalty question in February, 1943, were a number of men who had tried to volunteer for the Army earlier and had been rejected.

In Hawaii, a Nisei national guardsman was reported to have assisted in the capture of the first enemy prisoner, Ensign Kazuo Sakamaki, the skipper of the midget submarine that the Nisei coastguardsman, Toshio Shimabukuro, later escorted on a war bond drive in the United States.[9] Nisei soldiers performed heroic deeds at Pearl Harbor. A number lost their lives. Yet when the smoke had cleared, civilians and Army officials were suddenly uneasy because Japanese–Americans in the Territorial Guard were being entrusted to protect vital installations.

The Nisei therefore agreed to become inactivated, but 159 of them petitioned General Emmons, asking to be allowed to make some contribution to the war effort. "Hawaii is our home; the United States our country," they wrote. "We know but one loyalty and that is to the Stars and Stripes."[10] General Emmons converted the inactivated Nisei guardsmen into a labor corps, and they called themselves the Varsity Victory Volunteers. Some Hawaiian Nisei were on active duty with the 100th Infantry Battalion as early as February, 1942.

On the mainland Nisei soldiers complained that they were locked up or confined to barracks when an important official, such as the President of the United States, visited the Army camp. One group of Japanese–American servicemen were confined to quarters after captured American airmen were shot by the enemy following the bombing of Tokyo. They were told it was "for your own protection." One man disagreed. "I . . . know it is not for our own protection. . . . It is a punishment for what we have no responsibility for. I blew up when we got the order. . . . I don't want to feel this way toward this country and I honestly tried very hard to keep faith in her and believe in her, but I can't help it any more when things like this happen so often. I cried last night and I wasn't the only one either."[11]

Peter Nakahara, formerly of San Pedro, tells the following story of resisting discrimination in the Army:

Shortly after Pearl Harbor I tried to volunteer for the Marine Corps (they turned me down), for the Navy (they turned me down). Finally, I went to my draft board. They wouldn't accept me as a volunteer, but would take me as a draftee with a waiver from my parents. I was twenty. I went into service about January 9 and was sent to Fort McArthur for induction.

The first few days they had me filling sandbags all day. I looked around. Everyone else had a big "P" (for prisoner) on their fatigues. They were guys from the stockade. From there I went to Fort Ord. Some order came out. All Japanese Americans had their guns taken away, were sent to inland areas, to interior commands less vulnerable to security. I was sent to Wyoming.

I took my basic at Fort Warren. Orders came that my outfit were leaving. There were only two Nisei in the group and the orders omitted our names. When that regiment pulled out I cried to see them go without us. We had to shovel all the coal for the barracks.

They shipped us out too, put us all in the Quartermaster Detachment or Head Service Detachment. When I reported to the Company Commander for work, he addressed me in Spanish, found out I had taken statistics in college and could run a comptometer. He took me to a central office and I was assigned to work there. One day one of the supervisors asked me what nationality I was. I said, "I'm an American." "What's your racial ancestry?" I said, "Japanese."

The next day the Company Commander came to my barracks and said, "Well, I've got a new job for you." And he took me to the warehouse. "From now on you're going to unload boxcars." I looked at the guys that were doing the work. They were colored soldiers. I was the only non-colored soldier. We were the only group who worked Saturday afternoons and Sunday mornings, darn near seven days a week.

The other Nisei in the outfit were doing similar kinds of work. We used to get together in the evening and bitch and gripe about the discrimination. I remember one thing that caused me to get mad and disgusted. They'd post requests for volunteers on the bulletin board. We'd always volunteer and they'd never take us.

If you had an IQ of 120 or over you were automatically entitled to apply for OCS. I appeared before a board of three officers who started asking me questions. They had a dossier on my father, and the first question was about him. [His father had been held and questioned by the FBI and then released.] One Major asked questions that I felt impugned my loyalty because of my father. I turned to him and said, "Major, he is a poor patriot whose patriotism does not enable him to understand how all men feel about their altars and their hearthstones, their flags and their fatherland," a quotation from John Sommer.

Boy, when I made that remark, you could hear a pin drop and he said, "That'll be all, Private." About two weeks later I got my notice. I had been turned down. The thing that griped me was carrying groceries from the Commissary for the officers' wives. We just hated to do that work. I told the Company Commander, "I joined the Army to fight, not to carry grocery bags for the wives"; but he chewed me out and said, "Well, you're going to do the job that you're put on."

I got mad and wrote a letter saying that we were being discriminated against in the Army and suggesting that a special Nisei combat team be formed to fight in Europe. I addressed one copy to President Roosevelt, one to Secretary of War Stimson and the third to the Chief of Staff, General Marshall. Other Nisei boys chickened out and wouldn't sign the letters; so I signed them alone and marked the envelopes "Personal."

I thought the letters would end up in the wastepaper basket. I forgot all about them. A month passed. One day I was working in the warehouse and the Company Commander comes rushing in and he asks, "Nakahara, what the hell did you do?" I said, "I don't know." He said, "Well, you better hurry up. The Post Commander wants to see you right away."

The Post Commander was named Colonel Blair. I went to his office. Marshall had written a reply saying that regrettably there were unpleasant jobs in the Army, but the jobs had to be done. He sent the letter through channels so it came to the desk of Colonel Blair, who took the trouble to explain that he was of German ancestry and during World War I he was subjected to some discrimination, that this was an unfortunate thing, but nevertheless it did occur.

Then he told me he was going to send the letter back to the commanding officer through channels. My commanding officer misunderstood, because the next thing I was called into the Company Commander's office, and he really chewed me out because I sent the letter to a superior without going through military channels. He began reading me the Articles of War. I had violated this Article and that Article. Finally he said, "You understand that what you have done is almost tantamount to treason."

I could see myself being lined up against a wall. But he said, "I'm going to give you a break. Will you take general Court Martial or company punishment?" Naturally, I took company punishment. He put me on KP and cleaning detail for a week or two. But I remember about the third day, it was a Saturday, I was scrubbing the floor when Colonel Blair happened to come through on inspection. He recognized me and asked me what I was doing. I told him I was serving company punishment for writing that letter. Then I had the pleasure of hearing my own Company Commander called in and dressed down by the Colonel.

After that I was the fair haired boy. I got a reply from every one of the three letters that I wrote, one signed by Marshall, one by Stimson and a letter from Roosevelt signed by Steve Early, who said the President was very busy and regretted he personally could not take care of the problem. It really impressed me that I would get replies from these men. For a long time I had those letters. But we had to destroy all our important documents when our outfit was going into a forward position in New Guinea.

The JACL also wanted equal treatment for Nisei in the service as well as the restoration of full eligibility for the draft and the right to volunteer. Togo Tanaka recalls that some of the JACL pronouncements from Salt Lake City, that were aimed at the American public, to the effect that loyal Nisei were waiting to volunteer for the armed forces to prove their devotion to the United States, "had a different ring inside the camp. If someone had taken a Gallup Poll at Manzanar in the summer of forty-two when half the people were suffering from diarrhea, you wouldn't have found many 'loyal volunteers.' The embittered activists among the pro-Japan elements called JACLers who advocated volunteering 'liars and hypocrites.' The kindest thing the neutralists could say was that we were stupid." Yet in August, two hundred young men at Manzanar requested combat duty and asked the government to launch a "second front," a common plea of liberals who wanted to help Russia in the war against Germany.

During Thanksgiving week JACL leaders met with Dillon Myer and other WRA administrators in Salt Lake City and made the decision to ask for the reinstatement of Selective Service for Japanese–Americans. This is sometimes regarded as the historic first step that led to the recognition of the Nisei as Americans. Henry Shimizu, a delegate from Amache, recorded in the minutes of that meeting: "We have made a most significant decision and one which we will be proud to recall in the years to come."[12]

Masao Satow, now the national director of the JACL, also attended the meeting as a delegate from Amache. Twenty-four years later, he wrote, "This was not a popular decision at the time. The most we experienced on our return to Amache was to be tagged *Amerika kusai* [Stinking Americans], which we took as a high compliment, but other delegates returned to face physical beatings."[13] Three who were attacked partly as a result of participation in the JACL meeting were Dr. T. Yatabe from the Jerome center, Fred Tayama, in the incident that provoked the Manzanar riot, and Saburo Kido, a delegate from Poston. At an informal gathering in a men's room in the Salt Lake City hotel after the vote, representatives suddenly realized how difficult it would be to return to the prevailing sentiment in the relocation centers. Particularly uneasy were the delegates who had slipped out of camp surreptitiously and planned to reenter in the same way though their names were announced in the *Pacific Citizen*. The attack on Yatabe occurred in March, 1943. Kido was ambushed in his barracks apartment in January, 1943, after he had made speeches on JACL policy. Though special lights had been put up to protect him and special guards assigned, his silent assailants removed a door, entered the apartment, and struck him on the back with an ironwood club. After a month in the hospital he was released to Salt Lake City. In the face of evacuee hostility to the JACL and its decision, Mike Masaoka was moved to declare, "The Japanese–American Citizens League never has, and never will, acknowledge any other allegiance save that to the United States of America."[14]

But the Army did not immediately reopen Selective Service to the Nisei. A more controversial challenge was thrown out to them. Elmer

An UNIDENTIFIED American Japanese bride and groom in California around 1910. After a proxy wedding ceremony at home the "picture" brides, sometimes dressed like this one in *wa-fuku* (Japanese dress) arrived in Seattle, San Francisco, and Los Angeles to join the husbands they knew only through correspondence. West Coast anti-Orientalists insisted that the importation of wives violated the spirit of the Gentlemen's Agreement and the practice was eventually discontinued, but many Japanese–American families are descended from these marriages. *Photo courtesy of Hisory Division, Los Angeles County Museum of Natural History*

AN ISSEI FISHERMAN and his son on Terminal Island in San Pedro Harbor in the early days of Japanese immigration. At the time of World War II five hundred fishermen and their families lived on the island in shacks provided by the canneries, which they rented for $15 a month. This group probably suffered more financial loss as a result of the evacuation than any other segment of the American Japanese population. *Photo courtesy of History Division, Los Angeles County Museum of Natural History*

A FARM OWNED by an American Japanese family on the coast south of Los Angeles. Along with forty others, this farm was searched in February, 1942, by FBI men looking for devices that might be used to signal enemy submarines. *Acme News photo; courtesy of United Press International*

A SOLDIER SERVES an evacuation order on a Terminal Islander. Most of the men had been arrested by the FBI on February 1, 1942; at the end of the month their families were given forty-eight hours to move to the mainland. The island was considered to be too close to a naval base and other military installations. *Acme News photo; courtesy of United Press International*

A PADLOCKED STORE in Los Angeles' Little Tokyo in March, 1942. The Federal Reserve Bank failed almost completely in its assignment to protect evacuee property. Many people lost almost everything. *Acme News photo; courtesy of United Press International*

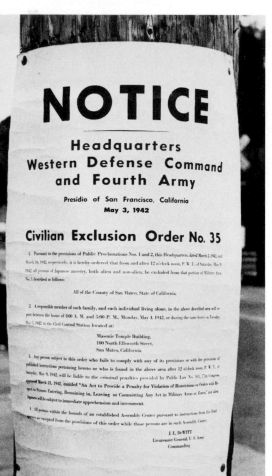

SIGNS LIKE this began to appear in store windows on the West Coast in early 1942. *Photo by Star Photographers; courtesy of the Hoover Institution on War, Revolution, and Peace, Stanford University, Stanford, California*

AN EVACUATION NOTICE nailed to a telephone pole. Between March and August, 1942, 111,000 people were sent first to hastily improvised assembly centers and later to more permanent relocation camps inland. *Photo courtesy of Burlingame (California)* Advance-Star and Green Sheet

A CARAVAN of American Japanese pioneers crosses the desert. In late March, 1942, a group of volunteers, accompanied by Army jeeps, drove to Manzanar near Lone Pine in eastern California to begin building a reception center, later a relocation center, which would eventually house thousands of evacuees. *Acme News photo; courtesy of United Press International*

SCHOOL CHILDREN walking near the tar-paper-covered barracks at Manzanar. Caucasian and evacuee teachers improvised classes in buildings like these without books, desks, or equipment of any kind. *Photo by Toyo Miyatake*

ORIGINAL DRAWING of a dust storm at Topaz, Utah, by the artist Miné Okubo, who lived for many months at Topaz. When the evacuees arrived at the desert camps in California, Arizona, Utah, Colorado, Wyoming, and Idaho, they encountered a hostile environment—fierce winds, ovenlike heat, and a barren landscape.

THE INTERIOR of a barracks at the Amache center, Granada, Colorado, in December, 1942. The Ninomiya family made their Spartan quarters homelike with curtains, bedspreads, and other amenities. *Photo by Tom Parker; courtesy of the Pacific Citizen*

YOUNG NISEI volunteering for Army service at Manzanar. In early 1943 the Secretary of War announced that the Army would enlist recruits for an all-Nisei combat team to fight in Europe. *Photo by Toyo Miyatake*

Brigadier General Frank D. Merrill in Burma in May, 1944, flanked by his Nisei interpreters, T/Sgt. Herbert Miyasaki (left) and T/Sgt. Akiji Yoshimura (right), both graduates of the Army's Military Intelligence Service language school which trained Nisei to be interpreters and translators in the Pacific. Fourteen Nisei fought with Merrill's Marauders in a hazardous campaign behind enemy lines in North Burma, and by the end of the war seven of them were commissioned. Yoshimura is today head of the organization of Nisei veterans who served in the Pacific. *U.S. Army photo*

Lieutenant General John L. DeWitt, head of the Western Defense Command, testifying on April 13, 1943, before a House Naval Affairs Subcommittee in San Francisco against allowing any American Japanese back to the West Coast. On this occasion he made his oft-quoted remark, "A Jap is a Jap." *San Francisco* Chronicle *photo*

SERGEANT HOICHI KUBO, who served with the Military Intelligence in the Pacific, comforts a Japanese child found abandoned in a field by infantrymen on Saipan in July, 1944. A few days earlier Kubo had entered a cave in the island and persuaded the natives and Japanese soldiers hiding there to give themselves up to the Americans. *U.S. Army photo*

NISEI VETERANS of the famed 442nd Infantry Combat Team present a check for $4,300 to the Franklin Delano Roosevelt Memorial Fund. Gathered for the ceremony in Washington, D.C., in September, 1945, are (left to right) Earl Finch, who befriended Nisei training at Camp Shelby, Mississippi, Pfc. George M. Tsujimoto, Pfc. Terumi Kato, Pfc. Jesse Hirata, Sergeant Yeichi Kuwayama, and Dillon Myer, director of the War Relocation Authority. *Photo by Gretchen Van Tassel; courtesy of the* Pacific Citizen

THE JEROME CENTER in Arkansas was the first to close. Here evacuees crate the family dog in June, 1944, for the move to the Gila, Arizona, camp. After a few months in the centers, residents were allowed to send for their pets. *Photo by Charles Mace; courtesy of the* Pacific Citizen

THE CEMETERY AT the Rohwer, Arkansas, center. In some camps the dead were cremated and the ashes kept for burial outside. While the evacuees were under WRA custody, there were 1,862 deaths, 5,981 births, and only four "unauthorized departures" of individuals who wandered into the desert and disappeared. *Photo courtesy of the* Pacific Citizen

MRS. HIDE KANOW stands surrounded by her possessions in July, 1945, shortly before the Rohwer, Arkansas, center closed. All four of her soldier sons were wounded in Italy. After the West Coast was reopened to people of Japanese ancestry in January, 1945, 54,127 returned there and 52,798 went to or remained in other parts of the United States or Hawaii. *Photo courtesy of the* Pacific Citizen

IN MARCH, 1945, vandals defaced the garage of the Cal Tech professor Dr. Linus Pauling, in Altadena, California, when he hired a Nisei gardener, George Mimaki, twenty-four, of nearby Sierra Madre. *Photo courtesy of the* Pacific Citizen

MRS. SHIGEO NAGAISHI and her three children returned to Seattle from the Mini-doka, Idaho, center in May, 1945, to find unwelcome messages scrawled in red paint on the side of their house and front steps, a skull and crossbones with "No Japs Wanted Here," "Beware," and "Death." Floyd Schmoe of the American Friends Service Committee gave the family moral support as they settled down to "ride out" adverse public opinion. *Acme News photo; courtesy of United Press International*

ISAMU NOGUCHI, the sculptor, at his studio in Long Island City, shortly before the retrospective exhibit of his works at the Whitney Museum in New York City in 1968. Noguchi's fame is indicative of the general esteem accorded to Japanese art and culture in the United States today. The sculptor has not forgotten the few months he spent in the Poston, Arizona, relocation center in 1942 where he felt "very deeply isolated from America." *Photo by Kaz Inouye*

THE ARTS OF JAPAN flourish in America today. Yoshiki Hirabayashi of Sunnyvale, California, donates countless hours to teaching *origami* (paper folding) and
judo to school children. Here he instructs a group of fourth graders at the Pippin
School where several children folded one thousand paper cranes apiece and sent
them to decorate the Children's Peace Shrine in Hiroshima, symbolizing present-
day amity between Japan and the United States. Hirabayashi, a Kibei, volunteered for the Army from Manzanar in the summer of 1942 at the risk of physical
attack by a dissident faction at the camp. *Photo by Rowe Photographers*

JOHN F. KENNEDY meeting with Nisei Democrats in Los Angeles before the 1960 election. From left to right, Tony Mitsumori, Ted Okumoto, Frank Chuman, Frank Kurihara, Senator Kennedy, Mary Jane Yokoi, and Kango Kunitsugu. Nisei are beginning to be active in politics. *Photo by Archie Miyatake; courtesy of the Los Angeles County Museum of Natural History*

MANZANAR twenty-five years later. Many evacuees feel impelled to return to see once again the wilderness prisons where they languished. The picture, taken in the summer of 1968, shows a corner of a burial ground left to the ravages of time and the elements. *Photo by Dale Mayer*

Davis, as director of the OWI, wrote the President in October, urging a voluntary enlistment program for Nisei as a means to counteract Axis propaganda which "insists that this is a racial war. We can combat this effectively with counterpropaganda only if our deeds permit us to tell the truth. Moreover, as citizens ourselves [he was speaking also for Milton Eisenhower] who believe deeply in the things for which we fight, we cannot help but be disturbed by the insistent public misunderstanding of the Nisei; competent authorities, including Naval Intelligence people, say that fully 85 percent of the Nisei are loyal to this country and that it *is* possible to distinguish the sheep from the goats." He concluded that, "It would hardly be fair to evacuate people and then impose normal draft procedures, but voluntary enlistment would help a lot."[15]

The Assistant Secretary of War, John McCloy, who had conferred with Dillon Myer, sent his administrative assistant, Colonel William P. Scobey to visit the relocation centers. After interviewing a number of articulate, patriotic Nisei, Scobey decided that the decision of the Washington military board which had ruled against accepting Nisei volunteers should be reversed. He persuaded McCloy to reconvene the board, and succeeded in convincing them that Nisei should be allowed to volunteer. The idea of forming a separate, all-Nisei combat unit is generally attributed to Colonel Scobey. At a later congressional hearing a senator asked Colonel Scobey, "Aren't you afraid of them [the Nisei soldiers]?" Colonel Scobey answered, "No, sir."[16]

Mike Masaoka says that the formation of the all-Nisei 442nd Infantry Combat Team Battalion was "a joint decision between the Army and the WRA, with the approval of the President and the Secretary of War." As for the often criticized segregated nature of the unit, he adds, "We called it congregation, not segregation." The unit was formed in part by bringing together on a volunteer basis Nisei servicemen dispersed in Army camps throughout the country, some of whom, incidentally, accepted a demotion in rank with the new assignment. "Our thinking was that we were inconspicuous scattered throughout the Army," Masaoka says. "Individual records wouldn't prove much. The Army had said that Nisei protestations of loyalty were so much hogwash. We had to have a demonstration in blood."

Actually, a proposal for a segregated unit had been introduced almost a year before by JACL leaders. In the spring of 1942, hoping to forestall evacuation, a Nisei group had met with Major-General Robert C. Richardson in San Jose and proposed that the Army should hold their parents as hostages and send the Nisei to fight the Japanese in the Pacific. General Richardson had replied that the Army did not believe in hostages, in segregated units (except for Negroes), or in a suicide corps.

January 28, 1943, at a press conference in his office in Washington,

Secretary Stimson announced that the War Department, after a study "of many earnest requests by loyal American citizens of Japanese extraction for the organization of a special unit of the Army in which they could have their share in the fight against the nation's enemies," would admit Nisei volunteers to a special combat team. The unit, to consist of 4,500 men, was to include the customary elements of infantry, artillery, engineer, and medical personnel. Stimson noted, "The new unit will be trained separately from the Battalion of Americans of Japanese extraction, the 100th Infantry Battalion—originally a Hawaiian National Guard organization—which is already a component of the Army." Elements of the 100th Battalion were training at Camp McCoy, Wisconsin, in the summer of 1942. Hawaiian Nisei also volunteered for the 442nd. Stimson decreed, "It is the inherent right of every faithful citizen, regardless of ancestry, to bear arms in the nation's battle."[17] On February 1, President Roosevelt, in a letter to the Secretary, commended his decision in an oft-quoted statement: "The principle on which this country is founded and by which it has always been governed is that Americanism is a matter of mind and heart; Americanism is not, and never was, a matter of race or ancestry."[18] A year after issuing the order permitting the head of the Western Defense Command to treat the Nisei as aliens, the President of the United States publicly recognized their claim to American citizenship. The change in attitude led to a clash with General DeWitt.

The War Department had demonstrated its conversion to the Justice Department viewpoint which favored "paroling" citizen evacuees. The creation of the 442nd was a form of parole since Nisei volunteers were to be accepted on a special basis with the suggestion that they must earn the privilege awarded them. President Roosevelt called it "a natural and logical step toward the reinstitution of the selective service procedures which were temporarily disrupted by the evacuation from the west coast."[19]

Even this step toward equality was protested by those who took the racial view of the Japanese. On February 19, Representative A. Leonard Allen of Louisiana spoke in Congress of his doubts "about the wisdom of that action. . . . When we place them in the Army they occupy a position where they can be of greatest harm to our Nation, and, incidentally, of greatest service to their own if they choose to pursue that course. . . . I doubt that the perfidy, the treachery, and the complete lack of elementary human principles which have been instilled into a people for centuries can be removed with one generation."[20] Some West Coast congressmen expressed somewhat similar views.

One of these critics of the Japanese, Representative Jack Z. Anderson of Gilroy, was a member of the House Naval Affairs Subcommittee which met in San Francisco on April 13. On that day General DeWitt launched his well-remembered broadside against the people he had evacuated a year before. California newspapers publicized his more intemperate remarks. The general said he "didn't care what they did with the Japanese as long as they don't send them back here. . . . It makes no difference whether the Jap is a citizen or not. He's still a Jap and can't change."[21] "A Jap's a Jap. There is no way to determine their loyalty. . . . This coast is too vulnerable. No Jap should come back to this coast except on a permit from my office."[22]

Representative Anderson later inserted a longer portion of DeWitt's testimony into the congressional record. The general told the subcommittee:

> I haven't any problems except one—that is the development of a false sentiment on the part of certain individuals and some organizations to get the Japanese back on the west coast. I don't want any of them here. They are a dangerous element. There is no way to determine their loyalty. The west coast contains too many vital installations essential to the defense of the country to allow any Japanese on this coast. There is a feeling developing, I think, in certain sections of the country that the Japanese should be allowed to return. I am opposing it with every proper means at my disposal. We can handle individuals if there aren't too many. No Japanese can come back now for any purpose except by permit from my headquarters. There are a number of Japanese in the area who are in hospitals, too sick to be moved, or in mental institutions, but very few. We let them come in in an emergency to visit the sick and those in mental institutions. We also let them come to relocation centers. The great difficulty is that if you let an individual Japanese in for any reason at all, you establish a precedent and the whole question begins to develop and ramify so you can't stop it.[23]

In mid-April, aside from hospitalized patients, and a few wives of Caucasians, only eight Nisei were allowed in an official capacity in the Western Defense Command. Seven were translators for the Federal Communications Commission, and one was an interpreter for the Immigration Department. All of them were required to wear identification at all times. Yet DeWitt felt it was necessary to investigate the past activities of the Japanese already evacuated from the West Coast. In the summer of 1942, a research division with a staff of over fifty people had been organized to study the group. Working with old vernacular newspapers, ship manifests, records of Japanese organizations and banks, the researchers, who were still at work when the war ended, recorded some 500,000 separate items of information on the dossiers of 115,000 persons.[24] There is no record of the use to which this great mass of material was put.

General DeWitt's testimony on April 13 did not go unnoticed. Representative Henry M. Jackson of Washington quoted his racial indictment with approval in Congress two days later. The editorial writer on the camp newspaper at Amache decided DeWitt was trying to justify the mistake he had made in evacuating the Japanese. "Pity him and don't waste your anger," he wrote.[25] On April 15 the Washington *Post* published an editorial entitled, "A Jap's a Jap," which gave the opinion that, "The General should be told that American democracy and the Constitution of the United States are too vital to be ignored and flouted by any military zealot. The panic of Pearl Harbor is now past. There has been ample time for the investigation of these people and the determination of their loyalty to this country on an individual basis. Whatever excuse there once was for evacuating and holding them indiscriminately no longer exists."

This was the opinion of the War Department. Colonel Scobey wrote a letter to the San Diego County Supervisors, in which he said, "The war Department feels that the retention of 100,000 people in relocation centers at the expense of the government in time of war is not only unjust to those who can establish their loyalty, but it is an unnecessary expense. . . . To condemn the Japanese in this country as a whole for the actions of the Japanese militarists does not seem to be just or appropriate."[26]

On April 19, less than a week after his statement before the House Naval Affairs Subcommittee, General DeWitt was forced to reverse his previous stand by issuing a proclamation allowing Nisei servicemen on furlough to enter the Western Defense Command. Cries of alarm greeted this proclamation, and the general's about-face was noted and commented upon. "What an utterly incomprehensible and contradictory policy for the War Department to adopt," Representative Jack Z. Anderson told the Congress on May 5. "Mr. Speaker, I am of the opinion that General DeWitt did not issue that proclamation of his own free will." At the April 13 hearing, a witness had asked, "What is the idea of putting the Japanese in the United States Army at all? Is that a matter of military policy? Did the War Department decide that? Not some civilian agency agitation?"

General DeWitt had answered, "I don't know anything about that. I have had nothing whatever to do with it. Manzanar and Tule Lake are kept under my observation as they are in the prohibited area. Recruiting parties were sent in by the War Department to obtain volunteers, and I do not want to be understood as in any way criticizing that action. At one time we had a great many Japanese in military units on the west coast. They were all, at my request, transferred out by the War Department to other organizations."[27]

Anderson charged that the general was coerced into issuing the proclamation and hinted that his impending transfer from the Western Defense Command was the result of his opposition to War Department policy on the Nisei issue. Another California congressman, Richard J. Welch, came to the same conclusion.[28] Secretary Stimson called these reports "nonsense" and praised DeWitt's handling of the evacuation.[29] His new appointment was as commandant of the Army and Navy Staff College in Washington, D.C. He was succeeded on the West Coast by General Delos Emmons, whose notably more moderate attitude toward the Japanese-ancestry population in Hawaii was being vindicated by events. Allowed to conduct themselves as free citizens, the Hawaiian Japanese had responded by making enthusiastic voluntary contributions to the war effort.

Seventy-five hundred Hawaiian Nisei wanted to join the 442nd, though the original quota called for only 1,500 men from Hawaii. By contrast, only 1,181 men volunteered from behind barbed wire in the mainland relocation centers, though the Army had hoped to enlist 3,000. The 100th Infantry Battalion, which was composed of Hawaiian Japanese National Guardsmen, acted as a lever to improve the service status of mainland Nisei. Their conduct while training at Camp McCoy, Wisconsin, in the summer of 1942 helped prepare the way for the creation of the 442nd Combat Team, and the 100th Battalion's record in Italy in late 1943 contributed to the War Department's decision to reopen Selective Service to the Nisei, as announced on January 20, 1944. Eventually, the Army went full circle in its policy. On November 24, 1944, it was announced that Japanese aliens would be allowed to volunteer. One of the first to sign up was Henry Ebihara, who had relocated in Cleveland from Topaz.[30] Certain branches of the Army, however, remained closed to the Nisei.

Japanese–Americans who held the JACL viewpoint greeted the announcement of the formation of the 442nd Combat Team with fervent gratitude. An evacuee in Minidoka said, "What we face is the acid test. If we flunk it, we damn ourselves and our posterity."[31] Mike Masaoka echoed these words. "I want to be able," he said, "in the years to come to know that my children and their children after them will not be forced to suffer, as we have suffered, because I was not visionary enough, or courageous enough to be baptised under the fire of enemy guns and to prove beyond all doubt that we who are Americans in spite of our Japanese faces are loyal to the land of our birth, even unto death. . . . I have a stake in America. I believe it is worth fighting for."[32] Larry Tajiri spoke for this opinion when he wrote that Secretary Stimson's announcement "was interpreted by the evacuees themselves as the answer of their American government to those individuals and forces within America who would deny the Japanese–American his right of participation in this struggle of the free world against the slave."[33]

In truth, many evacuees interpreted the Army's call for volunteers in an entirely different light. The controversial nature of the recruitment program might have been anticipated from the camp attitudes toward Nisei and Kibei who signed up for duty with the military intelligence from the relocation centers during the last six months of 1942. Eight Nisei who enlisted from Poston during the strike were subjected to threats from "pro-Axis sympathizers."[34]

Yoshiki Hirabayashi, a Kibei, left Manzanar on November 30, enlisting with a group of twelve Japanese–Americans. He had been working as a kitchen supply deliverer at the camp, a job which other evacuees coveted and tried to take away from him. An angry faction, consisting mainly of former fishermen from San Pedro and some gamblers from Los Angeles' Little Tokyo demanded to know why he was willing to work with *keto* (hairy foreigners) since the United States government had put him into a prisoner of war camp. Though Hirabayashi liked his job, he had never received a pay check, his savings were running low, and he had been wearing the same clothes and shoes for nine months. He decided that the only way to get out of Manzanar and earn some money was to join the Army. He also thought that if he volunteered he might have a chance to see his brother at Topaz, though this never happened.

One day towards the end of November he was called in to the administration office where two Nisei recruiting sergeants told him that the Army was looking for men like him who could understand the Japanese language. He told them that he was a Kibei with parents living in Japan and asked them whether they would trust his loyalty to the United States if he volunteered. They replied that he would be sent to the Japanese language school at Camp Savage, Minnesota, would receive his basic training afterwards and be assigned to duty in the United States. (In fact, he was shipped to the Pacific without basic training after several months in the language school.)

He agreed to enlist. On the way out of the office he was accosted by some Nisei from San Pedro and Los Angeles. As a volunteer for the United States Army he knew he would be put at the top of their black list of traitors to Japan so he had to think of a plan. He lied and told them that since he was a Kibei he didn't know enough English to be accepted by the Army. He told no one, not even his best friend, about signing up. He went on working until the day before it was time to leave, and the last day after finishing his job did not return to his apartment but went straight to the military police station and asked to be allowed to stay there overnight. An MP went to his apartment to pick up his suitcase and he left Manzanar safely.

As noted earlier, the months in camp had polarized opinion into extremes. Many evacuees interpreted any sort of cooperation with the government that had wronged them as a betrayal of the group. When Nisei soldiers came to the centers to recruit volunteers for the 442nd Combat

Team, people demanded to know, "What are you doing on that side?" The War Department had judged that the presence of Nisei on the recruiting team would stimulate enlistment, but the propaganda misfired. The fact that the Nisei were enlisted men serving under Caucasian officers was cited as proof of the Army's discrimination. At the Butte camp at Gila, the Nisei sergeant who presided at a meeting to explain the program "was greeted with howls of derision and was not allowed to present his prepared speech."[35]

Soon after Secretary Stimson's January 28 announcement, ten recruiting teams of four men each were hastily assembled in Washington for a briefing before being sent to the relocation centers. The War Department, expecting some adverse reaction to the recruitment program, prepared a statement of rebuttal to the question of whether it was fair to ask citizens to volunteer from behind barbed wire. The inequity of the Nisei situation was acknowledged, but young men were to be asked to look upon the evacuation and detention as a temporary sacrifice of the "best interests of the few . . . for what seems the good of the many," and to welcome the opportunity to serve as a partial restoration of citizen rights.[36]

The reaction at many of the relocation centers to this argument was much more hostile than the recruiting team was prepared for. At Poston as soon as the young lieutenant had finished his speech, the crowd burst on him with such questions as, "Why are the loyal Japanese–Americans not allowed to go back to California?" "My two brothers [in Army camps] have been denied permission to visit our sick father in the Los Angeles County Hospital. Why can't they, who are in the uniform of the U.S. Army, visit their dying father when Caucasians in Army uniforms may do so?" "What is the reason for giving some of us 4-C classification? We are without a country now." "Why were Nisei kicked out of the Army after December 7?" "Why can't Nisei soldiers visit this camp? Are you afraid they will see how bad conditions are in camp?" "Why were Nisei changed from combat duty to menial tasks after Pearl Harbor?" "Why are Nisei not accepted in the Navy?" "Why the Jim Crow decision?" "Why were the Nisei stripped of their ranks after Pearl Harbor?" "Why were veterans of the last war put in camps when they proved their loyalty then?" "If we volunteer, will our interned parents [in Justice Department camps] be returned to our families?" "May a Nisei apply for appointment to West Point?"[37]

The War Department's presentation was based on the assumption that the Nisei would respond to a patriotic challenge; the extent to which the group might react in the contentious spirit of their American upbringing was overlooked. The movie actor Lee Tracy arrived in uniform at Topaz and had considerable influence with the younger generation, though a newspaper editor commented that with "Armed guards around the fence being our only contact with men in uniform for nearly a year, it was difficult for the military team of four . . . to put over the idea that they were sincere in their attempt to assist the Nisei."[38] A petition was drawn up by a committee of Nisei asking that the Secretary of War allow evacuees cleared by the FBI and other agencies "absolute freedom of movement and a choice of returning to their homes"; that "security for the Issei be assured"; that Issei judged loyal be classified as "friendly aliens"; that the Nisei be dispersed throughout the Army rather than segregated; and "that the government, recognizing that we are fighting for the Four Freedoms as embodied in the Atlantic Charter, should apply these democratic principles to us here at home."[39] When answers came from Dillon Myer and the War Department urging cooperation in this "crucial test," the committee agreed to accept the registration and recruitment.[40]

The response to the call for volunteers was more affirmative at Minidoka than at any other center. The Nisei leaders, with the Army team and the administration playing self-imposed auxiliary roles, effectively convinced most of the evacuees that the future of the Japanese in America could depend greatly on the success of the recruiting program. In an editorial in the Minidoka *Irrigator*, Dyke Miyagawa applauded the chance to prove loyalty on the battlefield, but questioned the plan to set up a segregated Nisei combat unit. His criticism was censored by the WRA staff, but he published the commentary, leaving blanks where the words had been deleted. As noted earlier, the relationship between administrators and evacuees at Minidoka was good at this time. Five days of intensive discussion had preceded the arrival of the Army team. The staff forestalled a plan to put sentries in the watchtowers, and asked the Washington office "to take steps to improve the status and facilitate the release of Department of Justice internees whose sons volunteered for induction."[41] The Nisei responded affirmatively.

The same persuasions were not effective elsewhere. At Gila when the officer read the prepared statement and added that he expected to enlist 300 to 350 volunteers from the camp, the evacuees leaders pointed out that Japanese–Americans had already shown their patriotism by cooperating with the evacuation in which they had suffered a denial of all their rights and that asking them to volunteer for the Army under these conditions was not a privilege but a sacrifice.[42] Some of the Army recruiters conveyed the impression, "Uncle Sam doesn't particularly need you, but is giving you a chance to show your loyalty and vindicate your people." The Nisei reaction to this was, "If they don't need us, why volunteer?" If the response was poor, evacuees were sometimes reminded they might be drafted.

When a recruiting officer at Poston announced that the Army would accept loyal Issei, the crowd hooted, "Try and get one."[43] The Issei were in a morbid state as a result of incarceration in what an observer called an "ostrichlike community." Their security was threatened once again. It was unthinkable that their sons should go to battle against Japan. Above all, having lost so much else, they did not want to lose their sons. In the Japanese tradition, soldiers went to war expecting to be killed.

The Issei could not easily sacrifice the expectation of family continuity. Two sociologists described the predicament of the first generation. "Old-age security among the Japanese is institutionalized in the practice of *inkyo* (in which aged parents are relieved of economic and social responsibilities by the eldest son). Although the evacuation had swept away their hard-earned economic security, the security of the integral family unit had largely survived. In threatening to separate the Issei and Nisei . . . the registration program denied the Issei the secure present within which to adjust to a disrupted past and an uncertain future."[44] Issei were afraid of being deported or exchanged for captives while their sons were in the Army.

A young bachelor explained his feelings about refusing to go into the Army:

> My dad is fifty-eight years old now. He has been here [the U.S.] thirty years at least. He came to this country with nothing but a bed roll. He worked on the railroads and he worked in the sugar-beet fields. If I told you the hardships he had you wouldn't believe me. I owe a lot to my father. Everything I am I owe to him. All through his life he was working for me. During these last years he was happy because he thought he was coming to the place where his son would have a good life. I am the only son. I have to carry on the family name. You white people have some feeling like this but with us it is greatly exaggerated.
>
> I tell you this because it has something to do with my answer about the draft question. We are taught that if you go out to war you should go out with the idea that you are never coming back . . . That's the Japanese way of looking at it. . . .
>
> In order to go out prepared and willing to die, expecting to die, you have to believe in what you are fighting for. If I am going to end the family line, if my father is going to lose his only son, it should be for some cause we respect. . . . I would have been willing to go out forever before evacuation. It's not that I'm a coward or afraid to die. My father would have been willing to see me go out at one time. But my father can't feel the same after this evacuation and I can't either. . . .
>
> There isn't much I can do for my father any more; I can't work for him the way I used to. But I can at least quiet his mind on this.[45]

A Nisei woman thinks her mother had a minor nervous breakdown "after being thrown into camp and the boys taken one by one." There were five sons in the Army. All survived the war. In another family, the son did not volunteer, but agreed to be drafted. His parents would hardly speak to him for two months. Whenever his mother looked at him, her eyes would fill with tears. At the time George Aki signed up to become a chaplain with the 442nd, his mother said, "You're going to be mere cannon fodder. You have no gratitude to us." His response was, "No matter what has happened in the past, America is still my country. This is where my children will be born and will grow up." He thinks he was influenced by an awareness of some support from the Caucasian community. "People were sticking their necks out. They're the ones who made me see what America could be."

Wayne Kanemoto says, "I didn't feel outraged. I felt that this was war and war was an unreasonable thing. . . . So when they asked for volunteers for the Army, I volunteered. Lots of people said I was crazy, but thirty-three of us volunteered from our relocation center on the first trip out. I was in that first group. I thought, well, I'll do everything I'm supposed to do so that nobody could say afterwards that I didn't pull my share. When I volunteered and got ready to go, they said my draft board in Santa Clara County [California] hadn't changed my classi-fication from 4-c and they couldn't take me. I said, 'What do you mean you can't take me? You wanted me to volunteer and I volunteered. Now you tell me I can't go because someone has got me reclassified which I know nothing about.' So they wired and got my classification changed just barely in time to let me leave with this group."

A diametrically opposite opinion was expressed by a Nisei at another center. "What do they take us for? Saps? First, they change my army status to 4-c because of my ancestry, run me out of town, and now they want me to volunteer for a suicide squad so I could get killed for this damn democracy. That's going some for sheer brass!"[46]

The chief source of anger was the questionnaire that all volunteers for the Combat Team as well as all other center residents were required to fill out. The registration and the recruiting were conducted simul-taneously, with disastrous results. "The Army were cowboys, and the Japs were cattle," one protester said. The evacuees were being rounded up and separated, the good ones from the bad ones. "The whole thing was botched," according to Mike Masaoka.

The WRA, with JACL approval, was beginning an all-out effort to get the evacuees out of the camps, unaware that such a program would be very unpopular with the Issei in particular. At the time of the question-naire, only college students, farm workers on temporary leave, candi-dates for the military intelligence language school, and a few others had left the centers, but the WRA was trying to expedite a mass movement to the East and Middle West. People wishing to relocate had been frus-trated by delays of as much as three months on getting clearance from the FBI, in which time job offers were sometimes lost. The WRA therefore decided to take advantage of the Army's processing of citizen volunteers to register at the same time the entire evacuee population. Robert C. Cozzens, West Coast director of the WRA, now feels, "There was absolutely no need for it in my estimation. We had enough information on everybody in the centers at that time. The military could have picked out anyone they didn't want without any problem."

The loyalty oath demanded of all residents exploded an emotional holocaust and damaged the recruiting program. It is hard to explain how the WRA which had consistently opposed discriminatory screening procedures could have imposed such a cruel and meaningless test upon the captive American Japanese. The answer must lie in good part with the sentiment of the American people in 1943. Relocation and Army service for Nisei were unpopular at the outset. Incarceration being proof of guilt, a public fed on wartime propaganda was nervous about the release of potential spies and saboteurs. A technical affirmation of loyalty on a certificate offered a means to allay popular fears.

But the questions were devised without thought of their effect on the people who were required to answer them. Daisuke Kitagawa, who was at Tule Lake, wrote:

> . . . the whole program not only was based on muddled thinking, but also was executed with undue rigidity. . . . Their freedom having been taken away, the Issei in the relocation center were far from being free moral agents: they were psychologically incapable of making decisions freely any more, for they were collectively in a pathological state.[47]

Two registration forms were prepared in Washington, one for male citizens seventeen years or over, and the other for everyone else. The first twenty-six questions dealt with age, occupation, close relatives in Japan, foreign travel and investments, memberships in clubs and societies, dual citizenship, and newspapers and magazines customarily read.

The controversial questions were numbers 27 and 28. In Question 27, Nisei men were asked, "Are you willing to serve in the armed forces of the United States on combat duty, wherever ordered?" A different version of Question 27, intended for young women, was asked of all other adults, "If the opportunity presents itself and you are found qualified, would you be willing to volunteer for the Army Nurse Corps or the WAAC?"

Question 28 asked male Nisei, eligible for service, "Will you swear unqualified allegiance to the United States of America and faithfully defend the United States from any or all attack by foreign or domestic forces, and forswear any form of allegiance or obedience to the Japanese emperor, or any other foreign government, power, or organization?" All others, including Issei, were asked, "Will you swear unqualified allegiance to the United States of America and forswear any form of allegiance or obedience to the Japanese emperor, or any other foreign government, power, or organization?"

The only persons who were not required to fill out the questionnaire were those who had applied for repatriation to Japan. The compulsory registration of all other center residents ushered in a period of acute turmoil bordering on civil war in most of the centers. The Nisei were outraged that as Americans they were asked to repudiate Japan. The dilemma of the Issei was even more acute. Not allowed to become American citizens, they were asked, in effect, to relinquish Japanese citizenship, to become men and women without a country.

The questions were "a real trap" in the opinion of a WRA man. Eight staff members at Manzanar wrote an angry protest to the project director, demanding that "the answers to the so-called loyalty question, Question 28, be thrown in the waste-basket where they belong, and that any request for an affirmation on this subject, if one is thought necessary, or desirable, be divorced from any other kind of confusing or disturbing registration. We believe that loyalty is a matter of activity, behavior and record and that if there is nothing in these to prove otherwise, loyalty should and must be assumed. . . . We can recognize that no setting was more inauspicious for a determination of simple loyalty than the one into which the Nisei were injected. We can recognize that the answer wrung from them under the strains and perplexities with which they were faced is no more an evidence of witchcraft."

The question for Issei at most centers was eventually changed to: "Will you swear to abide by the laws of the United States and to take no action which would in any way interfere with the war effort of the United States?" This satisfied those who felt as one man did, "No Issei would disobey the laws of the United States. They've always been law-abiding. In that sense they can be called loyal to the United States. On the other hand, none of them are disloyal to Japan. You can't use the word "loyalty" or "disloyalty" for Issei because it just doesn't apply to them."[48] But another fear made many Issei hesitate to say "yes." Their questionnaire was called "WAR RELOCATION AUTHORITY APPLICATION FOR LEAVE CLEARANCE" and it was rumored that residents who answered "yes" to Questions 27 and 28 would be forced to leave the relocation centers whether they wished to go or not.

If the questions were a trap, the evacuees were not going to jeopardize their security by avowing a technical loyalty. As one woman said, "It was a question of lying or facing more hardship." A member of a family who signed "no" to Questions 27 and 28 interpreted their motives, "My family did not consider relocation at any time because we were so broke." His father ordered him and his brother to sign "no-no," and both complied. "When I signed 'no-no' on the questionnaire I did not know what patriotism meant," he said later. "I did not know what was going on and I did not know what to do. . . . My 'no' answer simply implied that I was not going to join the Army. It meant nothing else to me."[49]

The WRA offered relocation as a reward for loyalty but to many evacuees, it was a threat that caused them to avow disloyalty. At Gila when the recruiting officer said that families who had a son in the army would be given preference in the matter of relocation, "a hiss of protest went up throughout the audience. It was pointed out to him that he apparently did not realize that the average modal age of Issei was 56, of Nisei 21. The Nisei was the breadwinner of the family, and if he were drafted the family hope of resettlement would be gone."[50]

The fear of uprooting was very evident in the hearings that followed the registration, when those who answered "no" were asked if they wanted to change their answers. An Issei at Tule Lake failed to register "because of the rumor that those who registered would be forced to leave and he had no place to go."[51] Another Issei woman was asked, through an interpreter, "Will she abide by the laws of the United States and not harm the war effort?" "She says that if she answers yes, she might have to leave. . . . She says she can't do any harm anyway because she doesn't want to leave. She has that fear she can't squelch."[52] Another Tulean burst forth angrily, "Hell, you can't consider me disloyal. I've been loyal too long. But if I can't stay by being loyal, I'm going to be disloyal. I told the interviewer that I wanted to stay here, and he said that I could."[53]

For the very reason that they had been taught American principles in school, many Nisei answered "no" as a protest. An idealistic Kibei at Gila said, "I answered the loyalty questions in the negative. These were the days when I thought I had certain rights inherent in my citizenship and that I should demand them."[54] Another young man at the same center who signed "yes" to both questions "turned to the officer and said, 'And now, am I an American citizen again?' The officer replied, 'Of course you are.' The young man then asked, 'May I go to Phoenix?' and when the officer answered, 'Of course not, that's a prohibited area,' the young man tore up his questionnaire, saying, 'That's the way I feel about your attitude toward our citizenship!' "[55]

Other Nisei were afraid that if they volunteered for the Army they would be forced to fight against relatives in Japan. Some feared their relatives would suffer reprisals by the Japanese government if they pledged loyalty to the United States. Many Issei and some Nisei as well, felt that, as a result of their losses, there was no future for them in America. A number of Issei hoped Japan would win the war, or expected Japan would win, or were neutral, but had money or land in Japan and were reluctant to sever ties. Among some Issei and Kibei there was a long persisting dream, which enabled them to bear the humiliation of their prisoner's lot, in which a victorious Japan rewarded those who were faithful.

All of these feelings affected answers to the questionnaire, as did simple carelessness or bravado. A recruiter at Manzanar is said to have greeted a group of Terminal Islanders, "I suppose you are the 'no-no' boys." So they wrote, "no-no." In discussing the inadequacy of Question 28 as a test of loyalty, Morton Grodzins concludes, "In fact, it was not possible to separate those who answered 'No' for reasons of 'conviction' from those who did so as a means of protest or to maintain family units or attain security. The reasons were hopelessly intertwined, and all of them—or any combination—could go into a single 'No' response."[56]

His study of the answers at one center revealed, predictably, that Nisei were more likely to answer "no" if they had been educated in Japan, were Buddhists (rather than Christians or nonbelievers), if they came from an area unfavorable to Japanese before the war, or if their previous occupations had involved little contact with Caucasians.[57] In looking at the actual story of registration at the ten centers, it is clear that the influence of various factions upon one another and the reaction of the administration must also be taken into account. At several centers coercion, or attempted coercion, played an important role. A writer in the *Pacific Citizen* commented that in some cases, *"loyalty was to a degree dependent upon and relative to the amount of protection offered by the administration."*[58] Staff members at some centers acted to curb the threats of organized opponents to registration and recruiting. In addition to providing protection, the WRA also attempted to affect the outcome of registration by offering rewards and threatening penalties.

In at least two centers anti-administration ringleaders were removed. At Gila the chief agitator was warned by the project director that if he did not cooperate with the Army, he might be indicted under the Espionage Act. When negative answers continued, the FBI was called in and removed twenty-eight Issei and Kibei suspects, who were sent to internment and isolation centers. With the demonstrators curbed, registration became a matter of family decision.[59]

The initial response to recruiting was poor at Amache. Colonel Scobey telephoned Masao Satow, chairman of the Community Council, asking him to talk to fellow evacuees. Using Scobey's answers to the objections that were being voiced, Satow and his fellow council members called another mass meeting and later visited every Nisei in the center who had answered "no," persuading a good many people to change their answers.

At Jerome when George Aki went to the mess hall to register, the pro-Japan people were sitting outside the door waiting for him when he came out. "They jeered and called us traitors. One young man whose dad was ringleader came to me and said, 'You're a nut!' I asked him, 'Am I bothering you? You do anything you want to. Go back to Japan where your folks fled from years back. Your decision is yours. Mine is mine. Just mind your own business.' "

The emotion was most extreme at Tule Lake where registration had been poorly prepared for and the relations between evacuees and administrators were not conducive to cooperation. Rocks were thrown through windows and rebels threatened families with baseball bats. "People you knew before you left who had been your friends turned against you," said one man. Sada Murayama as an "unprotected woman" (her mother and two daughters were with her) was subjected to pressure from the anti-administration group. They wanted her to answer "no." She didn't feel she could do this. She was the mother of two Americans. "My children had had the benefit of living in this country." The hostile faction nailed her door shut so she couldn't get out. "They thought since I was friendly with the Administration I was telling tales. So they kept me, a possible informer, under restraint. I was very hurt. How could I turn against my own people?"

Opposition at Tule Lake took the form of refusing to register. In order to break the boycott against registration, the Army took cognizance of the real fears and motivations of the evacuees, which were to no small degree the reverse of government expectations, by posting the following information:

> Nisei and Kibei who answer "No" to questions No. 27 and 28, and who persist in that answer, *cannot anticipate that the Army of the United States will ever ask for their services* or that they will be inducted into the armed forces by Selective Service.
>
> A "No" answer on question 27 accompanied by a "Yes" answer on question 28, *is not regarded by the War Department as a proof of disloyalty* in the individual, or as bearing on that question . . .[but] these men have the minimum chance of being called into the military service.
>
> The "Yes" answer to both questions speaks for itself. . . . In case it is so filled, then *they are liable to induction* for general service elsewhere throughout the Army of the United States, in the same manner as any other inductee within the country.[60]

Some residential blocks pledged themselves to noncooperation. As a protest a large number of Nisei and Kibei applied for expatriation. Thirty-four ringleaders were arrested and taken by military police to county jails. The WRA threatened fines and imprisonment to those who refused to comply with registration, but 42 per cent of the residents either answered "no" or refused to register. The pressure of the staff in this instance, where there had been poor communication, served to harden the opposition. It was discovered, when Dillon Myer queried the War Department, that registration was not compulsory after all. "No announcement of this fact, however, was made to the evacuees, who were allowed to continue in the belief that they were violating the Espionage Act by failing to register."[61] They remained adamant.

An older woman Kibei at another center delayed answering until the last day. "One of the *hakujin* [whites] at the office asked me what I was going to do, and I was ashamed to tell him."[62] Her husband, an Issei, would not allow them to relocate as she wished to do. A Nisei said, "A lot of people were very bitter. I guess I was, too. But still, what can you do? We were not citizens of Japan. We had to make a choice."

Ironically, more of the aliens than the citizens pledged loyalty to America. Statistics gathered from all ten centers show that 25 per cent of Nisei men and 18 per cent of the women refused to swear allegiance to the United States; whereas only 10 per cent of the Issei men and 7 per cent of the Issei women answered "no" to the modified Question 28. This was a result not anticipated by the Army and the WRA.

Minidoka and Amache led the other centers in "yes" answers. In the ten centers several thousand people refused to register at all. At Tule Lake almost half of the residents either answered "no" to Question 28 or refused to register. At Manzanar and Jerome about 26 per cent of the evacuees answered "no" to Question 28. The Army recruitment program fell far short of expectation. As mentioned before, only 1,181 Nisei volunteered, though a quota of over 3,000 had been set. At Manzanar only forty-two young men agreed to offer their services to the Combat Team.

The eight staff members at Manzanar who protested the questionnaire, concluded that, "No segment of our population or of any population would have answered differently in the same circumstances. A much more pressing *question* is that of *America's Loyalty* to fair-play and the democratic credo." Yasuo William Abiko, describing the outcome of registration at Topaz, wrote, "As it was many were called upon to make decisions under great emotional strain, giving answers which they will regret or are already regretting."[63]

The uproar reached Washington. Harold Ickes, Secretary of the Interior, wrote the President in mid-April, 1943, about his concern:

> Information that has come to me from several sources is to the effect that the situation in at least some of the Japanese internment camps is bad and is becoming worse rapidly. Native-born Japanese who first accepted with philosophical understanding the decision of their Government to round up and take far inland all the Japanese along the Pacific Coast, regardless of their degree of loyalty, have pretty generally been disappointed with the treatment that they have been accorded. Even the minimum plans that had been formulated and announced with respect to them

have been disregarded in large measure, or, at least, have not been carried out. The result has been the gradual turning of thousands of well-meaning and loyal Japanese into angry prisoners. I do not think that we can disregard, as of no official concern, the unnecessary creating of a hostile group right in our own territory. . . .[64]

While the registration was in progress, Senator A. B. Chandler of Kentucky, led an investigation of the relocation centers by the Senate Committee on Military Affairs. The group traveled approximately 7,000 miles by train and auto, inspected six centers and held ten hearings, interviewing project directors, school superintendents at the camps, agricultural managers, the fathers of Nisei Army volunteers, and the fathers of Nisei who answered "no-no."

An evacuee described Chandler's survey of his relocation center, "Senator Chandler spent about two hours . . . riding through in a car with two armed soldiers on the running board to 'protect' him. These investigations were a hoax and we laugh about them whenever they come up in our conversation. But it's bitter laughter when we read in newspaper releases by the Committee: 'After careful investigation . . .' "[65]

The anti-Japanese press made sensational copy of Chandler's reports, which included the statistics, embarrassing to the government, on Nisei "disloyalty" in the registration. The figures were exaggerated by newspapers. It was reported, for instance, that of disloyal Japanese, 30 to 40 per cent were "definitely enemies of this country" and were counting on reparations they would extort "when Japan wins the war."[66] This alarmist tone was not characteristic of Senator Chandler himself.

Though his inspection of the centers may have been superficial, his committee's lengthy report is, for the most part, fair and factual, in notable contrast to the Dies Committee's strident distortions (in an apparent attempt to promote panic) on the question of un-Americanism in the centers. Senator Chandler's recommendations were essentially in harmony with the policies of the War Department and the WRA. He recommended that Nisei be drafted, that the "loyal" evacuees be released from the centers and the "disloyal" segregated, and that the centers be dissolved at the end of the war. A failure to separate the "loyal" from the "disloyal," he said, "will result in the continuation of this melting pot, which is not really a melting pot. We are making enemies for this country. We are making enemies of people who would otherwise support the country and be loyal to it. They are being made disloyal."[67] Some form of segregation had been contemplated by the WRA almost since its inception.

As early as August, 1942, before the Poston and Manzanar "incidents," Dillon Myer had indicated at a staff meeting that he was in favor of separating disparate elements in the center population. General DeWitt had wanted the Kibei isolated, and later proposed another scheme for separating "undesirables" which Dillon Myer blocked. Lieutenant Commander K. D. Ringle, who was assigned briefly to the WRA, suggested that Kibei and their parents be required to state their loyalties, but Myer had opposed a special policy for this group.[68]

The responses to the loyalty questionnaire provided a criterion though a manifestly unjust one, for judging the evacuees, and the turmoil in the centers at the time of registration created an additional impetus for a segregation program. The JACL favored segregation. "We thought if we could get the two groups separated, it would be easier to get the Nisei into the mainstream of American life," says Mike Masaoka. An editorial in the *Pacific Citizen* in March, 1943, approved Senator Chandler's recommendation. It spoke of the intimidation tactics of pro-Axis elements in the centers and the WRA attempts to control them, adding, however, that segregation of the disloyal was a sensitive task. The method of deciding who was disloyal "must not be determined in any arbitrary, mechanical way."[69] The writer implied that some evacuees had been coerced into giving disloyal answers.

On July 6, 1943, the United States Senate adopted a resolution requesting the WRA to segregate "persons of Japanese ancestry in relocation centers whose loyalty to the United States is questionable or who are known to be disloyal."[70] On July 15, Dillon Myer complied by announcing a segregation program. The Tule Lake center was chosen as the camp for the "disloyal." To it were to be sent:

> I. All persons who had formally asked for repatriation or expatriation before July 1, 1943, and did not retract their applications before that date.
> II. All persons who, during the February and March registration (a) answered question 28 in the negative, or (b) failed or refused to answer it, or (c) failed or refused to register at all and (d) had not changed their answers or registered affirmatively prior to July 15, 1943, and (e) were, in the opinion of the Project Director, loyal to Japan, and not loyal to the United States.
> III. All persons who were denied leave clearance after appropriate hearings. This category included (a) persons about whom there was an adverse report by a Federal intelligence agency; (b) persons who had answered 28 negatively and who changed their answers prior to July 15; (c) persons who answered question 28 with a qualification; (d) . . . persons who had requested repatriation or expatriation subsequent to July 1; (e) persons for whom the Japanese American Joint Board established in the Provost Marshal General's office did not affirmatively recommend leave clearance; (f) persons about whom there was other information indicating loyalty to Japan.[71]

The prospective expatriates and repatriates were not to have a hearing. Hearings were held for evacuees who answered "no" to see if they would reconsider. Those who had changed their answers were also questioned about their sincerity.[72] In the opinion of one Nisei, the project directors had an interest in lowering the number of "disloyal" because the figures reflected on the administration of the given center, "disloyalty" being often synonymous with dissatisfaction. On the other hand, the segregated group included people who had answered "yes" to Question 28, but who either wanted to return to Japan themselves or were the relatives of people who did. At the hearings WRA officials were made aware, if they had not been before, of the variety of motives that prompted the answers on which now so much depended.

A Kibei who did not change his "no" answer said, "I was asked at the hearing whether or not I was mad, and I said, 'Yes.' I have my citizenship and I was put in camp. They asked me why I don't go out, and I said that I have been living in camp so long that, financially, I would not be able to go out unless there is an assurance of a steady job. They asked me, if I go to Japan, would I serve in the Army over there? I said that I would, though I do not like war. Nevertheless, there is a law which says that I must if I am in Japan. . . . There was a time when I thought of resettling, but I gave that up due to insecurity and uneasiness."[73]

If the registration had taken place a year earlier while the Japanese were still free, the result might have been very different. Morton Grodzins reported the following testimony at other hearings.

> NISEI: We have citizenship and we are still in camps. We are treated just like aliens. So what's the use of talking about citizenship and being loyal citizens.
> HEARING OFFICER: But that's what this hearing is for, so that you can prove you are a loyal citizen and help free yourself of restrictions.
> NISEI: If we say "yes," can we go back to California?
> HEARING OFFICER: We can't promise anything like that. That is strictly up to the Army. . . .
> NISEI: If "loyal" citizens can't go where they want to it's discrimination. That's why we said "no" in the first place. . . .
> HEARING OFFICER: Don't you think you should consider what the question means? It's a loyalty question and if you say "no" to it you are saying that you are not loyal.
> NISEI: You people say that a Jap's a Jap. . . . You've ruined our future. We had something to look forward to; now it is all gone.[74]

Another Nisei, when asked if he was loyal to Japan rather than to the United States, answered, "The only way I can say is that my loyalty is more to Japan than to the United States. That's the way my conscience tells me to say. Before evacuation it was different. We were making a pretty good living. I was just beginning to get started. Then this thing came and took our property. It doesn't seem fair. A country that wants you or wants your loyalty doesn't treat you this way."[75]

Hime Enomoto, still in her teens, had made the decision to answer "yes." It was a decision to stay in this country. Her parents followed her example. In another family, the father wanted to go back to Japan "for America would not be fair." The mother and two children wanted to stay. The father said he would go alone. "They went round and round on it." Finally, the teen-age son made the decision that they would all go with the father. But segregation separated other families. In one, the oldest brother, a Kibei, and a member of the clandestine pro-Japanese organization in camp, was arrested and sent to an isolation center while two younger brothers answered "yes." In some instances, children either had to lose their parents or lose their birthright. Mrs. George Aki, in working for the Welfare Department at Jerome, encountered many agonizing situations. There was one case where the father answered for the whole family that they would all go to Tule Lake. He died before it was time to leave and the children came to her and asked to have the decision changed, which was arranged. When she called on another family, the Issei father upbraided her, because, having recently visited Japan herself, she urged him to wait until after the war to decide whether to return there. The son apologized to her later for the father's anger. They did not go to Tule Lake, either.

Another large family had two unmarried daughters. One was allowed by her parents to relocate in the Middle West, but they were determined to take their youngest child with them to Tule Lake as well as the families of two married children in camp. The younger girl objected so much that her father became afraid that she might try to run away. She did make two unsuccessful attempts to flee. Finally, she escaped with the help of the administration. While her father was visiting the latrine, she dashed out of the barracks, into the next block, and to the home of the project director. Without going through any red tape, he drove her to the Rohwer center nearby. She was given sanctuary away from her family for a week and was determined not to see them. They finally relented and let her join a married sister at Heart Mountain.

One boy wrote a Caucasian friend, "I trust the government more than my old man. I want to live here and they want to go back to the old country. As for me, I do not care if I am against my old man and the rest of the aliens. I'm sick of the old men telling me what to do. I hope you will understand me. I'm different from the other Nisei."[76]

Women whose husbands were in Justice Department camps had to decide whether to join them and face deportation (the Crystal City, Texas, camp had family quarters) or to relocate alone. And their children, if they did not accept unquestioningly a maternal edict, had to decide whether their future was with their family or with their country. Before they left the centers the people bound for Tule Lake were sometimes ostracized. A child who was going to leave with his family was tormented by his schoolmates in the playground. They would taunt him, shouting, "Akio was born in Japan! Akio was born in Japan!" "No! No!" he would answer, "I was born in Fresno. You *know* I was born in Fresno."[77]

The exchange of evacuees took place between September and October. Many Tule Lake residents refused to leave; over a thousand who had answered "yes" to the loyalty questionnaire would not consent to move again. Many Tuleans had written "no" in order to stay. Finally, 6,250 people left Tule Lake for six other centers, while some 12,000 people were transferred to Tule Lake.

Carey McWilliams, watching the departure of segregees from some of the centers, saw "the anguish, the grief, the bottomless sorrow that this separation occasioned . . . this was a final separation, a fateful farewell. Parents were being separated from children and children from parents; brother from brother, sister from sister. In these scenes was the stuff of timeless tragedy. . . ."[78]

The "no-nos," as they were called, were sometimes taken away at night. The story is told that when two trains passed each other, one filled with the "loyal," the other with the "disloyal," youngsters from the first group shouted at the others, "Go back to Tokyo, you Jap bastards!" One group was moving in the direction of America, the other toward Japan.

ELEVEN · THE CONSEQUENCES

AFTER SEGREGATION, the evacuees adopted three different life modes. The more restless and enterprising, who had the opportunity, left the centers under the relocation program. This had been happening since 1942, and the registration gave an increased impetus to the granting of leaves. These new settlers, widely dispersed, made a place for themselves in wartime America.

At the opposite extreme, the segregated "disloyal" evacuees at Tule Lake were cut off from the rest of the country, suspected and feared by outsiders and divided among themselves, at the mercy of "the undercurrents of terror and destruction."

The third group, who remained in the nine centers for the "loyal," set to work to establish more satisfying societies, also insulated from the world, also Japanese in character. The WRA described the period in these nine centers between November, 1943, and December, 1944, when the evacuation orders were rescinded, as one of "settling down." The community analysts concluded, "There was unquestionably, after registration, a larger area of common ground on which evacuees and staff could stand to deal together with common problems in the centers."[1] Paradoxically, this period was characterized both by a limitation of aims and an expansion of actual freedom. The staff came to accept the evacuee view of the centers as Japanese colonies rather than showcase American democracies. Having reached a *modus vivendi*, tension between the governors and the governed relaxed at many centers and some restrictions were lifted.

The greater leniency was noted with alarm by critics. The WRA was under constant attack in Congress in 1943. "We were the most investigated agency in government during that year," Dillon Myer said later.[2] Beginning with Senator Mon C. Wallgren's statement in January, hardly a month passed in which a legislator did not propose to transfer the American Japanese to the control of the Army or the Justice Depart-

ment. Even the Chandler Committee, which made constructive suggestions in harmony with the WRA objectives, was critical of its personnel.
Senator Chandler gave his opinion as follows: "I may say that generally,
from the top, that is from Mr. Myer on down through each one of the
officers, these people are sincere and God-fearing, honest, well-meaning
American citizens, but they are theorists, they are professors, they are
making a social experiment out of this thing."[3]

Of all the investigating bodies, the Dies Committee (the House Committee on Un-American Activities), which received a $75,000 appropria-
tion early in 1943, and its adjunct, the Costello Subcommittee, were the
most vocal. The Dies Committee was taking credit for having forced the
evacuation in the first place, though the claim has little validity in view
of the fact that the much-publicized "Yellow Book" on West Coast
spies was released to the press after Roosevelt had signed the executive
order permitting General DeWitt to remove the Japanese.

Dillon Myer called the Dies Committee probe of the WRA, which
began before the segregation of the "disloyal," in May, 1943, at the
instigation of Representative J. Parnell Thomas of New Jersey, "a smear
campaign."[4] The committee had decided that the evacuees were dangerous saboteurs who were being negligently guarded. Before the congressmen had visited a single relocation center, they announced that there
were 25,000 subversives in the camps. The evidence given at the hearings was often ludicrously irrelevant.

Actually, many of the shocking disclosures were wholly or partly true.
The evacuees were people and, for the most part, the WRA treated
them like people. Possessed of a growing amount of freedom and a great
deal of ingenuity, they began to create societies that certainly were
not typically American. But neither were they un-American, in the Dies
Committee sense. At the nine centers for the "loyal," the communal
life that evolved represented a cultural accommodation to circumstances
that was essentially nonpolitical.

The committee was concerned with "Americanizing" the Japanese,
yet members proclaimed to the public for its shock value the fact that the
evacuees had equal rights with the administration in the governing of
Poston. The WRA described the new collaboration differently: "Community government became in actuality an adjunct of administration."[5]
As mentioned earlier, the crises, particularly the Poston strike, had had a
catalytic effect on the working relationship of staff and evacuees. The
administrators had been forced to take into account the grievances,
the aspirations, and the life patterns of the people. One result was
the recognition of Issei leadership both by the WRA and by the Nisei,
who had hitherto been awarded most of the positions of responsibility.
After April, 1943, Issei were allowed to hold office in the centers. Though
the WRA curtailed the power of the community councils after the fric-

tion at Poston and Manzanar, as time went on both the block managers, who were employees of the administration, and the block councils became politically powerful.[6]

Another evidence of change was the relaxation in the attitude toward what was called "external security" at the centers. The number of guards was substantially reduced, except at Tule Lake where it was increased. The contrast was most notable after the West Coast was reopened to American Japanese. After April, 1944, the nine centers had only a few officers and from thirteen to sixty-four enlisted men, while Tule Lake continued to be guarded like a prison camp, which, in effect, it was.

The Dies Committee investigators noted, "At one camp the Japanese objected to a fence which confined them. They tore it down. It stayed down and the Japs are still roaming around there at will."[7] Dillon Myer explained, "It is true that a section of the fence surrounding the Minidoka Center has recently been removed and has not yet been replaced. . . . It was removed by evacuee labor crews working under orders of the War Relocation Authority and with the full knowledge and consent of the military authorities."[8] "The fence came down," said an evacuee, "because people wanted to use it for a clothes line. Who was going to walk out in the middle of the desert? There was no reason at all for that barbed wire."

At this time evacuees ignored the inner fences at many centers during daytime hours. Guards looked with tolerance at teen-agers who paired off and wandered away for a little quiet love-making. Miné Okubo, the artist, tells of scavenging expeditions by evacuees to the outer project area at Topaz.[9] A violinist named Niva, also at Topaz, hiked about sixteen miles from the camp to the base of Drum Mountain where he found a pair of Baltimore oriole nestlings, which he brought back to his barracks and tamed.[10]

Heart Mountain people went out with a lunch, climbed the mountain, and searched for rocks, fossils, or for evergreen trees to make *bonsai* (dwarf tree) specimens. A former Palo Altan became an amateur paleontologist. "Most Sunday I walk over 15 miles (one way)," he wrote to a friend, "and look for [fossils] and my goodness, I got very valuable one, no-one but me. . . . I discovered the lower mouth of *Coryphodon* probably 50,000,000 years old. . . . It is so very interesting. . . . Once walked 21 miles 6 A.M. to 8:30 P.M. Picked up petrified wood in Table Mountain about 11 miles from Center."[11]

While teen-agers at Gila went swimming in a canal, Poston residents fished in the Colorado River despite the opposition of the Arizona Fish and Game Commission and the Tenney Committee of the California legislature, which as part of an investigation of un-American activities, was checking on illegal fishing by residents of relocation centers. The chief administrative officer at Poston admitted that the WRA rented Japanese-owned trucks for from $75 to $175 a month and that evacuees had picnics on the banks of the Colorado. "But," he reassured the committee, "we have been tightening up right along."[12]

This was hardly true, but, as Shig Matsunaga said, "Nobody went A.W.O.L." Remarkably enough, when the WRA was compiling statistics on the 120,313 people in its custody, there were only four persons listed as "unauthorized departures, believed to have been deceased."[13] These were senile or deranged individuals who disappeared into the wilderness and were never found.

Only a few nature-lovers did not return to camp. At Manzanar a man who had gone out with a party to sketch in the mountains became separated from the group. "This was of course out of bounds," wrote a camp official, "but the back gate of the camp was often open; the farm hands went freely in and out and Mr. Merritt had looked with leniency upon recreational sorties, since they were no danger to military security." Eventually, the artist's corpse was found by two Caucasian travelers passing through the mountains and a group of his friends from camp went out to the spot described. "Lacking soil, the party built a cairn over the remains, gathered mountain flowers to add to those they had brought from the camp, took photographs of the decorated cairn and of the wonderful mountain views that the man might have been sketching there and carried them home to the widow. She was much comforted."[14]

A former Seattle man who had gone into the desert near Minidoka to look for greasewood specimens became separated from a companion and was found two days later "beneath a meager shelter of sagebrush" frozen to death. "It was stated that he had apparently become confused in the snowstorm which was then blowing across the rugged area of hills, gullies and lava outcroppings, and had walked parallel to the camp for about six miles instead of toward it." The project director, Harry L. Stafford, piloted a plane in an aerial search while more than a thousand volunteers covered the area around the camp.[15]

The evacuees also left the centers on day passes. Heart Mountain people took buses to sightsee in Yellowstone Park. People who owned cars and wanted to have them close at hand for use or safekeeping were sometimes allowed to go back to the West Coast to get them. At Topaz, car owners would take friends to the little town of Delta which was friendly.

Though evacuees ordered things from the mail order houses, many preferred to shop in the nearby towns. "They would let them go out after a while," a woman remembers. "At first the storekeepers looked on these strange dark faces with wonder. Then they got used to them and were friendly." Heart Mountain people found Cody "a little cool, but in general, as long as you're spending money they didn't mind too much."

A storekeeper from nearby Lake Village sent a bus to the Jerome center to pick up evacuee shoppers. Some of the local people near the Arkansas centers thought of the Japanese as "yellow Negroes" and were surprised when a Nisei driver defied Jim Crow treatment by refusing to move over when a Caucasian demanded the right of way.

The merchants at Parker solicited trade from Poston, but had to impose restrictions because the evacuees were buying up so much stock there was not enough left for regular customers. It was told that one man from the camp purchased $100 worth of soap, a story difficult to credit in the light of the monthly salaries paid by the WRA.

Senator Chan Gurney of South Dakota had called for more control over mail, telephone calls, and the forwarding of money at the relocation centers. "They may be sending money to other Japs or to Germans or to other spies or saboteurs," he said.[16] But the WRA announced that evacuees outside the Western Defense Command could apply to recover their cameras, short wave radio sets, and other items surrendered during the period when contraband articles were prohibited. When the contents of a warehouse in San Diego got mixed together, the owners were allowed to go back six at a time to sort through and pick out their own things. Until January, 1945, except for a few individuals, Japanese were allowed in the Western Defense Command only by special permission and under guard to conduct vital business.

Tales of unchecked thievery and hoarding at the centers were circulated before the Dies Committee by certain former WRA staff members. The reports were much exaggerated, but there was some basis for them. A Nisei, who was a child in one of the camps, wrote:

> Everyone was hungry during the first months. Children filched potatoes from the warehouse whenever they got a chance. They would pack them in mud and bake them in the desert. Stealing, if it was from government stores, was not only acceptable, it seemed to be everyone's primary occupation during the first weeks. Adults made nightly raids on government lumber supplies, with which they made furniture, shelves and closets. . . .
> Hiroshi's mother, like most others, turned her effort to the children still in her care. Every day she would save her share of bread from the mess tables, dry it in the sun and store it in paper bags. Food supplies would most likely be cut off when the United States began losing the war, she reasoned.[17]

The WRA's attitude towards the evacuees who helped themselves to the scrap lumber piles was sometimes to look the other way and sometimes to prosecute thefts. An engineer described his home at Amache as containing "folding cots and chairs, but no tables. We made those ourselves, but don't ask where we got the wood . . . Or the food."[18]

Though Dillon Myer objected that "simply taking the testimony of former employees is not a sound method of investigation,"[19] the Dies Committee put on the stand a former supply chief at Poston who linked the thefts with un-Americanism, claiming that supplies stored underground in the desert were destined for the parachute troops of the enemy invasion forces.[20]

Rumors of desert caches of food and warehouses full of rationed items continued to be subjects for gossip in the communities near the centers. When a staff member at Tule Lake went into a restaurant in a nearby town and told the girl that the hamburger he had just ordered was for a friend in the camp, she opened it up and spat on it. Jeannette Rust remembers that some of the local farmers, who formed their opinions outside the fence, were actively hostile. Other neighbors who went inside saw the people firsthand. "The schools were pathetic, the whole thing was pathetic," said Ruth Fischer who taught a class of eighth graders and helped with the loyalty registration. "The place was referred to as 'The Jap Camp' and was never known by any other term," said George Fischer. "Local people became accustomed to it and took it as a matter of fact."

John Kitasako served as a camp correspondent from Heart Mountain to a weekly newspaper in a neighboring town. He was paid for his 800-word column "written with an eye toward developing public relations in this area." He complained that the possibilities for mutual understanding suffered in April, 1943, at the time of the much-publicized execution of a group of General Doolittle's aviators in Tokyo. The day the news came, leaves were canceled, evacuees outside the camp were picked up by truck, and neighboring towns were placed out of bounds.[21]

About this time the Denver *Post* sent a reporter to Heart Mountain who wrote an exposé which was cited almost verbatim in the Congressional Record by Senator Edward B. Robertson of Wyoming. The reporter found both treason and administrative bungling at the center, and claimed that 70 to 80 per cent of the citizens among the evacuees were disloyal. The espousal of Japanese military control of Asia was the predominant concept in the camp. (Actually, only 7 per cent of the entire population of Heart Mountain had declared themselves "disloyal" or refused to register in February and March.)

The WRA personnel, he said, "is typical of the incompetent, wasteful, extravagant, spend-all-the-money-you-can type of administration which has grown up in the last ten years." He found "many signs of waste and incompetent ordering," including $12,000 worth of baby food, 268,293 cans of rationed vegetables, 86,480 cans of fruit, and 6,853 gallons of mayonnaise. "They apparently can get all the intoxicating liquor they want." He was particularly outraged to discover 120 sets of mule harness and not a mule in camp.[22]

The Heart Mountain *Sentinel* offered a vigorous rebuttal to those charges as "a vicious pack of half-truths drawn from the twilight zone of fact. . . ."[23] Two representatives of the Dies Committee promptly announced their intention of investigating the charges and the *Sentinel* welcomed them:

> We are glad that the Dies Committee has seen fit to look into the situation here. A forthright unbiased report from an American viewpoint can do us and the country at large a great deal of good by clearing up points of dispute. It can put to rest a large number of vicious rumors and assure the public that we are not guinea pigs for social experimenters, nor participants in thrice-daily orgiastic feasts. Neither are we a gang of cutthroats playing possum until Tojo flashes us the high sign. To this extent the Dies Committee can be useful to us and the nation's war effort.
>
> We are far from perfect here, but there is nothing to fear in the truth. We ask only that the truth and all the truth be made public by the officials the investigators represent.[24]

The *Sentinel's* faith in the impartiality of the Dies Committee was misplaced if, as officers of the American Civil Liberties Union charged, the relocation centers were not so much subjects of an investigation as "the target of a new attack."[25]

The WRA managed to enlist some support in high places to offset the bad publicity of the Dies Committee. The JACL asked Mrs. Roosevelt to visit a relocation center, and she came to Gila in the spring of 1943. "In a manner of speaking," wrote Damon Runyon, "she shed tears over the plight of the interned Japs in this country just about the time our captured aviators had been beheaded in Tokyo."

Mrs. Roosevelt was sympathetically disposed toward the evacuated people. Before the outbreak of war she had pleaded for tolerance toward enemy aliens and their descendants. Later she wrote that freedom from discrimination was one of the goals of the postwar world.[26] However, in a statement in *Collier's* entitled "A Challenge to American Sportsmanship," she evaded the central question of the right of the government to imprison citizens.[27]

However impolitic a contradiction of her husband's policy might have been, Mrs. Roosevelt's humanitarian instincts could be counted upon. She did not disappoint her sponsors. She spoke out in favor of relocating evacuees from the centers, which was at that time the chief issue on which the embattled WRA was being attacked.

No doubt Gila was chosen for her inspection because it was one of the more attractive centers. By the spring of 1943 the landscaping, the gardens, the vines, and porches with which the evacuees had embellished their quarters presented a pleasing appearance. One resident recalls that linoleum was put down on the floors in anticipation of the First Lady's arrival. "They let them use it afterwards." Salty herring was served that day for lunch, and after her visit the food improved.

In addition to government investigators, the most frequent visitors to the centers were clergymen and Nisei servicemen on leave. According to the *Pacific Citizen*, the first soldier to visit his family in a camp was Private Mataki Yeto who traveled from Camp Crowder, Virginia, to Gila in the autumn of 1942. A young doctor in the service visited his family in camp. "I'll never forget the winter that he came," says his sister. "He had to accompany one of his patients back to the coast, and he brought his little boy, and he stopped off to see us in the camp. It was rather ironic. He was a Captain in his dress uniform. Here he was, serving his country, and we were inside. He didn't say anything. He was a quiet one, very much like my father. I guess he thought it was ridiculous. That's what we all thought."

Yori Wada wrote about trying to find his family at Jerome:

> Arriving about midnight I sloshed around in the rain and red mud among black tar-papered barracks searching for 22–11–D. Half an hour later I found it. My knock, a light turned on, my sister's face in the half-opened doorway, and I was home.
>
> *Tadaima kaeri mashita* (I have just come home) has been my customary greeting whenever I came home from Cal. Now it came unconsciously from my lips.
>
> *Oh, kaite kitake* (oh, so you've come home) was Mother's greeting as she got up from the Army cot. It struck me suddenly and without warning that she had aged, aged ten years in two. Her face was covered with countless wrinkles, her former jet-black hair was streaked with gray, those deep brown eyes were tired, her body thinner. Oh, Mother, I wish I could have spared you this. Surely Americans couldn't approve of this. But Mother smiled at me and I answered.[28]

Gordon Adams, now a prominent San Jose businessman, followed the Okamoto family around the country during his brief Navy leaves. He had helped in their store while he was in high school. He felt so badly about the evacuation that he had donated extra hours of work during their last weeks in San Jose. Fuji (Okamoto) Takaichi recalls, "He hitchhiked out to Santa Anita to see us, and sat around for two days waiting for a pass and finally got to see Yuk [her brother, Yukio] for fifteen minutes. On a two weeks' leave before going overseas, he managed to save a few days to come out to see us at Heart Mountain. He got a ride to Salt Lake City and hitchhiked to Cody and he almost froze to death because it was winter and he was wearing his summer suntans from California."

He lived with the Okamoto family in their single room apartment. Adams remembers: "I ate in the mess hall, I participated in the camp activities. The four days I spent were fun-filled and enriching. It was unbelievable the way these people were reacting to this tremendous inconvenience. Had I not been acquainted with the circumstances I never would have known. . . . Heart Mountain was unlike anything I had ever seen before. I have since seen similar appearing camps on television—some of the prisoner of war camps in Europe."

A Mexican boy who came to Manzanar because he wanted to be with his Nisei chums, was elected student body president of the high school. Sheriff William Emig of Santa Clara County visited his friends, the Ai-hara family, at Poston. Dr. Harold Alexander, an ophthalmologist from Southern California, took his vacations at Poston in order to work on people's eyes. Esther Breisemeister was sent by the YWCA to visit all the centers, establish YWCA programs, and give help to the evacuees. "She was really remarkable," Dorothy Tada remembers. "She was one of us. She worked with us. She ate with us in the mess hall and shared the endless menu of turnips."

Shizuko Kajikawa, who was never evacuated because she had been studying in Chicago when the war started, was recruited by the WRA and sent to work at Amache as an interpreter between the administration and the evacuees. She lived outside the camp and ate in the staff dining room except when she got special permission to go to the evacuee mess hall to enjoy *tsukemono*, a pickle served with fish and rice.

The former president of Doshisha University, Dr. Hachiro Yuasa, came from a ministry in New England to preach at the centers. Bishop Charles Reifsnider visited his scattered Episcopal flock. When E. Stanley Jones, the liberal Methodist clergyman, came to Topaz in 1943, he said, "You Japanese are not a problem. You are possibilities." Presumably, he was referring to the challenge for America.

Protestant ministers at the centers were supported by their denominations. The Catholic church supplied chaplains. The Maryknoll Fathers from Los Angeles, who had maintained a mission for the Japanese in the prewar years, sent Fr. Clement Boesflug and nine other fathers to the camps to support the evacuated people. "Churches" were created in the barracks for Catholic, Protestant, and Buddhist services. The WRA allowed the free practice of all religions except Shinto, which had a political connotation. Professor Leonard Bloom has estimated that only one quarter of 1 per cent of the prewar American Japanese population were Shinto worshippers. According to WRA statistics, 55 per cent of the people were Buddhists, 28.9 per cent were Protestants, 2 per cent were Catholics, a few belonged to obscure sects, and about 13 per cent were nonbelievers or did not state an affiliation.[29]

One of the most faithful visitors was Herbert Nicholson, the Quaker missionary, who devoted the war years to helping the West Coast Japanese—those left behind in sanitariums and the uprooted people in the camps. With a truck he plied back and forth between Los Angeles and Manzanar and Poston. He writes:

It was on our first trip to Manzanar that I was asked to get the Yamamoto Dodge truck, and from that time I usually went up in that with loads of furniture, books, trunks, etc., for the internees. . . . The WRA would get these things, but it took weeks for each request to be carried through and the things were brought by a trucking company and were handled very badly and often deliberately broken. I had many experiences picking things up at the homes of Caucasian friends, or in churches or language schools.

Although I arrived in camp in my work clothes I was always busy on Sundays at church services, preaching in Japanese and English. I also conducted funerals and weddings at various camps. I was once asked to have the Japanese part of a preaching mission of one week at Hunt, Idaho [Minidoka]. Stanley Jones was speaking in English. At that time the high school teachers asked me to speak to the students on cultural things in Japan. They had no auditorium so I spoke to 250 or so at a time in a mess hall. Later I was asked to give the same sort of talk at LaJunta, Colorado, camp [Amache]. Afterwards, one of the teachers told me that his students said, "My, that fellow was a pro-Jap!"

The most exciting time was when I took Roy Smith and Howard Hannaford—missionaries who had returned on the Gripsholm from Japan. We had mass meetings to which everyone turned out, at Manzanar, the three camps at Poston and the two at Rivers [Gila]. This was the first news they had received from Japan since Pearl Harbor and the meetings were a great help to the spirit of the camp.

In 1942 Mr. Nicholson was barred from Manzanar for six months for bringing with him on one trip the Caucasian wife of an evacuee and a young conscientious objector. The FBI was upset to discover their names on the list of camp visitors. Later, regulations were more relaxed.

As Christians and Orientalists, former missionaries often sympathized so completely with the descendants of a people whose culture they loved that they entirely ignored the fact of war between the two countries. The story is told of a woman missionary at Tule Lake in August, 1945, who reprimanded the Nisei who too abruptly announced to their parents that Japan had lost the war. Such a blow should have been softened, she felt. She went about collecting pots and pans from the camp rubbish heap to ship to the defeated country. Two years before when some ministers had defended the American Japanese before the Dies Committee, the press conveyed the impression that they were irresponsible pacifists.[30]

Letters went back and forth between friends who could not visit. In general, Caucasians took the initiative. A Nisei woman said, "When I went into camp I never corresponded with any of my friends. I thought about them, some of the girls. I still know their names. We were friends, close in school, but we never visited in each other's homes." Her husband recalls, "We used to have neighbors that were awfully poor.

They were looked down on. A lot of people used to make fun of them. They were the only people that used to write to us. They had good hearts."

Mary Oyama Mittwer, a young intellectual, wrote to a friend outside, "Before I close, many thanks for the subscription to *Harper's*. You don't know what it means to us in this 'lonely outpost of civilization,' and especially when we are so financially low as we are now. . . . I am a one-woman circulating library around here. All the young Nisei come over to borrow my papers, books, magazines etc." She tells of drafting a letter to Pearl Buck in the hope of getting her to come to the center.[31]

A woman at Poston complained that radio reception was poor and newspapers hard to come by. Others thought they knew as much about what was going on in the world as anyone else. They read about the battles in the Pacific in the American press and in Japanese newspapers published in Denver and Salt Lake City. From short wave radio sets which were sometimes allowed and sometimes listened to clandestinely, they learned the Japanese view of the war. It was difficult to reconcile the two versions. An Issei wrote of this problem in a poem,

> Balancing the war news
> With his own future—
> Dilemma of dilemmas![32]

They were very much aware, from reading the West Coast papers mailed in and from the *Pacific Citizen*, of outside attitudes toward themselves. At Manzanar a bulletin for clippings was given the heading, "WHAT THEY ARE SAYING ABOUT US." To keep up ties with home communities, evacuees wrote to their local papers. Eichii Sakauye and Phil Matsumura sent Christmas greetings from Heart Mountain to the San Jose *News*. The first year, 1942, their message was printed without comment. The second year, 1943, Sakauye's message had an editorial comment attached: "Again on this Christmas *The News* was sent a touching little letter from a Japanese–American living in the Heart Mountain, Wyoming, relocation camp, voicing greetings from former Santa Clara County Japanese to the people of this County.

"The letter sounds, and undoubtedly is, wholly sincere. Reading it the thought might come to you that it is too bad. We have never said it wasn't. However, we have said and still say that so difficult is it to distinguish the loyal from the traitorously disloyal that all must continue to be kept away, at least until the war is over."[33]

The center newspapers varied in quality. In general, they were concerned with camp news, announcements, and outside developments relevant to the situation of American Japanese. Dyke Miyagawa, who was discovered on the Minidoka *Irrigator* by Larry Tajiri and hired as an associate editor for the *Pacific Citizen* in Salt Lake City, characterized them as "pretty myopic." One of the best was the Heart Mountain *Sentinel*, which was praised by Elinor Cogswell, at that time editor of the Palo Alto *Times*, one of the few West Coast papers to espouse the cause of the Nisei. She wrote, "The attitude of the *Sentinel* interests me greatly. I think it keeps a remarkable balance of candid recognition of unpleasant facts and optimistic determination to make the best of them. From it I get a picture of a real civilization being worked out in sweat and tears, if not blood."[34]

The WRA in principle guaranteed "full freedom of editorial expression" to center newspapers, though in fact censorship was occasionally imposed. The project director was given permission "to suspend publication of the newspaper at any time if this seems necessary in the interest of public peace and community security." The papers were encouraged to publish a section in Japanese and six of them did. The Poston paper announced the addition of a United Press wire service in August of 1942, to carry dispatches on the war, domestic news, and sports. In addition to the mimeographed tri-weekly *Times*, Topazians published a literary magazine called *Trek* containing short stories, poems, and articles illustrated by Miné Okubo. A short story in the February, 1943, issue called "Tomorrow is coming, children," by Toshio Mori, was later developed into a full-length book.

Creative writing by the Issei followed the traditional Japanese forms. Poetry societies flourished in all the centers and members produced *haiku*, *tanka*, and *senryu*, three different forms of Japanese verse. One of the new practitioners expressed the excitement felt by many of the Issei at spending their new-found leisure in pursuing the time-honored Japanese arts:

> Fortunate me! Indifferent
> To the fierce fighting
> All over the world
> Here I am, learning
> Flower arranging, writing and embroidery.[35]

The remarkable development of the arts at the centers has been commemorated by Allen Eaton in his book *Beauty Behind Barbed Wire*, in which he shows extraordinary examples of calligraphy, wood carving, miniature landscapes (*bon-kei*), polished wood (*kobu*), embroidery, weaving, pottery, stone-carving, and artificial flower-making. In addition, many turned to the creation of gardens, costume-making, flower-arranging (*ikebana*), and practiced the tea ceremony (*cha-no-yu*). The creation of miniature objects, *bon-kei* and *bonsai*, are stressed in traditional Japanese art, Japan being a small country.

The evacuees showed great ingenuity in finding materials for art in the crude and essentially savage surroundings in which they lived. They used sagebrush for flower arrangements, created cactus gardens, wove rugs from unraveled gunny sacks, and produced beautiful pieces of furniture from scrap lumber. Jeannette Rust was amazed at the work people did "with nothing"—with rocks, plants, with any kind of wood they searched out. Gardens, cupboards, and ingenious room dividers were created. A rivalry developed between craftsmen.

At Gila people carved birds from pieces of crates and wrote to the Audubon Society for pictures. The tiny birds were "a miracle of precision and accuracy," says Esther Sills, herself an artist. A fireman carved a beautiful fish from ironwood to which he gave a high polish by rubbing it with his hands, a task that required infinite time and patience. At Topaz, old men would cut out chain links from one chunk of wood, like a Chinese puzzle. They would make carving knives out of hay rakes found in the stables; carve tiny animals out of prune and peach pits. The *kobus* produced at Jerome were created from a tumor on the trees where lightning had struck. Roaming the woods with saw and axe, "We saw those portions off and shape and sandpaper the objects so that the end product becomes what we pictured mentally when we first saw the *kobu* on the tree," one man wrote.[36]

The art work was stimulated by the presence of a number of professionals at various centers. Chiura Obata presented two impressions of Topaz, silk screen prints, to President Roosevelt and Dillon Myer. Tamokichi Hibino painted an oil of Manzanar in the spring, showing Mount Whitney, trees, and desert foliage. A New York artist, Robert Minami, taught arts and crafts at Manzanar. Before cameras were allowed, Toyo Miyatake, the Los Angeles photographer, made one at Manzanar from a lens which he brought to the camp in his coat pocket, a lightproof box made in the carpentry shop, and a sink outlet into which he set the lens. A friend from San Luis Obispo supplied him with film, while camp officials "looked the other way."

But the art was for the most part spontaneous and untutored and developed with the later adjustment to center life by the Issei in particular. After months of exposure their surroundings became familiar, and less fearful. Some responded creatively to the infinite spaces of the wilderness.

> Standing
> On the wide desert,
> Before the silent wind,
> My body sank
> Into nothingness.[37]

> The lights have been turned off
> Here at the Relocation Center,

And I'll sleep this evening
With the voices of the migrating wild ducks
Passing through my heart.[38]

There is a Japanese tradition of "courtesy to nature," one manifestation of which is the enjoyment of stones in their natural state (*suiseki*). People would walk out after a dust storm and speak polite greetings to each other, bowing, "*Oyasumi nasai*" (Rest well).[39] After viewing a scene of this sort, John Collier is reported to have commented on the extraordinary psychological recuperative powers of the Japanese.

Esther Sills, who later assembled examples of what was produced for Allen Eaton's book, thought that at Gila the traditional art "carried dignity, simplicity and beauty," while the Western styles, particularly in drawing and painting, were childlike and crude. Japanese culture was heightened by the life in the center as some of the Issei reproduced a semblance of the Japan of their earliest years. It was natural for them to espouse Japanese culture she felt, "because they had every reason to want to discard ours."

The Nisei found themselves drawn in, moving back and forth between the traditional family observances and the world of dance bands, movies, and American slang. A former Hollywood actor, Teru Shimada, took charge of a drama group at Poston which presented skits on camp life, *Coming to Broilton*, *The Blockhead's Nightmare*, and *Blaze of Noon*. A show at Minidoka in March, 1944, was much more Japanese in character. The actors were mainly Kibei, and aside from a few songs in Spanish spoke only Japanese. The program included a modern comedy, a modern dance, and a classical drama. Esther Sills recalls theatrical performances outdoors at Gila. "To Western-trained ears, both music and the theatrical voices, particularly the female voices, had an eerie quality enhanced by the setting. Unable to decipher more than a very few key words, I had to guess at what was actually supposed to be the 'story.' The laughter of the audience suggested to my ears that jokes were made at the expense of the non-Japanese."

While the Nisei danced the latest jitterbug steps, the Issei practiced the traditional singing, *shigin* and *joruri*, or played the harp (*koto*). Both generations, as well as WRA staff members, joined in such festivals as the midsummer *obon* in which kimona-clad dancers performed the ritual steps to popular Western music played over the loudspeakers.

At the different centers *shibai* and *kabuki* dramas as well as *Bunraku* puppet shows were given with elaborate costumes that had either been made at the camp or brought from the outside. A woman in her seventies taught girls dressed in rich gold-embroidered robes to perform classical *kabuki*. A member of the audience said, "It was an astonishing feat. These Nisei girls could hardly understand what they were enunciating and here they were participating in classical drama which could only be seen in the larger cities of Japan and could not be fully interpreted by university graduates."[40]

The WRA approved the spontaneous bourgeoning of Japanese art. The Dies Committee investigators were not so enthusiastic. Representative Earl E. Mundt of South Dakota, reporting on a four-day tour of the centers, was strongly critical of the display of Japanese pictures and decorations in administrative offices. He reported that public funds were being used to pay instructors in judo, *goh,* and the Japanese language. "It is about as sensible as it would be to use taxpayers' money to provide textbooks in sabotage and give laboratory training in making nitroglycerin bombs to enemy prisoners of war being held in this country."

He wanted the centers to be converted into "Americanization units," with the government taking advantage of the opportunity to inculcate respect for American traditional ideals. This could be done through entertainment, scouting programs, and the schools.[41] Representative Herman P. Eberharter of Pennsylvania, also a member of the Costello Subcommittee of the Dies Committee, challenged this plan in a minority report. He wrote:

> Anyone genuinely interested in the problem of continuing the Americanization of the Japanese American population of this country must acknowledge that the greatest force for Americanization is free, friendly and continuous contact with non-Japanese Americans in normal communities. The evacuation and isolation of the Japanese population in relocation centers away from normal contacts is an almost overwhelming obstacle to the assimilation of the Japanese Americans, as it would be to any immigrant population. To say that "The War Relocation Authority had before it an almost unparalleled opportunity to inaugurate a vigorous education program for positive Americanism" is an almost complete inversion of the true situation.[42]

But to reassure his colleagues, Representative Eberharter pointed to the games of basketball, baseball, football, the Boy and Girl Scout troops, the Camp Fire Girls, and the Future Farmers of America, which he found were much more popular with young Nisei than *judo* and *sumo.* In Tule Lake, the only center where Japanese culture was fostered for political reasons, a corrupted form of Japanese English was used, particularly by Issei, with words such as "basuketto boro" for basketball, "sofuto boro" for softball. The Nisei slang was almost synonymous with general American usage. An attractive girl was "a slick chick" or "a rare dish." An unattractive girl was labeled "a rusty hen," "dog biscuit," and "seaweed." The Nisei predicament was reflected in the vernacular. Strict parents were called "curfew keepers" and youngsters explained what had happened to them by saying, "I was Pearl Harbored."[43]

The Americanization attempts of the WRA like those of the assembly center period were an interesting novelty for the Issei. The Topaz adult education department sponsored courses in American foreign policy and world affairs, American history, and current forums in Japanese. The occidental music that was played was "strange" and "unintelligible" to most of the listeners, though one man expressed an appreciation for the "Ballad for Americans" sung by Paul Robeson even though he couldn't understand the words.

Some of the Issei enjoyed the experiments in participatory democracy, particularly a few of the women who became fire wardens and representatives on block councils and were given a community recognition quite outside the customary Japanese tradition of the subservient female. An Issei from Heart Mountain wrote about his excitement in public affairs:

> We have Blk Meeting every Mon-day night which we talk about the welfare of our Community and discuss. This is first time I get express my opinion since last December 2 weeks ago first time (in 6 months) I ever talk to *outsider* the school teacher who came to my house after school.[44]

The ventures in adult education were intended to be a link with the world outside the center, but often that world blighted the brave hopes of reciprocal friendship. The president of the University of Arizona, appealed to for extension courses, library books, and faculty lectures for Poston, refused on the grounds that "We are at war and these people are our enemies."[45] He was rebuked by the Arizona *Daily Star*, published in Tucson. "If the University refuses such lessons to American citizens who happen to be of Japanese ancestry, then it can justifiably at some future time or even now refuse lessons to Jews, Italians, Chinese and others."[46]

Other institutions were not so inhospitable. The University of Chicago gave credit for courses in anthropology and psychology at Poston. UCLA offered extension courses to Manzanar residents. A junior college at Manzanar was formerly recognized and accredited by the California State Department of Education in June, 1943. The WRA did not support it financially, so evacuees and a few Caucasian volunteers comprised the teaching staff. Seventy students completed the first semester's work, mainly in business subjects.

Adult education at the centers was less successful in promoting "Americanism" than in providing what was more generally desired, training in skills and occupations. Some of the Issei were glad to learn basic English. Courses in drafting, welding, carpentry, sewing, and electronics were much in demand. A woman who now works in the yardage department of a large store feels she benefited vocationally from her dressmaking courses in the center.

Whereas the untrained had an opportunity to learn or upgrade their skills, professional men often found small scope for their talents. Though overworked in the hospitals, the evacuee doctors and dentists who were "artists at heart" were often circumscribed in the exercise of their specialties. Some of the more conservative Caucasian medical directors discouraged autopsies and even such simple surgery as the removal of hemorrhoids. Dentists were not permitted to undertake fancy gold inlay work in camp. One medical student reviewed his training by teaching classes in human physiology.

Though almost all able-bodied men, and many women, worked forty-eight hours a week, many did not work hard because of the poor pay or work for the full amount of time. A sociologist who studied the Issei in camp observed a deterioration of character as they lost their industrious ways and resigned themselves to being wards of the government. It has been said that camp life was a vacation for the hard-working Issei. It was also, as an observer commented, "a vacation from assimilation."[47] Some of the farm families found living conditions easier than they had known in the past. The women enjoyed the freedom from preparing meals and the sociability. They were very busy in their world in microcosm. They became insulated from envy of the wider world and its opportunities.

> Inured to penury
> The sixteen dollars
> Is more than sufficient[48]

Issei and Nisei who had important positions in camp government which kept them busy and for which they were respected also found camp life rewarding. Some were working at white collar jobs for the first time in their lives. Health standards improved. Despite the danger of epidemics, one mother feels that babies and small children were wonderfully provided for in the matter of balanced meals, orange juice, formula, and baby food.

Though outbreaks of children's contagious diseases continued to occur as well as a few cases of polio and sporadic mass attacks of food poisoning, a Nisei nurse who practiced at Topaz says, "Considering the circumstances, we did remarkably well. Today we would panic at such a prospect. Antibiotics were just beginning to be developed. We had available the early sulfa."

Medical care for expectant mothers was generally good, though one woman lost her first baby because, though a Caesarian operation had been prescribed in a prenatal examination, this was overlooked when she was in labor, and the baby did not survive a natural birth. "We couldn't blame the doctors," her husband says. "They were avalanched." During the period of roughly three years 5,981 births were recorded.

Young mothers continued to find life difficult without washing machines and the other conveniences of baby care. Women who had children under ten remember the camp years as a period of fatigue and drudgery as well as anxiety over the welfare of the family in a communal situation. There was a marked incidence of peptic ulcers, though very few nervous breakdowns were recorded.

Boys and girls enjoyed the proximity of many playmates as well as the enticements of the wilderness country. A year after Kenny Nakamura died of meningitis at the age of ten at Heart Mountain, his mother in Minneapolis sent back a poem to the *Sentinel* in his memory. She wrote, "The last year of my son's short life was a happy and interesting one, 'crammed full to the brim' with boyish activities. Cub scouting, collecting 'Indian-y' things, hiking, swimming, boxing and playing ping-pong were some of the things he loved to do. He had many friends of all ages. I have not forgotten, nor will I ever forget, their friendship and love that made the last year of his life so completely happy."[49]

Brides were content where centers had a honeymoon cottage. A couple who were married at Tule Lake, moved into a new apartment. "We probably had the cutest little room in the center. My husband put in a window and extended the house so that we overlooked the playground. And I made white frilly curtains, and he made covers for me, and I really enjoyed that little room. People used to drop by and say how cozy it was. It was perfect for me as a newlywed."

Fuji Takaichi, who had insisted on separate quarters with her new husband at Santa Anita, objected to living with strangers at Heart Mountain.

> I can remember being indignant only once. They wanted to move in another family in our unit. It was only one room. There was no way of barricading it. There was nothing to hide behind to get dressed or undressed.
>
> I went to the man in charge of housing to tell him I didn't want another family moved in with us. He told me that he and his wife lived in a one-room apartment and I said, "Well, that's different, because you can go out in the street or visit friends or go to a movie. You don't have to live there. You're living there by choice. It isn't the same thing with me. I don't want to live in this place anyway, but I have to live here. But you're not moving anybody else in!"
>
> He thought I was utterly unreasonable. I ended up by telling him, "You won't dare move anybody in. Because I will be at the door and I won't let anybody in!"

In the artificial situation of the relocation centers where the economic and social basis of the Issei's authority had been abolished by the welfare system under which all the residents lived, family solidarity depended on what the sociologists termed "affectional resources." The overcrowded apartments, the mess hall dining, and the allurements of a large peer group were factors that drew young family members away from parental supervision. The Issei were frightened at losing control over their teen-age children.

One girl used to sneak out to dances and stay at a friend's apartment. She didn't know how to dance, but she would stand looking through the window at the gaiety inside. One night when she came home the family barracks were brightly lit though it was late. She found that her sister had had a ruptured appendix and had been taken away in an ambulance. She ran crying all the way to the hospital and sat by her sister till morning, sponging her face, until she was sure she would recover. She felt "doubly guilty."

For many teen-agers center life was like being transported from the country to the city with new temptations for idleness and mischief. A few school age boys "played hookey" and went about in gangs. Miscreants at Gila had their heads shaved for punishment and were put to work on the garbage trucks by Caucasian officials. Parents worried because they felt that "the kids were just fooling around." Hard work had been a unifying influence in the American Japanese family, and now there was no incentive for it. Sometimes a child would leave his apartment early in the morning and not be seen again until bedtime. A few would sleep under the floor boards away from home. Norman Thomas commented that "the Government has to put in social workers to cure that which it has created."[50]

"It was difficult because we were sort of on our own," says Frank Bunya. "We didn't need our parents for money. The family didn't really break down. Children just had a little more independence, that's all. The family didn't fall apart. A lot of the parents were worried that it would. They were so used to being the dominant figures in the household. They feared we would just turn about face and become rabble-rousers, and cause lots of trouble, but that never happened. I guess we were so used to this family system. We didn't think about going out with our new-found independence and raising heck. . . ."

Estimates varied. A sociologist wrote, "In the past the Japanese on the Pacific Coast rarely appeared on the police blotters, but their incarceration in relocation centers resulted in a crime record comparable to that of any city of their size or with any Army camp."[51] But Representative Herman Eberharter in his minority opinion to the Dies Committee report found far less crime in the centers than in the average American community. A WRA man at Minidoka had the highest praise for the people. "Community conduct of this sort is not bought and paid for. It reflects the attitude of an unusually honest and upright people. It reflects composure and courage in the face of unbelievable social and economic chaos."[52]

Dr. Victor Goertzel at Topaz observed no juvenile delinquency, but noted a dramatic increase in adult crimes, particularly assaults. Domestic altercations were extremely rare, though Togo Tanaka, as an observer for the WRA at Manzanar, documented a "love triangle" murder in the summer of 1942. The young wife of a man in his fifties was having an affair with a sugar beet worker. The husband strangled her and then killed himself.

An adolescent girl at Gila was awakened one night by a noise outside. She and her mother went to the door and their flashlight revealed an astounding sight. The woman next door, a musical entertainer, though hardly in the *geisha* tradition, and her lover, who smuggled liquor to her when her husband was absent, were locked in each other's arms and rolling over and over beside the fish pond built by the father of the astonished teen-ager. The spectacle was unusual enough to make a deep impression on her, since relocation center life was not auspicious for extramarital philandering. The divorce rate continued to be very low during the evacuation period, although one woman is reported to have got rid of her husband because he was objectionable to the family who shared their apartment!

The discipline and self-denial of the Issei helped them in adjusting to the physical hardships as well as the psychological deprivations of center life. The farmers and their wives, especially, were inured to a pioneer existence. Many, who had been struggling fiercely in the tradition of American immigrants, were able to accept their fate with resignation that was characteristically Oriental. They gave themselves up to an existence without expectation or effort, enduring the period of exile by immersing themselves in the customs and attitudes of Japan. It is not surprising that the WRA's democratization programs had scant success with the older generation.

The irony of such schemes in relation to their predicament was not lost on the Nisei, though the schools were to some extent, as they were intended to be, an influence for "Americanization." They were organized with the hope that the 30,000 pupils enrolled and the 7,220 who graduated from the high schools would feel themselves a part of the greater United States. For this reason evacuee leaders had asked the WRA to provide as large a proportion of non-Japanese teachers as possible, and the curriculum was patterned on that of the schools "outside."

A Senior High Core Studies Group at Poston produced a massive report on "An Approach to the Problems of Postwar Reconstruction," with emphasis on "The Nine Freedoms." The final (1945) year book of Butte High School at Gila with its lists of activities might have been compiled by any graduating class in America that year were it not for the message concerning the Seventh Graders who would soon leave camp: "Fortunately, the remainder of their high school years will unfold in environments like those of other American youth," reads the caption.[53]

Adolescents at Poston were asked to comment on their life in camp. One seemed to be parroting a government manual when he wrote, "The government is democratic. The people are given a right to vote and elect their block managers and block representatives." Another decided that the MPs "are not there to guard us but to protect us from the people outside." "At first I thought that Poston was purgatory," wrote a fifteen year old, "but now I think we are out of danger by being at Poston."[54] Yet one young girl, at another center, not so resigned, said "We have unpacked our luggage but not our minds."

The young Nisei suffered from being isolated. A girl graduate of an eastern college, finding herself suddenly smothered in a monoracial atmosphere, asked despondently, "Whom do I marry?" Another Nisei wrote, "About the younger generation and their attitude toward camp life, it is a sad story. It is really disgusting to see maturing personalities disintegrating. The young people around seventeen and eighteen are getting lazy, ambitionless, satisfied and stagnating."[55]

They suffered from a feeling of having nothing productive to do, yet sometimes the longer they stayed in camp, the more helpless they felt themselves to move away. They were caught in the quagmire of isolated "circular thinking."[56] An educator at Poston warned of the danger of institutional apathy, not only for young people, but for everyone:

> The most evident effect which Poston has had on its evacuee residents is the lowering of working efficiency and industry. From a conscientious, honest, independent and industrious people, a majority has developed habits of carelessness, laziness, dependence and dishonesty. By the last I mean they are dishonest with themselves and they seek excuses for being dishonest with others with regard to property, responsibility, work, etc. The usual excuse for these habits is that there is no economic base for life in a relocation center, and therefore there is no incentive to maintain the habits learned on the outside. It took most of the people many weeks— and in Poston a week is a long time—to reach the stage of deterioration which is the life of a government ward.[57]

For many young Nisei, the dances, the clubs, the good times together were anodynes that made them forget that they had "become almost completely detached from American life, the war, the world." When the distractions stopped, in the words of an observer, "They brood vaguely and fearfully of the future."[58]

These problems of claustrophobia were compounded at Tule Lake which suffered the stigma of being the center for the "disloyal." Even before the arrival of the segregees from other centers, the Tule Lake community was seething with unrest in the wake of the registration crisis. One man had been a member of the internal security or camp police force. In his job where "something was brewing all the time," he had to go in and out of the administrative offices several times a day. It was also known that he answered "yes" on the loyalty questionnaire. Consequently, he was so unpopular that fellow evacuees announced they were not going to feed him in the mess hall. Warned that he might be attacked, he persuaded Harold Jacoby, the head of internal security, to send a car for him. One day in February, 1943, a leave permit was issued, and he left for Idaho "on a one-way ticket" immediately. When feelings calmed down, he returned to camp to get his family.

Ironically, he was suspected by the FBI of being unpatriotic because he had urged officials to abandon a projected camouflage net program at Tule Lake on the grounds that people would not work for $12 a month, and if they were paid more, the difference between wages for war work and camp wages would create an insoluble problem. When he left Tule Lake he was in trouble for being pro-Japanese in the eyes of one group and pro-United States in the eyes of another.

At Tule Lake the dissension after registration did not heal as in the other centers. The WRA considered it a special place where there were "people with problems."[59] Milton Silverman, a reporter on the San Francisco *Chronicle*, visited the center in May, 1943, and described his impressions in a series of articles. "The camp is a mare's nest of rumors, of suspicion and distrust. Many of the Japanese feel that the Government has not kept all its promises—and the Government certainly hasn't—and they wait apprehensively for the next blow to fall." He reported that 478 of the colonists, only 164 of them Issei, had asked to be sent to Japan. One of the WRA men told him, "There are petty misunderstandings out in the Jap colony that in any normal community would be cleared up over night. But here they grow and fester until we have a riot on our hands."

Professor Yamato Ichihashi spoke to him of the deplorable effect of camp life on young people. He reported "stealing out of stores and homes, smart alec thievery which we never had among Japanese children—and we cannot stop it. We no longer control our own families."

At that time Tule Lake was run with the same degree of freedom as any other center. Telephone calls to the outside were allowed, long wave radios were permitted, nothing in the incoming mail was censored except packages. The English-language newspaper was published without censorship; a Japanese-language paper was censored by two evacuees approved by the FBI. The colonists were restricted to the 1,500 acre compound at night, but during the day they could roam over 7,000 acres. Only signs, not fences marked the limits, Silverman reported, and the guards were lenient.[60]

During the autumn as the "loyal" Tuleans left, some 8,600 segregees arrived, who represented 58 per cent of the population of the center.[61] In early 1944 some 3,600 more people were transferred from Manzanar, Rohwer, and Jerome, which increased the proportion of newcomers to 66 per cent, but the incidents that followed the confrontation of old and new colonists in the new context of a segregation center began before the second wave of arrivals.

According to the Thomas–Nishimoto study the old Tuleans, including large families unwilling to move, immigrant bachelors, Kibei Buddhists, and "the dispossessed in general"[62] who had tended to be the anti-administration protesters in the first year of the center, eventually became the accommodators, at least by contrast with the arriving dissidents. They were accused of being "loyal" (only 2,000 of the 6,000 were legitimate segregees), and the people who had answered "no-no" wanted them separated. They wanted Tule Lake to be a center for people with a true affiliation to Japan. For a time, however, the tension that developed between the old and new Tuleans was forgotten in common anger against the administration.

The WRA insisted that segregation was not punitive. Nevertheless, the group at Tule Lake was treated differently from evacuees at other centers. As the segregees arrived the camp was being transformed physically. A double manproof fence, eight-feet high, was erected around the inner project area. The military police guard was increased to battalion strength, and "half a dozen tanks, obsolete but impressive, were lined up in full view of the residents."[63] Searchlights swept the center at night, and the segregees entering Tule Lake were fingerprinted. A number of the Caucasian personnel resigned in protest against the changes. The former project director, who had resigned, was replaced by Raymond Best, who had been in charge of the WRA center for troublemakers at Leupp, Arizona.

Some of the segregees presented an equally militant posture on arrival. A few extremists among them insisted that an American flag at the gate be lowered, others broke office windows, destroyed copies of the *Pacific Citizen*, and decreed that Japanese national music be substituted for American jazz. The troublemakers were both feared and despised by the old Tuleans, who characterized them as "a sad bunch of people" who would be "hard to handle."[64] The "Old Tuleans" were hated by the newcomers partly because they were not considered genuine "disloyals" and also because they had established themselves in the best jobs and apartments.

The extremists among the newcomers, by their aggressiveness and by exploiting the universal grievances against the WRA, succeeded in winning political leadership through a new organization known as the Daihyo Sha Kai and in establishing a Japanese nationalist atmosphere at the center. Buddhist religious ceremonies took precedence over Christian; Japanese language schools were established. A Young Kibei complained to his former English teacher, ". . . the people who came from the other camps are all rough. They shout loudly, 'Banzai to the Emperor!' and even the police, it seems, are afraid to cross them. If you are caught at anything like [American] dancing, you are likely to be practically killed. . . ."[65]

The nationalists were never the majority at Tule Lake, but they succeeded in coercing the large group made up of both old and new Tuleans who were by inclination nonpolitical and who were, like most of the evacuees in the other centers, simply desirous of being left alone to survive the war as best they could and to make a decision on their future course of action on pragmatic grounds. Throughout the evacuation and detention period, the government investigative committees and even the WRA to a certain extent ignored the real motivation of this majority by categorizing people in terms of whether they expressed loyalty to Japan or the United States.

As we have seen, at the nine centers for the "loyal," these people were allowed to develop a peaceful mode of life. At Tule Lake, however, because of the extreme dissensions, the nonpartisans were often forced into an anti-administration and/or anti-United States position by the agitators. Yet even at Tule Lake it was possible to adopt a passive role. "If you were pro-United States, you were in trouble," according to one former evacuee, "but if you were quiet they didn't bother you." Another man does not recall much difference between Tule Lake before and after segregation. "Our block was good, mostly Placer County people." A third, though he was only fourteen when he left Tule Lake in 1945, agreed that it was possible to live free of intimidation and coercion. As a boy with lots of friends and activities, he "couldn't wait for the next day for the sun to rise" so he could start playing all over again. The quality of life varied with the blocks. Some blocks were ruled by troublemakers, mostly Kibei and Issei bachelors.

The nationalists' fanatical behavior seemed to confirm the most dire warnings of the Dies Committee, perhaps intentionally. For it is interesting to speculate to what extent they were motivated by devotion to Japan and to what extent their treasonable actions were adopted to embarrass the WRA or to fulfill what they felt was expected of a stigmatized group of "disloyals." In the opinion of the social analysts, "A few of them were seriously interested in getting to Japan, but for the rest of them the dominant interest was in asserting themselves and their dignity in the face of mistreatment."[66] Their anger was typically American, but was expressed in Japanese symbols, which was an effective form of revenge against the government. By contrast some of the older people, who took pride in behaving as "true Japanese" in the Buddhist tradition, followed a code of "good," even submissive behavior.

In other centers incidents had occurred after several months of accumulated grievances had slowly fired the emotions of the people. But at Tule Lake where the administration had prepared itself for trouble with soldiers and fences, and segregees had arrived ready to do battle, an explosion occurred within a few weeks. On October 15, 1943, a farm truck driven by a minor overturned, seriously injuring five men, one of whom later died. This touched off a strike of eight hundred farm workers which jeopardized the harvest of many thousand dollars worth of crops. The strikers, aware of the power that time had put into their hands, asked the WRA to remedy some basic grievances in living conditions. The administration took a hard line, refusing to cooperate in arrangements for a public funeral for the victim and putting the responsibility for crop losses on the striking farm workers.

To break the impasse, "loyal" harvesters from Poston and Topaz were brought in at the wage of a dollar an hour in contrast to the $16 a month paid to Tulean farm workers. The disgruntled evacuee leaders expressed their resentment of the "double-crossing WRA" by refusing to transport the "strikebreakers" from the railroad station to the farm and organizing night watches on the warehouses from which food was being taken to them.[67]

In the midst of this tense situation Dillon Myer arrived and leaders of the Daihyo Sha Kai requested an opportunity to confer with him in the early afternoon of November 1. They were followed to the administration building by a crowd of several thousand people who had been ordered during their lunch hour in the mess halls to support their leaders by their presence. These men, women, and children stood for three hours surrounding the building while Dillon Myer and the staff conferred with the grievance committee inside. Meanwhile, a group of young hotheads on their own initiative had rushed to the hospital to recruit evacuees workers to swell the crowd and had had an altercation with the chief medical officer, Dr. Reese Pedicord, during which he was injured. The spokesman for the Daihyo Sha Kai, though he was not implicated in any way in the attack of Dr. Pedicord, asked for the resignation of the entire Caucasian medical staff, as well as the project director and other personnel. He accused Mr. Best of inhumanity in the funeral of the farm worker and protested the WRA importing "loyal" strikebreakers and feeding them "food belonging to us."[68]

Dillon Myer would not commit himself to any concessions to a group which he felt might not be representative of the 15,000 people at Tule Lake, but agreed to address the people outside after the two and a half hour conference. A religious leader then enjoined the crowd to patience, saying, "You people must remember that you are Japanese and must act as Japanese to hold together for the sake of the Empire and the Emperor."[69]

Though the crowd bowed and dispersed quietly, the Caucasian staff was frightened and tense, and a few of the men left for Klamath Falls where they contributed eyewitness accounts to lurid newspaper stories of "Jap riots" which crowded the front pages of West Coast papers. From this time on, events at Tule Lake would be complicated by the distortions of the press and visiting legislative committees. Robert Cozzens, a former associate of Dillon Myer's in the Department of Agriculture who served as West Coast head of the WRA, invited a group of San Francisco reporters to visit Tule Lake for two days and describe what they saw. At least two of them resigned their jobs on their return, because their papers insisted on reshaping their material to achieve a biased interpretation.

The tension at Tule Lake did not subside after Myer's appearance. On November 4 work began on a fence to create a barricade between the administration section (including the hospital and the warehouses) and the evacuee living quarters. Following the previous pattern, a group of young men reacted to this defensive move by an act of aggression. They crowded into the warehouse area and surrounded the home of the project director. He telephoned to Lieutenant Colonel Verne Austin, who was in charge of the military police, and asked the Army to assume control of Tule Lake.

A colonist remembers, "When the 'riots' started I saw the tanks right in front of the school. I didn't go out. I just looked from the window." His wife adds, "These tanks with the gun turrets were coming between the barracks."

The Army kept control of the center for two and a half months. "It looked tense as you drove by," Lucille LaValley, a resident of a nearby town, remembers. The local people referred to the disturbance as the "little war." It was actually a period of complete community breakdown, with the evacuees confined in "the colony" and the administration gathered behind the newly erected fence. For a brief period, there was not even telephone communication between the two groups. "At all points the line was tangible and unyielding," according to a WRA analysis, "and gave rise to attitudes of antagonism and suspicion on both sides."[70]

The general strike was called "status quo" and imposed grave hardships. The hospital was on the administration side of the fence, and the Nisei staff were temporarily trapped there. A girl worker volunteered to intervene with Colonel Austin when there was no longer any food for the patients, a courageous act, because even the Nisei who ministered to the sick were suspected by their fellow evacuees since they performed their duties on "enemy" ground. Eventually, the coal and garbage crews returned to their jobs in order to alleviate the general suffering, but Tule Lake struggled as a crippled community until January.

The breach between governors and governed was very wide. The Tulean *Dispatch*, published on the evacuee side, expressed confidence in the intercession of Japan. "The American Army has entered the Tule Lake Center with machine guns and tanks, and is intimidating the residents. Nevertheless, the Japanese in the center are holding out by displaying their *Yamato damashii* [Japanese spirit]."[71]

When Colonel Austin, head of the Army unit, came to address the colonists on November 13 to set forth the terms of the Army occupation of Tule Lake, his group was surrounded by a cordon of soldiers with drawn bayonets, yet not a single evacuee attended the meeting. Austin spoke to the empty air.

The Army had instituted a weapons search and imposed a curfew, but what really aroused the residents was the unannounced arrest without a hearing of a large number of anti-administration leaders. Not charged with any offense, they were nevertheless jailed in a stockade. When the WRA resumed control of the center in January, there were 352 men confined there. A few members of the Daihyo Sha Kai had managed to escape and hide out under the floor boards of apartments, sending directives to the people. But the "status quo" was working a real hardship on most of the residents and eventually a bare majority rallied behind a collaborationist negotiating committee and voted to end the strike.

A kind of normalcy was restored at Tule Lake under WRA control early in January. Meanwhile, Dillon Myer, caught between two fires, had been dealing with the wrath of the Dies Committee and other groups. His November 13 press release on the events that led to the Army takeover of Tule Lake was intended to dispel panic as well as false rumors, but he was castigated far and wide. When he wrote, "A large number of the evacuees at Tule Lake are citizens of the United States, with the constitutional rights of citizens. Many of them are children under 17, and they, together with a very large number of the adults, have no responsible part in the recent events,"[72] he was called "an appeaser."[73]

When Myer defended the use of evacuee police, Representative Karl Mundt asked, "Isn't that like hiring arsonists for the fire department?"[74] The Costello Subcommittee put a Tule Lake physician on the stand who accused Myer of dismissing the beating of Dr. Pedicord by saying, "It doesn't amount to anything."[75] Representative Clair Engle, in whose district the center was located, wanted Dillon Myer fired. Engle reported that evacuees had buried thousands of pounds of pork. (Concurrently, the evacuees had accused the administration of dumping 1,880 pounds of beef as unfit for human consumption.)

Engle said that there was sabotage in the fire department, that Japanese were using government tractors to play polo, and that they were stealing knives from the butcher shop and grinding down auto springs in the blacksmith shop to make weapons. He introduced a bill in Congress to keep Tule Lake under Army control. In the midst of general denunciation, a former military guard at Tule Lake sat down and wrote a letter criticizing segregation and defending the rioters, "They acted as any other American would have acted," he wrote.[76]

Joe Kurihara arrived at Tule Lake from the isolation center at Leupp, Arizona, while the Army was in control. He was immediately incarcerated, "this action placing the final stamp of 'bad man' on Joe." The project director, who had known him at Leupp, intervened in his behalf and secured his release. He urged him to take a leadership role but Kurihara found the atmosphere of Tule Lake alien to him.[77]

The Army control of Tule Lake was a sensitive international issue as the evacuees and the administration well knew. A statement came from Tokyo, "The Japanese government may have to reconsider the treatment which is now being given to Americans residing in Japan."[78] Francisco de Amat, the Spanish consul in San Francisco, went to inspect the situation for the Japanese government in the company of a representative of the State Department which was alleged to have asked the National Grange to withdraw a resolution advocating deportation of all American Japanese.[79]

Ray Cronin, an Associated Press correspondent interned at Santa Tomas in the Philippines, later told officers of the WRA that restrictive measures toward the prisoners at Santa Tomas were adopted for three days in response to the trouble at Tule Lake. Joseph Grew, the former ambassador to Japan, in an attempt to mollify Tokyo, publicly criticized distorted reports of incidents at Tule Lake and the consequent public uproar. Francis Biddle, the United States Attorney General, took the stand before the Dies Committee to warn that Japan was watching the treatment of the people at Tule Lake. He opposed permanent Army control of the center. In fact, he went so far as to say, "I know of no authority in any executive order to hold a citizen in a center."[80]

One of the chief grievances of the segregees at Tule Lake was that citizens were being held, not only in the center, but in a stockade within the center. Dillon Myer, in a statement to the public, justified this segregation within segregation.[81] The Army and the WRA defended the imprisonment on the grounds that neutrals deserved protection against gang rowdyism, intimidation, and assaults. Yet though the inmates of the stockade were, for the most part, anti-administration leaders, many of them were reasonable men, and the terrorism did not cease after they were put behind bars. The rioters were arrested presumably to protect the neutrals but no alternative leadership developed because of the pervasive fear of arrest by the government on the one hand and of accusations of collaboration with the government on the other.

The Daihyo Sha Kai, with many of its leaders in the stockade, had been replaced by a temporary coordinating committee. But it was unpopular because it had failed to fulfill its promises to get all the prisoners released and provide jobs for everyone who wanted to work. "Fielders" who were used for "intelligence work" were suspected of being *inu* (informers); yet the committee failed to win the full backing of the administration. In April its members resigned.

In vain the project director tried to get the blocks to elect representatives so that his staff would have some means of dealing with the people. The meetings called for this purpose were boycotted, and the nominees who had agreed to stand for election withdrew their names. The radicals were opposed to cooperation, and the moderates were afraid to cooperate. As a community analyst wrote, "Dealing with the administration had become impossibly dangerous."[82]

The only government thenceforth was the rule of the extremists. To forestall arrest they organized an underground movement and by what a Nisei girl called "Gestapo methods"[83] imposed their will on the rest of the people. No one was willing to risk cooperation and *inu* status where protection was not guaranteed. The sociologist Gladys Ishida wrote, "The cumulative tensions of living in a neurotic community such as Tule Lake mounted so that social acceptance by the majority was more desirable than being ostracized."[84]

The radicals were not the majority, as we have seen, but they *acted* as the majority in the absence of a group who were willing to defy them. In the spring of 1944 roving bands of "strong-arm boys" equipped with two by fours perpetrated a series of *inu* beatings. The reign of terror culminated in the fatal stabbing of an "old Tulean," the unpopular head of the Cooperative Enterprises. After his murder, never solved, the evacuee police resigned, and in some blocks no men would take their places. In other blocks members of the underground volunteered so as to carry on their activities without interference. The new police force was ineffectual and refused to become involved in controversial matters, with the result that lawlessness increased.

Tule Lake was isolated from the world in a way that augmented the internal strains. The willful distortions of the press made the administration reluctant to admit outsiders or to invite further criticism. When the manager of the Cooperative Enterprises was murdered, someone suggested keeping the news from the press, but Pat Frayne, the trenchant West Coast public relations chief for the WRA, disagreed. He predicted, correctly, that if the newspapers were given the facts, the story would be featured no longer than two days. As Robert Cozzens said, "It took a big battle in the Pacific to keep us [the WRA] off the front page" and Tule Lake provided most of the copy.

One of the visitors to Tule Lake, though he had difficulty getting permission to enter, was Ernest Besig, counsel for the Northern California branch of the American Civil Liberties Union, who was asked by their families and friends to investigate the imprisonment in the stockade of sixteen American citizens. Some of the men had been held as long as eight months. When Besig was given permission to interview them in mid-July, the WRA insisted that internal security officers be present when he took their depositions. The detainees had first called on the Spanish consul, representing the Japanese government, and getting no satisfaction, they turned to the American Civil Liberties Union.

Besig filed a complaint with Harold Ickes, charging that sixteen American citizens had been held for eight months without a hearing. Besig explained that he was not concerned with the morals, guilt or innocence of the persons of Japanese ancestry involved. "These people are entitled to a hearing and a trial," he said. "If they are guilty, put them in prison or anywhere. But they have the basic right of every citizen for a fair trial!"[85] Soon afterwards the prisoners staged a hunger strike. By August 24 all the men had been released, partly as a result of ACLU pressure.

The underground movement had been gradually coming into the open. The "resegregationists" wished Tule Lake to be divided again with those who planned to return to Japan separated from the "fence-sitters." An organization called Sokuku Kenkyu Seinen-dan (Young Men's Association for the Study of the Mother Country) was started in August, 1944, to educate Nisei for life in Japan. Members were compelled to attend lectures and to perform outdoor calisthenics which gradually became more militaristic with bugle calls and uniforms consisting of gray sweat shirts and headbands embellished with a picture of the rising sun. The Joshi-dan was started for young women.

Some Issei parents were pleased to have their children prepared for a life in Japan, though in fact there was only the most tenuous link between the activities of the Sokuku and the drab hand-to-mouth existence that the expatriates were to experience in the defeated country. Though many laughed at the noisy dawn rituals of the Sokuku, others looking for something positive to fill the vacuum of their days, were attracted by the slogan-shouting exhibitionism. There was a good deal of coercion, both indirect and overt, as Tule Lake espoused "the Japanese way of life" with WRA sanction.[86] In the expectation of their repatriation or expatriation, "Japanization" of the residents became an administration policy. Some observers felt that the government encouraged repatriation.

The Japanese arts flourished at Tule Lake as at the other centers and were enjoyed as pure recreation, but they were also encouraged by segregees for ideological reasons. American-style dances and sports were less approved than etiquette classes for girls and marching with shaved heads for boys. Attendance at the Japanese language school was compulsory, but at the American school was optional. A Nisei woman remembers that her father took down a picture of General MacArthur after his friends criticized him. Another woman recalls that they read news sheets in Japanese, monitored by members of the patriotic organizations, giving false optimistic news of the war. "I believed the propaganda of the Japanese radio, and the pro-Japanese organizations, since I didn't read any of the American newspapers."[87]

Yet about a quarter of the population of Tule Lake consisted of American-educated youngsters under seventeen, who, with no opportunity to make an individual decision in the matter, were forced to live with their parents in an atmosphere over which they had no control. When two members of the Society of Friends, Gerda Isenberg and Josephine Duveneck, visited Tule Lake early in 1944, Caucasian teachers begged them, "Talk to our children. The young people are so confused." These Quakers were the first visitors from the outside allowed to visit after the WRA resumed control of Tule Lake.

Mrs. Isenberg found that the most pitiable victims in the conflict of loyalties were the adolescents between sixteen and twenty. At the request of teachers, she talked to high school classes. "I used a very personal approach, telling them that I was a German-born, naturalized American citizen and that I had close family relations in Germany. This made an immediate and warm contact." She spoke of democracy and human rights. "Although evacuation seems to them a proof that democracy does not work, I tried to make them see that we have no right to lose faith in it. Like all other human institutions, democracy cannot be perfect and there is no justification in expecting it to be so." She told them that their situation could not be compared to that of the people in German concentration camps who might wonder, " 'Will I be alive tomorrow or the next day?' Though behind barbed wire, they were still members of human society under human law."[88]

Yet, when she went home she could not shake off the memory of the puzzled, diffident youngsters who were caught in a halfway country between Japan and the United States. As the months wore on, they in turn, must have doubted her words of hope. "There was an atmosphere of terror at Tule Lake in mid-1944," according to Frank Chuman. More and more, the administration left the colonists to govern themselves.

As the gulf widened, the "resegregationist" group insisted that Tuleans must proclaim their allegiance by renouncing their American citizenship. Congress cleared the way by passing a denationalization bill, Public Law 405. Whether the government was responding to pressure from the Nisei or from the American public, Public Law 405 was a fitting end to the process of evacuation, detention, and segregation, the final result of the persecution of a people.

TWELVE · RELOCATION

AMONG THE RENUNCIANTS at Tule Lake were a number of men who had served the American Army honorably in 1940, 1941, and 1942, only to be discharged during the period when Nisei were reclassified as 4-C, placing them in the same category with enemy aliens. A commentator wrote, "In this concentration camp an appreciative government permitted them to meditate upon the gratitude of the Government they had defended willingly and upon the 'Four Freedoms' for which they had fought but which were denied them and their families."[1]

Nisei who had remained at the "loyal" camps, affirming their patriotism, still protested serving in the Army. From January, 1944, when the draft was reopened to Japanese–Americans until November, 1946, about three hundred eligible men refused to report for induction. Some were influenced by their parents, yielding to their elders' fears for their safety. A former Boy Scout, who was remembered for having rescued the American flag when it dropped during a ceremony at his camp, was, according to a relative, "brainwashed" by his family who thought he owed nothing to the United States after the disgrace of being interned. After refusing the draft at their instigation, he spent two years in prison and on his release volunteered for the Army and was sent to Germany in the postwar era.

A few Nisei were conscientious objectors who refused to serve because of general convictions against war, among them, Gordon Hirabayashi, who figured in the curfew case before the Supreme Court. He had served nine months in a county jail in the state of Washington followed by three months in a federal penitentiary for violation of the curfew and evacuation orders. On his release he worked for the American Friends Service Committee both in Spokane and in the relocation centers under the direction of Floyd Schmoe, former professor of forestry at the University of Washington. Hirabayashi married Schmoe's daughter in July, 1944, and in September was in court again for refusing to fill out the special selective service questionnaire for persons of Japanese ancestry and for subsequently failing to report for his preinduction physical examination. As a Quaker, he refused service on religious grounds, but he also objected to the questionnaire as discriminatory. It was, he believed, "an outright violation of both the Christian and American principles of justice and democracy."[2] Since he refused alternative service in a make-work camp, entering a plea of *nolo contendere*, he was sentenced to an additional twelve-month term in prison as a conscientious objector. Another Nisei conscientious objector is mentioned as taking part in a strike against Jim Crow seating in the mess hall of a federal prison in Ashland, Kentucky.[3]

Other young evacuees, who would have served if they had been free, protested that the government had no right to induct them from behind barbed wire. At Poston an evacuee was charged with violating the wartime espionage act because he distributed a leaflet addressed "to the gentlemen of 17 yrs. to 38 yrs. of age" and another to "Niseis of Draftable Age" urging, "Those of you who have received notices for pre-induction physical: Cooperate and refuse to go until we have reached our goal. (Fighting for our rights.) Those who do not care for their rights and are willing to be drafted, please wait until our rights are granted or until we are all branded as pro-Axis elements."[4] He was exonerated by a federal district court in Arizona.

At Amache the privilege of freedom of assembly was suspended after a protest meeting of draft-age Nisei. The meeting was not illegal but the administration considered that the participants could be tried for sedition for urging resistance to the draft. At Gila a petition signed by 620 loyal Japanese–Americans facing immediate induction was sent to President Roosevelt. They asked for equal opportunity for Nisei in all branches of the service and for an early restitution of constitutional privileges denied as a result of the evacuation.

An evacuee at Heart Mountain wrote of a "small committee" that had been trying to "regain our rights as citizens," but he objected because the committee had "misguided youths into not reporting for their examinations and although they perhaps have a strong moral case, they are wrong in believing that now is the time to secure our Constitutional rights. They forget there is a war on."[5] Many of the protesters complied and were drafted, but others took the consequences of refusal and went to federal penitentiaries. Sixty-three were sentenced from Heart Mountain. The wife of one of these men wrote that he refused to report for his preinduction physical exam even though he would not have passed it. Instead, ". . . he stayed back to fight for his Bill of Rights and for the future of Japanese American[s] for this is his country and no other shall be his."[6] Three men from Minidoka were sentenced to two years and six months in prison and fined several hundred dollars. A man from

Amache wrote scornfully about the rebels at his camp in July, 1944. When five men were called up to take an Army physical examination, only one reported. "The rest didn't because you can guess??? Their faith in the emperor??? or is it thou shalt not kill??? They certainly got off easy by only 8 months for three of them. The fourth got two years. Their sentences should be more. Ask the 442nd and the 100th, they'll tell you."[7]

The draft resisters were supported by some members of the legal profession and in at least one instance their case was upheld in court. Federal Judge Louis Goodman of San Francisco, in Eureka, California, in August, 1944, dismissed indictments against twenty-six Nisei from Tule Lake who had refused to be drafted. He said:

> It is shocking to the conscience that an American citizen be confined on the ground of disloyalty, and then, while so under duress and restraint, be compelled to serve in the armed forces, or be prosecuted for not yielding to such compulsion. . . .
>
> It does not follow that because the war power may allow the detention of defendant at Tule Lake, the guaranties of the Bill of Rights and other Constitutional provisions are abrogated by the existence of war. . . . The due process, which is inalienable to the defendant in this proceeding, cannot be suspended because of the war or danger to national security, but only on a valid declaration of martial law. . . .
>
> The issue raised by this motion is without precedent. It must be resolved in the light of the traditional and historic Anglo-American approach to the time-honored doctrine of "due process." It must not give way to overzealousness in an attempt to reach, via the criminal process, those who we may regard as undesirable citizens.[8]

The segregees at Tule Lake, some of whom had renounced their allegiance to the United States, were in a special category, but the indictments against the draft refusers from the "loyal" centers were not dismissed. On March 12, 1945, a federal court of appeals upheld the conviction of the sixty-three men from Heart Mountain. Though A. L. Wirin, attorney for the ACLU, appealed for a reconsideration of the case, the United States Supreme Court denied a writ of *certiorari* on May 28. In early 1946 pardons were granted to almost all persons convicted of violating the Selective Service Act, and the rights and privileges of citizens were restored to them by the President's Advisory Board Proclamation of December 23, 1947.[9]

But the past was not so easily erased. The draft resisters who served prison sentences have a permanent "record." Moreover, they suffered hatred and persecution from Nisei veterans in the immediate postwar years. The hero of John Okada's novel, *No-No Boy*, spent two years in a relocation center and two years in a federal penitentiary. When he returned to Seattle, he hardly dared to show his face in town. A lawyer who worked with another stigmatized group, the repatriates, said, "Those of us in service felt bitter about those boys. We thought they made it tough for us."

The crux of the matter was that the American Japanese won acceptance in large measure through the feats of Nisei soldiers on battlefields abroad. The all-Nisei combat team was extraordinarily effective as a propaganda weapon. The WRA exploited the saga of the 442nd Combat Team to promote the relocation of civilians, first in the East and Middle West and finally on the West Coast when the rescission orders were issued.

The group that had been villified because of the war predictably won recognition in the same context. Since Nisei servicemen had been offered an unparalllelled opportunity to reverse public opinion by their performance on the battlefield, any deviation from the patriotic norm, even in the name of American principles, was considered detrimental if not treasonable to the group. Men who risked their lives against the enemy were not at that time likely to acknowledge that it also required fortitude to go to prison in protest against civil liberties betrayed.

A quarter of a century has put the matter in a different perspective. "They had the courage of their convictions," is the opinion on the draft resisters of Judge Wayne Kanemoto, himself a veteran.

The Nisei record in the service bolstered their status as Americans. Between November, 1940, and December, 1945, approximately 26,000 men volunteered or were inducted into the service, of whom 13,528 were from the mainland and 12,250 from Hawaii. More than 6,000 troops served in the Pacific theater and most of the rest saw duty in Europe. The all-Nisei 442nd Combat Team has been called the most decorated unit in the United States Army in World War II, its members winning over one thousand citations. They were preceded to the front by the Hawaiian 100th Battalion, which embarked for Africa in August, 1943, joined the invasion of Salerno, took part in four drives across the Volturno River, and aided in the capture of Cassino. On July 27, 1944, the 100th was awarded the Distinguished Unit Citation by Lieutenant General Mark Clark.

The 442nd trained at Camp Shelby, Mississippi, despite the objections of Congressman John Rankin. Earl Finch, a local [Hattiesburg] businessman and rancher, was renowned for befriending hundreds of the Nisei trainees. They also attended dinner dances at a USO at the nearby Jerome relocation center which was for a while directed by Sada Murayama. Young Nisei hostesses and their parents entertained 150 servicemen at a time.

Frank Bunya, who trained at Camp Shelby, said, "When we went into town we saw the signs in various places for 'Colored' and 'White.'

Naturally we were not white so we would go into the entrance marked 'Colored.' The Caucasians would tell us we were not considered colored so it was all right to use the 'White' entrance. This seemed strange because we had been forcibly moved out of our homes into concentration camps because we were not white. Off and on we would use the entrance marked 'Colored' which would upset the Caucasians. On the way to Mississippi we stopped at an overpass in Memphis, Tennessee. We had our caps and uniforms on and there was a girl who came walking down and looked at us and asked, 'Are you Japanese prisoners of war?' She had never seen Japanese–Americans. We razzed her to death." After the announcement of the execution of American aviators in Japan, Nisei soldiers at Camp Shelby bought $100,000 worth of war bonds in two days.

"Go for Broke" was the motto of the 442nd as the unit took part in the Italian campaign and went on into the drive into France. Their most notable exploit was the rescue of the "Lost Battalion," a Texas outfit, in Bruyeres, France, in 1944. An Hawaiian Nisei chaplain wrote an undated letter to George Aki about this exploit:

> . . . Though we had been fighting days on end, we were recalled to rescue the Lost Battalion. The 2nd Bn [Battalion] was commanded to make contact with the enemy; then the 100th and the 3d Battalions. The men are obedient and brave; they charge right into machine gun fire and are mowed down, but those who can get up, charge again and again in waves, like the waves beating on the shores. Our losses are heavy. The General himself has been directing the battle right behind the assault company, risking his life.
>
> And now Trench foot is setting in cutting down our men along with the wounded and the dead.
>
> My spiritual life is at its lowest ebb for I see so many of the men, close friends, who are giving their all; too many. The sacrifice is too great. . . .
>
> But despite my lamentations, our boys are brave and I am proud of them as they do their job with one mind and one spirit. . . . They are literally writing with their own blood a great chapter of democracy. . . .

Each October 30, on the anniversary of the rescue of the lost battalion the mayor of Bruyeres places a wreath in a local cemetery to honor the Nisei soldiers who died to liberate the town.

In this operation and others, the Nisei group acquired a formidable reputation among the other fighting men. An intelligence officer told George Aki, also a chaplain with the 442nd, that captured German prisoners said they feared the Japanese boys "because they never give up." An American colonel told him that when he met any of them, "I always salute first out of respect for their service." Another man remembers that when they were in a tough spot his commanding officer would put out an appeal, "Call in the Japs!"

The 442nd had a casualty rate estimated at 308 per cent! In the course of the European war, 569 of the men in the unit were killed outright, 81 died of wounds, 3,713 were wounded, and 67 were reported missing.

Frank Bunya was on a troop ship in the middle of the Atlantic when the news came that Germany had surrendered. "We got to Italy about the second week in May and the war was over. I was lucky. Several of the people that I trained with had been killed. A close friend was over there two days. The second day he was in the hospital. They had to take his leg off. The third day he headed back home. It happened that fast."

Sentiment in the relocation center changed as the men became heroes. The Issei who had often opposed the drafting of their sons began to express the feeling that "It's a man's duty to serve his country."[10] Sometimes inductees were given ten dollars by their block as they left the center. Memorial services were held for the dead. The *Pacific Citizen* kept the community informed about war news. Casualty lists were printed immediately because the JACL officials, who were on cordial terms with Colonel Scobey and John McCloy, obtained information from the War Department. Awards for heroic action were also noted.

The 442nd won its culminating honor when the unit marched down Constitution Avenue in Washington, D.C., on July 15, 1946, and received a presidential Distinguished Unit Citation from President Truman. The *esprit de corps* of the group has been attributed to a consciousness of racial ties as well as the Japanese sense of obligation (*giri*) and need to avoid shame (*haji*) which the Issei impressed upon the Nisei in spite of the cultural gap between them. The heroism was eventually rewarded. ". . . we were probably the only group of American soldiers in World War II who got what we fought for," Mike Masaoka said later.[11]

Much less known to the public were the exploits of the approximately 6,000 Nisei in the Pacific theater, because they were engaged in intelligence work, in translating documents, in interpreting, and other matters that were highly secret while the war was in progress. Most of the Nisei in the Pacific theater were in the Military Intelligence Service (MIS).

The Army did not use Japanese–Americans in a separate fighting unit in the Pacific. A military spokesman for the War Department explained that this policy was dictated for practical reasons and not because of discrimination. Lieutenant Colonel Harrison A. Gerhardt said the Army feared that the enemy might put on the uniforms of dead American soldiers in order to mingle with Nisei troops thereby "causing considerable confusion and increasing hazards of enemy infiltration." If Nisei soldiers were captured they might be subjected to "extreme torture. . . . If they were generally assigned to all units it would then be necessary to screen units which are to be employed in the Pacific theatre before such a unit could be shipped."[12] Nevertheless, approximately 3,700 Nisei served individually in combat areas in the Pacific where they were subject to some of the risks outlined by Colonel Gerhardt. There was such secrecy that some of the citations accompanying awards they received were not written up, according to Akiji Yoshimura who was an interpreter for the soft-spoken, somewhat scholarly Brigadier General Frank Merrill. (A 1962 Hollywood film on Merrill's Marauders erroneously portrayed Filipino interpreters.) Each Nisei was assigned a couple of Caucasian guards and Nisei were considered too valuable to be sent ashore in the initial landings in the central Pacific.

Hoichi Kubo participated in the invasions of the Gilbert Islands, the Marshall Islands, Saipan, and Okinawa. He was awarded the Distinguished Service Cross for having volunteered to "rope down" a one-hundred foot cliff and enter a deep cave on Saipan where a large number of civilians (of Japanese ancestry) were taking refuge with a group of enemy soldiers. He carried only a concealed pistol which, after gaining their confidence, he revealed. The Japanese soldiers had thought he was a spy. Pointing to the children in the cave, Kubo said he had come to persuade them to save the innocent.

When he was asked why he was fighting for the United States, he referred to an incident in Japanese history in which a hero turns against his father on the field of battle, saying, "I put my allegiance to my ruler higher than filial piety." His questioners understood, "We shouldn't have asked." (According to Akiji Yoshimura it was easier to explain to Japanese prisoners than to American troops "why we were in United States uniforms." The Japanese recognized loyalty to country whereas it never occurred to many Americans that Nisei would be loyal enough to serve against Japan.)

When it was time for the noon meal, Kubo shared his K-Ration with the others. Then he told them he must go back to his company. He said he would persuade the Americans to give them an hour to come out, after which the cave would be attacked. Before the time was up, they surrendered, thereby saving several hundred lives on both sides.

Yori Wada also found civilians hiding with the enemy soldiers on Okinawa. "We'd have to talk them out or go in after them." After capture, they were separated, the civilians released and the soldiers put in the stockade. It was the experience of Nisei interrogators that Japanese soldiers were not security conscious because they did not expect to be captured. According to Lieutenant Kan Tagami of Selma, California, "They talked their heads off."[13]

Yori Wada conducted the initial interrogation of prisoners. Another of his assignments was to intercept Japanese communications. He was on occasion attached to the Air Force to monitor messages from plane to plane and from ground to plane. He also intercepted ship to shore communications for the Navy. If the messages were in code they were rushed to cryptographers on Guam. Captured battle plans were translated by the valuable Nisei MIS men who were moved about wherever they were most needed. They were loaned to the British, the Australians, the New Zealanders, and the Chinese as well as to every branch of the American service, including the OSS and the OWI. A team of Nisei in Australia worked day and night for six days to translate documents captured after the Battle of Bismarck Sea which listed the past and present assignment of 300,000 Japanese military men. As a result, allied shipbuilding programs and selective service inductions which had been geared to an inflated estimate of the strength of the Japanese army were cut back to the benefit of the war economy.

A number of Nisei, including John Aiso, who emerged at the end of the war as a lieutenant colonel, were attached to MacArthur's headquarters. Sergeant Arthur Komuri, now a judge in his native Hawaii, served on the general's staff after escaping from the Filipinos who imprisoned him as a turncoat. His career in mixed identities began early, when in April, 1941, he "infiltrated the Japanese consulate in Manila by posing as a Japanese–American draft dodger."[14]

A third group served in the China–Burma–India theater. Sergeant Roy Matsumoto, "shy, slight, bespectacled," was a hero with Merrill's Marauders, besieged at Maggot Hill in Burma for fifteen days in the spring of 1944.[15] Under cover of darkness he crawled close enough to the enemy lines to overhear plans for a dawn attack which the Second Battalion was then ready to meet. In the thick of the fighting, he leaped to his feet and shouted, "Charge, you soldiers of Japan, charge, charge, charge."[16] The Japanese advanced straight to their death with a blind obedience.

The G-2 boys served to the end of the war, and afterwards Sergeant Fumio Kido risked his life right after the surrender of Japan when with four other Americans he parachuted from a B-24 bomber into a prison camp in Manchuria, on August 16, 1945, to rescue some United States citizens. He was the interpreter between the conquerors and the Japanese troops who were not yet aware that the war was over. Lieutenant Ralph Yempuko undertook a similar mission of mercy, also by parachute at about the same time.

The MIS men won the praises of their commanders in the Pacific, General Merrill, Major General Charles A. Willoughby, and General Joseph (Vinegar Joe) Stilwell, who said, "The Nisei bought an awful big chunk of America with their blood." Admiral Chester Nimitz declared, "Before World War II, I entertained some doubt as to the loyalty of American citizens of Japanese ancestry in the event of war with Japan. From my observations during World War II, I no longer have that doubt."[17]

Letters from Caucasian servicemen about Nisei comrades tempered the hate campaign in West Coast newspapers. A member of Merrill's Marauders praised Sergeant Hank Gosho, who translated orders foolishly shouted aloud by the enemy ("we call him Horizontal Hank because he's been pinned down so many times by Jap machine gun fire").[18] "I have a friend of Japanese ancestry and, I say it with pride, from the Pacific Coast," wrote a corporal on the Marshall Islands.[19]

A Nisei veteran of the 442nd, warned by local residents not to buy a farm in Harris County, Texas, wrote to the Houston *Press*, "What I would like to know is [is] this our answer for rescuing the 'Lost Battalion' of your proud 36th Division in the Vosges Mountains in France?" A story in the August 14, 1946, issue of the *Press* changed local opinion.[20]

A reader of the San Luis Obispo *Tribune-Telegram* who objected to a picture of a Nisei serviceman of the 10th Army greeting his father whom he discovered on Okinawa, was chastised by the following editorial comment, "T-4 Higachi was good enough for the United States Army, good enough for combat service in one of the most perilous spots in the Pacific war. That makes him good enough for our front page."[21]

Sergeant Ben Kuroki, of the United States Air Force, a veteran of fifty-eight bombing missions in Europe and the holder of the Distinguished Flying Cross, spoke to the Commonwealth Club in San Francisco on February 4, 1944. The "Boy from Nebraska," was held up for two months before being allowed to join the service. "I began to realize right then" he said, "that I had a couple of strikes on me to begin with, and that I was going to be fighting two battles instead of one—against the Axis and against intolerance among my fellow Americans. . . . Especially now, after the widespread publicity given the recent atrocity stories, I find prejudice once again directed against me, and neither my uniform nor the medals which are visible proof of what I have been through, have been able to stop it. I don't know for sure that it is safe for me to walk the streets of my own country. . . . I had thought that after Ploesti and 29 other missions so rough it was just short of a miracle I got through them, I wouldn't have to fight for acceptance among my own people all over again." He added, "In most cases, I don't. . . ."

Another group of ambassadors were the Nisei college students. At the time of evacuation, there were about 2,500 Japanese–Americans in West Coast colleges and universities. College administrators, who were impressed with the promise and ability of these students used their influence to get individuals transferred to inland institutions in order that they might be allowed to finish their education.

With the impetus of the college presidents, a Student Relocation Committee was formed on March 21, 1942, with headquarters in Berkeley and branch offices in Portland, Seattle, and Los Angeles. Joseph Conard, a member of the Society of Friends, was the executive secretary. Professor Claude Settles of San Jose State College worked at the Berkeley office in June and July of 1942. He had to write eight letters in behalf of each prospective student, including permission requests to the Army, the Navy, the mayor of the town in which the student hoped to live, the president of the college to which he was applying, the dean of admissions, and the local sheriff. Each group of letters had to be different in order to fit the particular student. "Once we broke the ice and got *one* student into a college (I don't remember which one now), we were able to say to the other colleges, 'Would you be willing to do the same?' We progressed rapidly after that."

In May, 1942, John M. McCloy asked Clarence Pickett of the American Friends Service Committee to form a National Japanese–American Student Relocation Council. The director was Robert W. O'Brien, who had been an assistant dean of arts and sciences at the University of Washington. The national headquarters were established in Philadelphia, with a distinguished group of educators and churchmen on the Board of Directors and serving in an advisory capacity. Thomas R. Bodine, who had been an investment researcher for the Connecticut General Life Insurance Company, was a field representative to the relocation centers. Because of the time involved in getting clearance for students and in counseling and encouraging the young Nisei in the choice of their colleges, the work moved slowly at first, but by the fall of 1943 students were attending 122 colleges in twenty-five states. Before the war ended, over 4,300 were in colleges and universities, more than twice as many as in the peak prewar years.

"The Council's most time consuming and challenging task these past two years," wrote Bodine in October, 1944, "has been to overcome the apathy, apprehensiveness and misconceptions that are so often a part of Relocation Center life. In its correspondence with students it has therefore tried to be warm and human. Each boy and girl has been thought of and written to as an individual person, worthy of careful thought and consideration."[22]

Military security restrictions were an exasperating hindrance in the beginning. In the summer of 1942, military authorities decreed that no evacuee student could attend a college that was within twenty-five miles of a railroad terminus. This was soon discontinued and a ruling was substituted that the names of colleges that had accepted evacuees would be submitted to the War Department for clearance. Later, clearance was waived except for institutions engaged in certain types of war work, and finally, on August 31, 1944, the War Department lifted all restrictions.

A former evacuee, speaking appreciatively of the detailed, painstaking work done by the council, wrote, "Being young we took all of this for granted at the time."[23] The council had to battle red tape but also student apathy, engendered by long residence in a relocation center, what Bodine described as "lose-fight." But in general, the response of the students and of the campuses to the students was extremely gratifying. Most of the Nisei earned their way, or a large part of it, through part-time jobs, but the council, supported by churches and foundation grants, awarded stipends for tuition averaging from $150 to $200 a year to students who needed financial assistance.

There were two unpleasant episodes in the early days of student relocation, referred to by the Nisei as "The Battle of Parksville" and "The Retreat from Moscow." Eight students arrived at the University of Idaho in Moscow in the spring of 1942 and were told that their admission had been canceled. Though the president of the university had expressed a willingness to accept Nisei students, the governor was hostile and a small group of aroused townspeople stirred up such a fuss that two girls in the group either asked for asylum in the local jail or were placed there by the sheriff for protection. One of them wrote from the jail: ". . . I feel very young and lost for once in my life. . . . Some of the townspeople are up in arms for our coming, and are threatening mob violence. . . . The jailer was talking to someone over the telephone, and said that he is afraid that a mob will come to lynch us tonight. . . . Please write. I'm scared."[24] The student newspaper attributed the uproar to "a combination of political haymaking and the threat of violence by a small group of local roughnecks."[25] Later, a number of evacuee students attended the University of Idaho without difficulty.

In the furor at Parks College in Parksville, Missouri, the president, Dr. William Lindsay Young, backed by the student body, refused to cancel the admission of seven evacuee students despite protests by the mayor and members of the American War Mothers and the American Legion. (An editorial in the *National Legionnaire* called student relocation ". . . a shocking injustice and breach of faith with our own American sons."[26]) Parks College social clubs "rushed" the Nisei newcomers, who were also given a hearty welcome by the campus newspaper, *The Stylus*.[27]

Lillian Ota, who won a Phi Beta Kappa award in her junior year at the University of California at Berkeley, left the Tanforan assembly center in August to finish her senior year at Wellesley on a scholarship. At the college she was feted. "Oh, yes, I had one nasty 'grilling.' One student accused practically all the Japanese in this country of being in some way connected with the 'sabotage and espionage network.' I argued against the misconception in the best way I could, but didn't finish my spiel as I had to return to my dormitory before lockout time. Later I sent her a copy of the *Pacific Citizen*. She then acknowledged she had been wrong."[28]

A graduate student taking anthropology courses at the University of Kansas wrote, "I must certainly have made some kind of impression by the very fact that I existed, good or bad as that impression may have been. . . . I came away feeling no different than if I had been at home or school in pre-war days. However, some went out of their way to be kind and helpful."[29]

In April, 1943, Dorothy Tada left Amache for Chicago where the National YWCA had arranged a scholarship for her graduate work at George Williams College, "a wonderful little college. People were most friendly, but I had a real need to understand a little better WHY we were put into centers, a real need to find out why in these United States these things happened to citizens." She became interested in the problems of minority groups in general. "I talked to Dr. Redfield of the University of Chicago (which restricted Nisei because of nuclear research), and he suggested I study with his father-in-law, Dr. Robert E. Park, dean of American sociologists, who taught at Fisk University in Nashville."

She received a fellowship as an assistant to Dr. Park and went to Nashville in the fall of 1943. "It opened my eyes to a great many things in terms of race relations in the United States. It was the most revealing experience. I had hitherto lived an isolated and sheltered life. I learned a great deal about other minorities in terms of feelings. I was very sympathetic because I had come through a devastating experience. I became aware that things people take for granted you no longer *can* take for granted. It wasn't easy." She later worked in a settlement house in Chicago, was a staff member of the National Board, YWCA, and pursued graduate studies at the New York University Center for Human Relations before returning to the West Coast.

Kenji Okuda, who had the second highest record in his Seattle high school class of five hundred, was elected president of the student council at Oberlin. He said, "I have met people who not only were interested but were going so far out of their way to help others that I felt small and cheap."[30] Kay Kikuko Murota, a graduate of Topaz High School, received the only all-A record at Wood Junior College in Mississippi. Because of her scholastic achievement, Topaz High School was trying to raise funds to send another student to the college.[31]

Nisei were also appointed to faculty posts in eastern and middle western colleges. An honor student at UCLA who had a PhD from Stanford had to get clearance from four federal agencies before he could accept a research position at Harvard, and he was denied permission to visit Niagara Falls on his honeymoon. A Japanese who had lived in Canada since infancy, and who was appointed to the physics department at Smith College, occasioned a minor uproar in the town of Northhampton, Massachusetts, where barbers would not cut his hair, and the custodial staff of the college threatened to resign until the president, Dr. Herbert

Davis arranged that the commander of a WAVE training program on the campus, Captain H. Underwood, address them and remind them of their responsibility to serve an institution where service personnel were being trained in wartime.

These stories reached the relocation centers through the *Pacific Citizen* and frightened many who from isolated incidents constructed a view of the world outside as a hostile place. "The journey out into America . . . was considered quite hazardous."[32]

Mixed reports came from another group of early relocatees, the men who answered the call for seasonal farm labor in the summer and fall of 1942. In response to urgent requests from Montana senators and their grower constituents about the labor crisis in the sugar beet field, Roosevelt suggested in a speech that schools could release students to save the harvest, to which Senator James Murray replied in a letter to Marvin McIntyre, the President's secretary, that, "The President seems to think that you can pick beets out of the ground just like you pick cherries off a tree."[33] He had written earlier, "We have got all these Jap evacuees, but the employment service under McNutt has failed to get them out on the farms."[34] A constituent had urged him by telegram, ". . . you should continue to hammer at the War Relocation Authority. They should force those Japs to take this work."[35] The first to leave were fifteen men from the Portland assembly center, on May 21, 1942. By September of that year a wholesale movement of evacuee workers was underway to the sugar beet fields of Utah, Idaho, Montana, and Wyoming. Approximately eight thousand men harvested around 915,000 tons of beets from 80,000 acres in western states, enough to produce 265,000 pounds of sugar, according to *Western Farm Life*.[36] S. J. Boyer, of the State Labor Commission in Utah, said, "We can just as well face the facts. If it had not been for Japanese labor, much of the beet crop of Utah and Idaho . . . would have been plowed up."[37]

Though California's sugar beets were harvested by Mexicans, General DeWitt, at the request of the War Department, lifted the ban against Japanese in that part of Arizona which was in the Western Defense Command so that evacuee harvesters could save the cotton crop. The western governors pleaded for evacuee labor (Governor Maw of Utah proposed some form of conscript labor), but almost simultaneously they opposed free colonization. E. P. Carvill, the governor of Nevada, wrote the Chandler Commission that he did not want Japanese unsupervised in Nevada.[38]

The governor of Arkansas expressed the same opinion.[39] Governor Nels Smith of Wyoming said, "The only condition under which we will have them is that at the conclusion of the war they shall be returned to the place whence they came," for which he was praised by Senator Edward V. Robertson, who said, "Governor Smith's attitude was straight-forward, it was western, and consequently thoroughly American."[40] The governor of Arizona told the Chandler Commission at a hearing in Phoenix that while "he would be glad to take back his 1,100 [the number of persons of Japanese ancestry in the state before the war], he certainly did not want to have 31,000 Japanese [from Poston and Gila] left on his hands."[41]

The evacuee workers noted this same ambivalent attitude in the communities they worked in. A man who was working in Los Animas, Colorado, wrote, "I'm afraid that the public opinion is none too favorable for Japanese in Colorado. It is really strange how they resent your presence when, after all, they asked for us to harvest the beets."[42] Another man wrote, "They treat us as if we had leprosy everywhere we go; we're being shoved around like so much cattle."

A worker in Valier, Montana, complained, "I don't see why in the hell the WRA let us come to such a damn place. . . . This trip really taught us a lesson. From now on before we take a job, we're going to find out how much prejudice goes along with it. . . . This region is more anti-Japanese than California. Our boss tells us that Japanese were actually run out of Great Falls, that is, not recently, but in the past. Prejudice runs high even among the wheat and sugar farmers. They don't like each other, so I guess that's why they didn't have any trouble getting to hate us."

However, other evacuees wrote, "It's better outside." "People have treated us fine." "Lewisville [Idaho] is a nice friendly small town." Ray Nash, the first director of Manzanar, was so anxious to see for himself whether or not 129 volunteer workers from his camp were laboring under decent conditions that he drove a dusty 1,200 miles to Idaho to investigate. The workers appeared quite moved by his demonstration of concern for them. A letter from an apple picker in Emmett, Idaho, said, "The people so far have been very nice to us. We are living in a fairly good American house. The inside sure is fixed good and clean. Everything is completely furnished as modern electric, range, new big refrigerator, heater, all the kitchen utensils, and even a console radio. Boy, it sure feels like a real home. . . ."[43]

But a beet worker wrote from Corvallis, Montana, "Our grand abode looks [like] something brought over from the Kentucky hills or the Oklahoma dust bowl. Our first impression when we saw it was that perhaps it may be haunted."[44] Shig Matsunaga was asked by the community council at his relocation center to check housing conditions on the sugar beet ranches in Idaho, Wyoming, Montana, and North Dakota. "Going from California looking at those places," he said, "I found the best of them were crude, but standard for the area. You lived in an old box car, an old shack. The bare necessities were all you got."

Some of the evacuee workers improved conditions on their own. David Sakai went out to Idaho to top sugar beets after only one week at Heart Mountain. "We contracted to top the beets. They were to furnish us a place in which to live, utilities, utensils and certain basic items, other than food and clothing. Of our group of six, five had had some college education (some had degrees), and we saw to it that they lived up to the agreement. Late October in Idaho requires fuel for warmth as well as for cooking. We repeatedly asked for coal. The boss was reluctant. We sawed and chopped all the used lumber and railroad ties in sight. We warned him that we would start on the northwest corner of the barn unless he provided coal. He did!"

Henry Tanda at Poston told his wife, "We can go to Montana if you'll cook for eight fellows." She agreed. The Tandas, with their two tiny daughters and eight young bachelors took a train for Harlem in the Milk River Valley just a few miles from the Canadian border. When the man who hired them showed the place where they were supposed to live, literally a chicken house with a dirt floor and cracked windows, Mrs. Tanda burst into tears. Her husband and the others said, "You don't expect us to live in here! How about that place over there?"

The large barnlike house they pointed to contained nothing but a wood stove. "We all slept on the floor that first night . . . on a straw bed and encountered bedbugs. They said it was sheep ticks, but we got rid of them. The boys made furniture. They built a Japanese bath house about six foot square, carried the water in a tank pulled by horses, heated it in a galvanized tub with a wooden rack on the bottom and a fire underneath. There was no running water."

Another group of boys in Idaho, spurning the creek offered to them by the boss, built a bath house with a tremendous tub big enough for a family which was filled by an ingenious arrangement from an aluminum trough. It was used by the other Nisei neighbors as well.

The farm work was strenuous. A man who was topping sugar beets wrote, "The very first day I worked I was so tired I just crawled into bed and fell asleep. Next morning my back was one big sore spot. Then I wondered why I left the easy camp life, but I realized only then how soft and useless camp life made me. . . ."[45] Seasonal work for Heart Mountain men, besides beet topping and apple harvesting included tearing down old deteriorating CCC barracks at Yellowstone Park, a project that allowed for trout fishing in the Shoshone River during the lunch hour. This was some time before a bill was introduced in the Wyoming legislature to deny fishing licenses to evacuees from Heart Mountain.

Though seasonal workers were often disappointed with the living conditions and the discrimination they encountered, the wages were good by comparison with those paid in the centers and the relative independence even more satisfying. "I shall never forget the feeling of breathing 'free' air . . ." one man recalled twenty-five years later.[46] Another said, "We went out to the farm on an old truck and we felt wonderful to have our freedom once more. It was such a good sensation to be moving along those dirt roads away from camp. As we traveled along further, I filled my eyes with the sight of green lawns, individual homes, paved streets, and actually water fountains. I never realized how much I missed those things that I had seen so often in San Francisco."[47]

There were varying degrees of freedom under the work furlough program. The only restriction imposed by General DeWitt was that the workers must travel to a single county. Many came and went at will between the farms where they worked and the nearby towns where they ventured for recreation. Others housed in Farm Security Administration camps were living under certain restrictions, such as a curfew. Sometimes they were not allowed to leave the farms except to accompany the employer when he was purchasing supplies. A resident of Poston complained, "Some individuals are being released from the confines of this reservation under strict regulations. However, as an American citizen, why should I be fettered with Federal shackles limiting my civil liberty when I am not a jailbird conditionally freed on terms of probation? I will not accept this type of quasi-liberty."[48]

But to many even limited freedom was sweet. A man who returned to Amache from the world outside wrote, "Now that I'm back the camp seems very disgusting to me."

The WRA, impressed by the success of the seasonal work leave program, began to set in motion the machinery for more permanent leaves. The farm workers on short-term leaves had not been carefully screened, but a more ambitious leave program, announced on July 20, 1942, imposed the following conditions on candidates for indefinite leave: the individual had to have FBI clearance, he could not have even visited Japan, he had to have a guarantee of employment outside the Western Defense Command and an assurance of favorable community sentiment at his destination.

Only a very few evacuees left the centers before these rules were modified on October 1 to extend eligibility to aliens as well as to citizens and to remove restrictions on destination, with the exception of the prohibited area of the Western Defense Command. Intended residence in the Eastern Defense Command (a strip along the eastern seaboard), however, imposed delays. By December 31, some 450 people had left the centers on indefinite leave, 250 of whom were college students though 414 student leaves had been granted. Of the 2,200 evacuees who had filed application for indefinite leave, the majority were waiting for clearance.[49]

As discussed earlier in chapter ten, the WRA's attempt to expedite the granting of leaves by a registration of the entire evacuee population over seventeen years of age had backfired disastrously, not least in its effect on the Congress. The Chandler Committee had recommended relocation of the "loyal" and segregation of the "disloyal," but Representative John Costello, chairman of the Dies Subcommittee investigating the relocation centers, was opposed to liberalizing the release procedures.[50] Of the members of his subcommittee, only Representative Herman Eberharter maintained that "the bulk of persons of Japanese ancestry are trustworthy."[51]

The agitation in the centers at the time of registration moved Costello to assert that the Kibei "have been especially trained in 'espionage, military tactics and Japanese propaganda' and virtually control the relocation centers."[52]

Before Tule Lake became a segregation center, Tony O'Brien, the project attorney, spoke his mind to a newspaper reporter on the subject of relocation and the public. "You Californians made a national issue of less than 100,000 people," he said. "We're doing the job you couldn't handle. We are dividing these people among 130,000,000 and we'd do it faster if the critics laid off. Leave them alone and we'll get rid of them for you. We don't want to be custodians—the WRA is supposed to relocate these people."[53]

In the same month, Representative J. Parnell Thomas of the Dies Committee had asked President Roosevelt to prevent the WRA from allowing, in his words, a thousand evacuees a week to leave the camps and resettle throughout the country. Actually, there were closer to five hundred departures a week in May and June of 1943, according to Dillon Myer. This normally mild-mannered man in July issued a stunning rebuttal at a hearing in Washington which "electrified" members of the Costello Subcommittee.[54] He accused them of creating dissension, inviting retaliation against captive Americans in enemy hands, and nullifying the objectives of the war.

Roosevelt promptly issued a statement supporting the relocation program and defending the thorough screening procedures of the WRA, which included information gathered at the January, 1943, registration, FBI reports, and an additional check by a Joint Board of the War Department, the Navy Department, and the WRA on evacuees wishing to work in war industries or enter the Eastern Defense Command. In the opinion of the American Civil Liberties Union, "The [White House] statement was needed to assure the country that Dillon Myer . . . had the backing of the Washington administration. . . ."[55]

(At a press conference over a year later, on November 24, 1944, Roosevelt said, ". . . and we all know that American citizens have certain privileges. And they wouldn't—what's my favorite word?—discombobulate? the existing population of those particular counties [in New York and Georgia] very much. After all, what? 75 thousand families scattered all around the United States is not going to upset anybody. . . .")

So, despite the Dies Committee, relocation proceeded. The evacuees may well have been the most investigated group of people in the history of the United States. Robert Cozzens of the WRA said that checking the records was like grading prunes. "I could look at the case histories, and they followed a line." But thanks to the Dies Committee furor, individual judgment sometimes abdicated to public prejudice in the matter of leave clearance. In the spring and summer of 1943 the project directors had the power to grant leave permits to applicants who answered "yes" to Question 28 in the registration form, but after the agitation the regulations were tightened and those who failed to qualify on nine particular counts had to have a hearing by an investigating board at the relocation center before they could get permission to leave.

The nine factors were: a negative answer to Question 28 even if subsequently changed; failure to answer Question 28; late registration; request for repatriation or expatriation, even if retracted; military training in Japan; employment on Japanese naval vessels; three trips to Japan after the age of six except for seamen; ten years residence in Japan after the age of six in the case of men not married to American citizens or with citizen children; or a connection with organizations that "intelligence agencies consider . . . to be subversive."[56] If the center committee denied clearance, the applicant could appeal to the Board of Appeals for Leave Clearance, which was established in July, 1944, and heard nineteen cases of which twelve were recommended for leave clearance.

The WRA also assumed the power to recall evacuees to the centers, but this was only invoked once in the case of a family group on work leave who innocently aided some escaped German prisoners. When recalled, they returned to the center. The WRA asked the assistance of the Justice Department to enforce a recall, should this be necessary, but Francis Biddle refused, saying he knew of no legal authority to do this.

The chief of the WRA Employment Division, Thomas Holland, readily admitted that the "security check system" which he devised was intended to reassure the public and to prove the loyalty of evacuees to prospective employers.[57] Though charged with no crime, the evacuees were in effect paroled rather than released by the WRA because of prevalent attitudes in the country.

"We were, I think, the first victims of the 'loyalty oath' hysteria," said Togo Tanaka. "Some evacuees didn't care what they signed—just so they could get out of the barbed wire encampment. Others balked, I was among those who refused to 'renounce allegiance' to the Emperor of Japan. Why? Because, we obstinately insisted, we never owed him allegiance. So how could we renounce it? So we refused to sign the stupid questionnaires and we were refused clearance to leave—until the [Manzanar] riot burst the bonds for us."

Though the leave clearance constituted a road block to some of the evacuees, the WRA was actively encouraging relocation. WRA field offices were established in many cities to help arrivals find jobs and housing. "Relocation teams" visited the centers to give movies and talks on opportunities outside. The agency adopted a program of "trial leaves." Those about to depart attended forums on "How to Make Friends" or "How to Behave in the Outside World." They were given coach train fare, $25 plus $3 a day for traveling expenses and a booklet of advice, called, *When You Leave the Relocation Center.*[58]

The WRA was anxious that people should become self-sufficient. When an Issei bee-keeper asked to have his eighteen hives moved from Manzanar to his new home in another state, an administrator ruled that while they were "livestock," they were also "livelihood" and should be considered in the same category as a pair of scales and a fish knife that had been given to a man who was going into the fish business.[59]

"I told my wife, 'I don't want to be in camp more than one year,' " said Kazuo Masuda of Livingston, California, who was at Amache. "I left one day before the year was up." Yet many evacuees were reluctant or fearful to leave. A medical student wrote from Manzanar in the summer of 1943, " . . . there are many evacuees whose only impediment to relocation is indecision, fear and uncertainty—fear and uncertainty largely fancied and born of the ignorance of the changing world outside."[60] Relocation was initially viewed with suspicion. Some of the early resettlers left quietly to escape the disapproval of the community.

Many more Nisei left than Issei. According to the Dorothy Thomas study on relocation, "Seven out of ten of the persons involved in the two waves of outmigration between registration and rescission were young people between the ages of 15 and 35."[61] Some of the older people protested a series of articles in the Denver *Rocky Shimpo*, written by one of their generation who had gone to Chicago, that urged that the future of the Issei was in the United States and that they should relocate and establish themselves in communities outside the centers. When the writer spoke on this subject at Heart Mountain and Amache, he did not elicit much favorable response.

But as the Pacific war news changed, the Issei attitude toward relocation—at least for the Nisei—changed also. By June, 1944, a staff member at Poston reported "a growing feeling in some Issei circles that there's just a little something wrong with a younger person who is still in the center."[62] Stories of successful relocation were also a contributing factor to the change in attitude.

An Hawaiian Nisei girl who was joining the WAC despite the disapproval of her friends complained, "You know how the Nisei are. They are very much on the defensive and when a good opportunity is opened up they are opposed to it. . . . They are waiting for a few guinea pigs to go in and send back a report."[63] People who left the centers ran the risk of experiencing hostility in communities outside. Fortunately, they also found sympathetic people to take their part. In Kansas City, when a little Sansei (third generation) boy was not permitted to enter the public school, a newspaper campaign pressured the school into taking him. In Denver when real estate agents and hostile neighbors threatened the owner of a house that had been leased to a Nisei family, a member of the Fellowship of Reconciliation leased the house herself and sublet it to the Japanese–American newcomers, living in it with them until the neighbors became friendly. After the execution of General Doolittle's fliers in Japan, the sheriff in a midwestern town ordered three relocatees working in a war plant to pack up and leave the area, but a town meeting of citizens, organized by local men of good will, voted to let them stay.

When the victory garden of four-year-old Teddy Matsumoto was destroyed by vandals in Larchmont, New York, a crowd of indignant townspeople offered to replant it for him, and a local paper published an editorial which began: "We're sorry about your garden, Teddy. . . ."[64]

As the Nisei were providing a test for the fairness of their fellow Americans, they were discovering the rewards of freedom outside. "Greetings from the FREE world!" jubilant Japanese–American friends wrote to Dr. and Mrs. Galen Fisher.[65] Just after Christmas in 1943, a former Manzanar resident wrote, "The outside world is so completely different from the camp community, so real and so cheerful, that we never tire of saying to each other, 'Gee, isn't it grand to be out of camp.' "[66]

Another man wrote, "It is good to have somewhere to go in the morning, a place to work—and in the evening, somewhere to return. That may sound strange, it is so commonplace. But it is not so for me. Only three weeks ago we were behind barbed wire of a War Relocation Authority Project, a drab desert city of tarpaper barracks."[67] The parents of a two-and-a-half-year-old who was taken to Twin Falls, Idaho, after a year in camp, noticed that when he stood under a tree, the first tree he could remember seeing, he had a look of awe on his face.

A young girl, who had lived a sheltered life, was amazed at the people she saw in a hotel lobby in Chicago where she was waiting for her brother. "There was a woman swearing. I was sure she was a prostitute. I was absolutely fascinated."

Fuji Takaichi got dressed up for a day's shopping in town after she and her husband had moved from Heart Mountain to nearby Cody where he had a job in a printing shop. "I had my best tweed suit on and my Dobbs hat and gloves and my alligator pumps. I can remember looking all around Cody, digging my foot in the dust and thinking, 'This is a lot different than San Francisco or even San Jose.' "

A family who went to American Fork, Utah, found "lots of prejudice at first, but every one of them [the townspeople] 'came around' when they got to know us and found we didn't have horns and a tail. It was a community where everything revolved around the church and they tried to make Mormons of us. They were all towheads in Utah. Our dark-haired son stood out like a sore thumb. He didn't want to leave and when he got back to California, he couldn't distinguish between Mexicans and Japanese for a long while."

In Cleveland where she spent two summers, Hime Enomoto was taken for an Indian, partly because she wore a pin with the name of her college, Muskigum in New Concord, Ohio. "I let it go at that," she said.

Pete Ida took coaching jobs in small towns in Nebraska after his graduation from the university at Lincoln where his sports prowess had attracted some publicity. The first superintendent who hired him told him he would like the town: 95 per cent of the people were Germans! "They had never seen Orientals. Here come two of us. But it was easy to win over the kids so we were accepted." When he traveled around the state with his teams, people would exclaim, "By golly, the coach speaks English!" In his first year of coaching his track team won the county championship, his basketball team placed third in the state, and his football team fifth. Once the coach of a rival squad accused him of teaching his boys *jiujitsu* because the backs were so effective in defense.

People came out of the relocation centers to take domestic jobs in nearby towns. Fuji Takaichi, who was living in Cody, near Heart Mountain, said, "Every woman in town wanted her houseboy or her maid. They met at their social clubs and bragged about their new servants." One of the most prestigious of these was a former butler named Henry from Beverly Hills or Bel-Air who had beautiful white hair and wore his life savings in the form of diamonds on his cuff links and stick pin. "When he was dressed up, he positively glittered. Because of his elegant appearance and manners he would lend 'class' to any establishment.

"All the women worried because the town offered so little in the way of recreation for their house servants. So I was approached because my husband and I were the only Japanese that actually had living quarters in the town at that time. They asked if I would mind if their servants came to call on their days off. It was thought we would have a lot in common. That wasn't quite the case, but it was interesting. Henry came and drank coffee. He was a fantastic person. We were also visited by a little Nisei woman who was the best cook in town. She would come bearing a seven-layer cake [or] a lemon chiffon meringue concoction on a tremendous platter for my husband. She wouldn't let the woman who was hiring her come into the kitchen while she was cooking. She had her completely cowed."

Sada Murayama was asked by a hotel in Chicago to recruit fifty or sixty girls from the centers as chambermaids because whole floors of the hotel had been closed for lack of help. The scheme of bringing the girls to Chicago worked out well. They were skillful, dependable, and intelligent. "But the girls were smart and were not going to make beds all their lives. They would hear of better jobs and would want to leave. The hotel put pressure on me to make them stay, which I could have done, perhaps, since the girls had faith in me, and were, naturally a little frightened in this new setup."

The hotel had paid their bus fare to Chicago, so they were under some obligation. When, as she had done before the evacuation, Sada Murayama hunted up the law governing the situation, she discovered that no one could force others to remain at a job they did not like. There was no question about it, she had to side with the girls. She told the hotel management that she could do nothing to deter them from leaving. The manager replied, "You should be working for a union, not a private company!" She left their employ soon afterward.

Other industries tapped the man and womanpower potential by recruiting at the centers. In late 1942 two transcontinental railroads filed an application with the WRA for a thousand maintenance employees. There were also requests for office workers, social workers, seamen in Atlantic shipping, hotel workers, science teachers, a *jiujitsu* instructor, wine chemists, a linotype operator, and a diesel engineer.[68] *Business Week* reported that several hundred Nisei were released as early as 1942 "to practice their skill of chicken-sexing in mid-western and eastern hatcheries."[69] They culled the roosters from batches of day-old chicks. The hatcheries had asked the WRA to release at least enough experts to teach Caucasians the skill, which was described as "a virtual Nipponese monopoly."

Recruiters from the frozen food industry at Seabrook Farms, New Jersey, came to the centers looking for workers. Eventually 2,600 American Japanese went to work in the tiny rural hamlet near the border of Delaware where the company provided housing. Later arrivals in the colony at Seabrook included aliens released after 1945 from the Crystal City, Texas, detention center run by the Justice Department, and some South American Japanese who had been sent to the United States during the war and could not get permission from their countries to go back. At one time there were so many workers that all the houses were filled and the overflow placed in a former CCC camp. As the Japanese stopped coming or moved away, their places were taken by European DPs. The number of Japanese has dwindled to around six hundred as people retire, move back to California, or the young people leave.

Today migrant workers augment the summer labor force. In the winter there is re-pack work which employs only a few. Members of the colony collect unemployment insurance and catch up on their hobbies in the winter. A Japanese store in nearby Bridgeton caters to the tastes of the elderly bachelors, mainly Kibei, who arrived twenty-five years ago and never left.

Two brothers from the Heart Mountain center, Henry and Ed Mitarai, organized a group of ten evacuee farmers to develop 150 acres of desert in west-central Utah in 1943. Their first crop of carrots was demolished by a sandstorm and a plague of crickets, but they persevered with a second planting of onions and peas. Mitarai "commended the friendliness of his neighbors in Beaver county."[70]

A group from Livingston, California, who had been at Amache, went to farm in Grand Junction, Colorado, where about fifteen California families had settled in the voluntary evacuation period and were raising cherries, peaches, and onions.

When Herbert Nicholson drove to Henderson County, Colorado, in an old car to hunt up a former Brawley, California, family, the Sonodas, he was awakened in the middle of the night while staying at a motor court, and clapped into the county jail. He had been overheard speaking Japanese and was held on suspicion of being a spy, but after some earnest talking he eventually changed the attitude of the local sheriff toward the evacuee newcomers and, incidentally, won his own release.

The evacuee internal security officer, who had left Tule Lake in a hurry when he was accused of being an *inu*, settled in the Snake River Valley in Idaho and talked his way into the management of 5,000 acres of potatoes. He went to a bank and told them he had a lease, but no money. "What have you got to put up?" he was asked. He answered, "Just the lease." The bank loaned him $80,000. Most of the potatoes he raised with evacuee labor were sold to the government to be dehydrated. Some years there were big losses; other years were good. He was well accepted in the community, where there were many Basque people.

A friend of his was recruited from Topaz for work in a cannery in Provo, Utah, where the crew lived in a tent city. One night two sailors who had gone AWOL went on a shooting spree through the camp. Miraculously, no one was injured though one bullet went over the evacuee's head and another passed between a neighbor and a book he was reading.

In some states, Colorado, for one, where there was prejudice against relocating evacuees, the American Japanese who had been living there since before the war were resentful that newcomers were creating a problem. But in Cleveland, Mich Kunitani found about ten long-established Issei whom he introduced to new arrivals "to tell them how to get along in the city." They were very helpful.

Yuri Katai, who was in her late teens, went to Minnesota with two other girls to work in the home of a judge. Though the people were "real nice," she was fearfully homesick and would cry herself to sleep every night. It took her hours to write a letter in Japanese to her parents back in the camp. The strange surroundings frightened her—the fireflies that looked like eyes blinking in the dark, the people that stared at her over the partition in a restaurant because they had never seen a Japanese face before.

After he graduated from high school in camp, Frank Bunya worked in

Salt Lake City for three months, washing dishes. "I was living with a friend of mine. Before we found jobs we ran out of money. We were subsisting on one hot dog a day, if we were lucky. I had to phone my sister who was working in a cannery in Ogden, and she sent me some money to pay my hotel bill.

"My roommate worked at night. I worked during the day. I never saw him. I didn't know anybody, didn't get around. So all I did was work, go back home, sleep, and work the next day. Every other week I would treat myself to a movie. I was only seventeen and it was very lonesome all by myself. So after three months I decided to go back to camp."

The WRA community analysts discovered that though many people on indefinite leave longed to return to the centers, few actually did except for visits to the families left behind. During the first weeks and months, many of the Nisei were uncomfortable outside. Their conversations when they met tended to be "gripe sessions." They didn't like their jobs, "the housing was terrible," "the climate was awful," "the city was noisy and dirty." They had a "sense of temporariness" and felt that the West Coast was still home. "They missed the old Japanese–American communities, their families, Issei support and direction, Nisei groups with established organization and ways. To a degree they even missed the discrimination they had lived with and under on the West Coast. Now, they were free to do many things they could not do before, but they did not know what they could and could not do."[71]

Sometimes their behavior toward other evacuees was self-conscious, because it was known that the WRA was anxious for them to make a good impression and to become assimilated into the new communities. Some clung together for security; others deliberately avoided each other. One Nisei was overheard saying of another, "Oh, yes, I know her. But I don't have much to do with her. She's not integrated, you know."[72]

The Nisei were discovering *hakujin* (Caucasian) friends, and some worked with Negroes and got along well with them. One man wrote of an interracial group in Chicago which sponsored a dance: " . . . it worked out very successfully. There were 35 Nisei, 40 Caucasians, 20 Negroes, 15 Mexicans, and a couple of Chinese present. The Nisei members in this group have become much more racially tolerant in the year I have been associated in the group. They mingle with the Caucasians now without feeling inferior and with the Negroes without feeling superior."[73] The world outside, once they had established a foothold with a job and housing, seemed to many to offer more opportunities and more diversity than they had ever known before. The high wartime salaries were a surprise to the Nisei who had had limited economic opportunities on the West Coast. Some practiced skills in which they had been trained but had had no chance to work at before because of discriminatory hiring practices in California.

One newcomer to Chicago was more than satisfied with his job in a garage where his employer had gone out of his way to help him get started and find a place to live, but he ran into discrimination in the AF of L. "They charged me $25 initiation fee and gave me a duration-working permit. I had to pay the regular $3 monthly dues like the members. I wasn't going to join it at all as I said I would only join if they gave me equal membership. Then the union representative went to the boss and told him that I would have to be fired or else become a member on their terms. If I refused to join, the union said there might be a strike against the shop. There wasn't anything I could do about it so I reluctantly joined up. The boss felt just as bad as I did about it and he paid half of the initiation fee. . . ."[74]

The Nisei were learning to stand up for their rights. A farm worker had an argument with his boss when he objected to digging potatoes in the snow. "He got sore as hell then and said we were not being patriotic. . . . What the hell, we told him that nobody was a sucker like that, and that even the defense workers were doing it for the dough. . . . Then he said that he was going to call the marshal and tell him that we were sabotaging his crop. . . . The Caucasian boss made us stay out in the field all afternoon in the snow just for spite. He lost money that way because we threw a helluva lot of his spuds away. Some of the guys went on and crushed them with their heels. We were all sore."[75]

In the summer of 1943 the WRA had begun a retrenchment program to encourage relocation. The evacuee labor force at the centers was to be reduced by one-third over a period of three months with only essential project operations continued. One project director interpreted the new directive from Washington as follows:

> While we have been in here for a year the situation outside has grown very acute. The war manpower situation has become critical. As a result we are shifting our emphasis from a sociological approach to an economic approach. This is absolutely necessary. We cannot provide other than bare essentials at public expense and we cannot keep any service which will encourage people to stay. . . .[76]

Relocation really took hold in 1944. A man at Heart Mountain wrote in April, "Young people are going out of here by the hundreds—into the Army, back East and to the farms. This will be a very quiet place in a few months."[77] In late 1944 the WRA discontinued the seasonal leave program in a further attempt to get people to leave permanently, though as long as the centers were open evacuees were allowed to return to them. Some wives returned to rejoin parents when their husbands were drafted. Some needed the security of being able to go back and forth. Others agreed with the Hawaiian girl who said, "Nothing could have ever gotten me back to camp again. I would have gone to any length to stay out of camp after I got out."[78]

The WRA had stimulated relocation by establishing hostels or encouraging other organizations to do so. Thirteen boys, the first to relocate without a specific job offer, left Manzanar on January 10, 1943, accompanied by Thomas Temple of the Community Service Section of the WRA, who acted as a "housemother" for them at a hostel in Chicago. Hostels were opened later in Des Moines, Cleveland, Cincinnati, Washington, D.C., Detroit, Philadelphia, Kansas City, Minneapolis, Boston, Spokane, Buffalo, Rochester, and Brooklyn. Plans to establish a hostel in West Branch, Iowa, had to be abandoned because of community attitudes.

A proposal for a hostel in Brooklyn in an old fraternity house caused a furor, partly because it coincided with a much publicized incident in Great Meadows, New Jersey, in which five evacuees sent by the WRA to work on a farm were forced by angry townspeople to leave town. The Brooklyn hostel story was carried in the Brooklyn *Eagle, The New York Times*, and *PM*. Some notable individuals were involved. The *Times* reported that Mayor La Guardia was understood to have filed a protest against the presence of Japanese–Americans in New York City or the eastern seaboard with the Army, the Navy, and other agencies in Washington.

Secretary of the Interior Harold Ickes, who had hired evacuees to work on his Olney, Maryland, farm, reprimanded the liberal mayor of New York City whom he accused of the same sort of prejudice shown by governors Walter E. Edge of New Jersey and John W. Bricker of Ohio. "This is a strange fife and drum corps to be playing the discordant anthem of racial discrimination."[79] The hostel was opened on May 10, 1944, after public hearings in Brooklyn. The twenty-five Nisei who eventually lived there were scarcely noticed, as an advocate had predicted, in a city of three million people.

In Colorado a tempest occurred following the arrival of relocating evacuees, though the issue was not housing but land. Relocatees—2,343 of them—had come to the state where there were already 2,261 persons of Japanese ancestry. Though the figures were small in comparison with the total population of the state, alarmists provoked the fear that "Japs are buying up our fair land." In January, 1944, pressure was put on the governor to call a special session of the legislature to put an amendment on the ballot to deny aliens the right to own property in Colorado. The National Farmers Union, which had pursued an anti-discriminatory policy in other states, was one of the chief opponents of the amendment, and supported the 146 Colorado farmers of Japanese ancestry. Of these eighty-two were citizens and only seven had been established since relocation, so that the proposal actually affected sixty-four people.

But Amendment Three, as it was called, was a test of attitudes in Colorado toward all resettlers from the relocation camps, most of whom had settled in the cities, particularly in Denver. The issue attracted nationwide attention. John R. Lechner, the Americanism spokesman for the American Legion, was called in to speak in favor of the amendment, and Carey McWilliams, whose book *Prejudice* was published almost simultaneously, returned to his native state to urge citizens to vote against it. "Keep Colorado American" was the slogan of the opponents. They were successful and the amendment failed. An analysis of the vote provides an interesting revelation of the attitudes of different groups. In Denver, Negro and Jewish precincts voted "no"; Italian and Spanish districts voted "yes." The vote of soldiers was markedly against the amendment. Grand Junction, where there were farmers of Japanese ancestry, voted for the amendment but even here servicemen opposed it.[80]

In other states opponents of resettlement introduced discriminatory measures of one kind or another which provided similar tests of public opinion. When an amendment was introduced in the Missouri House of Representatives which would have barred a Nisei doctor from practicing in a state tuberculosis sanatorium, Representative O. K. Armstrong addressed the chamber on March 30, 1944. "If interracial bigotry and intolerance raise their ugly heads and lift their reeking banners in other lands, or even in other states of this Union, let Missouri remain forever a refuge for tolerance, a haven of good will toward men," he said. Commenting a few days later on "the fight," he concluded, "we licked the proposition clean."[81]

When the city of Ogden, Utah, refused to grant business licenses to evacuees, Judge Tillman Johnson of the federal district court in Salt Lake City overruled the denial on May 9, 1944, and pronounced a similar decision against a ruling of the city of Layton on June 15. The Arizona *Daily Star* of Tucson called the public's attention to anti-Japanese prejudice in a report of a state fact-finding committee on relocation.[82] The *Daily Star* also commented on a law passed by the Arizona legislature that required persons doing business with Japanese (the euphemism employed was "individuals restricted in movement") to give notice of each transaction by triple publication in a county newspaper. Under this ruling the Standard Oil Company of California was fined $1,000 for selling $9.20 worth of gasoline to a farmer of Japanese ancestry in the Salt River Valley, which, in the opinion of the editorial writer, showed "the fantastic extremes to which civilians will go in time of war."[83]

The climate of tolerance in various cities and sections of the country was relayed to prospective resettlers in the centers by the WRA field offices and representatives of churches. Citizen committees for resettlement of Japanese Americans were ecumenical, including Protestants, Catholics, Jews, and nonbelievers. The Reverend Donald Toriumi and his wife surveyed the situation in different parts of the country in the spring of 1943. They found relocatees "satisfied" in Chicago, Cleveland, Dayton, Philadelphia, Boston, and New York. In general, employment was no problem, but housing was hard to find. Many expressed a desire to return to the West Coast. According to another minister, John Yamazaki, it was the churches "that turned on the green lights in the middle west and the east, opening up jobs and housing." Though a pastor in Denver asked a Nisei girl who attended his services, "Wouldn't you feel more at home in your own church?"[84] George Aki, who later became a chaplain with the 442nd Combat Team, felt, "If it weren't for individual church people, relocation wouldn't have even started."

Nevertheless, when the Reverend Aki went on a speaking tour around the country before going to Camp Shelby, most of the congregations refused to hear him. "They were afraid." George Aki addressed service clubs in Chicago, Minneapolis, St. Louis, and Baton Rouge. His purpose was to show people, "I am Japanese by ancestry but as American as anyone could be." Other attractive and articulate Nisei were chosen as ambassadors to the Caucasian public. In the New York and New Jersey areas Sada Murayama appeared before audiences, visual proof that, as she said, "all Japanese don't have bow legs, buck teeth and glasses."

Togo Tanaka told an audience in Chicago that he was "flabbergasted" at questions he was asked about "Japanese psychology." "I know I should be able to understand that it is perhaps natural for my fellow citizens to assume they are speaking to a foreigner, to a Japanese. Of course, they are not. But I am always more aware of my own personal feelings, whereas, at first meeting, they are more aware of my physical appearance, which you will agree is non-Caucasian. . . . I would certainly not attempt, on the basis of my experience, to pose as an authority on so-called 'Japanese psychology.' . . . I share the belief that my thinking processes are the product of our free and democratic educational system."[85]

Donald Toriumi said, "As a result of war dislocation the west coast Japanese came to know America for the first time." People were scattered far and wide across the country—36,000 of them—leaving some 18,000 at Tule Lake and 62,000 at the other nine camps. The artist, Miné Okubo, was one of the late departing ones from Topaz. "Here I was alone, with no family responsibilities, and yet fear had chained me to the camp."[86] A special assignment from *Fortune* magazine, to illustrate an article on the American Japanese, encouraged her to pack and leave for New York where she has remained ever since. She recalls the leave-taking. "I was now *free*. I looked at the crowd at the gate. Only the very old or very young were left."[87]

THIRTEEN · BREAKING THROUGH

THE RELOCATION PROGRAM in the Midwest and on the East Coast was being carried on with a minimum of unpleasant incident, due at least in part to the WRA publicity efforts to change people's ideas about the American Japanese as enemies. Dillon Myer said: "Relocation Centers are undesirable institutions and should be removed as soon as possible; they were a mistake in the first place, but cannot be abandoned tomorrow."[1]

But as opponents of the Japanese in California, Washington, and Oregon began to realize the next step in the relocation program might be the return to the West Coast, they renewed their efforts to "lock the door" against departed evacuees. The vigorous campaign of 1943 and 1944 to keep the Japanese from going back to their homes made the protests of 1942 seem insignificant by contrast.

A Gallup poll conducted in five western states at the turn of the year, 1942–1943, reported that while there was almost unanimous approval of the evacuation and detention of the Japanese minority, 53 per cent of those polled would allow citizens to return to their homes. Of this figure 29 per cent would include both citizens and aliens, and an almost equal number would oppose return of either group. A poll conducted by the Los Angeles *Times* at the end of 1943, on the other hand, revealed 9,855 readers would exclude American Japanese from the Coast as against 999 opposing exclusion. Furthermore, 11,203 readers favored taking concentration camp control away from the WRA and returning it to the Army; 1,139 would free loyal Japanese in the Midwest, 9,750 would not. It should be noted that the *Times* was asking questions of readers who had been subjected to months of the paper's propaganda on the subject. Commentators at the time also felt that the questions were stated in such a way as to influence the answers.

Nevertheless, there was a real change in opinion. In June, 1944, for example, a national survey of college students, who might be presumed to be better informed and more broad-minded than average newspaper readers, showed that half of them opposed return of alien evacuees, although only 14 per cent opposed the return of the Nisei. Professor Roger Daniels conjectures that evacuation, far from being ignored by apathetic citizens as some have stated, was actually one of the most popular acts of the war.[2]

Whether this is correct or not, the proposals made to restrict the West Coast Japanese ran the gamut from smiling cajolery and the appeal to "reason" to the extravagant threat. The California Joint Immigration Committee was still the primary force behind the anti-Japanese movement. Under the leadership of V. S. McClatchy, who in other matters of public policy tended to be fair-minded and progressive, this group took the most reasonable tone, was the best organized, and the most influential.

Nonpolitical groups sometimes caught the fever. Spokeswomen, perhaps self-styled, for the respectable California Federation of Women's Clubs voiced sympathy for their "sisters" in the East and Midwest whose "safety" and, in the words of Carey McWilliams, "presumably whose virtue," would be endangered by release of evacuees from the relocation centers.[3] A California district attorney, Fred N. Houser, attempted to appeal to the consciences of the members of the Women's Christian Temperance Union: "If you were called to serve as a juror at the trial of a serviceman who perhaps had been bombed or strafed by Japs at Midway or Guadalcanal," he asked, "how would you feel about enforcing the State law against murder? The possibility of having to answer such a question, should Japanese be allowed to return, is the foremost reason for working now to see that they be kept out."[4]

The Board of Trustees of the Los Angeles Bar Association, and numerous chambers of commerce were prevailed upon to pass resolutions against their former Japanese neighbors and associates. Several chapters of the Knights of Pythias, a social and fraternal order originally founded on the principles of "friendship, charity and benevolence," and with the idea of healing the wounds and allaying the hatreds caused by the American Civil War, passed resolutions asking that: " . . . the Legislatures of the several States and Congress be importuned to pass legislation which will exclude all American-born Japanese from entering into any business or from in any manner operating any orchard, farm, garden, nursery, or having anything to do in anyway with the cultivation of lands. . . ."[5]

Besides such established organizations which were drawn into the wartime hysteria, countless new groups sprang into being. Some towns boasted a number of them, their names often hardly distinguishable one from another. There was the California Citizens Association of Santa Barbara, the California Citizens Council of Los Angeles (which put out a windshield sticker showing a rat with a Japanese face), the American Foundation for the Exclusion of the Japanese, No Japs, Incorporated, of San Diego, and so on into the hundreds.

Lambert Schuyler circulated a hate pamphlet, *The Japs Must Not Come Back*, proposing one of the more extreme solutions to the Japanese problem—to send the Issei back to Japan and put all the Nisei on an island in the Pacific. His line of persuasion was as strange as his proposal: the presence of Japanese made for a "racially intolerant" community, he said. Caucasians did not want their "white bloodstream all muddied up. . . . They did not want any social or sexual mixing of 'Japs' with their own pure young people."[6] The idea of putting American Japanese on some Pacific island was picked up by such organs as *The American Legion Monthly*.[7]

Perhaps the most outrageous pamphlet was printed by an organization called the Home Front Commandoes. This leaflet, *Slap the Jap*, was subtitled, *No Jap is Fit to Associate with Human Beings*. Under a drawing of the Statue of Liberty trailed a list of adjectives supposed to apply to members of the Japanese race: treacherous, faithless, untrustworthy, irresponsible, inhumane, depraved, ungodly, soulless, disloyal.

Rumors common to wartime fed the fires of hatred. A letter from a seabee in the Pasadena *Independent* described American marines and sailors with their "guts blown out" at the mercy of hypothetical American-educated Japanese only pretending to give first aid. Advising exclusion from the East Coast, the writer warned, "Don't pull another Volstead Act on us!"[8] A similar letter related the "fact" that all residents on the Island of Oahu had been "vaccinated" because of the danger of the poisoning of the water supply by alien Japanese residents.[9] A Chico, California, citizen suggested keeping the absent Japanese in concentration camps until "they all die of old age," and a Drain, Oregon, man suggested turning the interned citizens "over to the Chinese for safekeeping" after the war.[10]

Because of the threatening nature of some of these expressions of feeling, many individuals within and outside the camps expected the worst if evacuees were released. The leftist-liberal newspaper *PM* feared the possibility of mass murder. In Los Angeles County the district attorney reported receiving letters from three organizations threatening to kill returning Japanese. After the war "our boys . . . will take care of them," said a mother whose son was captured at Corregidor.[11]

Fortunately, the most fanatical of the race baiters were more noisy than numerous. Furthermore, in few organizations, even where resolutions were passed, was the anti-Japanese point of view unanimous. Quite often stands taken by the leadership were either not known by the general membership or not accepted by it, and occasionally were actively fought by a member or two.

Some of the groups were economically motivated, some patriotically motivated, many had an economic bias with a patriotic overlay. As we have seen, the activities against Orientals by such groups as the American Legion, the Veterans of Foreign Wars, and the Native Sons and Daughters of the Golden West dated back many years.

In December, 1942, the California Department of the American Legion had appointed an "impartial committee," which included V. S. McClatchy and State Senator Jack B. Tenney, to investigate Japanese relocation. Within a short time the California Department had gone on record against return of Japanese to their homes, and a wide range of stock anti-evacuee proposals were adopted as policy by a number of Legion posts. Among these resolutions was a proposal that American Japanese who had "escaped" to east of the Rockies (meaning those who had left voluntarily) be apprehended and placed in concentration camps, too. The Hood River American Legion which deleted the names of Nisei servicemen from their roll of honor, advocated deportation of Issei and Nisei after the war. A Legion caucus in Glendale opposed release of Japanese from relocation centers and urged control under the Army. In some areas veterans resisted burial in national cemeteries for Nisei servicemen killed in action.

The economic groups fought for exclusion on more realistic, if selfish, grounds. The profit-motive was openly stated. A. L. Wirin continually tried to point out to the public that most of the clamor was coming from spokesmen for commercial interests. Clarence E. Rust and others had testified to this effect before the Tolan Committee. West Coast antagonism, Dillon Myer stated, was "economic rather than racial."[12]

The Associated Farmers, an anti-labor organization representing big corporation farming, and the Farm Bureau Federation were in the forefront of the restrictive movement. Local Farm Bureau meetings in Fresno, Colusa, Solvang, and elsewhere pressed for permanent removal of the Japanese, basing their reasoning quite frankly on economic competition. The California State Grange, consisting of smaller farmers, followed suit, its spokesmen asserting it would use "all peaceable but vigorous means" to accomplish its purpose against "the Japs."[13] Minor business groups such as the Dry Cleaners Association protested the possible renewal of competition.

In the ranks of organized labor, a resolution at the State Convention of the American Federation of Labor at Long Beach, California, urging revocation of Nisei citizenship rights was vigorously fought by John Shelley (later mayor of San Francisco) and John Wagner. The proposal was rejected by a wide margin during the fall of 1942, which was still a relatively quiet period. The Southern California Branch of the ACLU had protested, observing, " . . . organized labor has often suffered from unjust discrimination and should be the first . . . to spring to the defense of those who are oppressed."[14]

But the movement did not die. Japanese workers were still largely excluded from AF of L unions at this point, and many of the laboring people desired to exclude them still further—from the Pacific coast or even from continental United States. Various CIO unions accepted Japanese into membership, including Harry Bridges' Longshoremen's Union, which opposed the evacuation, but Dan Tobin's International Teamsters' Union, and Dave Beck, speaking for the West Coast teamsters, conducted a violently reactionary campaign against the rights of American Japanese.

A number of local labor unions limited their aims to preventive measures against Japanese entering certain trades (always their own) after the war. Others were more sweeping in their recommendations.

Throughout the history of the Japanese in the West we have seen that frequently they were attacked by members of racial and economic groups equally deprived and discriminated against, and of a lower educational stratum. When the Fourth Filipino Inter-Community convention in Fresno, California, stated as two of its objectives the mutually contradictory stands of, first, abolishing discriminatory legislation, and, second, providing for permanent postwar exile of all Japanese from the state the Nisei editor of the *Pacific Citizen*, Larry Tajiri, commented:

> . . . No one will put the full blame for this most recent "anti-Jap" resolution upon the Filipino residents of our western states. For they are only following a precedent set down by a long list of California chambers of Commerce, city councils, Legion posts, and other organizations. The Filipinos have fallen victim to a quite usual delusion of new immigrant groups and racial minorities which have known persecution—the desire to emulate popular "majority" opinion in a country where they are a minority. . . . This desire on the part of a persecuted minority to align itself with the majority is not a desire restricted to the Filipinos, but has been demonstrated time and again by all other minorities in the country, the Japanese American minority among them.[15]

Members of the convention later had second thoughts about their intentions and tabled the exclusion proposal.

Certain persistent individuals belonged not to one but to several bodies. V. S. McClatchy, for example, was able to express himself through his newspaper, the *Bee*, and through the Immigration Committee, which in turn influenced and was supposed to represent the American Legion, the Native Sons, and the State Federation of Labor. Legislators who used committees of various organizations they belonged to as investigatory bodies for their legislative activity were backed by anti-Japanese associations whose views they represented. Such "links" forming a seeming "network" and incidentally allowing for a great deal of guilt-by-association, would have delighted a Martin Dies of a different persuasion.

The letterhead of the Americans League of Los Angeles listed men prominent in the wholesale produce and floral industries of Southern California who had been in direct competition with businesses operated by persons of Japanese ancestry before the evacuation and who had subsequently profited to the extent of $26 million more business during the absence of their rivals. The membership of the Americanism Educational League included union leaders, real estate operators, Jack Tenney, the chairman of the "Little Dies" Un-American Activities Investigating Committee in the California Legislature, and its executive director, Dr. John Lechner, executive director and chief anti-Japanese standard bearer in the American Legion. Return of the evacuees was being planned by the WRA, these organizations warned, in the "VERY NEAR FUTURE."[16]

As with Lambert Schuyler, sex and subversion were twin fears in the mind of Charles M. Goethe, a Sacramento millionaire, treasurer of the Joint Immigration Committee, and one of the chief financial supporters of the Home Front Commandoes, who put out the *Slap the Jap* leaflet. Ironically, Goethe had also long been prominent in the Northern California Council of Churches. His own particular organization was the Eugenics Society of Northern California whose aim was to protect the purity of the Caucasian race. The American Quota Immigration Acts of 1921 and 1924, he was heartened to note in one of his pamphlets, were the first pieces of eugenics legislation enacted by a great world power, although Germany under Hitler was the "first nation of prime rank to enact a complete program of both negative and positive eugenics."[17] "Germany's plan is to eliminate all low-powers to make room for high-powers and thereby ALSO SAVE TAXES!"[18]

A minister-spokesman for exclusion relied on prayer to find the answer to the problem of Japanese return. After an hour of praying "in the privacy of that precious American heritage, the Christian home in a Christian city, in a Christian land of freedom," he had come to the conclusion, according to his testimony before a legislative committee, that it was his duty to urge the deportation of all persons of Japanese extraction from the American continent. Japanese Christians "ought to be glad to be shoved out anywhere that they can bear witness to the Kingdom of Christ."[19] The evangelist Aimee Semple McPherson added her voice to protest the return of the Japanese.

Both the plausible and the implausible groups put effective pressure upon members of the California legislature. Something similar was happening in Oregon where the Oregon Property Owners Protective League, the Portland Progressive Business Men's Club, and the Oregon State Legion were urging the same galaxy of restrictive measures against their departed residents. In the state of Washington, the Seattle Chamber of

Commerce went on record opposing use of Japanese for farm work "or any other supposed need" after release.[20] *Business Week* felt sympathy for the chamber of commerce businessmen who had voted this way, citing Depression days when Japanese "seemed to" do well while "Occidentals went broke."[21] The Washington Commonwealth Federation, representing, according to *PM*, "small New Dealish farmers" joined in the agitation, too, as well as the Mother Lodge of the Fraternal Order of Eagles, consisting of 15,000 members.[22]

The Northwest was fully as prejudiced as California, in the opinion of Robert B. Cozzens, Dillon Myer's top man on the Pacific coast. Speaking on a panel representing all points of view at a meeting in Washington sponsored by a group sympathetic to the American Japanese, he was challenged by one of the panelists as he discussed the role of the Nisei in aiding Army and Navy Intelligence. It was the only gathering he had ever attended where he thought he might be mobbed.

At the peak of the agitation, late in 1944, thousands of persons gathered in Auburn, Washington, for a mass meeting sponsored by the Remember Pearl Harbor League which advocated exclusion of persons of Japanese ancestry from the Puyallup and White River valleys. In 1943 the mayor of Kent, according to *Time* magazine, had printed up signs: "WE DON'T WANT JAPS BACK *EVER*." There were muttered proposals to "burn them out" but leaders advocated "means short of violence." The Nisei were not accused of disloyalty by this group, composed largely of small businessmen and truck gardeners, and their case rested squarely on the ground of economic competition. The Japanese who formerly resided there had controlled a large share of the agricultural enterprise of the valley. A similar meeting was held by the Remember Pearl Harbor League on Bainbridge Island, which had been a relatively friendly racial community. But the local newspaper, the Bainbridge *Review*, advocated fair play.

Not all the western presses were so benign. The Hearst papers in particular, in the words of *Time* magazine, were "vigorously stirring the witches broth"[23] which the agitators had concocted. In turn, local officials as well as state legislators were busily engaged in promoting measures to restrict Japanese. A particularly ugly diatribe by Westbrook Pegler in the Los Angeles *Times*, early in May, 1943, against allegedly drunken Japanese visiting "A.W.O.L." in Chandler and Casa Grande from their Arizona camp evoked a number of replies from readers. A letter from Glendale carried Pegler's point further: there was a big Army base near that relocation center, and furthermore, soldiers in training there were really "knuckling down" in camp after General Arnold "called upon them to think only of the day they can avenge their comrades executed by the Japs." What would happen, the Glendale citizen asked, if these boys just happened to run into evacuees in Chandler—within "spitting

distance of their post"? In heavy black print under the published letter
was an editorial comment: *"Wouldn't it be too bad!"*[24] The next day
Southern California papers carried a story describing how local authorities near Los Angeles were also displaying vigilance: 175 tubercular
patients of Japanese descent who were then in La Crescenta and Mon-
rovia sanitariums were to be moved inland by the Army on the urging of
the County Department of Institutions. The chairman of the County
Board of Supervisors explained that their "own citizens" were being
denied hospital care, because Japanese occupied sorely needed beds.[25]

In 1943 legislative activity increased, and there was a flurry of proposals in West Coast legislatures such as the Lowrey bill in California
which tried to tighten the Alien Land Law by prohibiting alien guardianship of their native-born children when children were the legal owners
of property and by making confiscation procedures easier by granting
injunction powers to government attorneys. Most of the bills died, but the
Tenney bill which incorporated the provisions of the Lowrey bill and
added more, was passed and signed by the governor. The Tenney bill extended escheat action to include even cropping contracts, and provided
sentences of ten years in jail or the penitentiary and/or a fine up to
$5,000 for violations, in addition to forfeiture of the property.[26]

In California, several legislative committees, principally the Joint Fact
Finding Committee on Un-American Activities, otherwise known as the
"little Dies" or the Tenney Committee, one in the senate and another in
the lower house, devoted themselves specifically to the Japanese question.
The house committee was headed by Assemblyman Chester F. Gannon.
These committees supplied the ammunition for dozens of bills representing a wide variety of proposals, some of which, though not all, were
introduced by men on their committees. There was a reciprocal agitation
between these legislators and their home communities, particularly Los
Angeles, a favorite location for special investigations. The Dies Committee also sometimes found it necessary to investigate Los Angeles, though
there were no longer Japanese there. Frequently these investigations
brought together people like Tenney, Mayor Bowron, representatives
Costello and Parnell Thomas, ex-Representative Leland Ford and
Gannon, whose performances made good copy for the newspapers.

In 1943, Jack Tenney, attorney and Democrat from Los Angeles
County, the head of the State Un-American Activities Committee as well
as chairman of Lechner's Americanism Educational League, was one of
the busiest men in the senate. A great many anti-Japanese bills came from
his pen alone. Chiefly interested in "red" disloyalty, at one point Tenney
directed the attention of his committee to the question of whether there
was a connection between teen-age Mexican–American "zoot suiters" and
Communist subversion. When not occupied with subversion, Communist or Japanese, the inconsistent senator drew up a number of bills to

prohibit discrimination in employment and housing on the basis of race, creed, or color, and his Senate Bill 36 would have provided a World Peace Planning Commission, with an appropriation of $50,000, the objectives being tolerance and the recognition of the rights of all peoples.[27] Another of his bills, SB 1017, more in the realm of thought control, would have required all delegates to political conventions to pledge support either to "Jeffersonian Democracy" or the "Republicanism of Abraham Lincoln."[28]

In the fall of 1943 Tenney was investigating not only American Japanese, but their sympathizers as well. In October, a Los Angeles superior court affirmed a misdemeanor charge against George Knox Roth, who refused to answer the committee's questions regarding American-born Japanese sponsors of his radio show, which had voiced opposition to evacuation.

In the same year the American Legion appointed two investigators to look into conditions at Tule Lake and Manzanar, Senator Hugh M. Burns and Assemblyman Nelson Dilworth, both of whom happened to be members of the Joint Committee on Un-American Activities of the state legislature. The chairman of the Legion committee which made the appointments was Jack B. Tenney. Subsequently, acting as senator rather than as Legion comrade, Jack B. Tenney read the Legion-sponsored report into the senate *Journal*. Like the Dies Committee, the Tenney Committee charged the WRA with "an overwhelming pampering of the Japanese evacuees" and recommended, among other measures, turning the camps over to the Army completely. Some time later, Robert B. Cozzens of the WRA described Tenney and Hugh M. Burns as spreading "fearless falsehoods" about the agency.[29] In a single two-year period the Tenney Committee which had been in existence before Warren became governor conducted eleven public hearings and filled sixteen volumes of testimony.

The Assembly Interim Committee on the Japanese problem, the Gannon Committee, was set up later, in August, 1943. Chester F. Gannon, a ruddy-faced Sacramento attorney, was the key Republican member of the assembly that year, and, like Jack Tenney, an active Legionnaire. Immediately after organizing, the committee adopted a resolution to keep all Japanese in concentration camps for the duration. Assemblyman Alfred Robertson of Santa Barbara, although voting in the unanimous proposal, voiced an objection to adopting a resolution before conducting the investigation. A past Imperial Potentate of the Shrine and Native Son of the Golden West took the witness stand after the resolution passed. Citing the increasing Negro population in the country as a comparison, he asserted that California had better keep the Japanese out, or "our children will damn us."[30] Chairman Gannon was then directed by the committee to contact high military and naval authorities in the area as well as the Fraternal Order of Elks in order to hear their recommendations for the direction of the probe.

In June "evidence" was uncovered by the Dies Committee—in Los Angeles—that numerous high officials, including Dillon Myer and John J. McCloy, were "working diligently" to bring about the return of American Japanese. Mike Masaoka was revealed to have written privately that the Nisei should "attempt to return" despite "the possibility of some bloodshed."[31]

A reassurance in July by James Byrnes, War Mobilization director, that the Japanese would not be allowed to return seemed to quiet newspapers for a time. Then in October, a lesser known group of the California legislature, the Senate Fact-Finding Committee on Japanese Resettlement, had four days of hearings in Los Angeles, during which Jack Tenney was called and, speaking under legislative immunity, attempted to label organizations which defended the rights of American Japanese as Communist controlled.

The spotlight was temporarily held, however, by Pearl Buck, popular author of *The Good Earth*, who had resided in both China and Japan for some forty-two years as the child of a missionary family and then as a missionary herself. She warned of the disastrous effects discrimination might have on international relations in the future, citing the Oriental Exclusion Act of 1924 as one of the causes of the current war, on the grounds that it had led to the decline of the liberal group in Japan which might have developed a democracy there.[32]

Soon afterwards, the Gannon Assembly Committee, not to be outdone, went to Los Angeles to conduct an investigation of its own. One of its members had returned from Washington, D.C., only three days before the hearings, after spending a month there as attorney for a group of vegetable packers whose funds had been frozen by the Treasury Department on the charge that these businessmen were dissipating the property of interned American Japanese.

At the December hearing the usual parade of anti-Japanese witnesses were presented, including a Veterans of Foreign Wars commander who assured the committee that returning Pacific servicemen would "take care of" any "Japs" who came to the Coast.[33] Horrible details of the "Rape of Nankin" in 1939 by soldiers of Japan were described. A former missionary claimed he had seen "Japs" take the body of a Chinese, cut out the heart and liver and eat them. The Hearst *Examiner*, featuring great headlines, ran sixty-two inches of this kind of testimony.[34]

Witnesses sympathetic to the Japanese were called but were consistently badgered. Even the Los Angeles *Times* cautioned, "Legislative Committees Should Not Be Bullies."[35] A. L. Wirin, who had been informed that his request to speak would be granted, was refused the opportunity to testify by the chairman. "I've had all I want of the Civil Liberties

Union," Gannon said. "Now you get out of here or I'll have an officer put you out."[36]

Gannon saw fit, however, to question members of two other organizations—the Pasadena chapter of the Committee on American Principles and Fair Play, and the Fellowship of Reconciliation. The original impetus for the hearings in Los Angeles had been a letter written by a serviceman circulated by the Pasadena Fair Play Committee which created a furor in the American Legion. Private Robert E. Borchers of Chicago, a marine had written from overseas after reading of the California Legion's "racial purge," and promised he would defend Japanese–Americans when he got home to insure that the soldiers "would not be sold out at home."[37] He was not summoned, but Mrs. Maynard Thayer, an eminently respectable member of the DAR and chairman of the Pasadena chapter of the Pacific Coast Committee on American Principles and Fair Play, was among those called to testify. Her organization could scarcely be described as militant. Once the evacuation had occurred, the group turned its efforts toward mitigating the hardships. Individual members varied in their views on return, some fearing that return of the Japanese to the West Coast would expose them to danger. William Carr, one of the founders, withdrew from the organization because he felt it did not go far enough, just as Clinton J. Taft, head of the local Civil Liberties Union, took a less accommodating position than some of the union's other spokesmen. After a series of witnesses had dispensed horror stories, Mrs. Thayer was put on the stand.

> GANNON: Do you want to champion the rights of people where different sexes do nude bathing together? . . . Mrs. Thayer, have you ever smelled the odor of a Jap home? . . .
> MRS. THAYER [attempting to bring in the subject of the Bill of Rights]: I have no interest in disloyal Japanese.
> GANNON: . . . . The Bill of Rights is not such a sacred thing after all. Don't you know that at the time the Bill of Rights was written we had 150,000 slaves in the United States?
> MRS. THAYER: I think we've made some progress since then. . . . It is of greatest importance that in time of war we do not go off into race hatred.
> GANNON: Are you a Communist? . . . This sounds like their doctrine.
> MRS. THAYER: I am registered as a Republican.[38]

Reading of the hearings, the Nobel Prize-winning scientist Robert Millikan telephoned a protest to the committee attorney. Gannon interrupted the reading of the Millikan statement to his committee. "Tell us who Dr. Millikan is," he demanded. "I don't know."[39]

The Fellowship of Reconciliation was cross-examined next. A former naval chaplain was on hand to testify that the group was one of the "chief organizations favoring aid to Japanese–Americans."[40] The hearing came to a climax during an argument that developed between Gannon and the Reverend Allan Hunter, the humane pastor of the Mount Hollywood Congregational church. The discussion began with the subject of American Japanese and ended with a theoretical invading army from Japan. In the words of Dr. Hunter, the chairman, in "trying to make a monkey out of me," asked him "What do you think about inter-marriage?" There was a law against intermarriage, and Dr. Hunter stated his belief that marriage was a sacred relationship, but Gannon pressed his point. Did he believe in the law or not? Hunter answered that he believed in changing the law. Gannon supposed that Hunter would go down and meet the invaders "with the Bible and a speech!" Hunter replied that he hoped he would do as he thought Christ would do.

"And what about the rest of us and the soldiers who resist with weapons?" Gannon asked.

"I respect the soldier who follows his belief and gives up his life," Hunter replied.

According to newspaper accounts, by this time Gannon had become enraged, both men were on their feet, and photographers' flashbulbs were popping, but Hunter "retained his poise as he answered question after question and met argument after argument."[41] Papers which nor-mally favored the committee covered the story with no criticism of Hunter. An investigator for Gannon later called on Hunter, took him for a walk in the park where they would not be overheard and told him, "I wanted you to know a lot of people feel as you do."

A few months later the Gannon Committee was back in Los Angeles, questioning Carey McWilliams, who had written extensively on minority problems, "Not about the evacuees and the WRA program, but about my views on 'racial integrity,' 'mongrelization,' 'mixed marriages,' 'mis-cegenation statutes' and similar fancy topics."[42]

Behind the scenes, Gannon had written a letter, presumably attacking the WRA, to Harold Ickes, the Secretary of the Interior, who was not inclined toward any sort of appeasement. Gannon received this reply from Ickes: "Your courteous and restrained letter has reached me. It is the kind of communication I would expect from a man who has taken an oath to uphold and defend the Constitution . . . and then foreswear himself. . . . I have no interest in bandying epithets with you or anyone else about loyal Japanese, who are born in this country and who are just as fully citizens as you or I." Assemblyman Randall Dickey of Alameda com-mented: "We should be in a position to take care of the situation after the war and not have to bother with a sociologist like Ickes."[43]

Gannon seemed by now to have forgotten completely that they were investigating the Japanese–Americans. The main purpose of still another hearing was, he said, "to smoke out pressure groups behind the move to return Japs to the West Coast in the face of majority opposition. . . ."[44] He blamed Communists, radicals in general, members of the CIO Political Action Committee, and a particularly suspicious group known as the JACL, which he had "never before heard of," and which in true western tradition he described as a "New York outfit" that claimed to have its headquarters in Salt Lake City.[45] Chester Gannon drew a line, however, on a proposal to bar all Nisei students from public schools, on the ground that such an action would be unconstitutional.[46]

Meanwhile in the legislature, Senator Tenney launched an investigation of the automobiles and tires that some of the evacuees had stored away to use in their return. The Fresno *Bee* carried an illustrated story of some of these cars jacked up on blocks in west Fresno garages. Representative B. W. Gearhart of Fresno criticized the Federal Office of Price Administration and the "rubber czar," William Jeffers, for failing to utilize an estimated 100,000 serviceable tires on evacuee-owned automobiles and trucks. An OPA agent who discovered what was described as a "cache" of tires in a farmhouse near Fresno, advocated investigating the evacuee owners of the stored cars and tires to see if they were subversives. When the war was over, Jack Tenney complained, these returned Japanese who had kept their automobiles would be able to motor again on "practically new rubber."[47]

On May 8, 1943, a joint resolution of the California assembly and senate memorialized Congress to make available to the civilian population such property as automobile tires, machinery and farm equipment, and other materials put in storage by evacuees. Later the same month the Lowrey bill was signed by Governor Warren, which provided for condemnation of Japanese farm implements and machinery, but commercial dealers in farm machinery were assured by the governor that this would not apply to them, and it was not put into effect.[48]

A number of bills were proposed attempting further harassment of the approximately 150 California state employees who had been suspended or dismissed previous to evacuation. The primary goal was to prevent their return and reinstatement, but, failing this, to penalize them in various other ways. Some of these bills were passed and signed, among them an act proposed by Assemblyman Nelson S. Dilworth, a Republican farmer from Hemet and a member of the Tenney Committee, which protected the State against collection of a possible total of $100,000 in back salaries. It further provided that if such back salaries should be paid anyway, that evacuation wages and cost of camp care were to be deducted from the total. The act of January, 1942, which had struck the civil service employees from the lists on the doubtful grounds of dual citizenship was tightened in 1943 to forbid future eligibility of persons so classified.[49] According to a ruling of the attorney general, however, one permanent civil service stenographic clerk, Misao Shiratsuki, was allowed accumulated vacation pay which she had forfeited in evacuating.

In Congress, while representatives Jack Anderson, John Costello, and other Californians persistently espoused the anti-Japanese point of view, Senator Sheridan Downey and Representative Jerry Voorhis more or less pursued a middle path. Other far western states contributed to the clamor. Republican representatives Mott and Angell from Oregon worked to restrict the Japanese group still further, and Pat McCarran assured fearful residents of Nevada, that he had obtained guarantees that Nisei teachers would be kept out of the Indian school system there.

Meanwhile, a handful of groups and individuals who might be described as the wound-binders, were keeping up contacts with the evacuees, doing what they could to prepare public opinion in their own towns and valleys to ease the way for return. Offshoots of the Pacific Coast Committee for American Principles and Fair Play began to appear in various communities—in Santa Barbara, Fresno, and elsewhere—under various names. Perhaps the most effective group of all was that which had been formed by Mr. and Mrs. William Carr in Pasadena called the Friends of the American Way, the organization that had been put on the carpet by the Gannon Committee. One of their projects was to locate people who could promise jobs and homes for evacuees whenever they would be able to come back. In June, 1944, 150 letters offering help were sent to relocation centers. A manufacturer offered to employ twenty to twenty-five former residents in his factory. The head of a Pasadena family wrote, "The house in which we live is large, and we will be glad to take care of four people, preferably men, until they are able to find employment and a place to live permanently. Also I pledge myself to assist in the securing of employment for these and others." A businessman wrote, "Whenever the War Department deems it to be advisable and safe . . . we would most gladly welcome them back to our employ."

While the Los Angeles Federation of Churches considered immediate return "most unwise," the Catholic Interracial Council in the same community advocated lifting the West Coast ban on loyal aliens and citizens. The *American Baptist Home Mirror* put out an illustrated flier for fair play. The General Council of the Methodist Church asked for freedom of movement for the American Japanese and denounced "the false principle of 'protective custody.' "[50] The California Christian Church conventions in San Jose and Los Angeles did likewise. As early as May, 1942, the Pasadena Council of Social Agencies had spoken in defense of the rights of the departed Japanese.

William Devin, the mayor of Seattle, warned that attacks on racial groups had no place in the American political scene.[51] In Campbell, California, a woman kept in touch with a former friend and employee, sending clothing and gifts, and promising a place to stay if and when she should come back. Josephine Duveneck in Los Altos and Gerda Isenberg in Palo Alto, California, were among those who kept up a heavy correspondence with their evacuee friends and with other evacuees whom they had not known before.

Win Freitas, a pear farmer near Hollister, California, carried on a correspondence with about 3,000 young people, which meant staying up to midnight to write six or seven letters each night. He had known a number of Japanese—as friends and as workers. "You could trust Japanese anywhere," he says. "You could leave anything around, and it was always safe." Before evacuation a Japanese man with a fruit stand had always given him gladiolas to take to his first wife, who had multiple sclerosis. A young Nisei girl who endeared herself to them had taken care of his wife, combing her hair, dressing her, doing the cooking. To his ever-increasing circle of friends in camp he tried to give courage: "America forgets," he would write. In World War I, he remembered, people were so hateful they would spit on the dress of a German mother walking down the street. After a few years everything was forgotten, and it would be the same for the Japanese. The Issei, too, he would tell them, were legal residents and had as much right to return as anybody else. Through correspondence he introduced two young people living near each other in camp who had not previously met.

As the possibility of release to the West Coast loomed, these helpful individuals were asked to supply information for their Japanese friends. In a typical letter, a Nisei technical sergeant inquired of Gerda Isenberg if he should move his "folks" back to the ugly atmosphere of California. If they did come back, would there be employment? Would there be housing? Mrs. Isenberg placed advertisements offering help in Japanese-language newspapers read by relocated persons. At the same time she sought out key people with ability to aid those who would return to the Coast.

Writers and other public figures brought into focus for the general public a more positive image of the evacuated people. Wallace Stegner in his book, *One Nation*, showed the American Japanese in a sympathetic light, along with other minority groups. *Born Free and Equal*, with pleasing shots of Manzanar and its residents by the author, the noted photographer Ansel Adams, gave an optimistic account of both the evacuees and the WRA. Carey McWilliams' book, *Prejudice, Japanese Americans, Symbol of Racial Intolerance*, was released in October, 1944. *The Christian Century*, *The Nation*, *The New Republic*, and Marshall Field's brief-lived, ultra-liberal newspaper *PM*, edited by Ralph Ingersoll, publicized the American Japanese predicament.

The national convention of the Socialist Party, meeting in June, 1944, in Reading, Pennsylvania, unanimously adopted a plank in its platform advocating "complete restoration" of rights of the Nisei, and a resolution by Anne Fisher of Seattle recommended reimbursement for losses suffered by evacuees. Norman Thomas spoke before an audience of 1,000 in Seattle.

In the entertainment world, Art Linkletter, Frank Sinatra, Bob Hope, Edgar Rice Burroughs, author of the Tarzan stories, and Joe E. Brown, who had visited physically shattered Nisei soldiers in European hospitals, publicly praised the American Japanese.

Resistance grew within some organizations as more moderate members began to exert an influence. In June, 1944, a convention of the California Baby Chicks Association withdrew a resolution for deportation at their conference in Fresno after listening to objections from such persons as Albert Bihn of San Jose, who argued that such a proposal was beyond the scope of the organization.

In the American Legion a good deal of resistance to the prejudiced stand was beginning to be felt, sometimes expressed in letters from soldiers overseas reacting against news of anti-racial activity. In October, 1943, *The American Legion Magazine* published a short article refuting charges against the evacuees by Claude Settles, who had resigned in protest from the Legion the previous year. In December, 1943, the California Legion, by a unanimous vote of its Executive Committee, passed a resolution of censure of their most notorious race baiter, Dr. John R. Lechner, who headed their committee on the Japanese problem. Lechner, who had influenced the passage of countless resolutions within the Legion, had overstepped the mark, according to the California *Legionnaire*, by representing himself in Washington, D.C., as having made the trip at the request of the Legion.

During the year following his censure, Lechner attempted to soften the opposition by some conciliatory moves. In a debate between the Reverend Fred Fertig and Attorney A. L. Wirin, speaking for the affirmative, and Attorney J. Wesley Cupp and Lechner, speaking for the negative of the question, "Would Prohibiting the Return of the Japanese to California be a Threat to Other Minority Groups?" over radio station KFAC, Lechner, while still opposing return at that time, conceded that loyal Japanese should be allowed to return to the Coast after the war was over.

Not originally anti-Japanese, Lechner had made a turn about face before, perhaps for opportunistic reasons, and the new change was therefore not too surprising. In a letter written December, 1944, to the editor of the *Pacific Citizen* he proposed a plan to "clear the atmosphere" and suggested gathering a number of JACL leaders together with Americanism Educational League leaders, recalling that at a talk in Brighton, Colorado, he had invited "Joe" [Joe Grant Masaoka] to say "anything he had on his mind" before the audience. Larry Tajiri photographed and published the letter and in a neighboring column reminded readers that while Masaoka had been allowed to speak in Brighton, he had been barred from even entering Lechner's public meetings at Denver and Grand Junction.[52]

A number of candidates taking anti-Japanese stands were defeated in the 1944 California primaries. While there were other factors involved, it was clear that Japanese-baiting did not insure election. But President Robert Gordon Sproul of the University of California declared that the dream of America would be dead when the color of men's skins determined the communities in which they might live. He feared that "the barometer of tolerance toward Japanese evacuees is still too low on this coast, and the opposition is still vehement and unscrupulous."[53] Noting the failure of important public figures to speak out for fair play for the Japanese, the *Pacific Citizen* editorialized on the "liberal collapse."[54] Behind the noise of the political struggle, the Nisei heard what someone else described as "the terrible silence of the decent."

The Jerome relocation center in Arkansas was closed in June, 1944, and its 5,000 residents were transferred to other camps. In addition to 2,400 persons on seasonal leave, over 22,000 former Pacific Coast dwellers had established new homes in other sections of the country— from Spokane to the eastern seaboard. As selected evacuees left in increasing numbers, stirrings both of hope and foreboding were heard from those still behind the fences. From Tule Lake, Professor Ichihashi pleaded that the American public should right its wrong, especially for the sake of the younger generation, lest this "so human a problem" breed yet another far more tragic one coming from a "philosophy of despair."[55] A group which called themselves the Council of Americans of Japanese Descent at Amache requested restoration of full rights as American citizens in a letter to Dillon Myer. Among eleven requests they asked for:

1. The opening of all branches of the armed forces.
2. The right of citizens to travel and reside anywhere in American territory.
3. Government protection in resettlement and the economic means to start life anew.
4. More rigorous efforts to enlighten the public on the difference between American citizens of Japanese extraction and the people of Japan.
5. Admission of students of Japanese extraction to schools on an equal basis with all others.[56]

Shunji Noguchi, an Issei incarcerated at Topaz, wrote an appeal to government heads of all warring nations:

> I am a Japanese subject living now at Topaz, Utah, U.S.A. I wish to make an appeal to the People of the World who are engaged in the present war. . . . As the war continues longer, the more human lives are lost. We

will lose our sons, father, husbands, and our friends. Some remain to live
as crippled and infirm. When we think of the dead, crippled or infirm, it
arouses thoughts of spite and hatred in our hearts. These bad feelings will
bring more grief to the minds of the people of every nation in the
world. . . .

War kills men.

. . . I just cannot watch the souls of a countless number of innocent
youths of the world today being led into the living inferno, and that is why
I composed this little thesis, had it translated, and now present it to each
respective prime minister of Japan, China, England, the United States,
Russia, Germany, and Italy.[57]

After having the manuscript translated, Mr. Noguchi asked the WRA to
mail it for him. Dillon Myer replied that they could not do that, but
Mr. Noguchi would be allowed to do it himself if he wanted to.

In March, 1943, Dillon Myer wrote to Secretary of State Stimson
recommending an immediate relaxation of the coastal exclusion orders,
but two months later the Secretary rejected his proposal. In June, 1944,
Secretary of Interior Ickes wrote President Roosevelt urging the revocation of exclusion, but the President still resisted any proposals for sudden change, because of fear of a "public outcry."[58] In a memorandum in
June to Stettinius and Ickes, the President, reiterating his disapproval of
proposals for rescission, replied: "As I said at Cabinet, I think the whole
problem, for the sake of internal quiet, should be handled gradually,
i.e., I am thinking of two methods: (a) seeing, with great discretion,
how many Japanese families would be acceptable to public opinion in
definite localities on the West Coast; (b) seeking to extend greatly the
distribution of other families in many parts of the United States. . . . in
talking to people from the Middle West, the East and the South, I am
sure that there would be no bitterness if they were distributed—one or
two families to each county as a start. . . . Why not proceed along the
above line—for a while at least?"[59] But to the public the President had put
the question on other grounds: evacuees could return to their homes
as soon as military conditions permitted.[60]

In July, 1944, three injunction suits were filed against Major General
Charles Hartwell Bonesteel, then Western Defense Commander, on behalf
of individuals desiring to return to their homes in Los Angeles. The government resorted to delaying tactics in order to prevent court testing.
Blocked in this direction, the Southern California ACLU urged a letter-
writing campaign appealing to the President in his capacity as Commander-in-Chief to proclaim the lifting of the ban against coastal return
and to assure evacuees of full protection against vigilante elements. They
also suggested sending messages to Congress asking special legislation to
reimburse evacuees for their fearful economic losses.

The Korematsu and the Endo suits testing evacuation and detention

which had been initiated earlier were still on their way up to the Supreme Court. The Korematsu, Hirabayashi, Yasui, and Regan cases had
all been heard about the same period of time by federal district courts
in 1943. *Hirabayshi* and *Yasui* had eventually been decided unfavorably
for the Japanese and the Regan citizenship case favorably.

The Endo case, unlike the others, began as a civil suit on a contract.
Mitsue Endo, a young, Sacramento-born Nisei stenographer was working
for the California State Highway Commission under civil service when one
of DeWitt's exclusion orders was applied to Sacramento. At the time of
evacuation she had not resisted the order, but soon found herself confined under armed guard, first at Tule Lake and later at Topaz. In
July, 1942, she filed a petition for *habeas corpus* through her attorney,
James Purcell of San Francisco, on the grounds that because of detention
and inability to perform her duties, she had been deprived of her civil
service rights by the State Personnel Board.

Her attorney did not focus on the evacuation or even the Army's
right to confine, but rather the lack of authority for continued detention.
Even if evacuation were valid, he argued, continued and indefinite detention was not authorized. Although the WRA was set up under presidential order and Congress allocated the money for running the camps,
it was contended that Congress had never meant to establish a provis-
ional government over these people. WRA regulations under which Miss
Endo was supposed to request leave were not valid. Thus, in effect,
neither the President, who had given authority to the Army, nor the
Army which had made the plans and transported the people, nor the
Congress were responsible for the decisions but rather the War Relocation
people who had been hired to implement the decisions.

The way the Army had carried out the orders was challenged—evacuation and detention had been accomplished without due process—without
hearings or criminal prosecutions. Citizens of Japanese ancestry had been
denied equal protection of the law by being treated on a different basis
than other descendants of enemy nationalities. Even during wartime,
Mr. Purcell contended, military power is subject to civil liberties guarantees.

Attorney A. J. Zirpoli, speaking on the concept of total war, argued
for the government that the West Coast was actually a theater of war,
and that while martial law had not been declared on the West Coast,
"Martial law proclaims itself."[61]

A full year after the case was filed, during which time the government
attempted to get the case dismissed before it could be appealed, federal
Judge Michael Roche of the United States District Court for Northern
California in which it had been instituted, denied Miss Endo's request
for discharge. According to Judge Roche the petitioner had not exhausted
her administrative remedies for release before asking for *habeas corpus*.
She made application to the WRA for leave clearance, but did not

request indefinite leave. In August, 1943, Mitsue Endo appealed to the Ninth Circuit Court. Almost another full year passed until in May, 1944, four basic questions and the entire record were ordered filed by the United States Supreme Court. Arguments were heard in the fall, and on December 18 the Supreme Court in a unanimous decision held that the indefinite holding in detention camps of citizens of Japanese descent who were of proven loyalty was not authorized by statute.

The Army, acting with the WRA, anticipated the Supreme Court decision and arrived first with their own announcement, twenty-four hours earlier, revoking the mass evacuation orders.[62] Since early in the year there had been numerous memoranda, proposals, and discussions within the WDC staff on the advisability of easing restrictions in order to avoid court decisions that might place limitations on military authority over civilians. In December, it seemed necessary to take immediate and drastic action in negating these orders in order to preserve the power of the military.[63] More than an affirmative decision in *Endo*, Army leaders had feared that the whole evacuation program might be declared unconstitutional by virtue of the Korematsu case to be decided the same day.

In the Endo case, William O. Douglas, writing the opinion of the Court, expressly indicated that they were not ruling upon certain constitutional issues involving the validity of evacuation and detention. At the same time he stated that such power as made evacuation and detention possible came from Executive Order No. 9066, which delegated authority to General DeWitt, and Executive Order No. 9102 creating the WRA. Prolonged detention was illegal, but the evacuation itself was not to be questioned.

Justice Owen Roberts, concurring in the decision, pointed, however, to the absurdity of pretending that the Executive branch of the government was unaware of what was being done and that some inferior public servant had merely exceeded the authority granted. Justice Murphy, also concurring, remarked that the "unconditional release" of Miss Endo implied she could go where she wanted to, presumably Sacramento, but that the Coast was in actuality still closed. The Endo case, however, set an important precedent because it established the limitation of the power of government over civilians.

Fred Toyosaburo Korematsu, who, it was conceded, was loyal like Miss Endo, and whose case was heard by the Supreme Court in October with hers and decided on the same day in December, had also been dwelling in a legal limbo. Mr. Korematsu, it will be remembered, had been arrested in May, 1942, on leaving a post office near Oakland, California. After undergoing plastic surgery, he had posed as a Spanish–Hawaiian and violated orders to report for evacuation. He was apprehended and, by 1944, when the case went to the Supreme Court, he was in the Topaz center in Utah.

The question in his case was the government position that evacuation had not implied detention—this despite the fact that preparatory camps (assembly centers) were built, and relocation camps for indefinite imprisonment were being planned and built. Since the President's Order 9066, according to this argument, did not contemplate evacuation (even though under its authority Japanese were evacuated), since Army orders for evacuation did not imply detention (even though Japanese including Mr. Korematsu were very evidently behind barbed wire), and since he, Korematsu, had been placed on "probation," his liberty to be enjoyed at Topaz rather than in jail, he was really free, yet not free to fight the Army evacuation in the sense of being transported into detention. Assembly centers were not really detention camps, in the government's argument. As Justice Hugo Black put it later, they were merely "part of the machinery for group evacuation."[64]

Another gap existed between civil and military responsibility. Korematsu had been convicted for violating Army Exclusion Order 34, but penalties for disobeying had been provided by congressional statute, Public Law 503, which was described by his attorney, Wayne Collins, as a "statutory monstrosity," entailing the involuntary servitude of thousands of Japanese-descended persons, and so vaguely and loosely framed as to make it possible for both military and civilian authorities to "blame each other" for the invasion of the constitutional rights of the people. This act would "one day be celebrated not only for its structural deficiencies but for the mailed fist" that it concealed, he said.[65]

Before the Supreme Court, Mr. Collins and Charles A. Horsky of Washington followed arguments similar to those used in the Endo case: General DeWitt and the WRA had exceeded their authority; due process was ignored; evacuation was executed along racial lines.

An exhaustive JACL *amicus curiae* brief was written for submission in the Korematsu case. For some time previously, Saburo Kido and other JACL leaders had been urging evacuated Nisei to take more interest in these cases being fought for their rights. The Nisei should know, Mr. Kido had pointed out in the *Pacific Citizen* in October, citing two San Francisco attorneys as examples, that counsel for some of these long, drawn-out cases sometimes spent thousands of dollars of their own money to carry them on. He had reminded his readers of the great financial sacrifices of the Issei generation in earlier years to combat legislative attacks on the Japanese group.[66] The primary purpose of the 120-page JACL brief, by going deeply into the history of the West Coast Japanese and into the racial question in general, was to refute the fallacies in the DeWitt report and particularly the contention of military necessity. But the majority of the Court upheld the government against Korematsu.

As the curfew was upheld in *Hirabayashi* and *Yasui*, the evacuation during the specific time of the military emergency was upheld in *Korematsu*. The important constitutional issues were left undecided. In the Endo case it had been argued successfully that loyal citizens could not be kept indefinitely in detention, which detention the WRA had abolished in any event. In *Korematsu*, the petitioner's counsel had attempted to persuade the justices that it was unconstitutional to put loyal citizens in detention in the first place, but the issue was by-passed by the Court.

Justice Hugo Black, who wrote the majority opinion, proclaimed the overriding authority of the military. The Japanese, he said, had not been excluded because of racial prejudice. "Pressing public necessity may sometimes justify the existence of such restrictions; racial antagonism never can." He rejected the assertion that the danger of invasion had disappeared by May, 1942, when the disobeyed order was promulgated. It was impossible to determine how many disloyal there were in a group. Congress and the Executive branch had not exceeded their war powers; the evacuation was constitutional, the Court stressed, *at the time the orders were issued.* (Italics authors'.)[67]

Three justices dissented—Roberts, Murphy, and Jackson. The evacuation was a "clear violation of constitutional rights," according to Justice Roberts. The petitioner was actually subject to arrest under two conflicting military orders, one telling him to stay where he was, the other telling him to leave—"a cleverly devised trap to accomplish the real purpose of the military authorities, which was to lock him up in a concentration camp." Justice Murphy reiterated the deeply felt arguments he had made in his *Hirabayashi* dissent. Evacuation to him was "the legalization of racism."

Associate Justice Robert H. Jackson, who had served as Franklin Roosevelt's Attorney General previous to his appointment to the Supreme Court bench and who in 1945 was to conduct the prosecution of Nazi war criminals at Nuremburg, was noted for his independent, incisive opinions. He wrote in his dissent:

> Korematsu was born on our soil, of parents born in Japan. The Constitution makes him a citizen of the United States by nativity and a citizen of California by residence. No claim is made that he is not loyal to this country. There is no suggestion that apart from the matter involved here he is not law-abiding and well disposed. Korematsu, however, has been convicted of an act not commonly a crime. It consists merely of being present in the state whereof he is a citizen, near the place where he was born, and where all his life he has lived. . . .
>
> Now, if any fundamental assumption underlies our system, it is that guilt is personal and not inheritable. . . . But here is an attempt to make an otherwise innocent act a crime merely because this prisoner is the son of parents as to whom he had no choice, and belongs to a race from which there is no way to resign. . . .
>
> The very essence of the military job is to marshal physical force, to remove every obstacle to its effectiveness, to give it every strategic advantage. . . . No court can require such a commander in such circumstances

to act as a reasonable man; he may be unreasonably cautious and exacting. . . .

I cannot say, from the evidence before me, that the orders of General DeWitt were not reasonably expedient military precautions, nor could I say that they were. . . .

No evidence whatever on that subject has been taken by this or any other court. There is sharp controversy as to the credibility of the DeWitt report. So the Court, having no real evidence before it, has no choice but to accept General DeWitt's own unsworn self-serving statement, untested by any cross-examination, that what he did was reasonable. . . .

Much is said of the danger to liberty from the Army program for deporting and detaining these citizens of Japanese extraction. But a judicial construction of the due process clause that will sustain this order is a far more subtle blow to liberty than the promulgation of the order itself. A military order, however unconstitutional, is not apt to last longer than the military emergency. . . . But once a judicial opinion rationalizes such an order to show that it conforms to the Constitution, or rather rationalizes the Constitution to show that the Constitution sanctions such an order, the Court for all time has validated the principle of racial discrimination in criminal procedure, and of transplanting American citizens. The principle then lies about like a loaded weapon ready for the hand of any authority that can bring forward a plausible claim of an urgent need. Every repetition imbeds that principle more deeply in our law and thinking and expands it to new purposes. All who observe the work of courts are familiar with what Judge Cardozo described as "the tendency of a principle to expand itself to the limit of its logic." A military commander may overstep the bounds of constitutionality, and it is an incident. But if we review and approve, that passing incident becomes the doctrine of the Constitution. . . .

It [the Court] argues that we are bound to uphold the conviction of Korematsu because we upheld one in *Hirabayashi* v *United States*. . . .

The Court is now saying that in *Hirabayashi* we did decide the very things we there said we were not deciding. Because we said that these citizens could be made to stay in their homes during the hours of dark, it is said we must require them to leave home entirely; and if that, we are told they may also be taken into custody for deportation; and if that . . . they may also be held for some undetermined time in detention camps. How far the principle of this case would be extended before plausible reasons would play out, I do not know. . . .[68]

In this eloquent dissent, Justice Jackson dissected the problem to expose its very heart and core. A rehearing of the Korematsu case was denied in February, 1945.

The *Endo* decision, while decreeing that loyal citizens could not be kept indefinitely in detention, did not immediately release Miss Endo or her fellow evacuees. The normal processes of individual relocation under the WRA now sanctioned by Army rescission continued to operate and accelerate.

For some time previous to the announcement on December 17, 1944, of the revocation of General DeWitt's 108 mass exclusion orders, the Army had been making exceptions and cautious experiments allowing certain individuals to return, including wives and widows of Nisei soldiers, wives of Caucasians, Chinese, and other non-Japanese racial groups, the children of mixed marriages, Nisei soldiers on furlough, and finally a few others on an experimental basis.

For the most part these rare returns attracted little public attention. The Assistant Secretary of War, John J. McCloy, termed "fantastic" politicians' fears that evacuees were a danger. A woman of Japanese descent who rejoined her Caucasian husband at his farm in Orange County in the fall of 1942 with her three-year-old daughter was checked on by a deputy sheriff who had received complaining telephone calls, but when he went to investigate he found her busily at work hoeing beans. Mrs. Lun Woo, a Nisei Phi Beta Kappa graduate of the University of Washington married to a Seattle Chinese restaurant operator, returned to pick up the threads of her previous life, along with several others in that city. Minor trouble occurred on the return of one evacuee wife of a mixed marriage, but it was smoothed over with outside help.

A number of California politicians became distraught over General DeWitt's edict of April, 1943, which allowed Nisei soldiers on furlough to go into the area of the Western Defense Command. But despite a few unpleasant headlines, such as the San Francisco *Examiner's* welcome, "SOLDIERS OF NIP ANCESTRY ALLOWED TO ROAM ON COAST,"[69] most Nisei soldiers, though sometimes anticipating reaction, attracted little notice except when seen by old friends in their home towns. Masao Kanemoto (now Judge Wayne Kanemoto) who had volunteered for the 442nd Regimental Combat Team, returned to visit exactly a year to the day after he had been evacuated. He was walking down the street in a uniform that did not fit very well, when he saw a Navy officer and saluted. It turned out to be an old school acquaintance, a football player who had gone to San Jose High School at the same time he had. The Navy man stopped and said, "Why you're Mas Kanemoto, aren't you?" They talked a while, and then the Navy officer remarked that he had heard all the people of Japanese descent and their families had been evacuated from their homes. "How are they treating you?" he wanted to know. Kanemoto, impressed by his concern, told him their treatment was satisfactory, that the government had restricted their freedom, but their treatment in camp was all right. The next morning, Kanemoto read in the paper that his friend had just returned from Guadalcanal and had almost lost his life in a dangerous patrol. Seeing Japanese transports coming, he had to give warning. The planes came after him, and he escaped only by skimming over the water. He was awarded the Navy Cross for gallantry. Kanemoto, thought, reading this in the paper, "If anyone had wanted to be prejudiced against the Japanese, I guess he had reason to be. But he was the one who came forward to talk to me. So I felt very good about that, and have never forgotten it." Kanemoto himself was on his way to India where he served in the China–Burma–India theater as an interpreter.

In August, 1944, Stanford University approved the hiring of fourteen Japanese language instructors who were to come from Manzanar. At the time the Army had decided to draft Nisei out of camp after the initial success of the volunteer divisions, Dillon Myer was in Pasadena where he met with a small group to discuss a number of matters relating to relocation. Herbert V. Nicholson, the Quaker minister and member of the Friends of the American Way, told him he felt it was absolutely wrong to draft men from concentration camps. The moment they started the draft, he said, they should open the camps and tell the internees they could leave and go back to the Pacific Coast if they wished. Myer agreed, but pointed out that one branch of the government could not tell another what to do. Nicholson asked who could then, and Myer said, "You," suggesting he go to the War Department to talk with John J. McCloy. Not long after, Nicholson was on his way to Washington, stopping at various relocation camps as well as Camp Shelby where Nisei soldiers of the 442nd—often called McCloy's "baby"—were in training.

During a forty-five minute interview with McCloy and two Army officials, the Assistant Secretary of War thanked Nicholson for his suggestions, but said that he received a constant stream of letters urging him to keep the Japanese off the West Coast. These letters were mostly mimeographed sheets with signatures, evidently distributed by organizations, but they had to be counted. McCloy pointed to two baskets, one for letters favoring rescission, which was empty, and one for letters against, which was full. According to Nicholson, McCloy then said, "If you'll fill this basket on my desk with letters from people on the West Coast urging the return of the Japanese, we'll do something about it."

Nicholson at once telegraphed the Friends of the American Way, and letters and telegrams began pouring in from Pasadena. Then he went to Philadelphia, asking the Friends' Service Committee to start letters, and to New York, contacting the Federal Council of Churches. On his way home he contacted Japanese in eastern cities and relocation camps and suggested they urge Caucasian friends to do the same thing. Letters which Issei could send to their friends were mimeographed. By July thousands of letters reached McCloy's office, and he wrote saying Pasadena had sent more letters than any other community. Would they sponsor a Nisei girl student from one of the camps?

Representatives of their group sounded out Pasadena Junior College, asking them how they felt. Polls of the student body, the faculty, and the school board showed that over 90 per cent favored the proposal.

Hugh Anderson, an officer in Friends of the American Way, requested of General Bonesteel, head of the Western Defense Command, that a Nisei college girl, a bright and attractive nineteen-year-old named Esther Takei, be sent from the Amache center. He had already conferred with the girl's parents in the camp. Ten days after the request was made, the young woman, who made the trip alone by train, was in the Pasadena home of Mr. and Mrs. Anderson.

She arrived on September 12, 1944, prepared to enter Pasadena Junior College. Despite her warm reception in most quarters and her subsequent popularity with the faculty and student body, a storm of protest broke out in the community and for five weeks it was not known what the outcome would be.

A parade of cars kept going by the Anderson house. Letters and phone calls made life tense for the family, but for every hostile message there were some of encouragement. Still, the pressure from the "domestic patriots" made it necessary for Anderson to remove Miss Takei and his wife and four children from the house.

Actually, California law was very specific on the right of all citizens to attend public schools, as was pointed out repeatedly by John W. Harbeson, principal of the junior college. But little support came from the Pasadena Board of Education, the ministerial leadership, or the Chamber of Commerce.

Although Miss Takei had been given advance clearance by the college, a member of the Board of Education advised Hugh Anderson, "Get her out of town. Send her at our expense to the University of Nebraska." Anderson, wanting to let the people of the community make the final decision, went instead to a local radio station owner and told him, "We're in trouble. An American citizen is trying to go to school." J. Frank Burke, the owner of the station went on the air and requested that sympathetic listeners call the manager of the Chamber of Commerce, who subsequently received fifty supporting calls at his residence over the weekend. These calls were influential.

A Navy serviceman hitchhiked from a veterans' hospital where he was confined to see Miss Takei and give her courage, and another took time off from night watch to write her a heartening letter. After a time the furor died down. General Bonesteel later said that this victory in Pasadena was the basis for opening the West Coast a year earlier than had been planned.

Several other certificates of exemption were issued by Bonesteel in the fall of 1944 to carefully screened Japanese who returned as advance scouts to test public reception. Miss Kaoru Ichihara, who had previously been allowed to relocate in Spokane, returned to Seattle, where she worked as secretary of the Seattle Council of Churches. Dorothy Tada returned to Los Angeles and YWCA employment. They needed people who "wouldn't scare anybody," she says. "In a city it's easier for people to be absorbed."

When a Japanese–American returned to his fruit farm in California, his congressman complained that he had not been contacted by the Army before permission was granted, and there was a flurry of letters, but neighbors and the local newspaper were friendly. By November some five hundred Nisei had quietly returned to their lives on the Coast. The first Issei reportedly allowed back was Kenematsu Osada, a handsome real estate man married to a Caucasian who owned a pet canary which, he boasted, could whistle "America."[70] Another Issei to return early was an elderly man of cheery disposition who made a point of going about looking up everyone he had known, even though returning aliens were subject to travel restrictions.

Dave Tatsuno had "taken a try" at writing government officials in the fall of 1944, saying he felt he and his family had been out on the desert long enough and should be permitted to come home. His brother was in the United States Army, he told them, and it was silly for him and his family still to be locked in. On December 15 he received a letter saying they would now be permitted to go back to their home in San Francisco, "a short lived triumph," according to Mr. Tatsuno, since two days later the general rescission announcement came.

As of midnight January 2, 1945, restrictions were officially removed from the Japanese group who had been excluded en masse from the West Coast, but with a large number of exceptions. In order to make distinctions between those who would be welcome and those who would not, the Army screened and classified the entire Japanese-descended population of the United States, according to three writers who studied military and government directives. Under the new program of individual exclusion some 5,000 male Japanese were catalogued as potentially dangerous and excluded from the Coast (they were called excludees) and another 5,000 persons called detainees were kept under detention and not allowed to relocate anyplace.[71]

At the time of the joint Army-WRA announcement that the Coast would be open in January, Dillon Myer publicly promised that centers would be closed within six months to a year. The WRA speeded its relocation efforts, giving assistance in the form of grants for travel and in the transportation of household goods. A schedule was set up for the proposed closing of the various camps.

A scattering of individual injunction suits had been filed against General Bonesteel some months before rescission, one by the widow of a Nisei serviceman who had died of wounds incurred in Italy. Suits were brought by a California dentist, a Los Angeles attorney, and an honorably discharged World War I veteran. In August, 1944, the Army allowed the widow and the veteran to return. The persistent dentist, who had been an active relocation camp leader and elected president of his evacuee governing council, was given a hearing and put into the category of permanent excludees, which was to include thousands. As was the case in other Army hearings of this kind, he was not allowed representation by an attorney, or to cross-examine witnesses, and did not know what evidence was used for the decision made against him. A Heart Mountain man wrote a friend that excludees were being placed in the same class as the "disloyal" segregees at Tule Lake. Later, approximately five hundred exclusion orders were revoked after board hearings, and still later in 1945, following the defeat of Japan, all outstanding individual orders were revoked.

In December and January of 1944–1945 a little of the opposition on the Coast began to fade, especially among public officials who now recognized that evacuee return would soon be a *fait accompli*. While Mayor Bowron of Los Angeles retreated from a position of implacable opposition to one of doubtfulness, Mayor Lapham, who had succeeded Rossi in San Francisco, welcomed those who wanted to come back. Governor Warren, who had actively resisted return, publicly announced that the rights of returning evacuees must be upheld, and Jack Anderson, while still objecting, asserted that those who were citizens must be given their full rights. John J. McCloy, who had long pled that there was no longer danger of large-scale invasion on the West Coast and for fair attitudes toward American Japanese, said, "We have every faith the people on the West Coast . . . will show their good citizenship by abiding by the military judgment and do their utmost to prevent any acts of discrimination against any of these people. . . ."[72]

But Dillon Myer estimated in September, 1944, that perhaps a fourth of the evacuees might never return to former Coast homes. Some specialists on minority race problems who looked at city racial concentrations as unhealthy were hoping this would prove true and that the Little Tokyos would not be formed again.

Miss Mitsuye Endo, whose test case before the Supreme Court had been decided in December, did not leave Topaz until the end of May, 1945. When she did leave, she went to the Midwest rather than back to Sacramento. Arriving in Chicago, she was met by newspaper photographers, and within a very short time she had been offered a half dozen stenographic jobs. She finally went to work for Mayor Kelley's Committee on Race Relations where she was reported happy in her employment, and her employers were happy with her. Her parents remained at Topaz (they were still there in July, 1945) until she could find housing for them.

The turning point had come, and the evacuation program was being terminated. But the Endo case, which might have opened a door for further legal testing of the right of the government to evacuate and detain citizens in concentration camps, had been undermined by Army rescission of the orders.

FOURTEEN · HOT SPOTS

THE GENERAL ANXIETY of the evacuees concerning their reception on return to the West Coast after rescission orders soon proved to have been well founded in reality. While mass vigilantism did not occur, there was a sufficient number of incidents of harassment and violence, particularly during the first six months or so of 1945, to make it seem to many evacuees there was no future on the Coast for them. Some sections turned out to be considerably worse than others—Hood River in Oregon, Salinas in California, the valley area around Fresno in California, these were some of the hot spots. Placer County, bordering Sacramento in Sutter County to the northeast, was one of the most difficult areas. Sacramento, itself, which was not only the home of the state legislature but also of the *Bee* papers, had seen many years of anti-Japanese agitation; yet long-standing working relationships existed between groups in the community.

Placer County, which had taken its name from a type of surface mining common during the Gold Rush era, is as rich in early pioneer history as it is in scenery. The eastern section goes into the high Sierra Nevada Mountains where it borders a considerable length of Lake Tahoe's shoreline. Here at the north fork of the American River, John Sinclair and a group of Indian retainers first panned gold in 1848. California gold, which had enriched the fortunate, eventually gave out, but the remnants of the culture are still to be seen: a hydraulic-scarred hillside here, picturesque buildings elsewhere. Old markers abound—Frytown, Dutch Flat, Spanish Corral, Secret Ravine. There are a few ghost towns. The Native Sons of the Golden West put up many of these markers such as the one at Emigrant Gap which points out the place where cross-country adventurers on their way to the gold fields had to lower their wagons by rope and tackle over a steep cliff after coming over Donner Pass. Auburn, the county seat, located in mountainous territory, was the turnpike for stage coaches and freight operations.

In Placer County towns with a sizable Japanese-descended population include besides Auburn, the tiny Penryn, Loomis, and Newcastle, and others which dot the countryside. In Loomis before Pearl Harbor about 65 per cent of the school children were of Japanese extraction. In 1940 there were 1,637 Japanese in the whole county representing 9½ per cent of the population. The schools were integrated.

The Japanese were orchardists rather than truck farmers. Like their Caucasian neighbors, they cultivated, pruned, and picked the trees and worked in the processing sheds of the fruit companies, packing peaches, almonds, plums, apples, and especially pears for shipment to other parts of the world. Fruit orchards covered not only the flatlands but some of the hill country as well.

World War II brought about more agricultural diversity. Cattle began to appear on the lands converted to grazing. During the war, too, DeWitt Hospital, named after the head of the Western Defense Command, was built four miles from Auburn. Today it is a mental hospital, but originally it served as a general Army hospital where wounded soldiers, including Nisei, were treated. During a blinding rainstorm one night late in November, 1945, a plane transferring Army personnel from Arizona to McClellan Field near Sacramento, crashed into a hillside near Auburn. Eight United States soldiers including six Nisei were killed; sixteen other Japanese–Americans were wounded. Survivors were searched out by lantern light and rushed to DeWitt Hospital.

This rather symbolic event occurred toward the end of a period of difficulty and trial for Placer-born Americans of Japanese descent returning home from evacuee camps. While colonies in Florin and Vacaville and other towns not far from Placer County had attracted national attention and been the subjects of attack and study by anti-Japanese writers and defenders, in the prewar era and while all these areas were served by the Sacramento *Bee* as well as the more neutral local papers, the Caucasian population and the Japanese population around Auburn had gotten along fairly smoothly.

"There was a harsh, miserable feeling at the time of Pearl Harbor," according to one Japanese–American resident, "even with some of our friends." But there were no pre-evacuation incidents.

In the prewar period, the Japanese-descended people in the area kept pretty much to themselves. While some older Nisei and a few Issei were active in the community, most were apolitical and not integrated socially. Most of the "old timers" were on the "poor to middling side" and did not "pull their weight" on charity drives, according to a Caucasian resident. "But they made a living, didn't bother anybody, got gypped plenty. We live in a competitive system, whether we like it or not."

Most Placer Japanese were a part of the working farm community, and they concentrated their energies on a few things: making a living for their families, saving their earnings, living for the future, raising their children to keep out of trouble and to get an education. The mother of one of the families who were leaders in the Japanese community (she had been a school teacher in Japan and her husband acted as a court interpreter in Placer County) wrote a message to her eight children in a little composition notebook which was found after her death in 1930. "Be sure that all of you finish high school," she told them, "because that will be the way to get along." Even when the children were small she had said: "You are all Americans. You have to make a place in this country. In order to succeed you have to work twice as hard and be twice as good to be accepted on the same basis as other Americans." All eight children did finish Placer High School and some acquired further education.

Most of the local Issei were Buddhists. A good number came from the kens of Hiroshima and Yamaguchi. They had a Japanese association and a language school. As elsewhere certain families sent their children to Japan periodically where a few were impressed into the Japanese army.

George Yonehiro of the justice court in Colfax, who was the first elected Nisei judge in the state of California, in a district where there were two voters of Japanese ancestry—himself and his wife—was brought up in the Newcastle area which had a larger number of Japanese. Not too many doors were closed in those days because of discrimination, according to Judge Yonehiro; more often Japanese were excluded for lack of the price of admission to local functions. Perhaps his father felt less of the usual West Coast discrimination than others because he, though an Issei, was a World War I veteran and one of the exceptional naturalized citizens. He loved to fish for trout and was able to do so, since the special licensing charges for ineligible aliens did not apply to him. He belonged to a number of civic organizations and later in life to a Legion post in Roseville.

"We had no such thing as interracial dating," a Caucasian businessman says, "and there was an unwritten and unspoken line of demarcation in the most important business area."

Bill Scott, the present sheriff of Placer County, was raised in the Long Valley where as a boy he knew many of the older Issei. He worked on ranches with them, cutting lumber, pruning fruit trees, and using prunings to burn under the Japanese bath houses to heat the baths. Sheriff Scott is known for a particularly good working relationship with the Japanese community. The Issei generation, he points out, were the 1941 adult generation. They were very old-country. Few could speak English. The second generation group were like himself "just kids" at that time.

The Issei farmers were great orchardists, according to another resident. They saved their money in the good years as a cushion for the bad years. Only in slack times could they afford to relax. Some local Caucasian ranchers resented the hardworking, thrifty Japanese, but the big packers liked working with them because they believed they brought in a better crop of fruit. The large farm entrepreneurs also found them desirable employees, because they gave full value in labor and sometimes more.

Because of Army zoning most of the Placer County Japanese went directly to Tule Lake, an assembly center at the time of evacuation. About 2,500 persons had to move, 1,500 from the Penryn and Newcastle sections. A good number of Placer County residents were among those who at the time of segregation decided not to make another move, but to stay in the center, thus becoming part of the group known as the "old Tuleans."

The Army's line of demarcation running lengthwise through the state separating prohibited Zone A from restricted Zone B had split Placer County in two. At the beginning of the "voluntary" evacuation period when there had been talk that people moving into Zone B would be left alone, several local families evacuated into their own orchards since the line ran through their property. A number of people came up from the Bay Area during this period of uncertainty, creating a housing problem. Makeshift quarters were arranged. Tents were pitched. The influx of newcomers may have increased the tension in the community.

A number of localities formed a volunteer, civilian militia to protect the east- and west-bound Southern Pacific railroad lines during a period of aroused feeling. They were later officially deputized by the Army.

A few of the older Nisei in the area had formed a charter group of the JACL in 1928 under the leadership of Tom Yego two years before the national organization was established. Its purpose was to educate for intelligent voting, to discuss public questions, and to take stands on local issues that concerned them. At the time of General DeWitt's West Coast zoning, this association announced that if there was any particular thing they could do or any way they could act to be able to stay even in a limited area they would do it. They wrote letters, appointed a committee to help the older generation, passed resolutions. They tried to communicate with the Caucasian majority in the area, but most people were a little frightened to come out too far. After evacuation was a fact, Kay Takemoto, who was president of this group at the time, and Hike and Tom Yego and other leaders operated on the premise that if they had to move they would do so in an orderly manner. They helped with registration in Lincoln, acting as interpreters.

The evacuation crisis struck hard at those who owned or were paying for farms. Many sold out at panic prices or made the mistake of leasing property to individuals for just the cost of taxes and insurance on the buildings; when lessees made high wartime profits during the absence of evacuees, some held to the letter of the contract and others turned money back to former owners. There were bound to be confusions and misunderstandings. Many of the farm families were working on crop mortgages, procuring advances from the food sheds, using perhaps seventy-five to one hundred dollars a month to feed their families. Credit came from packers; the banks offered little credit to the Japanese.

Evacuees who had been doing business with the Blue Goose Growers Incorporated (then the American Fruitgrowers) were given a good deal of help by this company in forming holding companies to take care of their interests while they were gone. Farrell Wrenn, the owner-manager of the corporation, one of the most prominent fruit growers in the county, says, "This way the properties were kept up, and crops were harvested though labor was scarce. Ten per cent of the profits were retained by packing houses. It cost a little money to form the holding companies, but the evacuating Japanese were advised by attorneys and government people to handle it this way. It was not mandatory. Sometimes we advanced modest amounts in expectation of earnings for their needs in camp. When the evacuees came home again, the property was turned right back."

Once the evacuees were gone, a movement to keep them from returning began to gain momentum for the usual reasons: general war hysteria, an identification of the local Japanese with losses suffered in the Pacific theater, and economic competition. When the Placer County Citizens Anti-Japanese League was formed, the keynote speaker, a prominent rancher, at a meeting of almost three hundred persons explained local opposition to Japanese ownership of farms: " . . . You and I know that we have absolutely nothing against the Japanese on account of either their color or their creed any more than we have against the Chinese, the Hindu or any other dark-skinned national. No, it is not his creed or the color of his skin that we object to, but the color of his heart that is black as ink and more treacherous than a rattlesnake."[1]

A local resident says, "It was just a minor group of people who weren't thinking. These people believed the Japanese were going to blow up the country and murder everybody." An observer who attended meetings of another anti-Japanese group formed in the area says: "My impression was . . . that they were frightened stiff of the 'yellow-peril.' " At one meeting an elderly retired state senator made a speech "so vituperative and so permeated with lies and half-truths as he told how he had fought all Japanese immigration since 1908 that [he] made me doubt the efficacy of democratic government." He was convinced the overwhelming motivation of the members was economic.[2]

Ordinary citizens began to echo the agitation group. The Board of Supervisors in Marysville in neighboring Yuba County as well as the Sutter County Supervisors went on record opposing return. In Colusa, Sutter County, a high officer of the Native Sons told a luncheon meeting of the Northern California Peace Officers Association of their intent to continue their program begun in 1876 to save California from Oriental invasion. The assemblyman representing Colfax, Placer County, offered a resolution in the legislature memorializing Congress to restrict Japanese. Clair Engle, by now a congressman, and Assemblyman Lloyd Lowrey from Yolo County were authors of anti-Japanese legislation. Fruit growers and businessmen's clubs in Loomis and elsewhere adopted resolutions. In a number of these places local officials and even occasionally peace officers were sometimes involved in the anti-Japanese movement.

Debate continued on return in the editorials and letters columns of the small local newspapers and especially those of the *Bee*. Prominent Auburn residents affirmed and reaffirmed the "unanimous" West Coast position against return. The fact that no more submarines had been sighted since removal was "sufficient evidence" to one of these writers that Tokyo had been relying on support from the local Japanese people.[3]

At the time General DeWitt opened the West Coast to Nisei servicemen on leave, a number came back to visit in this and neighboring areas. Some visits were uneventful. Other Nisei soldiers met with coldness. Hike Yego comments, "These servicemen visited at a bitter time." For Private Wilson Makabe the visit home to Loomis, after completing his basic training at Fort Douglas in Utah and before leaving for overseas, was a rude jolt. A son of the woman who had written advice to her children on participating in American life, he had been the first to volunteer for the 442nd in Idaho while working in the sugar beets. Two brothers also served in the United States Army.

Makabe was twenty-four years old. He had a number of friends he wanted to look up and say hello to, but everywhere he went for half a day people took him aside and told him they would like to be friendly and visit with him but were afraid of being accused of being "Jap lovers." Finally, when he went to the Nash De Camp Company's packing shed to see an acquaintance, a group of fruit packers left their tasks and, in a brief sit-down strike, refused to work. It was said later that relatives of two of the employees had been killed in action fighting Japan, and they resented the presence of any persons of the enemy race. Newspapers reported that Private Makabe was then put into the protective custody of Justice of the Peace Garrett Doty at the request of the company management.[4]

According to his brother, George Makabe, a social case worker in Public Assistance, the young soldier was so angry for the moment he almost ripped off his uniform. A corporal in an Army jeep was sent to pick him up. This soldier was very sympathetic and drove the private around before putting him on the train. Makabe picked up some fruit and spent the rest of his furlough visiting persons he knew at Tule Lake. "The attitude of my former neighbors was a great shock to me," he stated at the time of the incident. "I had looked forward to friendly visits with many of them."[5]

News of such incidents as this one carried to the relocation centers. A disheartened Tule Lake resident wrote, "All they could think about was what kind of reception was in store for them."[6] Privately, evacuees were writing letters after rescission to persons they trusted back home to see whether or not it would be advisable to come back. Some were discouraged; some decided to try, anyway. A Placer businessman, responding to queries from an Issei farmer whom he regarded with great affection, told the Issei he had found his ranch in a bad state of disrepair because tenants had allowed it to run down. The man wrote back asking if he "would then be put on some other ranch." The businessman wrote again cautioning him to wait thirty days until a full agreement could be worked out with the present tenants. Feeling was high, and he did not yet know how to handle it. But the first thing he knew, the farmer had come quietly back despite the advice and he and his family were scrubbing their house down, getting it in condition for occupancy.

Another early returnee who had formerly been active in the Lincoln community sent a friend back first to check on the situation. The report was that "things looked bad," but after making contacts the situation looked a little better, and he, too, took the chance and returned. He had been renting a fruit orchard—pears and peaches—in the mountain states and made the trip during the break in the fruit season there.

The Doi family was the first to return to California from the Amache center and the first family to return, on the fifth of January, 1945, to Placer County, where they had lived for thirty years before evacuation. The oldest son, Sumio, whose brothers were in the service, after first reporting to his draft board went to work reconditioning his home, milking cows, churning butter and pruning the trees for the first time in nearly three years. "I found the ranch in much better condition than I expected," he said. "However, there is much work to be done." He reported that people were courteous. At Amache the family had heard about agitation back home, but their neighbors had urged them to come back.

"The Army has carefully investigated each person to be permitted to return," Attorney General Robert Kenny had stated in alerting law enforcement officers and calling for full protection of the law for returning evacuees. "There should be no difficulty in this transition. . . ."[7] Nonetheless, a rash of violent incidents occurred throughout the West Coast during the last-ditch attempt to block evacuees from returning.

One of the first such incidents was the attempted burning and dynamiting of a packing shed on the Doi property and the firing of shots into their home. A few hours before the attempted burning, a group of area citizens, not involved in the incident and declaring themselves in favor of law and order, had announced a boycott of returning evacuees. The San Francisco *Chronicle* reported that the group, which proposed not doing business or fraternizing with returnees, had persuaded a number of local stores to post signs to this effect. A spokesman for the group stated that "fruit growers" did not want the Japanese back, though "the big packers did." Several of the women, according to the *Chronicle*, asserted at this time they would withdraw their children from schools attended by Nisei children."[8]

Doi, hearing cars that night and going outside to investigate, had managed to put out the blaze himself with the aid of his father and had not called the authorities immediately. Later, investigation showed the shed had been sprayed with gasoline; one wall was soaked.

In the early hours of the morning of the nineteenth, two days after the attempted burning of the barn, Doi, again hearing noises, opened the door to investigate. Shots were fired into the house. This time the family called the sheriff's office and reported that several carloads of persons were parked on the property and that shots were being fired. As a patrol car of deputies turned into the ranch, two cars were seen speeding away. Sticks of dynamite were found under a corner of the packing shed. Fuses attached to the sticks had burned out. Alongside was a litter of burnt matches.

Sheriff Charles Silva posted a twenty-four-hour guard at the premises, to prevent further intimidation. "The government is sending these people back here," he said. "The Constitution says they've got to have protection and under my oath of office I'm going to see that they get it."[9] The local district attorney's office promised vigorous prosecution of the molesters. The Anti-Japanese League made a public statement against the use of violence. An Anti-Japanese spokesman, deploring the violence, said that such acts might cause the Japanese army to retaliate on American soldiers held by them. "In the meantime, let us hope that the Japs will not always have American prisoners in their clutches. And that someday, may it come soon, we can declare ourselves free men and treat the Japanese menace as it should be treated."[10] The State Attorney General's office sent out their own investigators, one a laboratory expert. In Sacramento Governor Earl Warren condemned the violence as "atrocious." The *Chronicle* urged that the FBI look into the case, since the rights of the Japanese had been "disturbed in the first place by the Federal government."[11]

The Doi family managed to remain calm and kept to their occupation of caring for the farm. "They will have to blast me out," Doi commented.[12] His mother, Mrs. Masaru Doi, said that as more evacuees returned, there would be better community understanding. They owed it to their country of adoption, she believed, to claim their rights and responsibilities.[13]

An Auburn city police officer, Fred Adge, helped solve the case when he heard that a soldier who went AWOL had been habituating local bars dressed in a cowboy suit. Trying to escape through a glass door when asked for his identification card by military police he was caught and held. A local grower who saw the commotion reported that he had just purchased a rifle and a sack of dynamite from the young soldier. Two sets of brothers were arrested: the soldier and his eighteen-year-old brother, also an Army private and also AWOL, and a local bartender and his brother, both a good deal older than the soldiers. Later, three young women were charged with being in the night-riding party. According to the district attorney, the first soldier confessed on arrest and implicated the three other men. A confession by the bartender was announced by county authorities later. The older men, one of whom denied any part in the acts and was not brought to trial, lived on a ranch. At the preliminary hearing one of the women testified in detail concerning the attempts to destroy the packing shed. According to her testimony three separate trips were made the first night for sufficient gasoline to soak the shed.[14]

A technician with the State Bureau of Criminal Identification testified that the wrappings found with the explosives were from the ranch where the soldier was residing at the time of the raids, and positively identified the markings on the dynamite cap and fuse found in the blue Dodge sedan driven by the soldier at the time of arrest.

At the ensuing trial, the unsigned confessions were admitted by the Court after prolonged argument. The statement by the young soldier was read to the jury: one of the older men had asked in the bar room if they would "like to have some fun"; there were people out here he did not like. The statement went on to describe how they got the gasoline, soaked the rags, and set fire to them. The second night, according to the soldier, the bartender said that he "didn't like the job last night; no fun." He said, "Let's get some dynamite." On arriving at the ranch, the statement continued, a member of the party was asked if the dynamite would go off and the answer was, "It will; I lit it."[15]

No denial that the acts had been committed was put forward by the defense, and the defendants, who had pleaded not guilty, were not put on the stand by their attorney and therefore were not subject to cross-examination. Nor did the defense introduce witnesses.

Sumio Doi, who was the principal prosecution witness, says he "just wanted to get the case over with and wanted a civil judgment, not to send them to prison." He testified at the trial that he was unable to identify any of the raiders or any car. He was by this time—April, 1945—

waiting to report for a preinduction physical examination by the Army. During the trial against the alleged dynamiters, Doi was questioned concerning the family's title to their ranch property. How much did he pay down, the defendants' counsel asked him. "I don't have to answer that question. It has nothing to do with the case," Doi said, but he was required by the Court to answer the questions.

The defense attorney described the Death March on Bataan and appealed to the jury to keep the white man's country white: "The Japanese infiltrated into this county; we accepted them . . . we gave them the right to vote, never dreaming they would stab us in the back."[16] He described the trial as a battle between the WRA and the people of Placer County, since the WRA had sent an observer to the trial to determine whether all the facts were presented.

The case went to the jury of five men and three women after the judge gave lengthy instructions and warned them against "permitting prejudices, including those of race, creed or color entering into the deliberations." After two hours discussion with time out for lunch, the jury acquitted the three accused of the charges. The verdict was read aloud to the crowd of one hundred people who listened in silence, but when the session was adjourned the acquitted defendants were the center of a congratulatory throng.

Contributions for the defendants' attorney fees had been collected in March and ranged from fifty cents to one hundred dollars. Local residents would be proud of the jury decision "to the end of time," a correspondent wrote in the *Bee*.[17]

While most evacuees were returning without incident, approximately ten Japanese dwellings in the county burned mysteriously. Fire Chief Garrett Doty of Loomis reported in September that a number of threats had been made that farms that were occupied by "white families" during the evacuation would be "left in ashes" for the return of the Japanese. Some of these fires were probably accidental. George Makabe, whose family residence burned in 1944, says, "It could have been anything, defective wiring, a lampshade, something else." When a home in Rocklyn burned to the ground the day before one family returned, the Auburn Baptist Church presented a purse of $386.21 to help defray expenses in rebuilding. A structure used for the Japanese language school in Lincoln also burned down. It was insured.

A local Caucasian businessman lays the blame for some of these happenings on transient residents from depressed areas of the United States who are "not the best citizens in the world." "Apparently there are individuals in our state who cannot distinguish between Japanese militarists and loyal Americans of Japanese ancestry," commented Lieutenant Colonel Wallace H. Moore, an intelligence officer who had served in New Guinea, at the time of one of the burnings.

Minor incidents continued here and in nearby areas for about two years. A returned evacuee went into a Placer County hardware store to buy a necessity. There were other customers there, and the owner would not speak to him. The man did not give up but waited for half an hour. When the other customers were gone, the owner took him to the back of the store and was friendly. Later he sold him a washing machine. Others said no one would sell to them. A Nisei veteran in Walnut Creek, where schools were still segregated in 1940, was cursed by a local woman. In Vacaville, Solano County, the first man to return was refused service at two restaurants. In Penryn a Nisei ex-GI who had been decorated for heroism opened a store for business and had his window smashed.

The Placer County Anti-Japanese League, officially committed to law and order, in February, 1945, took a less belligerent title and became known as the California Preservation Association, simultaneously launching a program to expand into other towns with the object of becoming a statewide organization. In April the association claimed some three thousand members and held a joint meeting of Auburn, Winters, Sacramento, and Vacaville groups, where a member urged, "Treat them rough."[18]

But another member spoke for "soft-pedaling" the economic competition arguments and concentrating on the danger to national security.[19] While expanding their membership, the league attempted to restrict their meetings more carefully and to keep nonmembers from attending. When two prominent persons were asked to leave a meeting held in the county supervisor's room in the Sacramento courthouse on the grounds that they were not members, one of them, the vice-president of Sacramento Junior College, pointed out that the meeting was held in a public hall and he was allowed to remain.[20] Twenty people left a Marysville meeting when the chairman informed them that they had not met for the purpose of a pro and con discussion. The league was not aware, however, that Claude Settles, the San Jose State College sociologist who was working for the Red Cross in Sacramento, was attending meetings and reporting to the state attorney general, thus anticipating the organization's attempt to expand to other areas.

The Sacramento Council for Civic Unity and an ACLU branch in the capital city had also been keeping an anxious eye on agitation groups. When the California Preservation Association passed on a resolution to Congressman Clair Engle in March, 1945, requesting that every American citizen of Japanese ancestry be required to prove his parents were born in the United States or had entered the country legally, the Sacramento Council for Civic Unity suggested that members of the Preservation Association refresh their memories on the American Constitution, which was based on equal rights for all citizens, and that "any attempt to set up artificial tests or barriers against one group" would lead to a breakdown in the American system. The council urged all who had signed thoughtlessly to disavow their signatures.[21] During the same period the Council for Civic Unity sent its president, Rabbi Norman Goldburg, accompanied by Wayne Phelps of the WRA and Henry Tyler of Sacramento Junior College, to Auburn in an attempt to organize a group of peace-loving citizens in a local chapter. An Auburn high school and junior college teacher, Dr. Rufus Richardson, helped organize the unit.

Rabbi Goldburg, who had returned recently from Army service, had already protested vigorously against the local boycott as a dangerous, unfair, and subversive weapon which set up "a principle of private judgment and private vengeance as superior to the law of the land." The Fresno *Bee*, which had been unfriendly to the American Japanese return, supported the rabbi on this issue.[22] The league's proposal, which had spread to other towns, languished after a while and signs came down until only a few were left. Meanwhile Placer County churches were opened to house former residents who had not yet found permanent homes. A hostel was set up in one of the two Buddhist churches for fifteen or twenty families, and the Mikawa boarding house took in bachelors.

In September, 1945, the Placer County Board of Supervisors passed a resolution establishing a policy denying relief to alien Japanese after an elderly Issei requested it from the county welfare director. Two months previously aid had been denied a couple returning to their ranch near Loomis. Subsequently, the couple sold their property and left. The denial of aid was not unusual. Other welfare boards were also protesting the added burden placed upon them by returnees and attempting to shift the costs to state or federal agencies.

In September, the Pacific Coast Committee on American Principles and Fair Play, of which the Councils for Civic Unity were offspring, sent a questionnaire to Placer businessmen. Local citizens were still asking for imported Mexican nationals and school children from central California cities to help gather their fruit harvest, refusing the help of the agriculturally expert American Japanese. The businessmen were asked whether they really supported the local faction who were advocating paying the costs of transportation of substitute workers and buying or escheating Japanese property and selling it to returning veterans.

As public reaction to various incidents sharpened and as pressure from outside groups was applied, the Preservation Association lost many members. Judge Yonehiro comments that "little guys can push, push, push," but it helps when genuinely interested public figures work on problems.

There had been other appeals for fairness. January of 1945, the year of the Doi dynamite attempt, was also a month of extremely heavy American war casualties. In February Lieutenant Commander Roberts

Robinson of the United States Navy, a graduate of Placer Union High School, spoke before an assembly at the school and college, pleading for greater toleration, saying he knew personally of some of the contributions in the armed services made by county Japanese.[23] In Marysville, Lieutenant Robert Haines, a former officer in the 442nd infantry who was recovering from wounds at DeWitt Hospital, spoke with permission of the War Department and told a similar story. At the same meeting Claude Settles, who had published a poem, "The Restless Dead in Auburn," describing the vigil of unseen departed soldiers, also asked for fair play.[24]

Although the great majority of former residents of Japanese extraction eventually took up their lives again in Placer County, and most Caucasians felt like Farrell Wrenn who says, "You can't take people you know real well and discard them," trouble there lasted a long time.

It happened that Wilson Makabe, who had been spurned when visiting in 1943, was the most seriously disabled soldier of all those from the area who were injured. He lost a leg in the Italian theater and for a long time in an Italian hospital it was not known whether or not he would lose the other leg as well, or even his life. His brother wrote a letter to the Auburn *Journal*: "Wilson went through a lot of action, including the assault on 'Hill 140,' without getting hit," and at one time a shell landed within a few yards of his foxhole. He was injured in an accident while being taken back for a rest period. He was in good spirits and determined to get well, the letter concluded.[25]

In February, Wilson wrote the *Journal*, enclosing one dollar for a subscription. "Being a Placer graduate myself I am very much interested in Placer County news and especially reading articles about my various schoolmates." He praised the Thomas M. England General Hospital, which specialized in amputations and fitting artificial limbs and expressed gratitude for the twenty-five transfusions people had given him so he could live. He was hoping some day when the terrible war was over to carry on where he left off.[26] "He is not bitter," says his brother today. "He adjusted to his trauma. His life work is in prosthetics, and he has a good deal of understanding of the problems of other people adjusting to handicaps."

Some anti-Japanese spokesmen began to make exceptions of the Nisei war heroes. A past commander of the American Legion and of the Native Sons of the Golden West commented that Sergeant Ben Kuroki, who had flown thirty air missions over Europe, could live next door to him for the rest of his life. Robert B. Cozzens expressed the hope that the legionnaire "would also permit Ben Kuroki's father and mother, brothers and sisters, and—when he has them—wife and children to live next door to him."[27]

In Sacramento, state senator John Shelley introduced six Nisei veterans of the European theater to the legislature. When the group walked in, two on crutches, one without a leg, there was a hush in the senate chamber. A senator who had been proposing barring Japanese from California forever withdrew his resolution. Senator Shelley had spoken language they were able to understand. One of the legislators said, "That does it. We should never have let them into the Army."

A slight to Nisei servicemen when the sixteen names from the Hood River Oregon honor roll were removed in January, 1945, by the local American Legion Post, made headlines and received a good deal of attention in national magazines. *Collier's* termed the act "tops in blind hatred."[28] John Haynes Holmes noted a comparison: "When Hitler came to power he shocked the world by removing names of Jewish soldiers from the war memorials of Germany. . . ."[29] After six weeks of controversy, the names eventually were replaced on March 12, 1945, at the order of Edward N. Scheiberling, national commander of the Legion.

One of the servicemen whose name was removed had been awarded a Bronze Star for bravery on the western front. Another, technical sergeant Frank Hachiya, was killed while performing a dangerous mission in the Philippines. The first thing seen by a Caucasian infantryman returning to Hood River from Italy where he had fought alongside Japanese–Americans was a sign reading, "No cigarettes, No Negroes, No Japs."[30] Japanese soldiers were refused haircuts. A Caucasian customer who was a witness to one such refusal reasoned with the barber, who, persuaded, walked out on a cold winter day to find the Nisei and apologize.

The Hood River American Legion Post would not allow Nisei in their organization, and exhorted other posts as far off as Hollywood, California, to refuse them also. In February, 1945, the Post published a list of Nisei who were classified 4-c, which according to the Legion implied disloyalty. One retraction was made on threat of suit. Paid ads by the Legion post on the previous December had urged Japanese–Americans not to return.

While patriotism was the theme, the commotion was related to economic rivalry in the valley. Hood River, near the Washington border, was fruit country like Placer County in California. Growers specialized in apples and pears. Before the war a relatively small number of farms were operated by Japanese-descended producers (Hood River Japanese represented 10 per cent of the population before evacuation) though they contributed 25 per cent of the total fruit production.

In January, 1945, three hundred Hood River citizens signed petitions urging a gracious reception to returned Nisei. However, in February a group who called themselves the Oregon Property Owners Protective Association demanded mass deportation and enforcement of the old alien land laws at a mass meeting in Gresham near Portland. A Legion member, speaking at the meeting, discussed plans to investigate property titles of all land owned by local Japanese. In the same month, an advertisement in the Hood River *Sun* run by Kent Shoemaker, a legionnaire and chief agitation leader, listed the names of former residents of Japanese ancestry in Hood River Valley and noted the holdings of each property-owning family. "You Japs listed on this page have been told by some that you would be welcome back in Hood River. That is not true, and this is the best time you will ever have to dispose of your property."[31]

A full-page advertisement in the Hood River Oregon *News* for March concluded: "As evidence that the backbone of resistance . . . has not been broken, there is published, herewith, the names of about five hundred more Hood River people who do not want you back."[32] A convenient coupon was printed at the bottom of the page for additional persons to sign and mail in. One of Shoemaker's arguments was, "There are no Japanese in the United States navy. This is a proper evaluation of their loyalty."[33]

A great number of Hood River property holders of Japanese heritage heeded the warning and sold out. But there were offers of help. In March, a committee of five in the bar association of Multonomah County, which included Portland, offered to protect the interest of former residents "threatened by war hysteria."[34] A previous governor and publisher of the Salem *Statesman*, Charles A. Sprague, wrote in defense of the evacuees, while another ex-governor urged them to go back where they came from (presumably Japan) and leave the land to those who had pioneered it. By August, 437 persons had returned to Multnomah, many with agreeable reports, while only eighty-eight had returned to Hood River.

When a truck farmer living in Maryhill, Washington, and newly returned to a farm he had operated for thirty years before evacuation, took his first truckload of produce (parsnips, onions, and turnips) across the state line to the nearby Portland market, he and his son managed to sell only half the load. On two successive trips buyers refused to have anything to do with his produce. A large grocery chain was at first willing to buy, but later withdrew their offer. One of this farmer's isolated sales was to a Chinese huckster. The market master maintained the boycott was nothing personal, just an "economic measure."[35]

A young girl standing at her family's small market stall in Portland was challenged by a middle-aged Caucasian who demanded to know if she were Japanese. When the girl answered she was an American the same as he was she was told, "We don't want you here." After the girl tearfully but quietly reported the occurrence to the WRA representative in Portland, helpful people were found who began "digging up customers," and the little market prospered.[36]

There were no incidents of violence in Hood River, but for a while evacuees had a hard time getting fuel; they could not eat in restaurants; they could not buy groceries. The WRA and private groups got together and found a large store that would sell to anyone. Quakers and others helped paint and repair houses and clean up and revive gardens. A couple were warned not to return to a waterfront hotel they owned in another Oregon city because if they did all the help and fifty Caucasian guests would leave. They came back just the same. Nobody left. Some old men cried because they were so glad to see the proprietors return. Some brought them flowers.

When a boycott of Hood River apples in other parts of the country was advocated as a way of applying counterpressure, the *Pacific Citizen* editorialized that "such a campaign would punish the innocent as well as the guilty."[37] But the boycotting of apples in Cleveland and Chicago in addition to the withholding of credit to trouble-making Caucasian growers by a Portland banker did have some effect in changing the economic strangulation policies against Japanese though packing houses continued discriminatory tactics by postponing using Japanese grown produce until after the other produce was taken care of. The Nisei writer, Bill Hosokawa, termed the whole struggle a "tawdry drama of greed and hate."[38]

The city of Portland, which did not have a large Japanese-descended population like Seattle, was more tolerant than the farm areas except for the harassment of Japanese who tried to bring produce into market. A young mother who, riding on a bus, overheard a derogatory comment about her race recalls thinking, "My goodness, some people are so ignorant." But she found most people understanding. Japanese–American school children were popular and were elected to committees and organizations. Sometimes they were embarrassed by "special recognition."[39]

During a Seattle boycott, similar to that in Oregon, Dillon Myer suggested that anti-trust laws were being violated and protested vigorously that evacuees "must have complete freedom to earn their livelihood and contribute to the war food production program. Any efforts to hamper food products through normal trade channels, particularly at this time, would be tantamount to sabotage."[40] In July, Clinton Anderson, the Secretary of Agriculture, ordered the Northwest Produce Dealers Association to abandon the boycott. A Nisei charged that Seattle florists were refusing to purchase flowers, as well. A returned evacuee whose flowers were ready in July visited seventeen of his old florist customers, finding only two not "afraid" to buy from him. Florists who were interviewed gave varying reasons: remembrance of cut-throat competition, though they admitted this grower had never resorted to this, and fear of public sentiment. The flower grower cut all his flowers every day anyway, and took all the blooms he was not selling to the hospitals for enjoyment of the patients.[41] After ten months of goodwill work a number of anti-Japanese signs still remained in stores and in the public market of Seattle even after the boycott had been broken.

Trouble in the Puyallup, Wapato, and White River valleys of Washington repeated the Oregon pattern in Clackamas, Multnomah, and Hood River Valley—a few loud voices and much harassment, yet eventually a good deal in the way of aid and, if not welcome, at least neutrality.

Mass meetings of the Pearl Harbor League in the farm areas of Washington, at which members shouted for every means short of violence to discourage Japanese were responsible for the crippling boycott of flower and truck vegetables grown by persons of Japanese descent. The movement was promoted by a combination of farmers, businessmen, and teamsters. A group of college students pulled the rug from under the feet of the Pearl Harbor League when it attempted to spread the doctrine in Seattle. In a surprise move, 150 University of Washington students attended an April meeting, distributed pamphlets, and asked questions. A sociology professor who accompanied the group insisted the students were not "heckling," but admitted they laughed at a number of things the speakers said. It was reported there was a spontaneous outburst of laughter when one speaker asserted that pioneers had "taken this country away from the Indians and now the Japs are trying to take it away from us." The members of the Pearl Harbor League were taken aback by this unusual response from an audience: one wanted to "fight," though his invitation was not accepted.[42]

Down in California Attorney General Robert Kenny, apparently attempting to quiet with a few homespun phrases some of the passions aroused in the selfishly motivated boycotts, bemoaned the loss of the piles of tempting produce "which once made the shopper's mouth fairly water." He was criticized by letter writers who complained that he was inciting hatred "towards ranchers of Portuguese, Italian, Scotch, Irish, and plain Iowa American stock."[43] A member of an anti-Japanese group argued that persons who defended Japanese by describing their detractors as "barroom patriots" and those who "talked . . . bigotry" were themselves bigoted.[44]

Though there were two assaults in Seattle, one upon a Filipino mistaken for a Japanese, it was California which established the record for outright violence and terrorism. Dillon Myer had predicted that "incidents" would be the exception, rather than the rule.[45] Time proved him correct, but in the first half of 1945 there were more than thirty incidents of violence in California, thirty-nine by February of 1946, after which they almost entirely ceased. Twenty of these were shootings, the rest arson and other assaults. Shots were often fired into the air to frighten rather than to kill or maim, but sometimes people narrowly escaped with their lives. Hundreds of less serious incidents occurred, including the burning of a housewife's laundry on the line, which were nevertheless often traumatic to the individuals involved. February, March, and April of 1945 were the worst months, when agitators and hoodlums apparently felt if they frightened the first evacuees who came back, the rest would stay away. In April the United Press reported that Radio Tokyo propaganda was utilizing these incidents to the fullest.

The victims did not retaliate, although one interior valley merchant reported a knife attack after he told a Nisei he had no cigarettes to sell him. Numerous threats of violence were made. Sometimes men would call in the middle of the night. A young woman with three brothers in the Army and with parents still in camp was visited by five men who sought unsuccessfully to terrorize her into leaving a small town in Southern California. In San Juan Bautista Win Freitas was visited one night by a man who demanded to know if he was harboring any Japanese. He told him no, he was not. "But I should have been more firm," he said, "and asked him who he was." As the man turned, Mr. Freitas saw a pistol in his back pocket. He telephoned the sheriff the next day. He was later told that a group planned to burn his barn down but that the plan fell through.

Scattered incidents of varying seriousness occurred in Santa Rosa, Stockton, and other places in the northern part of the state, and in Orange and Los Angeles counties in the southern part. An apparently premeditated assault with intent to commit murder in Northern California ended with an easy sentence for two workers involved.

The "bad" areas were almost inevitably in farming country, and "good" areas tended to be the cities—principally San Francisco—and university or college towns such as Berkeley, Pasadena, Palo Alto, San Jose. But incidents occurred even in the "good" areas. In San Jose, one of the most auspicious places for return, there was vandalism, a shooting at an outspoken WRA man, the burning of a family home. The headrest of a barber's chair was hurled through the window of a candy store belonging to a Japanese who was too frightened to investigate.

Monterey, California, with its artistic and golfing crowd, its fishing industry, was generally hospitable; neighboring Salinas, in the same county, was hostile. The Monterey *Herald*, which served both towns, ran paid advertisements both by Salinas anti-Japanese spokesmen and by Monterey citizens, including Robinson Jeffers, Dwight Morrow, and Edward Weston, testifying to their belief in the resettlers. Editorially, the paper welcomed back the departed residents.

A Salinas national guard unit had been taken prisoner in the Philippines and many were lost in the Bataan Death March. Antipathy was expressed by some of the younger members of rival racial groups who worked the lettuce fields as well as the migrants from the southern United States. Feelings had festered during the war as wild stories of Japanese atrocities circulated. When the evacuees came back, church groups in Salinas were slow to offer aid. Returning scouts would check with Cottie Keltner, a distributer for the Hancock oil company, who has been described as "the best friend the Japanese ever had." They would call on him to see what conditions were like for return. Keltner says:

> Those who returned to Salinas would move into anything they could find, including two-room shacks. They couldn't get service, couldn't get their utilities turned on. They cooked on kerosene stoves but the companies wouldn't sell them fuel. I sold them kerosene in barrels for cooking and heating. Some white farmers said to me, "Well, if you serve Japs you'll be boycotted. It'll ruin your business." My brother was identified as a "Jap-lover" outside a store once. He called the fellow down and put a stop to that talk once and for all by saying, "These people are as good as you and I and are not responsible for what has happened in the war."
>
> Proprietors who had served them before they went away said, "We don't want your business," and turned their backs on them, refusing a handshake from a former friend. My brother and I bought groceries for the Issei who were out of funds and afraid to go into town. We picked up tools for them and did all we could to make them feel welcome. Old friends came from as far away as San Jose to get things from us.
>
> On oil deliveries my brother and I talked to all our ranch accounts, told them how unjust it was. All of our customers saw it our way except one whom we were glad to lose. Half a dozen Japanese started farming. As soon as the ball got rolling, this store or that would relent. It was just a short time until the major concerns were beating their brains out trying to get Japanese business.

Those who did return to Salinas sometimes found that tenants had let homes and businesses run down; one tenant family had cut the pipes and pulled away window ledges to use as firewood, and had given a party during which the barn burned down. According to Mr. and Mrs. Henry Tanda, who went back to Salinas because they owned a house there, a great many who did not own property never returned but went to more favorable areas such as Santa Clara County.

In neighboring Hollister the welfare board at first refused aid to elderly indigent Issei and two women were fined for assault and battery when they pulled a ladder from under a Japanese of the older generation as he was painting a house. There were those in Hollister, however, who assisted the arriving people.

By far the most dangerously hostile sections were the hot, inland valleys of the state, beginning in the vicinity around Sacramento, down into the Merced, Turlock, area, and farther south, around Fresno and the surrounding small towns and outlying farmlands—Madera, Fowler, Selma, Parlier, Tulare. Early Japanese felt they had pioneered these areas. They recalled the wooden sidewalks of Fresno, the barren land before it burst with vegetables, fruit, and vineyards. A strong anti-Japanese campaign persisted in Fresno during the war after evacuees departed. But since the Japanese owned a good deal of property which they had not sold on leaving, they returned there.

In these inland valleys in 1945 shotguns were fired into returned farmers' homes from speeding autos and from nearby orchards; eighteen Japanese and German graves were desecrated; rocks were thrown through windows of homes and of a Japanese sanitarium where three evacuees were staying. By the month of May, 1945, fifteen of the seventeen nightrider incidents in the state had occurred in the San Joaquin Valley. By June, of seventy such instances of terrorism and nineteen shootings, 90 per cent took place in Merced, Madera, Fresno, and Tulare counties. In one incident a bullet went into the wall over the bed of two sleeping children and missed a child just emerging from a bath, in another a bullet was fired six inches above the head of a discharged Nisei soldier. The discharged soldier who nearly met death at home as well as overseas was reported very surprised because his neighbors, who had nothing to do with the shooting, had been so exceptionally cordial on his return. A family that had refused to sell their property and a fairly large business despite pressure at the time of evacuation not only experienced a number of thefts during their absence, including the stripping of their automobile, but returned to have their home burned down by an arsonist.

Twenty years before a group of farmers in one hot valley community had actually turned Japanese away from the town of Turlock. In the period before the war, the other Japanese who lived there avoided further persecution by, as one resident puts it, tending to business, keeping more or less out of the way and not competing in certain economic fields. In Orosi similar incidents occurred in 1945 in a particular section of town when only a very few evacuee farmers had come back. In January a group of twenty-five ranchers and businessmen visited two returnees, advising them to leave the area and setting a deadline. The Japanese elected to stay, and the deadline passed without harm coming to them. A while later newly arrived returnees in the area were shot at, and a small house was burned, all within a brief period of time. Young hoodlums were blamed for writing epithets on windows. A patriotic rally in a neighboring town at which a school official decried exclusionist activities was followed by another meeting the same evening at which John Lechner spoke, asserting that appeasement in the handling of the Japanese might mean the end of Christianity.[46] Other Christians, however, went about reasoning in a friendly way with merchants who still had anti-Japanese signs in their windows, with the result that most of the signs were removed.

The climate of opinion is a determining factor in periods of racial tension such as the months that followed the rescission orders. If a sufficiently large segment of the population passively or actively approves a policy of injustice to a minority group, unpleasant or dangerous incidents are almost bound to occur and occasionally to get out of hand. It has been observed that sometimes the hoodlumism is perpetrated by youngsters who absorb adult attitudes, but who may carry them out in a direct manner which would not be countenanced by the prejudiced adults themselves. A sanctioning of intolerance also allows economically and educationally deprived persons to take out their generalized hostilities upon a scapegoat group. But the so-called respectable element of various communities have at times joined in the persecution of the Japanese.

As has been observed, the climate of opinion can also be decisively affected when prominent public figures work with persons of goodwill to lower the emotional temperature during periods of stress. One such person, Lowell Clark Pratt, recently retired as publications manager at San Jose State College and one-time crusading editor of the Selma (Fresno County) *Enterprise*, is content today with his stand in support of evacuees. "We opposed the movement to move them out of Selma," he remembers.[47] By calling attention to the community spirit and Americanism of the victims of hostile acts Pratt helped prevent more direct action by those he had once termed "historically (and hysterically)" opposed to the Japanese minority group.[48]

The quality of law enforcement sometimes affected and reflected community attitudes. A victim of violence in the San Joaquin Valley stated, "Whenever I look at the holes left by buckshot which ripped through my home I begin to wonder if peace officers really mean it when they say the equal protection of the law will be given to all."[49] Another man, surveying the damage three shotgun blasts had done to his attractive, two-story home, was more fatalistic. He said, "If someone plugs me, I'll just have to get plugged. . . . I'm not going to leave either."[50]

State Attorney General Kenny, a forthright man, jovial and energetic, met the problem of law enforcement head on. After shootings occurred in different areas he put the California highway patrol on the alert, and urged the chief to place on duty a special twenty-four hour guard though he was unsuccessful in this request. Kenny was constantly in contact with local enforcement officers, prodding them when necessary to follow up their cases. He also suggested offering rewards for the apprehension of wrongdoers. The ACLU posted a reward of $1,000 for information leading to the arrest and felony conviction of terrorists. The attorney general employed various approaches, from open condemnation to roundabout persuasion. Certain local enforcement officers gave him a particularly difficult time, but he praised all except two county sheriffs and spoke well of district attorneys who gave even a modicum of cooperation.

But law enforcement officers, even when doing their best as many did, could not prevent the more serious breakdown in civil justice that was occurring on a judicial level and in the body politic. The San Francisco *News* commented on the "almost total lack of convictions" of perpetrators of violence. The outcome of some of the court cases was "farcical" according to Dallas Wood, writing in the Palo Alto *Times*.[51] More dangerous than the vigilantism, in the words of Dillon Myer, was the "rationalization, public and private" which permitted such acts to go unpunished.[52] The fact that even after the war's end a national opinion poll showed 40 per cent of the American public were in favor of denying Nisei and 89 per cent of denying alien Japanese equal opportunities, suggest there was a climate of latent approval of acts of terrorism. Conditions were worst where the law-abiding men simply turned their eyes away. Probably few of those who passively stood by agreed with one of the representatives from Tulare, California, who had stated on the floor of Congress in 1943, "As I have said before . . . the only good Jap is a dead Jap, and that is just what is going to happen to everyone of them that is sent back there."[53]

When the offender in a shooting incident was let off with a sentence more in keeping with a misdemeanor charge than that of a crime, the justice of the peace in a strange interpretation of democratic theory stated that he believed he should consult the wishes of the voters before making a decision.[54] A majority of the people of the community felt the WRA was wrong in sending the evacuees back at this time, he said.[55] The defendant admitted firing four shots into a Japanese home, pleading that his motive was revenge for the slaying of a relative in the Pacific theater. It turned out that he received the letter announcing the death *after* his evening shooting spree. The local district attorney commented that the defendant had only used a shotgun, when he might have used a powerful deer rifle.

Eight other shootings occurred during these months within a fifty-mile radius. Perhaps coincidentally, the shootings ceased, according to Robert Kenny, on the eve of the exposure of a sponsor of anti-Japanese meetings. The man, a banker, had been managing a number of evacuee holdings at great cost to the Japanese involved. When the banker died of a heart attack the meetings stopped and the shootings stopped.

California's Earl Warren, who was strongly backed by the Hearst press and the *Bee* papers, had until December, 1944, when rescission of evacuation orders was announced, consistently acted in the anti-Oriental tradition as governor, signing restrictive legislation and making public pronouncements. But at the end of 1944 and during the year 1945, beginning with his call for cooperation in the orderly return of evacuees which set the tone for the vast majority of West Coast citizens, he began to demonstrate a change in position—not alone on the Japanese question, but away from his conservative orientation in general. Some have said

that his association with Attorney General Robert Kenny had something
to do with this new liberalism. Warren reacted with outrage and shock at
the flouting of the law by irresponsible individuals in the return period.
Law enforcement officers were urged by Warren and Kenny to adopt professional attitudes toward the returning citizens and nationals. A thirty-
eight page bulletin was published by the state setting up guidelines for
the handling of race relations problems.

The WRA worked from its offices in San Francisco to counteract the
injustices perpetrated upon returnees. Pat Frayne, an appealing individual, friendly but ready for combat, had been a sports writer before he
was hired by the WRA as public relations chief for the West Coast. Like
Dillon Myer and Robert B. Cozzens, he went about making speeches to
hostile groups. But 90 per cent of their work was behind the scenes.
When incidents occurred, they developed personal contacts to establish
more understanding, and then gave full public exposure of terrorist
activities through the press.

According to Pat Frayne, the tremendous opposition they had to face
did not personally disturb him, because he had been used to fights all
his life, and it was just another kind of fight. But the WRA work "took
something out of everyone."

Cozzens, who had worked in the federal soil conservation program
and who had once conducted a Farm and Home Hour on radio, recalls
that when trouble arose he would say, "Let's go see our friends." Frayne
would answer, "Let's go see our enemies." They would call on editors,
members of farm organizations and others and often made friends of
their enemies. They spent a good deal of time with Warren, who proposed
that they work in liaison.

When a newspaper editor accused the WRA office in San Francisco
of doing paid work for the Japanese propaganda machine, Frayne called
him on the phone, told him they were paid by Congress and that he
would sue for libel. "We had to act as tough as he." The editor printed a
retraction.

Once they warned a Jewish film maker who was producing anti-
Japanese–American movies, "This is just the beginning of attacking
minorities. If you let folks get away with this, what is the next minority
they would pick on?"

Perhaps the strongest ally the WRA had was Harold Ickes, Secretary
of the Interior. At a press club meeting one night in San Francisco,
Ickes expressed his philosophy. Pat Frayne recalls Ickes facing an antagonistic crowd and saying, "I'm a Constitution man, fair weather or
foul. Right now we're having foul weather." Ickes was responsible for
getting individuals and agencies together, insisting they help the WRA.
If they were not interested, he would scold them. According to Cozzens, one always knew where one stood with Ickes, and when they

were in difficulty he would back them to the hilt. In the terminology of a *Pacific Citizen* editorial, Ickes was a man "bristling with integrity."[56] Time and time again his colorful and succinct comments on the West Coast made the headlines of the newspapers—often arousing anger and opposition, but just as often, by describing a situation as it really was, bringing in supporters to work on behalf of evacuee interests. His analysis that West Coast agitators would grow more desperate as they saw they would not be able to "establish an economic beachhead on the property of the evacuees they vainly hoped would sell out or run out," was correct, as Dillon Myer was correct when he predicted that the flurry of incidents would last a few months only and then give way to an acceptance of general return.

FIFTEEN · BEGINNING AGAIN

AS THE WRA SET UP regional offices on the Coast during the early part of 1945, evacuees were given additional support and aid. Many of these offices were makeshift affairs, particularly at the beginning. Some opposition to their establishment arose, but they did not have to face the severe crises the parent organization had previously undergone. Housing and employment were the chief concerns, because the dislocated people, in addition to their other problems, were coming back to a severe wartime housing shortage.

The WRA work load was close to overwhelming. Nisei girls and young married women helped staff the offices as secretaries and helpers. Mrs. James Higuchi, whose husband was serving in Europe in the medical corps at the time, worked as a typist for James Edmiston, head of the San Jose office. She remembers all the anxious people arriving from the centers. "A lot of them were coming in without really a place to go to, so it was kind of rough. I had to make a card file and had to ask them questions. More questions! They were fed up with questions!"

The WRA worked closely with groups and individuals already in contact with evacuees, many of whom, like Gerda Isenberg in Palo Alto, had been working almost full time on a volunteer basis—finding homes and employment, speaking before groups—doing the same sort of thing the WRA did professionally. Under Mrs. Ruth Kingman, its executive secretary, the Pacific Coast Committee served to coordinate some three hundred organizations concerned with race problems on the West Coast. The WRA people worked also with cooperating government agencies such as the Federal Social Security Administration and the War Manpower Commission.

As evacuees returned, the railway coaches were often met by the same people who had gone down to see them leave. In Palo Alto members of the Fair Play Council, the Society of Friends, and former employers met the trains with more automobiles than there were passengers for them. In San Jose, members of the Council for Civic Unity took hot food to evacuees as they alighted from coaches. According to Mrs. Evelyn Settles, if a troop train happened to be going through at the same time as an evacuee train, in order to prevent trouble evacuees would disembark at the railroad yards in the nearby town of Santa Clara rather than the Southern Pacific station in San Jose. In March sixty Japanese returned to Santa Clara County. In June and July up to a hundred people were arriving at a time. Six months later, Santa Clara County had the largest percentage of returned evacuees of any county in the state.

Temporary quarters were sometimes found in private homes until more permanent housing could be arranged for or until household furnishings could be brought out of storage. Mrs. Isenberg wrote to one of her correspondents in a center, "It [housing] is one of the most difficult problems we have to face in relocating people. There are no houses to rent at all, so the only way to get families settled is to try to find places in which there are separate cottages for the helpers. . . . Of course, there are places that have single rooms. When your family is finally determined to come out, you can let me know and I will see what can be done. . . ."[1]

Before large numbers returned to San Jose, a corps of Negro and Caucasian women made a survey of the Jackson Street district where other tenants were lodged in homes formerly occupied by persons of Japanese descent. The survey workers told the tenants, often Negroes or Filipinos who had come in for factory and farm work, that the Japanese were coming back to their homes, but that nobody had to get out without a house to move into. This was a big promise, for housing, particularly for minority groups, was practically nonexistent. There had been no new building for four years and the city had condemned as substandard thirty-three residences and business properties owned or leased by Japanese. Yet the committee found places for these tenants all over the valley.

After writing a number of inquiries to find what other areas were doing to provide housing for returning Japanese, members of the local Council for Civic Unity obtained permission to open the Japanese language school building as a hostel. The school was located next door to the Buddhist church, which could not be used at the time because it was full of the stored possessions of evacuees. (These items, which had all been neatly wrapped in burlap and tied carefully, had been raided by vandals, and everything was in a bad state of disorder.) After gaining permission to open the hostel, the council had written to the Heart Mountain center, where many of the San Jose people were located, to see if the former San Jose Japanese Methodist church pastor could run it. He was unable to accept the assignment because the high altitude at Heart Mountain had damaged his heart. He died not long after. Mr. Torahiko Kawakami, an Issei much respected among the Japanese people, accepted the responsibility for managing the hostel, doing all the buying and bookkeeping. According to Mrs. Evelyn Settles, who was involved in the project, this was probably the only hostel to begin operation without any financial backing whatsoever. Mr. Kawakami and others paid the first expenses out of their own pockets. Furnishings were borrowed, the WRA located ample surplus equipment for the kitchen— large cooking utensils, huge pots and pans. Unemployed adults were charged $1.25 a day for room and board, employed adults $1.50, and children sixty-five cents. Originally it was thought only a few families would stay there but by the end of June when the first full trainload came home, it was found necessary to expand into an old corrugated metal gymnasium next door, which was hot in summer and cold in winter. The city inspectors were sympathetic and gave them much leeway; nevertheless they were not allowed to put in extra heating facilities because of the fire hazard. By fall they had expanded into the Japanese Methodist church as well as the Buddhist church. During a peak period the four buildings housed 370 persons.

"We tried to call a halt to the number of people coming in," Mrs. Settles says. "It just seemed inhumane to accept any more, but the relocation centers were getting ready to close at earlier dates than at first anticipated. The people were being forcibly put on trains and sent to their former homes; we just had to accept them and do the best that could be done for them. The cots were packed in there cheek by jowl." Finally, Marjorie Pitman, one of the Civic Unity Council members, and Don Hunter, a WRA official working in the area office on housing, reported the availability of some prefabricated houses. Then the Progressive Growers' Association bought some small units of the Camp Parks Federal Housing Project, which they moved to their farms in Santa Clara County. This helped relieve the shortage.

By the time the hostel closed after eighteen months of operation, it had served 1,423 individuals as a pausing place before they ventured out to pick up the threads of their lives again. Hostels served as centers for job recruiting and property counseling, as well as places from which returning evacuees could feel out the life of the communities they were reentering.

There were more than fifty such hostels on the West Coast, most of them operated by private groups. Some were quite small. A San Francisco hostel in a former language school on Bush Street housed twelve men. No meals were served, but the men could use the kitchen and prepare breakfast. Storage buildings as well as old rooming houses were widely converted to multiple housing. Eight hostels in Los Angeles were crowded to bursting.

The elderly stayed in these places as long as they could, according to Shig Masunaga, one of whose many postevacuation tasks in San Jose was to find friends such people could stay with or other places to which they could go. In Stockton, the Army had been slow to allow use of the church for a hostel and had put guards around it before public pressure removed them. Students at the College of Pacific and State Junior College at Stockton had been most helpful to arriving Japanese, transporting them and serving temporarily in the soup kitchen. Originally set up for families, the hostel was later occupied by elderly Issei farm workers who stayed on for reasons of personal convenience such as the proximity to Japanese activities and Japanese friends and access to Japanese grocery stores. Most hostels closed operations after about a year, but the Stockton hostel did not close until 1967 when the last of the residents returned to Japan, the others having passed away.

At first the WRA acted only as a clearing house for information and depended on volunteer groups for help, not assuming responsibility for finding jobs and housing. But as the problems multiplied it was forced into a more active role. Concerned citizens who previously had urged immediate and rapid emptying of the camps, now began to advise slowing up. The rush to home communities was imposing too much hardship. Friends of the Japanese protested that the federal government should not put the whole burden on individuals. Evacuees were being cast out of camps and expected to find their own housing. The federal government should provide housing for them in the same way it was providing housing for incoming war workers and veterans, they said.

The WRA, too, attempted to prevail upon Washington to take a more realistic view of the situation. The agency obtained permission to use vacated Army installations such as Camp Kohler near Sacramento and emergency barracks at the Santa Ana airport. Trailers or converted Army barracks were used to house 4,000 returnees in Los Angeles. Three hundred trailers in Glendale accommodated others despite the objections of townspeople. The Federal Public Housing Authority, which followed a policy of equal opportunity for all races, opened war housing developments to Japanese on the same basis as to war workers.

This was a period of tremendous migration to the West Coast, the most rapid population increase up to this point in its history. War workers and other families were pouring into California, from Arkansas, Louisiana, Oklahoma, and Texas, and other states. In 1944 a total of 1,113,874 persons arrived, as compared with 60,000 American Japanese expected in 1945. Moreover, the greatest influx occurred in areas of the greatest prewar Japanese concentration which tripled their population. Los Angeles County in particular grew rapidly.

Even before the war, housing was short in Central Valley towns in California where now air bases, training camps, and war industries taxed the available supply. Sacramento increased 16 per cent in population in four years. The presence of DeWitt hospital personnel caused an acute housing shortage in Auburn. Much of the shelter that existed was bare minimum. Lobbyists for real estate and landlord interests were nevertheless putting forth great effort in opposing government emergency housing.

Some citizen groups and government officials were more concerned about avoiding the creation of slums than in meeting the emergency housing needs of returning evacuees. In San Pedro a group of eighty-seven property owners protested against allowing returnees to live at Lomita Airstrip.[2] Many cities condemned buildings which could house Japanese. For a time Salinas intended to tax the Buddhist church—traditionally untaxed property—because it was to be used as a hostel.

Racism, which was as much traditional as war-induced was reflected in long-standing real estate practices, was written into property deeds in the form of restrictive covenants, and was everywhere apparent in the ghetto sections of even the most otherwise enlightened communities. Minorities including the Japanese, acceding to custom, did not ordinarily even try to get accommodations in hotels catering to the Caucasian trade until desperation drove them to it. In 1943, a Nisei woman at Topaz had received permission to visit her husband who had been ill in the hospital in San Leandro since 1938. On arrival, she was denied the hotel reservations which she had made in advance. A young Nisei mother with a five-month-old baby arrived in Pasadena after an exhausting drive from the East Coast. They were turned down at every hotel where they asked for a room. The woman became so upset she was taken to Emergency Hospital for treatment. Police found her lodging for the night, after which she and her child went on to Claremont where they had relatives. A Chinese hotel owner on the West Coast, asked by curious or antagonistic people if some of his tenants were Japanese, put them off by answering, "Hell, no! They're Chinese."[3]

Persons of Japanese descent were rarely shown houses for sale in Caucasian areas, and there were cases in which completed sales transactions were invalidated despite veteran status and strong financial standing. "If homes are available in the coastal areas, segregation will keep us from them," Dave Tatsuno, the Nisei businessman wrote in January, 1945, in the daily newspaper put out by the University of California. He saw that not only his own but other minority groups were affected. "If we have our own homes in these crowded areas, other minority groups are occupying them. It is a matter of who will be without a home."[4] The labor shortage during the war had been providential for the Negro people, who often for the first time were able to move into apartments and rent homes they had never been able to consider before. The Fillmore district in San Francisco which had comprised the Japanese section was filled in 1945 by Negroes who had come to work in the shipyards. Most of the seven or eight thousand American Japanese who returned during the next ten years spread throughout the city. A very small section of the district became Japanese again.

Evacuees sometimes found the new conditions in their old neighborhoods difficult to adjust to. One Issei returning to Los Angeles—to new sounds, new people, and new music—felt that Japanese were "a minority within a minority."[5] Russian Jews had moved into Boyle Heights in Los Angeles, Mexican–Americans and other minorities into the section near the railroad station in Sacramento where Japanese had formerly lived.

Some Japanese sued to regain possession of their homes. There was little of the expected trouble with evictions. For one thing, few Japanese were home owners at the time, but had been renters themselves. For another, there seemed no widespread desire among those faced with eviction to stir up antagonism on the issue. NAACP leaders took steps to calm what tension there was and to bring people together for the reconciliation of problems that arose from conflict of interest. Practically no incidents of violence arose in the large cities in contrast to the farming areas; most of the rebuffs and discourtesies, too, occurred in the smaller towns. Chinese–Americans who might have been expected to harbor animosity toward the Japanese–Americans because of the war and the supposed traditional coolness between the two immigrant groups were more notable for their helpfulness to evacuees than perhaps any others. Like the NAACP, Chinese organizations also held meetings, made pleas for toleration, and gave aid on an individual basis.

While housing problems caused very little of conflict, bitter feeling among the Japanese was aroused when they returned home to find their personal property lost, scattered, stolen, or damaged. Sometimes missing and damaged belongings caused more unhappiness than the larger injustices. There had been a tremendous amount of vandalism. Home owners often found tenants had broken into basements or rooms where they had stored their things. "I don't know what happened," one Nisei woman says of her experience in returning to find someone she had regarded as a friend refusing to give back a refrigerator and furniture. "Maybe it was because he had a new wife who put pressure on him. Maybe he was confused."

Cars disappeared or were stripped. In one instance a farmer returned to find his very house had been taken and moved away! "It wasn't much of a house," says the person telling the incident, "but it was his home."

The WCCA under the Army had been quite late in taking responsibility for evacuee property during the period of movement to the centers. Records of belongings were lost at this time and things neglected, all of which had to be straightened out later, when possible, by the WRA which did a tremendous job processing thousands of items in nine government warehouses, itemizing, packing, safeguarding, and later sorting out and seeing that every kind of possession, large and small, got back to the evacuees. All in all, missing or unclaimed items under WRA control from the beginning amounted to very little.

Discrimination in employment was never such a problem on return, principally because of the sizable labor shortage that existed. When Gerda Isenberg harbored a young Japanese mother in her home, she received threatening telephone calls. Gradually the phone calls changed in nature, and Mrs. Isenberg began to receive requests for household help instead of threats. In the first year of her work with the Palo Alto Fair Play Committee eighty evacuee families were placed in homes and jobs. In Beverly Hills, Bel-Air, Westwood, and Santa Monica near Los Angeles, wealthy residents were happy that thirty skilled gardeners had come back.

Harry Kingman, regional director of the Fair Employment Practices Commission, declared that the question of employment of the Nisei was a "hot potato."[6] On the whole, though, they did not expect real trouble. Few white collar jobs were open, but demand for women domestic workers was heavy. Gardeners and farm laborers usually found work, although the market for migratory farm labor had been filled with Mexican workers and wages were unsatisfactory. Openings in factories were few for persons of Japanese descent.

The Department of Employment attempted to place people in the vocations for which they were trained. But, while doing menial jobs was hard for persons with special training and education for other occupations, because they had to support themselves and their families they could not wait for jobs in their field. Evacuees did a good deal of job hunting on their own. The WRA, which, unlike the Department of Employment, worked from multiple listings, encouraged returnees to find war work and not to accept employment at substandard rates.

A Nisei druggist says that he and most people he knew found their jobs through the American Friends Service Committee. George Tsukagawa, then a flower grower and today a prominent restaurateur, was helped by Mrs. Isenberg and Mrs. Duveneck, both Quakers. He, in turn, helped other returnees to find jobs during these months.

The Interracial Committee at the University of California at Berkeley conducted a job and housing survey to help returnees. They distributed 4,000 questionnaries. As a result of this, a number found housing, forty-five persons found employment as domestics, forty-eight found non-domestic jobs, and twenty students, part-time jobs. The Berkeley Coop was one of the first businesses to hire Nisei in jobs in which they met the public. In Los Angeles, Lucius Lomax, editor of the Negro–American weekly, *The Tribune*, advertised for a Nisei reporter, and in June hired twenty-three-year-old Hasaye Yamamoto, an evacuee girl who had been editor of the Poston paper. In Portland, after some months, returnees began to be seen working in the public library, in art museums, stores, and offices, and even as kindergarten teachers, although teaching was still a field hard to enter. As reports of their competence began to spread, things became a little easier.

A number of counties refused relief to returnees and resolutions were made in the California legislature demanding that the federal government relieve the states of financial responsibility for them. Local agencies were eventually persuaded, however, to accept returning evacuees. Many appeared on relief rolls who had never been there before, not only elderly indigents but several hundred Nisei. A spokesman for the Naturalization and Immigration Service relieved anxious Issei by advising the WRA that no resident aliens of Japanese ancestry would be deported because they accepted public assistance. Alien Japanese were not eligible for social security.

Most employable persons found jobs after a few months, although several Nisei, growing despondent over their inability to find employment or homes for their families, committed suicide. There were instances in which trained nurses, and sometimes physicians, were barred from practicing in hospitals.

In a few plants workers threatened to quit their jobs if persons of Japanese-descent were hired. In San Francisco sixty machinist members of AF of L Local 1305 stopped work at a municipal railway bus barn when a Nisei reported for work. The thirty-seven-year-old Nisei who had been certified by the Civil Service Commission, considered resigning to avoid trouble, but was persuaded by others not to give in. Mayor Roger Lapham and state senator Jack Shelley went to the repair barn and made a personal appeal to the protesting workers, and the impending strike was called off. In a similar situation, a Los Angeles Aluminum Company acceded to protests and discharged a Nisei they had hired. When longshoremen in Stockton refused to work with Nisei in defiance of the International Longshoremen's and Warehousemen's Union's racial policy, the local CIO unit was suspended by the parent organization in San Francisco after a union trial.

With the exception of the Teamsters, most unions were accepting. Nisei plumbers and electricians who had joined unions in the relocation period in other parts of the country transferred into local unions when they came west. In Hawaii, American Japanese had always been an important part of CIO unions, and in 1945 it was reported that not one AF of L union discriminated against persons of Japanese origin.

Before fish cannery operations started in August, 1945, Louis Martin, president of the Monterey Fish Cannery Workers Union, announced that some five hundred returnees who had been members of the union before evacuation were still in good standing. Not only were persons of Japanese ancestry welcomed back to their old jobs (there was only one incident of unpleasantness), but union people helped them find housing during the shortage. The Fisherman's Union took a similar position, although Navy and Coast Guard restrictions prohibited Americans of Japanese ancestry from waterfront fishing until October. The San Diego CIO Food, Tobacco and Agricultural Workers Union as well as fishing unions in that city went out of their way to demonstrate their receptivity to returned evacuees. In February, 1946, Americans of Japanese descent returned to the tuna industry when the clipper *Costa Rica* went to sea with a full crew of relocated fishermen.

The question of civil service reemployment on the West Coast had been left in doubt. In the rush and uncertainty of evacuation some city employees had neglected to go through the necessary procedures for insuring their continued eligibility on return. Thus, some lost their jobs by default, some by discriminatory practice, while others retained their old positions. In the matter of some two hundred state employees who had been suspended from their employment several weeks before evacuation, eighty had attempted to fight the suspension through their attorney, James Purcell. In April, 1946, Wilmer Morse, deputy attorney general of California and legal representative of the Personnel Board, announced that charges of dual citizenship against them would be dropped. Those who had not defended themselves, however, failed to be reinstated. The United States Civil Service Commission gave assurances as early as 1943 that it would reemploy the evacuee group. Mich Kunitani, who had worked for the State Department of Employment, which became a federal agency in 1942 so that he was not affected by the state firings, was personally invited to come back to his old position.

Many persons of Japanese descent ran into trouble when they attempted to reenter or start businesses on the Coast. The power to grant or withhold licenses was an especially potent weapon in the hands of those who chose to discriminate. The city of Portland refused to issue any sort of business license to a Japanese national. Issei, unlike other alien enemies, found themselves extensively investigated by real estate boards on requesting licenses as agents for selling and renting property.

At a meeting in June, 1945, the California State Board of Equalization, which had the authority to issue or deny sales tax permits necessary to conduct retail business, established a policy of requiring that persons of Japanese descent procure written recommendation from the United States Navy or Army that they ought to engage in the businesses requiring such licenses. Hearing of this, spokesmen for both the Army and Navy stated they had no interest or authority to make any such recommendations, although the Army did clear all evacuees before they returned to the Coast. Further, the deputy attorney general advised the board that it had no such discretionary powers. The board then stated it would resort to delaying tactics for the purpose of discouraging returnees from staying in California and let the courts decide the issue. Ordinarily the securing of a permit was a routine matter on payment of a dollar fee.

In September, a Los Angeles optometrist, Kenzo Sugino, an Issei, with the aid of ACLU and Catholic Interracial Council attorneys, filed a petition for a writ of mandate in the Superior Court in order to get the necessary permit from the Board of Equalization for selling glasses and lenses. State Attorney General Robert Kenny declined to defend the Board in its position. In October, policy was changed before the mandate hearing, and licenses were granted Sugino and fifteen other Issei.

Small businessmen experienced great difficulty reentering their occupations. Few commercial sites were available to them. Many resettlers were depleted financially. Countless persons had been compelled to forfeit their insurance policies and mortage payments because they could not pay premiums out of the $12 to $19 a month they received in their camp employment. Loans were hard to secure chiefly because returnees now seemed a poor risk.

A woman evacuee at the Rohwer camp, anticipating the opening of the Coast, had applied early in 1944 to the Reconstruction Finance Corporation for a substantial loan for her greenhouse business in Orange County. She received no answer. Finally the WRA looked into the situation. After a lengthy delay, the RFC approved the loan in August, 1945, thus setting an important precedent for further loans.

When Yasuo William Abiko, publisher of the *Nichibei Times*, returned to San Francisco around the first of January, 1946, after being confined at Topaz and relocated in Philadelphia, he discovered all his printing equipment had been lost. His records had been chewed by rats; so he threw them away. After finding type in Sacramento and Fresno in garages, basements, and left over from extinct newspapers, he resumed publishing in May. Later he got new type from Japan. In Los Angeles, the *Rafu Shimpo* had resumed publication in December, 1945.

Despite the obstacles, scores of Issei and Nisei were beginning new businesses or reestablishing old ones. One man who had nine children and had always been poor had managed to save money during his stay at Tule Lake with which he started a small express company on his return. Restaurants, small drygoods stores, and repair shops began to appear. In Los Angeles, two Issei, Kyuji Hozaki and his wife, reopened their barber shop. "Business is good," they reported. "All our old customers have come back. People drop in to say, 'hello.' "[7] In the same city Nisei flower growers managed to raise $100,000 toward building a new wholesale market.

Legal obstacles due to misunderstandings and disagreements over contracts which had been made hurriedly in 1942 were numerous on return. Some of these questions were cleared up by the California Supreme Court decision in *Stockton Theatres* vs. *Palermo*. The right of a returning Issei to operate a theater he had built on leased commercial property in Stockton was challenged in the lower courts by the lessor who had been hired to run the business from 1936 through the evacuation period. On return of the Issei to the West Coast in 1944, the lessor had served him with a demand to vacate the premises. Losing in the lower court, the lessor appealed to the California Superior Court saying that the leasing contract was in violation of the California Alien Land Law. The Superior Court agreed, which meant that land restrictions under the Alien Land Law could be extended to include commercial and residential use. The California Supreme Court, however, reversed the decision, upholding the Issei, thus insuring the right of enforcement of such contract obligations for all returning Japanese nationals.

Owners of businesses or farm property who had not sold on evacuation were generally in a stronger position and had more motivation for leaving camp and returning to the Coast. "If you have property, you have roots," said George Tsukagawa, whose family had paid off the mortgage on their farm in 1941. Those who put their family business in escrow had protection in the law.

Some of these properties were managed well. A Palo Alto man who had a cleaning business was relieved to find it in better condition than when he had left it. The many cases of mismanagement were often the result of inexperience. A Mountain View chrysanthemum grower left unique strains in what he thought were expert hands and returned to find that they had all died. A San Jose orchardist, who had two pieces of property in different locations found one of the managers had done such a good job he only had to take up where he left off, but he lost a great deal of money on the other piece.

It has been estimated that at least one-third of American Japanese truck farmers were ruined by relocation—their farms run down or foreclosed, their machinery stolen, rusted, or seized for debts. Sometimes the agents entrusted with property, whether bankers, lawyers, respectable business men or mere speculators were reluctant to let go of the profitable enterprises they were engaged in on a temporary contract basis or verbal agreement. It was easy to take advantage of legal technicalities or to renege on verbal agreements. When five hundred persons joined the Japanese Exclusion League in Washington, they were told that the ten-dollar membership would be well worth their while. This was meant quite literally.

The Issei in particular were victims of nefarious practices. A lawyer solicited $7,000 from a frightened little woman on the grounds of "saving" her from deportation when she had already been aided by another lawyer. She refused to fight. An evacuee drug-store owner from Los

Angeles was visited in his relocation center by a prominent localite who offered to help him sell some of his property. The evacuee was grateful for the offer and agreed. The man made a second visit and told him he had found that all the evacuee's furniture and possessions had been stolen. He had a suspect in mind, but claimed he needed power of attorney before he could act. This was given him. The evacuee received no accounting of proceeds of any sales. In 1944 the WRA made a thorough investigation and, believing it had ample evidence the man was guilty of misappropriation and misrepresentation and had acted similarly with other evacuees, presented the assembled facts to the Los Angeles district attorney's office to be told that this office was not interested in filing charges.[8]

Two men representing themselves as FBI and secret service agents offering protection from molestation were convicted of swindling at least sixty-five Japanese in Phoenix, Arizona. They were caught when they tried to extort $250 from a farm family, promising to eliminate by death if necessary two Japanese "stool pigeons" who they said were responsible for causing the internment of others and were after the father of the family. A bank teller was indicted on nine counts of embezzling over $800 from evacuees' accounts. A Nisei returned to his home in a farming community was bilked of several thousand dollars by an attorney who told him he would help him reestablish himself in the seed business.

An early poll by the *Bee* showed Sacramento attorneys quite loath to give low-cost legal aid to American Japanese. Eventually, however, the WRA and the California Bar Association found more than eight hundred lawyers who would defend the rights of returned evacuees for minimal fees. In the over-all picture of farms and business properties, well over 50 per cent of American Japanese assets were lost in one way or another, amounting to many millions of dollars.

The closing of the world renowned and much loved Japanese Tea Garden in San Francisco's Golden Gate Park at the time of evacuation meant a great loss not only to the Hagiwara family who had cared for it for many years but to the public as well. Baron Makato Hagiwara, who had emigrated from Japan in the eighteen-seventies and had done landscaping and gardening for a number of San Francisco families, had designed and built the garden at the request of John McLaren, superintendent of the park. Makato Hagiwara had learned landscaping as a boy while watching the gardeners work on his father's estate. Not only was the garden of exquisite beauty, but it held many priceless objects of art which had come from Japan. Three generations of the Hagiwara family had cared for it primarily as a labor of love and as a gift to the city, built their home on it, and lived on the small proceeds from the tea house which they also ran, paying the city a monthly rate for the concession. One of the family, Mrs. Yamamoto, still today a San Francisco resident, baked the fortune cookies which they introduced to this country.

Three days before the evacuation deadline late in May, when it was known they were leaving, the city Park Commission served them with an eviction notice. When the five members of the Hagiwara clan evacuated, they left two large bronze lanterns and a large bronze eagle in order that the appearance of the shrine sitting by the *tori* gate would not be marred. They also left a large wooden Buddha and, on request of the park authorities, fifty potted plants so the garden would not look too bare. They removed some thirty-seven small loads of garden materials, shrubs, and dwarf trees and stored them in Mill Valley, where almost all of the plants perished during their absence from lack of water and care. Many of the art objects which they stored were also lost. Rare porcelains were broken in being moved.

After rescission, George Hagiwara and his family, finding out through an intermediary that there was no chance of returning to the garden (renamed Oriental Gardens during their absence), settled in Oregon for a time. Eight or nine years after legal action was started in 1948, a government evacuation claims settlement awarded them approximately 10 per cent of a $250,000 claim, which was the evaluation of their assets made in 1941 by the Alien Property Custodian. Carrying on further litigation would have been too costly and time consuming. After working in the motor pool for subsistence wages at the Topaz center, Mr. Hagiwara was faced with the more immediate necessity of making a living.

In the year after rescission numbers of evacuees remaining in the camps were slow or reluctant to venture home. In January, 1945, Dillon Myer had announced that all centers except the segregation camp at Tule Lake would be closed by January of the following year. "In all cases," he said, "a three-month notice of closing will be given."[9] In March a White House message to Congress asked for $25,140,000 (about one half the usual WRA appropriation), part of which was to be used for the operation of an emergency refugee shelter in New York and transportation and subsistence grants for relocatees. In May, 1945, the center schools prepared to close permanently. Various agricultural and group projects were shut down. Farm equipment at various centers was put on public sale in April.

In the same month the news of President Franklin Roosevelt's death shocked the nation. Among the many Nisei liberals who had admired and trusted the late President was Larry Tajiri, who wrote a front page editorial in the *Pacific Citizen*, recalling the great things Roosevelt had done for the underprivileged and then going on to describe him as a man who did not recognize limitations fixed by race, color, or creed. Saburo Kido, president of the JACL, sent a telegram to President Truman pledging the support of Americans of Japanese ancestry "in the unfinished business of victory and peace."[10]

Many of those still remaining in camps, particularly the elderly, were deterred from leaving by an extremely negative impression of community sentiment awaiting them. In their isolation, entirely dependent upon newspapers or reports of acquaintances, they had no way of testing the reality outside. In the centers they at least had the necessities—three meals a day, a place to lay their heads at night. A common question asked of one Topaz adviser was, "The government can't put us out, can they?"[11]

The Heart Mountain Community Council, composed predominantly of Issei, accused the WRA of getting them to leave "not by force" but by a "gradual process" of depriving them of essential services for living. An editorial in the center newspaper, however, said this was incorrect, that facilities were reduced as the population shrank.[12] A group of sixteen Issei community leaders at Minidoka, termed "not extremists" in a WRA publication, drew up a similar statement of objection and presented it to the Spanish consul for submission to the United States and Japanese governments.[13] Though at first embittered by the WRA euphemism "war duration homes" many Issei were now angry because the promise was not being kept.

The Pacific Coast Committee, social workers, and others pleaded with the WRA and with their congressmen not to close the camps so rapidly or to make the drastic cuts in allocations. A New York City conference on evacuee problems requested President Truman to provide funds for the Interior Department to complete the task on the Coast "if it is impossible to prevent the suicide of the WRA."[14] The Negro novelist, Richard Wright, asked for continued federal help for the Japanese; a government which could force migration of a whole section of the population should not then wash its hands of further responsibility.

Though few congressmen took notice, Dillon Myer and other WRA officials were sympathetic. Myer told evacuee audiences, "I have been asked many times . . . why we announced the policy to close relocation centers by next January. We didn't announce that because we were mad at you . . . I felt badly about some of you older folks and I realize you have your problems. . . ."[15] But the WRA believed the perpetuation of the camps was unhealthy. Evacuees should find their places in society as rapidly as possible before apathy set in.

Poston and Gila Rivers were to be closed down by October 1, 1945, Granada by October 15. The camp at Rohwer was scheduled to close on December 15. In June, Myer predicted that 24,000 evacuees would return in the final movement then getting underway.

A quota system was devised to force out evacuees who did not make their own plans for resettlement. The WRA announced: "In each case the resident shall be informed that he must choose a departure date. The Project Director shall follow through to see that each resident leaves on scheduled date of departure. If any resident shall refuse to arrange for packing of personal effects, arrangements for the packing to insure his leaving according to schedule shall be made for him. If the resident shall have refused to select a destination for relocation, transportation shall be arranged to his place of legal residence. . . ."[16] A few last-ditch resisters refused to pack and missed trains out.

The original formula for relocation, in which the individuals and the communities of their destination were checked before they were allowed to leave, was abandoned. Blocks of people were sent out en masse, without any check on particular prospects. Paternalism rather abruptly changed into *laissez faire*.

Active West Coast opposition to Americans of Japanese descent began to taper off in April, 1945, and showed signs of disappearing entirely by August. Mayor Fletcher Bowron of Los Angeles publicly recanted his former anti-Japanese position. A great many Caucasians went privately to their former Japanese friends and apologized for attitudes they had taken. As fighting men returned, numerous veterans groups— units of the Legion and of the Veterans of Foreign Wars as well as the new liberal organization, the American Veterans Committee—began to take aggressive stands in behalf of the Nisei. Yet on the Sunday before the United Nations Conference met at San Francisco to draw up a charter night raiders fired into the home of an American Japanese family.

Later some of the United Nation delegates objected to San Francisco as a permanent site for the organization because of the outbursts on the Coast. A number of newspapers editorialized that we could hardly expect to get along with the people of other shades in distant countries if we could not get along with different races here.

The UN Conference met from April to June. On May 8 Germany surrendered, and the war in Europe was over. President Truman signed the charter of the United Nations, which pledged respect for human rights and for fundamental freedoms for all "without distinction as to race, sex, language or religion."[17] As the charter came into being, Hiram Johnson, the promulgator of many progressive reforms, who yet opposed the League of Nations, the United Nations, and the Japanese in California, lay dying. He had served five terms in the Senate.

The war was being escalated in Japan. In March, 1945, the first night bombings on Tokyo and Yokohama took place. In a single bombing raid on Tokyo almost 125,000 civilians died, were wounded, or burned. On August 6 when the first atomic bomb was dropped on the city of Hiroshima, 20,000 people living within a radius of approximately 1,600 feet in what is known as the Atomic Dome disappeared. On August 9 the "Fat Man," an implosion bomb of plutonium, devastated Nagasaki, killing 40,000 residents and wounding 60,000. The two cities and their inhabitants were almost completely annihilated.

The military in Japan continued the war after the atomic bombings, against appeals to reason, until Emperor Hirohito, abandoning his purely ceremonial role, asked for peace. " . . . the time has come," he said, "when we must bear the unbearable."[18]

The news of the bombings came as a shock to those remaining in the relocation centers. One-third of Tule Lake segregees either were natives of Hiroshima prefecture or had relatives there. For a long time it was impossible for evacuees to communicate with surviving Hiroshima relatives or to get any personal news. The destruction of Hiroshima caused greater psychological disturbance at Tule Lake than Japan's offer to surrender. In fact, according to the project director, Raymond Best, the first reaction to surrender was one of relief. Nevertheless, a great many Issei who had clung to the myth of an invincible, all-protecting fatherland, refused to believe Japan had lost, even when they understood English and heard the news on the radio.

On V-J day, August 15, California's Attorney General Robert Kenny happened to have a trip scheduled to the Fresno area to visit evacuees who had received threats. He found it moving on that day to go to these homes where returnees were listening to the announcement.

Leslie Nakashima, a Nisei who had been a member of the United Press staff in Tokyo and was marooned there during the war, was the first reporter to describe the destruction of Hiroshima for American newspapers. Not interned, but kept under surveillance, he did translation work for the Domei News Agency. Going to the ill-fated city of 300,000 inhabitants to try to find out what had become of his mother, he discovered that she was one of the more fortunate ones. On that day she had been weeding the garden of a relative two miles southeast of the city. Seeing the tremendous flash of light which some have described as brighter than many suns, she threw herself face down. Afterwards she ran as fast as she could away from the city.

Later, Nisei soldiers in the occupation army tried to find what had happened to their mothers or fathers or other relatives. Second Lieutenant Harry Fukuhara of Chicago found his mother and her three brothers living in a neighboring area. She had seen the flash light up the sky and felt the terrific impact. All had scrambled for shelter. When they came out, "People by the thousands were walking and staggering along the streets and practically all were covered with blood." A Long Beach soldier, a technical sergeant, was among the many who could not locate his family in the ruins.

One of the chief characters in John Hersey's *Hiroshima* was Kiyoshi Tanimoto, the pastor of the Hiroshima Methodist church. In the book, Hersey describes what happened to him and to a number of people on the fateful day in August—how he threw himself between two big rocks in his garden at the time of the blast, how he wandered about afterwards trying as best he could to give aid to the myriads of injured whose skin slipped off their bodies, who vomited in the streets, how he had not been able to understand the clouds of smoke rising from the streets when there seemed to have been no bomb, or why the sky turned dark, why drops of moisture were falling on a hot day in August, why the fires started when no one had heard any planes.

Mr. Tanimoto had lived in the United States. He had studied at Emory University in Atlanta, Georgia, graduating in 1940. Hersey described him as a small man, quick to talk, laugh, and cry. He wore his black hair rather long, and he had an old-young look, boyish and yet wise. Just before the war and before returning from the United States to Hiroshima, he had served in the Hollywood Independent church, which was turned into a hostel in the return period. (The grandson of another former minister, Dr. Edwin Ryland, had been killed in the war by a Japanese zero pilot. Returnees asked Dr. Ryland, "Don't you hate?" He said, "No. Both were victims of the war.") As a way of expressing thanks for the hostel, the American Japanese gave a party for Hunter's congregation, presenting them with $100. After debating what to do with it, they wrote to Tanimoto requesting a piece of wood scarred by the atomic blast. A Japanese girl delivered a slab of wood from a camphor tree which was made into a cross, a symbol of reconciliation, and Tanimoto, sponsored on a trip to the United States by Norman Cousins, installed it. Kagawa, the pacifist Christian, also visited briefly once more.

During the American military occupation of Japan, the special skills of Nisei soldiers from the MIS were put to use. While there had been and remained a great deal of sentiment against Nisei and Kibei with their strange American ways choosing to live in Japan, and competing for the food supply, there was a fairly general acceptance of Nisei as well as Caucasian occupation troops.

Other Nisei "strandees," had been caught in Japan at the outbreak of war and forced to remain for the duration because they were unable to get transportation home. Few Nisei in Japan had been able to get on the exchange ships that went between the two warring countries. Some had been on the last boat which left Yokahama bound for San Francisco and had to turn back because of the war threat in November, 1941. Among the strandees were children taken by Issei parents to Japan, students sent to get part of their education there, and white collar workers and professional people who had been unable to find employment opportunities in line with their training on the West Coast and had taken what they often considered to be temporary employment with companies in Japan.

During the war some of the strandees were interned; most were allowed freedom to live and work in the community, though often under surveillance. One young man supported his family by playing violin in a movie house. A number were forced into military service. Those who fought the draft were ostracized or punished. Nisei living in the country villages rather than the cities were left pretty much alone, according to Mrs. Eiichi Sakuye who was among those caught in Japan while on a temporary visit to see her parents. Her brother was serving in the American Army. She and others were able to receive letters through the American Red Cross.

The use of English was prohibited during the war, but many Nisei met secretly and spoke it. A Los Angeles born Nisei recalls a time when a group spent the greater part of an evening talking about cokes, chocolate malts, and American foods. As before the war, many were ridiculed for their American ways.

A few did translating and other work for the government, among them the Nisei woman known as Tokyo Rose, who worked as a disk jockey playing American popular music and broadcasting insinuating propaganda aimed at demoralizing American troops in the Pacific theater. Actually, there were a number of women who conducted the record programs under this pseudonym, and it is quite possible that the young woman convicted in the United States after the war did not broadcast propaganda.

A number of strandees as well as repatriates were killed in the air raids on the cities. After the war some strandees taught English to Japanese, some did liaison work for the occupation agencies. Hundreds of others, mainly students, besieged General MacArthur's headquarters for permission to return to their homes in the United States. After hearings, it was promised that many would be permitted to return if they had no record of collaboration with the enemy.

By the middle of December, all the relocation camps except Tule Lake were closed, two weeks ahead of Myer's prediction. The WRA dissolved on June 30, 1946. The director of the WRA took pride in the early demise of his agency. He had reversed Parkinson's Law, "Work expands so as to fill the time available for its completion."[19]

In the spring of 1945, only 1,500 or so evacuees had ventured to return to the Coast out of 55,000 cleared for return; 40,000 were residing in other states. By August 5,000 were reestablished on the Coast, representing 5 per cent of the American Japanese population. By January, 1946, 50 per cent were back, and another 25 per cent were expected to come gradually from the Midwest and the East.

Canada was even more harsh in its dealings with its Japanese than was the United States. "In all, the Japanese evacuees in the United States should consider themselves fortunate by comparison," commented the Fresno *Bee*.[20] At the beginning of the war the Canadian government, after evacuating Japanese residents of British Columbia, sold their property at public auction, the liquidation carried out regardless of citizenship status.

In a work camp, the men, housed separately from their women-folk, were refused visitation rights.

In British Columbia Nisei, though they were citizens, were not allowed to vote, nor were Chinese–Canadians. When the Nisei were evacuated they were not allowed to vote in federal elections nor to serve in the army until the war was almost over. Some soldiers in basic training in Ontario voted for the first time in 1945. After Nisei were finally accepted in the Canadian army, W. L. McKenzie King, liberal Prime Minister from British Columbia, maintained a censorship policy which included a directive to the Canadian press not to release news of Nisei activities in the war. The intention of the Canadian government in its evacuation program and property seizure was permanent rather than temporary relocation east of the Rockies.

Four months after V-J Day, no Canadian civilians of Japanese ancestry had yet been permitted to return to British Columbia. In November, servicemen in the Canadian military intelligence were allowed to return, but a United States Nisei football star from Seattle was refused permission by the provincial government to go with his high school team to Victoria for a game.

Travel bans to British Columbia were not lifted for Canadian Japanese until April, 1946, and then just for veterans. In 1947 Canada still restricted the movement of Japanese. Compulsory deportation orders were finally officially revoked; however, 4,000 persons had felt the chill and left the country voluntarily.

The pattern in Latin America in relation to its Japanese residents varied. At the time of the Gentlemen's Agreement in the United States and after the passage of our 1924 exclusion law, Japanese immigration was diverted to Latin American countries. In Brazil, definite colonies of Japanese capitalists as well as laborers arrived for permanent settlement, bringing wealth and industry into the country. Brazil, like Mexico, took security measures against Germans, Italians, and Japanese alike. Enemy aliens had to have travel permits and were guarded in certain areas of large concentration. Those considered dangerous were interned. The story is told that Japanese fanatically devoted to the mother country hid out in the jungles of Brazil, refusing for some time after the war was over to believe that Japan had been defeated. Today Japanese are extremely well integrated in Brazil, a country notable for its lack of racial distinctions; many Brazilian Japanese are prominent in government. In Mexico, the Japanese border community was moved to the interior, and camps were set up.

Japanese had entered Peru early in the century as indentured labor to work on cotton plantations. They saved their money, established cafés, barber shops, and stores. Some became wealthy. United States anti-Japanese legislation was copied in Peru. Peruvians charged the Japanese with unfair competition. There was much economic jealousy. Anti-Japanese riots occurred in May, 1940, after the Peruvian wife of a Japanese alien reported that her husband was being deported to Japan against his will and named the ship on which he had been placed. Forty Japanese shops were damaged or destroyed in the riots, and the Peruvian government later paid for losses.

There was no sabotage or espionage by Peruvian Japanese, according to a man who was sent by the United States to Peru in 1942 to investigate those living in the strategic coastal area who were regarded as a potential danger. In a joint action by the American Justice Department and the Peruvian government, approximately eight hundred Japanese were arrested and sent to the United States.

Some of those seized were proprietors of cheap hotels in Lima and Callao, forty-three of which had been closed by sanitary authorities just previous to the arrests. Placed on the U.S. transports guarded by U.S. warships, they were sent to temporary internment camps in Panama, then transferred to Justice Department camps at Crystal City, Texas, and Missoula, Montana, and later to Santa Fe, New Mexico. Eventually about 1,800 were removed. These imprisonments were almost completely unknown to the general public.

According to a Caucasian observer in Peru at the time, during the whole program the Japanese were "pretty cowed." Some of the more affluent made efforts to get off the list and remain in Peru. One of the men seized later related how on April 24, 1944, agents of the Peruvian secret police took him to the station where he was held incommunicado. Then he and four others were taken to an aerodrome and delivered into the custody of the United States military police and forced aboard a military plane.

The families of the imprisoned men were "invited" to become voluntary internees of the United States, and many did. Some of these wives were Spanish or of mixed Spanish–Indian inheritance. All had Spanish-speaking children. In the camps the children, 145 in all, attended American schools, and soon they all were speaking English.

After the spokesman for the Chief Alien Enemy Control Section declared that none of these Peruvian Japanese could be regarded as dangerous enemy aliens, the Justice Department no longer wished to detain them. They were scheduled for deportation—on the grounds that they had violated our immigration laws, because they lacked the proper admission credentials. Peru did not want them back; so they were to be deported to Japan.

The Peruvian government had confiscated the property of all Japanese nationals, and many of the Peruvian citizens of Japanese descent had been forced by the government to liquidate their property. Some of the impoverished Peruvian Japanese wanted to remain in the United States. During the deportation crisis, many of them were sent with their families to Seabrook, New Jersey, where they worked in the frozen food packing plants and attended classes. Eventually, after extensive negotiations with the Peruvian government, a good number did return to Peru.

SIXTEEN · DEMOCRACY BEGINS TO CORRECT ITS OWN MISTAKES

''NO AMERICAN WILL CLAIM that democratic processes work perfectly or that there have not been errors of judgment. If the indiscriminate evacuation of Japanese from the West Coast was such an error in judgment, every American will be proud that democracy, in the midst of an all-out war, can begin to rectify its own mistakes."[1] Larry Tajiri, then editor of the *Pacific Citizen*, wrote these prophetic words early in 1943 when most of the people he spoke for were still interned. At that time the government's policy of paroling evacuees from the centers to the armed forces and to communities outside the Western Defense Command might have been regarded as a first step toward the restoration of the rights of citizens.

By a long, slow process in the twenty-five years since the end of the war, discriminatory laws have been abolished, and the shocking material losses suffered by the American Japanese during the evacuation have been at least acknowledged by acts of restitution. These changes were brought about, moreover, largely through aggressive action by leaders within the minority in the courts, the state legislatures, and the Congress. The victories of this quarter of a century of unrelenting effort, while they represent only a token atonement for wrongs inflicted, are a significant vindication for democracy in that the victims themselves achieved a measure of justice working through the established institutions of the country and by so doing contributed to the reversal of public opinion, silencing even the Tenneys, the Gannons, and the Lechners.

The abolishment of discriminatory laws has gone beyond the evacuation period to correct the restrictions that hampered the first generation though the reforms often came too late, for most of the Issei have died. Some are living to benefit from a freedom of opportunity undreamed of in the early years of the century, undreamed of particularly in the bitter postwar era when people leaving the camps found their livelihood threatened by boycott or legislative enactment, their right to own property challenged and the property itself in jeopardy. While the discriminatory action was most virulent in California, other states enacted or reactivated existing restrictions, most often in the form of anti-alien land laws. Sixteen western states had these laws. A number were introduced during the war, notably in Utah and Arkansas where relocation centers were located. As noted earlier, Colorado voters defeated a ballot measure aimed at preventing noncitizen Japanese from owning land.

The three West Coast states responded to the rescission orders by tightening or enforcing existing alien land laws. The Oregon law was amended in March of 1945 to make it more stringent, more discriminatory, though in the same month a Portland judge issued the first court order directing a Causasian to return to a Nisei lands leased during the evacuation period.[2] The March, 1945, amendment prevented Japanese aliens from living on or using land purchased in the name of a citizen relative. In November, 1946, through a ballot measure, California voters gave their approval to a program that had been underway even before the evacuation. Though between 1913 and 1941, the state alien land law had become a "paper dragon" with only a score of attempts at enforcement by escheat, after the outbreak of war, Earl Warren as state attorney general had undertaken a program to remove Japanese farmers from the vicinity of important military installations by activating prosecutions,[3] and had also used the issue, as noted earlier, in his campaign for the governorship.

His successor as attorney general, Robert Kenny, in his words, "inherited" a number of these escheatment proceedings. Though he seems not to have been enthusiastic about initiating actions against the absent Japanese (he expressed a nonpunitive attitude in a 1943 ruling that the evacuees were entitled to the customary $100 householder's exemption on property tax and in 1946 urged repeal of the Alien Land Law), he was constantly reminded of his duty to carry out the law by persons who stood to profit from the forced sale of Japanese-owned land acting through local district attorneys. A special state investigator arrived in Placer County at the time of the Doi dynamiting case to study reports on 183 parcels of land, including Doi's, which were registered in the name of people of Japanese ancestry. The prize was tempting: the county's wartime fruit and nut yield had been extremely profitable. But the investigation did not result in extensive escheat actions. In 1940, 5,135 farms valued at approximately $66 million were owned by American Japanese in California. With the wartime increases in the value of land and crops, this was a windfall awaiting those who could prove that the deeds were illegal. "One of the biggest land grabs in history is on in California," Larry Tajiri wrote early in 1946, "and the Great Golden State, now one of the richest, proudest and most populous in the nation, is in the uncomfortable position of being the grabber."[4]

Robert Kenny had warned that litigation would prove costly, but the California legislature appropriated $200,000 to prosecute escheat actions and passed a bill that would allow the costs to be subtracted from the proceeds of sales on the acquired property. At least forty cases were filed by the end of 1945, indicating a policy that the Nisei called "legal intimidation . . . an attempt to prevent the return of the evacuee farmers to the State's agricultural industry."[5] Larry Tajiri warned, "Virtually all real property owned by Japanese–Americans in the State is under investigation."[6] Businesses and leased property, as well as farms, were being examined.

The size and value of the lands varied enormously. One of the richest properties seized was a 3,000-acre section of a ranch near Dos Palos in the San Joaquin Valley, planted in rice, grain, and cotton. The owner, Keisaburo Koda, had started his immigrant life in America as a laborer on the railroad, a sardine fisherman, and an oil driller. In 1927 he bought some apparently worthless alkali flats from which he developed the largest rice-growing, milling, and packaging operation in the state. During the evacuation period he entrusted the mill, the machinery, and most of the land to a group of managers who had power of attorney and who disposed of all but 987 acres for their own profit. After an escheatment action, the land was sold in May, 1943. From the sale price, $100,000 was to go to the state of California, "but no share of the proceeds may be paid to any alien stockholder."[7] The $100,000 was returned to him by the state after the war, but Koda, who claimed a loss of $2.4 million, died before the government finally recompensed his family in 1965 for his other losses.

A deputy sheriff bought five acres of agricultural land confiscated from a farmer near Stockton for $3,500. A couple who owned 117 acres in San Diego County did not contest the suit brought against their ownership in 1944 when they were in Poston. Instead, they applied for repatriation and were sent to Japan in November, 1945. Six months later their property was auctioned and sold for $44,000. Many escheat actions were uncontested, the defendants being confined in relocation centers and without funds. Another case involved forty acres held in an agreement with a county by two Nisei serving in the Army. The local district attorney ruled that their father had no rights in managing the property on his return, though he did not have to forfeit it. He had requested permission to plow up alfalfa and plant his own crops.[8] In all, seventy-nine escheat proceedings were instituted after Pearl Harbor.

After the evacuees returned to the West Coast, the JACL decided to fight back. In December, 1945, the organization's legal defense committee met in Stockton to undertake a program to "defend their property rights in current land seizure proceedings by the State of California."[9] ACLU attorneys, continuing the advocacy of the evacuation period, represented the defendants in some of the cases. It was a long battle. After seven years of litigation the Alien Land Law was declared unconstitutional, not by the United States Supreme Court, but by the State Supreme Court.

It was first tested in the Oyama case, concerning land in San Diego County held in the name of a Nisei, Fred Oyama. In October, 1945, when the Los Angeles County Superior Court ruled against him, James Purcell, the San Francisco attorney, filed a brief for the JACL, and in a memorandum the ACLU declared, "It may be said without exaggeration, that the entire nation is entitled to know as soon as may be, whether the legislation which the anti-Japanese race baiting groups of California were successful in writing upon the statute books of California will stand up in the crucible of today's constitutional fires. . . ."[10]

The Supreme Court did not meet the challenge. The 1948 decision in the Oyama case was an evasion of the central issue of the constitutionality of the California Alien Land Law, the more remarkable because, unlike the Court's upholding of the constitutionality of the evacuation, the question of possible racial discrimination was not complicated by considerations of war and national defense. The Court ruled in favor of Oyama, but on the special grounds that an alien can make gifts of real estate to citizen children if they are for the benefit of the children. The alien owner was required to prove that his purchase in a citizen's name was not made to evade the law. Justice Frank Murphy objected to the way in which the Court sidestepped the issue. "He came out fighting," in the words of John P. Roche.[11]

The forty-year-old discriminatory *tochi-ho*, as the Issei called it, was reversed four years later by the California Supreme Court in the Fujii case with Chief Justice Phil S. Gibson presiding. Sei Fujii, an important figure in Los Angeles' Little Tokyo, had first arrived in the United States in 1903 at the age of twenty-one, had been at one time president of the Japanese Association, and had started a newspaper, the *Kashu Mainichi*, in 1933. He had acquired the property on which his right of ownership was questioned in 1948. On April 24, 1950, in *Sei Fujii* vs. *State of California*, a district court of appeals decided that the Alien Land Law was unenforceable under the United Nations Charter. The State Supreme Court struck it down in 1952 when Gibson concluded that it was "obviously designed and administered as an instrument for effectuating racial discrimination and the most searching examination discloses no circumstances justifying a classification on that basis."[12] The Oregon Alien Land Law was declared unconstitutional in 1948 by the State Supreme Court as the final outcome of the Namba case involving land leased to a Nisei and his alien father. The appeal for the plaintiffs cited Justice Murphy's opinion in the Oyama case that alien land laws were designed to effectuate a purely racial discrimination and concluded,

"Our country cannot afford to create, by legislation or judicial construction, a ghetto for our ineligible aliens."[13]

After the Issei were allowed to become naturalized in 1952, alien land laws in other states were of less significance since by becoming a citizen a Japanese could own land. In Washington, an alien who would file first papers could acquire property. Washington did not repeal its law until 1966. Overcoming a powerful real estate lobby, on the third presentation as a ballot measure, voters defeated the law by the hardly overwhelming majority of 413,996 to 391,216. Secure in his right of ownership, Uhachi Tamesa, a retired farmer and orchardist in his eighties, celebrated the victory by selling his land near Seattle and donating $10,000 to the JACL.[14]

Another long battle was concluded with the Takahashi fishing case decision in 1948 by the United States Supreme Court. Until evacuation the Japanese Association and the JACL had been able to block what they termed "nuisance bills" by the California state legislature against alien fishing rights, though the Dies Committee had accused the JACL of "supreme loyalty to Japan" for opposing a 1939 measure "designed to curb the espionage activities of alien fishermen."[15] With Japanese–American lobbyists out of the way, two measures denying aliens ineligible for citizenship the right to obtain commercial fishing licenses were passed in 1943 and 1945. The Supreme Court considered the question of whether these laws could be used to deprive a man of the chance to earn a living by his acquired skills. His attorneys insisted that the plaintiff, Takahashi, had no other occupation than that of commercial fishing and had tried but was unable to secure other employment. The Fish and Game Commission insisted that the denial was a proper conservation measure which would help maintain a balance of fish!

The Court did not equivocate as in the *Oyama* decision, but struck at the heart of the question. Justice Black said that denying citizenship to a class of aliens was not necessarily illegal, but denying aliens the right to earn a living *was* illegal. Justice Murphy was more vigorous in denouncing the motivation of race prejudice. "Legislation of that type is not entitled to wear the cloak of constitutionality," he said. Only Justices Reed and Jackson dissented from the majority decision which ended for all time this particular form of discrimination.

Though it was a victory of principle, the prewar Japanese fishing industry was severely dislocated by the evacuation, both because it had been a predominantly Issei occupation and the Nisei did not return to it in large numbers and because of the severe material losses in boats, nets, and equipment. In 1947 it was estimated that about one-tenth of the 550 prewar American Japanese fishermen in Southern California, where they had been concentrated, had reentered the industry and less than half of the Issei were prepared to return to it even if permitted by law.[16] They were too old or had lost too much to begin again.

A witness before a claims hearing said of the evacuation that it "was the first time in American history that any people have been asked to voluntarily bankrupt themselves and go to jail for national defense, because that is about what it amounted to."[17]

Eugene Rostow, professor of law at Yale University, had made a connection between the moral obligation to make amends for evacuee losses and another Supreme Court decision, *Duncan* vs. *Kahanomuku* (1946). Though unconnected with the Japanese–American cases, it restored the principle of the primacy of civilian rights in wartime which had been set aside in the Korematsu, Hirabayashi, and Endo cases. Interpreting the Court's decision as a reflection of a public change of heart, he judged the time auspicious to ask for material compensation for the West Coast group. "Until the wrong is acknowledged and made right we shall have failed to meet the responsibility of a democratic society—the obligation of equal justice."[18]

At its 1946 convention the JACL passed a resolution to ask Congress to compensate evacuees for losses estimated by the Federal Reserve Bank of San Francisco at $400 million. Harold Ickes had asked for compensation for damage inflicted on property during the owners' absence from the West Coast. J. A. Krug, his successor at the Department of the Interior, urged that Congress pass an evacuation claims bill, a proposal endorsed by President Truman in the same month that he awarded the seventh presidential Distinguished Unit Citation to members of the 442nd Regimental Combat Team at a parade in Washington. It took two more years for a bill to emerge from Congress. On July 2, 1948, Truman signed Public Law 886, "An Act to authorize the Attorney General to adjudicate certain claims resulting from evacuation of certain persons of Japanese ancestry under military orders."

Claims "for damage to or loss of real or personal property" were to be filed within an eighteen-month period. There could be no claims filed by people who had gone to Japan or for property confiscated by the Trading with the Enemy Act, for "damage or loss on account of death or personal injury, personal inconvenience, physical hardship, or mental suffering," or for "loss of anticipated profits or loss of anticipated earnings."[19]

Pacific coast offices were set up to process claims and Congress appropriated $38 million, authorizing payments up to $2,500 to each claimant. By the January 2, 1950, deadline, 23,924 claims for a total of approximately $132 million had been filed. Half were reported to be under $2,500 and 95 per cent were under $25,000. The smallest claim was for a child's tricycle, the largest for a little over a million dollars.[20]

In the year 1950 only 210 claims were cleared, and only seventy-three people actually received their money. Claims were being processed at the rate of four a month and if the process was slow, it was also expensive since at the outset it cost the government over a thousand dollars to handle a $450 claim.

The impasse was removed by an amendment that the President signed into law on August 17, 1951, which authorized the Attorney General to automatically settle all claims up to $2,500 or three-quarters of the amount of the compensable items, whichever was less. This expedited the theretofore lengthy process of checking every item individually, and by June 30, 1954, 19,750 claims (popularly called "pots and pans claims") had been settled for roughly $23 million though over $63 million had been requested. Lawyers were reported to be advising their clients to settle for 50 per cent of the loss. Since compensation was made on the basis of prewar prices, it has been estimated that the evacuees received on the average no more than ten cents on the dollar.

Many were asking, "What's the use?" The Issei were concerned with the question of time. A ninety-two-year-old man claimed $75,000 but accepted $2,500 since it was reasonably certain he would not survive years of adjudication. At least one petition had to be dropped because of the death of the claimant who had sole knowledge of his business loss. Lawyers pleaded for priority for cases where oral testimony had to be given by people in their seventies and eighties.

The requirement of records to prove claims was crucial, for in many instances they had been lost or destroyed in hasty departure from the Western Defense Command. A man who owned a trucking business in California was caught unprepared by the deadline to move into the so-called free zone in the spring of 1942. In the words of his lawyer, testifying at a congressional hearing, he "appealed to some of his acquaintances that he might entrust his properties to them. When one of the proposed custodians tried to induce him to sign general powers of attorney, the claimant changed his mind. In fact, he suspected that these people wanted written authority to dispose of these properties once he had departed. He figured that if he were to lose all his property, he might just as well leave the automobiles in front of the Buddhist Church, which he did." He never saw them again, nor could he get authentication for his claim from the Department of Motor Vehicles or his former insurance agent. The lawyer concluded, "This case . . . illustrates that the very atmosphere of the evacuation was that of chaos, hysteria. . . . When property itself was abandoned, indicia of ownership were of very little or no consequence."[21] Records were lost, because, as George Hagiwara said, "At the time of evacuation people threw away what they could, liquidated what they could, including bills and receipts." Getting evidence from the buyers who had profited from a hasty sale or disposal of items was difficult if not impossible.

The hearings held in 1954 and 1955 to amend further the Evacuation Claims Law brought forth testimony regarding the many extraordinary losses not covered by the original law in the stories of people forced to abandon the fruits of many years of skill and labor, a thriving business, an assured clientele, perishable nursery stock. Losses from many prewar business arrangements based on purely oral understandings were not recoverable.

The following exchange took place between John A. Gorfinkel, a law-yer representing claimants whose losses were not covered by the 1951 compromise settlement plan and a member of Congress:

> CONGRESSMAN USHER L. BURDICK: I remember one case last year where one of these citizens had planted oysters in the bay, and when he returned his oysters were gone. Now, didn't the government make any provision to look after that while he was incarcerated?
>
> MR. GORFINKEL: None.
>
> MR. BURDICK: Just free for all—anybody could get them who got there first.
>
> MR. GORFINKEL: Unless they were fortunate enough, as a few were, because I think we should have the record show that while many people took ad-vantage there were others—they were few, but they were notable—who stepped in and did their utmost to preserve the property and rights of their Japanese neighbors and friends. I remember the testimony of the gentle-man with the oysterbeds. They were all dredged up. He was unfortunate.

He cited another instance of a claimant who did not make his tenant sign a lease. "Shortly after their evacuation . . . the lessee walked out. They received word from their neighbors that the property was com-pletely uncared for, it was being subjected to the depredations of van-dals. The file that I had in my possession was replete with efforts to get either the War Relocation Authority to send somebody, or to provide a custodian at the expense of these people, to permit them to return and see if they could do something. They were not allowed even to re-turn in the custody of a War Relocation Authority officer to see if they could do something. When they returned, 4 years later, there was nothing left standing but some debris." Another of Gorfinkel's clients rented his four-acre tract of land with a four-room house and nine greenhouses for $50 a month, a loss not compensable under the original claims act.[22]

On July 9, 1956, President Eisenhower signed an amendment to expe-dite the settlement of the relatively few outstanding but very large claims and to correct some of the inequities in the 1948 law. This in-cluded allowing corporations with a majority of stockholders of Japanese ancestry to file for claims. People interned by the Justice Department were allowed to file and petitioners could ask compensation for property confiscated by the federal government under the Trading with the Enemy Act. Settling some of the remaining claims covered by this amendment took almost ten years.

One of the last claims to be settled was that of the Shibata family, owners of a large nursery in Mount Eden, California, who at the time of evacuation had 80,000 plants, mostly roses, in 125,000 square feet of greenhouses. At a 1954 congressional hearing, Yoshimi Shibata detailed the business losses in plants and equipment, all of which had to be replaced or repaired at higher postwar prices. It took the family between three and four years to get the nursery back to normal operation. During the first few weeks back on the place they had to sleep in a car because they could not get into their house, which was occupied by laborers. They claimed a loss of nearly $400,000.

The Koda family was awarded $362,500, about 15 per cent of a $2.4 million claim, for their Dos Palos rice growing business losses. They had made a new start after the war on the 987 which remained to them after escheat action of their original nearly 4,000 acres. Before Keisaburo Koda died in 1960 at the age of eighty-three, he said, "I have every bit of faith in American democracy. I have absolute confidence in American justice." *Newsweek*, in telling his story, estimated that he was 15 per cent right![23]

A move to impose a capital gains tax on payments to the recipients was stopped by a bill in Congress instigated by Senator Thomas Kuchel of California. The government through the Foreign Claims Settlement Commission awarded $213 million, tax free, to United States companies for property damaged abroad during World War II, an allowance of seventy-five cents on the dollar as compared to the average of ten cents on the dollar paid to Japanese–Americans for evacuation claims.[24] In all, 26,500 evacuees were given a total of $38 million. The lawyers who represented the claimants and the spokesmen for the JACL agreed that the program was fairly administered, though the law, even as amended, was not flexible enough to cover all the contingencies. Nor did it take account of intangibles such as the cost in human anguish, the damage to reputation, the missed opportunities, the lost years.

In many cases the compensation to the Issei came too late. An old man might stare at the government check in his hand and wonder what remote connection it had with the destruction of his life's work. The claimant who in desperation parked his fleet of trucks in front of the Buddhist church became a laborer after the war. Another who lost all his property is today a janitor. Men in their sixties who had by hard work achieved managerial or entrepreneurial positions could not begin again. "We haven't paid for these losses at all," is the opinion of an economist, Kenneth Hansen. "In fact, the bill gets bigger every day. It's not a question of their temporary loss of rights, but has to be thought of in terms of their whole lives. They are still being denied the fruits of their earnings. The Nisei are paying the price today in the loss of opportunity and gains which they would have made had we not taken this outrageous action. Losses are still being compounded because of constantly increasing evaluations of often valuable lands they were forced to let go."

The desire to do penance on the part of legislators representing American public opinion was evident in the hearings on the claims law, and the JACL was instrumental in channeling the nation's conscience pangs into concrete form. Non-Nisei lawyers, notably attorneys for the ACLU, volunteered their services in behalf of claimants. A provision in the 1948 law limited legal fees to 10 per cent of the amount awarded to the claimant so that the lawyers concerned were perforce motivated by altruism. Nor was a single case of fraud ever proved on the part of the petitioners.

A more complicated matter was the $65 million in Japanese holdings that had been seized at the outbreak of the war and put under the control of the Enemy Property Custodian. A treaty was signed with Japan on September 8, 1951, whereby instead of exacting war reparations it was agreed that the United States would sell the properties and use the funds to settle war claims of American prisoners of war and civilian internees. Yet some of the seized assets belonged to long-term residents of the United States. By the 1956 amendment to the Evacuation Claims Law they were allowed to petition to recover their losses. Domicile rather than nationality was established as a deciding factor in a 1951 court case, *Nagana* vs. *McGrath*, which restored some shares of stock to a woman who had announced her intention of returning to Chicago, though she had lived in Japan for twenty-nine years. In the same year a Nisei in Hollister was awarded $30,000 after filing a suit against the United States government which had appropriated his family business during the war.

One case handled by Wayne Collins took eighteen years to settle. An Issei had tied up all his worldly possessions in a bandana, including a watch, rings, and securities worth about $12,000. After the war the alien property division of the Justice Department, which was handling thousands of cases, was ready to confiscate this nest egg because the man's wife was in Japan. Collins replied, "The hell you will. This is community property." Collins "pried loose" the man's half and later half of the wife's assets.

Probably the longest drawn-out postwar reparation has been the litigation to get back over $11 million in yen deposits in California branches of the Yokohama Specie Bank. The funds of some 7,500 persons were held by the Alien Property Custodian after Pearl Harbor. At the end of the war Congress amended the Trading with the Enemy Act and appropriated money to repay the depositors, but it was decided claims should be paid on the postwar conversion rate of yen to dollars, which was approximately 2 per cent of the value of the deposits at the time they were seized. A suit filed to challenge this ruling resulted in the government settling 1,800 claims filed at full value, but the other claimants who had not filed during a prescribed sixty-day period were excluded by the Attorney General. A United States court of appeals in Washington upheld the decision, but four ACLU attorneys, A. L. Wirin, Fred Okrand, Joseph L. Rauh, Jr., and John Silard took a case representing five claimants before the United States Supreme Court. The attorney general for the state of California, Thomas Lynch, calling the lower court decision a "regression to an unfortunate era we hoped had ended,"[25] filed an *amicus curiae* brief which concluded: "California's concern is not solely with the claimants before this Court. They represent subsequent generations of Japanese–American citizens as well. Their attitudes toward and respect for the institutions of our society of law will be deeply affected by this Court's decision."[26] For a representative of the state of California to plead with the federal government on behalf of the Japanese was indeed an historic reversal of an old pattern.

Justice John M. Harlan wrote the opinion by which the Supreme Court in April 10, 1967, unanimously reversed the decision of the lower court and upheld the rights of the yen claimants. The defense attorneys, veterans of many battles in behalf of American Japanese, spoke of the day as one "of sadness and gladness for all of us. A quarter of a century is a long time to wait."[27] A later procedural decision decreed that payments would be awarded in the year ending July, 1968.

All depositors who had not done so were urged to file a notice with the office of Alien Property. The Justice Department, fearful that many had moved or died, published information in Japanese and English in vernacular newspapers. "Some of this $11,000,000 may be yours," proclaimed a large advertisement in the *Pacific Citizen*, signed by Mike Masaoka of the JACL and the three Hawaiian Nisei members of Congress.[28] One eligible recipient was Masami Ishida, a Nisei laundry worker in San Francisco, who found he would receive $600 from an account he had started in 1934. "It's been so long, we had almost forgotten about it," he said.[29] Fittingly, *Life* magazine, which had sounded an ominous note on the danger concerning Japanese on the West Coast in 1942, used the occasion to evoke the current national mood of self-excoriation about the evacuation; an editorial called the decision "the last quiet act in a shameful drama."[30] A *Pacific Citizen* columnist, quoting from the Langston Hughes poem about "a dream deferred," wrote, "Even in victory, however, it was at best a very small win for the Issei as most of them had died and the fruits of the claim passed on to the Nisei. That is the story of their life."[31]

But some of the Issei were able to "sing America," in the words of another Langston Hughes poem.[32] They were the chief beneficiaries of the postwar liberalization of the naturalization and immigration laws. In

1952, the same year that California declared its alien land law unconstitutional, the Issei ceased to be classified as aliens ineligible for citizenship. A 1943 wartime law had allowed Chinese to be naturalized and permitted a small yearly quota into the country. These privileges were extended to East Indians and Filipinos in 1946, but Japanese, Koreans, Siamese, and a few other Asian groups continued to be treated under the terms of the Oriental Exclusion Act until the Eighty-second Congress passed Public Law 414.

The first Japanese to become an American citizen had been Joseph Heco (Hikozo Hamada) who anglicized his name and was converted to Catholicism before swearing the oath of allegiance in Baltimore in 1858. He began his long career as an interpreter between Japan and the United States at the age of seventeen when he was rescued by an American vessel. Though he shook hands with three American Presidents, Pierce, Buchanan, and Lincoln, he died in Tokyo, where his memory is honored today by historians interested in Pan-Pacific relations. But the welcome extended to the chance voyager was denied to the immigrant stream, as we have seen, with the result that only a few Issei veterans of World War I were naturalized at the time of World War II.

Soon after the return to the West Coast, a few long-resident Japanese aliens who had been instructors in Army and Navy language schools or were fathers of servicemen, petitioned the government for the right to file first papers. Their small, individual suits were soon drowned out by the clamor of returning American soldiers who wanted to bring their alien brides, German and Japanese, home with them with the expectation that they could become citizens.

Liberalization of the national policy toward Orientals was one of the few good features of the controversial McCarran–Walter omnibus Immigration and Naturalization bill of 1952, which in other respects both endorsed old prejudices and offered nefarious remedies for new fears. Like Senator Patrick McCarran's 1950 Subversive Activities Control Act, aimed at protecting the United States against Communist subversion, the omnibus bill was widely criticized and was passed over President Truman's veto. The first large-scale updating of the 1924 immigration laws perpetuated the "doctrine of Nordic superiority."[33] Southern European countries had very small quotas (3 per cent from Italy, 2 per cent from Greece as compared with 41.4 per cent from Britain and Northern Ireland). Quotas in the Displaced Persons Act were frozen. Senators Herbert Lehman and Hubert Humphrey offered a substitute bill which would have made immigration laws relevant to the postwar world, but it failed.

Though McCarran is reported to have said he did not want "the opening of the gates to a flood of Asiatics,"[34] the omnibus bill made what was termed a "generous gesture toward Oriental countries."[35] Reasoning that half a loaf was better than none, the JACL lobbied strenuously for its passage and later helped to round up sufficient votes in Congress to override the presidential veto. Mike Masaoka wrote a long letter to a California congressman, Chet Holifield, in which he answered criticism, not always convincingly, on the undesirable features of the bill and made it clear why the JACL wanted it anyway. ". . . legislation of this magnitude and complexity is always a compromise. . . . the proposed legislation marks a significant advance by eliminating complete exclusion. . . . Insistence upon complete equality of immigration at this time means no legislation on this subject at all. . . . We sincerely feel that it is far more important to secure naturalization privileges for our 85,000 aged parents now. . . ."[36] If Public Law 414 was a reactionary symbol to many Americans, it was a hope fulfilled for the Japanese minority. Though only 185 persons a year were allowed to immigrate under the Asia–Pacific Triangle formula (which gave a low quota to Australia, China, India, Korea, and New Zealand as well), several thousand spouses and children of American citizens were permitted to come in yearly on a nonquota basis.

A majority of the Issei became American citizens at long last. One of the first immigrants to reach the mainland, Gentaro Kotashiro of Oakland, was naturalized at the age of ninety. Twenty-year residents who were over fifty could take the qualifying examinations in their native language, but many of the Issei attended English classes. "Mother was very proud to be able to take her citizenship tests in English," says a Nisei. The elders attended mass swearing-in ceremonies in high spirits. A group came back from San Francisco "trying to recite the Pledge of Allegiance. Some of it came out funny, but they were trying," said a friend.

The non-English speaking could not vote in California, however, because of a state requirement that they demonstrate ability to read the Constitution in English. A 1966 ballot proposition which would have removed this requirement, was not approved by California voters. In the same year the Supreme Court ruled that Puerto Ricans could vote in New York if they could read or write Spanish. California driver's tests can be taken in Spanish, but not in Japanese. Official forms will probably never be translated into Japanese characters to accommodate such a small minority so the Issei continue to study English with real incentive.

In 1965 the immigration laws were liberalized, abolishing the Asia–Pacific Triangle formula as well as the principle of national origins. As of July, 1968, a South American immigrant of Japanese ancestry comes in under the Peruvian or Brazilian quota. Unused quotas are pooled and allocated to countries like Japan whose allowance is oversubscribed, enabling family members who have been waiting for years to obtain visas. In the period from July, 1965, to June, 1966, when some features of the new system were in effect for part of one year, 3,261 persons came to America from Japan. From 1957 through 1966 visas were issued to 45,640 people from Japan. The figure will inevitably go down as the waiting list dwindles. After immediate family members, top priority is given to technicians, scientists, scholars, and artists; laborers must be approved by the U.S. Department of Labor. If there is discrimination in American immigration laws today, it is not racial. The Japanese are treated like everyone else.

The Nisei participated in the struggle against restrictive covenants in real estate and in another Supreme Court decision that declared miscegenation laws to be unconstitutional. The JACL legal counsel, William Muritani, the first Nisei lawyer to argue before the Supreme Court, was asked to give an oral presentation in the Loving case in March, 1967. The marriage of Richard Loving, a white man and his half-Negro, half-Indian wife was declared legal by the Court, overruling a Virginia injunction. Miscegenation laws in other states had been invoked against Nisei–Caucasian marriages. The JACL helped repeal statutes in Idaho, Utah, Nebraska, and Wyoming. The Nevada law was challenged by Harry Bridges, the labor leader, who married a Nisei in Reno.

• • •

The battles are won, or nearly won. After twenty-five years of lobbying in Washington and state capitals, the JACL is able to proclaim that more than five hundred discriminatory laws against Japanese–Americans have been removed from the statute books, except for one or two that are inoperative. Both international relations and the postwar emphasis on civil rights have been factors in this achievement. Negro demands for radical measures to abolish inequalities have lent some heat to the quiet battles of the JACL. The Nisei are beneficiaries of the government's response to those demands, culminating in the historic decisions of the Supreme Court under Warren. The ferment among the other minorities has swept Japanese–Americans into a relatively secure position, partly because they are no longer themselves a racial symbol. It is hard to believe that a quarter of a century ago some members of Congress were willing to twist, bend, or break the Constitution in their desire to rid the country of them. Their action set in motion during the war was finally concluded in 1968.

The forced renunciation of their citizenship by several thousand Nisei was the final compounding of the government's mistake in ordering the evacuation. Public Law 405, passed by the 78th Congress in July, 1944, gave *permission* to those who wished to do so to renounce their American citizenship, but in subsequent court actions to restore citizenship it was demonstrated that for many the renunciation was in a very real sense forced.

It is true that the Justice Department, which drafted the law, was acting in response to disillusioned and pro-Japan Nisei and Kibei at Tule Lake who wrote letters to Washington, saying "We don't want our citizenship." However, it must be considered whether Public Law 405 was not also a palliative for the groups which had been trying since 1942 to get rid of the Japanese permanently. In the debate on the bill in Congress in February, 1944, spokesmen for the Attorney General had to hold the line against those who would profit by the opportunity in order to broaden the coverage. Although as Eugene Rostow said, "No statute makes disloyalty a crime,"[37] Congressman J. Leroy Johnson of California wanted to take away the citizenship retroactively of a large group on grounds which were ominously vague. He argued:

> Here is what I conceive to be the joker in the bill, if you can call it that: The Attorney General has said that this only applies to renunciations made after the date when the bill is passed. The Japanese who signed a questionnaire in which they acknowledged their allegiance to Japan, can simply refuse to sign again and thus nullify this bill. We want to make it apply any time that a man made that sort of statement, either orally or written, or at any time his conduct showed that he did in fact renounce his citizenship, from the time of the adoption of the selective service law on September 10, 1940, up to and including the duration of this war.[38]

Francis Biddle denounced Johnson's bill (which was later incorporated into an amendment) and other clearly punitive measures. Leonard Allen from Louisiana, a member of the Committee on Immigration and Naturalization, who drafted the law approved by the Justice Department, warned:

> Bear in mind that this bill is general. It must be general. It would be unconstitutional otherwise. The amendment proposed by the gentleman from California in its present form would make oral testimony and all sorts of testimony admissible to take away the citizenship of any native-born American. Under that even perjured testimony could be used to strip a native-born American of his citizenship and he might be kicked out. Again bear in mind his amendment applies to everybody. Whose citizenship would be secure?[39]

Speaking of the bill he authored, he said, "Of course, we want to go further and we may find a way to go further. I hope the Justice Department can work out some plan to go further, but let us at least go this far now."[40] Johnson continued to press for his amendment which would take away citizenship from all who answered "no" on Question 28. "We will have conquered Japan so successfully," he said, "that we can dictate the terms of the treaty which will undoubtedly include a provision that all these people shall be taken back to Japan."[41] The Johnson amendment was defeated, but by a margin of only six votes. The Allen bill was passed by 111 to 33.

Edward Ennis, who was in the Justice Department at the time the Allen bill became Public Law 405, has made a commentary on the government's position:

> We felt that [relocation] could not be accomplished with public support during the particular anxieties of the first year of the war while several hundred young men in the camps were marching around shouting their loyalty to the Japanese emperor. Therefore, we devised the plan of amending the Nationality Act of 1940 to provide that a person could renounce his nationality in the United States in time of war, with the approval of the Attorney General, and we established the administrative machinery that anyone who wished to renounce would have to write to the Attorney General to obtain the official application form. Our plan was upon the renunciation of the few hundred openly pro-Japanese residents of the relocation camps, particularly the camp at Tule Lake, we would remove these renunciants to camps for Japanese alien enemies maintained by the Immigration and Naturalization service of the Department of Justice and then be in a position to declare that no detention restriction was necessary or would be maintained at any of the war relocation camps presumably cleansed of enemy sentiment and harboring only citizens and resident aliens loyal to the United States.
>
> Alas, this plan to preserve some constitutionality in the relocation program misfired because of our miscalulation that only a few hundred evacuees were sufficiently alienated to seek renunciation of citizenship. When thousands of applications for renunciation were received we debated . . . whether to scrap the whole program as a mistake or go ahead with it and attempt to persuade the applicants not to renounce. There was a division of opinion but the Attorney General concluded that since the law had been enacted we could not refuse its "benefits" to applicants and the application forms were sent to thousands of applicants and an administrative procedure was set up whereby hearing officers . . . were sent to the relocation camps to give hearings to applicants and, if possible persuade them not to renounce.
>
> This is an interesting example of a government procedure proposed to separate the presumably few goats from the many sheep which to our surprise resulted in many of the sheep insisting upon being classified as goats until after the war.[42]

The renunciants represented a complete cross-section of the Tule Lake society from the youth to the middle-aged, from the highly motivated to the mentally incompetent, and included draft dodgers, those intensely loyal to Japan, angry rebels, and minors who were following family dictates. Many of the young people were pushed and pulled by all but intolerable pressures from their families and their peers. As noted earlier, they received no support for their position as American citizens from the disintegrating society at Tule Lake over which the WRA had relinquished any real control. John L. Burling, the Justice Department official who arrived in December to hold hearings, testified later that, "It was a commonplace witticism among the officials at the camp at the time of these hearings that the population of the Center was largely mad and that the Center might properly be taken from the management of the War Relocation Authority and transferred to the Public Health Service to be run as a species of mental institution."[43]

The pro-Japan faction, the resegregationists, were allowed free rein. Though they had not succeeded in their aim of physically separating old Tuleans from "true Japanese," a Japanese spirit pervaded the camp with the approval of the center administration. Joining the Sokoku, which began as a society to study the culture of the mother country, was a way for an internee to avoid the harassment which was the fate of those suspected of being loyal to America. By September, 1944, the Sokoku, renamed Hokoku, was more militantly oriented and members of another organization, Hoshi-dan, pledged "to sacrifice life and property in order to serve our mother country in time of unparalleled emergency."[44] In October both groups began an intensive propaganda effort to influence and coerce young Nisei into renouncing their citizenship. The announcement in December of the rescission orders, the opening up of the West Coast, and the WRA's decision to close the camps within a year assisted the campaign. Army officers came to the center to clear residents for reentry into the Western Defense Command, and were reported to be asking, "Do you want to go out or do you want to renounce citizenship?" An observer wrote, "Mass hysteria came upon the camp and hordes of American youth who have never seen Japan, found themselves before the Department of Justice authorities signing away their American citizenship. Very few of these youth realized the seriousness of the thing which they did at the time. Some signed away their citizenship in five minutes. To many of them it was merely signing a piece of paper as they had already been deprived of their rights as American citizens. Those of us who have worked here know that renunciation in the great majority of cases had nothing to do with pro-Japanism on the part of the renuncees."[45] In January, 1945, applications for renunciation were mailed by 3,400 Nisei and Kibei.

The renunciations of about one thousand pro-Japan organization members were approved automatically by the Justice Department and the renunciants were removed to internment camps. The leaders were given a hero's farewell by families and friends as they left Tule Lake. Some of the members, expelled from Tule Lake later, were hangers-on who had joined the movement for excitement or because they were following the line of least resistance. Using Dorothy Thomas' term, they were the true "spoilage" of the evacuation. Some of them did not leave their prisons until they met their parents on the ships going to Japan.

After their departure the WRA began to suppress Japanese nationalistic activities at Tule Lake. Dillon Myer announced that Tuleans would not be put out of camp to shift for themselves until January, 1946. Burling instructed the hearing officers to be alert to signs of coercion when they interviewed applicants for renunciation. But the protective measures came too late. There were too many other factors involved, rational and irrational. A typical Nisei renunciant said, "I was so undecided that any little pressure one way or another swayed my decision."[46] The children in another family renounced to prove their devotion to their stepfather who wanted to go to Japan. "Because of my stubbornness I did great harm to my children's welfare," this Issei later said. A Kibei renounced because, "I am a Japanese with Japanese face and hair."[47] A twenty-one-year-old girl was slapped by her mother when she told the Justice Department official that she didn't want to give up her citizenship and go to Japan. She was told by her family to leave and never return, but her soldier-fiancée told the mother, "Your loss is my gain."

Most decisive was the fact that after two or more years spent in an atmosphere of what one observer called "generalized insanity," the evacuees had lost touch with reality. Many thought that Japan was going to win the war since false news of Japanese military victories had been circulated in the camp. People believed only bad stories about the West Coast and generalized from these about their position in communities outside. The "Old Tuleans," the original colonists, came from some of the most prejudiced areas on the West Coast. Many of the segregated group who joined them had chosen to be "disloyal" to escape relocation. They reasoned that by renouncing citizenship or persuading a member of the family to renounce, they would be assured of continued protection. Again, as at the time of registration, they made their own equations. Retaining American citizenship meant expulsion into a hostile America. Renouncing it meant they could stay at the camps.

In all, over 6,000 people, the majority from Tule Lake, 460 from other centers, and 125 who had relocated, applied to give up their citizenship. The Justice Department, whose hearing officers under Burling had taken a transcript from each applicant, approved applications from 5,461 individuals at Tule Lake and 128 from other centers. But shortly afterwards hundreds of people changed their minds and applied to rescind their applications. This developed into a mass movement like the original impulse to renounce and was no doubt influenced by, but not entirely the result of, the war news in the Pacific. Well before V-J Day, the renunciants were writing letters to officials of the Justice Department pleading to be allowed to withdraw an action undertaken in anger, defiance, or fear. They spoke of hysteria, temporary insanity. One man had succumbed to a rumor that those who did not renounce would be forced out as slave labor. "These people—all of them, whether they say so or not—were in a perpetual state of terror, doubt, and uncertainty. Not one of them could have been in his right mind. They were all in a boiling pot," said Wayne Collins, the lawyer who rescued them.

Ernest Besig, the counsel for the San Francisco office of the ACLU who had intervened in behalf of the men imprisoned in the stockade at Tule Lake, pleaded with officials of the Justice Department to rescind the renunciations, but was answered with "steely legalism." The department sent out a form letter to each renunciant who applied, saying that it was not within the power of the Attorney General to restore citizenship once lost in this manner. As summarized by tenBroek, Barnhart, and Matson in their study of the legal and legislative aspects of the evacuation:

> . . . the Department of Justice was moving to send them all to Japan. On July 14, 1945, under the authority of the Alien Enemy Act of 1798, President Truman issued Proclamation 2655 which provided that all interned alien enemies deemed by the Attorney General to be dangerous to peace and safety "because they have adhered to aforesaid enemy governments or to the principles of their government shall be subject . . . to removal from the United States." Regulations governing their deportation were published by the Department of Justice on September 26, 1945. On October 8 the department began the registration of the renunciants, who were finger-printed and photographed. They were informed that they were now classed as "native American aliens." On October 10 the department announced that on and after November 15 "all persons whose applications to renounce citizenship have been approved by the Attorney General of the United States, will be repatriated to Japan, together with members of their families, whether citizens or aliens, who desire to accompany them."[48]

At this point Wayne Collins, the San Francisco lawyer, entered the picture. Though he was counsel for the Northern California branch of the ACLU, Collins acted in a private capacity in this instance. The issue of the renunciants was a "hot potato" which the JACL decided to avoid on the grounds that to espouse the cause of the "disloyal" would be damaging to the "loyal" in this touchy period. Several individual pleas made to the ACLU of Northern California were referred to the headquarters of the national organization in New York, which also vetoed intervention. Therefore, Collins acted independently. He first came into direct contact with the situation in July of 1945 while visiting at Tule Lake. His reaction to the news of the mass renunciations was, "That's ridiculous! You can no more resign citizenship in time of war than you can resign from the human race."

When he discovered the circumstances influencing renunciation, he became indignant. The people he talked to felt themselves to be helpless pawns of fate. They doubted that anyone successfully could oppose the Army, the WRA, and the Justice Department. But in Collins they had a friend they needed, an angry man fiercely devoted to principle. Defying the government, he almost literally pulled people off the ships going to Japan. He became virtually a commuter between San Francisco, Tule Lake, Bismarck, North Dakota, Santa Fe, New Mexico, and Crystal City, Texas, in his efforts to release the renunciants and aliens and recover the citizenship of the renunciants. He made the cause of these discarded citizens his almost full-time occupation for some twenty-five years. He did not as much as take a vacation during the early years because he was fearful that something might happen to these people, who had no individual access to the United States district courts, in the event of his absence. "I was frightened stiff that if I was not able to be in my office every day early and late that the government might attempt to remove all of them to Japan." Some of his clients called him "a brave man"; others, including Nisei, said that he was a "fanatic" and a "maniac."

At Tule Lake in mid-1945 he talked to individuals (one woman came to see him every day) and to large groups of several hundred people. Because he was overwhelmed with numbers he advised renunciants to find other lawyers to represent them, but at this time only one other attorney in the whole country agreed to assist the newly formed group that called itself the Tule Lake Defense Committee. Nevertheless, the renunciants, though they suffered from the feeling that they had done something shameful, in Collins' words, "stood up on their hind legs and began to fight." Though at first they were considered to be "alien enemies" and later "native American aliens," they appealed to the democratic institutions of the country through the courts.

In November, 1945, two suits were initiated in the names of the first 987, and eventually over 4,000 plaintiffs were included. They asked that individuals be freed, that their removal to Japan under the Alien Enemy Act be prevented, and that renunciation applications be declared void and that their citizenship be restored. *Abo* vs. *Williams* was a petition for a writ of *habeas corpus* to free the petitioners from removal to Japan and set them at liberty, and *Abo* vs. *Clark* was a suit in equity to restore their citizenship. The argument used by Collins in these cases was that the evacuees had renounced citizenship under government duress to which they had been unconstitutionally subjected. An incidental argument was that the duress was two-fold: government duress which in turn induced coercion by a small group of aliens and renunciants who had been informed that they would be removed to Japan as undesirable persons and who pressured others to join them. Included in the evidence was a letter to Ernest Besig from Abe Fortas, then Under-Secretary in the Department of the Interior, stating that, "It was primarily due to the pressure of these organizations that over 80 per cent of the citizens [at Tule Lake] eligible to do so applied for renunciation of citizenship this past winter."[49]

The government was having second thoughts. After court action on Collin's suits in San Francisco, which halted the removal of the aliens and the renunciants to Japan, the Justice Department announced that "mitigation hearings" would be held at Tule Lake and later at the department's internment camps to enable renunciants and interned aliens to "show cause" why they should not be "removed to Japan." The hearings were not concerned with restoring citizenship, which could be done only in court, but with staying removal to Japan under the Alien Enemy Act. Even while the hearings were being held beginning in January, 1946, ships were leaving for Japan carrying persons who had not requested Collins to represent them. Collins got assurance from the government that there would be no forced removals of his clients pending the final outcome of the litigation. At the mitigation hearings the renunciants could not be represented by a lawyer, but could bring witnesses. More than 1,200 persons were released unconditionally. On June 29, 1946, the Ninth Circuit Court of Appeals in *Takeguma* vs. *U.S.* declared that though renunciants were not citizens, they were subject to induction into the armed forces.

Slightly over 1,800 renunciants, all dual citizens, were recommended by the Hearing Board for removal to Japan. "While in some cases this notification may not be final," they were told, "it is contemplated that those on the following list who do not apply for voluntary repatriation to Japan in the vessel sailing from San Pedro, California, on February 21, 1946, will be removed in the near future to the Santa Fe Internment Camp or the Crystal City Internment Camp."[50]

After this ultimatum was issued, two people attempted suicide and a mother who developed an acute mental disorder killed one of her children with a hammer and injured another. Those in this group who did not go to Japan, about three hundred people, continued to be held by the Justice Department in Crystal City, Texas, and Seabrook Farms, New Jersey, until the California Judge Louis E. Goodman on August 11, 1947, ordered the Immigration and Naturalization Service to release them. He held that, "Even if the renunciations were deemed to be valid, the mere renunciation of United States citizenship by detained native-born residents did not convert them into alien enemies subject to internment and removal under the provisions of the Alien Enemy Act."[51] Pending the taking of an appeal by the Justice Department from his decision, Judge Goodman on September 8 of the same year ordered them to be placed in Collins' custody. The government agreed to pay the cost of bringing them back to California in the event individual trials were to be given to them in the future.

The internees were thus freed from their anomalous status as detained persons and were no longer under the immediate threat of removal to Japan, but with the rest of the renunciants, they would have to wait for further court action to regain their citizenship.

The end of the war released the bonds of millions of prisoners over the world but kept others still fettered by the strange categories that fate and their nationalities had assigned them. Scheduled for deportation were the Issei who had entered the country illegally as well as a group of alien Japanese called "treaty traders," long-time residents of the United States who had lost their official status as a result of the war. Some of these individuals had aided the American military as translators or worked with the OWI so that if they were forced to return to Japan, they faced punishment, possibly even death, as traitors. They were saved from deportation by the efforts of the JACL, litigation initiated by Collins and others, as well as by the help of congressmen who passed bills in their behalf.

Another group of Japanese under special consideration were the parolees from the Justice Department camps. Among the first to be arrested, some right after Pearl Harbor, they were among the last to be freed, though a number had been released early to join their families in relocation centers. One who had reversed the process was the Stanford professor, Yamato Ichihashi, who was removed for questioning by the FBI *while* he was at Tule Lake. An authority on Japanese history, he was working on a cultural history of seventh- and eighth-century Japan and lecturing to camp audiences. "They asked me to lecture on current topics," he explained to a reporter, "but perhaps ancient matters can more safely be discussed."[52]

From Tule Lake he was first taken to a poorly heated local jail, "a terrible thing to do to a gentle, aristocratic person," in the opinion of a friend, before being taken to Sharp Park. Professor Ichihashi, as a scholar and an internationalist, had been an interpreter for Admiral Kato at a conference in Washington in 1921. The Stanford colleague who testified in his behalf at the Sharp Park hearing was told that Professor Ichihashi was only one of many Issei required to appear before a nonjudicial board for an investigation of their loyalty. He was cleared of any suspicion of disloyalty and returned to Tule Lake and eventually to Amache.

The last to leave Tule Lake were "segregated parolees," originally arrested by the FBI, who were given a hearing and unconditionally freed on March 18, 1946. Then Tule Lake, that small portion of hell, which had been transferred to the Justice Department in the autumn, finally closed on March 29.

About one-fourth of the approximately eight thousand people who went to Japan after the end of the war were renunciants. Joe Kurihara sailed on one of the first ships on November 24, 1945, expressing the hope that he could help build a "democratized Nippon." Raymond Best, the project director at Tule Lake, who was his friend, wrote, "Whatever Joe may become in Japan or whatever Japan may become during his lifetime, it seems inconceivable that he can be anything but an eloquent and determined force for what he believes to be right, and that his concept of what is right will follow the basic principles of the land of his birth, America."[53]

A number of alien Japanese had already returned during the war through exchanges on the neutral Swedish ship the *Gripsholm*. In November, 1941, when war seemed imminent, Japan sent ships to our shores for the purpose of evacuating diplomats, visitors, and other nationals. Significantly, in contrast to their attitudes after a few years of duress, not one Issei (as distinguished from transient Japanese) accepted the invitation to return at that time. Many "treaty traders," though not permanent immigrants, had put down roots in the United States, were raising families of American children, and did not want to leave either.

In the spring of 1942 after the war was underway Japan submitted the names of 539 selected aliens who would be acceptable for exchange. At this time a small number of Issei applied for repatriation and arrangements were made for their passage. Of two hundred Japanese interned at Sharp Park near San Francisco, only two asked to go to Japan. A young Stanford medical student, who was born in Japan and was in a relocation center at the time, "received a long wire from the State Department . . . informing that arrangements have been made for me and my immediate family . . . to be repatriated. . . . The offer was a big surprise to us. . . . We declined . . . for a number of reasons, largely political. I still have faith in what this country stands for . . . my dislike of Japanese fascism is as strong as ever. I guess I'm a political refugee in self-exile now. The way I feel about my decision is simply this: what I exiled myself from is clear to me, but what I exiled myself into puzzles me sometimes."[54]

In June, 1942, the *Gripsholm* sailed from New York with approximately 1,500 persons aboard bound for Lourenco Marques, a mid-point between Japan and the United States in Portuguese East Africa. There she was met by a Japanese ship and the two exchanged passengers. Among those returning to the United States were Ambassador Grew and some of his staff, others from Tokyo, seven hundred missionaries who had been incarcerated in Japan's prisoner of war camps. There were a handful of Nisei, mostly employees of the American embassy and the U.S. consular offices, as well as a small group who had gone to Japan to try to prevent the outbreak of war.

In the summer of 1942 the Western Defense Command and the WRA conducted a survey of evacuees in order to ascertain how many aliens wished to repatriate. In September, 1943, the *Gripsholm* sailed again to exchange repatriates for American prisoners of war. Aboard the ship were about 1,500 Issei, including 250 Japanese from South American countries and their children. Tec Winebrenner, a Los Angeles college student returning from the orient on the *Teia Maru*, went aboard the *Gripsholm* at the rendezvous point in Mormugoa and reported that most of the young Nisei were very unhappy at being forced to go along with their parents as well as very apprehensive about their future in Japan.

The young Nisei who left the West Coast ports in late 1945 and early 1946 to go to a defeated Japan were apprehensive also. With their parents they disembarked at Uraga where Commodore Perry had landed. The first impressions of life in the war-devastated country were a rude shock. "After I landed I realized for the first time that Japan had really lost the war," one person said; "it was then that I wondered why I had returned to this country and I repented. I walked through the streets and the stores had nothing in them. . . . There was hardly anything to eat. I wanted to return to America again, but, of course, it was too late."[55] The Issei, who had kept alive a picture of the homeland during their life in America, were even more shocked by Japan.

At first the refugees from America were housed in former naval barracks in one large room without partitions where they slept under thin blankets. A Hawaiian-born Japanese who never thought it would be so "terrible" expressed surprise that "the Americans had nothing to do with his troubles—that the Japanese government was running the dilapidated camp."[56] They remained in Uraga for a week or ten days for processing, were issued ration cards for rice, oil, sugar, fish, matches, and *shoyu*. The trains which took them to their destinations were dirty and slow; the people, staggering under the burdens of life in a defeated country were not welcoming, not anxious to have more mouths to feed. Some of the renunciants looked upon the discomforts as "in effect, an expiation for their fateful decision to leave the United States."[57] One man described the food at Kurihama, where his ship landed, as "like garbage." They had been allowed to bring 370 pounds of luggage and $60 to Japan out of which they had to pay freight charges to move their possessions. Their relatives were not cordial because the refugees did not bring presents. "We were never so broke, disheartened and disappointed as these first few weeks in defeated Japan."[58] A visiting teacher from America was appalled to see Japanese people with social standing begging for sugar.

A young high school graduate said, "Mother said that she felt as if she came to a foreign country, instead of her native land. . . . The first few years in postwar Japan was almost unbearable, and there was nothing that we could do but to endure it." Flower arranging and tea ceremony taught her patience.[59]

When a Nisei member of the U.S. Merchant Marine spent three days shore leave in Tokyo and Yokohama, his uncle, whom he visited, begged him, "For God's sake, go back to America and tell the people there not to come here."[60] A renunciant who arrived with the first group asked an Associated Press reporter in Japan to send a message to America, urging others at Tule Lake not to return.

The Japanese asked one repatriate, "Why did you throw your citizenship away to come to Japan?" Eventually, the ability to speak English helped the renunciants to get jobs with the Occupation government and privileges at the U.S. Army mess halls and post exchanges. Some Nisei working in the U.S. commissary sold goods on the black market. When a September, 1947, directive canceled the government jobs of renunciants, the Kibei felt this was the final rejection by the United States. In Tokyo, however, Nisei found jobs using English with the airlines and American insurance companies.

Eight years after they came to Japan, Gladys Ishida, a Nisei sociologist, studied twenty-seven renunciants between the ages of seventeen and forty with the purpose of comparing the accommodation and assimilation to Japanese culture of Nisei and Kibei. She found that the Kibei did not "lament the loss of their American citizenship but considered it gone forever." Said one, "There is no chance of my going back and forth, not being satisfied in either place. Now, it is absolutely clear that I must make the best of it here." The author's comment was that "Upon returning to Japan they merely picked up the threads of life from where they had left off [between the ages of twenty and thirty-four] when they went to America."[61]

They voted to look after their own interests and because they were expected to, not from a sense of civic responsibility. Their mannerisms were Japanese (formal bowing, shyness of the women). They did not brag about life in America, had forgotten the little English they knew. They showed a tendency to conform, especially the women, because an individualist would be ostracized. Their neighbors had forgotten that they had not always lived in Japan. One of the Kibei had gotten back her American citizenship and planned to return to the United States. She shocked her in-laws because she was not submissive and associated with the *eta* class, Japan's untouchables.

Many of the Nisei had returned as minors, accompanying their parents from Tule Lake. Most of them were restless in Japan and wanted to go back to America. At least one had filed for restoration of citizenship in Collins' mass suit. They still celebrated American customs, ate Western food when they could, had more informal manners, and spoke of the Japanese, whom they did not fully understand, as "nationals." They were homesick. One woman said, "We are going to take my mother's ashes back to America since she wanted to return."[62]

The cases that Wayne Collins started in 1945 dragged on for twenty-three more years. First, Judge Goodman restored the citizenship of all renunciants under twenty-one years of age, and thereafter gave all the renunciants in Collins' cases judgment canceling their renunciations and declaring that each of them was a native-born citizen entitled to all the rights, privileges, and immunities of U.S. citizens. But the Ninth Circuit Court of Appeals ordered some four thousand cases re-opened to enable the Justice Department to introduce additional evidence. The renunciants were ordered to submit affidavits which the Justice Department would have to refute. It took almost a quarter of a century to decide these cases on an individual basis. Judge Goodman would not countenance a proposal by a Justice Department representative on one occasion that the pending cases be dismissed. Another judge, William Denman, in a case involving the government's refusal to issue passports to renunciants, gave what the ACLU of Northern California described as "a scathing denunciation of unnecessarily cruel and inhuman treatment" of the evacuees at Tule Lake.[63] In both this case and the Abo case *The Spoilage* by Dorothy Swaine Thomas and Richard Nishimoto was introduced as documentary evidence by the government.

The original position of the Justice Department in a complaint filed on September 23, 1946, had been that evacuees renounced American citizenship because of loyalty to Japan, belief that Japan would win the war, desire to avoid the draft, fear of public hostility, anger and frustration at their treatment, family feeling, and the predominant atmosphere of the center. The department claimed that renunciants were not threatened by terrorist groups and that the isolation center at Tule Lake (where troublemakers were punished) did not constitute government duress. At that time the government was not accepting the fact that the evacuation itself was the main cause of the disaffection.

The Justice Department changed its mind as evidenced by the words of Assistant Attorney General George Cochran Doub at a ceremony on May 20, 1959, after citizenship had been restored to 4,978 of 5,409 renunciants. He said:

> We have assumed, unless the contrary was indicated, that the renunciations were not free and voluntary acts but were accomplished under duress

and we have given the benefit of the doubt in favor of citizenship restoration. . . . The only applications which we have denied are those where reliable evidence of disloyalty to the United States was found. Most of these were Kibei. . . . We will vigorously defend our adverse determination of these comparatively few cases in the courts where the renunciants are entitled to have our decision reviewed.

At that time 1,327 of the 2,031 renunciants who repatriated to Japan had had their American citizenship restored; 347 had been denied restitution. A few cases dragged on. The last plaintiff, when his case was brought forward in early 1968, changed his mind. Others had died and a few decided to stay in Japan. Most of the renunciants, in the words of Edward Ennis, had "sought successfully judicial baptism into their proper character as loyal Americans."[64] Wayne Collins was the agent for democracy in correcting this most disastrous of all evacuation mistakes. The trenchant San Franciscan took the case of some other victims of war displacement, the Peruvian Japanese who had been brought to this country by the Justice Department in 1942. The story is told that when Collins called a Washington lawyer in the Justice Department about the case, the man, in an audible aside to a colleague, said, "Oh-oh, Collins has found them!"[65]

SEVENTEEN · TWENTY-FIVE YEARS LATER

THE UNIVERSITY OF CALIFORNIA professor William Petersen wrote about the American Japanese in 1966, "Barely more than twenty years after the end of the wartime camps, this is a minority that has risen above even prejudiced criticism. By any criterion of good citizenship that we choose, the Japanese–Americans are better than any other group in our society, including native-born whites. They have established this remarkable record, moreover, by their almost totally unaided effort. . . . Even in a country whose patron saint is the Horatio Alger hero, there is no parallel to this success story."[1]

This statement is borne out by such primary evidence as the statistics of the United States census. (Since the census separates racial groups, but does not distinguish national origin it is impossible to compare the Nisei with other immigrant descendants who are classified with the white majority.) So by all sociological standards, the American Japanese "are better," using Professor Petersen's words, than any other segment of the population. They have an extremely low divorce rate, crime rate, and unemployment rate, have completed on the average 12.1 years of school (higher than the Caucasian average) and have shown a steady upward mobility in income and occupation since World War II.[2] As a group who are making recognizable contributions in many fields, they are increasingly esteemed by Caucasians. They were always self-sufficient contributors to the American economy, but the esteem in which they are held is a new phenomenon, stemming in part from what Professor Don E. Fehrenbacher of Stanford University has called "a revulsion" of feeling,[3] a collective guilt throughout the nation for the years of discrimination that culminated in the evacuation. The postwar popularity of Japan is a decided factor in the change in attitude. Some observers feel this change has taken place largely because Japan is now an ally of the United States.,

The census figures illustrate growth in numbers as well as success of

American Japanese, and throw some light on the evacuation as a force for distributing and scattering former West Coast residents. In the last census Hawaii had 203,455 persons of Japanese ancestry, roughly one-third of the population. This is a little less than half of the total for the entire United States. There were 157,317 persons of Japanese ancestry in California, about 1 per cent of the state's total population. They are more numerous in California than Chinese and Filipinos, of whom the 1960 census records 95,600 and 65,459, respectively. However, they are far out-numbered by Negroes (883,861 in 1960) and by individuals with a Spanish surname (1,426,538).[4] (These figures would be substantially higher today.)

The evacuation clearly affected the living patterns of American Japanese. Between 1940 and 1950 their number in California dropped from 93,717 to 84,956, but in the decade from 1950 to 1960 it has nearly doubled. According to Mike Masaoka, the theory of dispersal as one of the benefits of the evacuation "is another cliché. There are now more Japanese in California than ever before." Still, many remained in the areas to which they had relocated from the camps. In 1960, there were 14,074 in Illinois as compared with 16,653 in Washington, more in New York and Colorado than in Oregon.[5]

The close to doubling of the American Japanese population in California in the decade 1950 to 1960 was the result of the return of 14,461 people from other states and the arrival of an almost equivalent number from abroad, mainly immigrants from Japan, following the liberalization of the laws.[6] Some of these were relatives of citizens, some were new immigrants, and some were war brides, whose number is estimated at one-twentieth the total Japanese-ancestry in the United States.[7] Though throughout the country the average number of persons per household among American Japanese is 3.98,[8] according to a Nisei writer, "the infinitesimal 'Japanese' portion of the population is growing at a somewhat more rapid rate than the nation as a whole, and the 20,000-odd war brides and immigrants don't account for all the difference."[9] The increase in numbers as well as the return to California attests to the postwar policy of restitution and acceptance.

Though there has been some fear of "re-ghettoization" among the Nisei, the postwar living patterns are different from those of 1940 and reflect the change in occupations, the move to the cities, and increased affluence. In 1960, about 25 per cent of the group in California were engaged in agriculture, but, according to a survey made by the Japanese Chamber of Commerce in Los Angeles, one-half of the Japanese-ancestry population in the state now lives in the mostly urban Los Angeles–Orange County–Long Beach area.

The Los Angeles Little Tokyo is still a bustling small center of Japanese businesses, newspapers, and cafés, but at night it is all but deserted because the proprietors go home to the suburbs. Gone are most of the hotels, rooming houses, bath houses, and pool halls that catered to Issei bachelors in the early years of the century. As noted earlier, during the evacuation period, the dwelling places were occupied by Negroes who migrated west to work in defense industries. The biggest drygoods store, valued by Dunn & Bradstreet in the thirties at $125,000, became the Bronzeville Emporium.

After the war the Nisei scattered to Gardena, Sawtelle, the Crenshaw district, Monterey Park, and Boyle Heights, places which had immigrant colonies in the early days. They tend to cluster in these areas now more by choice than because of discrimination. People no longer need to travel each Saturday to East First Street for Japanese specialties since suburban chain stores carry *tofu* and other traditional foods. Except for special occasions like the annual Nisei Week parade, Little Tokyo lacks the color it used to have. The gambling syndicate which prospered in the twenties, and in the thirties helped patrons hard hit by the Depression, has disappeared. The story is told that when the boss became too obstreperous, the Japanese Association, which exerted the real control over the community, arranged to have him deported. Today the building that once housed the Tokyo Club belongs to the Los Angeles Police!

At least 16 per cent of California's Japanese-ancestry population lives in San Francisco, where the Japanese business district has been beautified by the creation of a $16 million cultural and trade center, but an equal number of people live in Oakland, San Jose, Berkeley, and other outlying cities and suburbs. A recent analysis of the distribution of Sansei (third generation) students in the Seattle public schools shows some residential concentration, but hardly represents the situation of *de facto* segregation faced by Negro students in large cities.[10]

The American Japanese are no longer "shoved into . . . unwholesome slums and industrial areas," as Mike Masaoka complained before World War II.[11] The present-day living patterns represent a freedom and mobility undreamed of in 1940. When he was the English editor of the *Rafu Shimpo* before the war, Togo Tanaka helped to promote a minority housing tract in the Jefferson Park district in Los Angeles which was being undertaken by a builder as a money-making proposition. The surrounding white community was outraged. Tanaka was sent to address a church group in the area, where he faced an embarrassed minister and a room full of fearful, hating people. He thought of those people when he decided to stay in Chicago after the war. Now that he is back in Los Angeles, he is again involved in the real estate field as a sideline as owner and principal in a firm specializing in income properties. "I returned to housing as the area of my trauma," he said.

Discrimination in housing was evident in the late 1940's and 1950's.

In 1946 an American Legion post in Portland denounced the real estate board's refusal to sell a home to a Nisei veteran. One California community (Glendale near Los Angeles) was advertised by its real estate board as being 100 per cent Caucasian.[12] In the same period, a sympathetic real estate man told a Nisei to whom he sold a home in an all-white suburban area of San Jose, "In the event you have any trouble, don't sell out. Stick to your guns." A teacher in a town south of San Francisco bought a home in a neighborhood of his choice in 1956 when realtors were showing houses only in certain prescribed areas to Orientals. There was what he called "a rumble on the block" when he moved in; a petition of complaint was circulated by a couple of people, but the other neighbors would not sign. Before he was even settled his children ran outside to make friends. Neither he nor his wife hid in the house. "You have to be out, working in the garden or fixing your car for people to get to know you, to find something in common to talk about." He has lived comfortably in the neighborhood ever since.

A woman remembers, "We were told in a nice way that we couldn't buy a home in San Carlos (a San Francisco suburb). Although we had quite a number of Caucasian friends who offered to act as a front to buy the house for us, we never discussed the matter any further since we felt that we had no right to live where we were not wanted. As time has gone by this problem seems to be dissolving. As long as you are financially well off you can live wherever you please. This is my feeling as of today."

It has been suggested that American Japanese were "shuttled upward" because of competition for housing with Mexican–Americans and Negroes when they came back to the West Coast. Henry Kuwada, who is president of the approximately 440-member Berkeley real estate board which has gone on record as refusing to accept discriminatory listings, says, "There's no discrimination that I can see. We're accepted." He concedes that, despite the United States Supreme Court decision of June, 1968, which prohibits discrimination in rental, leasing, or sale of real property, discrimination in some degree still exists for some Negroes. A complaint of discrimination was filed with the State Fair Employment Practices Commission in January, 1967, when the owner of an apartment house in San Jose was accused of admitting members of other minority groups including Japanese–Americans, but excluding Negroes.

Housing discrimination in the Los Angeles area is described as "very subtle." There are all sorts of possibilities, so rather than crash an all-white neighborhood the Nisei does not take it to court but asks a Nisei realtor to find him something comparable in another district. The Seattle City Council unanimously passed an open housing ordinance in April, 1968.

Partly as a result of their reputation for being neat, clean, law-abiding, and good gardeners, the American Japanese have led the way in opening up neighborhoods to minorities, but often an open occupancy policy has begun and ended with them. Several years ago a Negro, commenting on the oversimplifications inherent in racial labels, said ruefully, "It's too bad we can't be known as great with crabgrass or earwigs, then everyone would want to have *us* as neighbors."

Economics is at the heart of the matter. "Most Japanese–Americans have middle-class aspirations," a spokesman has said. Almost half of the group are members of the middle class as gauged by their occupations. There were in 1960 almost as many American Japanese in the professional and technical fields as in agriculture, more managers, proprietors, clerical workers, and sales people than there were craftsmen or foremen. Most significantly, considering that many of the first generation immigrants got their start in America in domestic service, there were far fewer in that category than in the professions.[13] A 1966 survey of Nisei employment in the Seattle public schools is an indication of the upward mobility of the group. Of ninety-five employees, sixty-four were teachers, four were librarians, one was a counselor, and except for one lunchroom attendant, the rest were in secretarial and clerical jobs,[14] showing that the successors to the employees fired at the instigation of the Seattle PTA twenty-five years ago were faring very well indeed.

The education with which the Nisei had prepared for future careers that seemed illusory a generation ago has placed them in a good competitive position now that the job market is relatively open. When Pete Ida returned to California in the summer of 1949 after almost a decade in Nebraska, he traveled up and down the coast looking for a post in the public schools. "Everywhere I went I was told the community wasn't ready for me." He worked first as custodian and shop teacher in a private school in Menlo Park. Then Gordon Parsons, principal of the Green Gables School in Palo Alto, hired him as a sixth grade teacher. He has been in the Palo Alto school system ever since as a teacher, a coach, and an instructor in driver education.

A woman with teacher training who had been prepared to accept a clerking job when she returned to San Jose in 1956, was chided by an old friend who told her she must not waste her credential. "How would they accept me?" she asked. "Just like any other person who applies," her friend answered. "Things are different now." She has been teaching kindergarten and first grade for eleven years. In 1967, 976 Nisei were teaching in the Los Angeles public schools.[15] There are a number of Japanese–American principals in California. Another field where there has been a spectacular breakthrough is civil service. Before 1941 it was estimated that five Nisei held federal civil service positions; their number is now estimated at 10,000.[16] According to a Civil Service Commission study, they tend to be in the upper middle category in the wage scale.[17]

In the professions, many Nisei have gone into architecture, dentistry, and optometry, fields in which they exercise the precision and artistry popularly attributed to Japanese. They are also working in new fields like data processing. Nisei doctors, dentists, and lawyers now serve a cross-section of the public and not simply a Japanese–American clientele. The competence of some of these professionals has been acknowledged by government appointments. Several Nisei lawyers are public defenders. There are four Japanese–American judges in California. John Aiso was appointed to the bench in Los Angeles by Earl Warren, when he was governor of the state, an act which was interpreted by some members of the Japanese community as an apology for Warren's part in the evacuation. During his term of office, Edmund G. (Pat) Brown appointed three Nisei judges in Orange County, San Jose, and Sacramento. Governor Reagan appointed a Japanese–American physician to the State Board of Medical Examiners.

In contrast to the period before the war when they were restricted to Japanese-owned businesses, the Nisei are now executives in general corporations. A man who works for an electronics firm expresses surprise at his opportunities: as a youth his highest expectation was to become an auto mechanic.

Even those who follow the traditional occupations have continued to add scientific knowledge and business acumen to diligence with profitable results in the postwar years. Some Beverly Hills gardeners take evening classes in agriculture at UCLA and occasionally earn up to $15,000 a year.[18] A San Mateo nursery manager comments on his success, "Since carnations sell for the same price today that they brought fifteen or twenty years ago, the only way we've been able to stay in business with costs going up is through better growing methods and better management techniques." Nisei growers working through their county farm bureaus have improved the long-range prospects for agriculture in California by instigating a plan to give farmers who intend to cultivate rather than subdivide their land a low tax assessment.

There are far fewer fishermen today than in 1940, since coastal fishing has declined. Many of the old canneries have closed. There is no longer a resident colony of fishermen and cannery workers on Terminal Island.

Hotel management was a prewar occupation of many of the immigrant generation in Seattle; in the postwar era the Issei and their children have expanded into apartment ownership on a large scale.

The historical discrimination of the unions is breaking down, but for various reasons not many Nisei go into craft work. A civic leader feels that "the Japanese have been helped by the militant stand of the Negroes," though it has been charged that Nisei have been used to effect token integration at the expense of the black man to which union spokesmen in California reply that Japanese–Americans and Mexican–Americans are more aggressive in applying for training and jobs.

"I am not naïve enough to think that discrimination does not exist," says a professional man. It is noted that for Nisei "the higher you go, the more difficult it gets." The chief executive positions, both in private industry and government service, are often closed to them. This may account for the fact that though Japanese–Americans have more education than the average American and a larger proportion of them are in professional or white collar occupations, their median income is lower. Izumi Taniguchi, an economics professor at Fresno State College, after studying this discrepancy, commented, "It appears that the Japanese male reaches a ceiling income, whereas for the white male the sky is the limit." On the other hand, women of Japanese ancestry earn more than Caucasian women. In employment and promotion, discrimination is described as "subtle."

Though there is not yet complete equality, the tolerance of today represents such a drastic improvement over the prewar treatment that some of the returned group have expressed the conviction that a Japanese name is an asset. A Nisei married to a Caucasian used her maiden name when she ran, although unsuccessfully, for the New York state assembly. Grayson Taketa, the first Nisei candidate in a congressional race in California, used his experience in a relocation center to political advantage to the extent that his opponent in the primary complained jokingly that he was feeling "the Japanese–American backlash." Taketa, a thirty-three-year-old San Jose lawyer, championed the cause of minority and low income families in his 1968 campaign in which he lost to the incumbent Republican.

Mainland Nisei are just beginning to enter politics for which their upbringing as children of disenfranchised immigrants had given them little preparation since the Issei dealt with the Japanese Association rather than with the American political system. "We're just beginning to get our feet wet," is the opinion of Judge Wayne Kanemoto of San Jose, one of the founders of the local Democratic club. Several Japanese–Americans have run, unsuccessfully so far, for the California assembly and senate. There have been several Nisei mayors in California and one in Teton, Idaho. There are a number of city councilmen and city attorneys. Colorado has a Nisei member in its legislature, and the directors of the Human Relations Commissions in Denver and Seattle are Japanese–Americans.

Hawaiian Nisei have achieved an outstanding record in public office. The fiftieth state is represented in Congress by a Nisei senator, Daniel Inouye, and two Nisei representatives, Spark Matsunaga and Patsy Mink. The two men ran on the record of their war service with the 100th Infantry Battalion in Europe where Inouye lost an arm. All three were active in Democratic politics in Honolulu where Matsunaga was a member of the Territorial Legislature and Mrs. Mink was an accomplished and articulate young attorney. The fourth member of the Hawaiian congressional delegation is a Chinese–American, Senator Hiram Fong, creating a situation which was very nearly predicted by John Rankin when he actively opposed statehood for Hawaii in the nineteen-thirties.[19] He had warned that there would be "two Jap senators."

The changing attitude toward American Japanese is confirmed, appropriately enough, by the Gallup poll. In 1942 they were regarded as treacherous, cruel, sly, warlike, and hardworking, the last attribute apparently the result of first-hand observation, the rest influenced by war propaganda. In a similar poll conducted in 1961 they were considered hardworking, artistic, intelligent, progressive, but still sly.[20] However, though their public image has altered, they cannot forget the past entirely, especially in areas where feeling against them ran high. Today Placer County has Nisei businessmen as well as farmers. An automobile salesman, an insurance man, and a securities broker serve a Caucasian in addition to a Japanese clientele. Hike Yego, who returned in 1948, is a school trustee in Penryn and the first Japanese–American member of the Placer County Democratic Central Committee. Kay Takemoto, who works for a fruit growing association, is on the coordinating committee for the Office of Economic Opportunity. The evacuees returned because they owned property and were attached to old friends and familiar surroundings, and they succeeded in making a place for themselves through a determined and sustained effort by their leaders to bring about better relationships in the community. An Auburn resident, formerly with the sheriff's office, expresses the general opinion on how well they have succeeded. "It's amazing what the Japanese have done with this country. Better than average homes, well-tended orchards, solid citizens."

A resident estimates that about two-thirds of the Japanese families have returned to Hood River, Oregon. One Nisei is now a county commissioner and head of the county civil defense. The Nisei chairman of the board of directors of the fruit growers cooperative is a member of the State Board of Higher Education as well as the president of the Pacific International Trap Shoot Association. Mits Takasumi directed the Cancer Crusade for Hood River County.

"How is Salinas?" visitors ask those who braved the first postwar months of ostracism. The answer is, "Salinas is fine now." Cottie Keltner, who used to receive letters in 1945 asking, "Would it be safe to come back?" says, "Things are back to normal *plus*. The *obon* festival sponsored by the Buddhist Church is patronized by hundreds of people. They can't make enough food."

In nearby Watsonville, where many of the people were very hostile, a Nisei sits with the Rotary Club. "Buddy" Iwata, the general manager of the Livingston Farmers Association, was elected a member of the Merced County Junior College District, which held its first classes in the fair grounds where he was interned in an assembly center twenty-five years ago. During the war Hoichi Kubo was stopped at the "gate" at Pearl Harbor by a sentry who said, "Hey, you, Jap, you can't go in there!" In 1968 his son was offered appointments to both West Point and Annapolis.

With the abolishment of anti-Oriental practices has come a change in emphasis in the American Japanese promotional organizations. The old Japanese associations are no longer very active. Many of the pioneer Issei whose interests they represented are dead now. Though the JACL is not universally popular, it has ninety-one chapters, over 22,000 members, and a half-million dollar endowment fund. There are those who feel that its sponsorship of social functions will ensure a continuing interest even as the political issues have less immediate impact for the Japanese group. The organization is promoting the concept of a "new Pacific era," a development which would have startled the "Yellow Peril" spokesmen of the prewar years.[21]

Conditions have never been more auspicious for friendship between Japan and the United States. The friendly reciprocity between the two countries has stimulated a belated interest on the part of the Nisei in the land of their ancestors. The prewar trips of their parents were undertaken mainly to keep up family ties, a journey of weeks paid for by years of industry and thrift. With ease and comfort the Nisei travel to Japan for business or pleasure, sometimes very frequently, by jet. They are now well accepted in the mother country. Many hold responsible positions in private business or as United States government officials. Fukuoka City has a Nisei consul. Hank Gosho, who was with military intelligence during World War II, is a high ranking officer of the United States Information Service in Tokyo.

"The pendulum has swung to the opposite pole." said a former evacuee in commenting on the cultural and political *rapprochement* between the two countries. Shame for the nuclear holocaust visited upon Hiroshima and Nagasaki has contributed to the fervor on the American side. Isamu Noguchi designed a bridge for the Peace Park in Hiroshima which he called *tsukuru*, meaning "to build." The Japanese architect, Yoshiro Taniguchi, created a Pagoda of Peace for the Japanese trade center in San Francisco "to convey the friendship and good will of the people of the United States." Canada, not to be outdone in expressing a change of heart, has erected a Japanese cultural center in Toronto.

The pacifism of Toyohiko Kagawa, distinctly a minority viewpoint in the Japan of 1941, today is widespread and to it can be traced a slight revival of anti-Western feeling connected with the United States involvement in Vietnam which Japan fears may widen into an Asian war. Critics think that Americans look down upon Asians since the United States dropped atomic bombs in Japan and is now using gas weapons in Vietnam.

For many years intercultural relations have been promoted in a schol-

arly way in the United States by such organizations as the Blaisedell Institute of Religion and Philosophy at Claremont, whose members have
included James Blaisedell, former president of Pomona College, John
Anson Ford, a Los Angeles County Supervisor for twenty-four years,
and Katsumo Mukaeda, general secretary of the Japanese Chamber of
Commerce. Some of the more obscure newspapers in the institute's Oriental studies collection, the second largest in the state, were scrutinized
during World War II by members of the military interested in psychological warfare.

Popular interest has now extended to the history of Japanese immigration to America, and Caucasians have contributed to research on
the "Mayflower of the Pacific" which brought the ill-fated Wakamatsu
tea and silk colony in 1869 to San Francisco and eventually to Placerville. The grave of Okei, one of the two who remained at Gold Hill, the
first Japanese girl to die in the United States, is being commemorated
by a state historical landmark plaque. An ambitious American Japanese
history project, financed by the JACL, the Carnegie Corporation, and
government funds from the Department of Health, Education and
Welfare, is underway at UCLA. The project will produce both a formal
and informal history of the Japanese in America and a sociological study
based on hundreds of interviews with Issei, Nisei, and Sansei. The
public has lately become aware that the Japanese immigrants, though
late arrivals to these shores, created a chapter of pioneer history in the
development of the West.

One of the more curious manifestations of the reversal of feeling is the
commemorations with much fanfare of once-traumatic events such as
the Goleta shelling in 1942, in ceremonies to which the Japanese consul
invariably is invited. The once-vilified Japanese language schools have
actually been recommended by a member of Congress for federal
support, and will be affected by a law passed by the California legislature granting public school credit for language courses completed in
private schools.[22]

Literature has reflected the shift, also. Twenty-five years ago books
and pamphlets about the American Japanese were frankly propagandistic. Their defenders made the point that despite race, they were Americans and then proceeded to show how American they really were. Only
writers like Pearl Buck, who had a long acquaintance with the Far East,
were undismayed by the possibility of Oriental characteristics in the
Nisei. Toru Matsumoto's *A Brother is a Stranger*, published shortly after
the war, is a personal and somewhat defensive attempt to set down
Japanese ways in such a manner that a prejudiced American viewpoint
will find them acceptable.

Twenty-five years have restored a balance to the consideration of
the events that followed Pearl Harbor and an acknowledgement of com-

plexities impermissible in wartime. Gene Oishi's semifictional, possibly autobiographical newspaper account, "Remember Pearl Harbor, and then . . ." shows how a child's easy acceptance of two cultures and two loyalties (riceballs and hamburgers, Admiral Tojo and President Roosevelt) was inexplicably interrupted by the war that forced Issei and Nisei to take sides.[23] Daisuke Kitagawa's *Issei and Nisei* is an eminently honest account of the tensions of relocation center life.

No-No Boy by John Okada analyzes divided loyalties and the anguish which was the consequence of decisions made in regard to them. The mother in the novel was one of the Issei who could not believe that Japan had lost the war. When, after receiving a letter from relatives in the defeated homeland, she at last acknowledged the truth, she killed herself. The characters of both generations seem to wander in a confused state of shock more appropriate to life in the smoking ruins of Hiroshima or Nagasaki than Seattle; the war had scarred them as irrevocably as if they were on the battlefield.

Hawaii, End of the Rainbow by Kazuo Miyamoto describes in fictional form the impact of war on the Hawaiian Japanese, who had established themselves so much more firmly than the West Coast Issei in their adopted land. In this novel of uprooting, the war imposes arbitrary, often irrational decisions on the lives of individuals, from which they try to salvage some autonomy related to their own needs and desires. So, at last, the truth is revealed, not of spies or sabotage, enemy or ally, but of the complexity of all human life. Both these novels, intended for an American reading public, were written in English by Nisei though published in Japan by Charles Tuttle of Tokyo and Rutland, Vermont.

A 1967 novel written in Japanese concerns the loyalty question crisis in the relocation centers. The chief character is modeled on Toyo Miyatake, the Issei photographer who built his own camera at Manzanar. The author compares the introduction of Question 28, in which the Issei were asked to renounce their connection with the land of their birth, to an incident in Japanese history, when converts to Christianity were forced to stamp on the cross to escape persecution.

The contemporary work of graphic artists of Japanese ancestry reveals an unself-conscious union of cultural influences. This is not a new departure, but the response of the public encourages artists to express themselves more freely than ever before. Miné Okubo, known for her realistic illustrations, full of amusing, homely details, has changed to a more impressionistic, more Oriental style of expression. Isamu Noguchi creates gigantic works in granite and metal, yet also constructs fragile Japanese lamps called *akari*. His simple, organic sculptures, such as his stage settings for Martha Graham, transcend any national influence.

The effect of lightness in massive forms, so apparent in modern architecture, owes a great deal to Japanese art, as do modern patterns in textiles and the widespread use of paper as a medium for decoration.

Today no one is surprised when California school children are taught *origami* (paper folding) by a kimona-clad Kibei or when *judo* and *aikido* (Japanese physical self-discipline) are offered in city recreation classes. Yoshiki Hirabayashi of Sunnyvale donates many hours to teaching these traditional expressions of Japanese culture to young Americans. There was surprise, but only approval, when Lucille Nixon, a Palo Alto school administrator, won honorable mention for her *tanka* verse in the Emperor's poetry contest in 1957 and made a trip to Tokyo to receive a beautifully calligraphed copy of her poem. She had learned to write *tanka*, first in *romaji*, and later forming the Japanese characters with a brush, from Mrs. Tomoe Tana, the wife of a retired Buddhist priest, who went to her home to do housework and stayed to become her teacher. From their collaboration came a volume of the *tanka* of West Coast and Hawaiian poets, *Sounds from the Unknown*, and a children's book, *Yoshiko and the Porcelain Fox*, as yet unpublished, completed by the novelist Janet Lewis and based on Mrs. Tana's reminiscences of life in a fishing village in Japan. Speaking of this fruitful cultural exchange which ended with Miss Nixon's death in 1963, Mrs. Tana said, "We gave something to each other. I wanted the Caucasian world to know about *tanka*, and now because of Miss Nixon, whose verse is still published in Japan, some word of it has gone forth."

Buddhism, as another manifestation of Japanese tradition, is flourishing in America. It has been estimated that there are close to 100,000 Buddhists in the United States today, the majority of whom are of Japanese ancestry.[24] Buddhism for many Nisei has become institutionalized following the Christian tradition, with Sunday worship, whereas in Japan it is a religion of the home with public services and celebrations only at special times of the year. By contrast, the more intuitive forms of Buddhism, particularly Zen, are enjoying enormous popularity with Caucasians. A Zen monastery, started in 1967 at Tassajara Hot Springs in the mountains near Carmel, California, has attracted more Caucasians than Orientals. The Japanese Zen Master Suzuki Roshi finds a freedom in America from century-old preconceptions that inhibit expression in Japan.

Shinto worship, which was outlawed during World War II in the relocation centers, also flourishes today. The first Japanese-constructed skyscraper in the United States was dedicated with a Shinto purification ceremony.

There is some universality in the experience of the Nisei who came to an appreciation of his ancestral tradition by seeing Japanese art in Caucasian homes. "I had never thought of it in relation to myself. I was too busy Westernizing." In his lifetime the Nisei has had to suppress his "Japaneseness" but the habit of implicitly asserting, "I am more American than you" in his way of life is giving way slowly to an acknowledgement of ancestry. Most Nisei homes contain a number of Japanese objects displayed with pride. "The Nisei are divided," says Keisho Motoyama, a Buddhist leader. "Some want to perpetuate the old traditions." The Issei had enforced a strict moral code based on such concepts as pride (*haji*), duty (*giri*), and human feeling (*ninjo*). Some of the Nisei, who see the value of these rules in their parents' lives and their own, want to pass them along to their children in the most appropriate way; others prefer to cultivate American mores. "I think in a way they feel no different than other Americans, but they call themselves Japanese–Americans. This is an interesting phenomenon. Maybe they are building *their own* American mores." One group says, "Why should we throw away everything?" Others feel that the old standards are no longer relevant to them as they were relevant in the immigrant struggle in America, which, in the opinion of Mr. Motoyama was quite similar to the struggle to adjust to Western culture in Japan since the beginning of the Meiji era.

Jeffrey Matsui, a JACL spokesman, has commented, " . . . as the years go by, we appear to feel a hidden pride in bringing to attention the fact that the values imported from Meiji Japan by our Issei and passed on to the generations of Japanese Americans are almost identical to those of the white Protestant population. This similarity not only seems to give us a sense of belonging, but also an illusion of being an inseparable part of the WASP community." This is the explanation he gives to the question, "So why does the Nisei community always seem to side with the establishment over the underdog?"[25]

The American Japanese reaction to the extremism and separatism of the Negro revolution and to the extralegal actions of peace advocates, though it can be explained by family conditioning, the emphasis on the importance of good behavior, of earning rewards, of obedience to authority, shows how far the group identifies with the white middle class. Some Nisei were asked, "What advice do you have for Negroes?" They answered: "Get education and training." "Respect the law." "The Negro shouldn't feel the country owes him a break." "The colored people have a chip on their shoulder; so others really jump on them." Many would agree with the businessman who said, "We've gone up in the world. Are we expected to step down now in order to pull the Negro up with us?"

Shig Wakamatsu, a Chicagoan, wrote, "The average Nisei is utterly naïve about civil rights as it pertains to the American Negro. . . . In our desire to become more 'Americanized,' the Nisei have absorbed—consciously or unconsciously—the prejudices of the white man towards the black man. . . . Over in Los Angeles, when they finally figured the damages around Watts, the Nisei's share was over a million dollars."[26]

With prosperity, some American Japanese have acquired a vested interest in property values and resent any threat to them. A number of Issei and Nisei landlords have been as reluctant to accept Negro tenants as any white landlord. Some have switched from the group's traditional Democratic party affiliation to Republican. One man expressed his political philosophy as being against government interference, "such as the government favoring labor unions so that you cannot hire or fire a man of your choice." The Hawaiian congressional delegation often speaks for West Coast Japanese interests, but they differ on certain issues, notably, in their attitudes toward farm labor. Many West Coast Nisei farm operators favored the bracero program of importing cheap Mexican labor on a seasonal basis.

When the veterans of the 442nd gather together to talk about their war experience, an observer says he asks himself, "What have you done since?" A newspaper reporter who has covered veterans reunions says it is hard to fit the men with their record. "They're in their late forties, early fifties now. Their community service consists of the usual token things."

A woman who is serving on her city human relations commission complained that her fellow Nisei whom she canvassed in regard to a school integration issue, were too involved with children's piano lessons and other family activities to take an active part. "Let me know how it comes out," was a typical response.

Dr. S. I. Hayakawa, the acting president, who is credited with settling the strife at San Francisco State College in 1969, is approved by the majority of American Japanese, partly, perhaps, because he is enjoying nationwide esteem for what is regarded as his successful resolution of a conflict. But some Nisei, and Sansei, have taken pains to affirm their independence, their sympathy and affiliation with the groups involved in the strike.

A minority of Japanese–Americans have committed themselves to an active role in civil rights. Nisei have been active in human relations commissions, in branch offices of the Office of Economic Opportunity, and with the Fair Employment Practices Commission. Through the many employed in social work the Nisei have a close contact with the problems of poverty and discrimination. Frank Chuman challenged the JACL to raise $2.5 million to help disadvantaged Americans. A number have gone to the South to offer their services as attorneys or to support the Southern Christian Leadership Conference. A few years ago, they contributed to the effort to integrate the universities. William Hohri of Chicago marched with James Meredith in Mississippi. Another Chicagoan, Harry Techima, an engineer, was instrumental in bringing a Negro to the suburb of Park Forest. While undergoing a family emergency, he loaned $2,000 to a young professor at De Paul University so that he could meet a down payment on a house near Techima's. He had become interested in the question of open housing as a member of a civil rights study group. He is quoted as saying, "After a year of studying and talking, I began to realize we were just talking and not accomplishing anything. . . . Nuts to having people sign pledge cards for open occupancy and nuts to preaching sermons. The way to have integration is to integrate."[27]

The Reverend George Aki was the only Japanese–American who picketed a postwar Ku Klux Klan rally in Los Angeles. He carried a sign saying, "Jesus was a Jew." He wanted to make his Congregational church in Hollywood a neighborhood church, which would bring in Negroes, instead of an all-Japanese church. After his daughter, Joanne, lived and worked in Watts one summer, she described the impact of her experiences to her father's congregation. "The shame is obviously here," she said. "It can be seen by anyone with normal vision as he drives down Firestone, or Manchester or Avalon Streets. Once the shame is our shame, we must be good listeners. We must hear the people of the ghetto speak their needs, their desires, their hatreds, their aspirations and ultimately work with them in rebuilding our society."

She reiterated an idea that is proposed from time to time, that yellow men might be arbitrators between white and black men. Another Nisei, a member of the radical movement in civil rights, feels it is already too late for this. "How easy to be molded into what this society wants you to be. How long can we go through life comfortably blind, imbued with illusions (or delusions), sheltered by being docile and 'acceptable,' while others are reviled? I'm so glad those days are over. I want no part of being cocooned in a society that extols its own image in magnitude while it has systematically destroyed and subordinated the cultures, mores, religion, politics and economy of all others who will no longer play puppets and wish to assert their own humanity. My salutes are to those who oppose the United States. Malcolm X was the turning point in my life. What he exposed of American life and thought, what he revealed of the proscribed life of Black people; what he taught of the greatest potentialities for Blacks, and the relationship of all oppressed people—had its impact on me that changed my life."

This attitude is atypical, yet the fact is that many Nisei, by tradition moderates, are feeling increasingly uncomfortable as the political movements of this country, in particular the civil rights movement, have become polarized. Many acknowledge that the rules which held for them in their upward climb from rejection to acceptance are not applicable to the explosive problems of the Negro in the sixties. The Nisei dilemma in this respect was noted by Jeffry Matsui:

> To experience frustration in its purest form, get involved in what is popularly known today as "Human Relations." . . . You discuss some of

the social problems which our future Sansei–Yonsei must be prepared to meet (even though these problems may be almost laughable by the previous speakers' standards) .

Then comes the audience reaction. Practically all the Anglos in the audience seemed [sic] obliged to protest your modesty by reciting all the virtues of the Japanese American and the great obstacles we've overcome. And on and on—and you cannot help but sense that each praise for the Japanese American is actually cowardly criticism of the other minorities present. . . .

So you sit there unable to shake this crazy dream that the whites have taken hold of your limp, neutral arms and are using them to slap and strike at the larger minorities. You want to stiffen your arms and pull it out of their grasp and tell them bravely, "if you want to hit somebody, use your own hands." But you can't. Or you don't.

This is frustration. Or cowardice?[28]

The Nisei leadership, particularly in the JACL, has moved ahead of the group as a whole on civil rights. The JACL president, Jerry Enomoto, says, "We cannot stand tall until all minority groups in this country stand tall. . . ."[29] Yet even as a defender of such moderate organizations as the NAACP and the Urban League, the JACL does not have the backing of the entire American Japanese community. That all Nisei do not support civil rights issues on election day was demonstrated in California in the vote on the 1964 ballot measure to block open housing in the state.

The JACL campaigned strenuously against Proposition Fourteen. Speakers told audiences, "The same groups that are asking to be allowed to discriminate in housing are the ones who put you into camps." Nevertheless, many Issei, Nisei, and even Sansei voted in favor of Proposition Fourteen. A UCLA professor found that only 52 per cent of the Orientals in Los Angeles County (the majority, Japanese–Americans) intended to vote against it. A graduate student at UCLA after a study concluded that there was in the Los Angeles area "minimal Japanese American involvement in civil rights activity at the local level and political segregation from the Negro community."[30] A Negro civil rights spokesman told a group of JACL members that the black people are not sure whether the Japanese–American is "white or non-white," that the Japanese–American takes whichever side that suits him for pragmatic reasons rather than principle.[31]

Yet the JACL, actively committed to promoting civil rights legislation, has been effective as a lobbying organization through Mike Masaoka in Washington as well as at the state level. Even in the relocation center period, the *Pacific Citizen* protested a U.S. senate filibuster that defeated an anti-poll tax bill. The JACL legal counsel, William Marutani, took part in a court case in Bogalusa, Mississippi. The organization has been accused, by a Nisei critic, of acting "in conformity with the accepted response to the turmoils of the time—that of accepting any social revolt in the name of civil rights, however far-fetched and anti-social it may have become."[32]

But the 1968 president reiterates the JACL tradition of working for reforms within a constitutional framework. "I abhor and I know JACL abhors violence and hatred regardless of who preaches and practices it. We don't like what Brown and Carmichael stand for any more than we liked the rantings and ravings of men like Gerald L. K. Smith, John Lechner and others who vented their race-baiting venom upon us. JACL has always stood with moderates and, incidentally, 'old pros,' in the national leadership of the civil rights movement, like Roy Wilkins, Whitney Young, etc. This, I trust and hope, is where we will continue to stand." But on the subject of civil disobedience, he writes, " . . . unlike people who confidently say they know it's always wrong, I am not that sure. It seems to me that judiciously applied use of this technique brought the Southern Negro unprecedented civil rights gains. It also helped bring the Nobel Peace Prize to Dr. Martin Luther King. Who can say with absolute finality that morally wrong laws that stand for a seeming eternity should not be fought with such a tool?"[33]

The espousal of a cause other than their own is a new phenomenon for Japanese–Americans. Accused of not participating in community affairs, their response has been that they were up until recently too involved with their own problems as well as afraid to venture into a wider field for fear of not being accepted. Harry Honda, editor of the *Pacific Citizen*, says the role of the JACL is to rock the Nisei out of his complacency. The Nisei has been described as a "cool" personality. "Being cool," according to a professor of sociology, Dr. Stanford Lyman, at Sonoma State College who analyzed the group, "means character control, inhibition of impulses, the control of one's personality so that it is not revealingly expressive."[34]

Some Nisei think that the second generation are more introverted than the first, that they "stick together" and are reluctant to risk a rebuff from the white community. "All persons of Japanese ancestry are humble or shy," says a farmer. A newspaperman in his thirties disagrees. He said he was in his youth one of "the angry young men." If anyone discriminated against him or his friends, "our reaction was to break up the place." He complains that the Japanese community puts on a façade for visitors: the same spokesmen always issue the same tired platitudes. Another Little Tokyo reporter feels, "Nobody will tell the truth about 'Jaytown.' All the vernacular newspapers have a policy of suppressing any news that would distress the family."

There is a conflict between the tradition of close community and family relations and the desire for greater freedom. Some Nisei have "pulled away" from the Japanese group. Their friends are Caucasians. They live in "white" neighborhoods; their families attend community rather than Japanese churches; they rarely meet other Nisei. The only "Japanese affair" they attend may be the annual *obon* festival at the Buddhist church. They see Nisei whose careers are advanced within the Japanese group to whom it is important to keep up contacts for professional reasons, but this is not a consideration for them.

The aging Issei, some in their eighties, are generally retired and many, following the Japanese tradition, are living with their children. They generally stay quietly in the background when visitors come. Some, like Harry Sotaro Kawake of Seattle, are still active. At the age of seventy-seven he is still pursuing a career as a financier, merchant, art collector, and community leader. About half the Issei have become American citizens and are becoming interested in elections and issues, read the newspapers carefully, and follow the endorsements of Japanese community leaders. They tend to be conservative in their outlook as expressed by reluctance in voting tax increases.

Some of the group lost everything in the evacuation period and were too old to start over again. A group of Issei bachelors were discovered in Chicago in 1949 living in substandard housing, spending their free time in bars, gambling, placing bets with bookies. Though before the war they would not accept charity, they had no hesitation in accepting or even demanding it.[35] Yet a cross-section of over one thousand Issei who responded to a Japanese–American research project questionnaire revealed little evidence of psychic wounds inflicted by their struggle in America. Three-quarters said they had achieved a satisfactory life in the United States and one-half said they felt more American than Japanese.

The Nisei attitude toward the older generation is ambivalent. Many remember the desire to get out of the culture, to assimilate, to free themselves of the stifling weight of age-old traditions. As descendants of an immigrant group, they are considered remarkable for having become English-speaking in one generation. Very few Nisei speak Japanese in the home unless there are Issei family members living with them. Some remember the discipline under which they grew up as tyrannical and oppressive. There is also, and often by the same people, a great respect for the accomplishments of the Issei, who managed to help them get an education and become good American citizens despite terrible odds. The virtues of the Issei—frugality, pride, perseverance, and hard work—are recalled with an emotion bordering on reverence, and the devotion is repaid by the traditional Japanese honor to the aged family members.

The degree of cultural attachment in the Nisei is to a certain extent measured by their attitude toward intermarriage which with the third generation has become an active issue. (The old system of arranged marriage [*baishakunin*] had been discontinued; it is now much less common even in Japan than before World War II. The custom of adopting a male, if none is born into the family, to continue the name, is not practiced by Nisei.) The majority of the Sansei marry "within the race" but interracial marriages, particularly with Caucasians, are on the increase. Before 1940 they were common only in a few places, such as New York City, where Issei men had immigrated alone. Prewar statistics showed about 1,750 interracial marriages in New York City and about five hundred in Los Angeles.[36]

Reactions today vary from those of the father who said before he reconsidered, "My daughter knew how I felt about intermarriage . . . as far as I'm concerned, she's dead,"[37] to parents who are proud of the fact that their children have married Caucasians; it seems a confirmation of their social acceptability. Others say, "It makes no difference" or "It depends on what the person is like." When the World War II hero, Ben Kuroki, speaking before a JACL group wondered why Nisei prefer blondes and complained that "we're losing our Japanese heritage through intermarriage," his comments were "greeted by chuckles combined with subdued shock," according to Ellen Endo, the English language editor of *Rafu Shimpo*.[38] The *Pacific Citizen* report elicited reader response, including a reply from James Michener, the novelist, who is married to a Nisei.

Intermarriage as a consequence of assimilation mainly concerns Sansei, the third generation, most of whom are in their teens, twenties, and early thirties. (There are already several hundred Yonsei, the fourth generation.) The Sansei, who have been described as "too good to be true," are measurably taller than their fathers, more self-confident, more indubitably American and, in the opinion of one sociologist, "less racially visible."

Though the Sansei are continuing the Nisei tradition of outstanding academic performance, they are acquiring some of the less desirable majority group characteristics with assimilation. According to a recent article, "They now face a strange and serious problem, without precedent here: the problem of a non-conforming excellence. The young of every other minority group have shown a pattern of escape from the ghetto whereby their academic record rises to meet the U.S. white middle-class standard even as their delinquency rate drops to meet it. But in the Los Angeles area, where Dr. Harry Kitano of UCLA has studied them, the Sansei in high school are exactly reversing this pattern: as their Americanization increases (measured by 'popularity'—club memberships, student body offices, etc.), their scholastic level is falling and their delinquency rate is rising to white American levels."[39]

A Nisei social worker links Sansei delinquency with affluence. "They think they have it made, and then they relax their standards," he says.[40] "We would never have been allowed to get away with such expressions of rebellion," a Nisei mother of a teen-ager comments. A father says, "I see the young ones growing up and I see how they are acting, and it kind of scares me. Even though we are getting more and more integrated in this country, we're still a minority. We still feel this and we need to feel it here and there. When you get to the point when you feel equal, you start losing some of the things you were supposed to be known for." He spoke about his upbringing. "The Japanese had a way, I call it a subtle way, of punishing you. They burned little bits of incense on your back—it didn't really hurt—it was just the idea of burning that scares you. It didn't leave a scar or anything. But that would hold you back for a while if you were bad."

Another Nisei worries about his children's lack of motivation and appreciation. "What they need now and then," he thinks, "is a kick in the pants." A Nisei sports writer complains that the Sansei are "pampered and coddled" which puts them at a disadvantage in competition with highly motivated Negro athletes.[41] Delinquency is not serious or widespread among the Sansei but the fact that it occurs at all elicits a vigorous response from the Nisei, who have formed study commissions which are modern variants of the Issei's pattern of imposing a collective community discipline on the recalcitrant.

The Sansei, like other members of their generation, protest status seeking and materialism in their parents and in their symposia discuss drugs, sex, the generation gap, the Vietnam war, and civil rights. Only a few are activists in the sense of public protest (four Sansei were arrested in the Berkeley demonstrations in 1964; Sansei seem less interested than members of other minorities in the campus Third World Liberation Front). But a great many Sansei have left their parents behind in their style of response to current problems. One family jokingly told the college student with revolutionary ideas, "If you don't like it here, why don't you go back to Japan?" Protest, in the case of Sansei, may be considered a proof of assimilation. They share more with their peers than with their parents.

"Why should I be Japanese in American society today?" one boy asked the family minister. Another protested that the rule of removing one's shoes at his home and the Buddhist family shrine in the living room embarrassed him when he considered bringing friends to visit. The Nisei have a nostalgic feeling that the Sansei do not know enough about their cultural heritage. Language school attendance is not mandatory for them as it was for the Nisei.

"Youth and Its Identity" was the subject of the 1966 Junior JACL Convention. As R. B. Read commented, "No subject could be more appropriate, or—for the Sansei—more poignant. Unquestionably, their collective superiority has somehow been linked with their 'Japaneseness.' But should they try to hold on to it? and if so, how can they? Must they inevitably melt into the pot and become like the rest of us—variously great and small, good and bad, but mostly that passable, fallible, likeable, middling creature beloved to his fellows as The Average American?"[42]

The Sansei and Yonsei are proving their assimilation by accepting the troublesome challenges of the sixties that the Nisei prefer to ignore. By traditional American standards the Nisei have earned their success, and though the critics among them feel it is precarious, they also acknowledge that the majority are not likely to change their patterns of thinking. This is more a matter of generation than of Japanese heritage.

EIGHTEEN · CONCLUSION

OCCASIONALLY THE SANSEI first learn of the evacuation at school —their parents have not told them. Some Nisei have simply put the experience behind them as the "bad dream which went by." Others feel so bitter they will not talk about it.

A few, from nostalgia or curiosity, have returned to the sites of the former camps. The Bureau of Reclamation gave most of the land near Tule Lake to veterans who drew for lots. They were permitted to buy the old barracks for $60 apiece and move them onto their homesteads. Migrant workers and weekend hunters intermittently occupy buildings near the original camp site which is still owned by the government. Indians are living at Poston once again. Manzanar belongs to the City of Los Angeles, which stores equipment used by its water department in what was formerly the recreation hall. The Arkansas State Public Lands and Park Commission recently sponsored a pilgrimage to Rohwer for former evacuees who wanted to plant some cherry trees, crape myrtle, and azaleas near memorials for the dead now maintained by the state.

A Californian, a former evacuee, visited Heart Mountain in the early nineteen-sixties and found only some remaining potato cellars by the railroad tracks. The land which had been homesteaded was planted in beans and alfalfa. Another, who was at Minidoka, remarks, "There were people who did go back, but there wasn't really anything to draw you back to it. Lately I've been tempted to go up there. I might get lost. I could get as far as Twin Falls, but from there I wouldn't know where to go, which road to take."

Where the buildings have been removed the traces of the past have almost disappeared. Yet some people feel impelled to return, perhaps with a sense of disbelief, remembering the watch towers, the barbed wire, the fire breaks, the dust storms, the tar-paper barracks, and all the human turmoil that took place within these wilderness prisons.

The chief figures in the evacuation are invariably remembered. Roosevelt is less blamed by most Nisei than General DeWitt, who revealed his racial prejudice, at first privately, later publicly. In 1944 DeWitt replaced Lieutenant General Leslie J. McNair in a European command after McNair was killed in Normandy. In 1946 DeWitt was awarded the Distinguished Service Medal. He never returned to California. "Maybe he was afraid we'd sue him," Nisei have speculated. Suits *were* initiated against him by a few Caucasians he banished from the Western Defense Command. His assistant chief of staff, Colonel Bendetsen, was the target of a profusion of protest letters from Nisei when his appointment was announced as an Assistant Secretary of the Army during the Eisenhower Administration. On the other hand, Dillon Myer, the well-loved chief of the WRA, is invited to JACL functions and revered as a trusted friend.

The crowd of public officials who offered their apologies after the war was predictably large, and included the former mayor of Los Angeles, Fletcher Bowron, and Justice Tom Clark. But Chief Justice Earl Warren has never retracted what a reviewer of a book about him called "the greatest gaffe of his life," his insistence, based on expectations of a second Pearl Harbor, that the West Coast Japanese were dangerous *because* they had committed no treasonous acts.[1] Thirteen years later an abject congressman tried to explain the tide of irrationality that swept over the people of California, Oregon, and Washington in early 1942: "We were hysterical on the Coast, sure, at that time, much more than perhaps people in other parts of the country. . . . The opportunity in those days for sabotage, if anyone wanted to create it, was so great. We had no security on the Coast."[2]

A certain amount of honor is now connected with having been a friend to the American Japanese when it was an unpopular position. On the national scene Norman Thomas was the first to speak out. On the West Coast a few public figures and private individuals rejected the mass indictment, as demonstrated at the Tolan Committee hearings, though by then it was too late to affect the decision. In the crucial period the American Japanese had more detractors than sympathizers on the West Coast, and they were practically unknown in other parts of the country. "If we had had only one Joe DiMaggio it would never have happened," was the but partly facetious comment of Dr. Harry Kitano, a social psychologist at UCLA.

The Nisei have reexamined their own behavior at the time. Their generally unquestioning cooperation with the removal program has been attributed by critics among them to the Japanese trait called *enryo*, which is defined as reserve, shyness, restraint, hesitation.[3] "There is no question in my mind," accuses Dr. Kitano, who experienced relocation center life as a youth, "that if the United States government wanted to run death ovens we would have marched quietly to our doom with only slight hesitation." Good behavior was more important, he suggests, than defending rights. Yet to the criticism that the Nisei capitulated too easily, there is an inevitable question: What choice did they have? To whom could they turn?

And if their accommodation was not courageous, it proved to be wise. In 1942 a commentator had written, "It is a pretty general conclusion in the West that it will be generations before Americans of Japanese ancestry will ever be assimilated into the nation—if ever."[4] But the war intervened and, in the words of Daisuke Kitagawa, "changed the entire situation so completely that it can almost be said to have served as shock therapy for the collective neurosis of the Nisei community."[5] Japanese–Americans were catapulted out of their old patterns. By accepting the evacuation as a challenge they won their goal of assimilation.

It is one of the ironies that the camp rebels who, in the group judgment, took the wrong road, were acting in the American tradition. For their deviation they suffered shame and ostracism. In some cases the scars have not yet healed. Lives have been blighted by actions taken twenty-five years ago.

But Japanese–Americans honor two men who set out to test the evacuation from the outset rather than submit to it and whose names are immortalized in Supreme Court cases. Gordon Hirabayashi, who spent a good many months in jail during the war for defying first the evacuation and then the draft, is today the head of the Sociology Department of the University of Alberta, Edmonton, Canada. Minoru Yasui, the Portland lawyer, who deliberately violated the curfew order and also went to jail, is now the chairman of the Human Relations Commission in Denver. Had it not been for Minoru Yasui, Gordon Hirabayashi, and others who deliberately challenged the curfew and evacuation orders, the implications of the orders would never have had a national hearing.

Supreme Court Justice Robert Jackson in his dissent in *Korematsu* warned that the Court's declaration that the evacuation was legal meant that something similar might occur again, the principle lying about "like a loaded weapon ready for the hand of any authority that can bring forward a plausible claim of an urgent need."[6] Having once been the victims, whether they acceded or protested, the Nisei are concerned about the possibility of any repetition of group internment in this country. At its 1968 biennial convention, the JACL voted in favor of repeal of an eighteen-year-old law which has been ignored or forgotten by most Americans, but which Nisei leaders feel has certain similarities to Roosevelt's Executive Order 9066. This is Title II, the so-called Emergency Detention Camp proviso of the Internal Security Act of 1950.

Aimed at American participants in "the world Communist movement," it was introduced during the period of Joseph McCarthy's influence by

Senator Pat McCarran and was passed over the veto of President Truman, who called it "a long step toward totalitarianism." It allows the President to declare an "internal security emergency" in the event of an invasion of the United States, a declaration of war by Congress, or "insurrection within the United States in aid of a foreign enemy."

> Whenever there shall be in existence such an emergency, the President, acting through the Attorney General, is hereby authorized to apprehend and by order detain, pursuant to the provisions of this title, each person as to whom there is reasonable ground to believe that such person probably will engage in, or probably will conspire with others to engage in, acts of espionage or of sabotage.[7]

For a number of years a half dozen camps were kept in readiness, one of them purportedly at Tule Lake, California, by the Bureau of Prisons for possible "detainees." Congress appropriated funds to maintain them. They were visited and described by a free-lance writer, Charles R. Allen, Jr., in a booklet called *Concentration Camps, USA.* The Justice Department declares that the project was discontinued in about 1957 and that no funds have been appropriated since for maintaining the camps.[8]

Nisei have publicized fears in some quarters that the camps might be used to incarcerate ghetto rioters as threatened by the chairman of the House Committee on Un-American Activities. The Army Corps of Engineers which built prisoner-of-war camps and the ten relocation centers of World War II denies the existence of contingency plans to this effect. Even if rioting were formally declared an insurrection, there is, according to a Justice Department spokesman, no evidence to date that it is or might be fomented "in aid of a foreign enemy," as required under Title II.[9] Military police officials at the Pentagon say that a limited, not a mass, application of federal detention could occur if martial law were declared, if, for instance, riots should expand into a civil war.[10] Former Attorney General Ramsey Clark, in an ABC broadcast on May 11, 1968, said: "There are no concentration camps in this country. There are no plans to prepare any concentration camps in this country. No concentration camps are needed in this country."[11]

Nisei leaders point out that the Attorney General avoided commenting on the question of repeal of Title II. A resolution framed by San Francisco Bay area JACL leaders states:

> . . . . In fact, this law can be applied to any group that is unlucky enough to be the target of hysteria. And never, never become so smug as to believe that it cannot happen to us again.
> Because we Americans of Japanese ancestry do not seem immediately threatened is all the more reason to lead a repeal fight. We are in a unique

position to refute all those who argue "it cannot happen in America so don't worry about concentration camps."

We are the only ones who can say with authority "Unfortunately, it did happen only twenty-three years ago, and let us make sure it does not happen again." When we Americans of Japanese ancestry were placed in concentration camps, the rest of the American people did not effectively protest. We understand the anguish of innocent victims of injustice. We, of all people in America, must never be guilty of the crime of silence, and must be first to protest a mass imprisonment without due process of law.[12]

The War Department has amassed some figures on the cost of the concentration camps of 1942. It took 223 days and cost $80 million to remove 109,659 American Japanese from their homes. The assembly centers cost $10.7 million to build, and the relocation centers cost $56.5 million. In 1944 alone, Congress appropriated $39 million to the WRA. The whole program required a bureaucracy of thousands of employees.[13] Approximately 45,000 working adults were withdrawn from normal productivity, at a loss to the economy which was estimated for the first year at $70 million.[14] If the evacuation was a mistake, it was an expensive one. The passing of a quarter of a century has shown its true and lasting significance.

When Roosevelt, in a broad interpretation of his powers as wartime Commander-in-Chief, signed over the rights of the West Coast Japanese to the control of the military, the action, approved by Congress and the Supreme Court, gave national and official sanction to policies pursued over the years by West Coast anti-Orientalists. One of the effects of the government's intervention was to lift the mask of patriotism from the faces of the agitators, who then argued more openly on the grounds of self-interest. "A full assertion of the ordinary rights of citizenship would have shamed and weakened the lynch spirit," Eugene Rostow wrote in 1945, assessing the role of the judiciary.[15]

At the time of the Supreme Court consideration of the evacuation, Justice Murphy in his *Korematsu* dissent called the majority decision "a legalization of racism." Korematsu's attorney argued, "If of *white pedigree* these [citizenship] rights are considered to be indestructible, if of *yellow*, destructible. . . . There is no higher title in America than that of 'citizen.' "[16] But to admit that race prejudice was a factor would seriously weaken the validity of the military judgment that the majority upheld; therefore it was discounted as the Court ruled on grounds of military necessity alone.

A 1942 legal opinion foreshadowed the Supreme Court argument which justified precautionary arrest: "Perhaps ninety-nine peaceful Japanese plus an unascertainable one who would signal to a submarine would add up to a sufficient reason to evacuate the whole."[17] Three years later

Eugene Rostow indicted the Supreme Court's endorsement of this doctrine. "The exclusion program was undertaken," he wrote, "not because the Japanese were too numerous to be examined individually, but because they were a small enough group to be punished by confinement. . . . The idea of punishment only for individual behavior is basic to all systems of civilized law. A great principle was never lost so casually."[18]

"In wartime judges wear epaulets under their robes," the attorney, Wayne Collins, has commented. Traditionally, the Court gives the military a free hand in time of war and restores the balance in favor of civilian rights in peacetime. After the subjugation of the South in 1866 a strongly Union Supreme Court issued a classic ruling in *Ex Parte Milligan*, a *habeas corpus* case involving a conspirator working for the South in Kansas. The ruling contradicted a wartime verdict approving a military trial for a group who conspired to assassinate Lincoln. In *Ex Parte Milligan* the Court decreed:

> . . . . The right of trial by jury is preserved to everyone accused of crime who is not attached to the Army, or Navy, or Militia in actual service.
>
> Martial law cannot arise from a threatened invasion. The necessity must be actual and present, the invasion real, such as effectually closes the courts and deposes the civil administration.
>
> . . . . Martial rule can never exist where the courts are open, and in the proper and unobstructed exercise of their jurisdiction. It is also confined to the locality of actual war. . . . [19]

In by-passing the implications of the *Milligan* ruling in the evacuation cases, the Court gave sanction to the idea of limited, undeclared martial law in three respects: extension in time of controls after the military crisis of Pearl Harbor was past; extension in space of controls covering a good-sized portion of the western United States; and in effect, by denial of various civil guarantees in areas where civil government was still in operation in most ways for most people.

Less than a year after V-J Day, however, the Supreme Court handed down a decision in *Duncan* vs. *Kahanamoku*, which modified the judgment in *Korematsu* and the other Japanese evacuation cases—that the military holds precedence over the rights of individuals in wartime— and restored the principle of *Ex Parte Milligan*. The Court decreed that while martial law could operate in a crisis such as Pearl Harbor when civilians could be tried by military tribunals, after the turbulence was over, the governor in conjunction with the military did not have the authority to keep up such controls "for days, months or years," closing all the courts.[20]

The implications for *Korematsu* were not mentioned, although some commentators feel that if *Korematsu* had been heard at this time, in

1946, rather than in 1944, the outcome would have been different. Justice Frank Murphy, concurring with the majority opinion written by Justice Black in *Duncan* came close to naming the evacuation question explicitly when he described the racial bias involved in *Duncan*: although one-third of the population in Hawaii was of Japanese ancestry, members of the group were not considered fit for jury service in the lower courts. He stated further, "Abhorrence of military rule is ingrained in our form of government. . . . This supremacy of the civil over the military is one of our great heritages. It has made possible the attainment of a high degree of liberty regulated by law rather than by caprice. . . . From time immemorial despots have used real or imagined threats to the public welfare as an excuse for needlessly abrogating human rights. That excuse is no less unworthy of our traditions when used in this day of atomic warfare or at a future time when some other type of warfare may be devised."[21]

Perhaps only a few students of the law such as Rostow saw *Duncan* vs. *Kuhanamoku* as a significant modification of the principles enunciated in the evacuation cases. But Justice Robert Jackson, who had dissented in *Korematsu*, wrote shortly before his death in 1954: "I think the Court can never quite escape consciousness of its own infirmities, a psychology which may explain its apparent yielding to expediency, especially during wartime,"[22] and Justice William O. Douglas, who concurred with the majority, later altered his judgment, writing, "The power in time of war to take those extreme measures was sustained in decisions of questionable authority."[23]

It has been said that any denial of the rights of a single group cheapens citizenship for all. Edward Ennis, formerly with the Justice Department, called the evacuation "one of the most spectacular breakdowns . . . of government responsibility in our history."[24] The destructive effect of the episode has been mitigated due to a favorable combination of international and domestic circumstances as well as to the actions of the persevering and the indomitable spirit of the Issei and Nisei. The apologies have been made, the reparations attempted, the claims settled, and the citizenship of the renunciants restored, but the evacuation cannot be relegated to a dusty corner of history. As a departure from American principles that was endorsed by the highest tribunal of the land, it will stand as an aberration and a warning.

Notes

Chapter One

1. Monica Sone, *Nisei Daughter*, Atlantic, Little, Brown and Company, Boston, 1953, p. 148.
2. The correspondents of *Life, Time,* and *Fortune, December 7 The First Thirty Hours,* Alfred Knopf, New York, 1942, p. 172.
3. *Pacific Citizen,* June 11, 1942.
4. *December 7 The First Thirty Hours,* p. 19.
5. Gene Oishi, "Remember Pearl Harbor, and then . . . ," Los Angeles *Times WEST* magazine, March 12, 1967.
6. *The New York Times,* December 10, 1941.
7. "Japanese Evacuation from the West Coast," *Guarding the United States and its Outposts,* by Stetson Conn, Rose C. Engelman, and Byron Fairchild, Office of the Chief of Military History, Department of the Army, Washington, D.C., 1964, p. 117.
8. Carey McWilliams, "Japanese Evacuation: Interim Report," McWilliams Collection, the Hoover Institution on War, Revolution, and Peace, Stanford University, Stanford, California.
9. Theodore H. White, ed., *The Stilwell Papers,* William Sloane, New York, 1948, pp. 3–5.
10. *The New York Times,* December 4, 1941.
11. Los Angeles *Times,* December 9, 1941.
12. *Ibid.*
13. Louis Fischer, "West Coast Perspective," *The Nation,* March 7, 1942.
14. Letter to *Rafu Shimpo,* December 19, 1941.
15. Los Angeles *Times,* December 14, 1941.
16. *Newsletter,* January 13, 1942, Conard-Duveneck Collection, The Hoover Institution on War, Revolution, and Peace, Stanford University, Stanford, California.
17. Editorial, *Rafu Shimpo,* February 19, 1942.
18. *Newsletter,* January 13, 1942, Conard-Duveneck Collection, The Hoover Institution on War, Revolution, and Peace, Stanford University, Stanford, California.
19. Howard Costigan, "The Plight of the Nisei," *The Nation,* February 14, 1942.
20. Francis Biddle, *In Brief Authority,* Doubleday & Co., New York, 1962, p. 224.
21. *Ibid.,* p. 209.
22. Sone, *op. cit.,* p. 156.
23. Conard-Duveneck Collection, The Hoover Institution on War, Revolution, and Peace, Stanford University, Stanford, California.
24. Conn, Engelman, and Fairchild, *op. cit.,* pp. 147–148.
25. Stetson Conn, "The Decision to Evacuate the Japanese from the Pacific Coast," *Command Decisions,* Office of the Chief of Military History, Department of the Army, Washington, D.C., 1960, p. 138.
26. "The Japanese in America; The Problems and the Solution," by an Intelligence Officer, *Harper's,* October, 1942.

27. Biddle, *op. cit.*, p. 215.
28. Statement before House Naval Affairs Subcommittee on Housing, April 13, 1943.
29. Conn, Engelman, and Fairchild, *op. cit.*, p. 118.
30. Laurence Hewes, *Boxcar in the Sand*, Alfred Knopf, New York, 1957, p. 164.
31. Morton Grodzins, *Americans Betrayed*, University of Chicago Press, 1949, p. 239.
32. John Bruce, "California Gets Tough," *The New York Times Magazine*, March 15, 1942.
33. Conn, *op. cit.*, p. 141.
34. *Life*, January 12, 1942.
35. Cecil Henry Coggins, "The Japanese Americans in Hawaii," *Harper's*, June, 1943.
36. *The New York Times*, December 23, 1941.
37. Grodzins, *op. cit.*, pp. 19–20.
38. *Pacific Citizen*, September 10, 1942.
39. Conn, Engelman, and Fairchild, *op. cit.*, p. 120.
40. *The New York Times*, February 5, 1942.
41. Howard Costigan, "The Plight of the Nisei," *The Nation*, February 14, 1942.
42. Ernest O. Hauser, "America's 150,000 Japanese," *American Mercury*, December, 1941.
43. Grodzins, *op. cit.*, p. 102.
44. *Ibid.*, p. 110.
45. San Francisco *Chronicle*, February 2, 1942.
46. Los Angeles *Times*, February 10, 1942.
47. Hewes, *op. cit.*, p. 161.
48. Lincoln Kanai, Letter, December 14, 1941. Conard-Duveneck Collection, The Hoover Institution on War, Revolution, and Peace, Stanford University, Stanford, California.
49. Louis Fischer, "West Coast Perspective," *The Nation*, March 7, 1942.
50. Frank J. Taylor, "The People Nobody Wants," *Saturday Evening Post*, May 9, 1942.
51. Testimony of Floyd Oles before the Tolan Committee, cited in *Gordon Hirabayashi* vs. *the U.S.A.*, *Minoru Yasui* vs. *the U.S.A.* brief *amicus curiae*, Japanese American Citizens League, New York, 1943.
52. Mrs. Esther Boyd before the Tolan Committee, *loc. cit.*
53. Grodzins, *op. cit.*, p. 94.
54. San Francisco *Chronicle*, February 21, 1942.
55. John Bruce, "California Gets Tough," *The New York Times Magazine*, March 15, 1942.
56. Grodzins, *op. cit.*, p. 242.
57. Conn, Engelman, and Fairchild, *op. cit.*, pp. 129–130.
58. Biddle, *op cit.*, pp. 217–218.
59. *Ibid.*, p. 217.
60. Grodzins, *op. cit.*, p. 96.
61. *Ibid.*, p. 258.
62. *Ibid.*, p. 243.
63. *Ibid.*, p. 263.
64. Conn, Engelman, and Fairchild, *op. cit.*, p. 132.
65. Grodzins, *op. cit.*, p. 266.
66. Biddle, *op. cit.*, p. 219.
67. *Ibid.*, p. 226.
68. San Francisco *Chronicle*, February 23, 1942.

Chapter Two

1. Norimasa Muragaki, diary, as quoted in the *Pacific Citizen*, July 22, 1966.
2. Norimasa Muragaki, diary from *The First Japanese Embassy to the United States of America*, translated by Shugehiko Miyoshi, Tokyo, 1920, p. 47, as quoted in Nobutaka Ike, *The Beginnings of Political Democracy in Japan*, Johns Hopkins Press, Baltimore, 1950, p. 29.

3. E. Manchester Boddy, *Japanese in America*, Los Angeles, California, copyright E. Manchester Boddy, 1921, p. 178.

4. *Ibid.*

5. *Ibid.*

6. Peter Clark MacFarlane, "Japan in California," *Collier's*, June, 1913, p. 6.

7. San Francisco *Chronicle*, March 13, 1909, as quoted in Roger Daniels, *The Politics of Prejudice*, University of California Press, Berkeley and Los Angeles, 1962, p. 10.

8. *Ibid.*, p. 23.

9. *San Francisco Relief Survey*, Survey Associates Incorporated, New York, 1913, p. 94 f.

10. *Japanese in the City of San Francisco, California*, Report by Victor Howard Metcalf, November 26, 1906, Appendix, Senate Documents, Vol. 3, 59th Congress, 2nd Session, Washington, D.C., Government Printing Office, 1907, p. 8.

11. *Ibid.*, p. 9.

12. *Ibid.*, p. 19.

13. *Ibid.*, p. 22.

14. San Francisco *Chronicle*, October 26, 1906.

15. Japanese–American Treaty of Commerce and Navigation, 1894, see Appendix, Document No. 1, this volume.

16. Daniels, *op. cit.*, p. 34.

17. *Ibid.*, Chap. III, p. 128, fn. 14.

18. San Francisco *Chronicle*, December 7, 1906.

19. *Message from the President of the United States*, Senate Journal, 59th Congress, 2nd Session, 1906–1907, p. 13.

20. San Francisco *Chronicle*, December 11, 1906.

21. *Ibid.*, December 24, 1906.

22. John Steinbeck, "America and the Americans," *Saturday Evening Post*, July 2, 1966.

23. Franklin K. Lane, *Letters of Franklin K. Lane*, Houghton Mifflin, Boston, 1922, p. 135.

24. MacFarlane, *op. cit.*, p. 5.

25. K. K. Kawakami, *The Real Japanese Question*, The Macmillan Company, New York, 1921, pp. 48, 49.

26. Japanese–American Treaty, *op. cit.*, Article II, see Appendix, Document No. 1, this volume.

27. MacFarlane, *op. cit.*, p. 5.

28. Montaville Flowers, *The Japanese Conquest of American Opinion*, George H. Doran Company, New York, 1917, p. 23.

29. "Amendment, California Alien Land Law, adopted November 2, 1920," from *Present-Day Immigration—With Special Reference to the Japanese*, Carl Kelsey, ed., Annals of the American Academy of Political and Social Science, Vol. XCIII, No. 182, Philadelphia, January, 1921, pp. 13–14.

30. Judge Edward E. Cushman, as quoted in *Documental History of Law Cases Affecting Japanese in the United States, 1916–1924*, Vol. II, pp. 21–25.

31. Eliot Grinnell Mears, *Resident Orientals on the American Pacific Coast*, American Group, Institute of Pacific Relations, New York, 1927, pp. 136–138.

Chapter Three

1. V. S. McClatchy, "Japanese Immigration and Colonization," a brief prepared for consideration of the State Department, Sacramento *Bee* Publishers, Sacramento, California, 1921.

2. K. K. Kawakami, "The Japanese Question," *Present-Day Immigration—With Special Reference to the Japanese*, Carl Kelsey, ed., Annals of the American Academy of Political and Social Science, Philadelphia, January, 1921, pp. 82, 83.

3. R. L. Buell, *Japanese Immigration*, World Peace Foundation pamphlet, Vol. VII, Boston, 1924, p. 371.

4. *The Japan American News*, March 6, 1927, as quoted in R. D. McKenzie, *Oriental Exclusion*, American Group, Institute of Pacific Relations, University of Chicago edition, 1927, pp. 48–49.
5. *Documental History of Law Cases Affecting Japanese in the United States, 1916–1924*, Vol. 1, pp. 1–120.
6. McKenzie, *op. cit.*, p. 79.
7. *Ibid.*, p. 48.
8. *The Life History of ———: A Sample Life History of a Californian of Oriental Parentage*, Institute of Pacific Relations, undated, pp. 2, 6, and 7.
9. Satoko Marakami, "I Am Alive," *Common Ground* magazine, Vol. II, No. 3, Spring, 1942, p. 16.
10. M. J. D. Negoro, "A Defense Against Unmerited Attack," *The Japan Review*, Vol. V, No. 14, pp. 254–255.
11. Topaz *Times*, March 3, 1945.
12. *Japan*, Encyclopedia Americana, Vol. 15, 1968, p. 628.
13. Shuji Kimura, "The Life Nisei Knew," in *A Tule Lake Interlude*, anniversary issue of *The Tulean Dispatch*, WRA, Newell, California, May 27, 1942–43, p. 9. The Hoover Institution on War, Revolution, and Peace, Stanford University, Stanford, California.
14. K. K. Kawakami, *The Real Japanese Question*, The Macmillan Company, New York, 1921, p. 89.
15. Monica Sone, *Nisei Daughter*, Atlantic, Little, Brown and Company, Boston, 1953, pp. 22–23.
16. James A. Michener, *Hawaii*, Random House, New York, 1959, p. 699.
17. Montaville Flowers, *The Japanese Conquest of American Opinion*, George H. Doran Co., New York, 1917, p. 200.
18. Eliot Grinnell Mears, *Resident Orientals on the American Pacific Coast*, American Group, Institute of Pacific Relations, New York, 1927, pp. 236–237.
19. Leonard Bloom and Ruth Riemer, *Removal and Return—The Socio-Economic Effects of the War on Japanese Americans*, University of California Press, Berkeley and Los Angeles, 1949, p. 160.
20. *Ibid.*, p. 161.
21. Mears, *op. cit.*, p. 237.
22. Yamato Ichihashi, *Japanese in the United States: A Critical Study of the Problems of the Japanese Immigrants and Their Children*, Stanford University Press, Stanford, California, 1932, pp. 201, 202.
23. Carey McWilliams, "Once Again the Yellow Peril," *The Nation*, June 26, 1935.
24. CREA News Bulletin, Vol. I, No. 1, October 1920, *CRE Magazine*, April 1930, and *CRE Magazine*, July, 1939, as quoted in *Bay Area Reporter*, May, 1967.
25. Ichihashi, *op. cit.*, p. 38.
26. *The New York Times*, February 22, 1942.
27. Mears, *op. cit.*, p. 201.
28. Frank J. Taylor, "The People Nobody Wants," *Saturday Evening Post*, May 9, 1942.
29. Shuji Kimura, "On Borrowed Time," in *A Tule Lake Interlude*, anniversary issue of *The Tulean Dispatch*, WRA, Newell, California, May 27, 1942–43, p. 19.
30. Mike Masaoka, as quoted in *Rafu Shimpo*, September 30, 1941.

Chapter Four

1. San Francisco *Chronicle*, February 19, 1942.
2. Morton Grodzins, *Americans Betrayed*, University of Chicago Press, 1949, pp. 209, 210.
3. *Life*, January 12, 1942.
4. *The Daily Californian*, February 11, 1942.
5. Los Angeles *Times*, February 19, 1942.

6. Seattle *Post-Intelligencer*, February 19, 1942.
7. Drew Pearson and Robert S. Allen, "The Washington Merry-Go-Round," Seattle *Post-Intelligencer*, March 8, 1942.
8. Los Angeles *Times*, February 21, 1942.
9. *Ibid.*
10. *Rafu Shimpo*, February 18, 1942.
11. *The New York Times*, February 21, 1942.
12. *Ibid.*
13. *Rafu Shimpo*, February 21, 1942.
14. Grodzins, *op. cit.*, p. 196.
15. *Ibid.*
16. *The Daily Californian*, February 20, 1942.
17. Seattle *Post-Intelligencer*, February 25, 1942.
18. *Ibid.*, February 28, 1942.
19. *The New York Times*, February 22, 1942.
20. Laurence Hewes, *Boxcar in the Sand*, Alfred Knopf, New York, 1957, p. 160.
21. *Impounded People*, U.S. Department of Interior, WRA, Government Printing Office, Washington, D.C., 1946, p. 15.
22. *Ibid.*, p. 17.
23. *The Daily Californian*, March 5, 1942.
24. George D. Nickel, "Evacuation, American Style," *Survey Midmonthly*, April, 1942.
25. Los Angeles *Times*, February 19, 1942.
26. San Francisco *Chronicle*, February 25, 1942.
27. *Ibid.*, February 21, 1942.
28. *Report of the Select Committee Investigating National Defense Migration*, House of Representatives, 77th Congress, 2nd Session, March 19, 1942, p. 16.
29. *Ibid.*, p. 15.
30. *Pacific Citizen*, undated issue.
31. *The New York Times*, February 22, 1942.
32. *Ibid.*, February 24, 1942.
33. *Gordon Hirabayashi* vs. *U.S.A.; Minori Yasui* vs. *U.S.A.*, brief, *amicus curiae*, Japanese American Citizens League, New York, 1943, p. 87.
34. Grodzins, *op. cit.*, p. 192.
35. *Report of the Select Committee Investigating National Defense Migration*, House of Representatives, 77th Congress, 2nd Session, March 19, 1942, p. 21.
36. *Ibid.*, p. 15.
37. *The New York Times*, February 26, 1942.
38. *Life*, March 9, 1942.
39. Los Angeles *Times*, February 23, 1967.
40. *Ibid.*
41. *Ibid.*, February 26, 1942.
42. *Ibid.*
43. *Ibid.*, February 23, 1967.
44. *Hearings Before a Special Committee on Un-American Activities*, House of Representatives, 77th Congress, 1st Session, Appendix VI, U.S. Government Printing Office, Washington, D.C., 1942, p. 1839.
45. *Ibid.*, p. 1825–1826.
46. *Ibid.*, p. 1826.
47. *Ibid.*, p. 1830.
48. Carey McWilliams, "California and the Japanese," *The New Republic*, March 2, 1942.
49. Letter to the authors, January 23, 1967.
50. Carey McWilliams, *Prejudice*, Little, Brown and Company, Boston, 1944, p. 196.
51. Letter in the Conard-Duveneck Collection, Hoover Institution on War, Revolution, and Peace, Stanford University, Stanford, California.
52. Leonard Bloom and Ruth Riemer, *Removal and Return*, University of California Press, Berkeley and Los Angeles, 1949, p. 163.
53. Seattle *Post-Intelligencer*, February 28, 1942.
54. *Ibid.*, March 3, 1942.

55. *Ibid.*, March 1, 1942.
56. *Ibid.*
57. *Ibid.*, March 3, 1942.
58. *Ibid.*, March 1, 1942.
59. *The New York Times*, March 4, 1942.
60. *Report of the Select Committee Investigating National Defense Migration*, House of Representatives, 77th Congress, 2nd Session, Appendix A, March 19, 1942. p. 27.
61. *Ibid.*
62. *Ibid.*, p. 28.
63. *Spokesman Review*, May 24, 1942.
64. "Aliens in Our Midst," University of Chicago round table radio broadcast, with Ernest Colwell, Carey McWilliams, Louis Wirth, May 10, 1942.
65. San Francisco *Chronicle*, March 23, 1942.
66. Lieutenant General J. L. DeWitt, *Final Report, Japanese Evacuation from the West Coast, 1942*, U.S. Government Printing Office, Washington, D.C., 1943, p. 106.
67. *Ibid.*
68. Figures taken from General DeWitt's final report differ slightly from figures given by other sources. Carey McWilliams at the time estimated that 5,396 Japanese left the Western Defense Command.

Chapter Five

1. *The New York Times*, March 29, 1942.
2. Unidentified newspaper clipping, March 17, 1942.
3. San Jose *Mercury-Herald*, March 25, 1942.
4. Letter, April 17, 1942, Carey McWilliams Collection, Hoover Institution on War, Revolution, and Peace, Stanford University, Stanford, California.
5. Laurence Hewes, *Boxcar in the Sand*, Alfred Knopf, New York, 1957, p. 164.
6. Letter to the Editor, San Francisco *Chronicle*, March 11, 1942.
7. Reprinted in *Special Information Bulletin*, National Refugee Service, May 29, 1942.
8. Statistics culled from *Pacific Citizen*, December 24, 1942, quoted in Carey McWilliams, *Prejudice*, Little, Brown and Company, Boston, 1944, p. 151.
9. *The New York Times*, May 23, 1942.
10. *Victory*, Reprint, September 29, 1942.
11. Joseph Grew, *Ten Years in Japan*, Simon & Schuster, New York, 1944, pp. 533, 534.
12. Harry Paxton Howard, "Americans in Concentration Camps," *The Crisis*, September, 1942.
13. Letter, April 17, 1942, Carey McWilliams Collection, Hoover Institution on War, Revolution, and Peace, Stanford University, Stanford, California.
14. Seattle *Post-Intelligencer*, March 8, 1942.
15. "A Nisei Diary," *A Tule Lake Interlude, The Tulean Dispatch*, WRA, May 27, 1942–43, Newell, California, p. 100.
16. *Rafu Shimpo*, March 16, 1942.
17. Seattle *Post-Intelligencer*, March 25, 1942.
18. Hewes, *op. cit.*, p. 171.
19. *Ibid.*, p. 166.
20. *Ibid.*, p. 169.
21. Lieutenant General J. L. DeWitt, *Final Report, Japanese Evacuation from the West Coast, 1942*, U.S. Government Printing Office, Washington, 1943, p. ix.
22. Hewes, *op. cit.*, p. 167.
23. Frank J. Taylor, "The People Nobody Wants," *Saturday Evening Post*, May 9, 1942.
24. Seattle *Post-Intelligencer*, March 4, 1942.
25. Shuji Kimura, "The Exodus: On Borrowed Time," *A Tule Lake Interlude, The Tulean Dispatch*, WRA, Newell, California, May 27, 1942–43, pp. 23–24.
26. *Impounded People*, U.S. Department of the Interior, WRA, Government Printing Office, Washington, D.C., 1946, p. 35.

27. Claude Settles, letter to the editor, *Survey Graphic*, March 6, 1942.
28. Oakland *Tribune*, May 14, 1942.
29. Kimura, *op. cit.*
30. *Pacific Citizen*, December 23–30, 1966.
31. Edwin McDowell, *Arizona Republic* article, reprinted in *Pacific Citizen*, May 26, 1967.
32. San Francisco *Chronicle*, April 9, 1942.
33. Kimura, *op. cit.*, p. 29.
34. Letter, April 20, 1942, Grace Nichols Pearson Collection, Hoover Institution on War, Revolution, and Peace, Stanford University, Stanford, California.
35. Fresno *Bee*, May 27, 1942.
36. San Francisco *Chronicle*, March 13, 1942.
37. *Life*, April 6, 1942.
38. *The New York Times*, March 24, 1942.
39. Modesto *Bee*, April 14, 1942.
40. Seattle *Post-Intelligencer*, March 24, March 31, 1942.
41. Thomas R. Bodine, letter, April 2, 1942, Conard-Duveneck Collection, Hoover Institution on War, Revolution, and Peace, Stanford University, Stanford, California.
42. *Life*, April 6, 1942.
43. Letter from Josephine Duveneck, April 6, 1942, *Bulletin on Minorities in the United States*, American Friends Service Committee, May 15, 1942.
44. Kimura, *op. cit.*, p. 28.
45. April 20, 1942, letter, Grace Nichols Pearson Collection, Hoover Institution on War, Revolution, and Peace, Stanford University, Stanford, California.
46. Kimura, *op. cit.*
47. Berkeley *Daily Gazette*, April 20, 1942.
48. *Ibid.*, April 16, 1942.
49. *Time*, April 6, 1942.
50. Kimura, *op. cit.*, p. 28.
51. Letter, April 1, 1942, Grace Nichols Pearson Collection, Hoover Institution on War, Revolution, and Peace, Stanford University, Stanford, California.
52. "Sunday Evacuation, May 10," report by anonymous Quakers, Conard-Duveneck Collection, Hoover Institution on War, Revolution, and Peace, Stanford University, Stanford, California.
53. Letter to *The Nation*, May 9, 1942.
54. Carey McWilliams, *Prejudice, op. cit.*, p. 133.
55. "Third Evacuation from San Francisco, May 10," Conard-Duveneck Collection, Hoover Institution on War, Revolution, and Peace, Stanford University, Stanford, California.
56. Letter, May 28, 1942, Conard-Duveneck Collection, Hoover Institution on War, Revolution, and Peace, Stanford University, Stanford, California.
57. "Report from Seattle," by anonymous Quakers, Conard-Duveneck Collection, Hoover Institution on War, Revolution, and Peace, Stanford University, Stanford, California.
58. Kimura, *op. cit.*, p. 30.
59. "Japanese Evacuation Report #11," May 11, 1942, Conard-Duveneck Collection, Hoover Institution on War, Revolution, and Peace, Stanford University, Stanford, California.
60. Letter from a student to Claude Settles, May 13, 1942.
61. From American Friends Service Committee Bulletin on Minorities in the United States, May 15, 1942.
62. Letter, May 19, 1942, Conard-Duveneck Collection, Hoover Institution on War, Revolution, and Peace, Stanford University, Stanford, California.
63. Carey McWilliams, *Prejudice, op. cit.*, p. 134.
64. Undated letter from Healdsburg, Grace Nichols Pearson Collection, Hoover Institution on War, Revolution, and Peace, Stanford University, Stanford, California.
65. Letter, May 27, 1942, Conard-Duveneck Collection, Hoover Institution on War, Revolution, and Peace, Stanford University, Stanford, California.

66. R. B. Read, "The Sansei," San Francisco *Sunday Examiner and Chronicle*, August 14, 1966.
67. Anonymous letter to Herb Caen, San Francisco *Chronicle*, April 12, 1942.
68. Oakland *Tribune*, May 21, 1942.
69. *Pacific Citizen*, June 18, 1942.
70. Evelyn Clement, Report, *Christian Century*, August 5, 1942.
71. Hewes, *op. cit.*, pp. 174–75.

Chapter Six

1. "Japs Transplanted," *Newsweek*, April 6, 1942.
2. Modesto *Bee*, April 2, 1942.
3. "Coast Japs are Interned in Mountain Camp, Manzanar, California," *Life*, April 6, 1942.
4. *Ibid.*
5. James Sakoda, "The Tule Lake Project," *The Tulean Dispatch*, p. 33.
6. American Friends Service Committee Bulletin, June 3, 1942, Conard-Duveneck Collection, Hoover Institution on War, Revolution, and Peace, Stanford University, Stanford, California.
7. WCCA release, March 19, 1942, Carey McWilliams Collection, Hoover Institution on War, Revolution, and Peace, Stanford University, Stanford, California.
8. *Christian Century*, May 6, 1942.
9. A Nisei letter to A. Hunter, *Christian Century*, May 6, 1942.
10. Letter, May 23, 1942, Conard-Duveneck Collection, Hoover Institution on War, Revolution, and Peace, Stanford University, Stanford, California.
11. Letter, *The Nation*, June 6, 1942.
12. Helen Aihara (Kitaje) letter to Miss Hinze, May 18, 1942.
13. *Ibid.*, May 10, 1942.
14. Letter #5, June 29, 1942, Carey McWilliams Collection, Hoover Institution on War, Revolution, and Peace, Stanford University, Stanford, California.
15. Los Angeles *Times*, April 2, 1967.
16. Letter, May 23, 1942, Conard-Duveneck Collection, Hoover Institution on War, Revolution, and Peace, Stanford University, Stanford, California.
17. American Friends Service Committee Bulletin, June 3, 1942, Conard-Duveneck Collection, Hoover Institution on War, Revolution, and Peace, Stanford University, Stanford, California.
18. Letter, May 18, 1942, Conard-Duveneck Collection, Hoover Institution on War, Revolution, and Peace, Stanford University, Stanford, California.
19. WCCA release, April 16, 1942.
20. WCCA rules, July, 1942, p. 8.
21. Seattle Office American Friends Service Committee Report #8, April 2, 1942, Conard-Duveneck Collection, Hoover Institution on War, Revolution, and Peace, Stanford University, Stanford, California.
22. Monica Sone, *Nisei Daughter*, Atlantic, Little, Brown Company, Boston, 1953, p. 173.
23. Joe and Betty Goodman, Report on Visit to Puyallup Assembly Center, July 1942, Conard-Duveneck Collection, Hoover Institution on War, Revolution, and Peace, Stanford University, Stanford, California.
24. Ted Nakashima, "Concentration Camp, U.S. Style," *The New Republic*, June 15, 1942.
25. *The New Republic*, January 18, 1943.
26. Japanese Evacuation Report #12, American Friends Service Committee, Conard-Duveneck Collection, Hoover Institution on War, Revolution, and Peace, Stanford University, Stanford, California.
27. American Friends Service Committee Report #11, May 11, 1942, Conard-Duveneck Collection, Hoover Institution on War, Revolution, and Peace, Stanford University, Stanford, California.

28. *Ibid.*
29. Letter, Western Defense Command and Fourth Army, Wartime Civil Control Administration, to Mr. Claude N. Settles, July 6, 1942.
30. Letter, June 6, 1942, Conard-Duveneck Collection, Hoover Institution on War, Revolution, and Peace, Stanford University, Stanford, California.
31. *Vignette: A Pictorial Record of Life in the Fresno Assembly Center,* Fresno Assembly Center, 1942, Hoover Institution on War, Revolution, and Peace, Stanford University, Stanford, California, p. 32.
32. *Pacific Citizen,* June 11, 1942.
33. *A Tule Lake Interlude,* first anniversary issue, May 27, 1942–43, *The Tulean Dispatch,* WRA, Newell, California, p. 102.
34. Helen Aihara (Kitaje), letter, May, 1942.
35. Letter, May 29, 1942, Conard-Duveneck Collection, Hoover Institution on War, Revolution, and Peace, Stanford University, Stanford, California.
36. Letter, May 6, 1942, Conard-Duveneck Collection, Hoover Institution on War, Revolution, and Peace, Stanford University, Stanford, California.
37. Letter, May 25, 1942, Conard-Duveneck Collection, Hoover Institution on War, Revolution, and Peace, Stanford University, Stanford, California.
38. FOR Bulletin, June, 1942, Conard-Duveneck Collection, Hoover Institution on War, Revolution, and Peace, Stanford University, Stanford, California.
39. *Totalizer,* May 23, 1942.
40. Helen Aihara (Kitaje), diary.
41. Letter, May 19, 1942, Carey McWilliams Collection, Hoover Institution on War, Revolution, and Peace, Stanford University, Stanford, California.
42. Army release, April 9, 1942.
43. Louis Obed Renne, *Our Day of Empire, War and the Exile of Japanese–Americans,* the Strickland Press, Glasgow, Scotland, 1954, pp. 129, 132, 137.
44. Letter, May 27, 1942, Conard-Duveneck Collection, Hoover Institution on War, Revolution, and Peace, Stanford University, Stanford, California.
45. Letter, May 18, 1942, Conard-Duveneck Collection, Hoover Institution on War, Revolution, and Peace, Stanford University, Stanford, California.
46. Richard Donovan, "Japanese at Tanforan Survey a Meager Present and Prepare for a New Life," San Francisco *Chronicle,* May 12, 1942.
47. WRA Information Circular.
48. Letter #5, July 3, 1942, Carey McWilliams Collection, Hoover Institution on War, Revolution, and Peace, Stanford University, Stanford, California.
49. Letter, June 6, 1942, Conard-Duveneck Collection, Hoover Institution on War, Revolution, and Peace, Stanford University, Stanford, California.
50. *Aloha, Tulare,* News Relocation Issue, Conard-Duveneck Collection, Hoover Institution on War, Revolution, and Peace, Stanford University, Stanford, California.
51. H. V. and M. W. Nicholson, "Evacuation," May, 1942, Conard-Duveneck Collection, Hoover Institution on War, Revolution, and Peace, Stanford University, Stanford, California.
52. Los Angeles *Times,* April 9, 1942.
53. *Ibid.*
54. Donovan, *loc. cit.*
55. *Business Week,* July 18, 1942.
56. Sacramento *Union,* May 14, 1942.
57. Fresno *Bee,* May 18, 1942.
58. Oakland *Tribune* photographs, July 16, 1942.
59. Unidentified newspaper clipping, Conard-Duveneck Collection, Hoover Institution on War, Revolution, and Peace, Stanford University, Stanford, California.
60. Undated clipping, *Christian Science Monitor,* Conard-Duveneck Collection, Hoover Institution on War, Revolution, and Peace, Stanford University, Stanford, California.
61. Thomas R. Bodine, "The Japanese Displacement," a mimeographed paper, Conard-Duveneck Collection, Hoover Institution on War, Revolution, and Peace, Stanford University, Stanford, California.

62. Letter, May 13, 1942, Carey McWilliams Collection, Hoover Institution on War, Revolution, and Peace, Stanford University, Stanford, California.
63. Letter, June 6, 1942, Conard-Duveneck Collection, Hoover Institution on War, Revolution, and Peace, Stanford University, Stanford, California.
64. Letter, May 6, 1942, Conard-Duveneck Collection, Hoover Institution on War, Revolution, and Peace, Stanford University, Stanford, California.
65. Unidentified newspaper clipping, May 11, 1942.
66. Los Angeles *Times*, March 5, 1942.
67. Letter to Tom Bodine, Conard-Duveneck Collection, Hoover Institution on War, Revolution, and Peace, Stanford University, Stanford, California.
68. John F. Embree, *Suye Mura—A Japanese Village*, Phoenix Books, University of Chicago Press, Chicago and London, 1939, p. 174.
69. May 9, 1942 Report, Conard-Duveneck Collection, Hoover Institution on War, Revolution, and Peace, Stanford University, Stanford, California.
70. *Nichi Bei*, May 14, 1942.
71. Donovan, *op. cit.*
72. Anonymous author, "A Nisei Diary," *A Tule Lake Interlude, loc. cit.*, p. 102.
73. Donovan, *op. cit.*
74. Letter excerpt, FOR Bulletin, June 15, 1942, Conard-Duveneck Collection, Hoover Institution on War, Revolution, and Peace, Stanford University, Stanford, California.
75. American Friends Service Committee Bulletin #12, May 20, 1942, Conard-Duveneck Collection, Hoover Institution on War, Revolution, and Peace, Stanford University, Stanford, California.
76. Yoné Noguchi, "The Sweet Cherubim," *The Summer Cloud*, The Shunyodo Press, Tokyo, 1906, p. 7.
77. Series of letters, Carey McWilliams Collection, Hoover Institution on War, Revolution, and Peace, Stanford University, Stanford, California.
78. Tanforan *Totalizer*, May 23, 1942.
79. Mimeographed copy of a speech given by Ernest Iiyama, August 2, 1942, Carey McWilliams Collection, Hoover Institution on War, Revolution, and Peace, Stanford University, Stanford, California.
80. Letter, June 6, 1942, Conard-Duveneck Collection, Hoover Institution on War, Revolution, and Peace, Stanford University, Stanford, California.
81. Thomas R. Bodine, "Japanese Evacuation," Conard-Duveneck Collection, Hoover Institution on War, Revolution, and Peace, Stanford University, Stanford, California.
82. *Ibid.*
83. Letter, May 30, 1942, Conard-Duveneck Collection, Hoover Institution on War, Revolution, and Peace, Stanford University, Stanford, California.
84. Excerpts from letters, May 25, 1942, American Friends Service Committee Report, Conard-Duveneck Collection, Hoover Institution on War, Revolution, and Peace, Stanford University, Stanford, California.
85. Helen Aihara (Kitaji), letter to Mrs. DeVoss, May 21, 1942.

Chapter Seven

1. Lieutenant General John L. DeWitt, *Final Report, Japanese Evacuation from the West Coast, 1942*, U.S. Government Printing Office, Washington, D.C., 1943, p. 205–06.
2. Letter, July 24, 1942, Claude Settles Collection.
3. Masamori Kojiima and Setsuko Matsunaga, *Summary of Events*—a report, Carey McWilliams Collection, Hoover Institution on War, Revolution, and Peace, Stanford University, Stanford, California.
4. *The Open Forum*, publication of the Southern California ACLU, August 22, 1942.
5. San Francisco *News*, May 7, 1942.
6. *Doho*, April 23, 1942.

7. Letter, June 15, 1942, Carey McWilliams Collection, Hoover Institution on War, Revolution, and Peace, Stanford University, Stanford, California.
8. Tanforan *Totalizer*, May 30, 1942.
9. Carey McWilliams, "Moving the West Coast Japanese," *Harper's*, September, 1942.
10. Santa Anita *Pacemaker*, May 15, 1942.
11. *Vignette: A Pictorial Record of Life in the Fresno Assembly Center*, U.S. Fresno Assembly Center, Fresno, California, 1942, p. 8.
12. WCCA Regulations, August 1, 1942.
13. Letter, August 19, 1942, Carey McWilliams Collection, Hoover Institution on War, Revolution, and Peace, Stanford University, Stanford, California.
14. Associated Press Report, Palo Alto *Times*, July 20, 1942.
15. *Pacific Citizen*, July 23, 1942.
16. Los Angeles *Times*, undated clipping.
17. *Pacific Citizen*, June 4, 1942.
18. *American Civil Liberties Union-News*, August, 1942.
19. *Ibid.*, July, 1942.
20. DeWitt, *op. cit.*, p. 218.
21. *Ibid.*
22. Letter to Claude Settles, August 18, 1942.
23. *The Open Forum*, November 21, 1942.
24. Letter to Clara Hinze, May 25, 1942, Claude Settles Collection.
25. Maureen O'Brian, "Bridge Has Invaded Realm of the Assembly Camp," San Francisco *Chronicle*, August 16, 1942.
26. Letter, April 29, 1942, from Manzanar, Conard-Duveneck Collection, Hoover Institution on War, Revolution, and Peace, Stanford University, Stanford, California.
27. Helen Aihara (Kitaji), diary.
28. Aihara, letter, June 4, 1942.
29. *Vignette, op. cit.*, p. 12.
30. Report, May 27, 1942, Conard-Duveneck Collection, Hoover Institution on War, Revolution, and Peace, Stanford University, Stanford, California.
31. *Business Week*, February 21, 1942.
32. *Pacific Citizen*, August 20, 1942.
33. WCCA Release, September 29, 1942.
34. *The Call*, March 7, 1942.
35. *Pacific Citizen*, June 25, 1942.
36. *Civil Liberties Quarterly*, March, 1942.
37. *American Civil Liberties Union-News*, March, 1942.
38. Arthur Garfield Hays, Osmond Fraenkel, and Roger Baldwin, letter to the editor, *The Open Forum*, March 18, 1944.
39. *American Civil Liberties Union-News*, April, 1942.
40. Inre Ventura, *Ex parte*, 1942, 44 Federal Supplement, pp. 521–523.
41. Lincoln Kanai, letter, March 28, 1942, Conard-Duveneck Collection, Hoover Institution on War, Revolution, and Peace, Stanford University, Stanford, California.
42. *Pacific Citizen*, September 17, 1942.
43. Lincoln Kanai, letter to Dr. Galen Fisher, August 2, 1942, Bancroft Library, University of California, Berkeley, California.
44. Lincoln Kanai, undated letter, Galen Fisher Collection, Bancroft Library, University of California, Berkeley, California.
45. Lincoln Kanai letter to Galen Fisher, *loc. cit.*, July 25, 1942.
46. *The Open Forum*, November 28, 1942.
47. Minoru Yasui, letter to James Otsuka, Multnomah County Jail, December 14, 1942, Galen Fisher Collection, Bancroft Library, University of California, Berkeley, California.
48. *Pacific Citizen*, December 3, 1942.
49. *Ibid.*, November 19, 1942.
50. Gordon K. Hirabayashi, "Why I Refused to be Evacuated," *Fellowship of Reconciliation Bulletin*, June 15, 1942.
51. Letter from Grace Nichols (Pearson), May 28, 1942, Conard-Duveneck Collection,

Hoover Institution on War, Revolution, and Peace, Stanford University, Stanford, California.
52. Bulletin #18, Japanese American Citizen League National Headquarters, July 1, 1943, p. 13.
53. *Ibid.*, p. 12.
54. Caleb Foote, "Have We Forgotten Justice?" *Fellowship*, May, 1942.
55. *Pacific Citizen*, August 20, 1942.
56. General DeWitt, *op. cit.*, p. 184.
57. *Pacific Citizen*, November 19, 1942.
58. *Vignette, op. cit.*, p. 5.
59. *Ibid.*, p. 71.

Chapter Eight

1. Helen Aihara (Kitaji), diary, July 1 and July 4, 1942.
2. Los Angeles *Times*, September 26, 1942.
3. Alexander H. Leighton, *The Governing of Men*, Princeton, New Jersey, Princeton University Press, 1945, p. 54.
4. *Ibid.*, p. 55.
5. *Ibid.*, p. 55.
6. *Ibid.*, p. 73.
7. *Ibid.*, p. 64.
8. *The War Relocation Work Corps—A Circular of Information for Enlistees and Their Families*, War Relocation Authority, Washington, D.C., 1942, p. 8.
9. Leighton, *op. cit.*, p. 65.
10. *Ibid.*
11. Translation of letter from Poston, July 20, 1942, Galen Fisher Collection, University of California, Bancroft Library, Berkeley, California.
12. *Ibid.*
13. Helen Aihara (Kitaji), diary, July 7, 1942.
14. *Ibid.*
15. Helen Aihara (Kitaji), letter to Miss Harvey, August 2, 1942.
16. *Ibid.*
17. Leighton, *op. cit.*, p. 63.
18. *Impounded People*, U.S. Department of the Interior, WRA, U.S. Printing Office, Washington, D.C., 1946, p. 41.
19. Letter, July 23, 1942, Pearson Collection, Hoover Institution on War, Revolution, and Peace, Stanford University, Stanford. California.
20. *Impounded People, op. cit.*, p. 41.
21. Tanaka Togo, speech in Chicago, September 23, 1943, before the Seventh Interdenominational Institute, McCormick Memorial YMCA.
22. Letter to Galen Fisher, October 17, 1942, Galen Fisher Collection, Bancroft Library, Berkeley, California.
23. "Lil Dan'l—One Year in a Relocation Center," undated, Bancroft Library, University of California, Berkeley, California.
24. Letter, undated, Grace Nichols Pearson Collection, Hoover Institution on War, Revolution, and Peace, Stanford University, Stanford, California.
25. *The War Relocation Work Corps, op. cit.*, p. 7.
26. Richard S. Nishimoto, *Firebreak Gang*, manuscript, Poston, Arizona, September 1942, Bancroft Library, University of California, Berkeley, California.
27. *Ibid.*
28. *Ibid.*
29. *Ibid.*
30. *Ibid.*
31. Oakland *Post-Enquirer*, June 6, 1942.
32. Letter, September 8, 1943, Grace Nichols Pearson Collection, Hoover Institution on War, Revolution, and Peace, Stanford University, Stanford, California.

33. Helen Aihara (Kitaji), letter to Miss Hinze, August 11, 1942.
34. Helen Aihara (Kitaji), letter to the Hinzes, September, 1942.
35. *Ibid.*
36. *The Heart Mountain Community*, a report, Bancroft Library, University of California, Berkeley, California.
37. Los Angeles *Times*, April 2, 1967.
38. *The Heart Mountain Community, op. cit.*
39. Letter, September 7, 1942, John L. Von Blon Collection, Hoover Institution on War, Revolution, and Peace, Stanford University, Stanford, California.
40. Evacuees from Palo Alto, San Jose, Southern California, and Yakima Valley, *Colonists in Wyoming*, Fellowship of Reconciliation, November 6, 1942.
41. Letter, January 21, 1943, John L. Von Blon Collection, Hoover Institution on War, Revolution, and Peace, Stanford University, Stanford, California.
42. Letter, December 17, 1943, Galen Fisher Collection, Bancroft Library, University of California, Berkeley, California.
43. Letter to Miss Stillman, October 24, 1942, Alice Hays Collection, Hoover Institution on War, Revolution, and Peace, Stanford University, Stanford, California.
44. Ed Takeshi, "Two Thousand Acre Victory Garden Rises in Midst of Desert," Heart Mountain *Sentinel*, May 8, 1943.
45. Bill Hosokawa, "From the Frying Pan," *Pacific Citizen*, April 8, 1943.
46. Caleb Foote, *Outcasts! The Story of America's Treatment of Her Japanese-American Minority*, Fellowship of Reconciliation, New York, undated.
47. Letter, October 24, 1942, Grace Nichols Pearson Collection, Hoover Institution on War, Revolution, and Peace, Stanford University, Stanford, California.
48. Letter, October 21, 1942, Alice Hays Collection, Hoover Institution on War, Revolution, and Peace, Stanford University, Stanford, California.
49. Helen Aihara (Kitaji), letter to Miss Hinze, June 29, 1942.
50. *Ibid.*, April 17, 1943.
51. Chiura Obata, letter to Grace Nichols, September 29, 1942, Pearson Collection, Hoover Institution on War, Revolution, and Peace, Stanford University, Stanford, California.
52. Letter, October 31, 1942, Alice Hays Collection, Hoover Institution on War, Revolution, and Peace, Stanford University, Stanford, California.
53. Miyuki Aoyama, "Picture," Heart Mountain *Sentinel*, January 1, 1943.
54. Sumio Doi, letter to Sacramento *Bee*, undated clipping.

Chapter Nine

1. Letter, August 9, 1943, Alice Hays Collection, Hoover Institution on War, Revolution, and Peace, Stanford University, Stanford, California.
2. Galen Fisher, "Are the Evacuees Being Coddled?" *The Christian Century*, September 1, 1943.
3. *Ibid.*
4. Undated letter to Carey McWilliams, McWilliams Collection, Hoover Institution on War, Revolution, and Peace, Stanford University, Stanford, California.
5. Togo Tanaka, speech before the Seventh Interdenominational Institute, McCormick Memorial YMCA, September 23, 1943.
6. Carl Mydans, "Tule Lake Segregation Center," *Life*, March 20, 1944.
7. Carey McWilliams, *Prejudice*, Little, Brown and Company, Boston, 1944, p. 132.
8. Laurence Hewes, *Boxcar in the Sand*, Alfred Knopf, New York, 1957, p. 174.
9. Milton Eisenhower, letter to "Americans of Japanese Ancestry," undated.
10. Report of the Subcommittee on Japanese War Relocation Centers to the Committee on Military Affairs, United States Senate, May 7, 1943, p. 17.
11. *American Civil Liberties Union-News*, February, 1946.
12. Alexander Leighton, *The Governing of Men*, Princeton University Press, Princeton, 1945, p. 139.
13. Chet Huntley, broadcast, CBS KNX Radio, Los Angeles, September 2, 1949.

14. *Pacific Citizen*, April 15, 1943.
15. Leighton, *op. cit.*, p. 179.
16. Dorothy Swaine Thomas and Richard S. Nishimoto, *The Spoilage*, University of California Press, Berkeley and Los Angeles, 1946, p. 260.
17. Grace Nichols Pearson, *Though All We Knew Depart*, unpublished manuscript, p. 34.
18. Letter to Miss Minna Stillman, October 24, 1942, Alice Hays Collection, Hoover Institution on War, Revolution, and Peace, Stanford University, Stanford, California.
19. *People in Motion, the Postwar Adjustment of the Evacuated Japanese*, War Agency Liquidation Unit, formerly WRA, 1947, p. 5.
20. James M. Sakoda, *Minidoka: An Analysis of Changing Patterns of Social Interaction*, PhD Dissertation, University of California, Berkeley, California, 1949, p. 104.
21. *Pacific Citizen*, March 18, 1943.
22. *Impounded People*, WRA Report, U.S. Government Printing Office, Washington, D.C., 1946, p. 45.
23. *The Honolulu Advertiser*, November 6, 1942.
24. Letter to Carey McWilliams, June 11, 1942, McWilliams Collection, Hoover Institution on War, Revolution, and Peace, Stanford University, Stanford, California.
25. Letter from Heart Mountain, October 8, 1942, Carey McWilliams Collection, Hoover Institution on War, Revolution, and Peace, Stanford University, Stanford, California.
26. Larry Tajiri, "Democracy Corrects Its Own Mistakes," *Asia*, April, 1943,
27. Letter to Carey McWilliams, June 11, 1942, McWilliams Collection, Hoover Institution on War, Revolution, and Peace, Stanford University, Stanford, California.
28. Gladys Ishida, "The Japanese–American Renunciants of Okayama Prefecture: Their Accommodation and Assimilation to Japanese Culture," University of Michigan PhD dissertation, 1955, Library of Congress Microfilm, p. 99.
29. Morton Grodzins, *Americans Betrayed*, University of Chicago Press, Chicago, 1949, p. 61.
30. *Pacific Citizen*, November 12, 1942.
31. *Congressional Record*, 77th Congress, 2nd Session, Vol. 88, Part 4, p. 5427.
32. *Pacific Citizen*, July 2, 1942.
33. *Ibid.*
34. *Rafu Shimpo*, editorial, March 13, 1942.
35. *Impounded People*, p. 36.
36. *Pacific Citizen*, July 2, 1942.
37. William Henry Chamberlain, "Why Civil Liberties Now?" *Harper's*, October, 1942.
38. *Pacific Citizen*, February 17, 1967.
39. Los Angeles *Times*, November 7, 1942.
40. *Pacific Citizen*, October 15, 1942.
41. *Ibid.*, August 13, 1942.
42. *Ibid.*, July 23, 1942.
43. San Jose *News*, editorial, June 26, 1942.
44. Jimmy Yamada, "Falderol," *Trek*, magazine published at Topaz.
45. San Jose *News*, editorial, June 26, 1942.
46. Ishida, *op. cit.*, p. 69.
47. *Ibid.*, Appendix.
48. Daisuke Kitagawa, *Issei and Nisei, The Internment Years*, Seabury Press, New York, 1967, pp. 13–29.
49. Letter to *The Nation*, October 24, 1942.
50. Kitagawa, *op. cit.*, p. 91.
51. *Ibid.*, p. 84.
52. *Prevalent Fears at Tule Lake*, WRA pamphlet, September 3, 1942.
53. *Impounded People*, p. 44.
54. *Pacific Citizen*, June 4, 1942.
55. Morton Grodzins, *The Loyal and the Disloyal*, University of Chicago Press, 1956, p. 105–106. (The author does not name Kurihara.)
56. Thomas and Nishimoto, *op. cit.*, pp. 369–70.

57. Sakoda, *op. cit.*, p. 129.
58. Leighton, *op. cit.*, pp. 79–80.
59. Ishida, *op. cit.*, Appendix.
60. Leighton, *op. cit.*, p. 170.
61. *Ibid.*, p. 173.
62. *Ibid.*, p. 190.
63. *Ibid.*, p. 203.
64. Helen Aihara (Kitaji), letter to Miss Clara Hinze, December 2, 1942.
65. Quoted in the Fresno *Bee*, June 10, June 13, 1943.
66. *The New Republic*, February 1, 1943.
67. Los Angeles *Times*, December 8, 1942.
68. Letter, December 30, 1942, Alice Hays Collection, Hoover Institution on War, Revolution, and Peace, Stanford University, Stanford, California.
69. *Ibid.*

Chapter Ten

1. Appendix F, Brief for the Japanese American Citizens League, *Amicus Curiae*, in *Regan* vs. *King*.
2. "Aliens in Our Midst," University of Chicago roundtable radio broadcast, May 10, 1942.
3. *Pacific Citizen*, August 27, 1942.
4. *Ibid.*, June 11, 1942.
5. Report to the Subcommittee on Japanese War Relocation Centers to the Committee on Military Affairs, United States Senate, May 7, 1943, p. 13.
6. Bill Hosokawa, "Our Own Japanese in the Pacific War," *The American Legion Magazine*, July, 1964.
7. *The Open Forum*, Los Angeles ACLU bulletin, August 26, 1944.
8. *Ibid.*
9. *Pacific Citizen*, March 18, 1943.
10. Galen Fisher, "Our Two Japanese–American Policies," *The Christian Century*, August 25, 1943.
11. Letter from a Nisei soldier to a Santa Maria, California, high school teacher, April, 1943, Galen Fisher Collection, Bancroft Library, University of California, Berkeley, California.
12. Mas Satow, Director's Report, *Pacific Citizen*, December 9, 1966.
13. *Ibid.*
14. *Ibid.*, December 10, 1942.
15. Letter from Elmer Davis, October 2, 1942, Franklin D. Roosevelt Library, Hyde Park, New York.
16. Report to the Subcommittee on Japanese War Relocation Centers to the Committee on Military Affairs, United States Senate, May 7, 1943, p. 13.
17. *Pacific Citizen*, January 28, 1943.
18. *Ibid.*, February 11, 1943.
19. *Ibid.*
20. *Congressional Record*, Vol. 89, Part I, 78th Congress, 1st Session, February 19, 1943, p. 1130.
21. Fresno *Bee*, April 14, 1943.
22. San Francisco *Chronicle*, April 14, 1943.
23. *Congressional Record*, Vol. 89, Part 3, 78th Congress, 1st Session, p. 4006, quoted by Rep. Jack Z. Anderson on May 5, 1943.
24. Jacobus tenBroek, Edward N. Barnhart, and Floyd W. Matson, *Prejudice, War, and the Constitution*, University of California Press, Berkeley and Los Angeles, 1958, pp. 159–160.
25. *Congressional Record*, Appendix, Vol. 89, Part 10, 78th Congress, 1st Session, p. A2810.

26. Galen Fisher, "A Balance Sheet on Japanese Evacuation," *The Christian Century,* August 18, 25, September 1, 8, 1943.
27. *Congressional Record,* Vol. 89, Part 3, 78th Congress, 1st Session, p. 4006.
28. *Pacific Citizen,* May 27, 1943.
29. *Congressional Record,* Appendix, Vol. 89, Part 10, 78th Congress, 1st Session, p. A2810.
30. *Pacific Citizen,* December 2, 1944.
31. *Impounded People,* U.S. Department of the Interior, WRA, Government Printing Office, Washington, D.C., 1946, p. 105.
32. Appendix B, Brief for the Japanese American Citizens League, *Amicus Curiae,* in *Regan* vs. *King.*
33. Larry Tajiri, "Democracy Corrects Its Own Mistakes," *Asia,* April, 1943.
34. *Pacific Citizen,* December 10, 1942.
35. Dorothy Swaine Thomas and Richard Nishimoto, *The Spoilage,* University of California Press, Berkeley and Los Angeles, 1946, p. 69.
36. *Ibid.,* pp. 59–60.
37. *Ibid.,* pp. 67–68.
38. Yasuo William Abiko, letter to Galen Fisher, March 12, 1943, Galen Fisher Collection, Bancroft Library, University of California, Berkeley, California.
39. Topaz *Times,* February 15, 1943.
40. *Ibid.,* February 16, 1943.
41. Thomas and Nishimoto, *op. cit.,* p. 66.
42. *Ibid.,* p. 68.
43. *Ibid.,* p. 67.
44. Leonard Broom (Bloom) and John Kitsuse, *The Managed Casualty,* University of California Press, Berkeley and Los Angeles, California, 1956, p. 27.
45. Thomas and Nishimoto, *op. cit.,* pp. 94–95.
46. Monica Sone, *Nisei Daughter,* Atlantic, Little, Brown and Company, Boston, 1953, p. 198.
47. Daisuke Kitagawa, *Issei and Nisei: The Internment Years,* The Seabury Press, New York, 1967, p. 119.
48. Thomas and Nishimoto, *op. cit.,* p. 101.
49. Gladys Ishida, *The Japanese–American Renunciants of Okayama Prefecture; Their Accommodation and Assimilation,* PhD Dissertation, University of Michigan, on microfilm at Library of Congress, Washington, D.C., p. 72.
50. Thomas and Nishimoto, *op. cit.,* p. 68.
51. *Ibid.,* p. 90.
52. *Ibid.*
53. *Ibid.,* p. 91.
54. Ishida, *op. cit.*
55. Esther Rhoads, letter, February 17, 1943, Conard-Duveneck Collection, Hoover Institution on War, Revolution, and Peace, Stanford University, Stanford, California.
56. Morton Grodzins, *The Loyal and the Disloyal,* University of Chicago Press, 1956, pp. 117–18.
57. *Ibid.,* p. 123.
58. *Pacific Citizen,* March 25, 1943.
59. Thomas and Nishimoto, *op. cit.,* p. 69.
60. *Ibid.,* pp. 79–80.
61. *Ibid.,* p. 81.
62. Ishida, *op. cit.,* p. 99.
63. Letter to Galen Fisher, March 12, 1943, Galen Fisher Collection, Bancroft Library, University of California, Berkeley, California.
64. Harold Ickes, letter, April 13, 1943, Franklin D. Roosevelt Library, Hyde Park, New York.
65. Letter, August 9, 1943, Alice Hays Collection, Hoover Institution on War, Revolution, and Peace, Stanford University, Stanford, California.
66. Fresno *Bee,* April 5, 1943.

67. Report of the Subcommittee on Japanese War Relocation Centers to the Committee on Military Affairs, United States Senate, May 7, 1943, p. 18.
68. tenBroek, Barnhart, and Matson, *op. cit.*, p. 161.
69. *Pacific Citizen*, March 25, 1943.
70. tenBroek, Barnhart, and Matson, *op. cit.*, p. 161.
71. Thomas and Nishimoto, *op. cit.*, p. 85.
72. tenBroek, Barnhart, and Matson, *op. cit.*, p. 162.
73. Ishida, *op. cit.*, p. 87.
74. Grodzins, *op. cit.*, pp. 111–112.
75. *Ibid.*
76. Letter, February, 1943, Galen Fisher Collection, Bancroft Library, University of California, Berkeley, California.
77. Grace Nichols Pearson, *Though All We Knew Depart*, unpublished manuscript, p. 132.
78. Carey McWilliams, *Prejudice: Japanese–Americans: Symbols of racial intolerance*, Little, Brown and Company, Boston, 1944, pp. 188–189.

Chapter Eleven

1. *Impounded People*, U.S. Department of the Interior, WRA, Government Printing Office, Washington, D.C., 1946, p. 115.
2. Speech at Topaz Relocation Center, April, 1945, quoted in Topaz *Times*, March 3, 1945.
3. Report of the Subcommittee on Japanese War Relocation Centers to the Committee on Military Affairs, United States Senate, May 7, 1943, p. 12.
4. Speech at Topaz, *loc. cit.*, March 3, 1945.
5. *Community Government on War Relocation Centers*, U.S. Department of the Interior, WRA, Washington, D.C., 1946, p. 5.
6. Jacobus tenBroek, Edward N. Barnhart, and Floyd W. Matson, *Prejudice, War and the Constitution*, University of California Press, Berkeley and Los Angeles, 1958, pp. 130–131.
7. San Francisco *Examiner*, May 25, 1943.
8. *Ibid.*
9. Miné Okubo, *Citizen 13660*, Columbia University Press, New York, 1946, pp. 202–03.
10. Allen H. Eaton, *Beauty Behind Barbed Wire: The Arts of the Japanese in our War Relocation Centers*, Harper & Brothers, New York, 1952, p. 84.
11. Letter from Heart Mountain, September 28, 1944, Alice Hays Collection, Hoover Institution on War, Revolution, and Peace, Stanford University, Stanford, California.
12. Los Angeles *Times*, June 10, 1943.
13. *WRA: A Story of Human Conservation*, U.S. Department of the Interior, WRA, Washington, D.C., 1946, Appendix, p. 196.
14. *Pacific Citizen*, December 23–30, 1966.
15. *Ibid.*, December 10, 1942.
16. Los Angeles *Times*, February 12, 1943.
17. Gene Oishi, "Remember Pearl Habor, and then . . . ," Los Angeles *Times WEST* Magazine, March 12, 1967.
18. Los Angeles *Times*, April 2, 1967.
19. Fresno *Bee*, December 7, 1943.
20. *Ibid.*, editorial, June 14, 1943.
21. Letter, April, 1943, Alice Hays Collection, Hoover Institution on War, Revolution, and Peace, Stanford University, Stanford, California.
22. Denver *Post*, April 23, 24, 1943.
23. Heart Mountain *Sentinel*, May 1, 1943.
24. *Ibid.*, editorial, May 29, 1943.
25. *The Open Forum*, June 26, 1943.

26. Eleanor Roosevelt, "Race, Religion and Prejudice," *The New Republic*, May 11, 1942.
27. *Collier's*, October 16, 1943.
28. Yori Wada, "Beyond the Horizon," *California Monthly*, December, 1943.
29. *The Evacuated People, A Quantitative Description*, War Relocation Authority, Washington, D.C., 1946, p. 79.
30. Los Angeles *Times*, June 16, 1943.
31. Letter, October 8, 1942, Carey McWilliams Collection, Hoover Institution on War, Revolution, and Peace, Stanford University, Stanford, California.
32. *Impounded People, op. cit.*, p. 154.
33. San Jose *News*, December 25, 1943.
34. Heart Mountain *Sentinel*, May 8, 1943.
35. *Impounded People, op. cit.*, p. 173.
36. Kazuo Miyamoto, *Hawaii, End of the Rainbow*, Charles E. Tuttle Company, Rutland, Vermont, 1964, p. 469.
37. Fumiko Ogawa, *tanka* from *Sounds from the Unknown, A Collection of Japanese–American Tanka*, trans. by Lucille M. Nixon and Tomoe Tana, Alan Swallow, Denver, 1963, p. 118.
38. Kojin Tahara, *tanka* from *Sounds from the Unknown*, p. 130.
39. Monica Sone, *Nisei Daughter*, Atlantic, Little, Brown and Co., Boston, 1953, p. 193.
40. Miyamoto, *op. cit.*, p. 444.
41. *Congressional Record*, Appendix, Vol. 89, Part 11, 78th Congress, 1st Session, pp. A3674–3675.
42. Report and minority views of special committee on un-American activities in Japanese Relocation Centers, 78th Congress, 1st Session, HR 282, 1943.
43. Topaz *Times*, August 31, 1945.
44. Letter, October 24, 1942. Alice Hays Collection, Hoover Institution on War, Revolution, and Peace, Stanford University, Stanford, California.
45. Salt Lake City *Tribune*, October 1, 1942.
46. Arizona *Daily Star*, editorial, November 5, 1942.
47. *Impounded People, op. cit.*, 173.
48. *Ibid.*, p. 170.
49. Heart Mountain *Sentinel*, September 18, 1944.
50. *Commonweal*, January 22, 1943.
51. Gladys Ishida, *The Japanese–American Renunciants of Okayama Prefecture: Their Accommodation and Assimilation to Japanese Culture*, PhD Dissertation, University of Michigan, on microfilm at the Library of Congress, Washington, D.C., pp. 74–75.
52. *The Open Forum*, November 13, 1943.
53. "Year's Flight," Butte High School, Rivers, Arizona, 1945.
54. Undated student composition, Edythe N. Backus Collection, Huntington Library, San Marino, California.
55. Letter to *The Nation*, October 24, 1942.
56. *Impounded People, op. cit.*, p. 158.
57. Bulletin to teachers on working hours and working habits by Arthur Harris, Superintendent of Education at Poston, May 15, 1943, Backus Collection, Huntington Library, San Marino, California.
58. "Issei, Nisei, and Kibei," *Fortune*, April, 1944.
59. *Impounded People, op. cit.*, p. 134.
60. San Francisco *Chronicle*, May 25, 26, 29, 1943.
61. Dorothy Swaine Thomas and Richard S. Nishimoto, *The Spoilage*, University of California Press, Berkeley and Los Angeles, 1952, p. 107.
62. *Ibid.*, p. 185.
63. *Ibid.*, p. 106.
64. *Ibid.*, p. 110.
65. *Ibid.*, pp. 111–12.
66. *Impounded People, op. cit.*, p. 137.
67. Thomas and Nishimoto, *op. cit.*, p. 130.

68. *Ibid.*, p. 135.
69. *Ibid.*, p 138.
70. *Impounded People, op. cit.*, p. 176.
71. Thomas and Nishimoto, *op. cit.*, p. 152.
72. War Relocation Authority Advance Release, Office of War Information, November 13, 1943.
73. *Congressional Record*, Appendix, Vol. 89, Part 12, 78th Congress, 1st Session, p. A4895.
74. Fresno *Bee*, December 6, 1943.
75. Los Angeles *Times*, November 30, 1943.
76. Letter to Fresno *Bee*, December 2, 1943.
77. *Joe Kurihara, repatriate*, as told to R. R. Best, Project Director, Tule Lake Relocation Center, Bancroft Library, University of California, Berkeley, California.
78. Fresno *Bee*, November 24, 1943.
79. *Ibid.*, November 19, 1943.
80. *Ibid.*, December 9, 1943.
81. *Ibid.*, December 3, 1943.
82. *Impounded People, op. cit.*, p. 182.
83. *Ibid.*, p. 136.
84. Ishida, *op. cit.*, p. 12.
85. *Pacific Citizen*, July 22, 1944.
86. Thomas and Nishimoto, *op. cit.*, p. 314.
87. Ishida, *op. cit.*, p. 100.
88. Gerda Isenberg, "I visited Tule Lake," *The Friend*, May 11, 1944.

Chapter Twelve

1. *Brief for Appellees* in Bruce G. Barber, As District Director of the U.S. Immigration and Naturalization Service for the Northern District of California—appellant vs. Tadayasu Abo, et al., appellees (No. 12, 195 in the United States Court of Appeals for the 9th Circuit) and *Brief for Appellees* in Bruce G. Barber vs. Mary Kaname Furuya, et al. (as ditto above) in *Habeas Corpus* proceedings (on appeals from Final Decisions of the District Court of the United States for the Northern District of California, Southern Division), 1951, p. 50.
2. Palo Alto *Times*, July 1, 1944.
3. *Pacific Citizen*, August 11, 1945.
4. *The Open Forum*, Southern California ACLU, August 5, 1944.
5. Letter, Heart Mountain, April 16, 1944, Alice Hays Collection, Hoover Institution on War, Revolution, and Peace, Stanford University, Stanford, California.
6. Letter, March 29, 1944, Alice Hays Collection, Hoover Institution on War, Revolution, and Peace, Stanford University, Stanford, California.
7. WRA pamphlet, Granada, Bancroft Library, University of California, Berkeley, California.
8. *The Open Forum*, Southern California ACLU, August 12, 1944.
9. Jacobus tenBroek, Edward N. Barnhart, and Floyd W. Matson, *Prejudice, War and the Constitution*, University of California Press, Berkeley and Los Angeles, 1958, p. 170.
10. *Impounded People*, p. 190.
11. Hearings before Committee No. 5 of the Judiciary, House of Representatives, 83rd Congress, 2nd Session on HR 7435, p. 14.
12. Palo Alto *Times*, April 27, 1944.
13. "Our Own Japanese in the Pacific War," Bill Hosokawa, *The American Legion Magazine*, July, 1964.
14. San Francisco *Examiner and Chronicle*, November 13, 1966.
15. Hosokawa, *loc. cit.*, July, 1964.
16. *Ibid.*
17. From *People in Motion*, WRA, U.S. Government Printing Office, Washington, D.C., 1947, p. 21.

18. *What We're Fighting for*, Statements by U.S. Servicemen about Americans of Japanese Descent, U.S. Department of the Interior, U.S. War Relocation Authority, Washington, D.C., p. 3.
19. *Ibid.*, p. 20.
20. *People in Motion, op. cit.*, pp. 23–24.
21. Editorial, San Luis Obispo *Tribune-Telegram*, July 17, 1945.
22. *Pacific Citizen*, October 7, 1944.
23. *Ibid.*, September 23, 1966.
24. Letter from Moscow, Idaho, jail, *Pacific Citizen*, June 11, 1942.
25. "Idaho Argonaut," April 23, 1942, as quoted in Robert W. O'Brien, *The College Nisei*, Pacific Book, Palo Alto, 1949, p. 87.
26. *Congressional Record*, Appendix, Vol. 89, Part 9, 78th Congress, 1st Session, p. A358.
27. *Pacific Citizen*, September 24, 1942.
28. Lillian Ota, "Campus Report," *Treg*, Topaz Center Magazine.
29. Helen Aihara, letter to Miss Hinze, July 22, 1943.
30. *Time*, June 21, 1943.
31. Topaz *Times*, March 3, 1945.
32. *Impounded People, op. cit.*, p. 219.
33. Letter to Marvin H. McIntyre, October 13, 1942, Franklin D. Roosevelt Library, Hyde Park, New York.
34. Letter to Marvin McIntyre, September 24, 1942, Franklin D. Roosevelt Library, Hyde Park, New York.
35. Telegram, September 24, 1942, Franklin D. Roosevelt Library, Hyde Park, New York.
36. "The Japanese in Our Midst," Colorado Council of Churches, Denver, Colorado, 1943.
37. *Ibid.*
38. Letter, March 8, 1943, Report of the Subcommittee on Japanese War Relocation Centers to the Committee on Military Affairs, United States Senate, May 7, 1943, p. 91.
39. Letter, January 29, 1943, Report of the Subcommittee on Japanese War Relocation Centers, *loc. cit.*, p. 92.
40. *Congressional Record*, Vol. 89, Part 3, 78th Congress, 1st Session, pp. 4040–4041.
41. Report of the Subcommittee on Japanese War Relocation Centers, etc., *loc. cit.*, p. 20.
42. Letter, October 24, 1942, Pearson Collection, Hoover Institution on War, Revolution, and Peace, Stanford, University, Stanford, California.
43. Tule Lake WRA Bulletin, October 7, 1942.
44. *Ibid.*, Report dated September 27, 1942.
45. Letter, Los Animas, Colorado, October 4, 1942, Pearson Collection, Hoover Institution on War, Revolution, and Peace, Stanford University, Stanford, California.
46. *Pacific Citizen*, December 23–30, 1966.
47. Dorothy Swaine Thomas, *The Salvage*, University of California Press, Berkeley and Los Angeles, California, 1952, p. 253.
48. Letter to Carey McWilliams, McWilliams Collection, Hoover Institution on War, Revolution, and Peace, Stanford University, Stanford, California.
49. tenBroek, Barnhart, and Matson, *op. cit.*, p. 149.
50. Los Angeles *Times*, May 7, 1943.
51. *Ibid.*, August 26, 1943.
52. *Ibid.*, June 29, 1943.
53. San Francisco *Chronicle*, May 28, 1943.
54. Los Angeles *Times*, July 7, 1943.
55. *The Open Forum*, July 24, 1943.
56. tenBroek, Barnhart, and Matson, *op. cit.*, p. 152.
57. *Pacific Citizen*, August 4, 1967.
58. Miné Okubo, *Citizen 13660*, Columbia University Press, New York, 1946, pp. 207–208.
59. *Pacific Citizen*, December 23–30, 1966.

60. Letter, August 9, 1943, Alice Hays Collection, Hoover Institution on War, Revolution, and Peace, Stanford University, Stanford, California.
61. Thomas, *op. cit.*, p. 115.
62. *Impounded People, op. cit.*, p. 193.
63. Thomas, *op. cit.*, pp. 319–320.
64. Mamaroneck (New York) *Daily Times*, editorial quoted in Toru Matsumoto and Marion Olive Lerrigo, *A Brother Is a Stranger*, Asia Press, New York, 1946, p. 261.
65. Letter, September 13, 1943, Galen Fisher Collection, Bancroft Library, University of California, Berkeley, California.
66. Letter, December 28, 1943, Alice Hays Collection, Hoover Institution on War, Revolution, and Peace, Stanford University, Stanford, California.
67. Robert Hosokawa "An American with a Japanese Face," *Christian Science Monitor Weekly Magazine*, May 22, 1943.
68. WRA Second Quarterly Report, July 1 to September 30, 1942.
69. *Business Week*, December 12, 1942.
70. *Pacific Citizen*, August 7, 1943.
71. *Impounded People, op. cit.*, p. 223.
72. *Ibid.*
73. Thomas, *op. cit.*, p. 231.
74. *Ibid.*, pp. 357–358.
75. *Ibid.*, p. 284–85.
76. *Minidoka Irrigator*, July 17, 1943.
77. George Kitasako, letter, April 16, 1944, Alice Hays Collection, Hoover Institution on War, Revolution, and Peace, Stanford University, Stanford, California.
78. Thomas, *op. cit.*, p. 317.
79. *Pacific Citizen*, May 6, 1944.
80. Toru Matsumoto, *Beyond Prejudice*, Friendship Press, Inc., New York, 1946, p. 95.
81. Letter, April 4, 1944.
82. Arizona *Daily Star*, editorial, May 28, 1943.
83. *Ibid.*, May 26, 1943.
84. Matsumoto, *op. cit.*, p. 68.
85. Speech, Seventh Interdenominational Institute, McCormick Memorial YWCA, September 23, 1943.
86. Okubo, *op. cit.*, p. 208.
87. *Ibid.*

Chapter Thirteen

1. *The Japanese in our Midst*, pamphlet, Colorado Council of Churches, Denver, Colorado, 1943.
2. *Pacific Citizen*, June 9, 1967.
3. Carey McWilliams, "Racism on the West Coast—Part 2," *The New Republic*, June 12, 1944.
4. Los Angeles *Times*, June 21, 1943.
5. Harold Lavine, "Japanese Americans Target of Coast Hate Crusade," *PM*, January 21, 1944.
6. Lambert Schuyler, *The Japs Must Not Come Back*, pamphlet, Heron House Publishers, Winslow, Washington, 1944.
7. "Japs in Our Yard," *American Legion Monthly*, June, 1943.
8. Pasadena *Independent*, November 1, 1944.
9. Los Angeles *Times*, May 24, 1943.
10. Morton Grodzins, *Americans Betrayed*, University of Chicago Press, Chicago, 1949, p. 118.
11. *PM*, January 21, 1944.
12. Associated Press report, Salt Lake City, undated.
13. *Newsweek*, May 28, 1945.
14. *The Open Forum*, Southern California branch of the ACLU, October 10, 1942, p. 2.

15. *Pacific Citizen*, September 23, 1944.
16. *Ibid.*, July 22, 1944.
17. Lavine, *op. cit.*
18. McWilliams, *loc. cit.*, Part 1, May 29, 1944.
19. *Ibid.*
20. *Business Week*, October 28, 1944.
21. *Ibid.*
22. Lavine, *op. cit.*, and *Time*, December 20, 1943.
23. *Time*, December 20, 1943.
24. Los Angeles *Times*, May 7, 1943.
25. Fresno *Bee*, May 18, 1943.
26. 1943 Statutes of California, California State Public Printing Office, p. 2999-3003.
27. Legislative Digest, January 4–January 31, 1943, California Legislature, 55th Session, California State Public Printing Office, SB 36, p. 13.
28. *Ibid.*, SB 1017, p. 112.
29. UP, July 7, 1945.
30. Los Angeles *Times*, August 4, 1943.
31. *Ibid.*, June 20, 1943.
32. *Ibid.*, November 11, 1943.
33. *Ibid.*, December 10, 1943.
34. *Time*, December 20, 1943.
35. *The Open Forum*, December 18, 1943.
36. Fresno *Bee*, December 10, 1943.
37. *Time*, December 20, 1943.
38. *Ibid.*
39. *Ibid.*, and *The New Republic*, June 12, 1944.
40. Fresno *Bee*, December 10, 1943.
41. *Ibid.*, December 10, 1943, and Los Angeles *Times*, December 10, 1943.
42. McWilliams, *loc. cit.*, Part 1, June 12, 1944.
43. Palo Alto *Times*, undated.
44. *Pacific Citizen*, October 14, 1944.
45. *Ibid.*, October 7, 1944.
46. *Ibid.*
47. Fresno *Bee*, January 28, February 2, February 14, 1943.
48. Joint Resolution No. 21 of the California State Legislature, May 8, 1943, and California State Assembly Bill 1975, signed May 19, 1943. See Statutes and Amendments to the Code, California, 55th Session, 1943, p. 2156.
49. *Ibid.*, pp. 2586–2590.
50. *The Open Forum*, June 24, 1944.
51. *Pacific Citizen*, October 28, 1944.
52. *Ibid.*, December 30, 1944.
53. *The Open Forum*, July 15, 1944.
54. *Pacific Citizen*, undated clipping.
55. *A Tule Lake Interlude*, first anniversary edition, *The Tulean Dispatch*, WRA, Newell, California, May 27, 1942–43.
56. *The Open Forum*, March 18, 1944.
57. Shunji Noguchi, "Supplication to the People of the World Now Engaged in the War," a petition sent to "Prime Ministers" of Japan, China, England, United States, Russia, Germany, and Italy, miscellaneous collections, Hoover Institution on War, Revolution, and Peace, Stanford University, Stanford, California, May, 1944.
58. Jacobus tenBroek, Edward N. Barnhart, and Floyd W. Matson, *Prejudice, War and the Constitution*, p. 172, as quoted from papers of Franklin D. Roosevelt, Franklin D. Roosevelt Library, Hyde Park, New York.
59. *Ibid.*
60. *Pacific Citizen*, February 5, 1944.
61. Summary of arguments before the U.S. District Court of Northern California, July 20, 1942, Conard-Duveneck Collection, Hoover Institution on War, Revolution, and Peace, Stanford University, Stanford, California.

62. Army proclamation, No. 21, December 17, 1944.
63. tenBroek, Barnhart, and Matson, *op. cit.*, pp. 171, 172, and footnotes 324.
64. Justice Hugo Black, majority decision, *Toyosaburo Korematsu* vs. *U.S.*, Vol. 65, Supreme Court Reporter, 1944, p. 197.
65. *Korematsu* vs. *United States of America*, Appellant's Opening Brief in the 9th Circuit Court of Appeals, filed December 9, 1942, pp. 41–49.
66. *Pacific Citizen*, October 21, 1944.
67. Justice Hugo Black, majority opinion, *Korematsu* vs. *United States of America*, *op. cit.*, pp. 194–197.
68. Justice Robert H. Jackson, dissenting opinion, *Korematsu* vs. *United States of America, ibid.*, pp. 206–208.
69. San Francisco *Examiner*, May 28, 1943.
70. Caption, Acme press photograph, unidentified Sacramento newspaper clipping, November 17, 1944.
71. tenBroek, Barnhart, and Matson, *op. cit.*, pp. 170, 171.
72. *Pacific Citizen*, December 16, 1944.

Chapter Fourteen

1. Undated clipping, camp newspaper.
2. Letter to authors from Claude Settles, April 2, 1968.
3. Letter to Sacramento *Bee*, June 14, 1943.
4. Unidentified clipping, June 12, 1943.
5. Unidentified clipping, June 12, 1943.
6. Letter to Sacramento *Bee* from Tule Lake, undated clipping.
7. Unidentified and undated newspaper clipping, San Francisco.
8. San Francisco *Chronicle*, January 18, 1945.
9. *Ibid.*, January 21, 1945.
10. Auburn *Journal*, January, 1945.
11. San Francisco *Chronicle*, January 22, 1945.
12. Sacramento *Bee*, undated clipping.
13. *Pacific Citizen*, February 3, 1945.
14. Clipping, McClatchy Newspaper Service, February 22, 1945.
15. Unidentified clipping.
16. *Pacific Citizen*, May 5, 1945,
17. Letter to the Editor, Sacramento *Bee*, undated clipping.
18. San Francisco *Chronicle*, April 12, 1945.
19. *Ibid.*
20. *Pacific Citizen*, May 12, 1945.
21. *Ibid.*, March 3, 1945.
22. Fresno *Bee*, January 25, 1945.
23. *Pacific Citizen*, February 17, 1945.
24. *Ibid.*, June 23, 1945, and July 21, 1945.
25. Auburn *Journal*, undated letter.
26. *Ibid.*, February 28, 1945.
27. Robert B. Cozzens, Assistant Director of the WRA, address, Southern California-Arizona Methodist Conference, Pasadena, California, June 26, 1944.
28. *Collier's*, editorial, January 20, 1945.
29. *Pacific Citizen*, March 31, 1945.
30. *Ibid.*, June 16, 1945.
31. Hood River *Sun*, February 2, 1945, as quoted in *Pacific Citizen*, March 3, 1945.
32. Hood River Oregon *News*, March 23, 1945.
33. Hood River *Sun*, February 16, 1945.
34. *Pacific Citizen*, March 24, 1945.
35. *Ibid.*, May 5, 1945.
36. *Ibid.*, February 16, 1946.
37. *Ibid.*, March 3, 1945.

38. *Ibid.*
39. *Ibid.,* November 24, 1945.
40. *Ibid.,* July 7, 1945.
41. *Ibid.,* July 21, 1945.
42. *Ibid.,* April 14, 1945.
43. Fresno *Bee,* March 29, 1945.
44. *Ibid.,* August 7, 1945.
45. *Pacific Citizen,* February 10, 1945.
46. *Ibid.,* August 25, 1945.
47. Unidentified newspaper clipping.
48. *Pacific Citizen,* December 9, 1944.
49. Fresno *Bee,* June 17, 1945.
50. *Ibid.,* February 13, 1945.
51. "The Prowler," Palo Alto *Times,* July 17, 1945.
52. *Pacific Citizen,* June 30, 1945.
53. Congressman Alfred Elliott of Tulare, California, *Congressional Record,* Vol. 89, Part 6, 78th Congress, 1st Session, October 11, 1943, pp. 8, 193.
54. Fresno *Bee,* June 17, 1945.
55. *Ibid.,* June 3, 1945.
56. *Pacific Citizen,* February 16, 1946.

Chapter Fifteen

1. Gerda Isenberg, letter to evacuee, April 6, 1945, Isenberg Collection, Bancroft Library, University of California, Berkeley, California.
2. *Pacific Citizen,* November 3, 1945.
3. *Ibid.,* May 5, 1945.
4. *Daily Californian,* January 26, 1945.
5. *Pacific Citizen,* undated clipping.
6. *Ibid.,* January 13, 1945.
7. *Ibid.,* June 16, 1945.
8. *Congressional Record,* March 29, 1948, Vol. 94, Part 10, 80th Congress, 2nd Session, Appendix, p. A2429, text of article, Mike Masaoka, "Evacuation Claims—Justice Delayed," *Christian Register,* February, 1948.
9. *Pacific Citizen,* February 10, 1945.
10. *Ibid.,* April 14, 1945.
11. AP report, February 23, 1945, Salt Lake City.
12. Heart Mountain *Sentinel,* March 24, 1945.
13. WRA, *Impounded People,* U.S. Department of the Interior, Washington, D.C., 1946, p. 145–146.
14. *Pacific Coast,* November 23, 1945.
15. Topaz *Times,* March 3, 1945.
16. *Pacific Citizen,* August 18, 1945.
17. *Charter of the United Nations and Statute of the International Court of Justice,* United Nations, New York, December, 1964.
18. William Craig, "The Fall of Japan," *Saturday Evening Post,* August 26, 1967.
19. C. Northcote Parkinson, *Parkinson's Law,* Houghton Mifflin, Boston, 1957, p. 2.
20. Fresno *Bee,* March 10, 1947.

Chapter Sixteen

1. Larry Tajiri, "Democracy Corrects Its Own Mistakes," *Asia,* April, 1943.
2. Portland *Oregonian,* March 23, 1945.
3. Jacobus tenBroek, Edward N. Barnhart, and Floyd W. Matson, *Prejudice, War and the Constitution,* University of California Press, Berkeley and Los Angeles, 1958, p. 267.

4. *Pacific Citizen*, February 2, 1946.
5. *Ibid.*, editorial, December 8, 1945.
6. *Ibid.*, February 16, 1946.
7. *Ibid.*, May 27, 1943.
8. *Ibid.*, undated clipping.
9. *Ibid.*, December 1, 1945.
10. *Ibid.*, November 24, 1945.
11. John P. Roche, *Shadow and Substance*, Macmillan, New York, 1964, p. 174.
12. *Pacific Citizen*, July 29, 1966.
13. *Kenji Namba, Etsuo Namba, and Florence C. Donald* vs. *John B. McCourt and George Neuner*, Appeal from Circuit Court, Multnomah County (Oregon), December 21, 1948, p. 25.
14. *Pacific Citizen*, September 1, 1967.
15. Report of the House Committee on Un-American Activities, 1942, p. 2008.
16. Leonard Bloom and Ruth Riemer, *Removal and Return*, University of California Press, Berkeley and Los Angeles, 1949, p. 196.
17. Hearings before Subcommittee No. 5 of the Committee on the Judiciary, House of Representatives, 83rd Congress, 2nd Session on HR 7435 to amend the Japanese–American Evacuation Claims Act of 1948, p. 12.
18. Letter to *The New York Times*, April 4, 1946.
19. See Appendix, Document No. 10, this volume.
20. As reported by Chet Huntley, ABC TV, Los Angeles, May 11, 1951.
21. Hearings on HR 7435 to amend the Japanese–American Evacuation Claims Act of 1948, *op. cit.*, pp. 206–07.
22. Hearings Before Subcommittee No. 2 of the Committee on the Judiciary House of Representatives, 84th Congress, 1st Session on HR 7763 to amend the Japanese–American Evacuation Claims Act of 1948, pp. 140–41.
23. *Newsweek*, October 18, 1965.
24. *Pacific Citizen*, letters column, June 2, 1967.
25. *Ibid.*, February 17, 1967.
26. *Ibid.*, January 13, 1967.
27. *Ibid.*, July 28, 1967.
28. *Ibid.*, September 29, 1967.
29. San Francisco *Chronicle*, April 11, 1967.
30. *Life*, April 28, 1967.
31. Jeffrey Matsui, "Sounding Board," *Pacific Citizen*, April 21, 1967.
32. Langston Hughes, "I, Too," *Anthology of American Negro Literature*, ed. by V. F. Calverton, Random House, 1929, p. 210.
33. *Commonweal*, June 20, 1952.
34. *Time*, June 2, 1952.
35. *Commonweal*, June 20, 1952.
36. *Congressional Record*, Vol. 98, Part 2, 82nd Congress, 2nd Session, pp. 2225–2226.
37. Eugene V. Rostow, "The Japanese–American Cases—A Disaster," *Yale Law Journal*, Vol. 54, June 1945.
38. *Congressional Record*, Vol. 90, Part 2, 78th Congress, 2nd Session, p. 1779.
39. *Ibid.*, p. 1787.
40. *Ibid.*, pp. 1787–1788.
41. *Ibid.*, p. 1986.
42. Letter to the authors, August 9, 1968.
43. Wayne Collins, brief for *J. Howard McGrath* vs. *Tadaysu Abo* and *J. Howard McGrath* vs. *Mary Kaname Furuya*, Nos. 12,251 and 12,252 in U.S. Court of Appeals for Ninth Circuit, p. 122.
44. Dorothy Swaine Thomas and Richard S. Nishimoto, *The Spoilage*, University of California Press, Berkeley and Los Angeles, 1946, p. 322.
45. Letter from Thomas W. Grubbs, Tule Lake, Christmas, 1945.
46. Gladys Ishida, *The Japanese–American Renunciants of Okayama Prefecture: Their Accommodation and Assimilation to Japanese Culture*, PhD dissertation on microfilm at Library of Congress, Washington, D.C., p. 71.
47. *Impounded People*, p. 211.

48. Jacobus tenBroek, Edward N. Barnhart, and Floyd W. Matson, *Prejudice, War, and the Constitution*, University of California Press, Berkeley and Los Angeles, 1958, pp. 178–179.
49. Letter, August 9, 1945, in *Pacific Citizen*, December 8, 1945.
50. *American Civil Liberties Union-News*, March, 1946.
51. Cited in petition for writs of *certiorari* to the United States Court of Appeals for the Ninth Circuit and brief in support thereof, *Aoki et al.* vs. *Barber* and *Wakabayashi et al.* vs. *Barber*, 1951, p. 8.
52. San Francisco *Chronicle*, May 29, 1943.
53. *Joe Kurihara, repatriate,* as told to R. R. Best, Project Director, Tule Lake Relocation Center, Bancroft Library, University of California, Berkeley, California.
54. Letter, June 17, 1942, Alice Hays Collection, Hoover Institution on War, Revolution, and Peace, Stanford University, Stanford, California.
55. Ishida, *op. cit.,* p. 106.
56. American Friends Service Bulletin, December 13, 1945.
57. Ishida, *op. cit.,* p. 108.
58. *Ibid.,* p. 76.
59. *Ibid.,* p. 124.
60. *Pacific Citizen*, January 5, 1946.
61. Ishida, *op. cit.,* pp. 103, 104, 105.
62. *Ibid.,* p. 133.
63. Louis Obed Renne, *Our Day of Empire*, The Strickland Press, Glasgow, Scotland, 1954, pp. 167–68.
64. Letter to the authors, August 9, 1968.
65. William Peterson, "Success Story, Japanese–American Style," *The New York Times Magazine*, January 9, 1966.

Chapter Seventeen

1. William Peterson, "Success Story, Japanese–American Style," *The New York Times Magazine*, January 9, 1966.
2. United States Census of Population, Non-White Population by Race, 1960, p. 16.
3. Don E. Fehrenbacher, *A Basic History of California*, D. Van Nostrand Co., Princeton, New Jersey, Toronto, New York, London, 1964, p. 81.
4. *Californians of Japanese, Chinese, Filipino Ancestry*, State of California, Department of Industrial Relations, Division of Fair Employment Practices, San Francisco, California, June, 1964, p. 65.
5. *Ibid.*
6. *Ibid.*
7. "The Ultimate City," *The New Yorker*, October 15, 1966.
8. United States Census of Population, Non-White Population by Race, 1960, p. 16.
9. Bill Hosokawa, *Pacific Citizen,* July 29, 1966.
10. *Pacific Citizen*, May 27, 1966.
11. *Rafu Shimpo*, September 20, 1941.
12. *California Real Estate* magazine, June, 1952.
13. United States Census of Population, Non-White Population by Race, 1960, p. 108.
14. *Pacific Citizen*, May 27, 1966.
15. *Ibid.,* February 24, 1967.
16. Albert Q. Maisel, *They All Chose America*, Thomas Nelson and Sons, New York, 1955.
17. *Pacific Citizen*, January 27, 1967.
18. *Newsweek,* June 13, 1966.
19. *Pacific Citizen*, December 29, 1945.
20. Professor Roger Daniels, UCLA Symposium of Evacuation, June, 1966.
21. JACL 19th Biennial Report, 1966, p. 34.
22. *Pacific Citizen*, October 28, 1966.
23. Los Angeles *Times WEST* magazine, March 12, 1967.
24. *Pacific Citizen,* undated clipping.

25. *Ibid.*, March 1, 1968.
26. *Ibid.*, July 22, 1966.
27. *Look*, May 16, 1967.
28. *Pacific Citizen*, July 21, 1967.
29. *Ibid.*, undated clipping.
30. *Pacific Citizen*, editorial, July 29, 1966.
31. *Ibid.*, September 15, 1967.
32. Letter, *Pacific Citizen*, August 5, 1966.
33. *Pacific Citizen*, November 3, 1967.
34. From an article in the *Hokubei Mainichi,* reprinted in the *Pacific Citizen*, September 16, 1966.
35. *Ibid.*, December 24, 1949.
36. *Ibid.*, undated clipping.
37. Joe Grant Masaoka, article, *Rafu Shimpo Supplement*, December, 1966.
38. *Pacific Citizen*, February 17, 1967.
39. R. B. Read, "The Sansei," San Francisco Sunday *Examiner* and *Chronicle, California Living*, August 14, 1966.
40. *Ibid.*
41. *Pacific Citizen*, March 31, 1967.
42. Read, *op. cit.*

Chapter Eighteen

1. Review of John D. Weaver, *Warren: The Man, the Court, the Era, The London Times Literary Supplement*, January 18, 1968.
2. 1955 Hearings before Subcommittee No. 2, Committee of the Judiciary, House of Representatives, 84th Congress, 1st Session on HR 7763 to amend the Japanese–American Evacuation Claims Act of 1948, pp. 136–137.
3. Professor James Sakoda thinks a more appropriate word is *giri*, which implies a sense of duty, a debt of gratitude, honor, or responsibility.
4. Jim Marshall, "The Problem People," *Collier's*, August 15, 1942.
5. Daisuke Kitagawa, *Issei and Nisei*, Seabury Press, New York, 1967, p. 31.
6. Justice Robert Jackson, dissenting opinion, *Toyosaburo Korematsu* vs. *United States,* 1944, Supreme Court Reporter, Vol. 65, West Publishing Co., St. Paul, Minnesota, 1946, p. 207.
7. Emergency Detention Act of 1950 (McCarran Act), Title II, U.S. Statutes at Large, Vol. 64, Part 1, 81st Congress, 2nd Session, pp. 1019–1030.
8. J. Walter Yeagley, Assistant District Attorney, Internal Security Division, letter to the authors, April 25, 1968.
9. The Washington *Post*, March 3, 1968.
10. *Ibid.*
11. *Pacific Citizen*, May 24, 1968.
12. *Ibid.*, August 16, 1968.
13. The Washington *Post*, March 3, 1968.
14. Galen Fisher, "A Balance Sheet on Japanese Evacuation," *The Christian Century*, August 18 and 25, September 1 and 8, 1943.
15. Eugene V. Rostow, "The Japanese–American Cases—A Disaster," *Yale Law Journal*, Vol. 54, June, 1945.
16. Brief for Appellant, *Fred Toyosaburo Korematsu* vs. *United States of America*, United States Ninth Circuit Court of Appeals, December 9, 1942, pp. 92–94.
17. Charles Fairman, "'The Law of Martial Rule and the National Emergency," *Harvard Law Review*, June, 1942.
18. Rostow, *loc. cit.*
19. *Ex Parte Milligan*, December, 1866, U.S. Supreme Court Reports, Vol. 18, Lawyers' Edition, p. 281.
20. Justice Hugo Black, majority opinion, *Duncan* vs. *Kahanamoku*, Supreme Court Reporter, Vol. 66, West Publishing Co., St. Paul, Minnesota, 1947, p. 611.

21. Justice Frank Murphy, concurring opinion, *Duncan* vs. *Kahanamoku, ibid.*, pp. 616–19.
22. Robert H. Jackson, *The Supreme Court in the American System of Government*, Harvard University Press, Cambridge, Massachusetts, 1955, p. 25.
23. William O. Douglas, *An Anatomy of Liberty*, Trident Press, Pocket Books, Inc., New York, 1964, pp. 32–33.
24. Hearings Before Subcommittee No. 5 of the Committee of the Judiciary, House of Representatives, 83rd Congress, 2nd Session on HR 7435, p. 35.

Appendices

1. 1894 TREATY OF COMMERCE AND NAVIGATION*

Concluded November 22, 1894; ratification advised by the Senate with amendments February 5, 1895; ratified by the President February 15, 1895; ratifications exchanged March 21, 1895; proclaimed March 21, 1895.

ARTICLES

I. Mutual freedom of trade, travel, etc.; taxes; exemptions.
II. Commerce and navigation.
III. Inviolability of dwellings, etc.
IV. Import duties.
V. Export duties.
VI. Transit dues, etc.
VII. Equality of shipping.
VIII. Tonnage, etc., dues.
IX. Port regulations.
X. Coasting trade.
XI. Vessels in distress, shipwrecks, etc.

XII. Nationality of vessels.
XIII. Deserters from ships.
XIV. Favored nation privileges.
XV. Consular officers.
XVI. Patents, trade-marks, and designs.
XVII. Abolition of foreign settlements in Japan.
XVIII. Former treaties superseded.
XIX. Date of taking effect.
XX. Ratification.
Protocol.

The President of the United States of America and His Majesty the Emperor of Japan, being equally desirous of maintaining the relations of good understanding which happily exist between them, by extending and increasing the intercourse between their respective States, and being convinced that this object cannot better be accomplished than by revising the Treaties hitherto existing between the two countries, have resolved to complete such a revision, based upon principles of equity and mutual benefit, and, for that purpose, have named as their Plenipotentiaries, that is to say:

* The Japanese immigrant case (189 U.S., 86).
Japanese–American Treaty of Commerce and Navigation, 1894 (from *Treaties, Convention, International Acts, Protocols and Agreements between the United States of America and Other Powers 1776–1909*, Vol. I., pp. 1028–1036, Document No. 357, Washington Government Printing Office, 1910).

The President of the United States of America, Walter Q. Gresham, Secretary of State of the United States, and His Majesty the Emperor of Japan, Jushii Shinichiro Kurino, of the Order of the Sacred Treasure, and of the Fourth Class; who, after having communicated to each other their full powers, found to be in good and due form, have agreed upon and concluded the following Articles:

ARTICLE I

The citizens or subjects of each of the two High Contracting Parties shall have full liberty to enter, travel, or reside in any part of the territories of the other Contracting Party, and shall enjoy full and perfect protection for their persons and property.

They shall have free access to the Courts of Justice in pursuit and defence of their rights; they shall be at liberty equally with native citizens or subjects to choose and employ lawyers, advocates and representatives to pursue and defend their rights before such Courts, and in all other matters connected with the administration of justice they shall enjoy all the rights and privileges enjoyed by native citizens or subjects.

In whatever relates to rights of residence and travel; to the possession of goods and effects of any kind; to the succession to personal estate, by will or otherwise, and the disposal of property of any sort and in any manner whatsoever which they may lawfully acquire, the citizens or subjects of each Contracting Party shall enjoy in the territories of the other the same privileges, liberties, and rights, and shall be subject to no higher imposts or charges in these respects than native citizens or subjects or citizens or subjects of the most favored nation. The citizens or subjects of each of the Contracting Parties shall enjoy in the territories of the other entire liberty of conscience, and, subject to the laws, ordinances, and regulations, shall enjoy the right of private or public exercise of their worship, and also the right of burying their respective countrymen, according to their religious customs, in such suitable and convenient places as may be established and maintained for that purpose.

They shall not be compelled, under any pretext whatsoever, to pay any charges or taxes other or higher than those that are, or may be paid by native citizens or subjects, or citizens or subjects of the most favored nation.

The citizens or subjects of either of the Contracting Parties residing in the territories of the other shall be exempt from all compulsory military service whatsoever, whether in the army, navy, national guard, or militia; from all contributions imposed in lieu of personal service; and from all forced loans or military exactions or contributions.

ARTICLE II

There shall be reciprocal freedom of commerce and navigation between the territories of the two High Contracting Parties.

The citizens or subjects of each of the High Contracting Parties may trade in any part of the territories of the other by wholesale or retail in all kinds of produce, manufactures, and merchandise of lawful commerce, either in person or by agents, singly or in partnership with foreigners or native citizens or subjects; and they may there own or hire and occupy houses, manufactories, warehouses, shops and premises which may be necessary for them, and lease land for residential and commercial purposes, conforming themselves to the laws, police and customs regulations of the country like native citizens or subjects.

They shall have liberty freely to come with their ships and cargoes to all places, ports, and rivers in the territories of the other, which are or may be opened to foreign commerce, and shall enjoy, respectively, the same treatment in matters of commerce and navigation as native citizens or subjects, or citizens or subjects of the most favored nation, without having to pay taxes, imposts or duties, of whatever nature or under whatever denomination levied in the name or for the profit of the Government, public functionaries, private individuals, corporations, or establishments of any kind, other or greater than those paid by native citizens or subjects, or citizens or subjects of the most favored nation.

It is, however, understood that the stipulations contained in this and the preceding Article do not in any way affect the laws, ordinances and regulations with regard to trade, the immigration of laborers, police and public security which are in force or which may hereafter be enacted in either of the two countries.

Article III

The dwellings, manufactories, warehouses, and shops of the citizens or subjects of each of the High Contracting Parties in the territories of the other, and all premises appertaining thereto destined for purposes of residence or commerce, shall be respected.

It shall not be allowable to proceed to make a search of, or a domiciliary visit to, such dwellings and premises, or to examine or inspect books, papers, or accounts, except under the conditions and with the forms prescribed by the laws, ordinances and regulations for citizens or subjects of the country.

Article IV

No other or higher duties shall be imposed on the importation into the territories of the United States of any article, the produce or manufacture of the territories of His Majesty the Emperor of Japan, from whatever place arriving; and no other or higher duties shall be imposed on the importation into the territories of His Majesty the Emperor of Japan of any article, the produce or manufacture of the territories of the United States, from whatever place arriving, than on the like article produced or manufactured in any other foreign country; nor shall any prohibition be maintained or imposed on the importation of any article, the produce or manufacture of the territories of either of the High Contracting Parties, into the territories of the other, from whatever place arriving, which shall not equally extend to the importation of the like article, being the produce or manufacture of any other country. This last provision is not applicable to the sanitary and other prohibitions occasioned by the necessity of protecting the safety of persons, or of cattle, or of plants useful to agriculture.

Article V

No other or higher duties or charges shall be imposed in the territories of either of the High Contracting Parties on the exportation of any article to the territories of the other than such as are, or may be, payable on the exportation of the like article to any other foreign country; nor shall any prohibition be imposed on the exportation of any article from the territories of either of the two High Contracting Parties to the territories of the other which shall not equally extend to the exportation of the like article to any other country.

Article VI

The citizens or subjects of each of the High Contracting Parties shall enjoy in the territories of the other exemption from all transit duties, and a perfect equality of treatment with native citizens or subjects in all that relates to ware-housing, bounties, facilities, and drawbacks.

ARTICLE VII

All articles which are or may be legally imported into the ports of the territories of His Majesty the Emperor of Japan in Japanese vessels may likewise be imported into those ports in vessels of the United States, without being liable to any other or higher duties or charges of whatever denomination than if such articles were imported in Japanese vessels; and, reciprocally, all articles which are or may be legally imported into the ports of the territories of the United States in vessels of the United States may likewise be imported into those ports in Japanese vessels, without being liable to any other or higher duties or charges of whatever denomination than if such articles were imported in vessels of the United States. Such reciprocal equality of treatment shall take effect without distinction, whether such articles come directly from the place of origin or from any other place.

In the same manner, there shall be perfect equality of treatment in regard to exportation, so that the same export duties shall be paid, and the same bounties and drawbacks allowed, in the territories of either of the High Contracting Parties on the exportation of any article which is or may be legally exported therefrom, whether such exportation shall take place in Japanese vessels or in vessels of the United States, and whatever may be the place of destination, whether a port of either of the High Contracting Parties or of any third Power.

ARTICLE VIII

No duties of tonnage, harbor, pilotage, lighthouse, quarantine, or other similar or corresponding duties of whatever nature, or under whatever denomination levied in the name or for the profit of Government, public functionaries, private individuals, corporations, or establishments of any kind, shall be imposed in the ports of the territories of either country upon all the vessels of the other country which shall not equally and under the same conditions be imposed in the like cases on national vessels in general or vessels of the most favored nation. Such equality of treatment shall apply reciprocally to the respective vessels, from whatever port or place they may arrive, and whatever may be their place of destination.

ARTICLE IX

In all that regards the stationing, loading, and unloading of vessels in the ports, basins, docks, roadsteads, harbors or rivers of the territories of the two countries, no privilege shall be granted to national vessels which shall not be equally granted to vessels of the other country; the intention of the High Contracting Parties being that in this repect also the respective vessels shall be treated on the footing of perfect equality.

ARTICLE X

The coasting trade of both the High Contracting Parties is excepted from the provisions of the present Treaty, and shall be regulated according to the laws, ordinances and regulations of the United States and Japan, respectively. It is, however, understood that citizens of the United States in the territories of His Majesty the Emperor of Japan and Japanese subjects in the territories of the United States, shall enjoy in this respect the rights which are, or may be, granted under such laws, ordinances and regulations to the citizens or subjects of any other country.

A vessel of the United States laden in a foreign country with cargo destined for two or more ports in the territories of His Majesty the Emperor of Japan, and a Japanese vessel laden in a foreign country with cargo destined for two or more ports in the territories of the United States, may discharge a portion of her cargo at one port, and continue her voyage to the other port or ports of destination where foreign trade is permitted, for the purpose of landing the remainder of her original cargo there, subject always to the laws and customs regulations of the two countries.

The Japanese Government, however, agrees to allow vessels of the United States to continue, as heretofore, for the period of the duration of the present Treaty, to carry cargo between the existing open ports of the Empire, excepting to or from the ports of Osaka, Niigata, and Ebisuminato.

ARTICLE XI*

Any ship-of-war or merchant vessel of either of the High Contracting Parties which may be compelled by stress of weather, or by reason of any other distress, to take shelter in the port of the other, shall be at liberty to refit therein, to procure all necessary supplies, and to put to sea again, without paying any dues other than such as would be payable by national vessels. In case, however, the master of a merchant vessel should be under the necessity of disposing of a part of his cargo in order to defray the expenses, he shall be bound to conform to the regulations and tariffs of the place to which he may have come.

If any ship-of-war or merchant-vessel of one of the High Contracting Parties should run aground or be wrecked upon the coasts of the other, the local authorities shall inform the Consul General, Consul, Vice-Consul, or Consular Agent of the district, of the occurrence, or if there be no such consular officers, they shall inform the Consul General, Consul, Vice-Consul, or Consular Agent of the nearest district.

All proceedings relative to the salvage of Japanese vessels, wrecked or cast on shore in the territorial waters of the United States, shall take place in accordance with the laws of the United States, and, reciprocally, all measures of salvage relative to vessels of the United States, wrecked or cast on shore in the territorial waters of His Majesty the Emperor of Japan, shall take place in accordance with the laws, ordinances, and regulations of Japan.

Such stranded or wrecked ship or vessel, and all parts thereof, and all furnitures and appurtenances belonging thereunto, and all goods and merchandise saved therefrom, including those which may have been cast into the sea, or the proceeds thereof, if sold, as well as all papers found on board such stranded or wrecked ship or vessel, shall be given up to the owners or their agents, when claimed by them. If such owners or agents are not on the spot, the same shall be delivered to the respective Consuls General, Consuls, Vice-Consuls, or Consular Agents upon being claimed by them within the period fixed by the laws, ordinances and regulations of the country, and such Consular officers, owners, or agents shall pay only the expenses incurred in the preservation of the property, together with the salvage or other expenses which would have been payable in the case of the wreck of a national vessel.

The goods and merchandise saved from the wreck shall be exempt from all the duties of the Customs unless cleared for consumption, in which case they shall pay the ordinary duties.

* See Convention of 1880.

When a vessel belonging to the citizens or subjects of one of the High Contracting Parties is stranded or wrecked in the territories of the other, the respective Consuls General, Consuls, Vice-Consuls, and Consular Agents shall be authorized, in case the owner or master, or other agent of the owner, is not present, to lend their official assistance in order to afford the necessary assistance to the citizens or subjects of the respective States. The same rule shall apply in case the owner, master, or other agent is present, but requires such assistance to be given.

ARTICLE XII

All vessels which, according to United States law, are to be deemed vessels of the United States, and all vessels which, according to Japanese law, are to be deemed Japanese vessels, shall, for the purposes of this Treaty, be deemed vessels of the United States and Japanese vessels, respectively.

ARTICLE XIII

The Consuls General, Consuls, Vice-Consuls, and Consular Agents of each of the High Contracting Parties, residing in the territories of the other, shall receive from the local authorities such assistance as can by law be given to them for the recovery of deserters from the vessels of their respective countries.

It is understood that this stipulation shall not apply to the citizens or subjects of the country where the desertion takes place.

ARTICLE XIV

The High Contracting Parties agree that, in all that concerns commerce and navigation, any privilege, favor or immunity which either High Contracting Party has actually granted, or may hereafter grant, to the Government, ships, citizens or subjects of any other State, shall be extended to the Government, ships, citizens, or subjects of the other High Contracting Party, gratuitously, if the concession in favor of that other State shall have been gratuitous, and on the same or equivalent conditions if the concession shall have been conditional; it being their intention that the trade and navigation of each country shall be placed, in all respects, by the other upon the footing of the most favored nation.

ARTICLE XV

Each of the High Contracting Parties may appoint Consuls General, Consuls, Vice-Consuls, Pro-Consuls, and Consular Agents, in all the ports, cities, and places of the other, except in those where it may not be convenient to recognize such officers.

This exception, however, shall not be made in regard to one of the High Contracting Parties without being made likewise in regard to every other Power.

The Consuls General, Consuls, Vice-Consuls, Pro-Consuls, and Consular Agents may exercise all functions, and shall enjoy all privileges, exemptions, and immunities which are, or may hereafter be, granted to Consular officers of the most favored nation.

ARTICLE XVI*

The citizens or subjects of each of the High Contracting Parties shall enjoy in the territories of the other the same protection as native citizens or subjects

* In effect March 8, 1897.

in regard to patents, trade-marks and designs, upon fulfilment of the formalities prescribed by law.

Article XVII

The High Contracting Parties agree to the following arrangement:—

The several Foreign Settlements in Japan shall, from the date this Treaty comes into force, be incorporated with the respective Japanese Communes, and shall thenceforth form part of the general municipal system of Japan. The competent Japanese Authorities shall thereupon assume all municipal obligations and duties in respect thereof, and the common funds and property, if any, belonging to such Settlements shall at the same time be transferred to the said Japanese Authorities.

When such incorporation takes place existing leases in perpetuity upon which property is now held in the said Settlements shall be confirmed, and no conditions whatsoever other than those contained in such existing leases shall be imposed in respect of such property. It is, however, understood that the Consular Authorities mentioned in the same are in all cases to be replaced by the Japanese Authorities. All lands which may previously have been granted by the Japanese Government free of rent for the public purposes of the said Settlements shall, subject to the right of eminent domain, be permanently reserved free of all taxes and charges for the public purposes for which they were originally set apart.

Article XVIII

This treaty shall, from the date it comes into force, be substituted in place of the Treaty of Peace and Amity concluded on the 3d day of the 3d month of the 7th year of Kayei, corresponding to the 31st day of March, 1854; the Treaty of Amity and Commerce concluded on the 19th day of the 6th month of the 5th year of Ansei, corresponding to the 29th day of July, 1858; the Tariff Convention concluded on the 13th day of the 5th month of the 2nd year of Keio, corresponding to the 25th day of June, 1866; the Convention concluded on the 25th day of the 7th month of the 11th year of Meiji, corresponding to the 25th day of July, 1878, and all Arrangements and Agreements subsidiary thereto concluded or existing between the High Contracting Parties; and from the same date such Treaties, Conventions, Arrangements and Agreements shall cease to be binding, and, in consequence, the jurisdiction then exercised by Courts of the United States in Japan and all the exceptional privileges, exemptions and immunities then enjoyed by citizens of the United States as a part of, or appurtenant to such jurisdiction, shall absolutely and without notice cease and determine, and thereafter all such jurisdiction shall be assumed and exercised by Japanese Courts.

Article XIX

This Treaty shall go into operation on the 17th day of July, 1899, and shall remain in force for the period of twelve years from that date.

Either High Contracting Party shall have the right, at any time thereafter to give notice to the other of its intention to terminate the same, and at the expiration of twelve months after such notice is given this Treaty shall wholly cease and determine.

Article XX

This Treaty shall be ratified, and the ratifications thereof shall be exchanged, either at Washington or Tokio, as soon as possible and not later than six months after its signature.

In witness whereof the respective Plenipotentiaries have signed the present Treaty in duplicate and have thereunto affixed their seals.

Done at the City of Washington the 22d day of November in the eighteen hundred and ninety-fourth year of the Christian era, corresponding to the 22d day of the 11th month of the 27th year of Meiji.

WALTER Q. GRESHAM   [SEAL]

SHINICHIRO KURINO.   [SEAL]

Protocol

The Government of the United States of America and the Government of His Majesty the Emperor of Japan, deeming it advisable in the interests of both countries to regulate certain special matters of mutual concern, apart from the Treaty of Commerce and Navigation signed this day, have, through their respective Plenipotentiaries, agreed upon the following stipulations:—

1. It is agreed by the Contracting Parties that one month after the exchange of the ratifications of the Treaty of Commerce and Navigation signed this day the Import Tariff now in operation in Japan in respect of goods and merchandise imported into Japan by citizens of the United States shall cease to be binding. From the same date the General Statutory Tariff of Japan shall, subject to the provisions of Article IX of the Treaty of March 31, 1854, at present subsisting between the Contracting Parties, so long as said Treaty remains in force, and, thereafter, subject to the provisions of Article IV and Article XIV of the Treaty signed this day, be applicable to goods and merchandise being the growth, produce or manufacture of the Territories of the United States upon importation into Japan.

But nothing contained in this Protocol shall be held to limit or qualify the right of the Japanese Government to restrict or to prohibit the importation of adulterated drugs, medicines, food or beverages; indecent or obscene prints, paintings, books, cards, lithographic or other engravings, photographs or any other indecent or obscene articles; articles in violation of the patent, trade-mark or copy-right laws of Japan; or any other article which for sanitary reasons, or in view of public security or morals, might offer any danger.

2. The Japanese Government, pending the opening of the country to citizens of the United States, agrees to extend the existing passport system in such a manner as to allow citizens of the United States, on the production of a certificate of recommendation from the Representative of the United States at Tokio, or from any of the Consuls of the United States at the open ports of Japan, to obtain upon application passports available for any part of the country and for any period not exceeding twelve months, from the Imperial Japanese Foreign Office in Tokio, or from the Chief Authorities in the Prefecture in which an open port is situated, it being understood that the existing Rules and Regulations governing citizens of the United States who visit the interior of the Empire are to be maintained.

3. The undersigned Plenipotentiaries have agreed that this Protocol shall be submitted to the two High Contracting Parties at the same time as the Treaty of Commerce and Navigation signed this day, and that when the said Treaty is

ratified the agreements contained in the Protocol shall also equally be considered as approved, without the necessity of a further formal ratification.

It is agreed that this Protocol shall terminate at the same time the said Treaty ceases to be binding.

In witness whereof the respective Plenipotentiaries have signed the same and have affixed thereto their seals.

Done at Washington the 22d day of November in the eighteen hundred and ninety-fourth year of the Christian era, corresponding to the 22d day of the 11th month of the 27th year of Meiji.

WALTER Q. GRESHAM   [SEAL]

SHINICHIRO KURINO   [SEAL]

2. STATUTES OF CALIFORNIA*

CHAPTER 113

An act relating to the rights, powers and disabilities of aliens and of certain companies, associations and corporations with respect to property in this state, providing for escheats in certain cases, prescribing the procedure therein, and repealing all acts or parts of acts inconsistent or in conflict herewith.

[Approved May 19, 1913. In effect August 10, 1913.]

The people of the State of California do enact as follows:

SECTION 1. All aliens eligible to citizenship under the laws of the United States may acquire, possess, enjoy, transmit and inherit real property, or any interest therein, in this state, in the same manner and to the same extent as citizens of the United States, except as otherwise provided by the laws of this state.

SECTION 2. All aliens other than those mentioned in section one of this act may acquire, possess, enjoy and transfer real property, or any interest therein, in this state, in the manner and to the extent and for the purposes prescribed by any treaty now existing between the government of the United States and the nation or country of which such alien is a citizen or subject, and not otherwise, and may in addition thereto lease lands in this state for agricultural purposes for a term not exceeding three years.

SECTION 3. Any company, association or corporation organized under the laws of this or any other state or nation, of which a majority of the members are aliens other than those specified in section one of this act, or in which a majority of the issued capital stock is owned by such aliens, may acquire, possess, enjoy and convey real property, or any interest therein, in this state, in the manner and to the extent and for the purposes prescribed by any treaty now existing between the government of the United States and the nation or country of which such members or stockholders are citizens or subjects, and not otherwise, and may in addition thereto lease lands in this state for agricultural purposes for a term not exceeding three years.

SECTION 4. Whenever it appears to the court in any probate proceeding that

* From *Statutes of California,* pp. 206, 207, 208.

by reason of the provisions of this act any heir or devisee can not take real property in this state which, but for said provisions, said heir or devisee would take as such, the court, instead of ordering a distribution of such real property to such heir or devisee, shall order a sale of said real property to be made in the manner provided by law for probate sales of real property, and the proceeds of such sale shall be distributed to such heir or devisee in lieu of such real property.

SECTION 5.   Any real property hereafter acquired in fee in violation of the provisions of this act by any alien mentioned in section two of this act, or by any company, association or corporation mentioned in section three of this act, shall escheat to, and become and remain the property of the State of California. The attorney general shall institute proceedings to have the escheat of such real property adjudged and enforced in the manner provided by section 474 of the Political Code and title eight, part three of the Code of Civil Procedure. Upon the entry of final judgment in such proceedings, the title to such real property shall pass to the State of California. The provisions of this section and of sections two and three of this act shall not apply to any real property hereafter acquired in the enforcement or in satisfaction of any lien now existing upon, or interest in such property, so long as such real property so acquired shall remain the property of the alien, company, association or corporation acquiring the same in such manner.

SECTION 6.   Any leasehold or other interest in real property less than the fee, hereafter acquired in violation of the provisions of this act by any alien mentioned in section two of this act, or by any company, association or corporation mentioned in section three of this act, shall escheat to the State of California. The attorney general shall institute proceedings to have such escheat adjudged and enforced as provided in section five of this act. In such proceedings the court shall determine and adjudge the value of such leasehold, or other interest in such real property, and enter judgment for the state for the amount thereof together with costs. Thereupon the court shall order a sale of the real property covered by such leasehold, or other interest, in the manner provided by section 1271 of the Code of Civil Procedure. Out of the proceeds arising from such sale, the amount of the judgment rendered for the state shall be paid into the state treasury and the balance shall be deposited with and distributed by the court in accordance with the interest of the parties therein.

SECTION 7.   Nothing in this act shall be construed as a limitation upon the power of the state to enact laws with respect to the acquisition, holding or disposal by aliens of real property in this state.

SECTION 8.   All acts and parts of acts inconsistent, or in conflict with the provisions of this act, are hereby repealed.

---

3. THE CREED OF THE JACL (JAPANESE AMERICAN CITIZENS LEAGUE)

I am proud that I am an American citizen of Japanese ancestry, for my very background makes me appreciate more fully the wonderful advantages of this nation. I believe in her institutions, ideals, and traditions; I glory in her heritage; I boast of her history; I trust in her future. She has granted me liberties and opportunities such as no individual enjoys in this world today. She has given me an education befitting kings. She has entrusted me with the responsibilities of the franchise. She has permitted me to build a home, to earn a livelihood, to worship, think, speak, and act as I please—as a free man equal to every other man.

Although some individuals may discriminate against me, I shall never become bitter or lose faith, for I know that such persons are not representative of the majority of the American people. True, I shall do all in my power to discourage such practices, but I shall do it in the American way; above board, in the open, through courts of law, by education, by proving myself to be worthy of equal treatment and consideration. I am firm in my belief that American sportsmanship and attitude of fair play will judge citizenship on the basis of action and achievement and not on the basis of physical characteristics.

Because I believe in America, and I trust she believes in me, and because I have received innumerable benefits from her, I pledge myself to do honor to her at all times and in all places, to support her constitution; to obey her laws; to respect her flag; to defend her against all enemies, foreign or domestic; to actively assume my duties and obligations as a citizen, cheerfully and without any reservations whatsoever, in the hope that I may become a better American in a greater America.

---

4. AUTHORIZING THE SECRETARY OF WAR TO PRESCRIBE MILITARY AREAS

Executive Order No. 9066

WHEREAS the successful prosecution of the war requires every possible protection against espionage and against sabotage to national-defense material, national-defense premises, and national-defense utilities as defined in section 4, Act of April 20, 1918, 40 Stat. 533, as amended by the act of November 30, 1940, 54 Stat. 1220, and the Act of August 21, 1941, 55 Stat. 655 (U. S. C., Title 50, Sec. 104):

Now, THEREFORE, by virtue of the authority vested in me as President of the United States, and Commander in Chief of the Army and Navy, I hereby authorize and direct the Secretary of War, and the Military Commanders whom he may from time to time designate, whenever he or any designated Commander deems such action necessary or desirable, to prescribe military areas in such places and of such extent as he or the appropriate Military Commander may determine, from which any or all persons may be excluded, and with respect to which, the right of any persons to enter, remain in, or leave shall be subject to whatever restrictions the Secretary of War or the appropriate Military Commander may impose in his discretion. The Secretary of War is hereby authorized to provide for residents of any such area who are excluded therefrom, such transportation, food, shelter, and other accommodations as may be necessary, in the judgment of the Secretary of War or the said Military Commander, and until other arrangements are made, to accomplish the purpose of this order. The designation of military areas in any region or locality shall supersede designations of prohibited and restricted areas by the Attorney General under the Proclamations of December 7 and 8, 1941, and shall supersede the responsibility and authority of the Attorney General under the said Proclamations in respect of such prohibited and restricted areas.

I hereby futher authorize and direct the Secretary of War and the said Military Commanders to take such other steps as he or the appropriate Military Commander may deem advisable to enforce compliance with the restrictions applicable to each Military area hereinabove authorized to be designated, including the use of Federal troops and other Federal Agencies, with authority to accept assistance of state and local agencies.

I hereby further authorize and direct all Executive Departments, independent establishments and other Federal Agencies, to assist the Secretary of War or the said Military Commanders in carrying out this Executive Order, including the furnishing of medical aid, hospitalization, food, clothing, transportation, use of land, shelter, and other supplies, equipment, utilities, facilities, and services.

This order shall not be construed as modifying or limiting in any way the authority heretofore granted under Executive Order No. 8972, dated December 12, 1941, nor shall it be construed as limiting or modifying the duty and responsibility of the Federal Bureau of Investigation, with respect to the investigation of alleged acts of sabotage or the duty and responsibility of the Attorney General and the Department of Justice under the Proclamations of December 7, and 8, 1941, prescribing regulations for the conduct and control of alien enemies, except as such duty and responsibility is superseded by the designation of military areas hereunder.

FRANKLIN D. ROOSEVELT.

FEBRUARY 19, 1942.

---

5. JAPANESE WAR RELOCATION CENTERS

Public Proclamation No. 5

HEADQUARTERS, WESTERN DEFENSE COMMAND AND FOURTH ARMY,
Presidio of San Francisco, California, March 30, 1942.
To: The people within the States of Washington, Oregon, California, Montana, Idaho, Nevada, Utah, and Arizona, and the Public Generally:

WHEREAS, by Public Proclamation No. 1, dated March 2, 1942, this headquarters, there were designated and established Military Area Nos. 1 and 2 and Zones thereof; and

WHEREAS, by Public Proclamation No. 2, dated March 16, 1942, this headquarters, there were designated and established Military Areas Nos. 3, 4, 5, and 6 and Zones thereof; and

WHEREAS, the present situation within these Military Areas and Zones requires as a matter of military necessity the establishment of certain regulations, as set forth hereinafter:

NOW THEREFORE, I, J. L. DeWITT, Lieutenant General, U.S. Army, by virtue of the authority vested in me by the President of the United States and by the Secretary of War and my powers and prerogatives as Commanding General, Western Defense Command, do hereby declare and establish the following regulations covering the conduct to be observed by all alien Japanese, all alien Germans, all alien Italians, and all persons of Japanese ancestry residing or being within the Military Areas above described:

Prior to and during the period of exclusion and evacuation of certain persons or classes of persons from prescribed Military Areas and Zones, persons otherwise subject thereto but who come within one or more of the classes specified in (a), (b), (c), (d), (e), and (f), below, may make written application for exemption from such exclusion and evacuation. Application Form WDC-PM 5 has been prepared for that purpose and copies thereof may be procured from any United States Post Office or United States Employment Service office in the Western Defense Command by persons who deem themselves entitled to exemption.

The following classes of persons are hereby authorized to be exempted from exclusion and evacuation upon the furnishing of satisfactory proof as specified in Form WDC-PM 5:

(a) German and Italian aliens seventy or more years of age.

(b) In the case of German and Italian aliens, the parent, wife, husband, child of (or other person who resides in the household and whose support is wholly dependent upon) an officer, enlisted man, or commissioned nurse on active duty in the Army of the United States (or any component thereof), U.S. Navy, U.S. Marine Corps, or U.S. Coast Guard.

(c) In the case of German and Italian aliens, the parent, wife, husband, child of (or other person who resides in the household and whose support is wholly dependent upon) an officer, enlisted man, or commissioned nurse who on or since December 7, 1941, died in line of duty with the armed services of the United States indicated in the preceding subparagraph.

(d) German and Italian aliens awaiting naturalization who had filed a petition for naturalization and who had paid the filing fee therefor in a court of competent jurisdiction on or before December 7, 1941.

(e) Patients in hospitals, or confined elsewhere, and too ill or incapacitated to be removed therefrom without danger to life.

(f) Inmates of orphanages and the totally deaf, dumb, or blind.

The applicant for exemption will be required to furnish the kinds of proof specified in Form WDC-PM 5 in support of the application. The certificate of exemption from evacuation will also include exemption from compliance with curfew regulations, subject, however, to such future proclamations or orders in the premises as may from time to time be issued by this headquarters. The person to whom such exemption from evacuation and curfew has been granted shall thereafter be entitled to reside in any portion of any prohibited area, including those areas heretofore declared prohibited by the Attorney General of the United States.

J. L. DeWitt,
Lieutenant General, U.S. Army, Commanding.

6. WESTERN DEFENSE COMMAND AND FOURTH ARMY WARTIME CIVIL CONTROL ADMINISTRATION*

Presidio of San Francisco, California
May 3, 1942

INSTRUCTIONS TO ALL PERSONS OF
JAPANESE ANCESTRY
LIVING IN THE FOLLOWING AREA:

All of that portion of the City of Los Angeles, State of California, within that boundary beginning at the point at which North Figueroa Street meets a line following the middle of the Los Angeles River; thence southerly and following the said line to East First Street; thence westerly on East First Street to Alameda Street; thence southerly on Alameda Street to East Third Street; thence north-westerly on East Third Street to Main Street; thence northerly on Main Street to First Street; thence northwesterly on First Street to Figueroa Street; thence northeasterly on Figueroa Street to the point of beginning.

Pursuant to the provisions of Civilian Exclusion Order No. 33, this Head-quarters, dated May 3, 1942, all persons of Japanese ancestry, both alien and non-alient, will be evacuated from the above area by 12 o'clock noon, P. W. T., Saturday, May 9, 1942.

No Japanese person living in the above area will be permitted to change residence after 12 o'clock noon, P. W. T., Sunday, May 3, 1942, without obtaining special permission from the representative of the Commanding General, Southern California Sector, at the Civil Control Station located at:

> Japanese Union Church,
> 120 North San Pedro Street,
> Los Angeles, California.

Such permits will only be granted for the purpose of uniting members of a family, or in cases of grave emergency.

The Civil Control Station is equipped to assist the Japanese population affected by this evacuation in the following ways:

1. Give advice and instructions on the evacuation.

2. Provide services with respect to the management, leasing, sale, storage or other disposition of most kinds of property, such as real estate, business and professional equipment, household goods, boats, automobiles and livestock.

3. Provide temporary residence elsewhere for all Japanese in family groups.

4. Transport persons and a limited amount of clothing and equipment to their new residence.

The Following Instructions Must Be Observed:

1. A responsible member of each family, preferably the head of the family, or the person in whose name most of the property is held, and each individual living alone, will report to the Civil Control Station to receive further instructions. This must be done between 8:00 A.M. and 5:00 P.M. on Monday, May 4, 1942, or between 8:00 A.M. and 5:00 P.M. on Tuesday, May 5, 1942.

2. Evacuees must carry with them on departure for the Assembly Center, the following property:

(a) Bedding and linens (no mattress) for each member of the family;

(b) Toilet articles for each member of the family;

* An Evacuation Notice Issued by General John DeWitt, May 3, 1942.

(c) Extra clothing for each member of the family;

(d) Sufficient knives, forks, spoons, plates, bowls and cups for each member of the family;

(e) Essential personal effects for each member of the family.

All items carried will be securely packaged, tied and plainly marked with the name of the owner and numbered in accordance with instructions obtained at the Civil Control Station. The size and number of packages is limited to that which can be carried by the individual or family group.

3. No pets of any kind will be permitted.

4. No personal items and no household goods will be shipped to the Assembly Center.

5. The United States Government through its agencies will provide for the storage, at the sole risk of the owner, of the more substantial household items, such as iceboxes, washing machines, pianos and other heavy furniture. Cooking utensils and other small items will be accepted for storage if crated, packed and plainly marked with the name and address of the owner. Only one name and address will be used by a given family.

6. Each family, and individual living alone, will be furnished transportation to the Assembly Center or will be authorized to travel by private automobile in a supervised group. All instructions pertaining to the movement will be obtained at the Civil Control Station.

GO TO THE CIVIL CONTROL STATION BETWEEN THE HOURS 8:00 A.M. AND 5:00 P.M., MONDAY, MAY 4, 1942, OR BETWEEN THE HOURS OF 8:00 A.M. AND 5:00 P.M., TUESDAY, MAY 5, 1942, TO RECEIVE FURTHER INSTRUCTIONS.

J. L. DeWITT
Lieutenant General, U.S. Army
Commanding

SEE CIVILIAN EXCLUSION ORDER NO. 33

---

7. JAPANESE WAR RELOCATION CENTERS

Public Proclamation No. 6

HEADQUARTERS, WESTERN DEFENSE COMMAND AND FOURTH ARMY,

Presidio of San Francisco, California, June 2, 1942.
To: The People within the State of California, and to the Public Generally:

WHEREAS, by Public Proclamation No. 1, dated March 2, 1942, this head-quarters, there was designated and established Military Area No. 2, and

WHEREAS, the present military situation requires, as a matter of military necessity, additional regulations pertaining to all persons of Japanese ancestry, both alien and non-alien, who are in that portion of Military Area No. 2 lying within the State of California:

NOW, THEREFORE, I, J. L. DeWitt, Lieutenant General, U. S. Army, by virtue of the authority vested in me by the President of the United States and by the Secretary of War and my powers and prerogatives as Commanding General,

Western Defense Command, do hereby declare and establish the following additional regulations covering the conduct to be observed by all persons of Japanese ancestry, both alien and non-alien, residing or being in that portion of the State of California lying within the Military Area above described:

1. Effective at 12:00 o'clock noon, P. W. T., June 2, 1942, all alien Japanese and persons of Japanese ancestry who are within the said California portion of Military Area No. 2, be and they are hereby prohibited from leaving that area for any purpose until and to the extent that a future proclamation or order of this headquarters shall so permit or direct.

2. No person of Japanese ancestry, whether alien or non-alien, who is now outside of Military Area No. 1 or outside of the said California portion of Military Area No. 2, shall enter either of said areas unless expressly authorized so to do by this headquarters.

3. The hours between 8 P.M. and 6 A.M. are hereby designated as the hours of curfew. Effective at 12:00 o'clock noon, P. W. T., June 2, 1942, all persons of Japanese ancestry, both alien and non-alien, residing or being within the said California portion of Military Area No. 2, shall, during the hours of curfew, be within their places of residence or, if any such persons have no places of residence therein, then they shall be in their temporary places of abode. At all times other than during the hours of curfew, or except as expressly authorized by order of this headquarters, all such persons shall be not more than 10 miles from their places of residence or, if any such persons have no places of residence, then not more than 10 miles from their temporary places of abode, unless traveling between such points and the places of their regular employment.

4. Nothing in paragraph 3 hereof shall be construed as prohibiting any of the above-specified persons from visiting, during non-curfew hours, the nearest United States Post Office, United States Employment Service Office or office operated or maintained by the Wartime Civil Control Administration, State and Federal courts and public offices, for the purpose of transacting any business or the making of any arrangements necessary to prepare for evacuation or to accomplish compliance with exclusion orders hereafter to be issued.

5. The following classes of persons of Japanese ancestry are hereby authorized to be temporarily exempted or deferred from future exclusion and evacuation upon furnishing satisfactory proof as provided in Proclamation No. 5, dated March 30, 1942:

    (a) Patients in hospitals or confined elsewhere, and too ill or incapacitated to be removed therefrom without danger to life;

    (b) Inmates of orphanages and the totally deaf, dumb or blind.

6. All alien Japanese and all persons of Japanese ancestry will be excluded from said California portion of Military Area No. 2 by future orders or proclamations of this Headquarters.

7. Any person violating this Proclamation will be subject to the criminal penalties provided by Public Law No. 503, 77th Congress, approved March 21, 1942, entitled, "An Act to Provide a Penalty for Violation of Restrictions or Orders with Respect to Persons Entering, Remaining in, Leaving or Committing Any Act in Military Areas or Zones." In the case of any alien enemy, such person will in addition be subject to immediate apprehension and internment.

J. L. DeWitt,
Lieutenant General, U.S. Army, Commanding.

8.

Exhibit I

WAR RELOCATION AUTHORITY

APPLICATION FOR LEAVE CLEARANCE

Relocation Center _____
Family No. _____
Center Address _____

1. Name _____
    (Last)   (First)   (Middle)

2. Name of wife _____

 Names and ages of children _____ _____

               _____ _____

               _____ _____

               _____ _____

               _____ _____

 List any other persons wholly or partly dependent on you for support at the time of your evacuation:

   Name   Address

 _____ _____

 _____ _____

 _____ _____

 _____ _____

 Indicate which of your dependents you propose to have accompany you on leave:

 _____

 _____

3. To the best of your knowledge, name the organizations to which your father belonged and the papers and magazines to which he has subscribed or which he has regularly read:

 _____

 _____

4. Have you ever been in Japan? _____ _____. If so, give dates and the purpose of the visit or residence: (Yes) (No)

 _____

 _____

5. List any other country visited, giving dates: _____

 _____

6. List all the addresses at which you have ever lived for a period of as much as 3 months during the last 20 years: _____

 _____

 At which of the above were you living with your parents? _____

 _____

7. To what extent have you been financially dependent on your parents during the last 3 years? _____

 _____

8. Give the names and addresses of references not to exceed five in number. These need not be Caucasians but good Caucasian references may be particularly helpful:

Name	Address
------------------------------	------------------------------
------------------------------	------------------------------
------------------------------	------------------------------
------------------------------	------------------------------
------------------------------	------------------------------

9. Have you ever been registered with a Japanese or Spanish consul? ____ ____
                                                                  (Yes) (No)
   If so, indicate which and give date:
   ----

10. Have you ever worked for or volunteered your services to a Japanese or
    Spanish consul? _____ _____. If so, indicate which and give date:
              (Yes)   (No)

    ----

11. Have you ever applied for repatriation to Japan? _____ _____. If so, when?
                                                      (Yes)   (No)

    ----

12. Have you ever announced an intention or desire to expatriate yourself from
    Japan? _____ _____. If so, when?
          (Yes)   (No)

    ----

13. Have you ever registered any of your children with a Japanese or Spanish
    Consul? _____ _____. If so, give names and dates:
          (Yes)   (No)

Names	Dates	Names	Dates
--------------------	-----------	--------------------	-----------
--------------------	-----------	--------------------	-----------
--------------------	-----------	--------------------	-----------

14. Have you ever sent any of your children to Japan? _____ _____. If so,
    give names and dates: (Yes)   (No)

Names	Dates	Names	Dates
--------------------	-----------	--------------------	-----------
--------------------	-----------	--------------------	-----------
--------------------	-----------	--------------------	-----------

15. Are any members of your immediate family (father, brother, husband, son)
    in the Japanese armed forces? _____ _____. If so, give relationship,
    name, service rank: (Yes)   (No)

    Are any members of your immediate family as so defined in the United
    States armed forces? _____ _____. If so, give relationship, name, service
    rank.   (Yes)   (No)
    Indicate those that volunteered.

    Are any members of your immediate family (father, mother, brother,
    sister, husband, wife, child) working for the Japanese Government?
    _____ _____. If so, give relationship, name, and situation.
    (Yes)   (No)

Are any members of your immediate family as so defined working for the United States Government? _____ _____. If so, give relationship, name, and situation.   (Yes)   (No)

Are any members of your immediate family as so defined now in Japan? _____ _____. If so, give relationship, name, and occupation.

(Yes)   (No)

16. Do you speak Japanese: [ ] fluently, [ ] fairly well, [ ] poorly, [ ] not at all?
Do you read Japanese: [ ] fluently, [ ] fairly well, [ ] poorly, [ ] not at all?
Do you write Japanese: [ ] fluently, [ ] fairly well, [ ] poorly, [ ] not at all?

17. List all the clubs and organizations to which you have ever belonged and state any offices which you have ever held in them:

        Clubs or organizations   Offices held

--   -------------------------

--   -------------------------

--   -------------------------

18. List the magazines and newspapers to which you have subscribed or which you have customarily read:

----

19. Have you ever been interned and paroled? _____ _____. If so, give date and place of parole: (Yes)   (No)

Have you ever been arrested or similarly detained? _____ _____. If so,
                                                (Yes)   (No)
state the circumstances and disposition of your case:

Have you ever been subjected to any disciplinary action since your evacuation? _____ _____. If so, state the circumstances and the disposition of
        (Yes)   (No)
your case:

----

20. What work have you done at an assembly center or at this or any other relocation center?

----

21. State any type of leave previously applied for, and indicate whether leave clearance has previously been applied for, giving date and place of application:

----

22. If employment is desired, but no definite offer has been received, list the kinds of employment acceptable in order of preference:

        First choice: _____

        Second choice: _____

        Third choice: _____

23. Preference as to location of employment:

        First choice: _____

        Second choice: _____

        Third choice: _____

NOTE.—Any person who knowingly and wilfully falsifies or conceals a material fact or makes a false or fraudulent statement or representation in any matter within the jurisdiction of any department or agency of the United States is liable to a fine of not more than $10,000 or ten years' imprisonment, or both.

_____

      (Date)

                                     _____

                                        (Signature)

EXHIBIT II

WAR RELOCATION AUTHORITY

APPLICATION FOR SHORT-TERM LEAVE

(Without previous leave clearance)

                              Relocation Center _____

                              Family No. _____

                              Center Address _____

1. Name _____ _____ _____

                    (Last)   (First)   (Middle)

2. Name of wife _____

   Names and ages of children _____ _____

                           _____ _____

                           _____ _____

                           _____ _____

                           _____ _____

3. Have you ever been in Japan? _____ _____. If so, give dates and the purpose of the visit or residence:

                          (Yes)   (No)

   _____

   _____

4. List any other country visited, giving dates:

   _____

   _____

5. List all the addresses at which you have ever lived, for a period of as much as three months, during the last twenty years:

   _____

   _____

6. Give the names and addresses of references, not to exceed five in number. These need not be Caucasians, but good Caucasian references may be particularly helpful:

              Names   Addresses

   _____   _____

   _____   _____

   _____   _____

   _____   _____

   _____   _____

7. Have you ever been registered with a Japanese or Spanish Consul? _____
_____. If so, indicate which and give date: (Yes)
   (No)

   ----

8. Have you ever worked for or volunteered your services to a Japanese or
   Spanish Consul? _____ _____. If so, indicate which and give date:
                    (Yes)   (No)

Exhibit VIII

War Relocation Authority

citizen's short-term leave

This is to certify that _____,
a citizen of Japanese ancestry residing in Block No. _____
within _____ Relocation Area is allowed to
leave such area on _____, 19____, to go to _____
----
for the following purpose:

----

and is required to return to such relocation area via _____
as soon as such purpose has been achieved, and in any event to reach such area
by ____ M., on _____, 19____. No delay and no
travel not necessary to the above purpose is authorized. This leave is subject to
the terms of the regulations of the War Relocation Authority relating to issuance
of leave for departure from a relocation area and subject to any special conditions or restrictions set forth on the reverse side hereof.

                                                    _____
                                                    Project Director.

[Reverse side]
This leave is subject to the following special conditions or restrictions:

Exhibit IX

War Relocation Authority

short-term leave

This is to certify that _____,
residing in Block No. _____ within _____
Relocation Area is allowed to leave such area on _____,
19 ____, to go to _____
----
for the following purpose:

----
and is required to return to such relocation area via _____

as soon as such purpose has been achieved, and in any event to reach such area by ____ M., on _____, 19____. No delay and no travel not necessary to the above purpose is authorized. This leave is subject to the terms of the regulations of the War Relocation Authority relating to issuance of leave for departure from a relocation area and subject to any special conditions or restrictions set forth on the reverse side hereof.

_____
Project Director.

[Reverse side]
This leave is subject to the following special conditions or restrictions:
_____
_____

EXHIBIT X

WAR RELOCATION AUTHORITY

ALIEN'S SHORT-TERM LEAVE

This is to certify that _____,
an alien of Japanese nationality residing in Block No. _____ within _____
Relocation Area is allowed to leave such area on _____, 19___, to go to:
_____
for the following purposes:
_____
_____
and is required to return to such relocation area via _____
as soon as such purpose has been achieved, and in any event to reach such area by ____ M., on _____, 19___. No delay and no travel not necessary to the above purpose is authorized. This leave is subject to the terms of the regulations of the War Relocation Authority relating to issuance of leave for departure from a relocation area and subject to any special conditions or restrictions set forth on the reverse side hereof.

Travel to the first destination shown above and return from the last destination has been permitted by the Department of Justice. Travel to the second destination may take place only with the permission of the United States Attorney at _____ and travel to other destinations shown above may take place only with the approval of the United States Attorney of the judicial district including the new point of departure.

_____   _____
(Date)   *Project Director.*

[Reverse side]
This leave is subject to the following special conditions or restrictions:
_____
_____

EXHIBIT XI

WAR RELOCATION AUTHORITY

CITIZEN'S LEAVE PERMIT FOR WORK GROUP

This is to certify that _____,
a citizen of Japanese ancestry residing in Block No. _____ within _____

Relocation Area is allowed to leave such area on _____, 19___, to go to
_____
and is required to return to such area not later than _____, 19___, unless
he is issued a written extension of leave. This leave is subject to the terms of the
regulations of the War Relocation Authority relating to issuance of leave for
departure from a relocation area and subject to any special conditions or
restrictions set forth on the reverse side hereof.

_____

Project Director.

[Reverse side]

This leave is issued subject to the following special conditions or restrictions:

1. The person granted this leave may not leave _____ County,
State of _____, unless he first obtains a written permit to do so from an
official of the War Relocation Authority. *No other person* has the authority to
grant such a permit. The only exception to this rule is in the case of an emergency where the services of a doctor or hospital outside the county are required.
In this instance, notice of the circumstances surrounding the case must be given
as soon as possible to the official whose address appears below.

2. If the person granted this leave changes addresses within _____
County, he must notify the official of the War Relocation Authority whose
address appears below:

_____

(Name)

_____

(Title)

WAR RELOCATION AUTHORITY,

_____

(City and State)

---

9. SEGREGATION OF LOYAL AND DISLOYAL JAPANESE IN RELOCATION CENTERS*

(S. Doc. No. 96)

The VICE PRESIDENT laid before the Senate a message from the President
of the United States, which was read by the legislative clerk, and, with the accompanying papers, was referred to the Committee on Military Affairs and
ordered to be printed, as follows:

THE WHITE HOUSE,
Washington, September 14, 1943.

Subject: Senate Resolution 166 adopted by the Senate on July 6, 1943.
THE PRESIDENT OF THE SENATE:

SIR: On July 6, 1943, the Senate considered and agreed to Senate Resolution
166.

* Message to the Senate from the President of the United States, September 14,
1943, relating to the Segregation of Loyal and Disloyal Japanese in Relocation Centers
(from the *Congressional Record*, Vol. 89, Part 6, 78th Congress, 1st Session, pp. 7521–
7522).

The resolution relates to the program for relocating persons of Japanese ancestry evacuated from west-coast military areas, and asks that the President issue an Executive order to accomplish two things— (1) to direct the War Relocation Authority to segregate the disloyal persons, and the persons whose loyalty is questionable, from those whose loyalty to the United States has been established, and (2) to direct the appropriate agency of the Government to issue a full and complete authoritative statement on conditions in relocation centers and plans for future operations.

I find that the War Relocation Authority has already undertaken a program of segregation. That program is now under way. The first train movements began in early September.

In response to the resolution I asked the Director of the Office of War Mobilization to issue a full and complete authoritative public statement on conditions in relocation centers and plans for future operations. A short preliminary statement on this subject was issued on July 17, 1943. A full and complete statement is being made public today. Copies of these statements are transmitted with this message.

Thus, both of the steps called for in Senate Resolution 166 have already been taken, and it appears that issuance of a further Executive order is not necessary for accomplishment of these purposes.

The segregation program of the War Relocation Authority provides for transferring to a single center, the Tule Lake Center in northeastern California, those persons of Japanese ancestry residing in relocation centers who have indicated that their loyalties lie with Japan. All persons among the evacuees who have expressed a wish to return to Japan for permanent residence have been included among the segregants, along with those among the citizen evacuees who have answered in the negative, or have refused to answer, a direct question as to their willingness to declare their loyalty to the United States and to renounce any allegiance to any foreign government. In addition, those evacuees who are found, after investigation and hearing, to be ineligible to secure indefinite leave from a relocation center, under the leave regulations of the War Relocation Authority, are to be included among the segregants.

While the precise number of segregants is not established at this time because a number of leave clearance investigations have not yet been completed, it is established that the disloyal persons among the evacuees constitute but a small minority, and that the great majority of evacuees are loyal to the democratic institutions of the United States.

Arrangements are being completed for the adequate guarding and supervision of the segregated evacuees. They will be adequately fed and housed and their treatment will in all respects be fair and humane; they will not, however, be eligible to leave the Tule Lake Center while the war with Japan continues or so long as the military situation requires their residence there. An appeals procedure to allow for the correction of mistakes made in determining who shall be segregated has been established so that the entire procedure may be fair and equitable.

With the segregation of the disloyal evacuees in a separate center, the War Relocation Authority proposes now to redouble its efforts to accomplish the relocation into normal homes and jobs in communities throughout the United States, but outside the evacuated areas, of those Americans of Japanese ancestry whose loyalty to this country has remained unshaken through the hardships of the evacuation which military necessity made unavoidable. We shall restore to the loyal evacuees the right to return to the evacuated areas as soon as the mili-

tary situation will make such restoration feasible. Americans of Japanese ancestry, like those of many other ancestries, have shown that they can, and want to,
accept our institutions and work loyally with the rest of us, making their own
valuable contribution to the national wealth and well-being. In vindication of
the very ideals for which we are fighting this war, it is important to us to
maintain a high standard of fair, considerate, and equal treatment for the
people of this minority as of all other minorities.

Respectfully,

FRANKLIN D. ROOSEVELT.

---

10. AN ACT*

United States Statutes at Large, 80th Congress, 2nd Session, Volume 62, Part 1, July 2, 1948, pp. 1231–1233

TO AUTHORIZE THE ATTORNEY GENERAL TO ADJUDICATE CERTAIN CLAIMS
RESULTING FROM EVACUATION OF CERTAIN PERSONS OF JAPANESE ANCESTRY
UNDER MILITARY ORDERS.

*Be it enacted by the Senate and House of Representatives of the United
States of America in Congress assembled.* That the Attorney General shall have
jurisdiction to determine according to law any claim by a person of Japanese
ancestry against the United States arising on or after December 7, 1941, when
such claim is not compensated for by insurance or otherwise, for damage to or
loss of real or personal property (including without limitation as to amount
damage to or loss of personal property bailed to or in the custody of the Government or any agent thereof), that is a reasonable and natural consequence
of the evacuation or exclusion of such person by the appropriate military commander from a military area in Arizona, California, Oregon, or Washington;
or from the Territory of Alaska, or the Territory of Hawaii, under authority
of Executive Order Numbered 9066, dated February 19, 1942 (3 CFR, Cum.
Supp., 1092), section 67 of the Act of April 30, 1900 (48 U. S. C. 532), or
Executive Order Numbered 9489, dated October 18, 1944 (3 CFR, 1944 Supp.,
45). As used herein "evacuation" shall include voluntary departure from a
military area prior to but in anticipation of an order of exclusion therefrom.

LIMITATIONS; CLAIMS NOT TO BE CONSIDERED

SECTION 2. (a) The Attorney General shall receive claims for a period of
eighteen months from the date of enactment of this Act. All claims not presented
within that time shall be forever barred.

(b) The Attorney General shall not consider any claim—

(1) by or on behalf of any person who after December 7, 1941, was
voluntarily or involuntarily deported from the United States to Japan or
by and on behalf of any alien who on December 7, 1941, was not actually
residing in the United States;

(2) for damage or loss arising out of action taken by any Federal agency

---

* Public Law No. 886 (Evacuation Claims).

pursuant to sections 4067, 4068, 4069, and 4070 (relating to alien enemies) of the Revised Statutes, as amended (50 U. S. C. 21–24), or pursuant to the Trading With the Enemy Act, as amended (50 U. S. C. App., and Supp., 1–31, 616);

(3) for damage or loss to any property, or interest therein, vested in the United States pursuant to said Trading With the Enemy Act, as amended;

(4) for damage or loss on account of death or personal injury, personal inconvenience, physical hardship, or mental suffering; and

(5) for loss of anticipated profits or loss of anticipated earnings.

HEARINGS; EVIDENCE; RECORDS

SECTION 3. (a) The Attorney General shall give reasonable notice to the interested parties and an opportunity for them to be heard and to present evidence before making a final determination upon any claim.

(b) For the purpose of any hearing or investigation authorized under this Act, the provisions of sections 9 and 10 (relating to examination of documentary evidence, attendance of witnesses, and production of books, papers, and documents) of the Federal Trade Commission Act of September 26, 1914, as amended (15 U. S. C. 49, 50), are hereby made applicable to the jurisdiction, powers, and duties of the Attorney General. Subpenas may be served personally, by registered mail, by telegraph, or by leaving a copy thereof at the residence or principal place of business of the person required to be served. A verified return by the individual so serving the same, setting forth the manner of service, shall be proof of service. The United States marshals or their deputies shall serve such process in their respective districts.

(c) A written record shall be kept of all hearings and proceedings under this Act and shall be open to public inspection.

ADJUDICATIONS; PAYMENT OF AWARDS; EFFECT OF ADJUDICATIONS

SECTION 4. (a) The Attorney General shall adjudicate all claims filed under this Act by award or order of dismissal, as the case may be, upon written findings of fact and reasons for the decision. A copy of each such adjudication shall be mailed to the claimant or his attorney.

(b) The Attorney General may make payment of any award not exceeding $2,500 in amount out of such funds as may be made available for this purpose by Congress.

(c) On the first day of each regular session of Congress the Attorney General shall transmit to Congress a full and complete statement of all adjudications rendered under this Act during the previous year, stating the name and address of each claimant, the amount claimed, the amount awarded, the amount paid, and a brief synopsis of the facts in the case and the reasons for each adjudication. All awards not paid under subsection (b) hereof shall be paid in like manner as are final judgments of the Court of Claims.

(d) The payment of an award shall be final and conclusive for all purposes, notwithstanding any other provision of law to the contrary, and shall be a full discharge of the United States and all of its officers, agents, servants, and employees with respect to all claims arising out of the same subject matter. An order of dismissal against a claimant, unless set aside by the Attorney General, shall thereafter bar any further claim against the United States or any officer, agent, servant, or employee thereof arising out of the same subject matter.

ATTORNEYS' FEES

SECTION 5. The Attorney General, in rendering an award in favor of any claimant, may as a part of the award determine and allow reasonable attorneys' fees, which shall not exceed 10 per centum of the amount allowed, to be paid out of, but not in addition to, the amount of such award.

Any attorney who charges, demands, receives, or collects for services rendered in connection with such claim any amount in excess of that allowed under this section, if recovery be had, shall be guilty of a misdemeanor, and shall upon conviction thereof be subject to a fine of not more than $2,000, or imprisonment for not more than one year, or both.

ADMINISTRATION

SECTION 6. For the purposes of this Act the Attorney General may—

(a) appoint a clerk and such attorneys, examiners, interpreters, appraisers, and other employees as may be necessary;

(b) call upon any Federal department or agency for any information or records necessary;

(c) secure the cooperation of State and local agencies, governmental or otherwise, and reimburse such agencies for services rendered;

(d) utilize such voluntary and uncompensated services as may from time to time be needed and available;

(e) assist needy claimants in the preparation and filing of claims;

(f) make such investigations as may be necessary;

(g) make expenditures for witness fees and mileage and for other administrative expenses;

(h) prescribe such rules and regulations, perform such acts not inconsistent with law, and delegate such authority as he may deem proper in carrying out the provisions of this Act.

APPROPRIATIONS

SECTION 7. There are hereby authorized to be appropriated for the purposes of this Act such sums as Congress may from time to time determine to be necessary.

Approved July 2, 1948.

Bibliography

BOOKS

Adams, Ansel, *Born Free and Equal,* photographs of the loyal Japanese Americans at Manzanar relocation center, Inyo County, California. U.S. Camera, New York, 1944.

Biddle, Francis, *In Brief Authority,* Doubleday, Garden City, New York, 1962.

Bloom (Broom), Leonard, *A Controlled Attitude-Tension Survey,* University of California Press, Berkeley and Los Angeles, 1948.

—— and Kituse, John, *The Managed Casualty,* University of California Press, Berkeley and Los Angeles, 1956.

—— and Riemer, Ruth, *Removal and Return: the Socio-Economic Effects of the War on Japanese Americans,* University of California Press, Berkeley and Los Angeles, 1949.

Boddy, E. Manchester, *Japanese in America,* E. Manchester Boddy copyright, privately printed, Los Angeles, 1921.

Bosworth, Allan R., *America's Concentration Camps,* W. W. Norton, New York, 1967.

Conn, Stetson, "The Decision to Evacuate the Japanese from the Pacific Coast," *Command Decisions,* Office of the Chief of Military History, Department of the Army, Washington, D.C., 1960.

——, Engelman, Rose C., and Fairchild, Byron, "Japanese Evacuation from the United States," *Guarding the United States and its Outposts,* Office of the Chief of Military History, Department of the Army, Washington, D.C., 1964.

Daniels, Roger, *The Politics of Prejudice: The Anti-Japanese Movement in California and the Struggle for Japanese Exclusion,* University of California Press, Berkeley and Los Angeles, 1962.

December 7 The First Thirty Hours, the correspondents of *Life, Time,* and *Fortune,* Alfred Knopf, New York, 1942.

Douglas, William O., *The Anatomy of Liberty—The Rights of Man Without Force,* Trident Press, Credo Series, Pocket Books Inc., New York, 1963.

Eaton, Allen H., *Beauty Behind Barbed Wire: the arts of the Japanese in our war relocation camps,* Harper's, New York, 1952.

Edmiston, James, *Home Again,* Doubleday, Garden City, New York, 1955.

Embree, John F., *Suye Mura—A Japanese Village,* Phoenix Books, University of Chicago Press, Chicago, 1939.

Fehrenbacher, Don E., *A Basic History of California,* Van Nostrand, Princeton, 1964.

Flowers, Montaville, *The Japanese Conquest of American Opinion*, George H. Doran Co., New York, 1917.

Fisher, Anne Reeploeg, *Exile of a Race*, F. & T. Publishers, Seattle, 1965.

Grew, Joseph, *Ten Years in Japan*, Simon & Schuster, New York, 1944.

Grodzins, Morton, *Americans Betrayed: Politics and the Japanese Evacuation*, University of Chicago Press, Chicago, 1949.

——, *The Loyal and the Disloyal*, University of Chicago Press, Chicago, 1956.

Gulick, Sidney Lewis, *The American Japanese Problem*, Scribners, New York, 1914.

——, *The East and the West*, Charles E. Tuttle Co., Rutland, Vermont and Tokyo, Japan, 1963.

——, *Japan and the Gentlemen's Agreement*, Federal Council of Churches of Christ in America, 1920.

Hersey, John, *Hiroshima*, Alfred Knopf, New York, 1965.

Hewes, Laurence, *Boxcar in the Sand*, Alfred Knopf, New York, 1957.

Hull, Eleanor, *Suddenly the Sun,* a biography of Shizuko Takahashi, Friendship Press, New York, 1957.

Ichihashi, Yamato, *Japanese in the United States; a Critical Study of the Problems of the Japanese Immigrants and their children*, Stanford University Press, Stanford, 1932.

——, *Japanese Immigration—its Status in California*, The Marshall Press, San Francisco, 1915.

Ike, Nobutaka, *The Beginnings of Political Democracy in Japan*, Johns Hopkins Press, Baltimore, 1950.

Ishida, Gladys, *The Japanese American Renunciants of Okayama Prefecture: Their Accommodation and Assimilation to Japanese Culture*, PhD Dissertation, University of Michigan, on microfilm at the Library of Congress, Washington, D.C.

Kawakami, K. K., *The Real Japanese Question*, Macmillan, New York, 1921.

Kelsey, Carl, ed., *Present-Day Immigration—With Special Reference to the Japanese*, Annals of the American Academy of Political and Social Science, Philadelphia, January, 1921.

Kitagawa, Daisuke, *Issei and Nisei: The Internment Years*, The Seabury Press, New York, 1967.

Leighton, Alexander H., *The Governing of Men*, Princeton University Press, Princeton, 1945.

Life History of—— A Sample Life History of a Californian of Oriental Parentage, The Institute of Pacific Relations, New York, 1927.

Lind, Andrew W., *Hawaii's Japanese—An Experiment in Democracy*, Princeton University Press, Princeton, 1946.

Matsumoto, Toru, *Beyond Prejudice; a story of the church and Japanese Americans*, Friendship Press, Inc., New York, 1946.

—— and Lerrigo, Marion Olive, *A Brother is a Stranger*, The John Day Company, New York, 1946.

McKenzie, R. D., *Oriental Exclusion*, American Group, Institute of Pacific Relations, New York, 1927.

McWilliams, Carey, *Brothers Under the Skin*, Little, Brown and Co., Boston, 1943.

——, *Factories in the Field*, Little, Brown and Co., Boston, 1939.

——, *Prejudice: Japanese Americans: Symbol of racial intolerance*, Little, Brown and Co., Boston, 1944.

Means, Florence Crannell, *The Moved Outers*, Houghton-Mifflin Co., Boston, 1945.

Mears, Eliot Grinnell, *Resident Orientals on the American Pacific Coast*, American Group, Institute of Pacific Relations, New York, 1927.

Michener, James, *Hawaii*, Random House, New York, 1959.

Millis, H. A., *The Japanese Problem in the United States*—An Investigation for the Commission on Relations with Japan, Federal Council of the Churches of Christ in America, New York, 1915.

Miyamoto, Kazuo, *Hawaii, End of the Rainbow,* Charles E. Tuttle Co., Rutland, Vermont and Tokyo, Japan, 1964.

Mori, Arinori, *The Japanese in America*, Charles Lanman, ed., Japan Advertiser Press, Tokyo, Japan, 1926.

Nisato, Kanichi, *Nisei Tragedy*, Shinpoha Nakano, Tokyo, Japan, date uncertain.

Nixon, Lucille M. and Tana, Tomoe, trans., *Sounds from the Unknown*, a book of *tanka* by Japanese Americans, Alan Swallow, Denver, 1963.

O'Brien, Robert W., *The College Nisei*, Pacific Books, Palto Alto, California, 1949.

Okada, John, *No-No Boy,* Charles E. Tuttle Co., Rutland, Vermont, and Tokyo, Japan, 1957.

Okubo, Miné, *Citizen 13660*, Columbia University Press, New York, 1946.

Pearson, Grace Nichols, *Though All We Knew Depart*, unpublished manuscript.

Renne, Louis Obed, *Our Day of Empire—War and the Exile of Japanese Americans*, The Strickland Press, Glasgow, Scotland, 1954.

Roche, John P., *The Quest for the Dream; the Development of Civil Rights and Human Relations in Modern Amreica*, Macmillan, New York, 1963.

———, *Shadow and Substance; Essays on the Theory and Structure of Politics*, Macmillan, New York, 1964.

Sakoda, James M., *Minidoka: An Analysis of Changing Patterns of Social Interaction*, PhD Dissertation, University of California, Berkeley, California, 1949.

Scalapino, Robert A., *Democracy and the Party Movement in Prewar Japan—The Failure of the First Attempt*, University of California Press, Berkeley, California, 1953.

Seidler, Murray B., *Norman Thomas: Respectable Rebel*, Syracuse University Press, Syracuse, New York, 1961.

Smith, Bradford, *Americans from Japan*, J. B. Lippincott Co., Philadelphia and New York, 1948.

Smith, Louis, *American Democracy and Military Power—A Study of Civil Control of the Military Power in the United States*, University of Chicago Press, Chicago, 1951.

Sone, Monica, *Nisei Daughter*, Atlantic, Little, Brown and Co., Boston, 1953.

Stegner, Wallace and the Editors of *Look, One Nation*, Houghton-Mifflin Co., New York, 1945.

Strong, Edward K., Jr., *Japanese in California*, Stanford University Press, Stanford, 1934.

tenBroek, Jacobus, Barnhart, Edward N., and Matson, Floyd W., *Prejudice, War and the Constitution*, University of California Press, Berkeley and Los Angeles, 1958.

Thomas, Dorothy Swaine, with the assistance of Charles Kikuchi and James Sakoda, *The Salvage*, University of California Press, Berkeley and Los Angeles, 1952.

——— and Nishimoto, Richard S., *The Spoilage*, University of California Press, Berkeley and Los Angeles, 1946.

WAR RELOCATION AUTHORITY PUBLICATIONS, PRINTED BY THE U.S. GOVERNMENT PRINTING OFFICE, WASHINGTON, D.C.

The Administrative Highlights of the WRA Program.
Community Government in War Relocation Centers, 1946.
The Evacuated People, A Quantitative Description.
Impounded People; Japanese Americans in the Relocation Centers, 1946.
Legal and Constitutional Phases of the WRA Program.
Myths and Facts about the Japanese Americans, 1945.
People in Motion: The Postwar Adjustment of the Evacuated Japanese, 1947.
The Relocation Program.
Wartime Exile, The Exclusion of the Japanese Americans from the West Coast.
Wartime Handling of Evacuee Property, 1946.
What We're Fighting For; Statements by U.S. Servicemen about Americans of Japanese Descent.
WRA, A Story of Human Conservation, 1946.

PAMPHLETS

The 1943 *Album* of the 442nd Combat Team.
The Military Intelligence Service Language School *Album,* 1946.
Douglass, Truman B., *70,000 American Refugees Made in U.S.A.,* Citizens Committee for Resettlement of the Congregational Christian Committee for Work with Japanese Evacuees.
Fisher, Galen M., *A Balance Sheet on Japanese Evacuation,* 1943.
Foote, Caleb, *Outcasts!* The Fellowship of Reconciliation, New York, 1944.
Flynn, John T., *The Final Secret of Pearl Harbor,* New York, 1945.
From Camp to College, the story of Japanese American Student Relocation, National Japanese American Student Relocation Council, Philadelphia.
"Issei, Nisei, Kibei," *Fortune,* April, 1944; retitled *The Displaced Japanese Americans,* circulated by the American Council on Public Affairs, Washington, D.C.
Johnson, Herbert B., *Documents Against Japanese in California—a Review of the Real Situation,* Courier Publishing Co., Berkeley, 1907.
McClatchy, V. S., Brief, *In the Matter of Immigration Quota for Japan,* December, 1931.
———, *California's Answer to Japan,* 1924.
———, *Japanese Immigration and Colonization,* Sacramento *Bee* Publishers, 1921.
———, *Our New Racial Problem,* Sacramento *Bee* Publishers, 1920.
McWilliams, Carey, *Japanese Evacuation: Interim Report,* a report to the American Council, Institute of Pacific Relations, New York, 1942.
———, *What About our Japanese Americans?,* American Council, Institute of Pacific Relations, May, 1944.
The Sunday Before, Sermons by Pacific Coast pastors of the Japanese race on the Sunday before evacuation to assembly centers in the late spring of 1942, edited by Allan A. Hunter and Gurney Binford (mimeographed).
A Tule Lake Interlude, first anniversary issue, May 27, 1942–1943, *The Tulean Dispatch* (mimeographed), Tule Lake Relocation Center.
They Work for Victory, The Story of Japanese Americans and the War Effort,

edited and published by the Japanese American Citizens League, Salt Lake City, Utah, undated.

Schuyler, Lambert, *The Japs Must Not Come Back*, Heron House, Winslow, Washington, 1944.

Thomas, Norman, *Democracy and Japanese Americans*, Post War World Council, New York, 1942.

Wada, Yori, "Beyond the Horizon," reprinted from *California Monthly*, December, 1943.

GOVERNMENT DOCUMENTS

Chandler Committee—*Report on the Subcommittee on Japanese War Relocation Centers to the Committee on Naval Affairs, United States Senate, May 7, 1943*, U.S. Government Printing Office, Washington, D.C., 1943.

DeWitt, Lieutenant General J. L., *Final Report. Japanese Evacuation from the West Coast, 1942*, U.S. Government Printing Office, Washington, D.C., 1943.

Dies Report (House Committee on Un-American Activities) Appendix VI, 1941 *Report and Minority Views of special committee on un-American activities in Japanese Relocation Centers*, 79th Congress, 1st Session, U.S. Government Printing Office, Washington, D.C., September 30, 1943.

Immigration and Nationality Act with amendments and notes on related laws, 5th ed., revised through December 31, 1965, U.S. Government Printing Office, Washington, D.C., 1966.

Japanese American Evacuation Claims, Hearings on HR 7435, U.S. Government Printing Office, 1954.

Japanese American Evacuation Claims, Hearings on HR 7763, U.S. Government Printing Office, Washington, D.C., 1956.

Naturalization Laws, compiled by Gilman G. Udell, U.S. Government Printing Office, Washington, D.C., 1964.

Tolan Committee—Hearings before the Select Committee investigating National Defense Migration, San Francisco, February 21 and 23, 1942, U.S. Government Printing Office, Washington, D.C., 1942.

Journal of the Senate of California, 55th Session, 1943. California State Printing Office.

Statutes and Amendments to the Codes of California, 55th Session, 1943, California State Printing Office.

Statutes and Amendments to the Codes of California, Extra Sessions, 1941–1943, California State Printing Office.

Treaties, Conventions, International Acts, Protocols and Agreements between the United States of America and other Powers 1776–1909, Vol. I, 61st Congress, 2nd Session, U.S. Government Printing Office, Washington, D.C., 1910.

To Improve the Relations of the United States with Western Germany and Japan, Hearings before the subcommittee of the Committee on Foreign Affairs, House of Representatives, 84th Congress, 1st Session, United States Government Printing Office, Washington, D.C., 1955.

Legislative Digest and Table of Sections Affected, January 4–31, 1943, California State Publications Office.

LEGAL DOCUMENTS

Abo   Brief for Appellees, *Bruce G. Barber* vs. *Tadayasu Abo et al.,* and *Bruce G. Barber* vs. *Mary Kaname Furuya, et al.,* Nos. 12,195 and 12,196, United States Court of Appeals for the Ninth Circuit, 1951.

Abo Appellees' Petition for a Rehearing, *J. Howard McGrath* vs. *Takayasu Abo* and *J. Howard McGrath* vs. *Mary Kaname Furuya, et al.,* United States Court of Appeals for the Ninth Circuit, 1951.

Abo Appellees' Petition for a Rehearing, *J. Howard McGrath* vs. *Takayasu Abo Abo, et al.,* vs. *J. Howard McGrath* and *Mary Kaname Furuya, et al.,* vs. *J. Howard McGrath,* Supreme Court of the United States, October term, 1950.

Aoki, Petition for Writs of *Certiorari* to the United States Court of Appeals for the Ninth District and Brief in Support Thereof, *Shinichi Jimmy Aoki, et al.,* vs. *Bruce G. Barber* and *Kiyoshi Wakabayashi, et al.,* vs. *Bruce G. Barber,* 1951.

Duncan vs. *Kahanamoku,* Supreme Court Reporter, Vol. 66, West Publishing Co., St. Paul, Minnesota, 1947.

Ex Parte Mitsuye Endo, Supreme Court Reporter, Vol. 65, West Publishing Company, St. Paul, Minnesota, 1946.

Hirabayashi vs. *United States,* United States Reports, Vol. 320, U.S. Government Printing Office, 1944.

Brief *Amicus Curiae,* Japanese American Citizens League, *Gordon K. Hirabayashi* vs. *United States of America* and *Minoru Yasui* vs. *United States of America,* Supreme Court of the United States, October term, 1942.

Documental History of Law Cases Affecting Japanese in the United States, 1916–1924, compiled by the consulate-general of Japan, San Francisco, 1925.

Toyosaburo Korematsu vs. *United States,* Supreme Court Reporter, Vol. 65, West Publishing Company, St. Paul, Minnesota, 1946.

Brief of State of California as *Amicus Curiae, Fred Toyosaburo Korematsu* vs. *United States of America,* United States Circuit Court of Appeals for the Ninth Circuit, 1943.

Brief for Appellee, *Fred Toyosaburo Korematsu* vs. *United States of America,* United States Circuit Court of Appeals for the Ninth Circuit, 1943.

Appellant's Opening Brief, *Fred Toyosaburo Korematsu* vs. *United States of America,* United States Circuit Court of Appeals for the Ninth Circuit, 1942.

Brief for the American Civil Liberties Union, *Amicus Curiae, Fred Toyosaburo Korematsu* vs. *United States of America,* Supreme Court of the United States, 1944.

Brief for the United States, *Fred Toyosaburo Korematsu* vs. *United States of America,* Supreme Court of the United States, October term, 1944.

Brief for Appellant, *Fred Toyosaburo Korematsu* vs. *United States of America,* Supreme Court of the United States, October term, 1944.

Appellants' Abstract of Record, *Kenji Namba, Etsuo Namba, and Florence C. Donald* vs. *John B. McCourt,* Supreme Court of the State of Oregon, October term, 1947.

John T. Regan vs. *Cameron King,* Federal District Court, N.D., Calif., S.D., Federal Supplement, Vol. 49, West Publishing Company, St. Paul, Minnesota, 1942.

Brief for Japanese American Citizens League, *Amicus Curiae, John T. Regan* vs. *Cameron King,* United States Circuit Court of Appeals for the Ninth Circuit, 1942.

Ex parte Milligan, December, 1866, U.S. Supreme Court Reports, Vol. 18, Lawyers' Edition.

Torao Takahashi vs. *Fish and Game Commission, et al.,* 68 United States Supreme Court Reporter, West Publishing Company, St. Paul, Minnesota, 1948.

Petitions for Writs of *Certiorari* and Brief in Support Thereof, *Kioyshi Wakabayashi, et al.,* vs. *Bruce G. Barber,* Supreme Court of the United States, October term, 1950.

Brief of State of California as *Amicus Curiae*. In the matter of the Application of Toki and Ernest Wakayama for Writs of *Habeas Corpus*, 1942.

Yasui vs. *United States,* 1943, United States Reports, Vol. 320.

Brief of the State of California as *Amicus Curiae, United States of America* vs. *Minoru Yasui,* United States Supreme Court, October term, 1942.

SPECIAL COLLECTIONS AND CORRESPONDENCE

Backus, Edythe, Collection, Henry E. Huntington Library, San Marino, California.

Conard-Duveneck Collection, Hoover Institution on War, Revolution, and Peace, Stanford University, Stanford, California.

Doi, Sumio, scrapbook.

Fisher, Galen, Collection, Bancroft Library, University of California, Berkeley, California.

Hays, Alice, Collection of letters from Evacuees, Hoover Institution on War, Revolution, and Peace, Stanford University, Stanford, California.

Isenberg, Gerda, correspondence and papers, 1942–1946, Bancroft Library, University of California, Berkeley, California.

Kitaji, Helen (Aihara), diary and letters.

McWilliams, Carey, Collection, Hoover Institution on War, Revolution, and Peace, Stanford University, Stanford, California.

Nishimoto, Richard S., *Firebreak Gang,* sixty-two-page manuscript on Poston, Arizona, Bancroft Library, University of California, Berkeley, California.

Pearson, Grace (Nichols), Collection of letters, Hoover Institution on War, Revolution, and Peace, Stanford University, Stanford, California.

Settles, Claude, Collection.

Sowers, Mrs. Roy V., Collection, Hoover Institution on War, Revolution, and Peace, Stanford University, Stanford, California.

Von Blon, John L., Collection, Hoover Institution on War, Revolution, and Peace, Stanford University, Stanford, California.

INDEX

DATE DUE

MR 8 '76			
OCT 1980			
APR 1 8 1994			

940.531
G

24870

Change Tab

Girdner

The great betrayal

SENIOR LIBRARY

DATE DUE

FEB 16
MAY 27 1997

2753

WASHINGTON

MONTANA

OREGON

■ HEART
MOUNTAIN

WYOMING

TULE LAKE

■ TOPAZ

COLORADO

UTAH

AMACHE

CALIFORNIA

MANZANAR ■

ARIZONA

NEW
MEXICO

■ POSTON

■ GILA